ADMINISTRATIVE DIMENSIONS OF HEALTH AND PHYSICAL EDUCATION
PROGRAMS, INCLUDING ATHLETICS

ADMINISTRATIVE DIMENSIONS OF HEALTH AND PHYSICAL EDUCATION PROGRAMS, INCLUDING ATHLETICS

CHARLES A. BUCHER, A.B., M.A., Ed.D.

Professor of Education, New York University,
New York, New York

Assisted by
LINDA M. JOSEPH
Instructor of Health and Physical Education,
Queensborough Community College of the
City of New York

THE C. V. MOSBY COMPANY

Saint Louis   1971

PREFACE

When this readings book, *Administrative Dimensions of Health and Physical Education Programs, Including Athletics,* was conceived it was known that many publications included articles relating to the subject of administration. However, after the project was under way and the literature was examined more closely, the available material proved to be voluminous. Over the course of a three-year period approximately 150 periodicals were examined in the search for suitable articles. About 500 articles were selected initially for consideration. These were read and reread and finally reduced to about 350 in number. At this point, the authors and editors of these publications were contacted to see if their materials could be used in this book. With this additional information the articles were reread and those kept that: (1) related to the five-part format developed for the book, (2) made a significant contribution to the reader's understanding of the many problems concerned with the administration of health and physical education programs, (3) contained current and up-to-date information, and (4) helped to provide the proper balance needed in such a publication, such as relating to boys', girls', men's, and women's programs, pertaining to the many areas of administration, and written in a length and style appropriate for such a text. After the various readings were selected and approval received for their publication, the other essential details were added. Introductions to each of the five parts of the book were written, and projects, thought questions, and references for each part were developed. After three years and much reading and work, the book was finally sent to the publisher. I wish to thank Miss Linda M. Joseph for her help in this project.

Administrative Dimensions of Health and Physical Education Programs, Including Athletics is intended as a source book for students in undergraduate and graduate professional programs as well as administrators and leaders on the job. It is an anthology that should be of great value to faculty members in general, but particularly to those who teach administrative courses to professional students. Leaders in youth agencies, recreational programs, schools, and other institutions should also find this text valuable in their work.

The readings included in each of the parts are grouped into five coordinated themes. The introductory sections preceding each of the five major divisions and each chapter present brief summaries of the scope of the parts and readings in each chapter. Projects and thought questions based on the readings and a list of suggested references complete each chapter.

Users of the book will find each article highly readable and thought provoking. Not all of the authors are health educators or physical educators, yet each selection has definite implications for health and physical education programs.

Many authors and publishers have made the completion of this book possible. Their recommendations for proper documentation have been followed in crediting each selection.

Charles A. Bucher

v

CONTENTS

PART ONE   THE NATURE AND SCOPE OF ADMINISTRATION

Administration is an important consideration for any organization that desires to achieve the goals for which it exists. It follows that administration is of vital importance to each member of the organization. Administration involves human beings and their desire to achieve personal and professional objectives through associated effort. The manner in which schools, colleges, youth agencies, and other organizations are administered will determine, in large measure, whether the hopes and dreams of the people who compose these organizations are realized.

Administration involves much more than just the duties of the director, chairman, principal, superintendent, dean, president, supervisor, or other person. It is the total process involved in directing, coordinating, and carrying out the functions essential to achieving the aims of the organization. Therefore, everyone should be acquainted with administration and what constitutes appropriate and inappropriate administrative principles, procedures, and practices.

Administration has been, and is, changing rapidly in today's world. The old, autocratic type of administration is going out of vogue, and a more democratic type of administration is taking its place. Administrators are being prepared for their roles much more thoroughly and scientifically than they were years ago. For-

merly, being on the job for several years and being popular with the other members of the organization were sometimes the main qualifications sought. Today we find that administrators are being prepared through serving in internships where experience can be gained on the job, much as doctors do as part of their preparation. In addition, persons training to be administrators study such areas as the social structure of organizations, the requirements for leadership, and the decision-making process. A body of administrative theory has come into being, the knowledge of which prepares a person to carry out administrative functions in a much more effective manner than formerly.

Part One provides the reader of this book with essential background information relating to this changing nature of administration. It also provides such foundational information as administrative relationships and objectives, some aspects of the administrative setting, and personnel administration of school and college health and physical education programs (including athletics).

The readings presented in Part One have been drawn from a large group of writings by outstanding educators and researchers who know the subject of administration, from the standpoint both of research findings and of experience on the job.

1

CHAPTER 1   THE CHANGING NATURE OF ADMINISTRATION

Chapter 1 sets the stage for this anthology of readings in the administration of school health and physical education programs by presenting some of the changes that will be taking place in these programs in the future, with implications for administrative action being drawn. Also discussed are the priorities that exist in education today and that have implications for health educators and physical educators, and the leadership role that educators can play in carrying out their role in schools, colleges, and youth-serving agencies.

America's current preoccupation with education is explored by Virgil E. Strickland with the underlying concept that this concern is healthy for any democratic society. Strickland believes that youngsters should be taught an "approach to life" rather than the minutia of subject matter. By developing desirable attitudes, learning to accept themselves, understanding freedom as opposed to control, and learning to live disciplined lives, our youngsters will be better prepared for the technological age and the strange tomorrow.

J. Lloyd Trump, Enid Von Bergen, and Harry E. Pike devote their efforts to the scheduling and utilization of facilities. Trump's article favors student responsibility in learning. He feels that participation in programs of health, fitness, and recreation is facilitated by the total schedule of the school. Innovative schools allow scheduling of instruction in large groups, small-group discussions, and required independent study. The motivating of large groups through awakening interest is followed by small-group discussions or skill development, after which the students advance their skill through independent study. This allows for more student responsibility and achieves better utilization of facilities by the students.

Von Bergen and Pike describe the innovative scheduling procedures at Poway (California) High School. Poway High School has modular, or flexible, scheduling: the time is allotted to fit the needs of each course rather than to give each class a fixed amount of meeting time each day. The main goal of the physical education program is to educate for the future with the inclusion of lifetime sports. Each sport is divided into skill levels, and no student may advance in a sport until achievement is gained in the preliminary skill levels. This flexible scheduling allows for instructor specialization as well as student involvement and the utilization of facilities to their fullest extent.

Sherman Tingey and Van R. Vibber point out the relationship of creativity and imagination learned in school to the changing aspect of management of a job situation. Society is changing, and the youth of today are challenged by the creativity and imagination offered by a job situation. The authors believe that intelligence does not necessarily lead to creativity on the job. Organizations must allow people to act more freely, permit contrary viewpoints, and get people involved.

As seen in this chapter, administration and its changing nature take on many aspects. Development of leaders and desirable attitudes, the proper utilization of facilities, innovative programming, and the challenge of creativity are some of the areas effecting the necessary changes of administrative policy-making today.

1 CURRENT PRIORITIES IN EDUCATION*

VIRGIL E. STRICKLAND
PROFESSOR OF EDUCATION AND INTERNSHIP COORDINATOR,
FLORIDA STATE UNIVERSITY, TALLAHASSEE, FLORIDA

The American scene is characterized by a unique emphasis and focus on education. This is good, for democracy, American style, can survive and develop only through an educated citizenry. Through individual and group action generated at local levels and through support and expansion created at state and national centers, the future of education in the U.S. looks promising. However, if America is to realize fully the worthy educational goals it has set, careful thought and planning must be exercised.

---

*From *School and Society* **95**:51, January 21, 1967. Used by permission.

On every hand, these questions arise: What will children and youth need most if they are to cope successfully with the problems of a yet unknown technological age? And, how can children be reared today so that they will be strong and ready for an unpredictable and strange tomorrow? From many quarters, including some educational, the very loud and immediate response has been: more education, especially, more mathematics, science, modern languages, and reading instruction through pre-school programs. Add to this the plea for increased homework, higher standards, and so on through endless minutia, and one will have the answer proposed by many self-appointed authorities for the problems of a coming generation. Many of these ideas may represent true needs. However, merely adding more of anything to the school curriculum will not, in itself, give the needed preparation for life in the world of the immediate tomorrow. In fact, it is rather doubtful that adequate prediction can be made as to just what mathematics, science, and so forth will suffice.

It is granted that the new advances in mathematics, science, and modern language content and methodology must find their place in the school's curriculum. No doubt, many of the contemporary proposals are good; however, most of them are far too specific and limited in point of view. In fact, one would conclude from such ideas that the shape of the future was known exactly. Such foreknowledge can be nothing more than sheer guesswork or, at best, qualified estimates with little or no certainty. On the other hand, there are some considerations which must receive top priority if the mathematics, science, or any other system of organized knowledge is to have full meaning and usefulness to the learner, no matter what may be the nature of his world. Hence, it is essential to identify and focus attention on those concerns that must be accorded top priority in America's educational endeavor.

Not knowing the future, it seems logical to determine what broad concepts, principles, skills, and attitudes best will serve the learner in facing a new and different world. For instance, the school must be concerned much more about the basic attitudes a child learns as he studies mathematics, science, and all the other subjects at school, and as he lives at home with his parents. These fundamental ways of feeling, a person's deep-rooted approach to life and people and problems, are his real equipment for living happily in any world order.

Thus, the first priority to which the school must give attention is the task of "attitude development." To this end, the teacher and the total school resources must give purposeful planning and direction. In the setting of institutional policies governing the way of work for both teachers and pupils, there must be a keen awareness of the nature and character of those feelings which such policies will promote. Each teacher must be sensitive to the many subtle and direct ways in which the subject content being studied can contribute to the establishment of desirable attitudes within his pupils. In all his personal and group interactions with pupils, the teacher constantly must be cognizant of his impact on attitude development. For, true education often is not so much learning what one does not already know as it is becoming aware of those inner feelings generated by what he has learned or by problems he has encountered.

Specifically, this means that, as children pursue their studies in the school curriculum, they must come to value Learning, Life, Liberty, and Law. These are the top priorities demanding the school's attention. For if such are not the discernible outcomes of the pupil's pursuit of his understanding of the measures of height, weight, and depth, the intricacies of language, the rhythm of sound, the marvels of the universe with all its physical phenomena, beauty, design, and color, then all his learning is in vain and will profit little.

An absorbing fascination for learning comes first. Children forever must be excited and challenged by a new fact, a new idea. They should experience a real thrill out of using what they have learned to work solutions and come to conclusions. In school they must learn to think, to investigate, to find out. This deep and permanent love of learning is not an instamatic thing. Neither does it emerge just through the process of hard work at school, or through doing homework, or passing tests. The significant outcome rests in how a child feels about his learning and why he studies. It should be a real concern of the teacher and home if the reason for learning is just to get a good grade, or to get on the honor roll, or to be promoted, or just to please adults. The measure of learning and the cause for satisfaction should come when a child learns and keeps on learning, because he wants to know.

Teachers and schools too often are guilty of stuffing children with subject content the teacher and school think are important. The sad truth, however, is that "stuffed children" are likely to be empty tomorrow, at the very time they will need most a dynamic enthusiasm for learning. The valuable teacher, then, is not necessarily the one who assigns the most, or demands the most, or grades the toughest. The really significant teacher is the creative person who searches for ways to help children to catch on fire—who will help them chase after facts they want to know and sharpen skills they want to master.

Educator and layman alike must work for the kind of schools where teachers are alive and imaginative, not dreary taskmasters who merely prod their pupils to study through fear of failure, or the promise of honor roll prestige. Today's generation is a demanding one, living in a demanding time.

A second priority is the "measure of life." Somehow, through the organized program of studies, the child must be helped to learn to love his own life first; then he will have the capacity to love life for all mankind. For the sake of tomorrow, today's child must be glad he is who he is—proud of himself, pleased with himself. Girded with this good feeling, he will be able to grow into the courage and strength to take the tomorrows in stride.

On the surface, this may appear to be a high self-centeredness and cocky conceit. It is not a support of conceit, for the child must want to change, to grow, and improve. In fact, it is impossible to stay put; one either grows up or shrinks downward. It is the unsure person who attempts to sit still, not the confident one. A child who has learned to accept himself is free to grow. Children who are convinced that no one loves or approves them can not love or approve themselves. When a child becomes sold on the idea that he has the wrong kind of intelligence, the wrong sex, the wrong speed, the wrong talents, he feels that he is just wrong. This is no feeling to carry into an uncertain tomorrow.

The uncertain child is afraid of others. He always must keep his guard up and be set to deliver the first punch. To this child, everyone who is different—different religious beliefs, different national origin, different color—is a threat. This shaky fear is the great barrier between persons and nations today, and will be the world's biggest obstacle in the future. Fear such as this is not inborn. The school and the home make children this way; when, just as easily, each could help them to value other people.

Those children who, in their homes and

schools, have known much love and laughter are fortunate. True, they must be called down when they do wrong; they must know correction, even punishment. But, if all the days of their childhood and youth teach them that people usually are pleased with them, they will learn to love life and feel no need to hide, or to hurt. Tomorrow's century will need such persons if a good tomorrow is to prevail.

The third priority is liberty. The school and the teacher must deal expertly with this most illusive and deceptive idea—freedom. Yet, all children must come to know a "decent freedom" and to treasure it. The child's concept and use of freedom well may be the central issue in his adult life. He must grow up knowing freedom; he can not begin to value it all at once when he is an adult.

Freedom should grow as the person grows. For instance, when he is two, he must have the freedom to touch and explore. When he is eight, he must have the freedom to make some noise, to play, to choose his friends. For it only is by being always "free for his age" that a person comes to know liberty in such a way that he forever will choose freedom. Children never are too young to learn liberty, nor is a person ever too old to cease growing in his concept and use of liberty.

The implications of this priority—liberty—for the teacher and school are clear. Both teacher and school must be careful, on the one hand, not to boss children too much; and yet, on the other hand, not to be too permissive. There must be a delicate balance between control and liberty, with both children and teachers knowing and accepting the limits of each. Over-regulated children today will become tomorrow's passive people; yet, totally uncontrolled, licensed children today will be tomorrow's insurrectionists.

The fourth and last priority suggested is a love of law. In far too many areas of society, the idea of discipline has become old-fashioned and has fallen into ill-repute. Many schools have become partners with society in avoiding the use of, or permitting any reference to, discipline. Yet, discipline seems to be a necessary ingredient of life. And, the chances are that children, in their adult life, will come to know discipline in a much larger realm than is true today. Perhaps, there will be a world government, or, even, planetary law exercising discipline over the individual and nations. Children must come to regard highly law today, if they are to choose the way of law and order as adults.

Society should view with alarm the large numbers of children today who "get away with murder" in both school and society. Granted that children must feel comfortable and reasonably free from tensions growing out of restriction at home and school; but, they must learn that other people have rights too—father, mother, kinfolks, neighbors, friends. They must learn about discipline, but not just that control which comes only from without and which is to be obeyed only when someone bigger, or when someone in authority, is present. The world of tomorrow will be safe only if today's boys and girls carry good discipline inside themselves. In all of its dealings with boys and girls, the school must so direct and plan for and with

its pupils that the way of law and order gradually becomes their way of life. For example, the school must set wise limits geared to each child, and his age and development. Also, the school must take the time and have the patience to let the pupils in on its thinking—to explain the why of a rule or regulation. Boys and girls must hear not just a verdict handed down from on high, but the whole case for law and order.

These represent some priorities in education with which the school must busy itself. The need is urgent and demands the full and immediate energy and dedication of all America's educational and societal resources. The need is actions, not words, philosophies, and vacilation.

2 ➥ NEEDED CHANGES IN SECONDARY SCHOOLS WITH SPECIAL REFERENCE TO HEALTH, FITNESS, AND RECREATION*

J. LLOYD TRUMP
ASSOCIATE SECRETARY OF NATIONAL ASSOCIATION OF SECONDARY SCHOOL PRINCIPALS

Class size in health, fitness, and recreation, as in other areas of the curriculum, varies with the purposes and content of instruction. There are three types of classes: 100—150 (more or less) students for large-group instruction; 15 or less for small-group discussion; and various sized groups, and at times individual study, for work in learning centers in and outside the school.

Large-group instruction. The most competent available person on the school staff or from outside the school will present ideas through talks and demonstrations to relatively large groups of students in order to save time and energy of staff as well as to make these "best persons" logistically available to *all* of the students. Mostly this instruction will be conducted in face-to-face groups with the aid of an overhead projector. At other times, it will take place via television, video tape, or films.

Recreation interests will thus be stimulated by putting students in contact with someone "fired up" with an area of interest. A respected physician will describe health practices. Physical fitness will be explained and demonstrated. The most competent teacher will show how to develop basic skills in a sport. Most of the time these large groups will be coeducational. Usually the make-up of the group will depend on past

training, knowledge, and skills. The purposes will determine the constituency of the groups.

Small-group discussion. Classes of 15 or fewer students will meet regularly with a professional teacher to discuss problems and programs. The group is small so all may participate in the discussions. The teacher acts mainly as a consultant and observer. The make-up of these small classes can be changed at will as the needs of students change. The small group combines therapeutic and instructional services to students.

Independent study. The health, fitness, and recreation learning resources centers are places where students individually, or in small or large groups, learn by doing. They will learn and practice physical fitness exercises which they can also do at home. They will learn the fundamental skills of games that can be played at other times in gymnasiums and on playing fields at school and in the community. They will practice hobbies that can be recreational interests at home and in the community.

The centers provide space for physical activities as described while other centers house automated learning devices (teaching machines for self-instruction by individuals and small groups). Also there are materials to read, films to observe, dial access systems, and the like. Students are able to tell immediately whether or not they have learned, and what they need to do next. Other appropriate supplies are provided so the varied needs of students can be

*From Secondary School Athletic Administration, January 1969. p. 7, American Association for Health Physical Education and Recreation. Used by permission.

served. Obviously, not all learning takes place in the school building. Libraries, recreation areas, museums, and a variety of other community resources also are utilized, especially by pupils with special projects.

The purpose of the program is to develop individual responsibility for the student's own learning. All students will be expected to follow systematic programs of fitness, games, recreation, and good physical and mental health habits outside these minimum times. Teachers will know about these practices of students as they listen to the discussions in the small groups, observe physical and mental adjustment and developments, and analyze records of home and community activities.

Some students will study in depth in these fields just as some other students concentrate on mathematics, science, or history. These students will spend many more minutes per week in large and small groups, in the learning centers, in the gymnasiums, and on the playing fields. Some of them will play on intramural teams and others will represent the school on interscholastic teams. Who participates and to what extent will be based on professional decisions rather than on clerical decisions as in today's school. (Arbitrarily limiting participation on an interscholastic team to those passing three subjects is an example of a clerical decision.)

Student participation in programs of health, fitness, and recreation will be facilitated by the total schedule of the school. In the future other subjects will not meet on a five-day-a-week basis, but like the health, fitness, and recreation classes will be related to the purposes and content of instruction. The average student will be in regularly scheduled groups no more than 8-10 hours per week. Greater flexibility in time use will result.

The building facilities for health, fitness, and recreation, like those for other subject areas, will be available to students more hours per day, more days per week, and for more weeks in the year. Students will be under the supervision of competent adults during these extra times, but not necessarily under professional teachers.

The United States leads the world in the proportion of its youth enrolled in secondary schools. More than 16,000,000 pupils are involved. What changes in these young people is their secondary education producing? And how may the schools themselves be changed to serve these students better?

Our experiences during the past 12 years in educational innovations have produced considerable knowhow in methods of changing schools. The concepts of team teaching, independent study, large-group instruction, small-group discussion, flexible scheduling, and the like, were *then* relatively vague. *Now*, we know how to do these things and how to relate them to each other. We understand better the evaluation process.

The health-fitness-and-recreation program

Teaching and learning in health, fitness, and recreation should be required every year a pupil is in school. The same situation applies to the other seven areas of human knowledge. For all pupils there are two regularly scheduled class meetings per week—one *large-group instruction* and one *small-group discussion*—each lasting 30 minutes. Also, each week there is some required independent study in the two learning resource centers for health, fitness, and recreation. The amount of time a given pupil spends in independent study varies with his needs, interests, and talents. Some will require as little as 90 minutes per week; others as many as 8–10 hours. Each pupil's program is designed especially for him. Flexible schedules make these arrangements possible.

The instructional staff

The school program needs to dramatically change the teacher's current role of teaching 25 hours per week in conventional classrooms (often with other assigned responsibilities). In the innovative school the typical teacher (with individual variations) is scheduled with groups of pupils about 10 hours per week. Having the rest of the time free from classroom routine is essential if the teacher is to prepare adequately for the new teaching methods to be used.

This typical teacher in the innovative program should have only one or two preparations per week. These preparations involve getting ready for large-group presentations which aim to give pupils information not readily available elsewhere that will help them to learn what they are supposed to learn, to motivate them by awakening interest, and to make assignments. The oral assignments are complemented by duplicated materials which tell pupils of diverse talents and interest what they are expected to know and how to go about learning it. Each of these presentations should last about 35 minutes. The teacher's schedule also includes sitting in with pupils in groups of 15 or less who are learning how to talk to each other, how to listen, how to discuss, and how to respect each other in the process. There will be 14-16 of these groups, each scheduled for about 35 minutes.

The rest of the teacher's day is spent in planning for the independent study of pupils, checking from time to time on the independent study centers to see what progress is occurring, preparing, conferring with colleagues, improving evaluation, and in other aspects of the teaching-learning process.

Some of the teacher's time is spent in seeing pupils who need special help as they are referred to the teachers by the person supervising the independent study centers. Each teacher also serves as a teacher-counselor for about 35 pupils. She knows these pupils as total human beings, collects information about them from their various teachers and from standardized tests and inventories given by the school, and learns about their home situations. She does not regularly meet the pupils as a group.

Of course, the teacher also participates in a variety of staff meetings and independent study activities designed to help her perform these various tasks well. The teacher's work week will be reduced to approximately 40 hours, of which 30 hours are spent on the school premises.

These professional teachers need to work with three kinds of assistants. Here we use the same three categories that we described more than a decade ago in papers and in a booklet, *Images of the Future:*

1. Instruction Assistants. Housewives, upperclassmen in teacher education programs, and retired teachers, each with the equivalent of about two years of college training in the subject field in which they help, supervise independent study areas, help with preparing materials and evaluating pupil progress. They work part-time, usually 10 to 30 hours per week —the number of hours per week is equal to 20 times the number of professional teachers in the school (for example, in a school with 36 teachers, instruction assistants work a total of 720 hours per week).

2. Clerks. High school graduates with skills in typing, duplicating, record keeping, etc., whose total number of hours worked per week equals 10 times the number of professional teachers. (For example, a school with 36 teachers has 9 full-time clerks assigned to the teachers.)

3. General Aides. Housewives lacking training in a subject field or clerical skills are employed to get materials out and put them away, sell tickets, supervise non-study areas, etc.

They work part time—the number of hours per week equals 5 times the number of professional teachers. (For example, 36 teachers have 180 hours per week help from general aides.)

The foregoing assistants are paid workers, selected with care to do specific tasks. At times their services are supplemented by *community consultants* who volunteer without pay for a specific assignment such as a presentation to a student group, service as a chaperone, or preparation of a special exhibit.

Each teacher needs an office with at least partial privacy. Nearby are work areas for clerks and instruction assistants, meeting rooms, and other work rooms where teachers can design instructional materials, keep records, and the like.

The pupil's program

The typical schedule of a pupil should include about eight presentations per week, one in each of the major subject areas of the school, each lasting approximately 35 minutes. Similarly, the pupil's schedule should include one small-group discussion session of about one-half hour with about 14 other pupils in each subject field. The balance of his time, approximately 60 percent of the week, should be spent in independent study.

We define "independent study" simply as what pupils do when their teachers stop talking. It is sometimes done individually, more often in various sized groups. Pupils read, view, listen, write, and do both what their teachers require and what is described as working in greater depth or being creative. There will be a substantial increase in the quality and quantity of independent study as schools develop better resource centers and other learning areas inside the school, and as effective arrangements are made with offices, industries, museums, institutes, and other learning areas in the community. Also, school programs will develop retrieval systems that make it possible for pupils to tap resources both in the storage places of the school and in the community.

The curriculum needs to be organized on a continuous progress basis so that pupils do not waste time waiting for other pupils to catch up or by being frustrated by work which is too difficult for them. In other words, each pupil is able to find quickly his place in the required curriculum so that he can move on from where he is now to an advanced program.

The foregoing arrangements will intensify pupil motivation, as will the fact that each pupil has time to devote to studies that are particularly interesting to him or helping him toward his future goals. Superior presentations and the opportunity to meet in a small group to discuss topics that interest him will provide added motivation. Evaluation will be based on individual pupil progress rather than a comparison of the pupil with the group he happens to be in.

Introducing different evaluative criteria

Innovative schools need new criteria to replace the usual criteria now being enforced by accrediting associations and state education departments. They need to evolve more valid ways of judging the excellence of the product, based on the goals of new teaching methods. The extent to which learning is individualized for pupils, that teachers become more professional, that curriculum is refined, and that facilities are better utilized should determine the worth of the program. These schools should receive permission from accrediting agencies and state education departments to be excused from existing criteria and in their place to provide more detailed evaluations.

What outcomes should be expected? Here is one example. Students who develop more responsibility for their own learning increasingly work in learning resource centers inside and outside the school with minimal faculty supervision. Not only do they learn the essential facts, concepts, and skills of each subject, they also go beyond these minimums to greater depths and creative approaches. They demonstrate effective skills in selecting special projects, utilize appropriate human and material resources, show self-discipline and persistence, evaluate their own productivity in relation to stated purposes, and show creative solutions.

Furthermore, pupils who develop better skills in oral communications and interpersonal relations express ideas frequently in discussion groups. When they speak, they build on what others say. They use accurate facts and ideas to support their own points. They respect and show understanding of what other pupils bring to the discussion. They relate better to other persons and evoke better reactions from them.

Pupils apply what they learn in new situations. The effectiveness of the school's intercultural education program is not measured merely by how well pupils perform on tests and attitude scales. Observations are made and reported about relations among cultural groups in the school and community environment. For example, do Negroes and whites still separate in the school cafeteria or in classrooms? How do various pupils cope with community problems?

Evaluation emphasizes in many aspects the behavioral or performance outcomes of education, in addition to the acquisition of facts and understandings. The old saying, "The proof of the pudding is in the eating," applies also to evaluation. Data should be collected regularly to reveal pupil accomplishments, costs, professional accomplishments of teachers, utilization of facilities, and the like. Comparisons should be made with conventional schools of similar size, composition, and other similar characteristics. Publications should be prepared and distributed regularly to show the school's progress in achieving the foregoing goals.

Advantages of innovative schools include:

1. All students every year they are in school will receive motivation and assistance from the most able persons on the staff or in the community.

2. The professional competences, as well as individual differences in strength, of the professional teachers will be utilized.

3. Individual differences among students will be recognized more quickly in discussion groups of 15, and in work in independent study.

4. Teachers will have more time to plan and evaluate instruction. Clerks, instruction assistants, and general aids will help them accumulate data and keep better records of individual student needs and accomplishments.

5. The purpose of instruction will be to develop individual responsibility on the part of students for personal programs.

6. What happens in health, fitness, and recreation outside of school will be integrated more closely with what happens inside the classrooms.

7. The playing of games in either intramural or interscholastic competition will be an outgrowth of instruction in the classroom rather than the major determinant of how time is spent in the classroom and the nature of the spaces where instruction occurs.

8. Some significant steps will be taken to raise the professional standards of teachers. Teachers will do the teaching, clerks the clerking, instruction assistants and general aides the subprofessional tasks, and machines will automate some parts of teaching.

SELECTED REFERENCES BY J. LLOYD TRUMP

Focus on change—guide to better schools. Chicago: Rand McNally and Company, 1961, 147 pp.

Focus on the individual—a leadership responsibility. Booklet, 33 pp. and Filmstrip, 135 frames, color with sound. Washington, D.C., 20036, National Association of Secondary School Principals, 1965.

Independent study centers, January 1966, pp. 45–51 and Secondary education tomorrow—four imperatives for improvement, April 1966, pp. 86–95. The Bulletin. The National Association of Secondary School Principals.

What is team teaching? Education. February 1965, pp. 327–332.

School buildings for modern programs—some informal comments on functional architecture. The High School Journal November 1966, pp. 79–86, or Education Digest February 1967, pp. 19–22.

The first 55. Booklet, 28 pp. Washington, D.C., 20036. National Association of Secondary School Principals, 1967.

Secondary school curriculum improvement. Chapters 1, 2, 17–27, 28, and 30. Boston: Allyn and Bacon, Inc., 1968, 408 pp.

Answers and questions. 16 mm. film, color and sound. 24 min. Washington, D.C. National Association of Secondary School Principals, 1968.

Multilithed unpublished papers available from the NASSP:

Presentations and other types of large-group instruction, 6 pp.

Small-group discussion, 6 pp.

Independent study, 6 pp.

Evaluating pupil progress in team teaching, 16 pp.

Are you asking the right questions? 2 pp.

How excellent are teaching and learning in your school? 11 pp.

Providing more equal educational opportunities for youth, 9 pp.

3 ⁊ FLEXIBLE SCHEDULING FOR PHYSICAL EDUCATION*

ENID VON BERGEN
CHAIRMAN, DEPARTMENT OF PHYSICAL EDUCATION, POWAY (CALIFORNIA) HIGH SCHOOL

HARRY E. PIKE
DEAN OF STUDENTS, MICHIGAN TECHNOLOGICAL UNIVERSITY, HOUGHTON, MICHIGAN

Increasingly, the nation's physical educators are facing the problems of providing physical education for students in schools operating under a flexible, or modular, schedule. A recent count showed that over 5 percent of the secondary schools in the United States had adopted this method of scheduling, and more are doing so each year.

The advantages to be derived in most areas of the curriculum are well known, but a significant number of physical educators believe that flexible scheduling cannot be adopted in their field. Some important innovations at Poway High School in Poway, California, have not only disproved this theory but have established flexible scheduling as an important new tool in the field of physical education.

Some of the problems arising under a flexible schedule are as follows: satisfying state and local attendance requirements, utilizing facilities, and achieving major departmental goals. In their attempt to satisfy these major concerns, the Poway High School physical education staff first found it necessary to define

basic objectives and arrive at a common rationale for the teaching of their subject. The major goal, they decided, was "to provide the instructor time to help students gain advanced skills in those areas which might carry over into their adult years."

Working from this premise, the staff developed a program which revolved around two major curriculum areas: team sports and individual sports. Examples of the latter type, as they appear in the Poway High School curriculum, include golf, tennis, gymnastics, wrestling, and several kinds of dance. Both types of sport were offered for the first time at the school on an elective basis. Since Poway's student body numbers only around 850 and the Physical Education Department has only four full-time instructors, any elective type of curriculum had heretofore been impossible under a traditional schedule.

Once the rationale and the course of study had been determined, it was necessary to adapt the methodology of flexible scheduling to the new program. It was discovered that team sports could best utilize large group instruction and small group instruction. Large groups, which may meet from one to two

*From JOHPER **38**:29, March, 1967. Used by permission.

hours, are used for actual play. Small groups, ranging in size from ten to twenty students, are used for skill building, practice, and scrimmages. The stress in small groups is on individual help rather than team play.

Individual sports are scheduled in a slightly different manner. They use large groups, as do team sports, but also rely upon the open laboratory concept possible under a flexible system.

Large groups in the individual sports are used for teacher-centered presentations covering the basic skills which that sport demands. Here the instructor may lecture, may demonstrate, or may utilize a wide variety of audiovisual aids to make clear to the students the concepts involved.

The instructor, using the student's master program, also schedules him for a physical education area during a portion of his open, or independent study time each day. In this lab time the instructor works with the student individually and allows him the opportunity for practice. Because of a California State requirement, care is taken to ensure that each student receives physical education daily. Thus, a student taking golf might meet in a large group on Monday and Thursday of a given week. On Tuesday, Wednesday, and Friday he would be working in an open lab practicing the concepts presented to him in the large groups.

Sports performance curriculums

To guide the student in the open labs, and to provide a basis for evaluation, Poway's staff has developed a performance curriculum for each sport. These contain a progressive list and description of the skills involved and a space for the instructor to evaluate the student in each of the skills. Evaluation is done on a "poor," "satisfactory," or "outstanding" basis. Not until a student has mastered a given skill well enough to receive at least a "satisfactory" is he allowed to move on to the next step in the curriculum. Such a system also provides the student with both a permanent record of his strengths and weaknesses and a guide to those areas requiring special concentration during his laboratory work. The student, in effect, is then able to participate in creating his own plan of action. Among the courses taught in this manner are gymnastics I and II, dance, tumbling and trampoline, golf I and II, tennis, and wrestling. Each of these electives are offered on a semester basis with advancement in the multistage courses depending upon skill acquisition. These courses, plus the team sports, demand

a maximum utilization of the department's facilities—which has proved to be a mixed blessing. While the philosophy at Poway is that facilities should wear out from overuse and not from overage, the open lab approach has taxed them to the limit. As a result, additional physical education facilities have been included in the school's master plan.

Increased effectiveness in faculty utilization, however, has more than offset any disadvantages caused by strained physical facilities. For the first time, physical educators are able to specialize in the areas of their own personal interests, and from this opportunity have gained a high degree of personal satisfaction. Students are able to draw upon the special skills of the department's teachers in a manner not possible in the past.

Heightened student motivation

Another major benefit derived from the program is the tremendously heightened student motivation, attributable to the fact that students can participate in sports which appeal to them personally and can acquire the skills which *they* desire. Teaching the virtues of physical fitness (an important goal of the department) has become easier, since the relationship of fitness to the goals of the student is now readily apparent.

The department also utilizes the independent study phase of the flexible system to good advantage. It has built a library of films for 8 and 16 mm loop projectors devoted to the improvement of specific skills. The student can use these films (available in the audiovisual center of the school) as well as a departmental library of several hundred volumes during his independent study modules. By directing the student to the material meeting his specific needs, Poway's physical educators are able to provide truly individualized courses of instruction.

Attendance procedures have been simplified by letting student assistants check attendance, both in the large groups and the open labs. These students also act as locker room monitors —a necessity, since traffic through the locker areas is extremely heavy throughout the school day.

Scheduling problems are soluble

The problems presented to a physical education department by this form of schedule, then, are not insoluble. Given careful staff planning and a clear understanding of departmental goals, the advantages—including total facility utilization, increased student motivation, efficient faculty utilization, and individualized courses of study for the student—far outweigh the disadvantages. Flexible scheduling may well prove to be as important an innovation for the physical educator as for his colleagues in other fields.

WHAT FLEXIBLE SCHEDULING IS ALL ABOUT . . .

The best way to examine a flexible, or "modular," schedule is by comparing it to the typical traditional schedule. The latter contains from five to seven periods in the school day, with each day's schedule resembling that of every other day in the week. Very little, if any educational rationale exists for this type of schedule, which is primarily an administrative arrangement by which students can be effectively organized within the school day.

This schedule makes two basic assumptions which the creators of flexible scheduling do not share. The first assumption is that all courses need the same kinds of time, i.e., exactly fifty-five minutes a day, five days a week. Yet physical education, obviously, does not need the same kind of time as English—or art, business, the sciences, etc. Fifteen minutes could conceivably be all the time needed by the English teacher, while the physical education instructor could often use an hour and a half to two hours. Nor does every course always need the same kind of time. A chemistry teacher might need half an hour today for a lecture but two hours tomorrow for laboratory experimentation. In other words, we have been tailoring our courses to fit an artificial time pattern, rather than making time fit the needs of our courses. The other traditional assumption is that all students are the same and that the slowest student in school should take as many courses as the brightest.

In contrast, a flexible schedule operates on the assumptions that different kinds of courses need different kinds of time, and that students of differing abilities must not be chained together in a lockstep dictated by the form of the school day.

Under a flexible schedule the school day is fragmented to a much greater degree than under a traditional schedule. A typical program will contain from thirteen to twenty units of time—called "modules" rather than "periods"—varying from eighteen to thirty minutes in length, and much resembling building blocks. By stacking one module on another, each teacher assembles his courses according to the kind of time needed for the type of educational activity planned. For example, a course with two lectures a week would use two modules for this activity—one for each lecture. Since the adolescent attention span is approximately twenty-five minutes, one module is about all the time that can be used effectively in a lecture situation.

For a lecture, all the students enrolled in a given class will be assembled, enabling the teacher to make the presentation only once to all the students enrolled in, for example, American history. This is far preferable to the traditional system, which forces the teacher to repeat a lecture to classes of forty or forty-five students over and over throughout the school day. The single presentation to a large group is generally far more dynamic and effective.

The same teacher may decide to use small groups within the course structure to give students an opportunity to discuss concepts, ask questions, and relate the study material to their own personalities, their own needs. These small groups would contain from eight to twelve students, a size ensuring maximum participation, and might last for two modules, or nearly an hour.

The course might contain "lab" work as well. For this type of activity three or four modules would be strung together, giving a total block of time from an hour and a half to two hours in length. Within this length of time meaningful activity, practice, or experimentation can be conducted.

A portion of the student's school day will remain unscheduled. This time is used for individual study, for the completion of what once was "homework," for the practicing of skills, and for individual conferences with teachers, who also have portions of their day unscheduled, giving them the opportunity to work on a one-and-one basis with students.

This unscheduled time has two major purposes. First, it gives the student a chance to use the resources, both material and human, available within the school. School libraries no longer stand empty throughout the day, because students now have access to them. Secondly, it provides the student with the opportunity to learn responsibility and the decision-making process. The unbelievable failure rate among our college freshmen and sophomores is a clear indication that students have not become acquainted with this process in secondary schools under traditional programs.

Schools operating under a flexible schedule usually open any facility which is not being used by a class to students in an "open lab" situation. Here the student may practice skills, pursue his own interests beyond the scope of the regular course outline, and, using a performance curriculum, can in many cases move through a course at his own rate rather than being tied to the larger class. With performance curriculums, specific objectives are outlined for each course. These, coupled with careful evaluation, enable the student to move through a course as quickly or as slowly as he desires. Time is no longer the criterion for course completion.

Under a flexible system, some students take as many as ten courses, while a great many take seven or eight. Conversely, some take only four; given a program they can handle, they do not drop out of school, but remain to complete the work required for their diploma.

A traditional schedule is complex enough to generate. It usually requires an entire summer for administrators scheduling by hand to place the right student in the right class in the right room with the right teacher. A flexible schedule is so much more complex that its generation manually would be all but impossible. For this reason, it is done by computer, usually in connection with a larger institution. Stanford University, for example, produces the schedules for a large number of schools using this type of schedule. The computer still leaves the power to make decisions in the hands of the school administrator; the machine is merely a tool acting upon the data fed to it.

The typical computer-produced flexible schedule is not truly flexible in the sense that it can be changed at random. It is produced for an entire semester or year, and recycles weekly. No two days of the week will resemble each other, but every Monday will be the same. Total flexibility may be an imposibility, given the size and scope of today's schools. A flexible schedule, however, is an important step toward individualized instruction and toward fully utilizing the teachers' knowledge, the time available each day, the students' abilities, and the school's resources.

Creativity—or original thinking—is perhaps more needed than ever before in business. Yet business may unwittingly hamper some of the conditions that can aid creativity. Here's what can be done to foster—

4 ❧ CREATIVITY IN MANAGEMENT*

SHERMAN TINGEY
ASSOCIATE PROFESSOR OF MANAGEMENT,
ARIZONA STATE UNIVERSITY, TEMPE, ARIZONA

VAN R. VIBBER
GRADUATE STUDENT, ARIZONA STATE UNIVERSITY

The Beatles, pop art, the psychedelic influence, and a changing sense of values among young people have made creativity a popular topic with them. Some of this emphasis has been carried over to the business sphere, since business is extremely interested in today's young people. In fact, business is quite alarmed at the large number of college graduates who enter areas other than business. In an effort to attract first-rate graduates college recruiters and employment advertisements alike are boldly proclaiming, "A job at XYZ Corporation offers you a chance to use your imagination!"

This article deals with creativity and its application and importance to management. It is intended to answer the questions: What is creativity? What are the characteristics of creative individuals? Is there a need for creativity in business? Can management foster creativity? Finally, some suggested managerial guideposts for increasing creativity are also presented in some detail.

What is creativity?

"Creativity is a mysterious force, responsible for pulling primitive man out of his caves into houses, turning his arrows into rockets, supplanting his bison meat with shrimp creole, and replacing his monoliths with skyscrapers."[1]

Whenever anything new is developed creative forces have been exerted. In other words, creativity is birth. It is a natural human process. It includes the process of becoming sensitive to problems, deficiencies, and gaps in knowledge. Creativity also includes identifying key issues, searching for solutions, testing and retesting the hypotheses, and finally communicating the results.

The essential tool of creation is original thinking—thinking that takes cognizance of what others have discovered but aims to proceed beyond the point they have reached. Significantly, there is no clear line of occupational demarcation for creativity. It can be found in sports or industry as well as the arts or university research. Whatever is new and has not previously existed, or whatever improves on previous achievements, is creative.

---

*From Management Services 5:44, July–August 1968. Used by permission. This article has many implications for the creative administration of health and physical education programs.

[1] Eugene W. Jackson, "Hunting Yardsticks for Creativity," *Management Review*, March, 1965, p. 38.

Creative individuals

The creative individual is characterized by his free use of imagination and his willingness to employ fantasy. He produces a fountain of ideas and may suggest alternative ideas with little regard for their practicability. Frequently others think of his guesses as mistakes. He is distinct from the less creative, highly intelligent person who would rather play it safe and produce fewer new ideas but ideas that are more likely to be accepted as logical and practical.[2]

Intelligent people are not necessarily creative people, and vice versa. However, in certain occupational fields that require creativity admittance is based in part on intelligence. This may lead people to the incorrect conclusion that creativity is the same as intelligence. To illustrate, a group of nuclear physicists will have a superior average intelligence quotient, but among them there is no correlation between creativity and intelligence.[3]

Typically, the creative person prefers complexity, as he has the ability to keep more ideas in his head at one time than the person who is not creative. He is more independent in his judgments and more open to new experience. He is more dominant, adventurous, and emotionally sensitive and is not always pleasant. In addition, he is often more open in his feelings and emotions.

Creativity in business

"Great industries . . . are all aware that however rich and prosperous they may be at this moment, they may wake up tomorrow morning to find that some new product has been invented which makes them obsolete."[4]

According to Peter F. Drucker, the only constant in business is change, and the only profitable way to react to change is to initiate it.[5]

Indeed, changes are so rapid that a company must adapt if it is to survive. If it is to adapt successfully, there must exist in the firm an attitude conducive to creative thinking and new ideas. An operation cannot be improved unless it is changed. Thus, creativity is *essential* for the long-run success of a business.

But creativity is not the miraculous road to growth. More often creativity in the abstract is confused with practical innovation in the concrete. Take, for example, two artists both of whom have great ideas for a painting. One tells all his friends; the other dons his beret and paints. Both might be called creative. What business needs is innovation in the action-producing sense. There appears to be an abundance of ideas but a scarcity of implementation. Business is action-oriented. Without follow-through, creativity is barren, for ideas themselves are useless.

Like anything else, however, creativity can be carried to extremes. *Getting the greatest creativity without sacrificing executive control* is the heart of a key management challenge. Management cannot afford a breed of creative anarchists, nor can management afford to nurture an organizational family more interested in repeating history than in creating it. Obviously, a dilemma exists—how can an organization maintain its flexibility through creativity yet maintain the needed stability and balance required for long-run growth and profitability? The proper balance may vary from industry to industry and even from firm to firm because of differing internal and external environmental constraints. Each firm will have to find its own balance, or optimal mix of creativity and conformity; however, it appears that at present most firms could benefit from more creativity at the expense of some conformity.

Unfortunately, business has not been very successful in relating the real excitement that it can offer to capable, imaginative people; specifically, the opportunity for creativity in business has not been communicated adequately. Instead, many perceive today's business environment as one in which individuality is muffled and creativity is stifled—the view popularized in William H. Whyte's *Organization Man*.

Fostering creativity

Often, early experiences in life enforce conformity rather than creativity. Altering these established patterns is a difficult task. Nevertheless, efforts in the following four areas may serve to develop an environment which can lead to increased creativity.

[2] For a more comprehensive description of the creative individual, see Arthur O. England, "Creativity: An Unwelcome Talent," *Personnel Journal*, September, 1964, pp. 458–461.

[3] Bernard Berelson and Gary A. Steiner, in their book *Human Behavior, An Inventory of Scientific Findings*, Harcourt, Brace, and World, Inc., Chicago, 1964, offer evidence that there is no correlation between creativity and intelligence via a number of studies.

[4] A.H. Maslow, "The Need for Creative People," *Personnel Administration*, May–June, 1965, p. 3.

[5] Peter F. Drucker, "The Objects of a Business," in *Management: A Book of Readings,* edited by Harold Koontz and Cyril O'Donnell, McGraw-Hill Book Company, New York, 1964, p. 50.

Firstly, the organization must allow people to act more freely. The creative individual is unique because he reacts differently than others react to the same social forces. For example, he might question the habit of equating the majority rule principle with the majority right principle. He must be allowed to do so if his creativity is to come to the fore.

Secondly, managers must welcome disagreement and contrary viewpoints. Potential creativity and uniqueness are stifled if management expects, or even permits, carbon-copy behavior. Risk and challenge are fundamental to growth, and controversy is inevitable. Too much emphasis on loyalty leads to the equation of loyalty with agreement.

The ominous result: the rapid development of the yes man.

Thirdly, subordinates must be made responsible for, and become personally involved with, change. Everyone in the organization must be encouraged to develop ideas and to take note of others' ideas. Only then will the creative effort overcome the natural tendency to resist change.

Finally, communications must be improved. Communication is often used as a scapegoat for all organizational ills. Nonetheless, one author estimates that fifty per cent of the creative ideas within major corporations are not communicated to the right people. One obvious method of improving communications is the use of suggestion boxes. Yet, surprisingly enough, few companies utilize the idea, even though it is not uncommon to average one hundred ideas per one hundred employees in a given year.[6]

Of course, this division of effort into four areas is somewhat arbitrary. It is only meant to serve as a base for analyzing what detailed steps need to be taken to actually increase creativity.

The question naturally arises whether emphasis in these four areas will lead to increased profits. In most cases where conscious attempts to develop creativity have been employed, companies report a positive impact upon profits.[7] Sikorsky Helicopter, for example, reports a saving of fifteen dollars for each dollar spent on its training program in applied imagination. Under a similar program, Sylvania Electric reports a twenty-dollar saving for each dollar spent.[8] It

seems, then, that management can foster creativity and that in most cases it is financially beneficial to do so.

Managerial guideposts

Because conscious efforts to increase creativity appear to be financially beneficial, perhaps it is wise to look at some specific features that might be utilized in a training program in applied imagination. The features listed here are not meant to constitute a complete program; they are merely specific features that might help in achieving the four broad goals outlined in the previous section.[9]

The organization must allow people to act more freely.

Allow freedom for individuals to guide their own work. Provide them with specified and formally agreed upon areas of freedom and self-direction, gradually increasing these areas if evidence of growth in maturity and self-reliance warrants it.

The organization structure should be kept flexible.

Individual differences should be recognized; each person should be treated as a person of worth in his own right. Personnel should be assigned to work where their backgrounds, skills, and interests fit the job rather than primarily on the basis of where they are needed.

Individual personalities should be considered in making assignments and picking leaders or supervisors. Those with special talents and aptitudes should be actively sought out.

Personnel policies and working conditions should be conducive to individual prestige and professional status.

Managers must welcome disagreement.

Lead and motivate by suggestion rather than by command.

Provide opportunity for a variety of experience, change, and learning. Allow people to try occasional pet ideas without premature prejudicial criticism.

Organize special experimental groups where constructive nonconformity and originality are the main goals to be pursued.

Constructive nonconformity should not only be tolerated but encouraged.

---

[6] Charles Gibbons, "Improving the Climate for Creativity in Your Organization," *Advanced Management Journal*, July, 1964, p. 47.

[7] Jere W. Clark, "Can Creativeness be Taught?" *Management Review*, June, 1965, p. 51.

[8] D. C. Dauw, "Creativity in Organizations," *Personnel Journal*, September, 1966, p. 466.

[9] Many of these features were adapted from the book *Managing Creative Scientists and Engineers,* by Eugene Raudsepp, The Macmillan Company, New York, 1963. Raudsepp discussed only technical personnel; however, the features apply to an applied imagination program for any employee.

Subordinates must be made responsible for change.

Personal recognition should be provided for accomplishment.

Excellence and extra effort should be rewarded, and special incentives should be established for achievers.

Competence should be the primary consideration for advancement.

A high value should be placed on creative effort. Management should provide inspirational beginnings for creative projects.

There should be continuous encouragement for personnel to take refresher and advanced courses. Nontechnical skills, such as human relations, should be taught within the organization.

Workers should be convinced that they, individually, are expected to take responsibility for initiating new ideas and that management will back them up.

Communications must be improved.

Individuals should be allowed to participate in decision making and long-range planning, particularly in areas which affect them. Personnel should be kept informed about important aspects of company operations, policies, and goals.

Interchange of information and opinion among groups and departments should be encouraged.

Groups should be made aware of the pressure they bring on individuals to conform.

Communication with management should be increased, with regular discussion panels for mutual problems. Personnel should at all times be kept informed as to how timing, budget limitations, and competition will effect the creative effort.

These suggestions should be useful for individual companies to use as a starting point in developing creativity training programs designed to meet their own needs.

PROJECTS AND THOUGHT QUESTIONS

1. What are some of the changes that are foreseen in health and physical education programs in the next ten years?
2. Identify the three most significant priorities that educators must be concerned with today. What recommendations do you make for health education and physical education in order to meet these priorities?
3. Investigate one research study on the subject of leadership. What were the purposes of the study, the procedures used, the findings, and the conclusions? What are the implications for leadership in health education and physical education programs?
4. Survey programs of health education and programs of physical education, and indicate whether you feel these programs are (a) meeting the priorities of education, (b) providing good leadership for the programs, and (c) developing up-to-date curricula. Support your findings with significant facts.
5. Contrast the type of administration one finds in our schools and colleges today with that which existed twenty five years ago.
6. What part should students play in the administrative process? Support your answers with good reasoning and a sound rationale.

SELECTED READINGS

Bucher, C. A.: Administration of health and physical education programs, including athletics, ed. 5, St. Louis, 1971, The C. V. Mosby Co.

Center for the Advanced Study of Educational Administration: Perspectives on educational administration and the behavioral sciences, Eugene, Oregon, 1965, The University of Oregon.

Goldman, S.: The school principal, New York, 1966, The Center for Applied Research in Education, Inc., The Library of Education.

Griffiths, D. E.: The school superintendent, New York, 1966, The Center for Applied Research in Education, Inc., The Library of Education.

Morphet, E. L., Johns, R. R., and Reller, T. L.: Education organization and administration, Englewood Cliffs, N. J., 1967, Prentice-Hall, Inc.

Simon, H. A.: Administrative behavior, New York, 1957, The Free Press.

Halpin, A. W., editor: Administrative theory in education, New York, 1958, The Macmillan Co.

CHAPTER 2 ADMINISTRATIVE RELATIONSHIPS AND OBJECTIVES OF GENERAL EDUCATION, HEALTH EDUCATION, AND PHYSICAL EDUCATION, INCLUDING ATHLETICS

As educators, we must consider, first, the broad field of general education and, second, how our special fields of health education, physical education, and recreation fit into the total scheme of education. Each of us is part of a whole and therefore should contribute to the objectives that have been established for education as a whole. Our programs need to be administered with this thought in mind, since this is the way the programs can contribute most to the boys and girls and men and women who participate in our offerings. It is important that in addition to contributing to education as a whole, we recognize the various parts of the whole and how all the fields of specialization that comprise education can work effectively together. This is particularly true of health education, physical education, and recreation, which represent distinct and separate fields of endeavor but at the same time are closely allied and related.

In the first article in this section, Franklin Parker researches the reasons why man plays. In an extensive history of sports in America, Parker explains the changes that occurred, starting with the Puritans and continuing through the opening of Springfield College, motion pictures, radio, the automobile, the spectator boom of the 1920's and up to participant sports of the 1930's. Today's problems can be associated with the fact that big-time sports have become an entertainment spectacle. Ancient philosophers could not explain why man plays, and educators today still cannot answer that question.

Madeline C. Hunter concerns herself with how man plays and learns to play. Movement is a common denominator of human expression, and physical education must be considered an opportunity for learning about movement. Movement theory, as explained by Hunter, identifies the content to be mastered, and curriculum theory directs the organization of the learning. Movement education theories are being researched extensively throughout America, and this article explains why physical educators are testing this new theory, with much success.

John L. Miller, in a brief article, explains

how the objectives of education involve health objectives. Health, as an expression of a behavioral science, should dominate the educational system. One problem arising in this area is that teaching health through a conceptual approach, as suggested by Miller, requires retraining of teachers and updating of the methods used in professional preparing institutions. There are no answers to the questions arising in education today with special reference to health. The health educators must be frank in discussion and open-ended in approach. This approach will upgrade the image of health education and provide a healthy outlook for students.

P. C. Bechtel suggests better training for health teachers through workshops, clinics, conferences, conventions, and in-service programs, in order to improve good health for all citizens through health education. Bechtel believes that more supervisors are needed and curriculum guides should be established; only then will the image associated with health instruction be improved.

Charles B. Wilkinson writes that the nation's destiny is in the hands of the educators, since education is the key to the future. Education should not be controlled by minority pressure groups because a quality education is for everyone. In his concern for physical education as an integral part of this general education, Wilkinson believes that people enjoy playing games throughout their lives, if playing the game is not a frustrating experience. The ability to play and enjoy an activity must be taught during the school years. Physical vitality, as a result of a good physical education program, promotes intellectual vitality.

In the last reading in this chapter M. L. Rafferty, Jr., states his belief that no "physical education" is being taught in this country and that physical educators and administrators are to blame—administrators for overcrowding the gymnasiums and physical educators for allowing their classes to be "free play" periods for the students. Physical education, as defined by Webster, is "instruction in exercise, care, and hygiene of the human body." Rafferty would like to see the instruction and education put back into physical education.

Health and physical education can play an important role in the education of the youth of today. The aims of education as a whole can partially be achieved through the objectives outlined in these articles.

5 ஃ PLAY AND EDUCATION*

FRANKLIN PARKER
BENEDUM PROFESSOR OF EDUCATION,
WEST VIRGINIA UNIVERSITY, MORGANTOWN, WEST VIRGINIA

In this anxious age we need to strengthen both body and mind. We need release to soar into space, fresh air to overcome mental torpor, insight to move in new directions. Inner form and beauty can help dispel outer dross and disarray. Whatever makes for play in man also offers the educator unusual opportunity. Play touches a deep well of interest. It is a taproot, rich and vibrant, awaiting only the touchstone of action.

Why?

Why does man play? Why does he engage in sports? Why does he dignify the practice of sports as physical education?

In the beginning Puritans frowned on sports in general and on Sunday sports in particular. In the language of the New England Primer "Your deeds to mend, God attend." In the North the sporting seed was lost on rocky Puritan ground. In the West, sports, play, and dancing to the fiddle were restricted to house or barn raising festivities. In the South, Virginians aped English Cavaliers in fencing, horse racing, and fox hunting. Early American sports were at first not of the common people nor of the frontier. In the middle Atlantic states and elsewhere boxing, card playing, even baseball were an upper-class prerogative. In 1845 when members of the exclusive Knickerbocker Club in Manhattan played baseball, it was a genteel game for genteel-men.

Sports—a safety valve

But times were changing. Between 1840 and 1880 America leaped from fifth to first place among industrial nations. Immigrants poured in by the tens of millions, half of them Germans and Irish and accustomed to the relaxed European Sunday. The Puritan Sabbath retreated before the laboring man's taste for Sunday picnics and ball games. With the frontier closed, rural agrarianism in decline, and urban indus-

trialism triumphant, sports rose swiftly. One historian, Frederic Logan Paxon, has suggested that sports were the safety valve that replaced the closed frontier. Surely in 1885 when the International Young Men's Christian Association founded Springfield College in Massachusetts as a training school for physical education teachers, sports in America had reached the age of consent. And by the turn of the century as the range of sports enlarged to include every known game, sports fed original ideas to serve the American drive for speed and efficiency.

Time and motion study

Sports had a marked effect on social custom and technological advance in late 19th century America. Frederick W. Taylor was a doubles tennis champion in 1881. Not long afterwards he established the time and motion study movement and fathered the scientific management revolution. In golf and tennis he first saw the value of analysis of motion, the importance of methodical training, and the worth of time study.

Photography

Leland Stanford, president of the Central Pacific Railroad and benefactor of Stanford University, bet a friend $25,000 that a trotter in gait lifted all four hoofs off the ground. He hired a photographer to prove his point. Photographer Muybridge set up trip wires for a 24-camera-shot sequence. He proved Stanford correct and laid the basis for motion picture photography. The first commercial motion picture ever shown on a screen was a six-round boxing bout in May, 1895. The filming of boxing events took motion pictures out of the peep show and into the big time.

Radio

Radio, too, received impetus from sports. As early as 1899 when Marconi desperately needed money to perfect his wireless, the *New York Herald* paid him $5,000 to transmit via radio the finish of America's Cup Yacht race.

*From The Physical Educator 26(1):3, March 1969. Used by permission.

Bicycling

Above all the bicycle had large influence. The cycling craze took hold after improved English bikes were shown in the Philadelphia Centennial of 1876. Lady riders shortened their skirts. The feminist movement had new support. And men became interested. The League of American Wheelman, one million strong at its peak, campaigned for better roads. By 1900 half the states had passed legislation for better highways. From improved bicycles came improved ball bearings, wire wheels, hub braking, the pneumatic tire, and variable speed transmission. The bicycle industry developed tubular nickle steel and played a key role in developing the motor boat, the motorcycle, and the automobile. Orville Wright was a bicycle racer before he was an airplane builder. He and his brother, Wilbur, operated a bicycle repair shop in Dayton, Ohio.

Automobiles

Henry Ford's first cars were racers. He needed financial backing. To get moneyed people interested, he needed publicity. Racing car winners gave him the public attention he wanted. The man Ford got to race his 80 horsepower "999" engine was a professional bicycle rider named Barney Oldfield.

20th Century boom

After the turn of the century, sports hit America with a bang. Teddy Roosevelt's Cabinet was often called the "tennis cabinet." By 1919, sports represented an annual expenditure of $73 million. By the 1920's, aided by radio, the spectator boom was on. Baseball, football, and boxing drew enormous crowds. During the Depression in the 1930's the trend turned toward participant sports. The Works Progress Administration alone built 10,000 tennis courts, 3,026 athletic fields, 2,261 horseshoe courts, 1,817 handball courts, 805 swimming pools, 318 ski trails and 254 golf courses. National and state parks and fish and game sanctuaries helped extol the outdoor life.

More participation

As direct participation rose, personal attendance declined. Radio and television in our time have aided this trend. Bigtime sports have become an entertainment spectacle, set up and arranged for home listening and viewing. Advertising has become the moneyed middleman. Wrestling, boxing, baseball, and football have become largely indoor TV spectator sports.

Conversely, swimming, boating, skiing, camping, bowling, skating—in short most par-ticipant sports whether private, school, or company sponsored—are on the rise. If this is a healthy trend, how can participant sports be encouraged? How can creative use be made of the participant trend to produce physically stronger and more mentally alert Americans?

Why does man play?

One comes back to the original question—why does man play? Why does he engage in sports? Why does he dignify the theory and practice of sports as physical education?

In the beginning, the amoeba stirred and all its descendants moved and crawled and ran and roamed the face of the earth *to find favorable life conditions.* For man from the beginning *bodily development was imperative since efficient movement meant survival.* The more efficient man, physically and mentally, led others out of danger (the root meaning of the word *education* is "to lead forth").

When danger was for the moment averted and food enough was at hand, prudence may have directed the channeling of surplus energy into preparation for tomorrow's challenges. From this surplus energy during earliest times of brief leisure, in imitation of previous battles, and in exultant hope for future achievement, youth may have learned to play and to engage in sports. Whatever the origin in the dim past, sports, play, and physical development are part of man's heritage and the necessary physical complement to his mind's search for understanding and meaning.

The *richest blending of physical and mental activity occurred in ancient Greece.* It was a rare and balanced blend. Can you remove the dance and not limit Greek drama? Can you take away running, jumping, and wrestling and not weaken Greek education? Can you subtract military training and not lessen Greek citizenship?

Physical movement and intellectual ideas may well be interrelated. Socrates hammered mallet to chisel on stone before he looked for virtue in men. Plato trod the sands and rocks of North Africa before he built the Academy. In the Lyceum Aristotle trained Alexander's body before he taught him philosophy.

It is challenge that prompts response, and physical-emotive stirring coincides with thought. No civilization, no people, rise except against adversity. It was in the desert that Moses gained his insight into the Ten Commandments. Along overflowing rivers man first controlled floods and developed agriculture.

Rome never accomplished balance of mind and body. Its overemphasis on military training and underemphasis on intellectual concern led to wanton luxury and eventual decline. Where there is no wonder and the future holds no promise, then people need circuses, and brute force provides grim spectacle to satisfy base appetites.

Unexpected good often comes out of supposed evil. With Rome in decay, the barbaric hordes broke through. It took several centuries, but the Teutons who swamped the Mediterranean into the Dark Ages fused their virility into the Greco-Roman world. Physically strong and vigorous, with large families of sturdy children, these northmen assimilated and ultimately surpassed the culture they had first smothered.

Much has been said in criticism of bodily neglect inherent in the early Christian search for man's eternal soul. But prayerful cloistered walks and Benedictine field labor surely aided spiritual insight. Even in ivory-towered medieval universities young scholars found physical outlets in exuberant pranks, boisterous tavern sport, and rowdy town-gown conflicts.

When knighthood was in flower, feudal obligation was joined to religious idealism. In tournament after battle, page, squire, and knight enjoyed sports and play.

Renaissance man turned from faith to reason, darkness to light, other world to this world. The blanket of ignorance that had hidden Greece and Rome was lifted and the humanists proclaimed man's uniqueness. In the new spirit, Vittorino de Feltre's court school at Mantus was called "The Pleasant House." Sports, play, and physical development were vigorously revived.

The Reformation that split the church may have briefly eclipsed this revival as Protestant groups disciplined themselves to find through Holy Writ the way to God. *Out of this reform came three thinkers whose ideas had profound impact on sports and play.* First, *John Locke,* the English Puritan, whose *tabula rasa* theory held that the mind is like a blank tablet on which experience writes. In his "Essay Concerning Human Understanding" Locke denied innate ideas. He threw doubt on the existence of Plato's divine truths, imbedded supposedley in rational thought, which by careful education in selected individuals could be nurtured to fruition. Locke's empiricism had several implications. If experience is everything, then all men are born with equal potential; human depravity is disproved; and man at birth is neither good nor bad but neutral, a being shaped by environment and experience. Locke's ideas influenced the English Enlightenment, the

French Age of Reason, the French and American Revolutions. From Locke flowed religious deism and philosophical skepticism.

Locke reopened an age-old philosophical problem: does knowledge come from the rational mind or from the objective world? This problem was examined by a small, frail man, *Immanual Kant* (1724–1804), German professor at the University of Königsburg. The objective world, said Kant, is indeed the source of much of our knowledge—but not all. Space and time do not exist as realities outside of the mind. Neither does the concept of God or religion or morality or the sense of duty or the sense of beauty. These the mind of man alone supplies. The senses may transmit the crude materials of knowledge but the mind has categories and structure which give meaning and understanding to complex impressions. In reinstating Idealism, Kant pointed to a connecting link between the physical world of things and the mental world of ideas.

Schiller ends this trilogy of great thinkers, Johann Christoph Friedrich Schiller (1759–1805), German poet, dramatist, historian, and philosopher who died in his 46th year. It was Schiller, following Kant, who gave us an aesthetic theory of play. His "Letters on the Aesthetic Education of Man" deserves to be studied by educators. It is profound and beautiful. Locke had said that the mind was passive and that sense impression was all. Kant had said that sense experience transmits crude impressions to the mind which through its own categories provides meaning and substance. Schiller said that in giving meaning and substance to sense impressions, the mind takes flight into imagination; he found the connecting link between mind and matter to be creative imagination. Aesthetics unites the sensory and the rational nature of man. It is this aesthetic link that evokes surplus energy, physical movement, and spontaneous play. It is an inborn desire to create form out of impressions. Beauty feeds the emotions, controls instinct, excites the soul, and sublimates passion. It explains the spirit of romance. It is the heart of the creative act. It is the sublime in education on which Pestalozzi, Froebel, Herbart and others have sought to build a better mankind.

It is easy to wax eloquent about Schiller's aesthetic theory of play. Philosophers have not dwelt sufficiently on it. Nor have physical educators, or their doctoral candidates. *More research is needed on why man plays and engages in sports. Perhaps he does so to recapitulate the cultural history of his species,* relive his ancestors' times of danger and victory, feel anew the struggles of old and gird himself for battle. This is one theory. Let us call it the *Recapitulation* theory.

Perhaps he does so because from infancy he has a will to power, to master his environment, to be aggressive and to win, to prove his superiority by competitiveness, for youth to emulate and to match adult strength. Let us call this the *Will to Power* theory.

Perhaps it is because he needs a catharsis, to let loose his animal instincts, to yell and push and kick and shove and snarl away his animal nature. Let us call this the *Catharsis* theory.

Perhaps, as Schiller has said, *man plays and engages in sports to give satisfaction to his creative imagination.* He plays and moves and strives somehow in some way to build and create beauty. Let us call this the *Aesthetic* theory.

Concluding statement

Why does man play and engage in sports? Probably for all these reasons. All of our theories may be but variations of one theme. Man is an unfinished creature placed on an unfinished planet in an unfinished universe. Even man's concept of God is unfinished. Up to now, work has necessitated education, or the leading forth of the young. Hereafter, in a technological age with increasing leisure, play must be the touchstone through which educators unlock the door to a creative tomorrow.

6 ❧ THE ROLE OF PHYSICAL EDUCATION IN CHILD DEVELOPMENT AND LEARNING *

Madeline C. Hunter
Principal, Elementary Laboratory School,
University of California at Los Angeles

Gone are the days when an overworked teacher could look forward to putting the children out to pasture with a ball and call the resultant activity "physical education." Gone are the days when "free play" was a sanctioned period during which the teacher sat on a bench and restored her nervous system to equilibrium. These are the days when physical education is no longer a respite *from* but an opportunity *for* learning. Physical education now has meaning as a sequence of skills, attitudes, and knowledge prescribed for the learner so he may achieve essential movement and other related objectives deemed appropriate for him by carefully trained physical educators.

The gap between theory and practice in physical education—what we know and what we do—remains large, but the contributions from movement theory, curriculum theory, and learning theory can rapidly close that gap. Movement theory identifies the content to be mastered. Curriculum theory helps us organize that content for learning. Learning theory suggests economical and effective ways of achieving movement objectives. As we discuss these three components of a valid physical education program, we shall see how each of them complements and supplements the others.

Movement theory provides content

I will not attempt to summarize current knowledge of the elements space, time, force, and flow as they are organized in movement theory, but it is essential to emphasize the importance of that knowledge. Most behavior is movement of one kind or another and consequently learning usually has movement as its foundation. Through movement the young child learns the difference between the "me" and the "not-me" which is essential to the ability to integrate form. Form perception, or his ability to assign meaning to form, is based on his posture, laterality (map of inner space), and directionality (map of outer space). His space perception or awareness of the relationships between forms is even more obviously developed by movement. His motor behavior is the primary channel through which cognitive and affective behavior are evident to others. Thus motor behavior provides the observable evidence of learning.

We hear a great deal these days about a child's readiness to learn. It is important to stress that readiness is not only preparedness to learn but is also the result of learning and consequently can be taught. For example, reading readiness is a complex cluster of more basic abilities, many of them grounded in movement, such as the ability to locate objects in space, track a line of type from left to right, and

* Speech presented at Southwest District AAHPER Leadership Clinic in Elementary School Physical Education, January 11, 1968, Phoenix, Arizona. From JOHPER 39:56, May 1968. Used by permission.

perform the transformation between space and time as words in space are transformed into sounds in time. All of this "readiness" is the result of appropriate experience in movement. If deficient, this readiness is responsive to remediation by movement education. Once we accept the fact that readiness is learned, we no longer fall into the trap of "give them more time and it will happen" or "send them home until they are ready" which has ensnarled or crippled so many in education. Better that we give the additional time at home to those who are "ready," for it's obvious that whatever they have done at home has been productive. Equally obvious is the fact that the "unready" should spend no more time at home on that which has demonstrably produced poor results; they need our immediate intervention at school to teach the movement and other learning that will "get them ready."

As we consider movement learning, we look to the theorists to analyze the locomotor, non-locomotor, and manipulative skills so that we know the components of such complex movements as skipping, twisting, and catching a ball. We also need to know the sequence of subskills which are essential to the accomplishment of a more complex skill. For example, catching is a more difficult task than throwing because it involves making both perceptual judgments as a ball is visually tracked and motor judgments to get the body in the proper position in space and time, plus closing the hands correctly at the appropriate second. Consequently, rolling a ball on the ground to a child who is learning to catch, reduces space to two dimensions rather than the three he must monitor if the ball is coming through the air and also eliminates the difficult problem of positioning his body in space. In like manner, the ability to deal in movement with the unseen space behind him is essential sublearning to running backwards or moving flexibly in all directions.

What curriculum theory tells us

Knowledge of curriculum theory helps us organize the essential content of movement into learning opportunities for children so an orderly, sequential, and more predictably successful program is developed. Simpson's taxonomy of the psychomotor domain and the Gutteridge rating scale of motor skills have supplied us with productive information at this point. As we plan to teach, we must first provide for the learner's perception of the movement task. Are the sensory stimuli actually being received and assigned significance, or are they being ignored

or rejected? From the universe of stimuli impinging on his consciousness is the learner selecting out the appropriate cues, such as the position of the ball and the thrower's feet, or is he focusing on the thrower's tongue or a bird in a nearby tree? Has he engaged in the mental process of translating these perceptions into movement? Only if these aspects of psychomotor perception are in process can we say the learner has perceived the movement task.

Our second concern is with the learner's set, or predisposition to act. Is he physically, intellectually, and emotionally ready and prepared to attempt the movement task? Third, we must provide an opportunity for a guided response, an overt movement which may be imitative, trial and error, or done with verbal or physical guidance of the teacher or another child. Only after these three steps have been successfully completed can a movement skill become a usable and habitual part of the learner's movement repertoire.

Finally, after these responses the learner achieves the complex overt movement response where all uncertainty has been resolved and his performance is automatically elicited in any situation where it is appropriate. It is interesting that we usually focus only on this terminal level of competence and think of such skills as racing, ball playing, tumbling, or swimming rather than the full spectrum of all levels of the taxonomy which are necessary to achievement of such an automatic skill. We assign academic tasks of varying difficulties to children in a classroom, yet it remains acceptable that they all engage in the same movement task in the physical education period. As a result we complain when a boy is standing on the sideline and insist that he "get in the game," hoping he will develop ballplaying skills. We wouldn't think of making this same pedagogical error by placing a poor reader in a research library hoping he will learn to read.

The current trend for individualizing instruction is pointing out the serious error of classroom practice which assumes that the same movement task is appropriate for all learners in a group. Contemporary theory mandates differentiating learning tasks on the basis of a diagnosis of each student's position in the sequence of learning. As a result, school organization for instruction must change: one classroom with one or two balls is no longer defensible.

Current curriculum theory is also demanding that we build precision in our instruction by specifying in behavioral terms our instructional objectives. "Enjoying team games" or "learning motor skills" will no longer suffice as our educational destination in a physical education program. Such unassessable objectives must be precise and specific objectives expressed in behavioral terms. "Catching a large ball when it is thrown with moderate force to a position between his waist and shoulders" or "catching eight out of ten baseballs thrown from any direction to his general position" tells the instructor the type of learning opportunity to plan and whether or not the objective has been achieved.

How learning theory contributes

As movement theory provides us with content to be mastered and curriculum theory directs us in its organization to attain clearly specified objectives, we turn to learning theory to enable us to accomplish those objectives. Here again, critically needed but currently little used knowledge is now available. Psychological theory is rapidly being translated into language intelligible to and therefore usable by teachers. Motivation theory has identified six variables which may be manipulated by a teacher so a student will more earnestly engage in learning movement skills. The factors which will increase the speed and degree to which he learns a skill have been identified. As a result, a teacher may make valid and productive decisions of how much to practice and for how long a time, what to reinforce and what to extinguish, and which sensory modalities will yield the greatest input, to mention only three of the many factors identified as important in rate and degree of learning.

Retention theory has specified five factors with which a teacher must be concerned to minimize the "fall out" of forgetting, and transfer theory guides the teacher in planning learning so it is available to the child and used in all situations where it is appropriate. The physical educator must become so conversant with this psychological knowledge that he too has resolved uncertainty and achieved the skill of automated valid performance in his teaching.

The current trend to move physical education from an activity whose purpose was to drain off fatigue from other learnings to a period for learning of the utmost importance is long overdue. However, still undiscovered by many who are designing education for the twenty-first century is the certainty that the learner will retain his own mind and body though all else in his environment may change. The physical educators are in the unique position of knowing that movement education, which includes the knowledge of the use of the learner's body, is sure to be necessary to the learner twenty or fifty years hence. In the art of movement we find the common denominator of all human expression, a foundation for learning, and a release from the damaging inner tension which is so pernicious in our society.

With this new prominence comes the responsibility for designing and executing a physical education program which incorporates present knowledge in movement, curriculum, and learning. The challenge is great. Are we up to it? I think so—let's get moving!

7 ❧ SHARED HEALTH OBJECTIVES FOR SCHOOL AND SOCIETY*

JOHN L. MILLER
SUPERINTENDENT, GREAT NECK
(NEW YORK) PUBLIC SCHOOLS

It is an acknowledged fact that schools are maintained in order that the interests of society may be served. We all recognize that a democratic society requires that the individuals within it must be strong both for their own sakes and for the sake of that society. It follows, then, that one objective of education must be the development of a healthy individual, possessed of adequate health knowledge, sound health attitudes, and satisfactory health habits, as well as a concern for a healthful environment for

himself and his fellow men. Such an objective is by no means new. It was voiced in 1910 by the first White House Conference on Child Health and Protection, found expression in the Cardinal Principles of Secondary Education in 1918, was endorsed by the Educational Policies Commission in 1938, and has been given lip service by countless school administrators. Further, it may be pointed out that satisfaction of other accepted objectives of education may be impaired unless the health objective is adequately achieved. What is the value of an educated person who, because of poor health, is unable to apply that which he has learned? Our

*From The School Health Review, p. 20, September 1969. Used by permission.

critics are quick to tell us that we are too ready to assume the responsibilities of society itself, but if we are to effectively educate the child, we must seek to have him in such a total state of well-being—physical, emotional, mental, and social—that he can learn within the limits of his capacity.

The problems of society are to a degree the problems of the school. Some of these health problems are as follows:

1. Narcotics and drugs.
2. Alcohol.
3. Tobacco.
4. Family situations—marriage, divorce, population explosion.
5. Poverty, poor housing, malnutrition.
6. Public and consumer health.
7. Epidemiology.
8. Catastrophe survival.
9. Mental health and personality development.
10. The "hippie" and his disregard for accepted health behavior.

Unrest on the campus—and even in the public schools—is a health problem in the broadest sense. Unfortunately, society too often looks to the schools to eradicate such problems via the educative process. Too often, the schools alone cannot meet the challenge. What are the problems that the schools face?

I. *Problems of Teacher Preparation*

1. Where do we find qualified health teachers? College emphasis on liberal arts makes them hard to find.
2. Who is teaching these teachers how best to teach children?
3. Even those teachers who *are* properly qualified often are geared to the anatomical and physiological fundamentals of health. Where is their self-training and insight in the behavioral sciences? Do they understand that their approach to pupils, especially in the secondary schools, must be dialogue-centered and open-ended? Do they understand that the "do's and don't's" that characterized the messianic technique will no longer be accepted by today's young people?
4. How do we retrain our present teachers?

II. *Problems of the Health Curriculum*

The biggest problem is not what to put into the curriculum but what to leave out, which has been commented on by John I. Goodlad in *Health Education,* a publication of the Bronfman Foundation's School Health Education Study. In describing today's educational dilemma, Dr. Goodlad says:

> The selection of most significant bits of content no longer is difficult; it is impossible. Consequently, teachers and pupils must seek out those fundamental concepts, principles, and methods that appear to be most useful for ordering and interpreting man's inquiries.

It is interesting to compare the approaches to health curriculum content that reflect Dr. Goodlad's statement in two of the studies with which I am most familiar. The School Health Education Study, under the leadership of Elena Sliepcevich, has moved in the direction of the *conceptual* approach as its materials were developed. John Sinacore, in his guides for the New York State Education Department, has structured his content on *strands* that run vertically through the grade levels. And yet Dr. Sliepcevich's ten concepts and Dr. Sinacore's five strands appear to be quite comparable in total scope and sequence. The problems raised for us as we look at these new materials are many. Some of the major ones are as follows:

1. How do we bend the techniques and procedures used by our present teachers to meet the new conceptual approach?
2. How do we achieve consistency in the educational background of our teachers of the future?
3. How do we maintain flexibility of our health content so that it will always be applicable to the local situation in which it is being taught?
4. How do we reach the pupil to the extent that his personal living habits are affected by the content under discussion?

An elaboration of this last point may be pertinent. Attempts to impress teenagers today with the dangers of experimenting with "soft" drugs—pep pills, depressants, and especially marihuana—are often greeted with derision. Teachers, who are considered out of tune with the times, are challenged with such questions as "How do you know? Have you ever tried it?" Arguments from students range from "Marihuana is no worse than alcohol," to "My civil liberties are being denied me and I am actively working for the repeal of the law that prohibits the sale of marihuana." Curiosity, also, may lead to experimentation, which often leads to outspoken antagonism to the teacher who is trying to emphasize its dangers. Few are prepared to teach about the use of drugs, and there is a paucity of valid materials and positive long-range programs in this problem area.

The teacher of health education often runs into a similar type of student reaction when dealing with teenagers on the topic of sex education. His ability to conduct frank and honest discussion is paramount, but care must be exercised lest he be drawn into a statement of personal experience, or lack of experience, when asked "How do you know?" or "Did you ever?"

I have raised questions and called attention to problems. It is to be hoped that through workshops and meetings, discussion will lead us to answers and solutions.

8 BETTER SCHOOL HEALTH INSTRUCTION—A CHALLENGE THAT FACES OUR PROFESSION *

P. C. BECHTEL
SUPERVISOR, HEALTH EDUCATION AND CIVIL DEFENSE,
OHIO DEPARTMENT OF EDUCATION

High on the priority list of American goals is good health for all our citizens. As the late President John F. Kennedy once said, "The strength of our democracy is no greater than the collective well-being of our people. The vigor of our country is no stronger than the vitality and will of all our countrymen. The level of physical, mental, moral, and spiritual fitness of every American citizen must be our constant concern."

Within the past two decades great strides have been taken for improving the health status of our population. This has been brought about by a combination of many factors—improved public health programs, new drugs and other medical discoveries, more and better equipped hospitals, better medical care, expanded health insurance plans, and improved school health programs.

But are we moving rapidly enough? Are we achieving the objectives which are expected of the school health program? Are schools lagging behind in making adjustments and changes in their curriculum to meet the health needs and problems of youth created by a rapidly changing society? Are we placing enough emphasis on the health education of our children and youth?

The answers to these and related questions vary, of course, with different school systems. Some are doing an outstanding job in health education. But obviously, in the one area of the total health education program for which schools are most responsible—health instruction—the results are not satisfactory. This fact is substantiated by several recent research studies, such as the Bronfman "School Health Education Study" and by the numerous physical and emotional health problems found today among our school population.

In two studies just completed in Ohio—one by Dr. John H. Williams, formerly of Bowling Green State University, but now at the University of California, and another by the Ohio Department of Education on "A Study of Attitudes and Knowledge of School Superintendents Toward the Public School Health Program" many of the school administrators expressed dissatisfaction with the results accruing from the health instruction program. At the same time, most felt that the program has great inherent values and that increased emphasis should be placed on this area of education. Here are just a few of the many statements taken at random from these studies:

"Presently, health is one of the most useless courses in our curriculum. This need not be true—it could be one of the most valuable."

"Our teachers have difficulty in making health interesting. It lacks challenge to the students."

"Before Sputnik, Rickover and Title III, I vaguely remember health education as one of the Cardinal Principles of Education. In general, I doubt if it is being treated as such."

"It would seem to me that health education is one of the more important areas of our curriculum. Much needs to be done in this area."

The results of these and other studies indicate that a concentrated effort needs to be taken for upgrading the health instruction programs in our schools. How can this be accomplished? Who should assume the leadership? Where should we start?

Below are listed six approaches which, in my opinion, should be used in attacking this important and pressing problems. Many other devices and procedures must be used also, but these are ones which deserve immediate and serious consideration in planning for better health education.

*From The Journal of School Health 35:419, November 1965. Used by Permission.

Number one—better prepared and more interested teachers

This should be our first concern and where our major emphasis should be placed during the next few years for improving school health instruction. In the majority of schools today the teaching of health is a secondary assignment for the teacher. Usually his or her major interest is in some other area—science, home economics, physical education, or coaching. True, these subjects make many worthwhile contributions to health but health understandings and attitudes are not the principal contributions they make to the development of the child. As long as this situation exists, high quality health instruction programs will be impossible.

Modern youth need adequately prepared health teachers just as badly as they need well-qualified teachers of science, mathematics, and English. This is essential for worthwhile results. It takes a person with a major interest and an adequate preparation in health education to make health challenging and vital to our students. But as long as teachers look upon health-teaching as something 'extra' and school administrators consider it of secondary importance, we can never achieve the potentialities of the program. This kind of a philosophy results in large classes, failure to provide teaching aids and sufficient time for the program, and a lack of interest and enthusiasm on the part of the teacher, administrative staff, and pupils.

At least three things need to be done for securing better prepared health teachers. First of all, state departments of education need to do whatever they can to promote workshops, conferences, prepare and distribute materials, interpret the program, and promote any other activities which will improve health instruction. Most important of all, they need to take a good look at their certification standards if they have not done so recently. Are state requirements high enough to prepare a person to teach health adequately? Are enough content courses required? Have the certification standards for health teachers been revised in recent years?

Second, teacher education institutions need constantly to evaluate their health education program. Is the professional library kept up to date? Are enough reference books and teaching aids made available to students? Are available community resources being used? Are well-qualified personnel assigned to teach the health education courses? Does the college have sufficient staff for preparing teachers in a field as broad as health, physical education, recreation and athletics and at the same time meet the requirements in these areas for the entire student body of their institution?

And last, health teachers themselves should grow on the job. They need to belong to our professional organizations, attend health conferences and conventions, keep abreast of the times by reading the latest professional books and magazines, and attend summer schools and health education workshops periodically. Only in this way can the health teacher become and remain qualified to do an adequate job in teaching health.

Number two—more extensive in-service education programs

This is a corollary to Number One. An effective in-service education program is one of the ways that schools can help prepare teachers for their responsibilities in health instruction. Even teachers with relatively broad backgrounds of preparation in health will find it difficult to keep abreast of the rapidly increasing fund of health knowledge unless the school promotes a well-organized in-service education program in school health.

Many schools have developed very worthwhile in-service education programs. Several schools have conducted clinics and conferences for teachers in such areas as smoking and health, teenage drinking, nutrition, family living, dental health, and traffic safety. On the other hand, many schools do very little in the way of providing in-service education programs for their health teachers. When well planned in-service education programs are made available to teachers, the quality of health instruction programs, in most instances, improves greatly.

Number three—more supervisory services

This is badly needed both on a state and local level. At the present time, many state departments of education have only one person to supervise the entire program of health, physical education and recreation. At least a dozen states do not have even one person assigned on a full-time basis to all these areas. When one considers the extent that health and physical education programs have expanded in the past thirty years, it becomes obvious that very few state departments of education have adequate personnel to fulfill all the functions and responsibilities required of a state supervisory staff. Increasing state supervisory staff would be very helpful in most states in improving health instruction programs.

Although several city boards of education have a larger staff of health and physical education supervisors than their state department of education, the need for more supervisory services on the local level is great in many communities. Most city school systems have only one supervisor of health and physical education. Often he is also the athletic director. When this is true, his responsibilities for making out schedules, planning tournaments, supervising the physical education program require so much of his time that he is unable to do a good job of supervising the health education program.

It is obvious that maximum contributions from the health instruction program will be difficult, if not impossible, to achieve until more supervision is provided both on a state and local level.

Number four—better coordination for health education

Health education today is very complex and involves many people and many agencies. For this reason, organizing for group planning should be one of the very first steps taken for developing a school health program. When this is done, much can be accomplished in the way of producing materials, promoting conferences and workshops, developing standards and teaching guides, and motivating interest in the programs.

In spite of its inherent values, schools have been slow to organize health committees or councils or appoint members from their staff to serve as health coordinators. Even many states do not have state planning committees for health education; yet these have proved invaluable in the states where they are organized in improving health instruction programs. Lack of group planning for health education is a major obstacle toward progress in school health.

Number five—curriculum guides

Effective health instruction programs do not come about accidentally. They are the products of careful planning and considerable work. Since health instruction can be incorporated in the curriculum in so many ways, more planning is probably required for this teaching area than for any other subject. Unless the program is carefully planned and built on sound principles of health education, no worthwhile results can be expected.

A carefully selected committee should be assigned to plan the program, with its work ultimately resulting in the development of a curriculum guide. This guide should be practical,

fairly detailed, and developed upon the following guidelines.

1. The development of a curriculum guide should be primarily the responsibility of the local community curriculum director, supervisors, teachers, local health personnel, parents and other local leaders. State and college health educators should be used as resource people whenever their services can be helpful.
2. Both the school administration and faculty must be willing to give time and effort to the project.
3. Careful attention must be given to the scope and sequence of health topics to prevent serious omissions and needless repetition.
4. Health educators should be represented on every school comiittee assigned to prepare to guide in health education.
5. The school should provide needed references for building a curriculum guide.
6. The guide should contain, in general, the following information:
   a) Philosophy of health education
   b) Health problems and needs of the pupils in the school
   c) Goals—in terms of understandings, attitudes, and habits to be developed at various grade levels
   d) Broad units of instruction for each grade level
   e) Teaching techniques
   f) How to motivate the program
   g) Suggested list of activities and learning experiences
   h) List of teaching aids
   i) List of resources
   j) Sample teaching units

Number six—a better image of health education

One of the greatest problems facing health education is to win support for the program from school administrators and the general public. To us in the profession this would seem to be a comparatively easy undertaking. Unfortunately, however, there exist many misconceptions regarding the value and place of health education in the school curriculum. Here are just a few of the several misunderstandings that school and lay people often have relative to health instruction.

1. There is no room for health instruction in a crowded curriculum, especially under mounting pressures for excellence in academic subjects.

2. Compared with science, mathematics and many other subjects; health education is relatively trivial and superficial.
3. Pupils get all the health instruction they need in other subject areas, such as biology, general science, and social science.
4. Health education is uninteresting, boring and a waste of time on the part of the pupils.

Correcting these misconceptions and building a better image of health education is a serious challenge facing our profession. Until we do,

health instruction will have difficulty in finding its rightful place in the school program; and without good health education programs our students will leave our schools not properly prepared to cope with their problems related to growth, development and adjustment.

These are some of the approaches which we must use in order to improve our school health instruction programs. But these are challenges which we must meet, and meet now, if we are to inspire children and youth to develop the kind of fitness we are asking of them today.

9 ᒣ QUALITY PHYSICAL EDUCATION—A SCHOOL RESPONSIBILITY*

CHARLES B. WILKINSON
SPECIAL CONSULTANT TO THE PRESIDENT

I recognize very clearly the complexity of the decisions you face. Education, like most human decisions, becomes a problem of priorities. What value do we place on our different responsibilities, all of which are clearly recognizable?

What I wish to talk to you about is the fact that not enough schools and administrators and not nearly enough school boards have recognized the vital importance of quality health education and physical education programs as part of the school curriculum. Part of this is past policy, I know. There is always a squeeze on dollars and it is difficult to change.

Dr. Cross who was president of the University of Oklahoma had a cartoon on his desk that I always enjoyed every time I went to see him. This showed an executive-type individual behind a desk, hitting it with great force, and underneath the caption it said, "Of course, there is no reason for it. It is just our policy".

I feel this has a certain degree of validity as to the way many school boards have looked at the health education and physical education programs.

You people do have what to me is an awesome responsibility. You have heard it said too often, but it still remains true that education is the key to the future. What this Nation will become in the decades ahead will be the direct result of the educational programs administered by you people and your counterparts throughout the Country.

I feel that the American ideal of equal educational opportunity is one of the most meaningful of all the convictions we have had as a society. I believe that we are making progress toward the realization of it even though, as you are well aware, we have not been able as yet to create actual equality of opportunity perfectly.

In this regard, I believe we must recognize clearly the obligation we have to provide quality educational opportunities for every youngster because this is the heart and soul of the American heritage.

I had this brought home to me very convincingly a few years ago. I was invited to attend the *Look* All-American Football dinner in New York. The All-American fullback was Jim Baktiahr of the University of Virginia and I had heard he was an Iranian prince. I thought of the oil wealth of the Near East and was anxious to meet this young athlete to learn more of his background. I didn't get a chance to meet him during the reception before dinner. Following the banquet, during the awards, to avoid the repetition of each player coming up, receiving his All-American watch and saying, "Thank you, I accept this on behalf of my teammates and coaches"; Mel Allen, master of ceremonies, asked each boy a question. When he introduced Jim, I was pleased that he asked him, "Is it true you are an Iranian prince?".

Jim Baktiahr said, "No, Mr. Allen, and I am glad you asked me because it gives me an opportunity to correct a misunderstanding that many people have. It is true that I am a native of Iran. My family was allowed to come to this Country as immigrants because of their skills. My father is a medical technician and my

*Address at the Annual Convention of NYSSBA, Syracuse, New York, October 24, 1967. From The Journal of the New York State School Boards Association, Inc. **31**:35, December 1967. Used by permission.

mother is a nurse. I was 14 when we came to America. I could speak very little English when we arrived eight years ago, but tonight you are calling me 'All-American'".

I think this story does indicate the faith this Nation has had in the equal opportunity for all. I think it is also self-evident that the quality of any nation depends on the quality of the individual citizen and that results only from the quality of his education.

What that means, again to put it very bluntly, is that our Nation's destiny is in your hands and those of your counterparts throughout the Country because you are the authorities that will determine the future.

I would like to add parenthetically to what the previous speaker, Dr. Brind, said and from what Dr. Allen said last night as I read his remarks. You people must maintain the judgment and decision controls that are vested in you. You must not be pressured by minority, self-interest groups. You are representatives of the citizens. It is your responsibility to see that education be conducted according to your best insights.

I would like to address myself to this physical education, health education problem, but I would like at the outset to be bluntly frank and say I want to sell you on the importance of this part of the curriculum. You control the administration of education. New York State school curricula will reflect your convictions.

As long as I have been acquainted with education, we have talked in terms of the whole child. I don't think anybody questions the validity of the statement, but, practically speaking, do we mean it?

Relating back to physical education, in a cursory examination we find we don't. Less than five percent of the elementary schools in this Nation have a gymnasium. Less than 14 percent of the secondary schools offer any instructions in the so-called "carry-over" sports. If you make a survey of health instruction, it is obvious also that, while we may have courses, they have not been motivating enough to convince some students that they should practice the principles taught. We face a hard, obvious, basic, but often overlooked, fact—man is a physical being.

Whether we like to accept it or not, we are physical beings and we function only as well as our good health, vigor, and vitality enable us to function. Our intellectual ability and our intellectual performance is based totally on our good health, vigor, and vitality.

Moving forward many centuries to a modern educator of stature, Dr. David Henry, president

of the University of Illinois, says, "The premise that physical vitality promotes intellectual vitality and contributes to academic performance as well as emotional stability is one that every school should embrace and implement. The notion that physical well-being will take care of itself among young people or that intellectual vitality is something apart from good health can no longer be tolerated as an institutional attitude in view of the overwhelming scientific evidence on the subject".

Again going back to the survey of what we have done, it is evident that we have not met our responsibilities in this phase of the curriculum.

Let me define terms quickly.

"Physical fitness" is a term everyone is familiar with. What is it? Some say freedom from disease. This is not inclusive enough. If you are physically fit, you must be free from disease, but you must also have the ability to perform. This quality, physical fitness, is analogous to a simple tripod—the three legs are a proper amount of rest; an adequate, well-balanced diet; and sufficient exercise. In our society we have severe problems in the areas of diet and exercise.

One more quick statistic: 54.8 percent of the deaths in America today are caused by cardiovascular diseases. The medical profession is unanimous in its opinion that proper diet and sufficient exercise will assist in delaying the onset and in controlling the factors which account for the majority of these diseases.

The problem, of course, is one of motivating the individual and motivation only can be achieved through good instruction. What your schools are able to do will depend on the value placed on this area of the curriculum.

You may agree fundamentally with some of the things I have been saying, but whether any change actually takes place will depend on the degree of motivation you possess.

Poor programs, I feel, to a degree have been caused by varsity athletics. Let me explain why, but, before doing so, let me make it clear that I am totally supportive of varsity athletics. It has to be an either or situation, or that you cannot have good health education and physical education and good intramural programs and also have good varsity programs. However, concentration on varsity athletics has allowed, unknowingly perhaps, those responsible for school programs to let this substitute for what should be done for the other children in the school system.

Let me be blunt. For example, if your basketball team is winning the state championship or playing a reasonably successful season, the average constituent assumes you must have a good physical education program for everyone. If this team is playing that well, it will draw enough in-gate receipts to pay for itself. Thus, you haven't spent any educational funds for a program that unknowingly substitutes for physical education for all students.

I would like to describe quickly what I think a good program ought to be in hopes you relate it a little to what is happening in your school today. I would like to preface it by saying I believe this should be compulsory. I make no apology for it. The reason I say it is because in this curriculum area the people who need it most are not the most likely to volunteer. At the outset they will not have good coordination and will not do physical things well. They feel embarrassed and won't want to participate, but we must remember that these children will function as adults or as well as their health and physical vigor permit.

If education does not condition people for the world they will actually be involved in, it has failed to meet its responsibilities.

Quickly, a good program of health and physical education would begin with adequate continuing health examinations for every child with dental and medical care provided in some manner, and I know it is a complex area, to remedy those deficiencies that are remedial; basic developmental programs to bring each child up to an adequate level of strength, coordination, and flexibility; instruction in the carryover sports or lifetime sports so these people will have a skill in sports, hopefully a variety of skills, that they will be able to use throughout their lives.

Let me expand on that quickly. You can achieve excellent condition by doing calisthenics, but I have never known anybody who maintained physical fitness by calisthenics alone throughout life because they become boring.

The Foundation I am associated with, the Lifetime Sports Foundation, has the following philosophy. People enjoy playing games if they play them well enough to derive satisfaction instead of frustration from the experience. If a game frustrates you, you obviously won't continue to play, and the key to avoiding frustration is good instruction at an age when the muscles are easy to teach, during the school years.

There is a physical quality which everyone possesses, kinesthetic memory or muscle memory. If you have learned physical skill, it stays with you. Riding a bicycle is a good example. If you ever learned to ride a bike, 40 years can go by without riding, but you can still get on and ride again. The same is true of swimming, skating, bowling, and golf.

Our Foundation's basic program provides workshops for in-service teacher training, recognizing the many problems which exist in this area of the curriculum.

First, the usual teacher-pupil ratio is about one to 50. How does one individual teach 50 children to play tennis?

Second, a teacher will not teach any subject if she doesn't feel capable.

However, by good methodology and good use of instruction materials that are available, the class can be diviided into different groups which rotate at teaching stations using available equipment and the lifetime sports skills can be effectively taught.

Whether they will be taught, however, remains a question of the priority you place upon it.

Most school districts are in the situation the 101st Airborne Division was in at the Battle of the Bulge. It is a favorite story of mine and very interpretive of a sound American attitude. The 101st was surrounded at Bastogne by the Germans. The German commander sent in a message: "Surrender or be annihilated!".

General McAuliffe replied, laconically, "Nuts!".

I think everyone remembers this, but his message to his troops was overlooked. The 101st was a proud outfit. They were the only group that jumped three times behind the enemy lines in World War II. After replying "Nuts" to the ultimatum, McAuliffe sent this message to his troops: "Men, we are completely surrounded by superior enemy forces. This is the greatest opportunity in the history of the 101st Airborne because we can now attack in any direction".

I know that some of you have excellent health education programs in your schools. I know that some of you probably have excellent physical education programs beginning in kindergarten and extending through the last year in senior high school. I am also sure many of you have inadequate programs.

What I am hopeful you will now do is to honestly analyze what your schools are doing in health and physical education and then take steps to change your program so it is one of quality and what to my way of thinking is the most basic area of education. Whether you will do this or not will depend on how important this is to you.

I used to question our Oklahoma football team in the following manner and it has relevance to what I have been discussing with you. At our first squad meeting, I would put it to them this way: "How good do you really want to be? You are going to make the decision. I can't make it. Our staff can help you develop your full potentials but you will decide where the limits are. How good do you really want to be?"

This is related to your obligations as school board members. How good do you want your programs to be? I know you want them to be excellent in science, math, modern language, remedial reading, all these areas which are highly necessary for quality education, but I hope you will also recognize the need for quality in your health and physical education programs.

I am in Washington much of the time now. There are many beautiful buildings in Washington. One of my favorites is the National Archives. Those of you who have seen it will remember the magnificent bronze doors and on each side there is a statue. Under the one on the left is the simple inscription, "Study the Past", and under the one on the right, "The Past is Prologue".

Historians have found a common pattern to the rise and fall of nations and civilizations, and have summarized it in a simple manner. Great nations rise and fall. The people go from bondage to spiritual faith, from faith to great courage, from courage to liberty, and from liberty to abundance, but, then, from abundance to selfishness, from selfishness to complacency, from complacency to apathy, from apathy to dependency, and from dependency back again into bondage.

I think if we were to pass a ballot among us today we would be in agreement as to where America stands in this cycle today.

The quotation ends "I am only one; but, yet, I am one. I cannot do everything, but I can do something. But because I cannot do everything, I will not refuse to do the something that I can do".

You can take a realistic look at what your curriculum in health and physical education is offering, hopefully recognizing the basic, fundamental importance of quality instruction in this area so that it will be motivating for the future living habits of your students.

10 ❧ A CRITICAL LOOK AT PHYSICAL EDUCATION *

Softball, horseshoe pitching, or bowling on the green

M. L. RAFFERTY, JR.
FORMER SUPERINTENDENT OF SCHOOLS,
NEEDLES, CALIFORNIA

A few high schools teach physical education. A few more make an attempt at it. But there is no such thing as physical education in the great majority of secondary schools.

1958

There is some excellent coaching being done in competitive athletics. There is good participation in many games and sports. There are recreational programs, and play days, and tournaments, and group activities, all cuddled coyly under the blanket labeled "physical education." But when all the excrescences have been scalped away, there is darned little physical education.

I can imagine the squawks which will no doubt go up from some of the zealous and dedicated physical educationists at the baldness

of this statement. They will point with pride to their gymnasiums, many of them veritable gleaming temples to the goddess Hygeia. They will stress the abundance of trained and experienced instructors who direct the multitudinous activities which justify the existence of these costly structures. They may extol their complex and ingenious devices, such as whirlpool baths, diathermic machines, and mechanical baseball pitchers. Finally, they will ask indignantly, "Where do you get this 'no physical education'?"

The trouble lies, as it so often seems to these days, in semantics. What a good many of us like to think of as physical education is really something else altogether. Let's see what Webster has to say:

"Physical education is instruction in the exercise, care, and hygiene of the human body."

Precisely . . .

*From the Education Digest 23:50, March 1958, as condensed from California Journal of Secondary Education 33:32, January 1958. Used by permission.

A brutally honest definition of what passes for physical education in most high schools today would go something like this:

"Take the roll. Check out a ball to a bunch of kids. Tell them to go ahead with the game. I'll referee."

I have often wondered why such a yawning breach has developed in this great instructional field between lip service on the one hand, and actual performance on the other. If English or geometry or shorthand were to be taught by dividing classes up into "teams" which competed against each other in "round robin" tournaments all year, we might rightly expect the results in terms of individual achievement to be something less than spectacular. If grades in physics or history or literature were to be given almost entirely on the basis of "participation," disaster might reasonably be anticipated in the not-too-distant future.

But before proceeding too far, let's get the hapless gym teacher off the hook, at least to some extent. A lot of the trouble lies with the administrator. He is the fellow who does the Horatius-at-the-bridge act to hold his academic classroom loads below 30 pupils, but makes up for it by pouring 50 or 60 kids into each gym class. This may not make the "grab the ball and let's play" routine inevitable, but it certainly helps. And the administrator is entirely too apt to consider his work done once he has hired several more or less muscular instructors, and bought some thousands of dollars worth of miscellaneous equipment. As he walks through the $150,000 gymnasium, hearkening to the happy shouts of the flushed youngsters and savoring the indescribable but unmistakable aroma exuded by all gyms, our administrator is all too likely to smile benevolently at the prospect of a job well done. This is about as justifiable as walking past a typing class and adjudging it a huge success on the basis of the clatter of the typewriter keys and the sight of the students bent over their machines.

However, the gym teacher cannot escape entirely scot-free from the general indictment. He, or she, has consented in all too many cases to compound the felony by equating in his own mind the dual concepts of "physical education" and "organized sports." Nomenclature is partly to blame for this situation. The physical education instructor is usually referred to as a "coach," which he certainly is not unless he is working directly with an organized competitive team. Too often, of course, he is doing this very thing, not only after school as a properly extracurricular activity, but all day as well,

bringing the highly specialized methods of the coach improperly to bear on unspecialized and heterogeneous masses of nonathletes. This works about as well as could be expected, that is to say about as effectively as a brain surgeon called in to treat a bellyache.

What is needed

What seems to be needed is a program designed to bring physical education out of its present equivocal status as a sort of "free period" play time. Inasmuch as most of us can agree that its main goal should be the continuing improvement of the child's muscular development, coordination, and general health over a set period of years, we should also be able to set forth the principles of a good physical education program.

Theory should be either implemented or discarded. A course of study is good only insofar as it is used. If calisthenics are scheduled somewhere along the line, they should be taught efficiently and constructively, not used as a disciplinary device to punish recalcitrants. A skill area should never be left in the written curriculum as padding, or because someone thinks it looks good there. Teach it, or take it out.

Repetition should be used only to insure adequate mastery. Letting a boy play softball every spring just because it happens to be softball season is indefensible. Once he has gained a reasonable proficiency in any area, let him be led into something else, whether it be horseshoe pitching, shuffleboard, or bowling on the green. The only criterions should be its desirability from the standpoint of individual needs, and the sequential position of the subject in the course outline.

Let us not confuse physical education with sports. Proper individual exercise, dietetics, hygiene, and care of the body are collectively far more important to the average adolescent's future than the whole galaxy of competitive sports. And it should be obvious that continuous supervision and evaluation of the whole physical education program are essential, if the relative importance of the several areas is to be kept in balance.

Many states require that physical education be taught to more boys and girls over a longer period of time than any other subject. This is expensive, in terms both of money and effort. It should long ago have produced results in terms of our young people's strength, ability, and general fitness commensurate with its universality and its cost. The blunt truth is that it has not.

Any one familiar with the Selective Service rejection figures and a report recently made to the President of the United States on this topic knows that our youth is becoming progressively less fit. While this decline may have its roots in causes outside the schools, it is nonetheless subject to diagnosis and treatment within the schools. We had better begin to administer the cure, or turn our money and facilities over to organized recreation, which is a horse of quite a different hue.

PROJECTS AND THOUGHT QUESTIONS

1. List the objectives for each of the following: (a) general education, (b) health education, (c) physical education. Show how each is related to the others.
2. Do a critical analysis of a program of health education and a program of physical education that you are familiar with, and identify the objectives that you feel these programs are attempting to achieve in practice. Compare these objectives to those the program planners have listed in their syllabi.
3. What do you feel is the true worth of health education and of physical education in today's society? Document your answer with significant facts.
4. Prepare a position paper on: "Play is an important part of the educational process." Present this position paper to your class.
5. Outline what you consider to be a quality program in physical education for the schools of today. Do the same for health education.

SELECTED READINGS

American Association for Health, Physical Education, and Recreation: Health concepts-guides for health instruction, Washington, D.C., 1966, The Association.

American Association for Health, Physical Education, and Recreation: Knowledge and understanding in physical education, Washington, D.C., 1969, The Association.

Bucher, C. A.: Administration of health and physical education programs, including athletics, ed. 5, St. Louis, 1971, The C. V. Mosby Co.

Bucher, C. A.: Physical education for life (high school text), St. Louis, 1969, Webster Division, McGraw-Hill Book Co.

Mayshark, C., and Irwin, L. W.: Health education in secondary schools, ed. 2, St. Louis, 1968, The C. V. Mosby Co.

Neff, F. C.: Philosophy and American education, New York, 1966, Center for Applied Research in Education, Inc., The Library of Education.

Oberteuffer, D. and Beyrer, M. K.: School health education, ed. 4, New York, 1966, Harper & Row, Publishers.

CHAPTER 3 THE ADMINISTRATIVE SETTING FOR HEALTH EDUCATION AND PHYSICAL EDUCATION PROGRAMS, INCLUDING ATHLETICS

To understand administration it is important to understand where it takes place. Programs of health education and physical education are not organized and administered in a vacuum. Several factors influence their operation. The nature of the community in which they exist, the type of school, college, or organization in which they are located, the key administrative personnel who are in charge of the organization, and many other factors play important roles in the administrative process. Thus it is important to be aware of the setting for our programs and some of the main factors that influence them.

Frederick W. Hill, in the first reading in this chapter, pinpoints 1841 as the year the first full-time position of school business administrator evolved. During the present century the position has increased in importance. The school business administrator today is a professionally trained person, or team of people, skilled in personnel administration, programming, fund allocations, and facility planning. He is the administrator of school business affairs and a leader in the school district.

Problems associated with the governance of schools are explained by Arthur H. Rice in his article about the changing responsibilities of a school board. He believes that the job of a school board should be to audit or approve decisions of those trained individuals who make them, to evaluate programs, and to concern itself with the interrelations of employees. Rice concludes that parent-teacher associations should list the qualifications of school board members and consider the role and job expectations in doing so.

Calvin Grieder believes that governing boards and administrators possess the power and responsibility to enforce the rules of education and should not bow to the demands of students. In the 1960's, changes were seen in schools; smoking rooms were allowed, athletic programs were overemphasized, and lax enforcement of rules was permitted. Administrators must enforce rules, but they must select a new approach to enforcement.

In the next reading Mildred T. Wilson and Samuel H. Popper offer differing opinions as to the purpose and structure of the middle schools. Wilson describes an ungraded school that admits students who would regularly be in the fifth grade. Students are assigned to courses in blocks, with the goal being improvement of personal responsibility, learning strategy, critical thinking, creative thinking, effective social behavior, and effective communication. It is said that the students feel safe and important and learn how to go about learning and that learning is proved to be worthwhile.

Popper, on the other hand, states that the advocates of the fifth-to-eighth-grade school claim that adolescence is attained at a younger age today and, therefore, youngsters are ready for this new approach earlier. The reasons for the seventh-to-ninth-grade school are more substantial, and, until research physiologists can show this downward shift to be a reality, the seventh-to-ninth-grade school is still needed. Teachers must be trained for early adolescent education so that innovative programs can be instituted without reeducating teachers involved.

In the last article in this chapter, Rebecca Dennard describes the twelve-month high school program presently in use in Atlanta, Georgia. Students attend for three out of four semesters each year, and the faculty is faced with the problem of breaking down requirements and subject matter. Teacher competencies are acknowledged; therefore, improved quality of instruction and improved teacher morale result. The health and physical educators find this a challenging opportunity for professional growth.

The administration and organization of school and college programs in health education and physical education are as varied and diversified as each location of schools in this country. The obligation of meeting educational objectives in all the various settings described in this chapter is one of the most difficult tasks facing administrators today.

11 ❧ WHO IS THE SCHOOL BUSINESS ADMINISTRATOR?*

FREDERICK W. HILL
ASSISTANT SUPERINTENDENT OF SCHOOLS, HICKSVILLE, NEW YORK

In the United States and Canada, public education is a multibillion dollar enterprise in terms of both the value of physical facilities and the amount of money required annually to operate the schools maintained in tens of thousands of school districts of varying sizes. The task of administering this vast complex is delegated to a variety of personnel of technical, professional and nonprofessional status; and, because the schools operate under the statutory requirements and limitations of the individual states or provinces, and often under policies established by local boards of education, there is no single pattern of supervision or control. In some small districts, there is little direct administration other than that performed by members, officers, or committees of the local board of education with, perhaps, some advice from a county superintendent of schools, or state or provincial educational official.

As districts increase in population a pattern begins to emerge. This pattern generally calls for a professionally-trained person or team of persons to provide the necessary administrative services of the school system. The chief interest of such person or persons should center in seeing that all parts and persons work together as a smoothly operating team, and contribute in the highest degree to providing pupils with the best possible educational program. This pattern of administration calls for a high degree of administrative skill, and such administrators must be aware of, but not encumbered with, the details of personnel, program, funds and facilities which are required to achieve the educational program. In most districts, the persons charged with the responsibility for the instructional program would have the title of Superintendent of Schools or Supervising Principal. Assisting them and cooperating with them are other persons to whom may be delegated specific responsibilities in particular areas of administration.

In some districts, the personnel caring for the business aspects are subordinate to the superintendent and directly responsible to him. In other districts, some, if not all of the em-

ployees caring for related business areas or services, are independent of the superintendent, so far as their official status is concerned. Throughout the United States and Canada as a whole, however, there generally is a good working relationship between the superintendents and the persons heading up the school business affairs, regardless of organizational status, as most of them recognize that all administrative functions are aimed at providing the highest standard of education that can be achieved within the limitations of the available financial resources. *Business administration serves, rather than controls, education.* This is as it must be, and the administrative structure and organization should be designed to achieve that end.

School business administration has existed since the beginning of the public school system, although originally it may not have been considered as important as it is today. Always, there were taxes or fees to collect for the support of the early schools, teachers to be paid, financial records to be kept, rents to be paid, and fuel to be supplied. At first, these duties usually were performed by local town or city officials, and later by members or committees of local school boards as they were established. Even today, in some communities, some of the business aspects of public education are handled by local municipal officials other than those directly associated with the schools, or by members or committees of local school boards.

Historically, it appears that the necessity for the appointment of a fulltime school business administrator was first recognized more than a century ago—in 1841—when the city council in Cleveland, Ohio, passed an ordinance providing for the appointment of an "Acting Manager" of schools whose duties would be "to keep a set of books, in which he shall open an account for each teacher in the employ of the city, and to make an accurate entry of all moneys paid out, . . . to keep an accurate account of each school district, whether for teaching, or rent, or for other purposes, . . . to provide fuel, take charge of the buildings and fixtures, and certify to the council the correctness of all accounts against the city for teaching, or for rents, fuel, repairs or fixtures on or about the school houses." It is also interesting to note that

*From The School Business Administrator, Association of School Business Officials of the United States and Canada-American Association of School Administrators. Used by permission.

Cleveland did not appoint a superintendent of schools until twelve years later. Likewise, Chicago and Philadelphia also appointed full-time school business managers several years before appointing their first superintendents of schools.

It appears clear that the men who were first appointed to serve as school business administrators were not primarily interested in the instructional program, but were appointed because of their knowledge of business.

In the 1880's, according to the published proceedings of the National Education Association, some professional educators of that period were emphasizing the importance of school business administration, and urged the creation of a business division in city school districts.

During the late nineteenth and early twentieth centuries, many school trustees and school superintendents recognized the importance of good business administration of the school system. They felt that the way to accomplish this was to employ a well prepared business administrator to whom important business management responsibilities could be assigned. Accordingly some school trustees employed a professionally-trained educator to be the superintendent of schools and a businessman was appointed to be the business administrator. Both individuals had equal status in the administrative hierarchy; each was directly responsible to the board of education for his own area. This concept of management commonly referred to today as "dual control" received favorable reception in some areas, among which New Jersey, Pennsylvania, and Canada are examples.

In most other areas, school trustees have adopted the "unit control" plan, which places all administrative responsibility under the superintendent of schools. The school trustees in those areas have delegated to the superintendent of schools complete responsibility for the administration of the school district, while they concentrate on policy development and determination.

We now recognize that decisions relating to curriculum, school organization, and personnel all affect and are affected by decisions on finance, buildings, equipment, and supplies.

By accepting the relationship between curriculum planning and schoolhouse construction, between classroom activities and textbook procurement, between budget planning and educational activities, and classifying all as administrative responsibilities, the school trustees have enhanced the professionalization of all school administrators, including the school business official, all of whom have achieved a status highly respected by the public and the teaching profession.

By the turn of the century, the administration of school business affairs began to have the "tone" of professionalization; that is, the leading school business administrators commenced to realize the importance of their duties, the effect their services would have on education, and the need for obtaining further information regarding the specifics of their various duties and responsibilities. In 1910, a significant step was taken by these leading business officials in the formation of the National Association of Public School Business Officials, which later became the Association of School Business Officials of the United States and Canada.

In the early part of the current century, some literature began to appear dealing with aspects of school business administration, chiefly in the areas of school finance and accounting. Literature dealing with the broad topic of school business appeared in the 1920's sparked by the writings and stimulation of Professor N. L. Englehardt, Sr., of Teachers College, Columbia University. He was the first instructor of a specialized course in school business administration which was offered in the summer school session of 1926. The first book devoted entirely to school business administration, written by the brothers, N. L. Engelhardt and Fred Engelhardt, appeared in 1927. Since that time, numerous volumes and articles have been published dealing with various aspects of school business administration, and it now may be said with full confidence that school business administration has arrived as a potent and positive force in American education.

At present, there is no single pattern of school business administration, no single pattern of administrative organization, and no one title applicable to the chief business official. It is of interest to note that since 1940, the presidents of the Association of School Business Officials have held the various titles of: Secretary-Business Manager; Assistant Superintendent-Business; Business Manager; School Architect; Business Administrator; Director of Vocational Education; and Director of Administrative Services.

Of greater significance is the fact that, over the years, the position of school business administrator has become increasingly important. The position more often calls for a person trained and experienced in the field of education, with emphasis on school business administration, or trained and experienced in various phases of business together with a knowledge of educational practices. In the unit control plan, this person is considered an associate of or assistant to the superintendent of schools and an important member of his cabinet. In both dual control and unit control plans, he is a powerful force supporting the improvement of educational opportunity rather than serving chiefly as a watchdog of the treasury, which too often was considered his chief role decades ago. He has the special responsibility to make business and financial operations accomplish most in operation and improvement of the schools. To him the Superintendent looks for leadership in making business affairs add to educational efficiency and progress.

Within the context of this publication, and in answer to the question, "Who is the School Business Administrator?", persons dealing with specific phases of school business administration will be referred to as SCHOOL BUSINESS OFFICIALS. Persons dealing with the total area of school business, and with subordinate school business officials, will be designated as SCHOOL BUSINESS ADMINISTRATORS.

Within the historic framework previously suggested, the school business administrator may therefore be defined as follows:

> The school business administrator shall be that employee member of the school staff who has been designated by the Board of Education and/ or the Superintendent to have general responsibility for the administration of the business affairs of a school district. In any type of administrative organization, he shall be responsible for carrying out the general business administration of the district and such other duties as may be assigned to him. Unless otherwise provided by local law or custom (as in dual control areas), he shall report to the Board of Education through the Superintendent of Schools.

12 ᴈᴗ SCHOOL BOARDS REACH NEW HEIGHTS OF IMPORTANCE*

ARTHUR H. RICE
PROFESSOR OF EDUCATION,
INDIANA UNIVERSITY, BLOOMINGTON, INDIANA

A short time ago I was asked to address a state group of school board members on the subject, "The School Board—Are Its Responsibilities Increasing or Decreasing?"

I was unable to accept the invitation (much as I would have enjoyed the occasion) because of a previous speaking commitment. My comment to those who invited me was that the responsibilities of the school board are not necessarily increasing or decreasing, but they are changing. And this is a thesis that I would like to defend in this discussion.

Audit, but don't administer

Never has public education meant more to a culture or a society than right now, and especially in these United States. And, consequently, never has the school board been more important. If we are to believe what is reported to us in the early history of school administration, school board members were selected for their business ability and entrusted primarily with the problems of hiring the staff, buying supplies, planning the construction of the

school building—mostly the material side of the public school operation. They also had the authority to hire personnel that they believed qualified to teach, and in many cases they had the sole or independent authority to levy taxes for the public schools.

It may be that in some small districts a few of these functions still remain in the hands of the school board, but in school districts that are large enough to be considered functionally efficient, the business of school operation should be in the hands of those who are professionally trained for it, and the school board should merely audit or approve. It should not be engaged in conducting the business management of the schools.

What, then, in a nutshell is the changing function of the school board, or what is its job today? Our thesis is that the biggest responsibility of the school board today is to evaluate the program that has been brought to it by its professional staff or the program that it, as a board, has helped to plan, and then to evaluate the activities of the staff in achieving that program.

A second responsibility which is coming more and more into the picture is to study the

*From Nation's Schools 80(3):10, September 1967, copyright, McGraw-Hill, Inc. Used by permission.

interrelations of its employes to ensure harmony, efficiency and fair play.

All this means that the superintendent who secretly would like to have his board operate as a rubber stamp or would have the board see the operation of the schools only through his eyes is encouraging a fatal kind of myopia. A school superintendent who is really competent will want his school board members to look at what is going on within the school system in terms of their experiences and judgments and values, and then share with the superintendent and the board members their points of view and recommendations.

What evidence is there that these roles are changing? One big accumulation of evidence is the manner in which state law has taken over a lot of the functions that were once exercised by the school boards. For example, the school board may no longer hire anyone it considers capable of teaching. It may hire those who are certified in accordance with state law. Tenure in many states is a state law. The state exercises many other controls over the school program, including the length of the school year. Another activity of the school district for which standards are determined by the state is the transportation services.

Other groups set standards

In other words, the school board no longer is allowed or expected to set up many kinds of standards and policies. It still remains, however, as the representative of the community in terms of what that school district wants to achieve with its own educational program and in terms of the satisfactory or unsatisfactory performance of its total personnel.

The question then follows:
Where and how does the community obtain school board members having the qualifications?

One thing is certain. It is a fatal mistake for an organized teacher group to nominate or support or presume to put into office a school board member. Groups who attempt it will live to regret the day they ever hatched the idea.

A school public relations leader whose integrity I greatly admire looks at this issue differently. He comments: "I can't say I agree with your hands-off attitude in regard to political endorsements. Political endorsements are rife with hazards, but the biggest enemy, I believe, continues to be head-in-the-sand apathy. Politicians thrive on disorganization and splintered allegiances." On this issue, we'll agree to disagree.

It has been traditional for parent-teacher associations to more or less stay away from the idea of endorsing individuals for school boards. I think a parent-teacher association should at least set forth the qualifications it expects of a school board member and then interview all possible prospective candidates, so that all parents may know as much as can be learned about these individuals as potential members of the school board.

Civic groups should care

Why shouldn't every civic-minded organization take a special interest in the election of school board members, unless, of course, the board members are elected on a partisan political basis. (If such is the case, then the concern of every citizen should be to get the school board out of politics.) A good school system is one of the greatest assets of a good community. And an inept school board is a community calamity.

This kind of nonpolitical interest is appropriate for labor unions, professional and religious units, industry and business, luncheon clubs, women's clubs and, in fact, for any organized group that is concerned with the improvement and growth of its community.

Whether any organization wants to endorse a candidate or group of individuals for membership on the board is a matter of policy for that organization. But certainly all of these groups should see and hear those individuals who seek to determine policies and represent them in the control of the public school system.

There is an alternative. Citizens can ignore the election of school boards and the efforts of the board to retain local control of the public school system. This apathy will be rewarded—sooner than you think—by federal domination of the schools of this nation. A shocking example is the recent decision of Judge J. Skelly Wright, circuit court judge of the District of Columbia circuit, in which he outlawed the four-track system that has been used so successfully in the school district of Washington, D.C., for the last several years. His decision usurps the prerogatives of the educator and of the school board. Note how easily and quickly a court can make sweeping decisions affecting public school policy everywhere.

Well, this wasn't intended to be a chapter on school administration. It was intended to develop the thesis that today the school board is more important than ever before. Its functions are (1) to know the program of the school, (2) to know the educational wishes and needs of the community, (3) to be well informed as to what the school actually is doing, (4) to be thoroughly cognizant of personal and professional relationships within the staff, (5) to be independent of and at the same time cooperative with members of the official planning and advisory group that works with the superintendent and his administrative staff, and, of course, (6) to perform assigned legal responsibilities.

13 ❧ CAN OUR PUBLIC SCHOOLS SURVIVE STUDENT UNREST? *

CALVIN GRIEDER
PROFESSOR OF SCHOOL ADMINISTRATION,
UNIVERSITY OF COLORADO, BOULDER, COLORADO

The late 1960's and early '70s may be remembered for a generation or two as a decisive period on the question of which shall prevail: law and order and orderly procedures for change, or anarchy with each individual deciding for himself which laws, rules and regulations he will observe.

Both school and society seem at this time to be falling short, in some ways, of doing their part in extending the rights and opportunities which we cherish in American life, and at the same time preserving the sense of duty and the obligations which are attributes of good citizenship.

Pampered pupils test rules

The all-too-often successful challenging of parental control by children of elementary and secondary school age inevitably affects the schools. School people find it difficult to maintain a classroom and school climate conducive to learning and wholesome development. And in too many communities they have pandered to pupil's demands (stimulated or at least supported by parents) for such anti-educational measures as smoking rooms, overemphasis on athletics and lax enforcement of rules.

Teachers and principals have, probably unwittingly, abetted their charges by accepting as fact the pupil's unwarranted assumption of maturity. For instance, the term "pupils" used to be universally applied to boys and girls in both elementary and secondary schools. It is still used in the arts for even adults taking lessons from their masters, as "a former pupil of Nadia Boulanger," or "a pupil of Yehudi Menuhin." The term "student" was reserved for those in college or university with the connotation of greater maturity than pupils had. Now everyone's a student, even in kindergarten. "Commencement exercises" with caps and gowns for tots completing kindergarten are held in some schools—that's really the height of absurdity, isn't it?

*From Nation's Schools, **82**:6, July 1968, copyright, McGraw-Hill, Inc. Used by permission.

Governing boards and administrators of schools, colleges and universities assuredly possess not only the power but the responsibility to make and enforce rules and regulations for the conduct of their institutions and the conduct of those who attend them. The courts have consistently upheld rules and regulations made by boards and administrators if such rules are reasonable, not arbitrary or capricious, and are not discriminatory, whether or not pupils or students have participated in formulating or adopting them. Pupil's and students need not be consulted, although they probably should be, and avenues for their suggestions and limited participation in management are desirable as part of the educational process.

But they are mere transients in institutions which presumably will live on for generations. No group of pupils or students has the right to change the provisions governing their school or university. They do not have the right to enforce their demands by illegal or violent methods, or to decide for themselves which rules and regulations they choose to obey.

It's a new ball game

How schools and higher institutions will come out of the present unstable period is hard to estimate. Some new administrative concepts and procedures undoubtedly will take shape. An interesting paragraph from a letter written recently by the superintendent of a large midwestern district points out:

"The administration and supervision of schools are entirely different than 15 to 20 years ago. About six weeks ago I took approximately 100 books on school administration and put them in the trash can to be hauled away. Any superintendent who attempts to operate on the principles that were advocated 25 years ago is lost. We are playing a new ball game today. However, the basic rules of fielding, hitting and running are the same as they have always been. It is a matter now of a new attack and a new approach on the problems."

14 ॐ WHAT ABOUT THE MIDDLE SCHOOL? *

SAMUEL H. POPPER
PROFESSOR OF EDUCATIONAL ADMINISTRATION,
UNIVERSITY OF MINNESOTA
MILDRED T. WILSON
PRINCIPAL, CONWELL MIDDLE MAGNET SCHOOL, PHILADELPHIA

ॐ *"Fifth graders are ready for individually tailored experiences,"* says
Mildred T. Wilson.

The term "middle school" has suddenly become fashionable in educational jargon. It has been used rather freely to describe various grade combinations—5 through 8, 6 through 9, 6 through 8, 4 through 7, and even, usurping the range sacred to junior high school, 7 through 9. Many of us, however, feel that the middle school is not dependent upon grade combinations but is really a completely new approach to the education of young people between the primary and the high school years. Grade combinations are much less important than the focus and spirit of the whole operation.

My not very original theory is that the early years of a youngster's schooling should be devoted to making the tools of living and learning familiar to him. He needs to learn the basics—reading, writing, and arithmetic—and to have the experiences that lead to social learning. In the late school years, he needs to gain the specialized and basic knowledges that will be vital to his career and to his whole adult life. The experiences of the years between—the middle school years—must be uniquely and individually tailored to each individual so that the tools may become the skills he needs in order to realize his full potential, and the fifth year is none too early for these tailored experiences to begin.

We at Conwell Middle Magnet School have had the opportunity of developing a school that offers such experiences. The school, which offers such experiences. The school, which draws from all sections of Philadelphia, is completely ungraded. When students apply for admission we screen them carefully in order to determine their present skills and attitudes. We use this information to guide us in planning each student's program so that it will provide

the sort of initial support important to his development.

We believe that young people during these in-between years are very different from those in any other period and also that they differ from each other to a greater degree than do members of any other group. At this stage, erratic physical and emotional growth patterns are usual and have definite effects on learning. During these years, when attitudes are formed, uncertainty as to abilities and values often keeps a young person off-balance, ill-equipped to profit from the traditional structured group learning process. The school's first responsibility seems to be to create a climate where it is possible and satisfying for each student to develop his own potential.

At Conwell, we have gone about this in many ways. Naturally, staff is of primary importance; not only must teachers measure up scholastically; they must also be able to see each student as an individual and really want to help him to make the most of himself.

The members of the staff must learn to work together in various team combinations. They must be willing to learn to give up the center of the stage and use their talents as directors and managers of learning experiences—to set the stage, even present the script, and then get out of the way and let the student learn.

The fundamental administrative unit at Conwell is the cross-discipline team made up of five teachers and about 180 students. These five teachers and two others from the labs each serve as adviser for a group of about 25 students, and the team is collectively responsible for the appropriateness of every student's program. We have four such teams, with an overlap of year levels in each one.

Every student on the roster is assigned a large block of "team time." The roster indicates lab assignments as well. (The term *lab* is used to designate any time assigned outside the team program, and covers physical education, art, science lab, business lab, journalism, TV pro-

Samuel Popper is the author of *The American Middle School: An Organizational Analysis,* Waltham, Mass., 1967, Blaisdell Publishing Co.

* From NEA Journal **58**:52, November 1969. Used by permission.

duction, foreign languages, various music offerings, the learning laboratory, and any other individually prescribed activity.)

The teachers in the teams are specialists in the basics—social studies, mathematics, science, and the communicating skills—and have complete autonomy within the team assignments over how each student's time is used. The scheduled daily team meetings make immediate adjustments possible as required.

Since it is more important for students to learn a skill thoroughly than to meet with a teacher a given number of times a week, the whole range of organizing for learning is at the disposal of the team teachers. This can result in teachers' having a realistic amount of time for planning and working.

As a school, we have focused our attention on six major areas for development—personal responsibility, learning strategy, critical thinking, creative thinking, effective social behavior, and effective communication. Our goal is to provide students with an environment where it is almost natural for every youngster to develop to the highest degree of which he is capable.

The general atmosphere of the school is friendly and busy. Visitors often remark that the many students moving about all seem to be going somewhere to do something. No demonstration classes are conducted, but visitors are free, after an orientation tour (often student-led), to spend time anywhere that particularly interests them. In the team rooms, they see various combinations of youngsters operating with or without teacher guidance and usually a sizable number working with some of the machinery designed to spread the influence of a good teacher and bring out independence in the student.

In the classrooms, teachers are available for consultation, but they hold back to give the student a chance to discover for himself or to learn from his errors if he's working on a specific skill. Teachers watch how a particular youngster goes about learning and plan his future course according to his specific needs and not on the basis of "what all twelve-year-olds require." Conwell students display a professionalism that is certainly not to be expected in the light of their ages, the broad range of their measured potential, their achievement records, their economic and social backgrounds, and their general behavior history.

Our experience indicates that middle school doesn't depend on grade range or team teaching or any specific administrative method. We have found that getting the youngster at fifth

year instead of at the seventh is good because it gives us a head start on thwarting the potential dropout, and we have found teaming important because more of us get close to every youngster and our pooled caring leads to understanding and confidence—students feel safe and important.

We have found that by relating the general curriculums to actual essentials for surviving in the society at a basic level and adding however much an individual student can master confidently, we can cut to a minimum passed-over subject matter and poorly learned skills. We hope to send off each student secure in the knowledge that he can learn, that he knows how to go about learning, and most of all, with a feeling that learning is really worthwhile. That will beat out mere Carnegie units anytime!

"I believe that it is an institutional corruption," says Samuel H. Popper.

No one professionally active in education has to be told that all American education, public and private, is troubled today. But early adolescent education has been troubled almost since its inception.

Now, some educators say that junior high schools of grades 7-9 are on the way out; middle schools of grades 5-8 are on the way in. These people frequently claim that everything that has gone wrong in junior high schools can be made right in the 5-8 middle school.

Things have gone wrong in junior high schools, but every learning objective, every innovation which is proposed for the 5-8 middle school—team teaching, modular flexible scheduling, nongradedness, computer terminals, talking typewriters, independent study—can be actualized in the 7-9 structure without compromising its institutional integrity. Indeed, I believe that the middle school composed of grades 5-8 is an institutional corruption. It is at once corruptive of early adolescent education and of childhood education in the elementary school.

The established institution for early adolescent education has been in a consistent state of growth since its beginning about 60 years ago, despite having been called "tramp steamer of the educational fleet," "stepchild of public education," "a school without teachers," and "a stepping-stone organization." Obviously, something in the cultural environment of American society is responsible for this growth. What is the something that generates such a powerful pressure on the school system that even an admittedly malfunctioning junior high school organization is better than none at all?

As I see it, the "something" is the need for an educational organization specially designed to meet the developmental requirements of early adolescence, the most difficult period of all human growth.

Kindergarten is the boot camp of formal education. Family and school join in an effort to introduce society's very young to the importance of achievement and the rewards of performance. By means of gold stars, appointment to the honored position of monitor, and other bonuses, pupils soon learn that a system of differential rewards for different levels of effort and achievement is a classroom norm.

When pupils reach high school, performance pressures intensify. Scholastic standing, college boards, and such things as competitions sponsored by industry and government are the visible evidence of this.

Elementary and high school students are, for the most part, physiologically and psychologically capable of satisfying school and family expectations. But in between, in early adolescence, a physiological revolution begins. Pupils, heretofore well-composed, encounter difficulty in conforming to performance expectations. At this point, they need the special school organization we traditionally called "junior high school."

Ideally, this special school organization is oriented to the pupil as a human being as well as to the pupil as a learner of cognitive skills. The learning of cognitive skills is not overlooked, but during this time of physiological and emotional stresses and strains, the pupil is granted a psychosocial moratorium from those cultural disciplines that school, as a socializing agent of society and as a social system, imposes.

Few disagree with the concept that early adolescents need a special unit of school organization in which they are to be exempted temporarily from the achievement and performance pressures of our society—an organization in which they can survive the turbulence of an "ego resynthesis" (a reference to Erik Erikson) without embarrassment and fear of failure. Disagreement arises, however, over what age brackets constitute early adolescence.

Advocates of the grades 5-8 middle school claim that the onset of adolescence has shifted downward because of a changed climate, improved diet, sharply modified social relations, and a host of other natural and cultural influences. However, during nearly six months of reading the research literature in reproductive physiology at the medical library of the University of Minnesota, I have found no substantive evidence in support of this claim. On the contrary, a 1968 publication of the Committee on Adolescence of the Group for the Advancement of Psychiatry is supportive of both general and specialized literature bracketing the early adolescent period as about age 12 to 15—the age bracket that has been institutionalized in American early adolescent education from the beginning.

Of course, more extensive research might lead to a different conclusion. To end argument, could we not ask specialists in reproductive physiology to determine the age for us? If their studies conclusively showed that the onset of adolescence has been accelerated since 1910, lowering the age brackets served by early adolescent education would be justified. Otherwise, to adopt the grades 5-8 middle school structure would be to ignore the raison d'être of this special kind of school. It would compromise the institutional integrity of the organization.

In my opinion, the ills that beset schools for early adolescents do not arise because of the ages of the pupils they enroll but because the schools seldom succeed in offering the special kind of education young adolescents need.

Anthropologist Margaret Mead sets the special case of early adolescent education in a revealing perspective when she notes that in our type of culture, early adolescents need ". . . freedom from pressure—freedom from choosing their careers, freedom from being told that if they don't pass this exam or that exam they won't ever get anywhere." She concludes, "The junior high school was set up to protect young adolescents."

For the most part, however, the junior high is not fulfilling its protective mission. In my research material, I have junior high report cards indicating a grade of D- in physical education, a C- in home economics. On a trial basis, Yale University has discarded the traditional grading system, but anyone who suggests that a junior high school teacher or principal follow this lead is usually made to feel like a thief separating a blind man from his guide dog. These educators agree, in principle, that junior high schools exist to satisfy the needs of early adolescents, but they go right on calculating grade-point averages to the last decimal point and otherwise turn their junior high school into a pressure-cooker microcosm of society.

The crux of the problem, it seems to me, is a failure to have special preparation programs for those preparing to teach early adolescents. Today, most junior high school teachers are trained in so-called programs of secondary education that are geared to prepare high school teachers.

Schools of education differentiate preparation for other units of public school organization. Why can't they do the same thing for early adolescent education?

15 ❧ THE 12-MONTH SCHOOL YEAR: AN OPPORTUNITY FOR HEALTH AND PHYSICAL EDUCATION PROGRAMS*

Rebecca Dennard
Director, Health and Physical Education,
Fulton County Schools, Atlanta, Georgia

The most exciting, stimulating, and challenging school year in all of my teaching experience began in the fall of 1968. With the opening of school the four quarter high school program was introduced in the Fulton County System and 4 other Metro-Atlanta systems. Such a program had been under study, investigation, and consideration for several years; a complete and total curriculum change was developed over the past year. Here are the highlights of the program, with particular emphasis on the effect on the programs of health and physical education.

Structure of the new school year

The school year will consist of four quarters with approximately the same amount of time in each quarter. The first quarter begins in September and the fourth quarter ends in August. This schedule allows for a few days between each quarter and for the usual holidays.

The student is required to attend school three of the four quarters. The student may, however, exercise an attendance option. He may elect to attend all four quarters or any three of the four quarters. This is his and his parents' decision.

A teacher's salary is based on a three quarter year. If a teacher works for a fourth quarter, he is paid extra for that period.

Philosophy and rationale

Why did we change to such a program? The answer and basic concept is simple. The purpose of the four quarter plan is to improve the educational opportunity for our boys and girls. We believe that it can do this. This four quarter plan is not a program to save money, to use the school plants on a year round basis, to relieve over-crowded conditions, or to accelerate students through high school to an early gradua-

tion. Some of these may be by-products of such a program but they were not the forces behind the planning and development of our program.

With increasing numbers of students attending school in the summer months, one major reason for the development of the four quarter plan was the need for a quality summer program. With this in mind, we have developed a program that offers the student the quality courses he needs in any of the four quarters.

Subject reorganization

In every area of the school program a completely new curriculum was designed and developed and all teachers and administrators had a part in this. This was a tremendous undertaking but it was the basis for building the kinds of programs needed. Without the development of this completely new curriculum, this twelve-month program would be doomed to failure as others in the past. The courses are designed on a quarter basis or unit of time independent of each other. Flexibility was the key and any rigid sequence of courses was held to a minimum.

Now specifically, let's review what happened in the programs of health and physical education. Our high schools in Fulton County, numbering 15 at present with new ones opening each year, include grades 8 through 12. In our previous structure, students were required to take health and physical education daily in grades 8 through 11 and could elect it in grade 12. Students were scheduled according to grade level in order to provide for progression in the program. All eighth graders took the same program, all ninth the same, and so on. Within the four years we tried to introduce the student to as many different activities as possible, and we offered a very broad and comprehensive program.

When we began to study the four quarter plan, we approached it with a completely open

*From Proceedings of the Sixth National Conference of City and County Directors, December 1968, p. 42, American Association for Health, Physical Education, and Recreation. Used by permission.

frame of mind. We evaluated our program under the semester structure and identified our concerns. We spent considerable time with our philosophy and beliefs about health and physical education. With this background we began to look at how the quarter plan could improve our programs, and we became more excited with the possibilities with each passing day.

As a result, for the first time we feel we really are providing for the needs and interests of the individual student. A basic change in our philosophy was made. We agreed that all eighth graders, or all ninth graders, do not need the same thing nor have the same interest so why make them all take the same courses. We concluded that our program was teaching a little bit about a lot of things and nothing in any depth and so we arrived at a basic belief that we would allow the individual to choose the activities about which he wanted to learn and offer him in-depth experiences in these activities.

In the new program the student is required to take two quarters of health education, a five day classroom subject. One quarter is required at the eighth grade level and one quarter at the tenth grade level. Ten quarters in physical education are required. This requirement is further broken down as follows: one quarter in personal fitness at the eighth grade, three quarters in team sports, three quarters in individual sports, and three quarters elective from either category. Beyond the requirement there are ample opportunities for the student who desires to elect additional physical education courses.

For the most part two activities were combined into a course. There are some exceptions to this where it was felt an activity would not need as much time and then three activities were combined. Courses are set up at beginning level, intermediate level, and advanced level, and not by grade level. Eighth graders, with two of their quarters determined in the health and fitness requirement, do stay together. Beyond this a class may include students of various grade levels. The homogeneous grouping of students now is not in their grade level but in the skill level of the course.

A numbering system was devised for courses with the first digit indicating level: 100—beginning, 200—intermediate, 300—advanced, 400—student assistants; the second digit indicates to whom the course is open: 0—coeducational, 1—boys, 2—girls, and the third digit helps to differentiate specific courses. For example, Physical Education 111 is a beginning level course for boys in soccer and volleyball. Physical Education 201 is an intermediate level

coed class which includes intermediate archery, and the one time offering of angling and casting, and camping. By the way, the interest in this particular course which for the first time offers angling and casting and camping to our students has been tremendous. Physical Education 325 is an advanced course for girls in gymnastics. Some activities are offered at only one level, as an example the course that includes angle ball, flag football and softball. These activities are offered only once. Most activities are taken through the intermediate level; only a limited number are offered at the advanced level.

Student assistants

For years we have had student assistants but there has been no specifically designed program to prepare them for this role. Now we offer in the spring quarter to students having successfully completed their health requirement and nine quarters of physical education and upon approval of the department a course, Physical Education 302, which is preparation for the student assistant's role. We feel that not only will this prepare students ready to be of real help and assistance to the teacher but that it will also give these students an insight into the profession and may influence some of them into choosing our field for their life's work. After completion of this course, the student is assigned to one teacher for one period in the day as an assistant and this student gets credit for each quarter so assigned at the 400 level.

Credit

A word of explanation about credit is of interest. The carnegie unit has been abandoned in favor of a more flexible credit hour system. Any course meeting five hours a week carries five credit hours regardless of whether it is physical education, English, art, science, et cetera. Some courses may be designed to meet only two or three days a week and would thus carry two or three credit hours respectively. This is a real accomplishment. No longer are we considered a minor subject and given less credit than an academic one. We feel this can have far reaching effects in student attitudes about the courses they take.

The carnegie unit was abandoned with the approval of the southern accrediting association for high schools and colleges.

The summer quarter

Just a special word about the fourth or summer quarter. First, we can offer any course offered at any other quarter as long as there are enough students interested in taking it. This quarter also offers some special opportunities for us. We may offer some courses here that we could not offer during the other three quarters for various reasons. Of particular note would be swimming and boating courses. We dreamed in planning this program, dreamed realistically, and planned a course, coed, in boating (power boats, sailboats, canoes) and water skiing that may very well become a reality this coming summer. Because of the summer heat and the fact that our older buildings are not air-conditioned, the fourth quarter classes may begin earlier in the morning and finish earlier in the afternoon. In our boating and water skiing course, we would organize differently. Rather than the usual daily one hour class, we would schedule this course at the last period of the day which might be 1:00 P.M. for only two days of the week. On these two days the class would be transported by school bus to the lake site, possibly forty miles away. Here they would spend several hours of the afternoon in class and would receive the five credit hours. This is just one example of some new ways of programming which we have never tried before.

In our curriculum guide, the courses are set up and the skills and knowledges to be covered are listed for each course. This is a definite program with, for example, Physical Education 212 meaning the same course in all schools. In the past our teachers have had to be able to teach all the activities in the program. Now their interests and competencies can be considered in assigning courses to them. The effect this can have on the improved quality of instruction is unquestioned. Likewise as a school needs new staff, it can look for teachers with particular talents. Our discipline is like so many of the others, so very broad, that it is most difficult for a teacher to do a good job in all activities.

A progress report

We have now completed the first quarter. Of course it has not been all smooth and easy. Any program of this magnitude requires time, patience and additional work in getting it implemented. Scheduling alone is a mammoth task. However, the results of one quarter make all our efforts worthwhile. The enthusiastic response and interest on the part of students and the decrease in disciplinary problems in our classes are just two of many positive results already recognized.

There are many new possible structures and organizational patterns on the horizon in education. As some of them come into being in your system, don't be tied to the old way and reluctant to take a look at the new and the possibilities they offer to the programs of health and physical education. Who knows, you may find yourself in the midst of the most exciting and challenging opportunities of your professional life.

PROJECTS AND THOUGHT QUESTIONS

1. Diagram what you consider to be a typical administrative structure for (a) a school system, (b) a college or a university, (c) a youth-serving agency such as the YMCA.
2. Survey a community, and identify what you consider to be the main ways in which the community influences health education and physical education programs. How can a community help or deter the growth of our programs?
3. What are the principal functions of (a) a school board or committee, (b) a board of trustees in a college, university, or youth agency?
4. What do you feel are some of the main reasons why student unrest exists today in many of our educational institutions? What do you feel are some of the realistic ways to cope with the administration of educational programs where student unrest exists?
5. To what extent does the social structure of a community affect the achievement of goals of health and physical education programs? Justify your answer.

SELECTED READINGS

Blackwell, T. E.: College and university administration, New York, 1966, The Center for Applied Research in Education, Inc., The Library of Education.

Brickman, W. W.: Educational systems in the United States, New York, 1964, The Center for Applied Research in Education, Inc., The Library of Education.

Bucher, C. A.: Administration of health and physical education programs, including athletics, ed. 5, St. Louis, 1971, The C. V. Mosby Co.

Getzels, J. et.al.: Educational administration as a social process: theory, research, practice, New York, 1968, Harper & Row Publishers.

Gauerke, W. E.: School law, New York, 1965, The Center for Applied Research in Education, Inc., The Library of Education.

Neilson, N. P., and Bronson, A. O: Problems in physical education, Englewood Cliffs, N. J., 1965, Prentice-Hall, Inc.,

CHAPTER 4 PERSONNEL ADMINISTRATION

Programs of health education and physical education cannot operate without personnel; thus personnel management is an important administrative function. The recruitment, selection, orientation, assignment, promotion, and termination of staff are a few of the responsibilities involved in administration. These duties must be carried out properly, or the organization will collapse. The principles governing personnel administration are very important for all health educators or physical educators to know. The readings in this chapter provide some key insights into many aspects of personnel administration.

Willard J. Congreve, in the first article in this chapter, reports on research studies of social interaction in the schools between administrators and staff members. Some administrators utilize a formal approach to their jobs, keeping social distance from other staff members, whereas others administrate on an informal level, becoming "friends" with the staff members. Staffs that have been surveyed for these studies preferred the formal administrative procedure. The responsibilities of the administrator can be handled effectively in either manner.

Research studies that explain the conflict among teachers, arising from the community's expectations of the teacher's proper role and from the teacher-administrator relationship, are explored by Charles E. Bidwell in the next article. He concludes that administrators, to control and avoid conflict, must assist teachers

in gaining confidence and security on the job and must be aware of tension causing problems in teachers.

Charles F. Austin devotes his writing to the problem of educating for leadership. He lists various examples of wrong practices of bossism and questions the present system of one "boss." No overnight changes are possible to solve the problem; the only solution feasible is the education of future leaders.

In the next article, Auren Uris defines the complexity of the executive position as a problem with four prongs: paperwork, planning, procedures, and people. The solution offered to the problems of administrative practices is self-improvement. The administrator must find his high performance areas, must reinforce weak areas, must delegate responsibilities, and must plan for the future.

Following these articles showing the problems of administrator-teacher relationships, Robert C. McKean explains how the gap between teachers and administrators is harmful to the educational process and decision-making process. Alternatives offered by McKean are collective bargaining and setting up school systems in which there are two chief executives for each school.

Education is being pressured for change, and change in administrative practice is a necessity to meet this demand. The duties of an administrator, although complex, must be met properly, in order to maintain a functioning educational system.

16 ADMINISTRATIVE BEHAVIOR AND STAFF RELATIONS*

WILLARD J. CONGREVE
FORMER STAFF ASSOCIATE, MIDWEST ADMINISTRATION CENTER,
UNIVERSITY OF CHICAGO

Early studies in administrative theory viewed administration largely as a process for allocating and coordinating the resources of an enterprise to facilitate its effective and efficient progress toward defined goals. This conception of an

enterprise as essentially a mechanical functioning of men, materials, and machines changed when research findings indicated that the human work unit itself is a highly developed and complex social system: The enterprise was conceived to consist not only of the formal pattern of jobs and job relationships within the organization, but also of an intangible series of human relationships. These relationships

*From Administrator's Notebook 6(2), October 1957. Used by permission.

[1] Footnote 1 deleted in proof.

set standards of work, levels of output, and modes of conduct within the work group which could not be accounted for by the organizational structure alone. Thus the concept evolved that an enterprise consists really of two organizations—the formal and the informal.

The schools have adopted many principles and findings of administrative theory and research to meet their needs and problems. Studies have been made, for example, of the functions performed by the school administrator and their relationship to current theories of administration.[2] Other studies have compared patterns of school organization with those that have developed in the military, government, industry, and business.

While many studies have been made of the structure, organization, functions, and related aspects of the formal organization of the school, research studying the sociological framework of the school has been given increased emphasis only recently. Most of the studies in this area have been concerned with such aspects of human interaction as patterns of leadership, individual satisfaction, and role expectations.[3] For example, the Midwest Administration Center has studied the effect of the leadership style of administrators upon the interaction among staff members.[4]

The school as a social organization

Boyan made one of the earliest attempts to study the school as a social system. Borrowing his models from industry, he studied a junior high school as a social organization composed of a formal and an informal organization, and described the interaction between them.[5] Cornell and Jensen, among others, have also suggested that the school social organization can properly be studied as a series of relationships and have suggested the importance of the informal organization to an understanding of the

effect of school organization upon administrative behavior.[6]

Congreve, in a more recent study, has examined further the social organization of the school.[7] This study was based on the hypothesis that the formal-informal organization concept developed in industrial settings was not applicable to an enterprise which demanded a high degree of social interaction. Consequently, Congreve felt that a careful study should be made of school staffs to determine the nature of their social organization and the effect of administrative behavior upon this organization.

The study was conducted in two schools which were matched in respect to size and population characteristics, but which were under the leadership of administrators with different behavioral styles. The case study method was used in conducting the study. This involved visitation and observation in the schools, focused and nondirective interviews with staff members, and the collection of data through the use of various instruments. From these data it was possible to describe the formal organization, administrative behavior, and the social organization of each school. The findings of the subjective observations and interviews could also be corroborated by data secured with the objective instruments.

The administrator's behavior

Differences in administrator behavior exist, of course, and this study confirmed previous findings in this field. Some administrators prefer a formal approach, relying heavily upon formally stated procedures and extensive written communications. While on a friendly basis with staff members, such administrators tend to keep a social distance between themselves and their teachers. Almost all personal contacts concerning school business occur in the administrative offices, and the job specifications and authority relations are specifically designated and respected.

---

[2] American Association of School Administrators, Staff relations in school Administration, Thirty-third Yearbook (Washington: The Association, 1935), pp. 9-29.

[3] "Who should make what decisions?" Administrator's Notebook, III (April, 1955).

[4] Egon G. Guba and Charles E. Bidwell, Administrative relationships: teacher effectiveness, teacher satisfaction, and administrative behavior. Studies in Educational Administration, Monograph No. 6 (Chicago: Midwest Administration Center, The University of Chicago, 1957).

[5] Norman J. Boyan, "A study of the formal and informal organization of a school faculty" (unpublished Ed.D. dissertation, Graduate School of Education, Harvard University, 1951).

[6] See, for example, the following:
Francis G. Cornell, "Socially perceptive administration," Phi Delta Kappan, XXXVI (March, 1955), 219-23.
Gale F. Jensen, "The school as a social system," Educational Research Bullentin, XXXIII (February 10, 1954), 38-46.

[7] Willard J. Congreve, "A study of the interrelationships existing between administrator behavior and the social systems of the adult population in two selected secondary schools" (unpublished Ph.D. dissertation, Department of Education, University of Chicago, 1957).

On the other hand, some administrators prefer an informal approach, relying heavily upon face-to-face contact with staff members, and following a rather highly personalized approach with some. Much of the business of the school is conducted outside the offices. These administrators tend to express a great deal of concern about the human idiosyncrasies of their staff and problems of human relations.

When the responses to administrator behavior by the staff members in Congreve's study were analyzed several findings seemed to emerge. Staff members tended to prefer the formal, impersonal approach to administration rather than the informal, personal approach. They also described the formal administrator as being more consistent, more positive in his approach, and as satisfying more of their basic professional needs.

Social interaction in the school

In studying the social interaction in the school, Congreve conceived of the social organization as functioning at three different levels of interaction. These levels he defined as follows:

1. *Universalistic* interaction was defined as being highly general in nature, evidencing no personal involvement of either interacting party, and usually confined to institutional requirements.
2. *Particularistic* interaction was defined as being highly personal in nature, evidencing great personal involvement of both parties, and embodying any possible matters including institutional requirements.
3. *Discretionalistic* interaction was defined as lying somewhere between the extremes with the participants demonstrating a balance between institutional requirements and personal involvement.

The schools in the study showed differences in the percentage of staff members who could be classified into these interaction categories. Under a highly formal administrator, a large proportion of the staff tended to interact at the in-between or discretionalistic level. Under a highly informal administrator, a large proportion of the staff tended to interact at the particularistic level. The groups at the various levels also differed in the purposes they served. Under formal administration the groups tended to satisfy personal needs and to provide for the satisfaction of individual inadequacies. Under informal administration the groups tended to champion causes and sought to satisfy profes-

sional needs which they felt were not being satisfied by the administrator.

The sex of the teacher appeared to have only slight effect at all levels of interaction. However, at the particularistic level there seemed to be a tendency on the part of teachers to select their friends from among others of the same sex. At every level of interaction, too, the teachers rated highest by their administrators were also the ones most favorably regarded by their fellow teachers.

The power structure in the school

Membership in the power structure of the schools studied tended to be a function of both personality and ability, which resulted in influence over persons in the formal administrative hierarchy, as well as over the other members in the organization. Older staff members, those rated highest by the administrators, and those who had served on the staffs for the longest periods of time, tended to occupy power positions in the school. Under informal administration the teachers who were most popular at the particularistic level of interaction tended to be the most influential over both teachers and administrators. Under formal administration there seemed to be no relationship between popularity and power influence.

The administrator's responsibility

The study summarized above has pointed to several hypotheses concerning the informal organization of the school which are of particular significance to the school administrator. Because the findings in this study are based upon an examination of only two schools, they must be considered tentative. However, careful consideration and evaluation of them by an administrator in terms of his own situation can provide him with additional insights into the social "climate" in his school.

1. Administrator behavior has an effect upon the informal organization of the staff. If this behavior statisfies the professional needs of the teachers, then the informal organization will tend to satisfy individual needs. If this behavior fails to satisfy the professional needs of the staff, then the informal organization will champion those needs, and, in doing, may divide the school into opposing camps.

2. There appears to be a definite relationship between leadership style and the informal organization of the school. The formal administrator will tend to encourage the development of a high degree of discretionalistic behavior on the part of the staff. As the administrator's

leadership style becomes more informal it will tend to encourage the development of a greater degree of particularistic behavior among the members of the staff. Since no administrator can make provision for the personal needs of every staff member, some members will tend to be overlooked. Thus, over a period of time, there will develop groups of staff members who feel close to the administrator and other groups who do not.

3. Teacher effectiveness does not appear to be greatly affected by the nature of the informal organization of the school. Unlike industrial organizations, where a direct relationship has been found to exist between the informal organization and productivity, no such relationship seems to exist in the school.

4. The school is not a family. Teachers do not look toward the administrator to satisfy their personal needs or to be treated with a great deal of personal attention. They tend to prefer the administrator who plans, organizes, and communicates in such ways as to ensure that all are informed; that those affected by pending changes are consulted; and that the professional needs prerequisite to effective teaching are satisfied.

5. The administrator must not become overly concerned with the personal feelings of staff members. The more formal, impersonal, bur friendly, administrative style appears to be the most effective. Furthermore, it is not who

associates with whom which is of importance to the administrator; rather, it is the nature of the needs which this interaction proposes to satisfy which is important. If all teachers feel secure in their position and their professional needs are being provided for, then the personal need satisfaction of the informal organization should be of no concern to the administrator.

6. Admittedly, the administrator faces a difficult task. The effective administrator must initiate structure in the interaction among staff members. At the same time, he must show consideration toward the group members upon whom he depends for the accomplishment of goals. His principal concern should be to maintain the proper perspective. When he becomes deeply imbedded in the highly personal interaction of the informal organization of his staff, he may confuse satisfaction of individual needs with organizational goals, lose objectivity, and, because he cannot interact at this level with all staff members, lose effective contact with many members of his staff.

For your own planning

1. In what respect, if any, would you expect the findings of similar studies conducted in your school to differ from those reported in this article?
2. What can an administrator do to utilize the informal organization in his school more effectively in the administrative process?
3. How deeply should an administrator concern himself with the individual needs of his staff members?

17 ♥ SOME CAUSES OF CONFLICT AND TENSIONS AMONG TEACHERS *

CHARLES E. BIDWELL
EXECUTIVE ASSISTANT, MIDWEST ADMINISTRATION CENTER,
UNIVERSITY OF CHICAGO

Ineffective teaching is often the result of tenseness and uncertainty on the part of teachers who are unable to determine what is expected of them or who cannot reconcile the conflicting expectations of different individuals and groups. Therefore, any administrator worthy of the title must assume a considerable amount of responsibility for assisting teachers in developing a sense of confidence and security. He must have a knowledge of the factors which result in conflict and tensions in faculties. He must attempt to alleviate the tensions and conflicts which exist or appear to be developing.

Recent studies completed at the University of Chicago point to two possible sources of conflicts centering around the teacher's role in the school and in the community. One source is the expectations held by community members regarding what they believe to be proper behavior on the part of teachers. The other is the nature of the teacher-administrator relationship.[1]

Conflict and community expectations

In one of the studies, Jacob W. Getzels and Egon G. Guba attempted to determine the

*From Administrator's Notebook 4(7), March 1956. Used by permission.

[1] Other issues of the *Administrator's Notebook* also have dealt with these relationships. See the issues of May, 1952; November, 1952; March, 1953; April, 1953; March, 1955; April, 1955; and September, 1955.

various kinds of expectations which typically are used in a community to define behavior appropriate for the teacher as a *teacher* and as a *member of the community*. They were especially interested in learning whether or not the various expectations were in conflict and, if they were, how the conflicts affected the attitudes and actions of the teachers.[2]

Extensive interviews were held with forty-one teachers from four school systems in two states. On the basis of information gathered in the interviews, a questionnaire was constructed which was designed to measure various aspects of the conflicts possible between what the community expected of the teacher as a teacher and what it expected of him as a church member, family member, voter, etc. The questionnaire and a personal information blank were sent to 344 elementary- and secondary-school teachers in eighteen schools of different types and locations in the Midwest. One hundred and sixty-six teachers returned the questionnaire.

Analyzing the information provided by the teachers, Getzels and Guba found that conflicts appear to center largely around three major roles occupied by the teacher. The first major group of conflicts involves the teacher's *socioeconomic role*. Community members usually expect teachers, as members of a professional group, to live according to the middle-class standards generally accepted in their communities. Compared with others who live according to these standards, however, the teacher often is not sufficiently well paid to undertake the responsibilities which accompany middle-class life. Many of the strains which teachers feel in this area arise not out of the fact that they believe that they are underpaid but from the realization that they are simply unable to maintain the standards of living which are expected of them.

The second major area of conflict is concerned with the teacher's *citizen role*. The assumption is generally made that adult members of a community are responsible citizens whose judgment about their own conduct is a private matter and may be trusted. Frequently the teacher does not enjoy this same confidence. For example, he may be expected to undertake church activities with more vigor than his fellow citizens while, at the same time, he is expected to take part in political affairs with less vigor than would be required by his own beliefs or even by good citizenship. Thus, his role as a

citizen is somewhat different from the citizen role enjoyed by most other members of the community.

The third major area of conflict involves the teacher's *expert or professional role*. Supposedly, the teacher is a professionally-trained person with expertness in his own field of specialization. Furthermore, his expertness has been certified by a state agency. The school administrator, however, may narrow the area of a teacher's professional initiative by making more or less specific requests regarding the performance of the teaching responsibilities. Even more important, the community itself may set up specifications regarding the content and methods of teaching without consulting the teacher and, indeed, often in direct opposition to the teacher's professional judgment. In many cases, therefore, the teacher is expected to be a competent professional with a wide range of professional initiative and freedom of action while, at the same time, he is expected to submit to the dictates of persons lacking his special training and experience.

Conflict and personal characteristics

Personal characteristics seem to influence the degree to which teachers are disturbed by the conflicts described above. Getzels and Guba found that different individuals react differently to the same conflict situation according to certain personal factors. Furthermore, because these different reactions followed a systematic pattern, some general conclusions regarding them may be stated.

Male teachers appear to be more disturbed by the conflicts than do women teachers. For women, more often than men, teaching is a respected and high-prestige profession. This fact tends to make women more tolerant toward various inconsistencies in expectations regarding their behavior. Men are inclined to feel the conflicts more severely because they often do not look upon teaching as a highly-valued occupation.

Teachers with one dependent are more likely to be disturbed by the conflicts than are those with no dependents or those with more than one. Teachers with several dependents are usually older and have had the opportunity to become adjusted to the conflicts; furthermore, they tend to receive higher salaries than do other teachers. Teachers with no dependents are generally single and, therefore, they are better able to maintain middle-class living standards than are other teachers. On the other hand, younger teachers with small families usually

[2]Jacob W. Getzels and Egon G. Guba, "The Structure of Roles and Role Conflict in the Teaching Situation," *Journal of Educational Sociology*, XXIX (September, 1955), 30-40.

do not enjoy either of these sets of advantages and, as a result, they are often disturbed by the conflicts in expectations regarding their standard of living. They are likewise more often employed in part-time jobs in addition to their teaching duties. Teachers who hold such jobs, according to Getzels and Guba, are more sensitive to conflicts regarding their socioeconomic status than are other teachers.

Teachers who do not identify themselves with their community, who perceive the community where they teach as being considerably different from that in which they were reared, who find it difficult to make friends in the community, and who feel that their social life is restricted, seem to be most disturbed by the various conflicts centering around the different roles performed by them. In other words, it is the group of teachers that feels it is "outside" rather than "inside" the community that is most likely to have difficulty in adjusting to conflicting sets of expectations about proper behavior.

The degree of satisfaction expressed by a teacher with his profession and with the leadership provided by his administrators is also related directly to his tendency to be disturbed by conflicts. Those teachers who are dissatisfied with their relationships with administrators, and who say that they would not again enter the teaching profession, appear to be the teachers most likely to experience emotional strain within the three major conflict areas.

Tensions and administrative behavior

The teacher's relationship with the administrator seems to be an important source of feelings of tension arising out of inability to cope with conflicting or ambiguous expectations. Evidence of the importance of such relationships was indicated in a study completed by the writer three years ago.[3] One hundred and ninety-five teachers in five suburban school systems of varying characteristics surrounding a large midwestern city participated in the study by completing a questionnaire regarding the desired and the actual behavior of their administrators. The data gathered in this manner were supplemented by intensive interviews held with a sample of eleven of forty-five teachers in one of the school systems.

The interviews revealed processes which are relevant to the problem of faculty tensions. Dis-

satisfied teachers said that they could not predict how their administrators would act. They felt that the administrators shifted their procedures from day to day and that they held ambiguous and sometimes conflicting expectations regarding behavior appropriate for their teachers. The teachers felt extremely tense about their relationships with their administrators and said that because they could not predict what their superintendent or principal would expect them to do, they could not determine how to act toward their administrators or in other professional activities. They were conscious of no clear area of professional initiative. Furthermore, they said that they were not able to discover any clear specifications of content or method of teaching desired by the administrators. Their resulting feeling of tension and insecurity was generalized into a widespread dissatisfaction with the school system in general, including relationships with fellow teachers, pupils, and patrons.

On the other hand, satisfied teachers felt quite secure in their relationships with their superiors. They could predict easily how their administrators would act and what would be expected of them as teachers by the superintendent and principal. They saw their administrators behaving consistently, holding clear and consistent expectations of teacher behavior, and giving ample warning of changes in procedures which would affect teachers. They felt that the expectations regarding their behavior which were held by their administrators were stable. They believed that they occupied a definite and secure professional role in the school system. They displayed a notable absence of tension regarding their relationships with the administrators. Their security in the relationships often was generalized into a feeling of satisfaction with the operation of the entire school system and with their role in it.

In the school where the interviews were held, the *same administrator* worked with both the satisfied and dissatisfied teachers. In other words, the same behavior on the part of the administrator resulted in both feelings of security and those of tension on the part of the two groups of teachers; the role of the administrator was spelled out differently by the two groups. Obviously, therefore, no single set of actions by the administrator could have produced a feeling of confidence and security in both groups.

There is no doubt that the teacher's feeling of security or of tension regarding his own behavior is very closely related to his view of

[3]Charles E. Bidwell, "The Administrative Role and Satisfaction in Teaching," *Journal of Educational Sociology*, XXIX (September, 1955), 41-47.

proper behavior on the part of the administrator. If he feels that the administrator is acting in suitable ways, the teacher will tend to feel that the administrator's expectations regarding his teaching are clear and unambiguous; he will feel comfortable with them. On the other hand, if he feels that his administrator is not doing his job properly, he will often feel that the administrator's expectations are conflicting and ambiguous; he will feel tense and disturbed by them. Thus, the administrator is faced with the problem of attempting to reconcile in some way the differing expectations of the teachers in order that there will be a general feeling of confidence and security among his faculty.

The administrator's responsibility

The two studies summarized above have pointed to two of several sources of tension and conflict centered around the role of the teacher in the school and in the community. Important work remains to be done in identifying others. In the meantime, the administrator can do much to remedy tensions and conflicts springing from the known sources.

First, he must always remain conscious of the fact that teachers occupy several community roles in addition to their professional role. When community expectations regarding the behavior of teachers becomes inconsistent, the administrator must help the teachers reconcile the conflicts by assisting them to think through the rights and obligations which are an integral part of being a teacher. There are, of course, few specific guides to help him in assisting the teachers with this problem. The personal characteristics of a teacher and the characteristics of the community will make every teacher's solution of such a dilemma a unique one.

Second, the administrator can make a significant contribution toward minimizing conflicts by interpreting to the community the rights and duties of teachers as professional workers in the community. Conflicts can be lessened only through community understanding of the nature of the teacher's job and of the conditions in the schools and the community necessary for enthusiastic and effective teaching. Modification of inconsistent and unreasonable expectations regarding both the professional and nonprofessional activities of the teacher will occur only when the community has such an understanding.

Third, the administrator, by his own behavior, can help reduce tensions which teachers experience concerning their jobs. By understanding how each teacher views his own role

and that of the administrator, and by incorporating these understandings in administrative actions and communications which indicate clearly the nature of the behavior which is expected of the teachers, the administrator can contribute to a secure and satisfying administrator-teacher relationship. If the faculty members have conflicting ideas of proper administrative behavior, the administrator has an additional responsibility. He must work with the teachers whose views of the proper role of the administrator are clearly inappropriate in an effort to produce a desirable change in their point of view.[4] Such a change, of course, cannot be dictated. It must result from a cooperative appraisal of honest differences of opinion.

For your own planning
1. How can an administrator really interpret to his community "the rights and duties of teachers as professional workers"?
2. How can an administrator help teachers modify any inappropriate views they may have regarding his proper role?

---

[4] For a more detailed treatment of this problem, see Francis S. Chase, "How to Meet Teacher's Expectations of Leadership," *Administrator's Notebook,* I (April, 1953).

18 ᴥ WHERE BOSSES FAIL*

CHARLES F. AUSTIN

Suprisingly, 60 to 90 per cent of all bosses are not regarded as organizational assets by their equals and their subordinates.

Probably, if you look back, more than half of your bosses had plenty of faults if they were typical bosses.

If you are a typical boss, therefore, you are probably regarded as something less than perfect by your equals and your subordinates.

---

*From Nation's Business 54(10):21, October 1966, copyright, Nation's Business—the Chamber of Commerce of the United States. Reprinted by permission. Charles F. Austin is an experienced executive, educator, lecturer, and consultant in executive development, human relations, and organizational behavior. He serves on three graduate faculties in Washington, D.C., and as a guest professor at many universities. This article is excerpted from his book, *Management's Self-Inflicted Wounds: A Formula For Executive Self-Analysis,* published by Holt, Rinehart and Winston, Inc., New York, 1966, and TOKUMA SHOTEN Publishing Co., Tokyo, 1970. Each type of boss failure is given detailed treatment in the book. Copyright 1966 by Charles F. Austin.

However, you can be a better leader.

One good administrator for 25 years, who has been bossed by many during that time, is very pessimistic and not at all hopeful that there will ever be any improvement in the present low state of the art of bossing. He said recently: "You're wasting your time. I refuse to believe that bosses will ever be any better than they are now."

If most bosses are not good bosses, why aren't they? The answer is not simple, but we could conjecture two reasons, or a combination of them:

1. We have not yet learned to educate for leadership.

2. The boss system of organization is not the best way to organize.

While we could spend a long time arguing the second item, this article is devoted to the former, that we have not yet learned to educate for leadership. The word educate is used in its broadest sense, to include self-education.

Galileo once stated, "You cannot teach a man anything—you can only help him to find it within himself." In today's world of executive-developmental education, the most accepted truth is, "Executive development is self development."

Another widely held belief in the field of boss education is that "developing requires action," on the basis that human behavior stems from attitudes; that behavior will not change unless attitudes change; that attitudes will not change unless the individual becomes emotionally involved in the subject he is studying; that this involvement can best be brought about by experiences which induce or cause the individual to act or react mentally or physically, or both.

This method of learning has been dubbed gut-level learning because of the belief that you are not truly involved in something unless you can feel it inside.

Let's accept that belief and examine ourselves as a boss, first by looking at the behavior of other bosses and then determining whether you yourself are guilty of the same type of undesirable boss behavior.

The most universally known and recognized (though not most understood) relationship in the world today, second only to the husband and wife relationship, is the one between the boss and the bossed; the superior and the subordinate.

In this boss/bossed relationship there are many situations in which the boss behaves in the "wrong" manner. It has been said that few men can define justice, but any man can define injustice. One executive says, "I may not know anything about management, but I sure know how I *don't* like to be managed."

Take a look at this listing of the wrong kinds of bosses and see how many of them you know:

His jobs are never completed before the deadline. He is a crisis manager.

He never passes along a memo without making changes. He is a nit-picking manager.

He doesn't understand the workings of other divisions in his company. He is a parochial manager.

He never receives both sides of a problem from his subordinates. He is a defaulting manager.

He never frankly tells his subordinate what he is really after. He is a hidden agenda boss.

He has an executive assistant, a right-hand man by any other name. He is a boss with a deputy complex.

He never defends his employees in front of his superiors. He is a one-way loyalty boss.

He procrastinates decisions until they no longer are decisions. He is a no-decision boss.

He feels personal contact with his employees doesn't befit his position as a manager. He is an unnecessarily lonely boss.

His door is open but he's guarded from contact with his employees by a series of complex procedures. He is a shielded boss.

He only wants to see his subordinates when he chooses to do so. He is a closed-door boss.

Many of his important projects seem to get lost in the press of daily business. He is a boss who does not know what to neglect.

He is often surprised by unanticipated events. He is a boss who is not ready for the unexpected.

He has not identified his inadequacies. He is a boss who doesn't know what he doesn't know.

When he has a leadership problem, he refers to a handful of tried and true rules. He is a boss who manages by rule-book.

When something goes wrong, he wastes time wishing he hadn't. He is a boss who only wishes things were different.

Members of a committee that he appoints always seem to endorse his ideas. He is a boss who sabotages his committee.

He does not know the detailed characteristics of highly effective groups. He is an unaware-of-groups boss.

He frequently vetoes a younger man's suggestion to substitute his own with words: "Experience is the best teacher." He is a handicapped-by-experience boss.

He really believes that all problems can be

solved by mathematical equations. He is a slide-rule manager.

He can never catch up with the work load. He is an after-the-fact manager.

Integrity is a word that he defines to suit his immediate needs. He is a shades-of-integrity boss.

He wants to take credit for all work done in his department. He is a grab-the-credit boss.

Even when his reprimands are justified, they are met with resentment. He is a negative-criticism boss.

He doesn't feel that a subordinate deserves praise "just for doing his job." He is a slow-to-praise boss.

He thinks that the only reason that a job gets done is because of the threat of punishment he uses in line with his authority. He is a boss who leans on the crutch of authority.

He uses the written disapproval because he doesn't have the nerve to do it face-to-face. He is a boss who lacks courage.

His secretary takes care of those letters of anniversary congratulations and even signs his name. He is an insincere boss.

He doesn't believe that anyone can effectively carry out his plans unless the person agrees with them. He is a brainwasher boss.

He keeps his official ratings of his staff a secret from them. He is a secret-performance-appraisal boss.

He will dismiss any disapproval of his actions with the words, "I'm not running any popularity contest." He is an unpopular boss.

He thinks he can "handle" his staff without their realizing it. He is a manipulator boss.

He doesn't care who does the job as long as it gets done. He is a boss who allocates the work unfairly.

He thinks looking busy is being busy; he thinks being busy is looking busy. He is a don't-let-me-catch-you-thinking boss.

He thinks that pinning the blame on someone will prevent future mistakes by his subordinates. He is a witch-hunter boss.

He uses memos for orders rather than face-to-face discussion. He is a one-way communication boss.

He makes up for his small physical stature by belittling others. He is a runt-complex boss.

He is intent on proving that every man has a breaking point. He is a human-erosion boss.

He is reluctant to promote anyone on the grounds that he's not ready for the job. He is a boss who neglects the development of his subordinates.

He always uses profanity in talking to his

employees because he feels it's more effective. He is a vulgar boss.

He believes that disagreement among his staff is unhealthy business. He is a boss who doesn't want conflicts.

Anything that he does is right because he's the boss. He is a boss who is drunk with power.

He doesn't contribute as much effort as he should to his organization. He is a lazy boss.

He believes the only time anything gets done is when he's around. He is a breathe-down-their-necks boss.

He believes threats and fear are the only way to get the job done. He is a manage-through-fear boss.

Every project that he gives out has equal importance at any given time. He is a horizontal-priority boss.

He knows how to do the work but he doesn't know how to get it done. He is a boss who doesn't use his staff.

He believes that as long as he gets rid of a symptom the illness will disappear with it. He is a boss who treats the symptom and ignores the real cause of problems.

His employees know that whatever proposal they offer, it will be watered down by everyone else's proposal. He is boss who manages by compromise.

The loneliest man in his organization is the man with the new idea. He is a boss who stifles creativity.

He feels that all problems can be solved according to standard policies he's set up. He is a policy manager.

He believes that, if you concentrate on the smallest details, the whole will take care of itself. He is a boss who strains at gnats but swallows camels.

He believes that intangible rewards are hardly important in a corporate system. He is a boss who misuses recognition and awards.

He demands flattery and deference from your employees—even in a social situation. He is a boss whose boots must be licked.

There is no doubt that he can solve any problem before anyone can say "think." He is a solve-the-wrong-problem boss.

He knows that his decisions are often retractable because he often makes decisions just to pacify one subordinate. He is a yo-yo boss.

There is no such thing as an honest mistake in his organization. He is no-freedom-to-fail boss.

He wants all your people to act and think alike. He is a boss who craves conformity.

All he is interested in is results, he doesn't

care what methods his subordinates use to get them. He is a results-at-any-price boss.

He believes that it is better to make a wrong decision than no decision at all. He is an often-in-error, never-in-doubt boss.

He surrounds himself with many assistants with no thought of its effect on the organization. He is a high-overhead boss.

Supervision is an absolute; it cannot vary in kind with different organizations. He is a boss who worships the unity of command concept.

He tried to solve your problems by reshaping his organization. He is a reorganizer boss.

He's the first one to say that informal personnel relationships have no bearing on the job he's doing. He is a boss who ignores the informal organization.

What his organization does is its problem—he declares himself innocent of any action by higher-ups. He is a boss who does not carry the conscience of his organization.

You probably agree that one or more of the bosses you have had or observed along the way has had each of these faults. Further, if you have looked into the mirror, you have by now identified and located a significant number of these faults on your executive anatomy.

Further still, you are probably asking yourself the final and most important question: "How can I correct them?"

Mending your ways

There is no easy, magical solution. You are what you have been thinking and doing a long time. You are not going to change overnight, and you are not going to be a perfect boss tomorrow.

However, you have already made progress if you have identified and located some of your faults.

Another suggestion is in the form of a methodical scorekeeping system on yourself as a boss. People like to keep score on things, whether it is a sporting event, a weight reduction program or some other activity. Furthermore, in any self-improvement program, it is the trend that counts. You can periodically check up on yourself, and score yourself from time to time as a boss.

The frequency with which you need to conduct these self-examinations depends upon you as an individual. The minimum probably would be every six months, with a more frequent process until you have your trend line well under control.

There is one principle of management which cannot be debunked. It was written about 2,000 years ago: "Do unto others as you would have others do unto you." Another is:

Success is a journey, not a destination. If we took these two rules to live by, we might not need so many other formulas for living. However, things do not always follow the ideal path, and there may be times when, upon checking out your executive score card, that you are not happy about your progress, nor about the direction of your trend line.

But any progress at all should be a source of satisfaction, and should inspire you further in your difficult program of executive self-improvement.

How to rate your boss

Something you have done regularly as a subordinate, and which your subordinates do all the time with you as a boss, is to make a boss performance appraisal.

Judge the bosses you have had along the way, including the present one.

You can use the following five measurements:

1. As a professional person (did he know his job?).

2. As a human being (did he behave like a human being and did he seem to recognize that you were also a human being?).

3. Did the organization make progress because of him or in spite of him?

4. Did you learn from him more things to avoid doing or more good things to copy in your own behavior as a boss?

5. When you refer to him in retrospect, are those references primarily positive or negative?

In applying this rating to the bosses you have had along the way, give equal weight to the ratings. It is helpful if you will select an odd number (3, 5, 7 and so forth) of bosses, placing plus or minus signs beside each of these ratings for each boss. Then total the plus and minus signs and arrive at a net negative or net positive figure for each boss.

This makes the scoring process relatively simple in that each boss comes out with either a net negative or net positive score, and each group of bosses also comes out either negative or positive. Please do not read further here until you have performed this rating process.

Having prepared these ratings of your bosses, if your bosses have been typical of that parade which has passed in review all too clearly in your mind's eye, 60 to 90 per cent now have a minus sign beside their images. If you are one of the few whose bosses scored a net positive rating, you're lucky. How would your subordinates rate you?

---

19 ❧ MAKE THE MOST OF YOUR WEAKNESSES*

Weighing your strong and weak points is first step toward self-improvement

Auren Uris

Everyone recognizes that an executive's job is complex. Most people—especially businessmen—will agree that the manager must have on tap a wide range of skills for satisfactory performance.

But we continue to think of the job as though it were a single monolithic thing. The oversimplification has costly consequences:

It prevents managers from understanding the true nature of the demands being made upon them.

It probably accounts for more cases of managerial failure than any other single cause.

The expectation of uniformly high levels of performance in all managerial activities is, in part, based on faulty observation. As a practicing manager, stand off and look at your own activity. For the most part, the job components —paperwork, planning, procedures, people— blend smoothly. There is seldom a distinction made by the executive: "Now I'm supervising my people, now I'm doing paperwork," and so on.

Precisely because the areas seem to merge without any joining marks showing, we overlook a crucial fact; there are major gaps among the four major managerial areas, in terms of what it takes to deal with them. For example:

Paperwork: This segment of your job requires an accountant's approach, an eye for detail. You must have the capacity for sticking with a procedure, following it down the line. A good memory, an ability to take pains, the ability to "think small" is essential.

Planning: This area of activity demands imagination and creativity. You must be able to conceptualize and visualize, both in abstract and practical terms. Here the ability to "think big" is mandatory.

Procedures: Executives in charge of production processes, with electronic data processing systems, men who must understand financial matters such as cash flow, are involved with intricate systems that they must understand and master. Here the executive has a need to "think technical."

People: Dealing with people requires sensitivity to their feelings and attitudes. You must be able to distinguish between Subordinate A, who can be motivated by putting him on his own and challenging him to produce, and Subordinate B, who will only get off the ground by encouragement and the reminder that you're at hand to backstop him if he needs help.

Working in a context of individual values and aspirations means that you must have the emotional reflexes that will respond properly to the leadership needs of those around you.

This aspect of the job requires the ability to "think human."

Are you a four-way expert?

Once the requirements are spelled out, it becomes clear that few people possess the four qualifications to an equal degree.

Most men function very well in one area— for example, an executive may be a whiz at handling people yet be only fair in the paperwork and planning areas. Occasionally, one comes across an executive who performs very well in two areas, and scrapes by in the other two.

An executive is supposed to think big and think small, think technical and think human. Unfortunately, few of us are flexible enough or have the universal genius that can encompass such opposite qualities. The man who is capable of thinking big usually has difficulty in thinking small. The executive who's a master at thinking human somehow finds that the intricacies of thinking technical elude him. In short, the human personality and the human intellect almost invariably fall short of the ideal—an executive sufficiently well rounded to perform at high levels in all four basic areas.

The question is: How does the typical executive manage to perform as well as he does? There are three answers:

One is the suitable job. This usually happens unconsciously, though it may also happen by choice. The executive gravitates to the type of job that best suits his capabilities.

While every executive must operate in each of the four areas to some extent, particular management functions tend to weight the de-

*From Nation's Business 55(4):74, April 1967, copyright, Nation's Business—the Chamber of Commerce of the United States. Reprinted by permission.

mands unevenly. For example: Finance and accounting are heavy in the paperwork element. Marketing is heavy in the planning element. Production is heavy on the procedures element, particularly if the process is complex.

But a vice president of personnel or an executive involved in recruitment or development must have both a knowledge of and a sensitivity to the individual human being.

The second way the executive can solve the dilemma is to put his major effort into the aspects of his job that he can handle at his highest skill level.

The second way the executive can solve the dilemma is to put his major effort into the aspects of his job that he can handle at his highest skill level.

This adaptation of one's capabilities to the task at hand is almost universally practiced. It explains the executive who gets the reputation of being a good desk man, who can skim a report and digest its essential contents in a fraction of the time it takes his colleagues. It explains the executive who gains a reputation as a people-builder, based on his concentration on the development of subordinates.

As a consequence of this emphasis approach, an executive tends to create a halo effect that favors his performance as a whole. He's so outstanding in the areas of his strength that he gives a general impression of outstanding performance.

Delegation is the third way in which an executive can get all facets of his job done well. Shifting to the shoulders of others the parts of a job in which one under-performs is a widespread and usually successful practice.

There's nothing wrong, for example, in handing over some paperwork detail to a subordinate if it's the kind of chore that bores or bothers you. There's nothing wrong in handing over to a small team of subordinates a major planning project, if planning is not your strong point.

Steps to better performance

With the awareness that the four-way analysis of executive activity brings, it is possible to develop a series of steps that can lead to improved achievement:

1. Spot your high-performance areas. A combination of thoughtful self-analysis and observation of your job activities can help you decide which of the four areas—paperwork, planning, procedures or people—are your fortes.

If you're in doubt about how well you do in a specific area, ask yourself questions along this line:

Do I like the activities that fall in the given area?

Do I solve the problems that arise in this area easily?

Have I, in the past, been able to score notable successes in a given area?

2. Pinpoint the job elements in your areas of greatest strength. Let's say, for example, that planning is one of your strong points. Isolate the procedures in your job that involve planning—for example the development of an agenda for a sales or production conference, a safety campaign, cost-cutting program and so on.

The purpose of this pinpointing is to increase your awareness and thereby your self-confidence and aggressiveness in these job aspects. Not an unusual case is that of a brilliant young executive in his early 40's who, in a period of about 12 years, gradually found his niche as a result of greater self-awareness. An M.I.T. graduate, he started as an industrial engineer, then worked into warehousing and traffic, made a switch to research and development, then finally into sales.

This was all with one firm—and he's still there—but now in a $40,000-a-year post as a marketing manager. He's supremely happy and successful in marketing—in a post quite different than might be expected from his education and early industrial experience. He has at last come to realize his strong capabilities in the planning-creative aspects of his work.

3. Reinforce weak areas. Don't set yourself the unreasonable goal of trying to bring your performance in the weak areas up to those in which you're naturally strong. A more realistic objective is to try to strengthen weak-area performance to an acceptable level or, as one merchandising executive puts it, "I want to perform well enough to stay out of trouble."

Once you're satisfied in your own mind that you are comparatively at a disadvantage in a particular job area, make a conscious effort not to avoid activities that fall within it. This is an unconscious pattern with many executives and usually only compounds the difficulties.

An awareness that he is weak in the procedures area, for example, should lead a manager to devote a little more of his time to studying the problems, digging into the facts and figures that occur on this part of his job.

Through the traditional techniques of delegation and the assignment of tasks to subordinates, get the assistance needed to maintain high performance levels in weak areas.

Some maintain that executives should not even be judged on their own abilities as such. Instead, they measure an executive's qualities by the conglomerate accomplishments of his entire group.

In some cases where the executive is in the position to modify the content of his own job as well as that of colleagues, extremely constructive results may be derived from this procedure. Like a jigsaw puzzle, it is a matter of fitting existing forms together harmoniously.

4. Devise a plan for the future. The insights that may come about through this approach to the executive job lend themselves particularly well to your own career planning.

Viewing your areas of strength and those in which you perform less well, you may be able to come up with a new and more realistic pattern for your own self-development. Questions like these can help you reassess your personal objectives:

Do my career plans depend on high performance in weak areas? If the answer is "yes,"

what implications does this fact have for readjustment?

What courses of study or practice can I undertake to strengthen myself in vital but weak areas?

Are any of my weaknesses so crucial that I should consider rethinking my career objectives?

Considering my strong points, do they suggest some career objective different from the one I now have?

Considering my strong points, are there courses of study I can pursue that would help make me a specialist or even more expert in an area I naturally favor?

Finally, it's important to remember that the flexibility and adaptability of the individual is tremendous. Psychologists assert that the capacity to learn never stops.

These facts all favor whatever measures you devise for the improvement of your job performance in the present and future.

20 ❧ DECISION-MAKING*

The administrator needs a new outlook

ROBERT C. McKEAN
PROFESSOR OF SECONDARY EDUCATION,
UNIVERSITY OF COLORADO, BOULDER, COLORADO

The problem of improved decision-making is one of the really crucial issues in public education at this time. Our concern about the changing relationships between teachers and administrators stems from the ominous specter of an emerging and possibly irrevocable cleavage between these two groups, a cleavage which cannot possibly lead to anything but harmful effects on the decision-making process in particular and public education in general. It is clear that we must discover a new pattern of organization which will make it possible for teachers and administrators to work productively together in making important judgments and solving significant problems in our schools.

Basic assumptions

At this point it might be well to lay out a handful of basic assumptions which seem to represent the realities of the present situation.

First: The right and proper function of the school administrator is to facilitate the primary

*From The Clearing House 41:285, January 1967. Used by permission.

work of the school which is teaching and learning.

This is a basic truth in administration; the administrator has no reason for being except for this supportive function. As the teacher is responsible for facilitating the learning of the pupils, so the principal is responsible for facilitating the work of the classroom teacher. Yet the danger exists that school administration may become an end in itself. And, of course, this is exactly the criticism most often leveled by teachers.

Second: Decision-making in the schools at the present time is unsatisfactory.

It is unsatisfactory for a number of reasons, but the most central is that it fails to meet several of the basic principles of decision-making. For example, quite typically the process does not now involve meaningfully those who will be affected by the decision. A decision made by the official leader, even though it may rest upon information contributed by the instructional staff, is still *his* decision and not a shared decision. It leads to manipulation or to outright coercion as the administrator seeks to implement it. In addition, decision-making has become more and more an exercise in expendiency. When the designated leader makes a judgment and must lay his "head on the block" each time, the real significance is one of survival.

Third: The present organization of the school and the approved operational style of administrators are retarding the development of professional teachers.

The traditional hierarchial power structure in the schools places the classroom teacher at the very bottom of the pecking order. This system is based on a concept, according to Staff Clayton of Indiana University, of *power over others,* a concept which is a matter of dominance and submission by its very definition. Furthermore, its nature depends upon a theory of scarcity (whatever power is added to one position or group is taken away from another) and a policy of exclusion (power must be guarded lest it slip away). Thus it should come as no great surprise that the theory of democratic administration is so seldom successful in practice; democracy cannot flourish in such a climate. Clayton suggests that professionalism demands *power with others* in a context of participative control and shared responsibility.

We have become committed somehow to the idea that teachers must be told, convinced, cajoled, and, if necessary, forced into doing what is best. Teachers typically are not given a real part in decision-making. Certainly, in an endeavor as large and diverse as public education, there are some avocational teachers, lazy teachers, and incompetent teachers. However, a system is indefensible which *prevents* the great bulk from becoming self-directing, professionals.

Fourth: Classroom teachers increasingly are demanding a real part in making decisions which affect themselves directly and their work in the schools.

As Benjamin Epstein points out in a recent NASSP publication, teachers are "no longer satisfied with mere permission to petition and be heard." They want to be involved in making the decisions. Teachers make the valid point that they are now well qualified to participate in decision-making in the schools. The import of the ground swell among the teachers is that they feel that they are ready and able to share in this process and, most important, it is a vital aspect of their perception of professional status. The thrust for a real role in decision-making comes from this striving for professionalism.

Moreover, this push is so great that it cannot be ignored. The teachers are on the move and we had better accommodate them to the advantage of education if we can.

If these four statements have any validity at all, it is not difficult to understand some of the changes which are taking place today. At any rate it is clear that change is underway, change which will significantly affect the relationships of teachers, administrators, and school boards.

Alternatives

There seem to be at least three possible alternatives to the present situation.

(1) Already underway is the movement toward professional negotiation or collective bargaining. No matter which term is used, it is certain to develop into a massive power play between the organized teachers on one side and the top administrator and school board on the other. Clark's study in Illinois and Epstein in the NASSP publication are just two of many sources which confirm that the superintendent is perceived by both teachers and school board members as primarily an agent of the board—certainly this is so in the districts wherein professional negotiation has been instituted.

Many view with alarm this development which places teachers and top administrators on opposing sides, which more often than not completely bypasses the building principal, which may make it forever impossible to achieve an all-staff community of interest, and which leads to decision-making based on power relationships rather than consideration of the best solution of the problem from the point of view of the youth enrolled in our public schools.

This is an approach which has been pursued by teachers because apparently we have not been willing to seriously consider other alternatives. Moreover, it is apparent that for all but the most militant teachers this step is distasteful. In reality it is a nonprofessional means to gain the professional status which they desire.

(2) A second alternative which apparently is being given some thought is the possibility of choosing two co-equal principals in a school building—one for business and supportive administration and the other for instruction. The latter would presumably be chosen because he is the instructional leader of the school, a person who can and will share decision-making responsibilities with the instructional staff.

The real danger here is that this dual principalship concept would result in the neutralization of leadership at the building level and encourage domination by the lay school board in areas of decision which rightfully belong to the professional staff.

(3) A third approach would involve the reorganization and readjustment of power relationships within building units in order to achieve what Dean Campbell of Chicago University and Willard Spalding call "collegiality" —a situation wherein staff members work together as colleagues. (Incidentally, a similar experiment was proposed more than 20 years ago by Calvin Grieder in an article in *Nation's Schools.*) In such a situation the building administrator would take his place as a co-equal *member* of the professional staff. He would be a specialist in supportive administration among other specialists in guidance, the teaching of English, the teaching of mathematics, and the like.

Authority for appropriate decisions would rest, not with an official leader, but with the staff as a whole. Leadership would be by consent—delegated to the emergent leader who would be elected by the staff itself. Decision-making would be broadly based, a product of wide involvement.

One might well ask, "What will this do to the profession of school administration?" It seems clear that an administrator is no less a professional if he participates as a member of the staff rather than as the official leader of the staff!

Conclusion

Insistent pressures for change are with us, indeed dramatic change is now underway. Our most productive approach at this point is to search for a school organization compatible with the new conditions emerging today. We must seek to find an alternative or to invent an alternative which will be best for public education in general.

PROJECTS AND THOUGHT QUESTIONS

1. Develop a list of principles for personnel administration. Document these by reference to the professional literature. Obtain at least two references to support each principle.
2. What do you think are some of the reasons for conflict and tensions among teachers?
3. Under what conditions do you think a health educator or physical educator should be dismissed from an organization?
4. Prepare a set of criteria which could be used for the promotion of health educators and physical educators.
5. Write an essay of 250 words on the subject: "The Importance of Democratic Procedures and Good Human Relations in the Administration of School Health and Physical Education Programs."
6. What conditions are important in establishing a high state of morale among staff members?
7. What constitutes the role of the personnel administrator in the power structure?

SELECTED READINGS

American Association of School Administrators: The American school superintendency, 30th yearbook, Washington, D.C., 1952, The Association.

American Association of School Administrators: Roles, responsibilities, relationships of the school board, superintendent, and staff, Washington, D.C., 1963, The Association.

American Educational Research Association: Teacher personnel. In Review of Educational Research, vol. 33, Washington, D.C., 1963, The Association.

Bucher, C. A.: Administration of health and physical education programs, including athletics, ed. 5, St. Louis, 1971, The C. V. Mosby Co.

Kindred, L. W., and Prince, W. B.: Staff welfare practices in the public schools, New York, 1963, The Center for Applied Research in Education, Inc., The Library of Education.

Moore, H. E.: The administration of public school personnel, New York, 1966, The Center for Applied Research in Education, Inc., The Library of Education.

National Education Association: The morale of teachers. Prepared by Dr. Frederick C. Redefer, Research Memo 1963-18, Washington, D.C., 1963, The Association.

National Society for the Study of Education: Behavioral science and educational administration. 63rd yearbook, Chicago, 1964, The University of Chicago Press.

PART TWO THE PHYSICAL EDUCATION PROGRAM

Administration is an essential concern when one is considering the various aspects of the physical education program, namely, (1) the basic instructional program, (2) the adapted program, (3) the intramural and extramural programs, and (4) the interscholastic and intercollegiate athletic programs. Administrative considerations are implied in such questions as the following: What constitutes a good program for each of the components of the physical education offering? What constitutes a sound program for boys, girls, men, and women? What are the various components of each phase of the program? What are some of the new developments in each area? What contributions should each of these programs make to each student? What does the future hold for each area? What is the role of leadership in the physical education program? What policies and procedures should one follow in order to have well-administered programs? What are some of the problems involved in the conduct of each program?

The sound organization and administration of physical education programs can result in significant contributions being made to the many human beings, young and old, who participate in these educational offerings. Unsound organization and administration, on the other hand, will result in harm with consequent loss of status and prestige to the profession.

Readings have been selected for Part Two that indicate the present status of physical education programs; also included are a discussion of some of the new developments in these programs and a critical look at some of the possibilities for expression of these programs in the future. A careful study of these selections should help the reader to better understand how such programs should be organized and administered to take advantage of recent trends in physical education and education as a whole.

CHAPTER 5 THE BASIC INSTRUCTIONAL PHYSICAL
EDUCATION PROGRAM

The basic instructional physical education program should provide students and participants with the opportunity to receive instruction, develop physical skills, acquire knowledge, and have a worthwhile social experience. It is in this phase of the total physical education program that student opinions are formed and attitudes are developed in respect to this field of endeavor. The fact that some persons grow into adulthood with indifferent or unfavorable attitudes toward physical education may often be traced back to the type of program they were exposed to while they were in school or college.

It has been said that if students are exposed to a sound physical education program during their formative years there will be little necessity for required physical education programs in later years. The reason for this statement is that the individual would develop skills and attitudes toward the physical education experience that reflect joy and satisfaction from participation; therefore, he or she would continue such enjoyable experiences without being required to do so.

The basic instructional phase of the total physical education program is, as the term implies, an instructional program. This means good teaching takes place, not free play. Skills are taught from a scientific approach utilizing the most recent knowledge about motor learning. The programs are progressive in nature, following the developmental aspects of human growth and development. Standards are established for student achievement. The class period involves more than physical activity. The student is also provided with experiences to help him understand such things as what physical activity does for his body and total health, the importance of sports and physical activities throughout a lifetime, the history of selected activities, and the role of sports in the various cultures of the world. Textbooks are used, tests given, and concepts taught. Records are also kept on each student so that physical educators can know what progress is being made and so that repetition is avoided.

The articles in Chapter 5 provide insights into various aspects of the basic instructional physical education program and what is needed to improve them.

Gordon Jensen feels, as he states in the first reading, that the time has come for physical education to inspect its merits. Basically, physical education improves a child's self-concept, thereby creating improved academic achievement. Physical education should be offered from kindergarten through the twelfth grade, with the instructional program being sequential and varied and with constant evaluative procedures being used. Jensen believes that, if this basic premise is carried out, then physical education will achieve its full potential.

In the next article, Adah Maurer implies that women's physical education programs are antiquated and suggests major changes in sports activities for women. Such major changes require training of teachers in cultural anthropology, group dynamics, psychology of exceptional children, sociology, and methods of play therapy. The fields of psychology, sociology, and physical education and recreation should overlap and supplement each other.

Coincidental with the recent upswing in criticism of physical education programs in our nation, Joseph B. Oxendine conducted a study on the status of required physical education in the spring of 1968. His results, reported in the reading in this chapter, are compared to those received in a similar study conducted in 1960, with some interesting changes noted.

Dance, as a unique expression of physical education's art, is explored by Betty Toman in the fourth article. The elements of art and the science of human development, as expressed through dance, become the responsibility of educators and should be taught from kindergarten through high school. Students will learn how to guide self-expression, with the possible outcome being better communication between students and teachers.

Communication is also the subject of an article by Aileene Lockhart, who believes that the best learning takes place through communication, which is necessary so that the students gain the idea of a problem and practice a situation in the best possible physical and psychological condition. Educators should provide the best models for each learning situation in order to achieve effective motor learning.

In the first of two articles by David Reams and T. J. Bleier, team teaching and the innovative reorganization necessary for team teaching are discussed. The method of organization that is utilized will help determine the results that will be achieved. Varying of the teacher-student ratio with each activity and effective utilization of teacher talents will help the learning process. Pupils will benefit from exposure to more than one teacher. Added pupil motivation, participation, interest, and improvement will make the extra administrative effort worthwhile.

In their second article Reams and Bleier discuss the impact the technological age has had on physical fitness. With the development of urbanization, the automobile, television, and other technological innovations, America has become a lazy society. Students who are physically fit take instruction more readily and have a greater desire to achieve. Physical fitness should not be overlooked in today's physical education programs.

Many educators—physical educators included—are critical of the programs offered in educational institutions today. The authors' ideas expressed in this chapter bring some of the main areas of criticism to the forefront.

21 ❧ PHYSICAL EDUCATION TODAY—TOMORROW'S OUTLOOK . . .*

GORDON JENSEN
SUPERVISOR, HEALTH AND PHYSICAL EDUCATION,
WISCONSIN DEPARTMENT OF PUBLIC INSTRUCTION

The growing body of knowledge in most academic areas and the demands for time in the school day by new subject matter fields have resulted in a close inspection of all curricular offerings. The field of physical education, among others, has taken its position on the inspection line to stand on its merits or move aside for more purposeful programs.

Any scrutiny of physical education necessitates a prior agreement as to what the program actually is. What constitutes a purposeful physical education program? Is it recreation, physical fitness training, athletic competition, or a combination of all these and more?

As a point of departure, perhaps we should follow a typical Wisconsin student through his 12 years participation in an average physical education program, beginning with kindergarten games, rhythms and mimetic activities.

Through the primary grades this student is taught by a certified physical education teacher two days per week, and three times per week by his classroom teacher. The physical education period is 30 minutes in length, consisting of 10 minutes for calisthenics and 20 minutes for rhythms, practice in basic skills and/or low-organized games.

If he is the typically normal, active, enthusiastic boy, our student enters the intermediate grades with a fairly good background of basic skills. He is now able to build upon his experiences and make good progress through a program of soccer, lead-up skills for football, basketball fundamentals, tumbling, rhythms, fitness activities and softball. His time with the physical education specialist is increased to three days per week in sixth grade, and once a week he is able to participate in an intramural athletic program after school.

Beginning in seventh grade and continuing through twelfth grade the typical student is assigned to a 50-minute physical education class three times per week. Gym uniforms are required and showers are provided. Traditional skills are stressed, but attention is also given tumbling, apparatus, fitness activities, square and social dancing, track and field, and selected aspects of health.

Some instruction is given in golf, tennis and volleyball. A variety of opportunities for varsity sports competition exists in both junior and senior high school. Intramural activities are offered weekly in grades seven through twelve, but rural students find it difficult to participate because buses leave immediately after school.

Although the program just described is not a poor one, it should be pointed out that better programs exist in many Wisconsin schools, as

*From Wisconsin Journal of Education 98:12, February 1966. Used by permission.

a result of curriculum planning by committees of teachers, administrators and consultants.

The outlook for physical education in future years is very promising. The traditional program was based partially on what seemed logical; science and research will determine tomorrow's needs. Already, findings such as the following have either assured the validity of present teaching or pointed the way toward new practices.

• It has been demonstrated that a child's self-concept, improved through skills gained in physical activities, can result in improved academic achievement.

• The work of Doman and Delacato indicate possibilities of reading and speech improvement through practice in certain motor patterns.

• The harmful effects of tobacco have been proven rather than "agreed upon."

• Traditional claims for the beneficial effects of vigorous exercise have been substantiated. Cardiologists recommend regular exercise for the young and old. Even cardiac patients benefit from prescribed exercise.

• A new unanimity among physicians in regard to physical education is exemplified by a quote from a national panel of outstanding medical leaders:

> Physical education, involving vigorous exercise adapted to individual needs and capacities, is so essential to optimum growth, development and health of pupils that it should be required daily in kindergarten through sixth grade, junior high schools and high schools.

If physical education is to fulfill its promise for the future, emphasis should be given to strengthening some well-known concepts and developing certain new ones. Specifically, the following points seem to need attention:

1. Physical education should be started in kindergarten and continued through the twelfth grade. Primary children need the program as much as secondary pupils. Classes should be scheduled daily in elementary schools and a minimum of three 50-minute periods per week in junior and senior high school. Regular opportunities for intramural activity should be provided for both boys and girls.

2. The program should be instructional and sequential, based upon the best current knowledge of growth and development. Children should be considered as individuals who stand at different levels of maturity, skill and experience. Every school's program should be available in written form.

3. Physical education activities must be varied to permit maximum benefits to children. All students need experiences in movement exploration, rhythms, game skills, fitness activities, aquatics, self-testing exercises, and competitive activities. Secondary students should receive instruction in more depth and in a wider range of activities.

4. Every graduating senior should leave school with sufficient competence and interest in several vigorous physical activities to insure his continued participation in adult life. For most students such competencies will necessitate more than a casual exposure to such sports as tennis, golf, swimming, skiing, hiking, bowling and the like.

5. School people, particularly physical educators, need to identify students with handicaps, physical defects, poor physical condition, and marked lack of coordination. Once the identification is accomplished, an adaptive or remedial program—planned jointly with the family doctor—should be provided to fit individual cases. An appropriate physical education program should be provided for every child in attendance.

6. Physical educators have a responsibility for teaching students the "why" of physical education. Compulsory fitness programs, practice techniques, specific training rules and endorsement of strenuous activity make little sense to students without supporting evidence and knowledge. The physically educated students should be conversant with appropriate aspects of anatomy, physiology, physiology of exercise, kinesiology, nutrition and first aid.

7. Curriculum content, methods of instruction, and pupil progress need constant evaluation. Experiments and changes, based on evaluation, should be commonplace in a healthy program.

Physical education as a curricular offering has a rightful place in the total education of children. Like all dynamic programs, it is striving for improvement. With the solution of such problems as transportation for intramural participants, lack of trained personnel, poor facilities, and crowded schedules, physical education will be able to approach its full potential.

22 ᴫ PHYSICAL EDUCATION: MODEL "T" IN THE SPACE AGE*

ADAH MAURER
PSYCHOLOGIST, CONTRA COSTA
COUNTY (CALIFORNIA) DEPARTMENT
OF EDUCATION

The present program in physical education for girls is as antiquated as the washboard. Based on the premise (important before 1920, when the women's suffrage amendment was finally passed) that women are "just as good as men," girls' physical fitness activities tend to be ambitious imitations of the program for boys.

It was historically necessary for women to rid themselves of the sidesaddle and the smelling salts, of second-rate status in a man's world. But the battle is won; the war of the sexes is over. The boyishform bra, the necktie severe, all of the badges and purple hearts of the forgotten fray are mouldering in old-fashioned attics. But in the athletic arena, the one place where women are most obviously outclassed, the futile posturings and protestations go on. The only change was the switch from middy and bloomers to romper suits.

Strange and irrelevant as it may seem, the typical session in far too many gymnasiums still begins with military drill. The mindless four-four beat permits no impertinent questions as to what goal girls shall forward march toward. The original purpose, training for obedience in the Kaiser's army, has been forgotten in failure. Training for obedience for its own sake, it has been agreed long since, would, if successful, leave the trainee at the mercy of any loud insistent voice. Training for intelligent followership that discriminates between causes and takes responsibility for choices, the educational corollary of political democracy, undergirds the modern courses of study in most classrooms and no one dreams of going back to the lockstep uniformity of authoritarianism—except in R.O.T.C. and in girls' gym.

Formal setting-up exercises ordinarily follow. High school girls have passed the stage of needing to romp out the stiffness of the sedentary school day and are ready to walk sedately and dance seductively. For them the stride position, the knees apart stoop, the prone support, and push-ups are graceless and without purpose. A useless chore that adds nothing to the store of knowledge, these mimetics provide no social interaction, correct no character, satisfy no aesthetic longing. Nor do they improve the physique. Posture improvement geared to the West Point ideal last seen in *Vogue* in the early Thirties has abdicated to the easy stance of the dancer and the controlled efficiency of the stewardess. But dancers and modeling experts are not normally certified. Schools continue to applaud the stiff upper backbone and the double chin tuck. A well proportioned figure that moves easily and gracefully is an asset every girl covets, but mass calisthenics are not, alas, the recipe. Heredity, good nutrition, a comfortable mattress, freedom from eyestrain, pleasurable participation in swimming or dancing, a feeling of pride in personal worth, and a few little tricks in walking and standing are quite enough.

From calisthenics, the lesson most often degenerates into a game, one in a round of seasonal sports: soccer, speedball, captain basketball, some version of baseball—watered down adaptations of the moral equivalent of gang fights: competitive athletics. In a 40- or 50-minute period, budding young women are required to undress, romperize, run or stand about for half an hour while a handful of adepts batter themselves into a lather, shower, pretty up again, and race to algebra or advanced Spanish. A horrendous nuisance, the daily, legally required performance neither relaxes nor revitalizes; it does not make childbirth easier nor prevent breast cancer. If all this expensive space and equipment are offerings on the altar of physical fitness, is it irreverent to ask: "Physical fitness for what?"

The decrease in the death rate during the twentieth century is creditable to medical discoveries, a fair distribution of medical facilities, and affluence generally. Superior performance in so-called fitness tests depends mostly upon body build and motivation to compete. It provides no insurance against coronaries or cancer which attack deskbound drudge, happy housewife, and teachers of physical education alike. "Fitness" for girls is a bit of folklore unrelated to genuine health.

---

*From The Clearing House **40**:210, December 1965. Used by permission.

Then what of character education? Historically, athletes have a few proud firsts, especially, in race relations. The Little League and the Globetrotters were long regarded as the prime preventives of delinquency until slum clearance promised more fundamental reform. Since both have failed, we are back at the beginning. Any possible civilizing influence that amateurism might have brought about has been thoroughly sabotaged by the record of collegiate sports in the last decade or two. The normal share that girls have played in the sports spectaculars has been limited to curtain raisers and sexy strutting. This may amuse or brighten the proceedings, but would have a difficult time fitting into the pigeonhole "Character education."

What excuse is left? The legislative lobbies that have rammed through mandatory periods of instruction in physical education have leaned heavily on the delinquent vs. the good soldier stereotypes. Persuasive arguments, if any are needed, are couched exclusively in terms of the male, and the girls are tossed in for makeweight. Required participation has withered from the college curriculum and ought to lose its categorical character on the secondary level as well. If considerations of policy and good sense do not dictate this, shortage of teachers may force it. The melange of skills from those of a top sergeant, a winning coach, a stage manager, a model, an acrobat, a dancer, a teacher of physiology, hygiene, manners, morals and public health, a life guard, an expert in first aid, a sanitary engineer, a square dance caller to those of a playmate, adviser, and confidant, attact fewer women each year. The lack of prestige afforded the low lady on the totem pole, the lack of a feminine identification, the lack of a conviction of usefulness, the resentment of growing numbers of students combine to make the position too unattractive to find many takers.

Health education, usually a once-a-week and somewhat peripheral responsibility of the physical education teacher, has similarly failed to respond to the differences that 40 years have made since the subject was first introduced. Rules for healthy living—wash behind the ears and don't take dope—are greeted with groans by television-sophisticated students. Attenuated dabs of physiology, hesitant sex education, side excursions into applications of the triangular bandage, and the rules of the road make a hodgepodge of material, often scuttled in favor of blackboard diagrams of tactics in tennis. It is safe to say that such a mulligan changes few attitudes to any measurable extent.

Most recently the surge to add mental health to the curriculum has replaced the highly unpopular lessons in etiquette. A delicate art, that of dealing with psychiatric problems, one that calls for many years of graduate training. Yet to whom is it delegated? To the one member of the faculty most highly trained in the nuances of cheerleading. Lessons in mental health, under these circumstances, tend to rely on the naive assumption that illegal pregnancies and the various addictions happen because young people have not been told no. The difference between the ability to recite the virtues and the willingness to practice them disappears in a hurried blur. Except for the rare, accidentally gifted, naturally understanding individual, lectures in mental health by the physical education staff are likely to be of the bagpipe type: an ill wind that nobody blows good.

Physical education for the future needs complete reevaluation and overhaul. Two major changes recommend themselves at once. First, sports activities for girls, divorced from the military manpower needs of the nation, should become optional. The girl who owns her own horse, the one who swims at the Y.M.C.A., the student of the ballet, all those who have access to private and out-of-school opportunities for physical expression could be freed from additional requirements. An optional program, especially in schools that serve the socially mobile, will continue to be appropriate. But the frenetic rush, the outdated routines could give way to a more flexible and realistic set of offerings.

Second, if mental health is deemed a proper and useful subject in the secondary schools, distinct from counseling and from academic psychology, and if how to handle one's emotions in emergencies seems on a par with how to handle one's car on the road and one's feet on the dance floor, then by all means let the teacher of physical education expand in still another direction. But let us be realistic in planning the curriculum for the training of such paragons of all the off-center skills. Training for this grab bag profession will need to concern itself less with the fine points of competitive athletics and more with a variety of social studies, including cultural anthropology, group dynamics, psychology of exceptional children, sociology, and methods of play therapy. Master's theses will bypass such virile topics as "Strength Decrement of Muscles of Trunk and

Lower Extremities from Sub-Maximal Treadmill Running" and attempt something real such as "Fear as a Factor in Clumsiness," or "Therapeutic Aspects of Folk Dancing," in which

psychology, sociology, and recreation overlap and supplement each other.

Enough of antiquated antics. Let's make it real or eliminate the waste motion!

23 ❧ STATUS OF REQUIRED PHYSICAL EDUCATION PROGRAMS IN COLLEGES AND UNIVERSITIES*

Joseph B. Oxendine
Professor, Department of Physical Education,
Temple University, Philadelphia

The status of required physical education in colleges and universities is of continuing interest, and occasional reports of changes in requirements or practices lead to suspicions that important trends are developing. Consequently, there is a need for periodic determinations of the status of the required program, also referred to as the "service," "basic instruction," or "nonmajor" program. While such information will not indicate what a particular institution's program should be, it does facilitate comparison with the general norm and reveals trends which may not be readily apparent.

The present study was designed to determine the status of physical education requirements and program practices in four-year colleges and universities in the United States during the spring of 1968. The results were compared with those of recent status studies by Hunsicker (1954), Cordts and Shaw (1960), and Oxendine (1961).[1]

A four-page questionnaire was prepared to gather information regarding requirements, credit, evaluation practices, and recent trends in physical education programs. The questionnaire and covering letter were mailed to the chairmen of physical education departments at the 1,046 institutions which the *College*

Blue Book (12th edition, Volume 1, 1968) lists as four-year institutions accredited by the regional accrediting agency and having an undergraduate enrollment of 500 or more. Very specialized institutions listed as "seminary," "conservatory," "mortuary science," or similar terms were omitted. Unlike previous studies in which differing techniques were used to select samples, this study included the total population meeting the established criteria. Of the 1,046 questionnaires, 723 (69%) were completed and returned. This number is compared with 265 returns out of 345 in the 1961 Oxendine study and 184 out of 300 in the Cordts and Shaw study.

Institutions returning the questionnaires were categorized into five groups according to size of undergraduate enrollment, four groups according to public or private affiliation, and three groups according to the sex of the student body. This information was provided by the person completing the questionaire. All tabulating and statistical work was done by hand or desk calculator. Since the number of institutions within each category varies, and since not all questionnaires were completed in their entirety, information is presented in percentages based on the number of institutions responding to each particular question.

Perhaps the most important single finding in the study deals with the overview of requirements and practices. Of all 723 institutions, 632 (87%) reported a physical education requirement for all undergraduates. (This figure exceeds that reported in the studies used as comparisons.) An additional 7% require physical education for students in certain departments or colleges. Only 6% of the 723 institutions reported no physical education requirements for undergraduates. Of 576 institutions responding to a later question, 74% indicated that requirements have remained unchanged during the past five years, while

*From JOHPER **40**:32, January 1969. Used by permission.

[1] H. J. Cordts and J. H. Shaw, Status of the physical education required or instructional programs in four-year colleges and universities, Research Quarterly, October 1960, p. 409-19.

Paul A. Hunsicker, A survey of service physical education programs in American colleges and universities, Fifty-Seventh Annual Proceedings of the College Physical Education Association (Chapel Hill, N.C., 1954), p. 29-30.

Joseph B. Oxendine, The service program in 1960-61, Journal of Health, Physical Education, Recreation, September 1961, p. 37-38.

15% reported an increase and 14% reported a decrease. These facts along with findings of previous studies reveal no reason to suspect any reduction of requirements during the past 15 years.

As was true in the earlier studies, the two-year physical education requirement was found to be the most common. Of the 677 institutions responding to this question, 66% require a two-year program. This figure exceeds those of the 1954, 1960, and 1961 studies which reported 57%, 61%, and 60% respectively. The question concerning required class time revealed that 92% of 683 schools require a minimum of one and one-half hours per week. Nearly half (46%) require two hours or more of class time per week, and only 4% require less than one hour a week.

In those institutions allowing exemptions for part or all of the physical education requirement, physical handicaps and psychological problems were found to be the most frequent reasons. Forty-two percent allow exemptions for military service or ROTC. This figure indicates a considerable reduction in such exemptions during the past ten years and may reflect a smaller number of student veterans as well as a decrease in military training programs on campus. The number of exemptions (44%) for intercollegiate sports participation has also decreased since 1958. Twenty-eight percent reported exemptions for marital status, 10% for intramural sports participation, 2% for age, and 29% for other reasons. Decision to exempt students from courses is most often made by the physical education department or the health services division and, in fewer cases, by the academic dean, counseling department, dean of students, or other personnel.

The percentage of institutions (74% of 669) reporting that credit is given for physical education courses has not changed appreciably in recent years. Comparative studies show that 77% allowed credit in 1954 and 76% in 1961. Concerning graduation requirements, more than half (55%) of the 567 institutions responding require four semester hours (or equivalent) of physical education. Earlier studies also found this to be the most common requirement. Twenty-eight percent reported a two semester hour requirement, 7% require three hours, and 4% require five hours or more. Of 469 responses, 41% allow one-half semester hour of credit for each clock-hour of class time per week; 32% allow one-fourth or one-third hour of credit; 17% allow one full hour of credit. A few (18%) of the institutions reported that students

may be allowed to meet course requirements and receive credit through proficiency exams rather than through regular class enrollment.

The great majority of institutions (77% of 691 responses) continue to give letter grades for physical education, and 82% (of 596) reported that the grading system is consistent with other courses. These figures are slightly higher than those reported in the earlier studies. A pass/fail grading system is used by about one-fifth of the schools, and a numerical system by the remaining 2%. Most institutions (63% of 651) also continue to count physical education marks in point-hour ratios; 60% (of 589) include such marks in honors for graduation. Evaluative practices for physical education courses were found to be similar to those of previous studies. Half of the institutions give written final exams in all courses, 34% give such exams in some courses, and 16% reported such exams were not given. Nearly half (46%) use identical exams in all course sections. Final exams are given prior to the regular exam period in most cases (61%) and in 61% of the schools, skill and fitness tests are given in all courses. Only 12% do not give skill and fitness tests. Knowledge and proficiency or skills are the criteria most often used as bases for the final mark.

While the course requirements have remained stable or shown slight increase during the past five years, a majority (59%) of institutions reported an increase in the size of teaching staff in relation to enrollment, and 8% reported a decrease. Nearly half (48%) have increased the adequacy of physical education facilities in proportion to enrollment; 39% indicate that facilities have remained constant.

Program changes appear to have been reasonably moderate during the past five years. The institutions were asked to indicate an increase or decrease in the following types of activities: recreational activities, fitness and weight control, gymnastics, aquatics, rhythms, team sports, adapted, and other. When the reported number of increases are compared with decreases, only activities categorized as "recreational" and "fitness and weight control" have shown significant gains. The most obvious shift of emphasis is the decrease in team sports, with more than half of the institutions reporting a reduction. Another detectable trend is the increase in coeducational courses at schools of all sizes. Thirty-seven percent of 334 institutions indicate that less than one-fourth of all physical education courses are coeducational; 21% report one-quarter to one-half; 18%, one-half to three-quarters; 22%, over three-quarters. Of 634 institutions, 47% offer such courses as electives, and 22% require them. The remaining 31% do not offer coeducational courses.

The number of class absences allowed is uniform for all courses in 64% of the schools and is determined by the instructor in the remaining schools. About one-third allow students to make up class absences while at other institutions excess absences result in automatic failure or a lowered grade in the course.

Comparison of institutions by size

To facilitate comparisons based on size, institutions were organized into five groups according to the number of undergraduate students: (A) 500–1,000; (B) 1,000–2,500; (C) 2,500–5,000; (D) 5,000–10,000; (E) over 10,000. One hundred and ninety-one questionnaires were returned from Group A, 258 from B, 117 from C, 86 from D, and 71 from E. The fact that a higher number of completed questionnaires was received from smaller institutions is due primarily to the fact that there are fewer large institutions to which questionnaires could be sent.

Reported figures indicated that smaller schools have a tendency toward an absolute requirement for all students while larger schools allow for greater variation in requirements among departments or colleges. The percentage of institutions requiring physical education for all students decreases steadily as enrollment increases and ranges from 94% of Group A to 72% of Group E. The number of schools requiring physical education in some departments or colleges increases with enrollment, ranging from 1% of Group A to 20% of Group E. This may be due to the fact that larger schools more

often have specialized departments or programs of study which assumed greater autonomy. As mentioned earlier, the two-year requirement is most common among all institutions, but it is most prevalent at smaller schools. Of the first four groups, 65% to 70% require two years, and 25% to 35% require one year of physical education. In Group E, 53% require two years and 45% require only one year. Larger schools are less likely to excuse students because of physical or psychological problems, but allow exemptions for age or proficiency exams more frequently than do smaller schools.

Academic status more prevalent in large institutions

The study reveals that large institutions count physical education as a regular academic course more readily than smaller schools. This tendency is reflected in the awarding of credit, consistency of grades with other courses, counting of grades in point-hour ratios, and the administration of written final examinations.

In regard to developments in the area of physical education during the past five years, course requirements at larger institutions have tended to remain constant while smaller institutions have shown a somewhat greater increase in such requirements. Program changes and the status of staff and facilities in proportion to enrollment are similar in all groups and consistent with the overview of developments mentioned earlier. While institutions in all groups report an increase in coeducational courses, a majority of schools in Groups D and E offer such courses as electives. Coeducational courses are not offered at 44% of Group A institutions.

SUMMARY OF THE MOST IMPORTANT FINDINGS

1. Seven hundred and twenty-three institutions returned completed questionnaires. This represented 69% of the 1,046 questionnaires mailed.
2. Eighty-seven percent of reporting institutions have a physical education requirement for all students. An additional 7% have a requirement for students in certain departments or schools. This represents a slight increase in the requirement as reported eight and ten years ago.
3. Among those institutions with a requirement, two-thirds mandate physical education for a period of two years.

4. Physical education is established on a sounder academic basis at large institutions as compared to small ones, at public institutions as compared to private ones, and at coeducational institutions as compared to segregated ones.
5. Physical education courses showing the greatest gains in program emphasis are "recreational" and "fitness" activities.
6. There is a rather strong tendency toward the the reduction or elimination of team sports.
7. Institutions of all sizes have shown coeducational classes during recent years.

Comparison of institutions by affiliation

Occasionally views are expressed that physical education practices at public institutions differ from those at private institutions and that private church-related schools view physical education differently than do private nonsectarian schools. Therefore, sample schools were asked to indicate their affiliation as public (state, federal, city, etc.), private sectarian, or private nonsectarian. Since many private institutions failed to indicate nonsectarian or sectarian, a fourth group listed only as "private" was also established for use in the analysis. Two hundred and ninety-four completed questionnaires were received from public institutions, 154 from private sectarian schools, 61 from private nonsectarian, and 214 from private institutions not reporting affiliation.

Public and private schools follow similar practices

Generally, suspicions regarding wide variations in physical education practices among public and various types of private institutions are not borne out in this study. An examination of the requirements and types of activities included reveals a high degree of consistency among the different types. Approximately 90% of institutions within each group require physical education for all students, and 61% to 70% of each group require a two-year program. A one-year program is required by 26% to 34% of each group. At least 90 minutes of class time per week is required at about 90% of institutions within each group, the most common requirement being from one and one-half to two hours per week. Public institutions are more likely to award credit toward graduation than private schools. Less than half of the private nonsectarian schools allow credit while 87% of the public schools do so. A graduation requirement of four semester-hours of physical education remains the most common among all groups; however, public schools tend to allow somewhat less credit per clock-hour in physical education than do private schools. Forty-three percent of public institutions allow one-third to one-fourth credit per clock-hour while about 45% of all private school groups allow one-half credit. Also, public schools more consistently give physical education grades similar to those in other courses and are more likely to give written final examinations in all courses. Grades are given on a pass/fail basis at 40% of the private nonsectarian schools, and letter grades are given at 87% of the public schools and 79% of the private sectarian schools. Of the public schools, 79% count physical education marks in the point-hour ratio, and 71% include them in graduation honors. Fifty-eight percent of the private sectarian, 32% of the private nonsectarian, and 52% of the other private institutions include such marks in the point-hour ratio and in graduation honors. More than half of the institutions within each private school group give identical final examinations in all course sections, but only 38% of the public institutions give identical tests.

Physical and psychological problems remain the most common reason for exemption from physical activity courses in all groups. Public institutions allow exemptions for age more frequently than do private schools, which, in turn, more often allow exemptions for intercollegiate sports participation. All groups reported that exemptions were most often made by the physical education department or the health services division.

The common practice among all groups is the administration of final exams prior to the regular exam period. Over half of the public schools give skill and fitness tests in all courses. Of the private school groups, 39% to 44% give such tests in all courses, and 42% to 46% in some courses. In all groups, proficiency or skill and knowledge are given the greatest emphasis in determining the final mark. Less than 25% of each group allow students to meet course requirements and receive credit through proficiency examinations. Over half of the institutions within each group reported that the number of class absences allowed is uniform in all courses, but more public schools (43%) than private schools (29% to 33%) reported that the number is determined by the instructor.

Physical education requirements remain constant

Findings of this study reveal that during the past five years, physical education requirements have remained constant in about 70% of institutions within each group; increased and decreased requirements were both about 11% for all groups. The size of staff in proportion to enrollment has increased in 67%, and remained constant in 26% of public schools. Of the private school groups, 47% to 56% reported an increase and 37% to 40% reported that the proportion has remained unchanged. Although the adequacy of facilities in relation to size of student body has increased in at least 40% of all institutions within each group, public schools have shown a greater increase than

private schools in comparison to those reporting that the relationship has remained constant. The proportion of coeducational courses
has remained static in 58% and 52% of the private sectarian and private nonsectarian schools
respectively, while 55% of the public schools
and 60% of the other private schools reported
an increase. Coeducational courses are not
offered at 63% of the private nonsectarian
schools. Of the public schools, 55% offer such
courses as electives and 25% offer and require
them.

Among private institutions, those classified
as sectarian more closely parallel the practices
of public institutions than do the others. Nonsectarian institutions often do not count physical education as a regular college course. This
is reflected particularly in the awarding of grades
which are often inconsistent with those in
other courses, a tendency not to include them
in grade-point averages or honors for graduation, and a greater reluctance to give credit for
physical education.

Comparison of institutions by sex of student body

To compare physical education practices on the
basis of sex of the undergraduate enrollment,
returned questionnaires were divided into
three groups. Of the 723 institutions, 604 were
classified as coeducational, 83 as all female,
and 36 as all male. Since the great majority are
coeducational, the matter of comparison
presented some problems but, nevertheless,
revealed some interesting observations.

More women's schools require physical education

The all female group has a higher percentage of
schools which require physical education for
all students and also a greater tendency toward
at least a two-year requirement. Ninety-four
percent of the women's colleges require physical education for all students, as compared with
78% of the men's colleges and 87% of the
coeducational schools. A two-year requirement was reported by 71% of the women's
group and 67% of the coeducational group. Of
the men's group, the number (39%) requiring
a two-year program is identical with the number
requiring only one year. However, the men's
institutions generally require a greater amount
of class time per week; two to three hours in
42%, and over three hours in 36% of men's
schools. One and one-half to two hours of class
time per week; two to three hours in 42%, and
over three hours in 36% of men's schools. One

and one-half to two hours of class time per
week is required by 53% of the women's
schools and 48% of the coeducational schools.

Coeducational schools more often give credit
for physical education courses than do all male
or all female schools. Credit is given by 80%
of the coeducational schools but by less than
half of both men's and women's colleges. Of
the coeducational schools, 43% give one-half
semester-hour credit per clock-hour of class
time per week, 33% give one-fourth or one-
third hour of credit, and 15% give full credit.
Of the women's group, 24% allow one-fourth
or one-third hour of credit; 29%, one-half
credit; and 33%, full credit. Twenty-four percent of the men's group allow no credit for
physical education courses; 47% allow one-half
credit; and 18%, full credit.

Physical education courses are graded on a
pass/fail basis at 61% of the all male institutions,
while letter grades are given at 73% of the
women's and 80% of the coeducational schools.
Of the coeducational schools, 85% reported
that physical education grades were consistent
with those given in other courses; 70% include
them in point-hour ratios, and 66% include
them in graduation honors. Of the all female
institutions, 73% report marks consistent with
other grades, but only 23% to 24% include
them in grade point averages and graduation
honors. Physical education marks are consistent with other courses in 57% of the men's
schools, included in grade point averages at
33%, and included in honors at 29%. Final
examinations are given in all courses by over
half (52%) of the coeducational schools, 37%
of the women's schools, and 23% of the men's
schools. Thirty-four percent of both coeducational and women's schools report final exams
are given in some courses, and 55% of men's
schools report that final exams are not given.
Of those schools giving final exams in physical education courses, most administer such
exams prior to the regular exam period. The
final mark is most often based on knowledge
and proficiency or skill at coeducational or all
female schools while men's schools reported
"other factors" received most emphasis. The
number of absences allowed is uniform for all
courses at nearly all (93%) of the men's colleges
who also report automatic failure as the most
frequent result of excess absences. Sixty percent of coeducational and 75% of women's
schools report a uniform number of absences
for all courses. Students may make up excess
absences in 48% of the women's schools or
receive a lowered grade at 32% of women's

schools. Make-up of absences is allowed by 30% of coeducational schools; lowered grades and automatic failure are each reported as practices by 35%.

Exemption from physical activity courses for reasons of physical or psychological problems is most common in all three groups. Almost all (92%) of men's schools and 48% of coeducational schools allow exemption for intercollegiate sports participation. Exemptions for age are more common at coeducational schools than at men's or women's schools, and exemption for proficiency exams is more readily allowed by women's schools.

Coeducational course opportunities vary

Of the all male institutions questioned, none offer coeducational physical education courses. Eight percent of the women's institutions offer coeducational courses in cooperation with neighboring institutions. Of the coeducational institutions, 54% offer them as electives, 23% offer and require them.

During the past five years, course requirements have remained constant at 73% of the coeducational schools, 71% of the women's schools, and 63% of the men's schools. Coeducational institutions have shown the greatest increase in size of staff in proportion to enrollment, while the all male institutions show the greatest increase in adequacy of facilities. Of the coeducational schools, 62% indicated an increase in staff in proportion to enrollment; 50% of the men's schools, and 40% of the women's schools reported such an increase. An increase in facilities in proportion to enrollment was reported by 60% of the men's schools, and by 50% of the coeducational and 38% of the women's schools.

24 ❧ DANCE—PHYSICAL EDUCATION'S ART FORM*

Betty Toman
Professor and Dance Coordinator,
Iowa State University, Ames, Iowa

Physical education is more than fitness; more than play. It is movement; it is sport; it is dance. Physical education is also learning, sharing, experiencing and creating. The specific concern of the physical educator is the human body: physiologically, psychologically, sociologically and aesthetically. Dance is a wonderful hybrid of two equal parental lines: the art and the science of human movement; the physical and the aesthetic. This is the physical educator's unique art form.

_____

*From Iowa Journal of Health, Physical Education, and Recreation, November 1969, p. 10. Used by permission.
Miss Toman received the B.S. degree in dance under Margaret H'Doubler at the University of Wisconsin and the M.S. degree from Iowa State University. She has served the IAHPER often as a program participant and as Vice President for Health, adviser to the Student Section, Chairman of the Professional Preparation Section and State Dance Chairman. In 1967, she received the IAHPER Honor Award. She has served the Dance Division of the AAHPERS in many capacities: presently as Chairman of the Heritage Committee, a member of the Curriculum Committee and past Chairman of the Theater Section. In 1969, she received an Outstanding Teacher Award from Iowa State University and is well known for her Graduate Dance Workshop for Physical Educators held in Ames every summer.

Man has danced almost since the world began. He has danced for joy; he has danced for hate; he has danced for love, for anger and for fear. Dance has been related to his religious life and to his social life. Almost every occasion has called for dance, and some dances existed for no reason but to use stored up energy and emotion. The art of dance has lived through the centuries, and probably as long as man can move, man will dance. Dance has had a long and honorable history in education, and the values of dance to a total education are numerous and varied. Here is a subject that not only is an excellent physical activity but can be a creative art experience as well.

Art—I keep using that word. It is not difficult to pronounce or hard to spell. It is a simple three letter word used by almost everyone, yet it is most difficult to define. We attend an elementary school exhibition of pictures drawn by fourth graders and call this an art exhibit. We hear a concert at Carnegie Hall and call the pianist an artist. We eat a wonderful meal at the home of a friend and say that our hostess is skilled in the art of cooking. From such statements a child might define art as a picture, music or good food. Although this definition sounds silly, is it really so far from wrong? Careton Noyes stated, "Art is creation. It is the combination of already existing material elements into new forms which become thus the realization of a preconceived idea."[1] The fourth grade child in his crude design was creating. He was working from an idea with the elements he had in his capacity. Naturally, his expression would not be equal to Rembrandt's, for his experiences and knowledges were limited. Yet, he certainly was creating a child's form of art. The housewife in preparing her delicious meal selected carefully the ingredients she would use, pictured in her mind the way she wanted things to look, hoped that it would please her guests, and worked with the idea of creating a meal fit for a king. Can we deny that this is art? The musician playing a Brahms concerto is only an artist to the degree in which he brings to the music something of his own. He plays the written score but it is his interpretation of it, his expression, and his ability to bring across his feelings about it to his audience that makes him an artist. Otherwise, he is merely copying, creating nothing, adding nothing, feeling nothing and is less of an artist than the housewife and the school boy.

Too many people think of art just as expensive paintings in museums, classical music played in huge symphony halls and famous sculptured figures in Greece. They do not think of art in the local gym. No! Never! Actually, art should be a part of all our daily lives. We all have the artistic need for self expression. Every man is an artist. It is nothing more than a matter of degree that makes the great artist. The art spirit is possessed by all! Movement is certainly a form of self expression, and since dance is expression through movement, it is easy to see that the claim of dance as a basic art form is a strong one. Art in the gymnasium—yes—yes—a thousand times yes!

In this rapidly changing world, I believe the real need is for broadly educated persons who are physically fit, who are able to adjust to new situations and who are able to think imaginatively and creatively. Science and the arts should not be competitive, but complementary; both should expand in union in our educational system. I believe that teaching dance creatively to all boys and girls is even more important today than when dance as a creative art experience was initiated into the academic curriculum years ago. Fortunately,

the last few decades have seen an increasing development and expansion of dance in education. Unfortunately, this expansion has been much greater in many of the other states than it has been in Iowa. The majority of Iowa students are graduating from high school viewing dance not as a part of their educational curriculum, but as something the few *girls* able to afford it, did outside of school at a private studio. After twelve years of education most students do not think of dance as a basic art form, for their art classes were limited to painting, literature, music and/or drama. They do not think of dance as an important part of a total physical education program. Margaret H'Doubler has stated "If dance is to function again as a vital experience in the lives of our people, it must be the responsibility of our educators."[2] Are we ready to accept this responsibility?

I believe we must view dance as an indispensable component of a well-rounded physical education program, recognizing the unique contribution of dance as a form of self discovery that cannot be measured competitively against a set standard or even the achievement of others. Serving as a member of the Curriculum Committee of the Dance Division of the AAHPER, I have worked on preparing supplementary guidelines for institutions applying for accreditation programs for the preparation of teachers of dance. In this committee report we state that the dance educator should be responsible for bringing well conceived programs of dance into the elementary and secondary school systems. The teacher of dance must be aware of the proper dance activities appropriate for students at various stages of their growth and emotional development. The dance teacher must be throughly familiar with the various dance forms (for example, the recreational and social forms of dance as well as an understanding of dance as a basic art form) to effectively present a progressive program of dance activities. Dance should provide an understanding of the psycho-physical instrument, a development of aesthetic values, encouragement of the creative attitude and recognition of individuality to aid in the physical, social and psychological maturing of all students.

I endorse in its entirety the philosophy of

[1]Noyes, Careton E. The gate of appreciation. Boston: Houghton Mifflin Company, 1907. page 5.

[2]H'Doubler, Margaret. Dance a creative art experience. New York: F. S. Crofts and Company, 1940. page 59.

these recommendations. Yet, there are just not enough dance-artist-educators to provide a dance specialist for every school. In many cases in Iowa, if dance is to be taught, it becomes the responsibility of the physical educator. Yet, have many of us in higher education tended to focus our attention on just the talented few? Have we been so concerned about where dance is taught—in a fine arts department, school of performing arts or physical education department—that we have failed to be concerned with whether or not dance is being taught at all at the K-12 levels? Have we been so concerned that dance be considered an art form and not just a "rhythmic sport" that we have *failed* to be concerned with whether or not dance is even being considered?

I believe that physical education is more than fitness and sports: it is dance. The gymnasium is the place for learning, sharing, experiencing and *creating*. As Margaret H'Doub-

ler so beautifully stated, "Dance—freeing the body from needless inhibitions and breaking down some of the unessential reserves, frees the personality for a wider and more satisfying life."[3] As teachers interested in youth we must be concerned with significant contemporary problems. Students today have a real need for self expression. Guiding them into healthy ways of expressing themselves is a challenge and a privilege. It constitutes hard, earnest work and a belief in youth, but it can reap a truly satisfying reward. Teaching should not be something static or passive but as active as art and life itself—an endless search and a continous creating. As Snoopy so often has said, "To dance is to live and to live is to dance." Maybe we do not have to go that far, but maybe dance could be one means to help us think more creative thoughts, do more imaginative things and communicate better with our students.

---

[3] H'Doubler, Margaret, op. cit., page 66.

25 ❧ CONDITIONS OF EFFECTIVE MOTOR LEARNING*

AILEENE LOCKHART
PROFESSOR OF PHYSICAL EDUCATION,
UNIVERSITY OF SOUTHERN CALIFORNIA,
LOS ANGELES

A wide variability is to be expected within any physical education class. Many dimensions account for the wide range of observable differences: differences in maturity and development, abilities and capacities; previous experience; ways of relating to the group; energizing structure, set, and goals; and perception—particularly self-perception and self-expectation. Effective learning depends mostly on the learner himself. The first and final and most indispensable requirement, the sine qua non of success, is that which coaches call *desire.* Though the above are crucial factors, nevertheless there are also certain conditions under which learning can best be accomplished and

---

*Adapted from an address given at the 1965 Fall Conference, the Fiftieth Anniversary, of the Eastern Association for Physical Education of College Women. This copyrighted material, used here by permission, is from a forthcoming book by Aileene Lockhart, Joan Johnson, Bonnie Purdy, and Waldean Robichaux on motor learning and motor performance, to be published by William C. Brown Company, Publishers. From JOHPER **38**:36, February 1967. Used by permission.

performance facilitated. The purpose here is to consider these conditions. Under what circumstances can we expect best learning? What knowledge can the instructor use to help students learn motor skills? Certainly one of the teacher's important roles is to help students short-cut the learning process, to reduce the price of pure trial and error learning. How can he do this?

1. *Communicate with the learner.*

The problem must be set. It must be clear and relevant. The teacher then helps to speed up the learning process by supplying external cues which trigger internal cues for action, cues which the student might or might not discover himself.

We have to communicate in some way with the performer in order to get the cues across. The usual external cues fall into two categories: verbal and visual. Thus we verbally explain the purpose of movement, we describe, we analyze, we suggest, we correct. In this way we hope that the student will understand what he is to do and will develop a concept of the problem.

Visual cues may be supplied through demonstration, visual aids, and films. Visually we attempt to show the learner how a movement looks and hope to give him a visual self-concept of how his body will look as he performs the movement. Sometimes a third method of guiding the performer is used. We attempt to move the learner through the sequence of a desired movement, hoping that in this way he will "get the feel" or "get the idea." Giving the learner a directional set in this manner is called manual guidance. Sometimes we merely put a hand on one spot to isolate the point of action for the learner, again to "give him the idea" (and also for safety purposes). It is certainly not the purpose in some of our teaching to direct the performer toward a specified response. It is not appropriate to show or tell the performer specifically what to do when the purpose is to develop original expression, or when problem-solving is itself the goal.

When movement exploration is the objective, when kinesthetic awareness of the quality of movement is sought, or when movement becomes the medium of communication (as in dance), stereotyped movement response is the very antithesis of the purpose of teaching. In these cases that which follows regarding communication with the learner is not applicable. Even when we attempt to elicit a formalized movement pattern, for example, the pattern of the American slice serve in tennis, the learner's response will not be identical to that which we preconceive nor can the performer, even if he tries, ever respond in exactly the same way twice even though automaticity of pattern, without conscious control of the higher centers, is the final objective of highly skilled performance.

Verbal communication

In general, we can say these things about verbal communication. Explanations should be kept at a minimum during the early stages of learning. It is not necessary, in fact it is confusing, to go into the fine details of performance at the beginning levels of learning. Direct the learner's attention only to the basic essential aspects of the movement problem. Do not analyze excessively. As skill increases, however, and when learners are highly motivated, we can communicate more and more via verbalization.

Visual communication

Most frequently we try to give the learner an idea of a formalized movement pattern by showing him what it looks like. The easiest way to achieve a specific motor goal is to follow a good example. Demonstrations, therefore, should be well done. Despite the fact that beginners do not perceive all the details of performance, demonstrations should be executed as perfectly as possible, because some learners are more apt and more movement-oriented than others and these students may pick up some of the details. Since we do not want learners to develop inefficient movement habits, every portion of a demonstration should be performed as well as possible. Demonstrations should be presented more than once. In general, we should not try to demonstrate in slow motion for it is practically impossible to perform in slow motion without destroying or distorting the desired movement—that is, the movement as it should be when performed at normal speed.

Manual guidance

Manual guidance, except when spotting a performer, is a last resort. Some authorities do not believe that this technique aids motor learning at all. All agree, however, that whatever advantages may accrue are limited mostly to initial learning trials. Manual guidance may be effective when used with the poorly skilled student, the slow learner, the very young, and the very old. For each of these, such guidance appears to be helpful presumably because it gives them confidence. Manual guidance is annoying to some students, and consequently the teacher should be sensitive to the student's response. If the learner does not respond well, then this kind of guidance may harm rather than aid the learning process. Though putting a learner through an action can never truly and completely duplicate a self-initiated movement, it may give some learners a specific concept of what to do and at what time to do it.

When we generalize, of course, a few exceptions to the contrary are temporarily ignored. Though we have said that manual guidance (guiding the learner through a whole pattern of action) is a last resort, no intent has been made to rule out the spotting one gives to a gymnast, for example. Highly proficient gymnasts are often aided greatly by isolating one crucial point in a performance; this is often done by touching the performer at a critical instant and at a decisive point in an action.

All of these—verbalization, demonstration, and manual guidance—are good methods if properly used, but apparently they are not equally effective. Considering the evidence now available, evidence from several disciplines, we may conclude that demonstration and manual guidance are in general of greatest help during the introductory stages of learning, while verbalization gains in value after the learner has developed a reasonable amount of proficiency and understanding both of the movement and of the terminology associated with the specific sport being learned. Demonstration is valuable at all levels of ability; learners at different levels of skill, however, derive different values from demonstration. It should be remembered, that the pupil learns only if he actually perceives, thinks, and plans during instruction. Words often are most inadequate substitutes for motor cues.

2. *Provide suitable conditions for practice.*

Having derived some idea of what is to be done, the learner then must practice. The teacher cannot do this for the learner. Motor learning results from meaningful practice, the aim and the result of which are known to the learner and accepted by him. Significant improvement will come only if these are honest attempts to improve. Many students just go through the motions. It is not surprising, therefore, that they make little progress. Practice alone will not result in proficiency.

The conditions and circumstances under which the learner practices can be more or less controlled by the instructor. It is the instructor's business to make the conditions for learning as favorable as possible. Quite a bit of information has been amassed regarding these conditions.

Should practice be distributed or massed?
Determination of the length and distribution of practice periods depends upon many variables, such as the nature and difficulty of the learning task, the age and maturity of the learner, and the degree of mastery which will satisfy the learner. It is obvious that no one recommendation can ever be made regarding the exact length of the practice period. "Long" and "short" are relative terms; the requirement of different learning tasks vary, and individuals differ. It is quite well established, however, that distributed practice is, in general, much more effective and economical for *learning* than massed practice. This statement is true provided, quite naturally, that each period is long enough for the learner to become oriented to the task—that is, warmed up to it—and long enough so that some progress can be made.

If the skill level is high and mastery is the goal, then performers will profit more from massed practice. Probably the most profitable

arrangement is one of progressive increase: Practice new motor tasks often, in short practice periods; as the length of practice sessions increases, as it should with increased ability and motivation, the length of the rest intervals between practices should be extended. The optimum arrangement obviously is one in which two extremes are avoided: the disrupted learning of too short periods and the loss of gains which result if practice sessions are too widely separated.

Should an activity be practiced in its entirety or broken down into parts?
Many studies, ever since the latter part of the nineteenth century, have dealt with the relative merits of part versus whole methods of learning. The results are vague and conflicting, largely because of terminology: what is a whole? and what is a part?

It is possible to hazard some educated guesses about the most effective methods of practicing gross motor activities. The whole method is preferable when the activity to be learned is composed of continuous or serial movements which form a chained sequence, in activities where timing and speed are fundamental in order not to destroy the structure of the total pattern, and where the proper relationships and coordination of the total pattern would be destroyed if various bits of the total pattern were isolated. Many movement patterns fall into this category. Some skills—take the tennis serve again as an example—are composed of an almost unbreakable coherence. The serve is continuous, one phase of it blending into and providing the cue for the next phase in sequential fashion. Present the serve as a whole; have students practice the complete action. Do not break it down unless the total pattern (in this case, the total serve constitutes the complete whole) obviously is too large a whole for the specific learner. It sometimes takes twice as long to combine the various parts of a serve into one unified, smooth act if the parts have been learned separately. The most important characteristic of a skill is its wholeness, its entity. The instructor should teach, therefore, the largest whole which he thinks his students can manage. After this, one part certainly may be singled out for special attention and practice, but only in understandable relation to the whole pattern.

If the final performance is complex but is composed of a number of sub-skills each of which can be considered to be a complete meaningful unit, then the part method of practice may be superior. Softball, for example, is a complex sport which answers this description. Many team-type sports fall into this category. There is evidence that after the learner achieves a general idea of the object of the whole complicated game, then he must learn the individual skills in relation to the total game, in relation to teammates and opponents, and with reference to the complex rules which govern the sport. All of these parts must be systematically and continuously put together to make up the whole game. When the part method is used, to be successful it must always be with reference to a concept of the whole. The learner must have at least a general picture of the final total objective—a general orientation—if he is going to learn the total act or, indeed, be motivated to attempt to do so.

What about so-called "mental practice"?

Motor learning and improved motor performance result from purposeful practice but there are many ways of practicing, many roads to learning. That anyone is surprised to learn that progress can come from "mental practice" is astonishing. All motor learning is perceptual. There is constant communication between brain and muscle. The human organism is delicately integrated and basically inseparable; consequently activity anywhere affects the whole. Both learning and performance can be improved by the intense stimulation of thoughtful rehearsal; indeed it is unlikely that much improvement can be achieved otherwise.

It seems completely clear that this type of practice is effective, but it is also equally clear that this method alone is not as effective as physical practice alone (if indeed this were possible). It is true that rehearsing the "feel of a movement" and going through the pattern of a movement awakens a kinesthetic image of that pattern, but the image cannot be identical with or as intense as that experienced during full-scale performance. Rehearsing movement in this way, however, can help in the attainment of smooth, coordinated performance.

What aid can we give the learner? Suggest that he *focus attention* on that which he wishes or needs to improve. Get into an *activity attitude;* a "set" for performance and a concept of it can be established by "feeling through" the performance. The learner should attempt to see himself in his mind's eye going through the action as he imagines himself performing it, as he observes others doing it, or as he reads about it. He should try to imagine himself going through the action as *vividly* as possible

and go through patterns of *total* action, not just isolated movements.

All of this should be done, however, prior to or between actual trials. During performance, concentrate only on the objective of the action, never on the mechanics of a skill. Although the higher centers are required during learning and during attempts to improve performance, the final objective is to be able to perform the skills involved in a sport in an automatic way. In the middle of a tournament, if the performer starts thinking about "how" to perform he will completely wreck his game. He should by then so well know how, that his mind is left free to concentrate on strategy.

3. *Provide appropriate learning experiences.*

It is not profitable to try to learn several activities simultaneously if they involve similar but conflicting elements. This is explained by our knowledge of the specificity of motor learning. For example, there may be conflicting transfer effects if one attempts to learn badminton and tennis at the same time.

4. *Provide good learning tools.*

Good equipment should be provided even for beginners. Favorable working conditions and tools have much to do with efficiency and effectiveness of motor learning.

5. *Group students for learning.*

It is probably best to group students homogeneously for instruction and practice. Since it is impossible to predict from performance in one activity what one may do in another, assignment to groups should be made on the basis of ability in a specific activity. Institutions of higher learning usually accomplish this assignment reasonably well, with beginning, intermediate, and advanced classes in dance, badminton, and fencing, for example. Junior and senior high school classes are not as well grouped. Often they are assigned on the basis of grade alone.

6. *Use specific warm-ups.*

Despite some suggestions to the contrary, warming up still seems to be a desirable practice. To be most effective, warm-ups should be closely associated with—that is, they should directly lead up to—the specific activity which is to be performed.

7. *Provide good models.*

Emphasize good form. Learn an activity correctly from the start. It is difficult to change form, and poor form imposes a barrier which limits the ultimate potentialities of a performance. This does not mean that there is but one way of reaching a goal. Performing within the large confines of good mechanical principles, however, results in most effective action, and it is this that we call "good form." Good form makes possible the greatest amount of precision, force, ease, and poise—thus skill. Since the structure of the human body remains relatively constant, since the tools which are used in a given sport at any one time are limited (that is, the approximate size, shape, and weight of the rackets, balls, bats, etc.), and since we move within the limitations of forces which we cannot alter (the laws of gravity, velocity, etc.), the best methods of using the human body vary little.

Differences in *style* are quite possible while still adhering to the principles of good form and are, of course, to be expected. Students should practice within the general limits of basic good form, but should not imitate some specific style. No matter how successful the idiosyncracies of style seem to be for another performer, style should develop individually and uniquely for each performer.

Best motor learning occurs within the limits of good form. When learning, the student should practice in ways which offer the greatest possibilities of not only immediate but continually spiraling success. "What" the objective is must be clear; "why" must be accepted; but it should be remembered that there is no exact "how."

8. *Provide realism in practice.*

Whenever possible, practice should be conducted at the normal speed of the activity, certainly as close to that speed as performers can *control*. When speed is essential to proper execution of a motor skill, it should be practiced from the beginning. (Note: "wild" speed is not recommended.) If accuracy is the final goal, this should be practiced from the first. If both speed and accuracy are equally important in final performance, then both should be stressed equally during the course of learning.

9. *Provide knowledge of results.*

The learner must know how he is doing, whether the direction of his effort is correct. Knowledge of results increases the rate of learning and its accuracy. It is essential to the maintenance of motivation.

10. *Provide for use of skills.*

In order to retain that which is practiced, there must be overlearning. This does not mean learning too much! It means that, up to a point, the more an activity is practiced the better and longer it will be remembered. It means practicing beyond the point of original learning—practicing to the point of automaticity of action. Teaching and learning would be fruitless unless at least some memory resulted from practice. The superior retention of motor skills (in comparison with the retention of other kinds of learnings) is largely accounted for by the greater overlearning customarily associated with motor performance. Overlearning accounts for the fact that patterns can be so well established that it is not necessary to think of the details of performance. Overlearning is the way to establish motor habits. Motor memory may or may not be brought to the conscious level. Just as a composition is remembered in the hands as well as the head of a pianist, so too is the approach and delivery of the bowler's hook ball retained. Consistency of performance—dependability, accuracy, nicety of coordination, and other qualitative characteristics such as precise timing and rhythm—results from repeated specific practice. Thus the principle of specificity is crucial. Advanced levels of ability gradually result from application of the principle of gradual progression. Finally, the ability to retain and repeat performance results from overlearning.

26 ❧ DEVELOPING TEAM TEACHING FOR ABILITY GROUPING*

DAVID REAMS
PHYSICAL EDUCATION INSTRUCTOR,
PARKWAY JUNIOR HIGH SCHOOL,
MIAMI, FLORIDA

T. J. BLEIER
SUPERVISOR, HEALTH AND PHYSICAL EDUCATION, DADE COUNTY
(MIAMI, FLORIDA) PUBLIC SCHOOLS

The traditional organization of physical education classes requires reevaluation with the inception of new approaches to the planning and conduct of the overall school program. Innovations must be continually applied, evaluated, and modified if physical education is to keep pace with the ever-increasing school population and with the changing demands of our school society. Ability grouping is a major step in this new approach. This has resulted in special grading procedures. The next concept that seems to follow is that of team teaching.

For the past three years a number of secondary schools have been carrying on team teaching. The term "team teaching" is applied to a wide variety of procedures. However, a generally accepted definition is any effort to improve instruction by reorganization of the teaching staff so that two or more people work together and are jointly responsible for all or a significant part of the pupils' instruction. By this definition, there are many types of team teaching situations presently in use. They may involve large class situations, seminars, independent study, and flexible scheduling for the total school situation.

One factor that must be taken into account in all team teaching programs in physical education is that, although many activities can be presented to large groups, some units of instruction are best suited to small groups and can be taught effectively only to classes of limited size. Secondly, the length of time required to master sports skills is not the same for all pupils. A third factor is that the ability to understand the complexities of sports strategy is not the same for all pupils.

Team teaching, combined with flexible scheduling offers the greatest advantage over traditional programs. However, team teaching within the boundaries of the traditional time schedule still provides an instructional environment with opportunities for improvement of the physical education program. The primary advantages are:

1. Instructor-pupil ratio may be varied with the type of activity, ability level, or facilities available.

2. The department is able to utilize the talents and interests of individual staff members to the best advantage.

3. The pupil has the benefit of the talents of several instructors rather than being limited to one person during an entire year.

4. Adaption to abilities can become a reality rather than a desire. Each level should have specific lesson plans based on the general abilities of that group. This enables the pupils to better establish goals for their progression through the physical education program.

All of the advantages of team teaching are not directly related to the pupils, but they do improve the total program and this eventually affects the individual pupil. These include:

1. Flexibility, although limited by the regular class period, can be gained by varying the level of instruction and adjusting the time spent on developing skills according to the ability of the group.

2. A cohesion of staff members can be obtained that is nearly impossible to achieve under the traditional program. The instructors play an integral part in the function of each class. This means that all policies should be group policy.

3. Supervision and control become easier. It has often been the policy to assign instructors specific areas of between-class supervision, such as locker room, office, and outside areas. However, there is a feeling by the pupil that only his instructor must be obeyed. In the team approach, there is no one instructor.

4. Variety in instruction is accomplished through the rotation of groups. No instructor will be working with the same ability level all year. Each new group necessitates a new approach.

*From JOHPER **29**:50, September 1968. Used by permission.

New concepts, new techniques

Team teaching, to be effective, requires concepts different than those applicable to the traditional program. This is true of pupils, staff, and school administration.

One of the first steps in preparing for team teaching is to develop departmental aims and objectives. These should be the unified thoughts of the entire staff and should be in writing. All new instructors should be aware of the reasoning on which the aims and objectives were developed. A unified method of grading, acceptable to all instructors, must be developed and adhered to by the staff. This should be detailed enough to cover such areas as improper dress, tardiness, and unexcused absences, as well as other components of the grade. The pupils should be aware of the grading system and of the fact that it is a departmental policy. The same approach should be taken in administration of the program.

One of the major deviations from the traditional approach is that of grouping. It would be good to have all pupils of the same grade level and same ability in one group, but since this is often impossible, it is much better to have pupils grouped by ability than by grade level. For many years teachers have been told during their college preparation that grade levels should not be mixed. However, those instructors who have mixed grade levels, while keeping ability level constant, have found much success with ability grouping. The arguments generally advanced for not combining grade levels are answered here:

"The younger pupils are not as emotionally mature." Since the pupils' grade span in most schools does not exceed three years, and since there is a wide range of ages within a grade level, there is no assurance the same spread will not exist in a traditional class.

"The smaller pupil cannot compete against the larger." In ability grouped classes the size is more often equal than in grade level classes since age is no assurance of specific size. Most activities in physical education are non-contact sports so the disadvantage of size is lessened. With instructor supervision, the smaller pupils can be distributed among the teams.

"Lower grade level pupils do not usually get along with upper grade level pupils." Since these groups must come together in the crowded locker room, exposing them to each other during controlled instruction and supervised play actually seems to lessen disagreements.

"The lower grade level pupil in the high group does not have the advantage of individual instruction given the low group." This might be a valid argument. However, actual practice has shown that the more experienced pupils are willing to aid pupils of like ability with less experience. Less formal instruction is usually given in this group, allowing the instructor more time to work with the potentially skilled but younger pupils in the group. Generally, these pupils are able to become proficient in skills in a much shorter time.

The suggestions outlined here are only a few approaches possible for an effective team teaching situation. They have proved successful in operation. In large school situations more than one physical education team may be used. A minimum of three teachers should be assigned to a team. If any of the suggestions made are to be considered imperative, it is the assignment of at least three instructors per team.

Four instructors on a team allows rotation of planning periods so that three staff members are on duty at all times. For three instructors to be present in a three-staff department, provisions must be made for a common planning period. This has been done at the junior high school level and scheduling difficulties were found to be minimal. Both the boys' and girls' schedules must be correlated so other departments are not overloaded during the physical education closed periods.

Planning time needed

The time required to plan and administer the team approach is greater than that required by the traditional method. This is especially true during the first year when each team should plan to meet at least once a week. This can be done before or after school or on a common planning period, if one exists. This meeting should be in addition to regular departmental meetings.

Each team should have a lead teacher, but this is not necessarily the same person throughout the year. It is usually better to rotate this duty according to the experience and interest level of the instructors in each activity. The lead teacher is responsible for guiding the team and for assisting less experienced teachers. Unit objectives for each level are usually established during the first year and are reevaluated yearly. The instructor or instructors assigned to each level within the class develop their own lesson plans to accomplish these objectives. The lead teacher then compiles these to form the team plan.

Lead teachers do not replace the department head. The department head often functions as a lead teacher, but he is also responsible for the normal administrative duties. In addition, he assumes the final responsibility for coordination between teams, as well as the responsibility for the proper functioning of teams in both instructional and supervisory capacities.

A large class formation at the beginning of each period aids in building class unity. In situations where there is more than one team in a period, these may form separately or together as a massed class. Even though varied facilities are being used, this large class concept may be employed to begin each period. There are a few instances when a portion of the team might not form with the rest of the class (swimming, bowling, dance, etc.). In such situations, the instructors working with that group are responsible for such items as roll call and uniform check.

The duties of each member of the teaching team during class formation and class change should be definitely outlined and the lead teacher should accept the responsibility for assuring that these are carried out.

EXAMPLES OF TEACHER DUTIES

Pre-class

TEACHER A: When dismissal bell rings, report to area where class will form.

TEACHER B: Supervise locker room until tardy bell rings, then report to class formation.

TEACHER C: Handle office problems and close locker room after last student is out.

Exercise

TEACHER A: Make announcements and lead class exercises.

TEACHER B: Supervise roll call and any special exercises if they are used that day.

TEACHER C: Assist with supervision of exercises as needed.

TEACHERS A, B, C: Conduct assigned activities.

Post-class

TEACHER A: Release pupils (method should be varied, but all pupils should run from formation to locker room). Last teacher to leave will supervise area where pupils wait for the dismissal bell.

TEACHER B: Stationed near locker room entrance until last pupil enters, then supervise locker room.

TEACHER C: First teacher in locker room supervises until teacher B enters, then takes office duty.

The large class requires an efficient use of student leaders. These pupils need to be screened by the entire teaching team and thoroughly oriented in duties expected of them. They should be given some special consideration for the extra duties performed. Such duties include roll call, uniform check, and recording skill tests scores. Instructors should always assume the supervision of duties performed by student leaders.

The large class lends itself to variety in exercises. Different types of exercises may be given the entire class or specific groups may be placed in special exercises. Team members are assigned by the needs of each individual exercise program.

Pupils should be aware of the grouping criteria and there should be adequate opportunity for advancement to higher groups. Conversely, pupils that fail to meet desired standards should be placed in lower groups. The large class formation and the use of student grade cards facilitates this interchange. Although several different arrangements may be used in transferring pupils, one of the better methods seems to be on the last day of each unit. This allows continuity in evaluation through an entire unit. It also increases the motivational value of the team approach since the pupils soon learn that effort and improvement will be promptly rewarded.

Many new approaches to class organization fall under the title of team teaching. The methods listed here cover only a few of the possibilities. These have been used and found to be successful when applied within the limits of the regular class period. A true team approach will probably use each of these methods during the year, depending on the specific activity being taught. Each school must evaluate its own needs and develop a program to meet them. The following approaches can serve as a foundation for developing the program.

The explanation assumes that three teachers are available for each team. If more are assigned, they should be used as assistants with the lower skilled group or with one of the upper groups if either was exceptionally large. When a fourth teacher is used to cover planning periods, he should remain with the same skill level insofar as possible for each unit. Every effort should be made to assure a minimum of three teachers since this seems to be the fewest number of skill levels that can effectively function in the large nongraded class.

Single activity—instructors assigned to skill levels

This is one of the more common approaches and works particularly well with team activities. Two instructors may be assigned to the low group and one to the two higher groups. There are major variations commonly employed in this approach.

The accelerated group may be placed in tournament play with minimal supervision while skill drills are taught to the general group. After a specific time, the general group joins the high ability group in tournament play.

The two groups may alternate between tournament and skill drills on a daily or weekly basis. The skills or strategy taught should be based on the skill level of the group. The accelerated group usually spends less time in skill development than the other groups.

The accelerated group is placed in tournament play for the entire unit while the general group alternates between skill drill and tournament play during each week of the unit. The tournament games may be seperate or combined.

The lower group works to develop basic skills and engages in game situations separate from the two higher groups. This group may be taught as one large section by the two instructors assigned, divided into two groups by skill level, or as one large group with one instructor making general corrections while the second instructor works individually with small groups taken from the larger class. These are pupils who need special help in specific skill areas.

The number of pupils in each level will determine the assignment of instructors. In some rare cases, two instructors may be assigned to the upper groups and one to the lower group. This should only be done if it still provides for a substantially lower teacher-pupil ratio in the basic group than in the other two.

Single activity—instructors assigned to specific phases

This method is best used in individual activities where facilities are not a limiting factor. Each member of the teaching team is assigned a specific phase of the activity, based upon his knowledge and interest. The groups then rotate from teaching station to teaching station. If more than three instructors are available, two different organizational approaches may be used: (1) three teaching stations with one instructor assigned to each while additional instructors move with the largest group or groups, and (2) as many teaching stations as there are definite components to the activity and teachers to maintain them. In this method the larger groups are divided into sections.

Exchange of groups may take place any time

desired, but less than one week total instruction time at each station would probably be of little value. Some instructors have found that an effective procedure is to rotate pupils through the stations more than one time, spending fewer days at each station. This seems to keep interest level higher. The instructor must use an entirely different approach with each different level. The amount of time spent in drills and the level of skill drills taught must be correlated with the skill level involved. This method is particularly adaptable to swimming, golf, tennis, gymnastics, and tumbling.

Multiple activity—instructors assigned by activity

Individual activities are often taught in this manner. If more than three instructors are assigned to a team, extra instructors may move with the larger groups, or other activities may be used for larger groups divided into subsections. It is especially necessary to consider the interest and ability of individual instructors when developing activity grouping for this particular method. It may not be possible to lessen class size by this method, but the ability grouping does allow more efficient lesson plans to be developed.

One instructor teaches all groups in the activity to which he is assigned. It is imperative that an entirely different series of lessons be developed for each group. The varied lesson plan provides true progression by ability level and maintains the interest of the pupils.

Specialist—pupils drawn from large class

Programs of this nature are applicable only in the large school situation since a large physical education staff is required to operate effectively. Regular teaching teams are used in addition to specialists assigned to activities such as gymnastics, tennis, wrestling, weight training, conditioning, and dance to work with small groups. This requires detailed planning in the use of staff, facilities, and equipment.

All pupils will not be able to receive instruction from every specialist during one year. Two commonly used methods of pupil assignment are: (1) specialists are available only to the upper group or groups while basic skills are taught to the low group by regular team teachers, and (2) students in upper grade levels are given priority in activities in which they have not previously had special instruction, but they should still be assigned by skill level.

Assignment to specialists by either of these

methods may also require pupils to miss instruction in the activity being taught to the remainder of the class. Care should be taken not to allow an activity to be missed more than once during the pupils' required physical education program.

The methods of rotation are many. Two that may serve as foundations from which a school may develop its own approach are:

1. Lower groups are instructed in individual activities with the advanced groups divided among the specialists. The lower classes are usually larger, have more instructors assigned, and spend a longer period in the activity. The advanced groups have smaller class sizes but spend a shorter time in the unit. A specialist might teach two different groups during the same time allotted for instruction of the lower group. When specialists are not teaching within their specialty, they assist other members of the teaching team. This is usually in team sports. The use of this method is often limited by the facilities available since all groups are in the same activity at the same time.

2. When the specialist is used only for upper grade level pupils and teachers all ability groups, the pupils are assigned from the large class to specific activities by ability groups. In this method pupils will often miss instruction in some team activities during the year.

Coeducational—elective

This is not intended as an organization to be used throughout the year, but as an innovation employed with special units when both the boys' and girls' programs are being team taught. It is possible to adapt this program to as few as six instructors. If more are available, the program becomes more flexible. The following is an example of a simple six teacher arrangement. A five week unit is employed with all groups.

The boys' lower group receives instruction in wrestling with one instructor. The girls' lower group receives instruction in softball with one instructor. The boys' general group receives instruction in tennis with one instructor. The girls' general group receives instruction in deck tennis. The accelerated groups, both boys and girls, are in coeducational volleyball, tournament play. This group is jointly supervised by the two instructors assigned to tennis and deck tennis.

The two additional instructors offer, on an elective basis, coeducational golf, archery, and tennis. These activities are open only to the accelerated groups. At the beginning of the unit, pupils must elect the activities in which they wish to participate. A pupil may elect either one or two of the activities, or remain in coeducational volleyball for the entire unit. After the pupils have made their selections, the instructors must set up the volleyball teams and the method of rotation to elected activities. The number of days each pupil will spend in each activity is based on the number of pupils requesting instruction in that activity.

Special classes

Some special classes are better suited for assignment to one instructor rather than instruction by the team approach. These include corrective classes for pupils on limited activity, special classes for physically underdeveloped, leadership classes, and electives offered pupils who who have completed regular physical education requirements.

The first two groups need to identify with one specific teacher. This person must be able to establish and follow through with special individual activities designed to meet the needs of each student. Leadership classes function in a manner that requires one instructor to coordinate their activities with other classes. Elective classes are taken by pupils with special interest in the activities offered and should be taught by instructors with special training and interest in them.

Assigning individual instructors to these classes does not preclude the use of other instructors with them. The team teaching approach in regular physical education classes makes this interchange easier. The regularly assigned instructor may temporarily exchange positions with any member of the teaching team when his special talents are needed.

Almost as important as the opportunity for better teaching through grouped skill levels, true progression units, and compatible teacher assignment is the increased interest and motivation of the pupil. The desire to improve and progress must be present before any teaching program can be truly successful. If full value is to be gained through the ability grouped team teaching program, as many motivational approaches as possible should be used.

The first and most important need is for truly different lesson plans for each group, based on skill level, which provide for progression from the basic skills through the complex. If this is not done, the primary reason for the program is lost. Also, there would be little incentive for pupils to extend themselves to advance to a higher group.

The method of grouping should be known to

all pupils and provisions should be made for pupils to advance from one group to another during the year. If the pupil has no opportunity to advance, there is little motivation to improve performance except during the test period.

Each school must develop the team teaching concept in the light of its own situation—the competencies of the individual staff members: the physical facilities, equipment, and supplies available; and the overall organization of the pupils' school day. To be effective and achieve the objectives of both teacher and pupil, joint planning and cooperative effort by all instructors involved is required. Dade County physical education teachers who have experience in team teaching agree that the rewards in pupil motivation, participation, interest, and improvement far outweigh any extra work.

27 ❧ AN APPROACH TO DEVELOPING PHYSICAL FITNESS AS AN INTEGRAL PART OF THE PHYSICAL EDUCATION PROGRAM*

T. J. BLEIER
SUPERVISOR, HEALTH AND PHYSICAL EDUCATION,
DADE COUNTY (MIAMI, FLORIDA) PUBLIC SCHOOLS

DAVID REAMS
PHYSICAL EDUCATION INSTRUCTOR,
PARKWAY JUNIOR HIGH SCHOOL,
MIAMI, FLORIDA

The needs of today's youth for the vigorous physical activity necessary for optimum development of their circulatory, respiratory, and organic bodily systems cannot be adequately met by the traditional sports oriented physical education program. Urbanization, the automobile, the television set and the automation characteristic of our technological society today obviate the necessity for the kinds of activity that these systems require for the growth, development, and maintenance which will insure the physical health of the body. The recognition of these facts demands changes in school physical education programs.

Physical fitness activities must be planned for, and, based on these plans must be the efficient, effective conduct and organization of this kind of activity to provide the highest motivation and greatest benefit to the individual student. However, physical education programs are still responsible for developing sports skills, as well as physical fitness. Although the development of fitness should be a prime objective in physical education, it must not be the entire program. Any so designed does an injustice to the students involved.

The plan

Fitness is a highly transient factor and calls for continued activity if it is to be maintained. The premise on which the Parkway program is based is that the student who is physically fit takes more readily to instruction, develops a much higher degree of sports skills, and has a greater desire to achieve and maintain his fitness potential. The traditional approach to physical education often seems to inhibit rather than enhance obtaining the balance of activity required if the above hypothesis is accepted. The Dade County Department of Health and Physical Education has initiated many innovations to the traditional approach.

The Parkway program has expanded these ideas and added others to move far from the usual approach. The methods involved include: level grouping with special grading criteria and graphic identification of each level, progression of instruction through various levels, team teaching, specially designed activities for developing or maintaining a high fitness level in a relatively short daily period, and special recognition as a motivator.

Grouping

It is administratively impractical to regroup students by skill with each new unit. Class size, available facilities and equipment, and limitations on time prohibit the use of certain accepted motor ability tests. Because of this, schools within Dade County use a minimum standard for grouping—the seven item battery of Youth Fitness Test of the American Association for Health, Physical Education, and Recreation. Parkway has chosen to refine grouping procedures still further in an effort to secure more selective grouping. Students are grouped using a twenty test fitness battery. The complete

*From The Physical Educator 25:164, December 1968. Used by permission.

battery of tests is administered three times during the year. Test administrations occur after a three-week conditioning unit at the opening of school, at the beginning of the second semester, and during the last six-week unit of the year. In addition, at least three of the tests are administered as part of each six-week test cycle. The test may also be taken at scheduled times after school. Cumulative record forms are kept of each individual's progress during his enrollment.

Costumes

Students entering Parkway are placed in the basic group and may progress through the general and accelerated category to the special group for students exhibiting an exceptional level of fitness. Each group is identified by a different colored T shirt: white, red, blue and gold. The instructional approach is varied with each of the color groups. The students in the basic group (white) devote two days per week to conditioning, two days to fundamental sports skills and one day to game play. The students in the general group (red) spend two days per week in advanced skills and strategy, two days in game play and one day in conditioning. The students in the accelerated groups (blue and gold) spend four days per week in games and one day in conditioning activities. In addition to these regular classes, there is one remedial group containing those seventh grade students identified by the feeder elementary schools as physically underdeveloped.

A standard county procedure is used for this purpose. Any student failing to score above the 15% ile on three or more of the seven AAHPER Youth Fitness Tests is considered underdeveloped. A form—93P—is filled out and filed in that student's cumulative record folder, the transmittal card is specially marked and a list of these students is forwarded to the receiving school. The objective of this class is to improve the level of physical development through special programs and activities. These activities are integrated with low level game play in specific sports with limited emphasis placed on sports skills.

The learning plan

Each period of physical education is considered one large with three instructors assigned rather than three small classes each assigned to one specific instructor. This allows the instructors to work with different levels so that any special talents or interests may be most effectively utilized. Prior to each new unit, a staff meeting is held in which the instructors are assigned the

level with which they will work. The general skills which are to be taught each of the levels are discussed. Specific lesson plans are then developed and incorporated into a departmental plan.

Team teaching

The team teaching approach employed in tennis, wrestling, gymnastics, varies from that used in other activities. These units are taught concurrently. One instructor teaches each unit to all levels as they rotate from one activity to the other. The instructor varies the skill level to coincide with the ability of the group being taught. All levels are in a track unit during the same period just as in other team sports. However, each instructor teaches specific events to all groups, varying the instruction to fit the needs of the specific level.

Squad and class procedure

The large class formation allows the use of the more experienced and capable students as squad and class leaders. These students meet with their squads for roll call and remain with them during test cycles although they travel with their particular color group at all other times. The large class system allows students to be moved to a higher level with little loss of class time. Students who have completed the requirements for a higher level are reclassified each Monday. This entails only the movement of the student from one squad to another and the transfer of his individual grade card from his old squad to the new one. These cards are punched to fit a standard loose leaf notebook. Such a notebook is maintained for each squad during all periods of the day.

Exercises

Each period begins with an exercise formation lasting from eight to twelve minutes. This exercise period follows specific guidelines. Each week four of these periods are devoted to continuous exercise by the basic group, while the fifth day a formal exercise routine is done. The general and accelerated groups alternate between continuous exercise and the obstacle course four days a week, and on the fifth day, both groups engage in formal exercise with the basic group. Continuous exercise, often referred to as "grass drill", uses specific exercise routines divided by bouts of running in place. The formal exercise routine employs the same general exercises administered at a slower tempo with more repetitions, thereby requiring a longer time period.

COLOR PROGRAM REQUIREMENTS

Test item	Red	Blue	Gold	School record*
Pull ups	7	12	20	51
Push ups	20	32	50	360
Bar dips	10	16	28	67
Rope Climb	1 trip	1 trip	7 sec.	4.0 sec.
		(no legs—from a sitting position)		
Agility run	16 sec.	13 sec.	12 sec.	11 sec.
Man lift and carry	600 yds.	1050 yds.	1500 yds.	No rec.
Peg board	1 trip	1½ trips	3 trips	4¾ trips
Sit ups (1 minute)	35	43	51	75
600 yd. run	2:30	2:10	1:55	1:25
Extension press ups	1	4	20	103
1 mile run	complete	complete	6:15	5:38
Distance run	no requirement	2 miles	5 miles	No rec.
Hand stand push ups	no requirement	6	12	No rec.
Two arm hang	no requirement	1:15	2:30	No rec.
Alternate arm burpee	no requirement	15	20	No rec.
300 yd. shuttle	no requirement	60 sec.	48 sec.	37 sec.
Hanging sit ups	no requirement	15	25	112
Obstacle course time	no requirement	——	7 min.	3:54
Grade level	no requirement	——	8 and 9	——

*Due to the nature of the event, records are not established on some test items. Records listed are as of June 6, 1967.

Obstacle course

The obstacle course contains thirty-four stations situated to form a 600-yard circuit. The apparatus, constructed by the physical education staff and industrial arts teachers, includes a forty-foot overhead ladder which rises from eight feet at the ends to twelve feet in the center, a fifty-foot parallel bar rising from four feet to eight feet, four fifteen-foot pegboards, balance beams, parallel bars, stall bars, and a twenty-foot "milking machine". The course is used by all four groups on conditioning days, as well as by the red, blue, and gold during the daily exercise periods.

After the exercise period, the large class breaks into smaller groups, by levels. Instructors are assigned according to their interest and ability in the activities and the needs of the students. The instruction and practice in skills is specifically geared for each level.

At the end of the period, the class reforms and runs a specific supervised course on the way to the locker room. This distance will vary between 600 and 1000 yards, depending on the class location.

Motivation

Motivation is an important factor in the overall function of the physical education program.

Several avenues are used to reach as many students as possible. The identification of levels through colored shirts and the progression of instruction offered the groups encourages many boys to extra effort. In addition, a four foot by eight foot record board is maintained on which the best scores on certain color program tests are recorded. Individual period records as well as yearly and school records are maintained. Many boys strive to hold a class record, although they may not better the year or school record. During the last six weeks of school, competition is held in an after-school "Obstacle Derby" between teams representing the different periods of the day. Competition is held on various pieces of apparatus and on the entire course. Winners are awarded trophies in the form of miniature replicas of the particular apparatus. A regular trophy is awarded to the student with the best course time.

Awards

Presentations are made at the annual awards assembly. At this time certificates are also awarded to students attaining an average above the ninetieth percentile on the AAHPER Fitness Test. This past year the Presidential Fitness Award was presented for the second time. One hundred and thirty-one boys were recognized with the patch and certificate for their achievement in physical fitness.

Concluding statement

No program is so perfect that it can not be improved nor is any completely free from problems. The staff at Parkway feels that the methods described allow a closer approach to fulfilling the objectives of the physical education program than could be attained through traditional methods. Physical fitness is an important factor in the program but does not eclipse the teaching of sports skills, rather it enhances it.

PROJECTS AND THOUGHT QUESTIONS

1. What is meant by motor perceptual learning, and how does it relate to the basic instructional physical education program?
2. Outline a progressive program of physical education from kindergarten through college.
3. What is the present nationwide status of physical education at the (a) elementary school level, (b) secondary school level, (c) college and university level?
4. Read a book on motor learning, and list and discuss five important principles that should be observed and followed in the teaching of physical activities.
5. Why is it important to get at the "why" of the activity as well as the activity itself?
6. Read *Physical Education for Life* (see selected readings), and report on this publication to your class. How can it be used to provide a meaningful physical education experience for high school boys and girls?
7. What should be accomplished in the physical education class besides the helping of each boy and girl to become physically fit?
8. How should physical education classes be scheduled and participants grouped for physical activity experiences?

SELECTED READINGS

American Association for Health, Physical Education, and Recreation: Knowledge, and understanding in physical education, Washington, D.C., 1969, The Association.

American Association for Health, Physical Education, and Recreation: Perceptual-motor foundations: A multidisciplinary concern, Washington, D.C., 1969, The Association.

Bucher, C. A.: Foundations of physical education, ed. 5, St. Louis, 1968, The C. V. Mosby Co.

Bucher, C. A.: Physical education for life. A textbook for high school boys and girls, St. Louis, 1969, Webster Division, McGraw-Hill Book Co.

Bucher, C. A.: Administration of health and physical education programs, including athletics, ed. 5, St. Louis, 1971, The C. V. Mosby Co.

Bucher, C. A., Koeing, C. R., and Barnhard, M.: Methods and materials for secondary school physical education. ed. 3, St. Louis, 1970, The C. V. Mosby Co.

Bucher, C. A., and Reade E.: Health education in the modern elementary school, ed. 3, New York, 1971, The Macmillan Co.

೨

CHAPTER 6 THE ADAPTED PROGRAM IN PHYSICAL EDUCATION

The adapted program refers to the phase of physical education that meets the needs of the individual who, because of some physical inadequacy, functional defect capable of being improved through exercise, or other deficiency, is temporarily or permanently unable to take part in the regular physical education program. The adapted program also refers to a significant number of school, or college, students who do not fall into the classification "average" or "normal" for their age or grade. These students deviate from their peers in a physical, mental, emotional, or social measure or in a combination of these traits.

Many times health examinations, such as the medical or physical fitness types, indicate that some pupils are not able to participate in the regular physical activity program. For example, those students with organic weakness and functional or growth abnormalities need special attention. Other atypical students are the culturally disadvantaged, the mentally retarded, the emotionally disturbed, the poorly coordinated, and the gifted and creative. Special adaptations also need to be made for these students.

Individual differences are being recognized increasingly by educators. Education is for each and every person in a democracy. The identification of and concern for the individual differences of students have resulted in special provisions in the schools for backward as well as for superior children, for those with heart disturbances as well as for those with defective sight, for those who are crippled as well as for those who have other deviations from the normal, and for those who are culturally deprived as well as for those who are emotionally disturbed.

The concern for individual differences that applies to education as a whole needs to be applied to physical education also. As long as a student can come to school, he should be required to participate in physical education. If this principle is adhered to, there must be programs adapted to individual needs.

Discussed in the first reading in this chapter is a program undertaken in Dayton, Ohio, for brain-damaged children or children with perceptual-motor problems. This program, in kindergarten and the first grade, concentrates on basic movement and movement education. Children in these categories of developmental problems often are underachievers in school. The skipping of any portion of the early stages of concept development, as is the case with these youngsters, results in difficulty in other learning areas as well as physical education.

New Trier High Schools, East and West, have developed an adapted physical education program for all who require it. The program outlined in F. Glen Loyd's article is for any student who "may not safely or successfully engage in the vigorous activities of the general physical education program."

In the Marple Newtown School District (Pennsylvania), under the direction of Dale F. Strawbridge and H. Lee Brubaker, a district-wide screening of all students was undertaken for selection of those students in need of adapted physical education. The program, as described in the reading, consists of students in the regular physical education classes who have modifications in their activities program. In addition, corrective activity classes are provided for those students who might be harmed socially or psychologically if they participated in the regular program of physical education.

The college level is not exempt from meeting the needs of those students who cannot participate in the regular physical education program. The University of Wisconsin program, described by Allan J. Ryan, Karl Stoedefalke, and Bruno Balke, places all students classified as "restricted from all activity," in an adapted program to see if they can benefit from a program designed to take into account their specific handicaps. The program is aimed at encouraging them to become physically active within the limitations of their functional capacity, with emphasis on cardiorespiratory endurance activities rather than on perfection.

Developing the potential of each child, as a challenge to American education, is discussed in the next article by Hally B.W. Poindexter. Ten percent of American school children are emotionally disturbed, unhappy, or insecure within themselves. Results of studies show that special classes in psychomotor development should be provided. The emotionally disturbed child needs a structured setting and teacher support, and he benefits from most of the activities appropriate to normal children a year or two younger.

The special children of Webster, New York, under the direction of Marion G. Noble, Joyce Maunder, and David G. Stryker, benefit from an adapted program. Overweight children exercise to music, the physically handicapped work with their peers as much as possible, the poorly coordinated practice exercises for hand-eye coordination, and the underdeveloped, immature, underweight, socially backward, and afraid youngsters work together to try to determine reasons for their problems.

Adapted physical education, that is, adapted to students' individual needs, is as varied as the physical and emotional problems that occur in those students needing this type of program. These programs, necessary at all grade levels, should be required of all school systems.

28 ✌ A FIRST CLASS APPROACH TO MOTOR PERCEPTUAL PROBLEMS*

Dayton's body management program attacks the root causes of under-achievement in elementary school children

NISSEN CORPORATION

In just five years, the body management program in Dayton, Ohio, boasts 17 full-time teachers and unusually successful results with nearly 3,000 students.

Some of the children affected by the program are brain damaged, but many others simply have missed one or more steps in the early development of the brain and thus have perceptual-motor problems which cause under-achievement. In the Dayton program the two types of children are not separated, since body management training has proved to be helpful to both the brain-damaged child and the child with an "under-developed" brain.

Dayton inaugurated what is believed to be the first extensive program of this type with personnel paid with Board of Education funds after an impressive guest lecture and demonstration sponsored by the system's curriculum and psychology departments back in 1963. Members of the audience, primarily kindergarten and first grade teachers, were so greatly impressed, it was immediately decided that a body management program should be considered for Dayton.

The lecturer was Dr. Newell Kephart of the Purdue University Achievement Center for Children. The subject was "Perceptual Motor Problems That Cause Children to Under-achieve."

Dr. Kephart's influence has led to the screening of more than 5,000 Dayton youngsters and a program operating in 25 of the city's schools, effectively utilizing such varied aids as balance and walking boards, outline templates, marble tracks and trampolines and an astounding variety of simple exercises. These exercises train the children in basic readiness skills which normal achievers have already mastered at home before reaching kindergarten age.

Motor learning is basic

Dr. Kephart, whose work served as a guideline for the Dayton teachers in the beginning, had begun experimenting with a group of mentally retarded children in 1958. Certain that these youngsters were capable of achieving more in the classroom, Dr. Kephart decided to base his experiments on a time-honored theory of learning: *All learning is motor and all subsequent learning is based on the initial motor learning.*

A newborn baby can thrust with both arms and both legs. Given the proper impetus, he then learns to reach toward objects with only one side of his body at a time.

To learn about his environment, he explores, first by looking around, using only his eyes. Later he learns to crawl and to creep. (Crawling is moving forward on the stomach; creeping, which has been found to be one of the most important stages of skill development, is moving forward on hands and knees.)

He next learns to balance in a sitting position, then in a kneeling position, and a standing position, and finally he learns to walk.

Dr. Kephart found that most of the mentally retarded children in his group had skipped portions of the developmental stages that most children go through. His approach was to put these children through a series of motor activity programs for a year, emphasizing the movements that babies normally engage in during their development. He wanted to show that movement is very important in a child's learning and that skipping any of the early stages of movement exploration and development will

---

*From the Nissen Corporation, Cedar Rapids, Iowa. Used by permission.

usually result in difficulties in other learning areas later.

At the beginning of the experiment, Dr. Kephart's staff tested the mentally retarded children with classroom work. Then, following a year of motor learning, during which time the children were led through the basic sequences of development, they were tested again. The improvement in academic performance was so great that Dr. Kephart immediately began to consider other applications.

'Normal' children also improved

His next experiments involved "normal" children from "normal classroom situations" who were having academic troubles for no apparent reason. Using the same plan—a program of motor learning—he again saw impressive classroom improvements.

The same results have been evident in Dayton. According to James C. Wheeler, coordinator of primary physical education for the school system, "The individual help that the body management teacher gives and the many varied activities in which the youngsters participate seem to strengthen the children's self-confidence and self-image enough to allow them confidently to go ahead on their own in classroom tasks."

The Dayton body management program has often been referred to as the Kephart program because of the great influence of Dr. Kephart's work in the instrumentation of the program in Dayton five years ago. Of course there are other programs around the United States that have been implemented with the same ultimate goals, but with slightly different approaches.

Two-fold program

The program in Dayton is two-fold. The first part is preventive; the second is therapeutic.

In the preventive part of the program, all of the pre-school and kindergarten children are given opportunities for movement—activities that teach them how their bodies work and what they can do in space. These children participate in group activities for 45-50 minutes twice a week, either in their classroom or in the gymnasium, when it is available.

For the therapeutic aspect, all of the kindergarten students are screened to determine those who have problems with gross motor skills, form perception, hand-eye-mind coordination and ocular pursuits. In the last three years, of the more than 5,000 children who have been screened, 50 to 60 percent have needed help in the body management area.

Once the children are selected for the program, the plan is to develop specific behavior characteristics in the four major problem areas.

(Before actual instruction begins, children must be able to interpret verbal directions and instructions. Thus, youngsters first are taught concepts of "up," "down," "in back of," and other terms referring to relationships between the body and its place in space. Participants are "told" rather than "asked" to follow a verbal direction so that they realize they must perform a task rather than assuming they may or may not comply.)

I. Gross motor skills

Developmentally, a baby first learns to move his head; then he learns to move his arms and legs. In the body management program the same developmental order is followed.

The child begins by lying on his back and rolling his head from side to side, touching each ear to the floor. When that is mastered, he progresses to the next exercise, eventually to a great number of movement and balance exercises, each slightly more complex and taxing than the exercise preceding it.

For example, bilateral arm movements are introduced by having the child slide his arms in unison over the head until they touch, then sliding them back to his sides. The child progresses to sliding his legs apart as far as they will go and slowly returning them together until the heels touch. The arms and legs next are moved simultaneously and then alternated. The child then takes up rolling movements and eventually leads into jumping, hopping and skipping.

Movements in this category help the child understand the interrelationship of the two sides of his body and the combination of movements and visual directions that are involved in balancing and in coordinating. To accomplish this objective, teachers use a list of 51 walking board activities. Actually, the use of the walking board and such conventional items as broomsticks and bean bags in developing gross motor skills is limited only by the imagination of the teacher.

II. Form perception

This area involves skill in the spacial relationships and the visual discrimination of figures and forms, perceiving size, contour, shape, likeness and difference, and being able to recall these characteristics accurately.

In this training the peg board and templates are used. The child is shown a shape or form such as a circle, square, triangle, rectangle or one of the many combinations of these and is asked to duplicate it on the peg board. If he cannot, he then traces the inside of the template figure with chalk or his finger. Finger paints also help those who need to "feel" the figure as well as draw it.

III. *Hand-eye-mind coordination*

Coordination of the body, eye and mind is essential in developing a relaxed and confident child. The child is saturated with experiences he has not previously experienced because the self-confidence he gains is a prerequisite in learning.

The trampoline plays a major role in the program. By counteracting the force of gravity, the child can find a new freedom of movement and orientation to his body, a great help in the area of coordination and muscular control. On the ground the child can adjust his rhythm to the neuro-muscular patterns he chooses. On the trampoline, such an adjustment is not possible since the rhythm is controlled by the trampoline.

"The trampoline has become our most valuable piece of equipment for developing balance, coordination, body image, laterality, directionality, and most of all, self-confidence," says Wheeler.

"Alternate foot hopping in different combinations and jumping jacks are the main trampoline activities, but knee and seat drops, quarter, half and full turns, and other simple stunts also are taught."

IV. *Ocular pursuits*

Control and accuracy of eye movement are required in learning tasks. Children first work on developing the near-far eye fixations. In a simple exercise, for example, they may be told to look at one thumb nail and then another and then at their teacher.

Some of the items used in the more advanced exercises are a pencil, penlight, swinging ball and marble track. The latter is a series of troughs that slope alternately downward. Each trough has a hole in it to allow the marble to drop to the next trough. Tilting the apparatus at the right end will make the marble roll more slowly to the right and much faster to the left, thus simulating the reading movement of the eyes with the quick return sweep to the next line.

Hand-eye coordination enters in if the child watches the marble as he points to it with his fingers or is asked to take if off a trough.

The apparatus is placed 12 to 15 inches from the child's eyes during these exercises.

"The doctors tell us that the two most important activities we can give earthbound children and children with ocular pursuit problems are swimming and trampolining," says Mrs. Karol Lee, a body management teacher. "Since most of our schools do not have swimming pools, we use the trampoline every day with every child."

Combining four major areas

Children are asked to perform their requisite exercises over and over until the movements become automatic, but without creating a splinterskill—a skill that has no carry-over value in other activities. By working next with combinations in the four major areas, teachers can then broaden the children's skill in continuity and rhythm of hand movements, in awareness of change in direction, in closure of figures, and in perception and completing of a form.

Eventually the children exhibit the skill of being selective in responses to changing stimuli and can make their responses automatic ones.

Advice from Wheeler to those conducting the body management programs includes the suggestion to support the child through new tasks and activities which he may fear. "Do not be afraid to 'get close to' the child."

If a child is having trouble moving his arms and legs, hold his hand, lift him up, put your arms around him, etc., but do not overdo this "helping hand." "Children will not learn if they do everything on the first try. Let them fail a few times, but always make sure that they complete the activity even if you have to help them."

Kindergarten and first grade

In the Dayton program, emphasis is placed on kindergarten and first grade children; second through sixth graders are included in the program as space becomes available.

Shortly after the beginning of each school year, a Perceptual-Motor Screening test is administered in the participating schools. Youngsters who qualify for the program have weaknesses in one or more of the following areas: balance, coordination, low achievement with normal intelligence, eye movement, span and fixation, fear of the unknown, development of the large muscles, ability to follow oral directions, attention span, coordination of hand-eye-mind and form perception.

A participant spends 20 to 30 minutes daily, five days a week, with his body management teacher. He may stay in the program anywhere from two weeks to the entire school year.

Older children needing body management instruction aid the teacher with younger groups and receive body management training at the same time. This procedure helps to eliminate self-consciousness on the part of the older youngsters.

At present, the body management program is concerned chiefly with those pre-school and primary age children who are experiencing difficulty in the learning situation because of the lack of physiological readiness. It does not deal with those who are disabled because of extreme physical or mental deficiencies.

Parents involved, too

The individually oriented techniques used in Dayton are most successful when parents are integrated into the program.

The present project attempts to involve parents and volunteers, both as aides in the school and in continuing their own youngster's body management program at home. In addition to the parent conference prior to actual student participation in the program, parent conferences and home visitations help to determine the extent of personal achievement made by the child and the degree of assistance given by the home.

Film, tours available

Many other educators and school systems are interested in Dayton's successful body management program, too.

"By the end of the first year (1965–66), there were so many requests for information on what we were doing in the perceptual-motor area that two services were instituted to satisfy these requests," says Bill Marquardt, Dayton's Director of Physical Education and Athletics.

"First, we made a film showing some of the problems that have been found and some of the training techniques that we use. A longer, more detailed film is planned for the fall.

"Secondly, we began offering a tour twice a month. During the tour the original film is shown, as are demonstrations of individual and group training techniques. More than 2,000 educators have already taken advantage of the tours."

Future plans for Dayton include maintaining the present program, increasing the size of the teaching staff and expanding to include the services of several other disciplines. Dayton teachers already have school doctors, dentists and psychologists to whom they can turn for help. The services of a neurologist, pediatrician and an eye doctor are proposed.

29 ॐ NEW BREAK FOR THE GYM DROPOUT*

Adapted-physical-education programs for the long-ignored handicapped and underdeveloped students are rippling in a number of states and could be a wave of the future.

F. Glen Loyd
Associate Editor, *Today's Health*

Darwin's theory of the survival of the fittest is usually taught in biology classes. But most students experience it firsthand in physical education.

Like nature's annihilation of the clumsy dinosaur, physical-education classes often strangle the spirit of the unfit.

Let's tune in an Eastern teen-ager who has turned a Darwinian eye on his physical-education period:

"When it's time for wrestling and other sports which quickly and brutally determine who the better man is physically, an epidemic seems to seize about 10 percent of my gym

class. These are the uncoordinated kids and the fat and frail ones. I mean there is nothing wrong with them—they just aren't good in sports. You see them cutting up as usual in the corridor leading to the boys' dressing room. But when they get there, they start coughing, sniffling, or limping and give the physical-education teacher an excuse from their parents or doctor. The teacher puts them to work in the equipment room for the whole period.

"There are some guys who work in equipment room year around during their PE class or take an extra study hall. They are handicapped in some way and have a permanent excuse. 'Boy, they're lucky,' an uncoordinated friend tells me all the time. That always kills me."

In practice, physical-education programs

---

*From Today's Health **47**:38, March 1969, published by the American Medical Association. Used by permission.

are almost always geared to the gifted, says O. William Blake, physical-education coordinator, Contra Costa County, California, "The highly skilled children usually dominate and monopolize the learning activities to the detriment of the less skilled. As a result the skilled become more skilled and the less skilled fall farther behind."

"According to the best estimates available, there are about four million children of school age in the United States with physical, mental, or emotional handicaps," says Julian Stein, director of Programs for the Handicapped, American Association for Health, Physical Education, and Recreation (AAHPER). They represent 10 percent of the total school-age population. A vast majority of these children are attending regular schools. In far too many school systems the handicapped child—who is likely to have a lower level of physical fitness than the average child—is ignored when it comes time for physical education. He is automatically excused and sent to a study hall or to an academic class.

"In addition to the handicapped, there is another often-ignored segment of students— those with poor motor ability, low physical fitness, or weight problems. Handicapped students and the latter represent between 20 and 25 percent of the total school population."

Charges that the nation's school physical-education programs weren't helping students most in need started snowballing during the administration of Pres. John Kennedy. The President's Council on Youth Fitness conducted a survey which indicated that more than 10 million of the nation's 40 million schoolchildren were unable to pass a test which measured only a minimum level of physical fitness, while almost 20 million would be unable to meet the standards set by a more comprehensive test of physical strength and skills.*

In 1961 the President urged "each school to adopt . . . the specific recommendations of my Council on Youth Fitness: Identify the physically underdeveloped and work with him to improve his physical capacity."

The call has been largely ignored. Specifically, the Council recommends that all students in

grades one through six be given at least one class period of vigorous exercise a day, five days a week; and that all students in grades seven through 12 exercise vigorously for one standard class period, five days a week.

Today 14 percent of America's schoolchildren do not participate in any physical education whatsoever. And another 27 percent are in programs rated less than adequate. Only a few states require daily physical-education classes for all grades. Although most other states have some physical-education requirement, the standards are all too often vague and enforcement of them frequently is lax.

Yet not all is gloom. Thirty-two states have improved general physical-education standards in the past seven years. And the torch has been passed in the fight for physical-education programs to benefit every student.

Physical education has techniques for working with the handicapped and underdeveloped. For many years, physical educators have been doing remarkable work at schools and other institutions for the physically handicapped, deaf, mentally retarded, visually handicapped, and emotionally disturbed. Physical education for such special students is called adapted physical education, defined by the AAHPER as games, sports, and exercises "suited to . . . students with disabilities who may not safely or successfully engage in . . . vigorous activities of the general physical-education program."

"Adapted techniques have been applied successfully in a number of general public schools," says Stein, "for those with major and minor handicaps, the overweight and underweight, the weak and poorly coordinated, the temporarily injured, the psychologically disturbed, and other special students.

"But these efforts have required communication and cooperation between local physicians and physical educators in finding the students in need and classifying them for activity. And in too many school districts, the only link between the two groups is one-way excuse notes written by the doctor and given to the physical-education teacher by the student."

Real communication has begun to develop on a nationwide basis,* though, paving the way for more adapted programs.

---

*In 1955 the Kraus-Weber survey indicated that American youths lagged far behind young Europeans in basic levels of physical fitness. Almost 58 percent of Americans were unable to pass these tests, while only 8.7 percent of Europeans failed. Concerned by evidence of declining vigor in American youths, President Eisenhower created the President's Council of Youth Fitness.

---

*In recent years, the classification of students for physical education and possible adapted programs has been discussed frequently at the National Conference of Physicians and Schools, held biennially in Chicago under the auspices of the American Medical Association. In 1965, the AMA Committee on
continued

Representative of a growing number of schools with adapted programs are New Trier High School East and New Trier West in Illinois. Forming New Trier Township High School District, they serve the Chicago suburbs of Winnetka, Wilmette, Glencoe, Glenview, Kenilworth, Northfield, and Northbrook.

Gary Clark, 27, and former major league baseball player Pete Burnside, 37, teach boys' adapted physical education at New Trier High School East.

It is two P.M. on a crisp winter day and Clark is waiting for an afternoon class to come down from the dressing room to the indoor track underneath the gym. Slim and handsome, he looks and speaks like a junior executive. You get the feeling that he has just dropped in for some jogging. His teaching credentials include a bachelor's degree in physical education and a master's in guidance and counseling.

"Among the students in this period," he says, "are an overweight boy, several poorly coordinated boys, an emotionally disturbed boy, a knee-surgery convalescent, and a boy with cerebral palsy."

Here they come. Frank, the boy with cerebral palsy, sways and walks knock-kneed. He falls several times before he gets to the weight-lifting room.

"Frank [not his real name] recently completed a four-week period of swimming with a regular PE class," says Clark. "Quite a few of my boys participate in some portions of the regular program. Frank wasn't able to take the 50-yard free-style test with the rest of the boys on the last day of his swimming class but he wanted to try one length of the pool which is 25 yards. While the other boys were on the deck drying off at the end of the period, Frank gave it a try. It was a struggling effort—almost like a dog trying not to drown—but he made it all the way. His peer group—the freshmen—gave him a standing ovation for his courage and determination.

"I've had Frank for several weeks. We're working on his upper body now—he's very

weak in the arms. With advice from his physician, we've modified the weight-training program so he can sit down while he's doing some of the exercises—he has a balance problem."

"This is a lot better for me than regular gym," Frank says, putting down the weights for a rest. "Because [he laughs] I really kill myself in regular gym."

"This boy over here is a sophomore—Ed had knee surgery about a year ago," says Clark. "His physician asked us to put him on some leg-strengthening exercises with weights."

"When I got my cast off," says Ed as he lifts a heavy weight with his leg, "I had a hard time bending my leg and it was real small and everything. For the last year I've been working down here and it helps a *whole* lot in building up my leg. I like sports and I think I might be able to go out for track soon."

"That boy running on the other side of the track," says Clark, "is on a 1300-calorie-a-day diet. He weighs about 230 and the doctor wants to get him down to 175—so it's going to be a long-range proposition."

"I've lost about 20 pounds so far," says the boy, his baggy gym suit soaked with sweat. "And I think I can lose more. I feel a lot better now and my folks are happy about it, too."

"That fella over there," says Clark, "came down in his freshman year because he scored low on the physical-fitness tests. He's very quiet and does not like the regular classes. He doesn't like to pit himself against other people.

"Before I came down here," says the boy, "I could only do 12 push-ups and three chin-ups. Now I can do 36 push-ups and eight chin-ups. Today I'm running a mile and a half. I feel a lot better down here rather than being in a regular class. I'm not fond of athletic competition. I'm more interested in individual things. I can work out here by myself and keep in shape."

"Those two boys skipping rope," says Clark, "are working on coordination. We have them play handball, too. Handball's good for improving hand-eye coordination."

Clark starts to walk over to the pair, but a bell rings and the whole class heads for the shower.

Wally Gart, a kind, soft-spoken man with a graying crewcut, has been an important force behind the boys' adapted physical education programs at both New Trier high schools. (There is a similar adapted program administered by the girls' physical education departments.)

Gart received a master's degree in health

Exercise and Fitness suggested to educators the use of the Recovery Index to determine physical fitness. The National Education Association's *Journal of Health-Physical Education-Recreation* published the statement, which also urged coorperation between schools and local physicians. And in a 1967 issue of the *Journal of the American Medical Association,* the Committee stressed the value of adapted physical education, urged physicians to encourage school administrators to set up such programs, and suggested guidelines for the classification of students for adapted programs.

education at the University of Illinois and worked with handicapped students at the university's therapy center. In 1960, he started the boys' adapted physical education classes at New Trier East. He is now director of the boys' adapted program at three-year-old, $10 million New Trier West. Gart is also national chairman of the AAHPER Section on Adapted Physical Education.

"Virtually all New Trier high school boys participate in physical education," says Gart. "At the beginning of the year, they are given medical examinations and physical-fitness tests. Those in need of modified activity as the result of a handicap, illness, injury, poor coordination or muscular development, or obesity are assigned to adapted classes at both schools where we give them individual attention. We have an adapted class at both schools every period."

A student excused from a regular class because of a permanent or temporary physical handicap is given a form to be filled out by his physician. The form lists activities offered and explains the program. On the basis of the physician's recommendations, the student is assigned to an activity or schedule of exercise.

Other students are put in adapted classes on the basis of their physical-fitness scores and upon observations of their performance in regular physical-education classes.

"If vacancies exist in adapted classes," says Gart, "we accept self-referrals who want to improve their strength and coordination."

"The physicians in the area have given their blessings to our adapted program. When we were developing it, we met with orthopedists at a local hospital and benefited from their suggestions."

Clark and Gart both have a file full of letters of appreciation from parents. In a letter to Gart, a father recently wrote, "Having been plagued with serious allergy and asthma problems all his life, Tommy [not his real name], understandably, had come to fear physical-education classes because of the unfavorable effects which the exertion caused. However, under your tutelage, and with the understanding and confidence you have instilled, Tommy has come to look forward to your classes, and his improvement is outstanding."

While there have been isolated adapted programs in practically all states for a number of years, now some state departments of education are promoting adapted physical education throughout their school systems. Such is the case in California, New York, and Pennsylvania —the first, second, and third largest states in population.

"In a state-wide survey of New York public schools, 10 percent of 3110 elementary schools reporting and eight percent of 1898 secondary schools reporting said they had adapted physical education programs," says Gerald Hase of the Division of Health, Physical Education, and Recreation, New York State Education Department.

With the help of the state medical society, American Medical Association, and prominent experts in adapted physical education, the Pennsylvania Department of Public Instruction has compiled and distributed to all of its physical education teachers a thick manual entitled, "Guidelines for Adapted Physical Education." In addition, the Department—working with Pennsylvania State University's College of Health and Physical Education and the University's educational television station—has produced a 17-program TV series and written supplement to help elementary and secondary physical-education instructors identify and work with disabled students. The series is being shown on the state educational TV network.

"In the past five years the growth of adapted-physical-education programs in Pennsylvania has been phenomenal," says Michael Flanagan, coordinator for health and physical education, Pennsylvania Department of Public Instruction. "To date, 89 percent of our public secondary schools and 58 percent of our public elementary schools have instituted adapted programs. Over 25,000 students who formerly were eliminated or excused from physical education, either temporarily or permanently, are now participating."

The California State Department of Education has published an adapted-physical-education manual similar to that of Pennsylvania's.

"Some two percent of pupils in general public schools in metropolitan areas of California participate in state-funded adapted programs for the severely handicapped," says Carson Conrad, chief, California Bureau of Health Education, Physical Education, and Recreation. "And many more students are in nonfunded programs for students with minor handicaps, or those found unfit."

Adapted physical education has taken hold in the United States. The following developments suggest that such programs may become more common in the future:

• The University of Illinois, University of Wisconsin, Pennsylvania State University, and many other institutions of higher learning have developed adapted programs for handicapped college students and are offering more courses in adapted physical education to physical education majors. At many universities, all physical-education majors must take courses in adapted physical education. And 36 states now require at least one course in adapted physical education for certification of physical educators. As a result of these developments, a growing number of teachers know how to work with special students.

• "The AAHPER Section on Adapted Physical Education and Programs for the Handicapped," says Gart, "are filling hundreds of requests for information from school districts throughout the country. The state department of education in Pennsylvania has distributed several thousand of its 'Guidelines for Adapted Physical Education' outside of the state. And college and universities such as the University of Illinois, University of Wisconsin, and Pennsylvania State University are also supplying information."

• The Elementary and Secondary Education Act and the many federal programs designed specifically to aid the handicapped have made funds available to state and local educators and private institutions for pilot adapted programs and for training physical educators to work with the handicapped.

• "Handicapped children these days are being kept in public schools with normal kids when at all possible," says Stein. "Adapted programs are needed now more than ever before."

Like a Tiffany lamp, however, the future of adapted physical education is bright but fragile. The stone throwers in Pennsylvania—which has more adapted programs than any other state—are numerous.

In 1965, the Pennsylvania Board of Education decreed that adapted physical education be provided in every elementary and secondary school. "Regarding the response to the mandate," says Edward Norris, associate professor of physical education at West Chester (Pennsylvania) State College and consultant to the Pennsylvania Department of Public Instruction, "honesty compels me to state that, in my judgment, the response has been mixed. This mixed reaction applies to physicians, administrators, and physical educators."

Norris says that the majority of physicians and school administrators have moved energetically to initiate programs.

"While we had anticipated some minor opposition from the physicians and school administrators, many of us were surprised if not shocked at the amount of resistance or lethargy on the part of physical educators.

"It is my opinion that some [physical educators] lack professional zeal or to put it bluntly they are too damn lazy.

"Secondly, some are already overloaded in numbers and size of classes. . .

"Thirdly, many of our physical educators lack confidence in the area of adapted physical education or in their ability to communicate with physician or both."

"The need for adapted physical education in our nation's public schools has been clearly established," says Gart "And pioneering programs are proving successful. It is time for physical education to stop being merely a proving ground for varsity athletes, and to start bending over backwards to benefit all students."

FOR FURTHER INFORMATION

Adapted physical education: a practical overview and guidelines, a booklet published by Programs for the Handicapped; American Association for Health, Physical Education, and Recreation; 1201 16th Street, N.W., Washington, D.C., 20036.

Guidelines for adapted physical education, a manual costing 25 cents, Bureau of Public Information, Box 911, Pennsylvania Department of Public Instruction, Harrisburg, Pennsylvania, 17126.

30 ⚕ ADAPTED PHYSICAL EDUCATION*

Dale F. Strawbridge
Director, Adapted Physical Education,
Marple Newtown School District,
Newtown Square, Pennsylvania

H. Lee Brubaker
Director, Pupil Personnel Services,
Marple Newtown School District,
Newtown Square, Pennsylvania

Marple Newtown School District initiated its existing adapted physical education program last September. Although physical education programs fitted to individual pupil needs had been in effect in varying degrees throughout the school district prior to this program, a systematic district-wide screening of all students was undertaken to establish the frequency of significant student problems requiring corrective or modified physical education programs.

In preparation for initiation of this program, the school nurses and physical education staff heard appropriate speakers during in-service days, attended a seminar germane to this matter, and met with the district's orthopedic consultant and personnel from neighboring school districts which are currently conducting adaptive physical education programs.

In addition, communication took place both with area physicians to determine recommended physical activity for students under their care who had been excused from the regular physical education program, and with district residents which permitted parents to express their preferences about their children's participation in the initial screening program.

During a carefully planned screening phase, where school staff worked closely with physicians and parents, 3058 elementary and 3134 secondary students were examined. Of this number, 379 elementary pupils (12.3 per cent) and 343 secondary students (10.9 per cent) were referred for rescreening by an orthopedic surgeon.

The surgeon's recommendations included general postural exercises, specific corrective exercises, orthopedic treatment, X-rays, corrective shoes or arches, or, in one case, surgical correction.

Adapted physical education—definition of the program

The program is one of physical education which is designed to meet the individual needs

*From Pennsylvania School Journal **116**:518, May 1968. Used by permission.

of boys and girls who are handicapped in some respect, who have functional defects or deficiencies amenable to improvement through exercise, or who possess other inadequacies which interfere with their successful participation in the diversified and vigorous activities of the general physical education program.

Two types of activities are included in the adapted physical education program: modified and corrective. Modified activities are selected from the regular physical education program and selection is based upon the particular needs of a handicapped student. Corrective activities involve the scientific use of specific body movements in order to restore normal strength and function to affected body parts.

The program

The modified physical education program in grades 1 through 6 is handled by individual class-room and elementary physical education teachers under the supervision of the elementary physical education consultant. The adapted physical education teacher outlines appropriate student activities based on the family physician's recommendation and consent. The school nurse provides the adapted physical education teacher with a complete list of all students evidencing disabilities requiring unique programming during period of physical exertion.

In the junior and senior high schools, modified physical education is conducted through the office of the chairman of the physical education department. Recommendations for appropriate student activities are obtained from the adapted physical education teacher and are based on the family physician's diagnosis and consent.

The modified program is intended to permit the pupil to participate, on a limited basis, in the regularly scheduled physical education classes. Special classes should be established only when the handicapped child cannot participate to his advantage in the regular course; when the regular class cannot provide the improvement of skills, attitudes and physical condition; or when participation in the regular class is detrimental to the social and psychological adjustment of the pupil.

Corrective physical education is conducted only by the adapted physical education teacher employed by the district as an adapted physical education specialist.

The district's evaluation of this program after a relatively short period of trial is one of enthusiasm and positive outlook. It is felt that the staff approach to such a program should be followed.

Relationship with the medical profession at the community level obviously has to be favorable if the program is to succeed. The use of one specialist (orthopedic surgeon) for all final evaluations permits "standardization of diagnosis" over the entire school district.

Nurses and physical education staff members should be required to perform considerable counseling of parents and students, particularly at the junior and senior high school levels as the psychological sensitivity of the teenager to anything different has to be adequately weighed against the severity of the disability.

It is strongly recommended that this approach, truly a consideration of all student factors, be used by all staff in the process of soliciting pupils to enter an adapted physical education program.

31 ⮞ THE WISCONSIN PROGRAM IN ADAPTIVE PHYSICAL EDUCATION*

ALLAN J. RYAN, M.D., KARL STOEDEFALKE, PH.D. AND BRUNO BALKE, M.D.
UNIVERSITY HEALTH SERVICE, UNIVERSITY OF WISCONSIN,
MADISON, WISCONSIN

There is a one-semester requirement of physical education at the University of Wisconsin for undergraduate students. All students are required to present a completed medical history and physical examination form made out by their personal physicians prior to admission. The form contains a space for recommendations regarding physical activity from the examining physician. These forms are reviewed by one of the members of the department of Student Health who then grades the student for the physical education requirement, intramural sports, and varsity sports activity according to one of three grades. Grade A indicates that the student may participate in any physical activity without restriction. Grade C indicates that on arrival at the University this student must be examined to determine whether he or she may participate in physical activities or should be restricted. Grade D indicates that the student is restricted from all activity.

At the beginning of 1965, it was decided to take a limited number of students who had been classified D for physical activity to see if they could benefit from a program designed to take into account their specific handicaps but aimed at encouraging them to become physically active within the limitations of their functional capacity.

Medical evaluation

The program of adaptive physical education began at the University of Wisconsin in the Spring Semester of 1965 with three students enrolled. The first had an S-shaped scoliosis of the spine secondary to congenital subluxation of the right hip. The second suffered from moderate impairment of the lower extremities following poliomyelitis at age five. The third had an unstable right knee following a football injury in high school.

In the fall semester of 1965, eight new students were enrolled whose ages varied from 18 to 22. Four had unstable knees, two from injuries sustained while playing football, one following an accident and one from an unknown cause. One had had recurrent shoulder dislocations following a high school athletic injury. There was one boy who had a flaccid paralysis of the right lower extremity following poliomyelitis at the age of four, one with weak abdominal muscles who had had a recent hernia repair and one who was an extreme ectomorph with a previous history of pneumonia and had a record of very limited physical activity.

In the fall of 1965 a detailed medical evaluation was made of 28 male freshmen students who had been classified D on the basis of recommendations by their personal physicians or at their own request and after review by a physi-

*Presented before the Section on Athletic Medicine, American College Health Association, Forty-fourth Annual Meeting, San Diego, May 4, 1966. Used with permission from the Journal of the American College Health Association 15(4):351, April 1967.

Table 1. Age distribution of students in adaptive physical education program

Age	Number
17	3
18	21
19	4
	28

Table 2. Causes of disability in 28 students in adaptive physical education program

Sports	18	Others	10
Football	11	Congenital deformity	3
Basketball	3	Automobile accident	1
Boxing	1	Fall	1
Hockey	1	Bicycle hit by car	1
Skiing	1	Kicked by cow	1
Skateboarding	1	Chronic arthritis (?)	1
		Spondylitis (?)	1
		Asthma and obesity	1

Table 3. Parts of body affected in 28 students in adaptive physical education program

Knee	13
Shoulder	3
Back	3
Ankle	2
Toes and Foot	2
Wrist	1
Hip and Thigh	1
Multiple Bones	1
Nose	1
Lungs	1

Table 4. Sites of injury by sport in 18 students in adaptive physical education program

Sport	Knee	Ankle	Shoulder	Wrist	Nose
Basketball	2	1	–	–	–
Boxing	–	1	–	–	–
Football	7	–	2	1	1
Hockey	1	–	–	–	–
Skateboarding	1	–	–	–	–
Skiing	1	–	–	–	–

cian in the Student Health Service. All but one of this group had defects primarily affecting the musculo—skeletal system. In only 16 instances had a recommendation been made by the personal physician on either the admission form or by a supplementary letter. These recommendations ranged from "no physical activity" to prohibition of specific sports or types of activity.

The examination form (see Appendix 1) used for the medical re–evaluation covers four pages and is folded so that it may be used in the file which contains the student's activity records.

The age distribution of the students is shown in Table 1. The greatest number fall in the age group corresponding to the average for the entering class of freshmen.

The causes of disability are shown in Table 2 and are subdivided into those obtained in sports and those acquired in other ways. It is interesting to note that if the four disabilities definitely due to sports injury from the first two groups are added on the left side of the table and the seven others on the right side, approximately 60 per cent of the disabling conditions which were considered to be so serious and of such a permanent character that no or very limited physical activity was recommended, were the aftermaths of participation in high school sports. This table also shows that among high school sports, football is responsible for the majority of the disabling injuries (more than two-thirds if the three football injuries from the first two years are added in).

Table 3 shows the part of the body where the disability existed. Knee injuries make up about 40 per cent of the total and this percentage is increased if the five knee injuries of the first two years are added. The shoulder is second in importance if the one case from the first two groups is added. The lower extremity was responsible for 26 out of the total of 39 disabilities encountered.

In Table 4 the sites of injury are classified according to the sport in which they were sustained. Adding three more football knees and one shoulder from the first group shows that football was responsible for 10 of 14 knee injuries and three of four shoulder injuries. Of those knee injuries not due to sports, three were due to accidents and one to an unspecified cause. There were three cases of recurrent dislocations of the patella including two sustained in football.

Table 5 shows the number of students from the last group of 28 who had surgery. Two of the knee operations were performed on one boy since both his knees had been injured. The boy with congenital deformities of the great toes had had multiple operations as had the boy with the congenital bone cysts.

Table 5. Sites of surgery in 10 students in adaptive physical education program

No. of operations	*11*
Knee	8
Wrist	1
Toes (Mult.)	1
Bone Cysts (Mult.)	1

Review of the histories of the 13 boys in the fall of 1965 who were suffering from disabilities caused by knee injuries reveals: (1) a tendency to recurrence following the supportive therapy given for the first and sometimes subsequent injuries; (2) failure in some instances to receive any specific therapy in spite of what was apparently a severe injury; and, (3) the failure in these cases of surgery to restore stability to the knee.

No other significant abnormalities were found in the histories and examinations of the third group with the exception of one boy with recurrent dislocation of the patella who also had a small asymptomatic inguinal hernia.

Following the initial examination to determine eligibility for the adaptive program, the students were referred for xray examination where indicated and for orthopedic consultation in a number of instances. The student with asthma and obesity was referred for medical consultation. Following the receipt of these consultation reports, the examiner then reviewed the whole situation and, in some cases, saw and talked with the student again before he was sent to the specialist in adaptive physical education. During the course of the program informal contact was maintained between the medical examiner and the physical educator to ascertain progress. One boy with a chronic back disorder had to discontinue the program because of back pain. He will be re-evaluated following physical therapy and a second attempt made in a subsequent year.

Adaptive physical education program

The Wisconsin Adaptive Physical Education Program is a cooperative effort between the Department of Student Health and the Department of Physical Education—Men. The admission criteria are:

1. Students with any type of functional incapacity of a chronic nature which does not require medical treatment, but which is severe enough to interfere with the student's participation in an activity program designed for "normal, healthy" students.

2. Students with any type of residual functional limitation after an otherwise sufficient and adequate recovery from disease, injury, or surgical treatment.

The objectives are not to provide a substitute for a therapeutic treatment which the student would receive from an established medical facility, but rather:

1. To provide an activity program designed to affect the student's general physical condition (physiological goal).

2. To help the student explore and widen the potential range of body movements and physical skills (physical education goal).

3. To supplement, on the request of a physician, a strictly therapeutic treatment with exercise and activity of an enjoyable and conditioning nature (therapeutic goal).

4. To provide an opportunity for the student to gain confidence in his own physical proficiency and in the institution which permits him to cope with his own handicap complex (psychological goal).

5. To discuss with the student the nature and limitations of the handicap and the possible effects of exercise and activity (educational goal).

We believe the Wisconsin program is unique because it is a dynamic program. It is dynamic because it places emphasis upon cardio—respiratory endurance activity, play rather than perfection, and "fun". Handicapped students who have been previously excused from physical education classes, now have an opportunity to express themselves in a wide variety of physical activities.

After the previously described medical evaluation which determines the enrollment of the student into the adaptive program, the accepted student is scheduled for a test of his functional adaptability to increased energy demands of athletic activity. Depending on the nature of the student's handicap, this test is performed either on a motor—driven treadmill or on a bicycle ergometer. This assessment of the student's capacity for circulatory and respiratory adjustments to physical exertion allows for more individualized treatment of the student during the activity program, with respect to the duration and intensity of certain exercises. It also serves as a baseline for further evaluation and enables us to follow his progress in developing functional competence. Other assessments taken at this time include selected measurements of girth, fat folds, and strength. In addition, each student's swimming competency is evaluated. The entire battery of tests can be completed in fifty minutes and is scheduled at the student's convenience.

The students use the facilities of the University of Wisconsin Athletic Department. These consist of a 220 yard indoor running track, basketball court, indoor tennis courts, a weight training room, and a university swimming pool. All students attend the adaptive class two times weekly. A session for swimming on Friday is optional, but recommended. Each class session is thirty minutes in duration. This excludes dressing and showering time or that time required to complete a resistance exercise routine. Resistance exercise programs are dynamic, supervised by physical educators and prescribed for students in need of increased muscle strength for joint support. These routines precede or follow the thirty minute class.

The components of the thirty minute sessions are perspiration, skill, motion and fun. Students are led through a variety of physical activities including: running, jogging, and walking, (forward, backward, sideward). They skip, hop, lunge, crawl, roll and jump. Furthermore, this may or may not be done with objects. Medicine balls of from five to twelve pounds, as well as volleyballs, soccer, or basketballs, are carried or passed between students. Emphasis is placed on endurance or sustained physical activity. Where applicable, these forms of movement are performed by the entire class. Each student, according to his handicap, functional capacity and skills, receives constant direction and instruction from the physical educator. This has been possible with small classes of from four to eight students. Students are taught to recognize the signs of fatigue, decrease in activity levels owing to the presence of discomfort, excessive perspiration, and labored breathing. Of maximum concern are activities which require more physical stamina and endurance than shuffleboard, table tennis, or horse shoe pitching, but which are at least as enjoyable and safe. The progress in covering considerable distances with increasing speed—a good criterion of increasing physical capability—is slow, but it is realistic to report that after twelve weeks of classes, twenty handicapped students "warm up" with a run of from three-quarters to one mile in length.

Early in the program which employs any conceivable mode of movement in an on-and-off-rhythm of exertion, also using gymnasium equipment or the participants as natural obstacles, the students become familar with the handling of different types of balls and are eventually introduced to simple ball games.

The rules and regulations of such ball games are frequently waived to ensure the most efficient participation and the optimum competitive spirit of all the students present. These games consist of striking, batting, throwing, and catching activities, and are modifications of the net game, volleyball. In one game a medicine ball of five or more pounds is substituted for the volleyball. The ball is thrown over the net and caught and returned by the opponent. "Bounce ball" is a popular activity and a net of tennis height is used. A volleyball is struck with the fist, but must bounce one time on the server's side before going over the net. Air dribbles and passing the ball to teammates are permitted and the entire basketball court is the field of play. Another well received game incorporates both volleyball and bounce ball skills. A side may not strike the ball more than three times before it is hit over an eight-foot net; however, the ball may bounce on the floor before being struck or passed and the entire gymnasium is "in" play. These are active games and a single eleven point game may have a duration of fifteen minutes. Single wall handball, paddleball, and tennis are also taught and have been enthusiastically received by the students.

During the last week of the semester, the adapted group is retested for endurance and strength and a medical examination is scheduled. After the medical evaluation, the student is reclassified and given a health grade indicative of his current health status.

Summary

At the University of Wisconsin there is a requirement of one semester of physical education for men and women students. Physical examinations are performed by family physicians prior to admission. All records are graded for purposes of classifying the student in the physical education program A, C, and D. Those graded D were formerly considered unsuitable for any sport or physical education program.

All D classifications are now reviewed and the student re-examined to determine whether he can be placed in the adaptive program. So far, only those with orthopedic handicaps have been accepted. A functional test of cardio-respiratory and muscular endurance is performed by all students entering the program. They are then given individual and group instruction in a basic activity session for eight weeks which stresses continuous activity for a period of 30 minutes supplemented by special corrective exercises as necessary. One period of aquatics, which includes instruction for those who are unable to swim is given each week during this time. This is followed by a program in which the development of appropriate individual skills in sports is taught for future use.

The Wisconsin adaptive program is a cooperative effort of the Student Health Services and Physical Education Departments. It is medically supervised and places emphasis upon cardiorespiratory performance, physical skill, and fun.

Appendix 1

ADAPTIVE PHYSICAL EDUCATION PROGRAM EVALUATION FOR UNDERGRADUATES

NAME _____   DATE _____
       Last   First   Middle initial

ADDRESS _____   AGE _____
       University

_____   STUDENT HEALTH
       Zip code   NUMBER

_____
       Home

_____
       Zip code

I. Reason for referral
   (Give exact diagnosis if possible, but express in terms of physical and/or functional defect rather than symptoms.)

II. History relative to defect
   A. Origin
   B. Duration
   C. Status (stationary or progressive)
   D. Treatment
      1. Past
      2. Present
         a. Medication

III. Physical examination and testing
   A. General appraisal
      (Include specifically evaluation of cardiac and pulmonary status as capable or not capable for exercises.)
   B. Specific defect
      (Include measurements.)
      1. Loss of structure
      2. Loss of function
   C. Laboratory examinations
      1. Hematology
      2. Urinalysis
      3. Blood chemistry
      4. X ray

IV. Examination of functional deficit
   A. Individual's own appraisal
      (Use his words where possible)
   B. Family physician's appraisal
      (Direct quotes if available)
      (Give physician's name and address)
   C. Examiner's appraisal
   D. Specific muscle testing
      (By physiotherapist)

V. Reports of consultation regarding correction of defect or deficit
   (Medical, surgical, orthopedic, etc.)

VI. Re-evaluation after correction of defect or deficit

VII. Recommendation of examiner
   (Underline one.)
   A. Acceptable for normal physical education
      Acceptable for adaptive physical education
      Not acceptable for adaptive physical education
   B. Reasons for acceptance or rejection

DATE FINAL EXAMINATION _____

EXAMINER'S SIGNATURE _____

32 &> MOTOR DEVELOPMENT AND PERFORMANCE OF EMOTIONALLY DISTURBED CHILDREN*

HALLY B. W. POINDEXTER
PROFESSOR, HEALTH AND PHYSICAL EDUCATION,
RICE UNIVERSITY, HOUSTON, TEXAS

One of the accepted challenges of American education is that of preserving and developing the potential of each child. Various studies estimate that 10 to 15 percent of the elementary school population has physical, social, emotional, and perceptual learning problems which require specialized facilities and personnel to offer an appropriate learning environment for these children. A conservative estimate indicates approximately one-third of the children who fail to benefit from a normal classroom setting are classified as socially-emotionally disturbed. In a large group study, 10 percent of school children were found disturbed to the extent of needing psychiatric help (2). He identified only 0.5 percent so severely handicapped emotionally that they needed intensive treatment or special placement.

Emotional disturbance is an encompassing term including such diagnosed categories as neurologically impaired—hyperactive, phobias, psychoses, and behavior disorders. The causes for such emotional disorders range from malnutrition, chemical imbalance, and neurological impairment to psychologically determined factors. The etiology of disturbance is beyond the realm of this article. Observation and clinical studies identify the emotionally disturbed child as one who is unhappy and insecure within himself, who has poor relationships with other people and with his environment, who has excessive hostility or fears or fantasy life and may evidence too many nonorganic physical complaints or too little control over his bodily functions without organic cause. They are readily identified by a classroom teacher for not only do they fail to benefit from the educational situation, but they often prove disruptive and destructive in such a setting. Some of these youngsters exhibit clumsy and awkward movement patterns; nearly all reflect learning disabilities.

It is suggested that the normal social adjustment of a child depends upon basic skills or performance in the area of perception which would allow the child to adjust to concrete objects. We must perceive the same things that others see prior to social contact (4). Thus, any lack in the perceptual ability would most likely hinder the child's performance in his social interactions and easily become a source of frustration to the child. It is not easy to determine, in individual cases, if the inability to perceive causes the emotional disturbance or outside influences encourage the disturbance which results in perceptual handicaps. Recent studies in personality and perception with children indicate that a child has a tendency to function in a differentiated manner, having developed a self image through various aspects of his total psychological activity, and obtaining a consistency of behavior is usually able to attain and maintain the desired level of adjustment (6, 7, 8).

There are several prominent theoretical pronouncements made for the relationship of perception and basic motor ability and there is increasing evidence that motor proficiency and mental ability are somehow related *if* the total range of mental ability is considered. There is extensive disagreement about the degree and kind of relationship that exists between intellectual and motor performances. There are numerous studies dealing with perceptual-motor abilities of mentally retarded children but few investigators have concerned themselves with the relationship between the occurrence and existence of emotional disturbance and perceptual-psychomotor abilities and disabilities. An investigation of the psychomotor abilities of normal and disturbed children has been in progress for three years.[1]

The following comments are broad generalizations gleaned from both experimental and

---

*From JOHPER **40**:69, June 1969. Used by permission.

[1] Findings of the study of the "Perceived and Actual Psychomotor Ability of Children: A Study of Normal and Emotionally Disturbed Children Ages 7-10," sponsored by the Department of Health, Education, and Welfare, Office of Education, will be available in late spring 1969 from the author.

empirical evidence and selected for their seeming interest to physical educators and special educators.

The child: The emotionally handicapped child, like other children, comes from various socioeconomic backgrounds, exhibits a range of intelligence similar to normal children, and generally lives with his parents in families of various sizes. In the age range of 7-10, more boys evidence disturbance than girls. They differ from other children in their emotional handicap and educational retardation. The severity of the disturbance has often led to an incorrect diagnosis of mental retardation. Emotionally disturbed children, as a group, evidence more measurable neurological impairment than the "normal" group; although approximately 10 percent of the latter group indicated brain disfunctions as measured by the electroencephalogram. As expected, the disturbed child reflects more deviations from the normal in developmental history, training routines, and behavioral patterns.

Disturbed children, contrary to expectation, were not significantly hyperactive in gross motor responses in the "activity room." This observation is made by exposing a child for a five-minute period to a room of appealing toys. The child's unhindered behavior patterns in handling toys, general activity, and intensity of the activity are measured by electronic computations.

The disturbed child, with no serious limitations of neurological impairment, reflects similar reaction and movement time responses when given a visual stimulus. The digital timer begins with the presentation of the light stimulus and stops with the release of the reaction key. The speed of movement time is then activated and is deactivated as the terminating button is contacted. Reaction time and movement time seem to be more related to a slow response function of mentally deficient (5), rather than emotionally disturbed.

Emotionally disturbed youngsters seem to score less well than their normal age mates on measures of strength, power, agility, coordination, balance and speed. Strength was evaluated by (1) grip—three trials with each hand using a hand dynamometer, (2) knee extension, and (3) shoulder arm strength as recorded by use of the Elgin table.

Power measures include the distance on three trials of the standing broad-jump; abdominal strength was evaluated by the performance on the Kraus-Weber test and bent knee sit-ups. Speed was assessed by time on a 30-yard dash

and agility by a shuttle run task and performance on a walking beam. In addition to time and distance measures, some of the performances were recorded on film and movement patterns were later analyzed and evaluated. Coordinated locomotor patterns of hopping and skipping and trampoline performance indicate further differences between the groups. Balance, both static and dynamic, was deficient in the disturbed group.

Further monitoring of the child's respiration, heart rate and blood pressure was accomplished under conditions of rest, stress, exercise, and recovery. An interesting response was seen in many of the emotionally disturbed subjects and recorded by the Galvanic skin response preamplifier under conditions of "academic" stress. When they were asked to accomplish a mirror tracing pattern in a limited period of time, normal children most frequently responded by anxiety and a corresponding resistance change. Many disturbed children, quite contrary to expectation, showed little resistance change. They did, however, respond to physical threat and stress much as the normal group. It seems reasonable to conjecture that the emotionally disturbed child is unaccustomed to "success" and anxiety created by stress makes failure more likely. If the child cannot muster an adequate response to a situation, he may create an anxiety state that blocks clear thinking. Such confusion precludes deliberation and destroys the ability to formulate an appropriate course of action. Excessive motivation or anxiety seems to narrow perception and therefore limits the response. Thus the child "turns off" his response.

The Kephart Perceptual-Motor Survey was administered to each child. This perceptual test has five major sections concerned with balance and posture flexibility; body image and differentiation; perceptual-motor match, concerned with drawing rhythmical and coordinated circles and vertical and horizontal lines, and rhythmically reproducing displayed motifs on a chalk board; ocular control section dealing with elementary ocular pursuits; and form perception involving the reproduction and organization of seven geometric forms on a single sheet of paper. The maximum individual score is 92 and in a random group of disturbed children the mean was 55.33; the normal (random) group mean was 79.77. This was found significant at .01 confidence level and supported the belief that emotionally disturbed children could be identified by the preceptual-motor survey. This should not be surprising as emotionally disturbed children are frequently identified by their emerging perceptual problems.

A battery of psychological tests relating to self-concept, body image, and level of aspiration need more intensive investigation but there are indications that the results will support Ayres' findings (1), using 150 neurologically handicapped, of deficits in body image, hyper-activity-destructibility, and figure-ground discrimination (inability to select superimposed figures out of confused backgrounds).

Although the analysis and interpretation of findings are incomplete and limited, there are some obvious implications for *motor programs.* Cratty notes that a group of educationally handicapped he investigated exhibited motor competencies typical of well-functioning children two to four years younger (3); emotionally disturbed children do not seem to reflect this large a performance deficit. Unlike some diagnosed handicaps, emotional disabilities are not necessarily permanent and are more modifiable than many other conditions. The earlier the identification of the child and modifications made in his educational and environmental setting, the more opportunity for improvement.

Special classes in psychomotor development should be provided. Because the disturbed child does reflect a motor performance deficit he should be protected from more advanced performers for his safety as well as his behavior. A disturbed child must experience success, and a motor program in which he is made aware of his relative inability tends to create stress and disruptive behavior (which often takes the forms of withdrawal or aggression).

Flexibility is required in program planning for the disturbed child is not in a static condition. His hourly experiences and changing environment result in changes in his behavior and personality.

Two things seem certain: the emotionally disturbed child needs a structured setting and teacher support. A structured approach involves rules and routines to facilitate action, not prevent it. Learning seems to take place best under conditions of moderate motivation in "uncharged" settings focusing on the immediate. A period of hyperactivity is not the time to ask for creative movements, but the time to channel movements. At these times the child seems to strive to bring order out of chaotic action and he often turns to the teacher for stability and a statement concerning parameters of behavior. He *want* and *expects* the teacher to prescribe and direct the task.

Contrary to general opinion, the "steam valve" theory, often used with normal children, in which vigorous gross motor activities are encouraged as a release of tensions, aggression, and hostility, there seems to be little value in such activity for the disturbed child. This activity often heightens general excitability, confusion, hostility, and irritability. Physical activity should be alternated with quiet periods of perceptual-task development. It is possible that a youngster "highly charged" should not participate in gross motor activities for a day or more. A child's ability to benefit from activity is directly related to his response. In cases of hyperactivity medication in the form of tranquilizing drugs has proved helpful in reducing behavioral symptoms and enabling the child to participate in instruction and socialized play.

Activities should be included in the motor program which aid in perceptual development. Indications are that balance, agility, coordination, and manipulative skills are among the desired activities. Ball skills involving catching, throwing, kicking, and tracking (ocular) are desirable. Fitness development may be important for the weak child and for enchancing a child's concept of his body. Simple trampoline tasks encourage the child to free his body in space. Swimming has proved an important skill for development of contralateral movements, relating to a new environment and using the body in a new spatial relationship.

The emotionally disturbed child benefits from most of the activities appropriate to normal children a year or two younger. He does not seem to get the same benefits from highly competitive activities or undirected movement. When possible, physical activity should augment the "subject matter" program which is geared toward relieving the perceptual distortion rather than toward remedying the academic retardate.

BIBLIOGRAPHY

1. Ayres, A. Jean. Patterns of perceptual-motor dysfunction in children: a factor analytic study. Perceptual Motor Skills, I-V 20:335, 1965.

2. Bower, Eli M. The education of emotionally handicapped children. Sacramento: California State Department of Education, 1961.

3. Cratty, Bryant J. Perceptual-motor behavior and educational processes. Springfield, Illinois, Charles C Thomas Publisher, 1969.

4. Kephart, N. C. The slow learner in the classroom, Columbus, Ohio, Charles E. Merrill Co., 1960.

5. Malpass, Leslie F. Motor skills in mental deficiency. Handbook of Mental Deficiency. Norman R. Ellis, ed., New York, McGraw-Hill Book Co., 1963.

6. Werner, Heinz, and Wapner, S. The body percept, New York, Random House, 1965.

7. Witkin, H. A., and Asch, S. E. Studies in space orientation and further experiments on perception of the upright with displaced visual fields. Journal of Experimental Psychology. 38, 1948.

8. Witkin, H. A. Cognitive development and the growth of personality and perception. International Congress of Psychology, 1960.

33 ᴥ HEALTH EDUCATION: PRESCRIPTION FOR SPECIAL CHILDREN*

MARION G. NOBLE, JOYCE MAUNDER, AND DAVID G. STRYKER
PHYSICAL EDUCATION DEPARTMENT,
CENTRAL SCHOOLS,
WEBSTER, NEW YORK

Overweight

The overweight child is a prevalent health concern. In Bay Road Elementary School, Webster, N.Y., two or three out of every class of 30 pupils can be considered overweight. Over fifty children in the school have an overweight problem. The key to helping these children is their parents. If the school is to do anything worthwhile in trying to help the obese child, it must have their cooperation and support.

• Where there are two or more overweight children in the same class, suggest they work together to lose weight. The nurse-teacher can talk with them without the rest of the class being aware of what is happening. They can set up exercises to do together after school; they can make a chart to compare weights with each other and with their previous weight; they can evolve menus for nutritious breakfasts and lunches; and so on. If possible, keep them together the next year so they can continue their weight-losing program.

• Many school cafeterias offer a salad plate lunch for their faculty members in place of the regular lunch menus. If your cafeteria follows this practice, recommend that overweight pupils also be permitted to have this salad lunch.

• Have everyone in the room make a personal chart for recording every bit of food eaten one day a week, for four weeks. Besides recording the three meals, have them indicate any between-meal snacks they eat in a day. Make this an all-class activity, then discuss charts with individual pupils.

• Some of your overweight pupils may want to form a Club 15. Any group of four or more pupils may form their own exercise and weight-losing group. Each member will receive a Club 15 booklet with exercises, food discussions, and breakfast and lunch menus. The group receives a free 33 1/3 record of exercises and the leader is sent a monthly newsletter to share with others. To register for this club, sponsored by Campbell Soup Company, send the names and addresses of each member (at least 4) to Club 15, Box 1515, Maple Plain, Minnesota 55359.

• Have the class do exercises to the tune of catchy rhythms from musical comedies. Select such records as "Hey, Look Me Over," "Hello, Dolly," "I Ain't Down Yet." From the Junior Chamber of Commerce you can get the record "Chicken Fat," composed by Meredith Wilson for the President's Physical Fitness Program. Encourage the class, especially those who are overweight to exercise at home to their favorite records.

Physically handicapped

Unless a doctor specifically orders a child not to do so, most schools insist everyone take some part in physical education classes. Some adaptations in the program are necessary but the person is still a member of the group. The more a child can be with his peers, the more likely he is to want to join them. Even a cardiac or an asthmatic can usually do part of the activities, but even if his role is merely to watch, sitting in the sun as an interested observer is better than not being there at all.

• Often a handicapped person can take part in the regular program with only a few modifications. A child with a useless arm, for example, might still be able to play a good game of volleyball if, when serving, he is given three tries

*From The Instructor 77:94, August 1967, copyright, Instructor Publications, Inc. Used by permission.

instead of one. A person with a crippled leg may become an excellent batter and a first baseman if he has a stand-in to make his bases for him and a shortstop who can run for the "long ones." If someone cannot do a push-up, substitute another exercise. Let your class and the child involved decide what modifications need to be made, but keep him in the group.

• Use your handicapped youngster as scorekeeper, manager, umpire, referee, and so on. Such jobs force him to be even more familiar with the rules than those playing, since he must make decisions concerning acceptable practices.

• Often doctors do not realize the many facets of a school's physical education program. When he specifies that a child is not to take part in phys-ed activities, he may not realize that there are many areas that would be beneficial to the child. The Webster schools send a form to the doctor asking him to check such conditions as cardiac, bone injury, postoperative, and so on, and then indicate if there is an activity the pupil can safely engage in—*observation only, leadership activities involving little or no activity, quiet activity, mild activity, moderate activity, vigorous activity.*

• A word of warning—even though you want to encourage the children to take part in normal class activities, do not let the handicapped child endanger his health and become exhausted. The family physician should determine whether a child with a heart condition may or may not run. The one with only one strong arm should not be allowed to climb too high. These youngsters want to do everything like others. Appreciate this but keep them from being too rash for their own good.

Poorly coordinated

The poorly coordinated child seems to be always stumbling over his feet; he cannot climb a ladder easily; he misses the ball when he swings his bat; he cannot catch a ball. He may be having difficulty learning to read. In other words, his eyes and muscles are poorly coordinated and he needs practice in developing ocular control and sensorimotor skills.

His poor coordination may be because of immaturity, or lack of practice in good posture and exercise habits, or it may be due to some physical problem. Before embarking on any kind of strenuous program to help the uncoordinated child, check his medical records to make sure the activities will not be detrimental.

• Arrange a playground obstacle course to give children practice in developing and coordinating

muscles. Everyone will enjoy it but the poorly coordinated especially will gain from this activity. There is much commercial apparatus available, or the maintenance department can make some simple equipment—balancing board, sloping board, ladder, parallel bars, jungle gym, and so on.

• When he can walk with ease on a balance board or slant board, a child may try other tasks on it such as jumping rope or bouncing a ball and catching it. Begin with a large ball and then progress to smaller ones as the child becomes proficient.

• To develop coordination between vision and arm and hand movements, try exercises where children move hands and arms in accord with certain directions and then follow these movements with their eyes. Place right hand on left shoulder, then move it to right slowly, straightening arm as it begins to move. Good for helping pupils create quick left-to-right eye movements necessary when learning to read.

• Kicking a soccer ball down the field helps develop agility and good foot movement. Hopscotch encourages coordination with both feet. For one foot activities try rope jumping, skipping, hopping, and walking on stepping stones (pieces of cardboard placed in an irregular path a footstep apart).

• Having children walk, march, or do simple exercises to music helps them achieve rhythm in their total body movements. The trampoline is also excellent for total coordination. Observing children's actions on the trampoline often helps you spot the child who has an eye problem.

Underdeveloped

Underdeveloped children may be characterized as immature, underweight, socially backward, and often afraid to take part in phys-ed activities. Such a child usually has poor endurance and a general lack of strength. Because of his fear of not succeeding, a child may even become an emotional problem as he finds himself unaccepted by his peers. More and more he will withdraw and refuse to even try.

Before beginning a corrective program, try to determine the reason for underdevelopment. Here a professional medical report is needed. If existing health records do not explain his condition, perhaps an examination by a physician should be scheduled. If there are no physical defects or conditions present, the problem is evidently poor health habits and little or no physical exercise and activity.

• Arrange a consultation with the parents to

evaluate the child's health habits. Is he getting enough sleep, well-balanced meals, sufficient fresh air and exercise? Does he have a good chair and proper lighting for reading? Is there a friend or pet he plays with actively outdoors? What procedures can be developed to change his habits?

• A chart listing everything a child eats in a day(see Overweight section) is also useful with this child, for he can see just how much he does or doesn't eat. This is a good clue for the teacher, too. If the child seems to be eating enough, there are probably other reasons why he is underweight.

• Encourage interest in good posture (poor posture is often a characteristic of this child) by a bulletin board containing slogans, pictures taken from magazines, or better still actual photographs of the children themselves taken at work and play. Have children practice good posture at home before a full-length mirror. Form a Password Club. The class decides on a secret word to be whispered to anyone who is seen slumping in his seat or not standing straight.

• For the child afraid to tackle the balance beam, let him practice on it alone, with no one from his class to see and laugh. Suggest he practice at home on this or a similar activity. As soon as he becomes adept at something, let him demonstrate his prowess to the class. Once he has won back the respect of his peers, he will be more willing to try a new thing in their presence.

PROJECTS AND THOUGHT QUESTIONS

1. Outline what you consider to be the minimum essentials for an adapted physical education program for (a) an elementary school, (b) a high school, and (c) a college or university.
2. Survey ten school systems and determine the type of adapted physical education program they provide for their students. Prepare a summary report of your survey and present to class.
3. As a physical education teacher, what type of physical education program would you provide for a class of culturally disadvantaged students? Document your program with facts from the professional literature.
4. Identify the chief characteristics of the following: (a) physically handicapped, (b) mentally retarded, (c) emotionally disturbed, (d) culturally disadvantaged, (e) poorly coordinated, and (f) gifted or creative. Outline the type of physical education program you, as an administrator, would recommend for each of these groups.
5. What research findings can you uncover that support the need for physical education experiences for the mentally retarded?
6. Do a case study of a student in an adapted program, citing the activities that were provided, the contribution made by each, and the progress made by the student as a result of being exposed to such a program.

SELECTED READINGS

Bucher, C. A.: Administration of health and physical education programs, including athletics, ed. 5, St. Louis, 1971, The C. V. Mosby Co.
Conant, J. B.: Slums and suburbs, New York, 1964, New American Library.
Cratty, B. J. Social dimensions of physical activity, Englewood Cliffs, N. J., 1967, Prentice-Hall, Inc.
Daniels, A. S., and Davies, E. A.: Adapted physical education, New York, 1965, Harper & Row Publishers.
Fantini, M. D., and Weinstein, G.: The disadvantaged: challenge to education, New York, 1968, Harper & Row Publishers.
Kretchmar, R. T.: The forgotten student in physical education, Journal of Health, Physical Education, and Recreation 31:21, May–June 1960.
Stein, J. U.: A practical guide to adapted physical education for the educable mentally handicapped, Journal of Health, Physical Education, and Recreation 33:30, December 1962.

CHAPTER 7 INTRAMURAL AND EXTRAMURAL PHYSICAL EDUCATION PROGRAMS

Intramurals and extramurals refer to that phase of school and college physical education programs that is geared to the abilities and skills of the entire student body and consists of voluntary participation in games, sports, and other activities. The intramural program offers activities within a single school or college, and the extramural program offers such activities as Play and Sports Days that bring together participants from several schools or colleges. These programs are laboratory periods for sports and other activities, whose fundamentals, skills, rules, and strategies have been taught in the physical education basic instructional program. They afford competition for all individuals: the strong and the weak, the skilled and the unskilled, the big and the small. They include both sexes, separately and in corecreational programs. They are characterized by an absence of the highly organized features of varsity sports, including commercialization, large numbers of spectators, publicity, and stress on winning.

Intramurals and extramurals represent important parts of the total physical education program. The manner in which they are organized and administered will determine the degree to which they make a contribution to all the students in a school or college.

Articles selected for this chapter discuss some of the administrative principles that should guide these programs, the role that these activities can play in the junior high school, the organization of Sports Days for girls, and other aspects.

David O. Matthews, in the first article, writes that administrative principles and policies regarding intramurals and extramurals should be carefully thought through and be put in written form. These principles and policies should include the best interests of the individual students, good human relationships, and student leadership, provide for the welfare of the participants, equalize competition for the skilled and the less skilled, provide a variety of activities, allow expression of grievances, set rules of eligibility, describe financing of activities, and allow equal use of the facilities by

both the men and the women. With this monumental task to be accomplished, the administrator of the intramural and extramural programs must be well versed in all the areas of involvement.

Frank D. Lindsey, in the next reading, explains how difficult it is to start an intramural program, but yet how beneficial such a program can be. The dominant objective of intramurals is social adjustment, with intramurals giving athletics a dignity and purpose by helping to educate the whole student.

A successful intramural program involving junior high school boys in Shaker Heights, Ohio, is explained by E.W. Nieman, Merl F. Garner, and Gerald Mayer. Boys wishing to learn how to play and boys just wanting to play, regardless of their athletic ability, are included in this program. The areas included are tackle football, soccer, basketball, swimming, wrestling, softball, track, hardball, basketball, and tennis, with wide participation as the underlying theme.

In the next article, M. Corinne Clark and Margaret Johnson differ in opinion as to the value of interscholastic competition for girls. Clark explains that, although the Illinois High School Association forbids interscholastics for girls except in archery, tennis, golf, and badminton, Sports Days are beneficial to the physical education program. She asks that if interscholastic competition for girls is allowed in music, art, speech, and science, then why is it not in physical education?

Johnson feels that Play Days and intramurals offer enough activity for the girls. They are times of competition, fun, social activity, and personal satisfaction. She believes that interscholastics lead to financial problems and offer participation to those limited few who are highly skilled and that Intramurals are for everyone.

In the last reading in this chapter, Don R. Andersen describes a public junior high school's intramural athletic program, which includes seventh- and eighth-grade parochial school students. The public school could accommodate the extra boys and girls in its program and believed it should provide the best in educational experiences to *all* the children of the community.

Intramural and extramural programs evolve from student interest and can prove to be beneficial to all involved: students, coaches, administrators, and the community at large.

34 ❧ INTRAMURAL ADMINISTRATION PRINCIPLES*

DR. DAVID O. MATTHEWS
DIRECTOR OF INTRAMURAL ATHLETICS,
UNIVERSITY OF ILLINOIS, URBANA, ILLINOIS

It is perhaps axiomatic to say that all intramural programs should be governed by a set of administrative principles, but how many intramural directors (men or women) have put into writing and have distributed their principles? Only when one's philosophy, principles, and policies are put into the printed word and made available to all concerned with the intramural program can a director really plan for the future, evaluate the present, and assess the worth of the past.

Leo Staley, director of intramurals at Ohio State University, at one time taught a course in intramural administration in which he emphasized certain administrative principles. We have borrowed the ideas expressed and at times even the words from that Staley course.

It shall be the aim of the administrative personnel to:

1. Establish policies consonant with the best interests of the individual and the total school welfare.

One of the most devastating things a director can do to kill off his program is to institute policies which are unworkable and entirely foreign to the philosophy of the school or school system. The everyday interests and welfare of the students must be uppermost in the mind of the director as he plans and executes those plans daily.

Specifically, if all indoor contests were held in the evenings during the week and the season were long and with numerous games scheduled, the academic program of the students would be adversely affected. Or in selecting units of competition if religious or racial groups were pitted one against another, possible smoldering ill feelings could be caused to flare into open animosity with resultant breakdown in the school spirit and harm to the total school welfare.

2. Develop good human relationships and attitudes by stressing sportsmanship at appropriate opportunities.

One of the traditional objectives of intramurals is the enhancement of fine social rapport. If the director hopes to achieve a high level of social cooperation between groups or individuals, he must at all times be on the lookout for opportunities where he can stress the values of good sportsmanship. Whether the emphasis on good human relationships comes through rating plans, supervision, officiating or special meetings makes no difference as long as something is done to keep in the forefront the importance of good sportsmanship. Slogans, rules, lectures, conferences, and assemblies are other means through which some degree of cooperation between competitors may be achieved.

The director must never hesitate to stop a contest in order to point out to the players that certain behavior patterns or overt actions are not in the best interests of anyone. He should constantly search for opportunities to stress ideal behavior on the part of the participants.

Written rules regarding sportsmanship are desirable but not absolutely necessary. Sometimes it is better to cope with undesirable conduct as it arises, and to match the offense with the punishment. One practice might be if a boy deliberately fouls to issue a warning. With a second offense, he is ejected from the game and prevented from competing in the next contest. Further misbehavior may bar the offender for the remainder of the season.

3. Develop student leadership by offering opportunities for student planning and management.

*From the Athletic Journal 46:82, April 1966. Used by permission.

Dr. Dave Matthews has written numerous articles on sports and intramurals and coauthored the text, "Athletic Injuries: a Trainer's Manual and Textbook," published by Wm. C. Brown Company. He has also edited three intramural manuals for The Athletic Institute. Matthews is currently devoting most of his time to the planning of the new $6,500,000 co-recreational, all-sports building soon to be built on the Illinois campus.

Intramural programs offer a tremendous opportunity for the development of leadership qualities. Areas of administrative responsibility range from those demanding much work and experience to those of relatively little importance.

The administrative council consisting of both students and faculty or of students alone may handle amendments to the constitution, settle protests, and make special rulings. It may even have the power to overrule the director in situations involving the eligibility of players, the settlement of controversies, and the presentation of awards. In most instances, such a council is chiefly an advisory group which has little to do with the details of administration. Its jurisdiction lies in the broad areas of guidance, legislation, and planning.

The most important job that a student can hold is that of student director. During his term of office, usually one year, he relieves the director of many administrative duties. He may be assigned to substitute for the director at any time although he takes no part in matters relating to policy or procedure. Although a student director never knows when he will be called upon to take the director's place, he can be responsible for field and floor supervision during games. This involves readying the play area, seeing that the games are run off smoothly, maintaining order, settling disputes as they arise, and clearing the area afterwards.

Each sport requiring team participation calls for team managers who assist the director by assuming direct control of the teams. They are usually appointed by the unit they represent. To encourage students to volunteer for team management, awards may be given in recognition assemblies. The responsibilities of the team managers or captains may be as follows:

1. Check on the eligibility of each of his team members.
2. Aid in selecting team members.
3. Coach the team.
4. Know and follow the schedule of games for the team.
5. Know the rules of the game.
6. See that the team members are properly dressed for the games.

Other intramural managers act as scorers, timers, doorkeepers, and referees for the various sports. Their jobs are often rotated throughout the year in order to give a maximum amount of experience in many areas. Scorers are not required to have previous experience and their training can be provided by a special program.

The timer's duties are simple and well defined. He may have to pick up a clock and horn, before a game. The actual job includes starting and stopping the clock upon signals from the referees, and blowing the horn at the end of the time periods.

Doorkeepers supervise the entrance and exit of students. They make themselves useful before the game by helping to get the equipment ready. Moreover they assist in keeping order among the spectators. In case of a disturbance, they are often fully authorized to act in behalf of the administration.

Most of the officiating may be done by students. If the system of training and selecting officials is effective, there is never any shortage of volunteers. If a student is really interested, he is asked to attend clinics for detailed explanations and demonstrations of the rules. The various officials receive careful instruction from the director throughout the school year.

Other areas of responsibility may include equipment, publicity, statistics, facilities, records, first aid, and scheduling.

4. Protect the welfare of all participants by examination, regulations, removal of hazards, first aid procedures, and insurance.

Ethical standards dictate that the participant should be the first concern of the director. If the director feels this, he will seldom be caught in a position where he may be blamed for negligence.

With the ever-increasing number of liability suits being decided in favor of the plaintiffs, the intramural director should be extremely concerned about the health and welfare of the intramural participants.

All physical educators would agree that periodic physical examinations are mandatory. The interval between and the means of getting the students examined will depend upon local policies.

Close and constant inspection of the facilities and equipment is the most important means of eliminating hazardous conditions. If a director can show in a lawsuit that he was not negligent in his obligations to provide safe play areas and sound equipment, he is less likely to be held responsible for injuries that are the basis for the suit.

First aid procedures such as those advocated by the American Red Cross or the American Association for Health, Physical Education, and Recreation should be followed by trained supervisors.

5. Equalize competition where practical so that success may be within the reach of the less skilled. Keep intramural competition for the students below varsity caliber in each sport.

One of the most prevalent reasons for teams or individuals forfeiting contests is the unequalness of competition. If the caliber of the skill ability can be adjusted so that the outcome of the tournament is always in doubt, interest will be sustained for a longer period of time and the participants will enjoy themselves much more. A constant loser will soon abhor competition and an easy winner oftentimes will become bored because of the lack of competition.

Intramural programs present a unique opportunity for students to experience losing as well as winning with no undue emphasis put on either one. If a novice, through handicap devices, stands a chance to defeat the more highly skilled, he remains enthusiastic about the game and will continue play until the tourney is over. He will have fun. He will be the best publicity medium a director can find.

6. *Offer a variety of activities within the limits of sound administration to as many students as possible.*

The director would do well to consult with the students to make sure that their interests are of prime consideration in the choice of activities in the program.

A well-balanced program would include both strenuous and non-strenuous sports; also both team and individual sports. A program of at least five different sports should be the minimum offered, with at least one of these being a co-recreation activity.

Diversity of programming will encourage many more students to enroll in the program especially if more is offered than the traditional football, basketball, and softball. It is well to remember, however, that it is better to have a few well-administered tournaments than to have many poorly run contests.

7. *Provide the best officiating possible through training and supervision.*

Seemingly, the most persistent problem in intramurals relates to the recruiting, training, and assigning of good officials whenever they are required. Ideally, officials should be supplied for every contest that is scheduled. However, practicality dictates that it is impossible to reach such an ideal. Therefore, the sports that are usually officiated by persons assigned by the director are touch football, soccer, volleyball, basketball, softball, track, swimming, and wrestling. Individual activities are on the whole officiated by the contestants themselves for such games as tennis, badminton, handball, and table tennis.

If a game is to be refereed, it should be refereed well. This connotes training and super-vision. A program of orientation, testing, and observation of techniques aids considerably in the preparation of students to officiate.

8. *Give fair or equal treatment and consideration to all in the redress of grievances.*

Along with providing leadership opportunities which permit students to have a voice in the administration of the program, there should always be an avenue open through which persons with a complaint, gripe or any criticism may express their opinions. By allowing an outlet for emotional build-up and by giving all equal treatment and consideration for the redress of grievances, participants will soon feel that the program is their program thus ensuring a reasonable degree of success and satisfaction for all concerned.

9. *Establish, publish, and enforce simple rules of eligibility and procedures consistent with democratic practice.*

Rules and regulations governing intramural competition are generally of two types: first, rules governing individual sports; and second, those dealing with general conditions prevailing in all sports. Both types of rules and regulations ought to be put into printed form and made available to all managers and participants.

The first type of rules is derived mainly from standard game rules which are widely accepted among high schools. It may be expedient at times to make changes to suit local conditions. This usually involves simplification of rules, time periods or other minor items.

The second type deals with general matters such as the eligibility of players, forfeits, and protests and is compiled by the director after consultation with the student intramural committee or managers. These should be re-evaluated each year by committees.

At most schools, rules dealing with eligibility are somewhat general and govern the players in all activities, although they are directed more specifically toward team sports. After the director has distributed the mimeographed or dittoed set of rules, he can have the student director furnish the team managers with eligibility sheets. Then the managers can check the members of their teams and fill out the forms.

10. *Finance the program through means consistent with school policy.*

With respect to financing, the intramural programs of high schools ought to conform to recommended practice which would be for the boards of education to appropriate funds.

In most instances, the cost of operating intramural programs is notably low since in many cases equipment used belongs to the physical education departments, maintenance costs of field, pools, gymnasium, and courts are borne by the school, referees are generally not paid, and extra remuneration for the director's services is paid as part of the salaries.

It would be hoped that school policy does not permit funds to be collected through such things as paper and scrap drives, carnivals, bake sales, and solicitations from merchants. The intramural program is a vital part of the total educational picture and should be supported finanically through monies allocated by the board of education.

11. Cooperate fully with the girls' (boys') program in the sharing of time and facilities for the joint development of corecreational activities.

No longer are there many schools where boys and girls are not permitted to play together on teams in sports such as volleyball, softball, and tennis. Same, well-planned, well-directed, and popular programs of co-recreational sports are being administered in thousands of schools throughout the country.

Consequently, no intramural program is complete unless some provision is made for co-recreational activities. A universally popular game is volleyball and perhaps this should be one of the first team sports to be introduced. Individual games such as tennis, golf, archery, and table tennis are found in many programs and these seem to be well received.

The women/girls director and the men/boys director should work closely in the administration of the co-recreational program. The joint use of facilities with perhaps the setting aside of one afternoon per week for the co-recreational activities appears to be acceptable in most situations.

An intramural program evaluation check list

A program can be evaluated in terms of the stated principles and objectives or according to prevalent acceptable standards.

How does the intramural program measure up to acceptable minimum standards? By taking a few minutes to check off the items listed below, a quick evaluation can be made of the present status of the excellence of the program.

YES NO PHILOSOPHY AND OBJECTIVES

☐ ☐ 1. Is a written philosophy or a set of objectives available to the participants?

YES NO ORGANIZATION AND ADMINISTRATION

☐ ☐ 1. Is the director professionally qualified to administer the program?

☐ ☐ 2. Does the director devote at least 75 hours per week to administering his program?

☐ ☐ 3. Are students included in the management of the program?

☐ ☐ 4. Is there an advisory committee composed of students and faculty?

YES NO UNITS OF COMPETITION

☐ ☐ 1. Are students classified according to ability, age, height or weight within the competive unit?

☐ ☐ 2. Within the basic unit, are students permitted to choose the members of their teams.

YES NO PROGRAM OF ACTIVITIES

☐ ☐ 1. Does the director consult with the students to make sure that their interests are of prime consideration in the choice of activities in the program?

☐ ☐ 2. Are there both strenuous and nonstrenous sports in the program?

☐ ☐ 3. Are there both team and individual sports in the program?

☐ ☐ 4. Are there at least five different sports making up the program?

☐ ☐ 5. Does at least one co-recreational activity make up part of the program?

YES NO TIME PERIODS

☐ ☐ 1. Does the hour immediately after school receive top priority for scheduling?

☐ ☐ 2. Is the noon hour utilized as a time period for intramurals?

YES NO METHODS OF ORGANIZING COMPETITION

☐ ☐ 1. Is the round robin tournament used whenever possible in perference to others?

YES NO POINT SYSTEM OF AWARDS

☐ ☐ 1. Is recognition of any kind given to the participants for their achievements?

☐ ☐ 2. Is the award primarily for achievement instead of incentive for participating?

YES NO RULES AND REGULATIONS

☐ ☐ 1. Are the rules defining such things as eligibility, health, safety, forfeits, postponements, and team membership distributed to all participants?

☐ ☐ 2. Is the lack of good sportsmanship regarded as a rule violation?

☐ ☐ 3. Is equipment provided for all of the activities offered?

YES NO PUBLICITY

☐ ☐ 1. Is there a special bulletin board for intramural information?

YES NO FINANCES

☐ ☐ 1. Does the board of education through the school budget provide funds for the operation of the program?

EACH YES ANSWER IS WORTH FIVE POINTS
Use the following table to determine how the program measures up to acceptable standards.

Excellent	88 to 100
Good	80 or 84
Fair	72 or 76
Poor	64 or 68

Intramurals in high school provide . . .

35 ❧ SOCIAL ADJUSTMENT VIA ATHLETICS*

FRANK D. LINDSEY
INTRAMURAL DIRECTOR,
L. D. BELL HIGH SCHOOL,
HURST, TEXAS

An attractive 17-year-old girl sat quietly in an isolated corner of the suburban bowling center, tears slowly streaming down her youthful face.

Her family had just recently moved to Hurst from an adjoining state, and this was her fourth week at the new L. D. Bell High.

She was lonely!

The week before she had signed an intramural request form to join a school bowling league. Although she now regretted that she had done so, her mother had insisted that she honor the request and had driven her to the bowling alley. Only after her mother's persistence would she bowl.

However, a remarkable transition began to take place. Laughter soon replaced her tears as she began to take an active part in the game and an interest in those around her. She became one of the group. And, needless to say, her grades improved with her new social adjustment.

The citizens of our country recognized the need for equality in education early in our nation's history, and our present educational system is a credit to their integrity. However, athletics is still striving for this equality.

The gifted few so often receive all the athletic attention, leaving the masses of our student body stagnated. The psychological association of one's self with a winner breeds this unfortunate situation.

Count the attendance in your stadium the last game of a season. If you won all games or lost all games, the difference in the two attendance figures will be the difference in those interested in our youth and those interested in self-satisfaction. It is this self-satisfaction group that so often dictate our athletic policies and keep our athletic system from reaching its true potential.

Newell Odell, Hurst-Euless-Bedford's superintendent, recognized the need for an athletic program that would reach all the students in our school system, and with the cooperation of the principal and athletic director, devised

the position of intramural director to meet this need. They approved the program, then we all waited to see the results.

Any program needs a start, and like the self-starter on your automobile, bowling was a natural to play this part.

The Texas Association of Bowling Youth had the organization, the facilities, and the willingness to help. All these ingredients were in operation and needed only a request to begin.

With the help of our physical education department, we soon had over 200 students bowling. This was the nucleus around which our program began to develop. Competitive teams were organized and enthusiasm began to generate in all phases of program.

Our present program is nearing the half-way point and has already reached 1,427 of our 2,600 students.

Previously, we had 20 students representing our school in volleyball. We now have approximately 225 students taking part in intramural volleyball competition.

Where many schools have one bowling team, we have 52, involving 541 students. Social adjustment is the dominant objective in our intramural program; not adjustment for a few, but for the entire student body.

If every student were to participate in a competitive team sport, we know we would have a more normal socially adjusted student body. This would mean a higher academic standing and healthier bodies. This, of course, is why we are interested in numbers.

The present program offers a wide variety of sports and activities from which a student may choose, including bowling, archery, riflery, volleyball, basketball, touch football, handball, softball, weight lifting, gymnastics, tennis, and a course in the art of self defense.

A student needs only the desire and interest to find a constructive, enjoyable sport.

The team sports compete for a championship trophy in each sport, and also compete for the coveted all-sports trophy given to the team compiling the most points in all sports.

The student governing body of the L. D. Bell

*From the Texas Outlook **50**:22, July 1966. Used by permission.

program is the Intramural Council, whose members organize, officiate, compile records, and take part in all activities.

They spend hours working on various parts of the program, for which they receive points which count toward letter sweaters and also determine next semester's officers on the Council.

Working in conjunction with the Intramural Council is the Intramural Parents and Teachers Organization, whose primary objectives are coaching, promotion, participation, and fellowship.

Each community has many gifted adults who are willing to help our youth, and we find they are not only willing to help, but enjoy it as well. One may lecture on safety in riflery while another may coach archery, but all are

helping to promote student social adjustment and healthier bodies.

Our goal is to reach all the students in our school system. We realize that we never shall, but the higher the percentage extends toward this goal, the higher educational level we can obtain.

Intramurals belong in our educational system. They give athletics a dignity and purpose by helping to educate the whole student.

The satisfaction of seeing athletics accomplish the end you always knew it should is a joy I would love to share with every coach.

A 17-year-old girl finding her place in society is the type of reward any educator recognizes as absolute value.

36 ❧ JUNIOR HIGH SCHOOL BOYS BENEFIT FROM AN INTRAMURAL PROGRAM*

E. W. NIEMAN, MERL F. GARNER AND GERALD MAYER
RESPECTIVELY, PRINCIPAL, ASSISTANT PRINCIPAL, AND
HEAD OF PHYSICAL EDUCATION DEPARTMENT,
BYRON JUNIOR HIGH SCHOOL,
SHAKER HEIGHTS, OHIO

For the past thirty years, in the Shaker Heights, Ohio school system, we have had a coached, intramural athletic program at the junior high level. We have provided participation for all boys wishing to learn how to play and wanting to play on a team, regardless of their athletic ability. This type of program was developed to conform with the recommendations of leading educators and the medical profession.

An interscholastic program was dropped in the spring of 1936 because of several factors. Financing athletics at this level was a problem, since state law did not permit use of tax moneys for interscholastics. There were difficulties in getting competing schools to adhere to standards of age, weight, and scholastic achievements of players. The use of playing fields and gyms by the varsity teams restricted the programs that could provide experiences for many more pupils than those out for the varsities. Finally, and most important, medical reports and the recommendations of health and physical education teachers indicated that the pressures of interscholastic competition in contact sports were not advisable for this age level.

The Board of Education, citizens committees, the administration, and teaching staff have evaluated our intramural program periodically and each time have concluded that the above four factors are still valid reasons for continuing our broad program, rather than re-establishing an interscholastic one.

About ten years ago a second junior high school was built in Shaker Heights and an intramural athletic program that included both schools was begun. Now each school has its own teams in tackle football, soccer, basketball, swimming, wrestling, softball, track, hardball baseball, and tennis.

(In each of the two junior high schools there is less formal coeducational homeroom sports program, conducted by the physical education teachers, as well as the broad, coached after-school intramural program. However, this article deals only with the after-school program.)

The coaches of the athletic teams—12 to 14 men during the school year—are faculty members and may be teachers of mathematics, science, English, social studies, etc. Similarly, the officials for the games are members of the faculties of the two schools. All effort is made to employ enough teachers with athletic experience and interest in working with boys so

*From The Clearing House 43:52, September 1968. Used by permission.

that help is available for a successful program. There is a coach for each team. The teachers are paid a differential for the coaching and officiating.

In tackle football, we establish lightweight squads (under 100 lbs.), middleweights (110–125 lbs.), and heavyweights (125 lbs. and up). We have enough boys for at least two teams in each weight bracket at each of our two junior high schools. Each boy provides his own equipment, which is checked for safety by the coaching staff. Game jerseys are provided by the Dad's Club.

All squads begin practice sessions during the first week of school in September. All weight squads have conditioning sessions, instruction, and practice for several weeks before playing their first games. The lightweight and middleweight groups have three sessions per week, and the heavyweights have five sessions per week. Each session is from about 3:45 P.M. to 5:15 P.M. The football season runs nine weeks.

Every boy who reports regularly for practice and carries out his training obligations gets to play the equivalent of at least one quarter in each game. The two lightweight teams play each other in four or five games. The two middleweight teams play each other in five games, and then a middleweight "all-star" team is picked to play the "all-star" team from the other junior high school in one game. There is no lightweight all-star game. The two heavyweight teams from the two junior high schools make up a four-team league and all play each other once. Then an all-star team is picked at each school and these two teams play two all-star games, one at each school.

Soccer season runs concurrently with football for boys who do not play football. Enough boys are interested to have at least two teams at each school. These two teams play each other most of the season. An all-star team is picked at each school near the end of the season and two or three all-star games are played.

There are 12 basketball teams at each school —4 teams in each of the 3 squads, which are set up on the basis of ability, not weight. After several weeks of practice, the four "heavyweight" teams at each school play each other. Two teams are then taken by bus from each school to the other where two games are played. At the close of the season there is a week of practice for the all-star teams before an all-star game is played at each school.

The four "middleweight" teams in basketball play a double round robin tournament at each school and then play an all-star game with the other junior high to wind up the season. The "lightweights" play only the teams in their own school.

The new junior high school has a swimming pool and a swimming squad. This squad is divided into three teams that compete against each other and has several meets each year with the high school's junior varsity team. This year a meet is planned with the other junior high whose swimmers have been able to practice in the high school pool. It is hoped that the older junior high school will soon have its own pool.

Each school has a wrestling team and two coaches. In addition, the high school wrestling coach and assistant coach divide their time between the two schools for about five weeks. This season is climaxed by a wrestling match (officiated by the high school coach) at each school.

Track is run similarly. Each school has its own competition and then there is one meet (on the high school track) between the two schools at each of the three grade levels. Each meet is a two-day meet with field events one day and running events the second day. This competition is between teams of each grade.

As early in the spring as the weather permits, baseball gets underway. The 8th and 9th grade boys play hardball baseball. There are six teams at each school. These six teams play a schedule among themselves. There is no all-star game between the two schools. Baseball practice and games are held three days a week.

Seventh grade boys form a softball league at each school. They play a schedule of games at their own schools only. Softball sessions are held twice a week.

Tennis includes girls and boys, and the match between the schools at the end of the season is, in reality, two matches—one for the girls and one for the boys.

We feel there are many advantages in a joint intramural program such as ours. Wide participation is the theme of the sports program. Every interested boy gets an opportunity to participate in competition with others of fairly equal ability. We try to provide experiences in a variety of sports for as many boys as care to participate. For some boys this may be their last opportunity to play on a team in tackle football or in the other sports. For the potential athletes, the opportunities are intensive enough to prepare them well to play junior varsity and varsity sports in our senior high school.

The question is often raised as to how this program affects the senior high school interscholastic teams. Shaker Heights High School is in a highly competitive suburban league. The other high schools, with one exception, have larger enrollments and are in districts where there are interscholastic junior high school programs. Our high school teams in the various sports usually have better than 500 seasons and many years are near or at the top of the league. One reason may be that the program helps keep the "latebloomers" interested and participating, so that they can be developed later when they are more mature.

37 ❧ SPORTS DAYS FOR GIRLS? *

Yes

M. Corinne Clark
Chairman, Health, Physical Education, and Recreation,
Wisconsin State University,
Whitewater, Wisconsin

James B. Conant once said, "A clash of opinion has often been the prelude to a fruitful development of new ideas." Let us hope this is what is transpiring in Illinois regarding the desire of many physical educators to expand programs to include more extramural activities.

A committee of interested physical education teachers, now some 200 in number, is working to develop and promote an expanded sports program for high-school girls. Since 1962 many attempts have been made to have the constitution of the Illinois High School Association amended to include Sports Days. The IHSA legislative commission has refused to clear this for a vote by the member schools. The Committee To Develop and Promote a Desirable Sports Day Program for High School Girls in Illinois continues to work toward this goal.

"Sports Day" is not a term to be omitted from our vocabulary. Play Day, an informal type of competition in which teams are formed from representatives of each school attending the program, has been a part of the program of the Girls Athletic Association of IHSA for many years. Sports Day is an informal type of extramural competition in which each school participates as a unit. This is an occassional event with two or more schools meeting simultaneously. More than one sport is represented and each girl participates in only one event. No championship is involved; Sports Day simply broadens competition and provides activity for the skilled and the interested. In no way does this take the place of Play Day; it expands the program with more activities for more girls.

If education is for all, if education aims to help each individual develop to the full extent of his potentialities, then physical education, properly organized and administered, can make a significant contribution to the individual's ability to live a meaningful and satisfying life. All phases of the physical education curriculum —regular activity program, adapted program, intramural program, and extramural program— should be included; balanced attention should be supplied with no phase being over-emphasized at the expense of the remainder.

In other areas of education, the girl of today is given many opportunities to compete: school against school, individual against individual, group against group. In music, there are IHSA-sponsored music contests. In speech, there are IHSA-sponsored debates held according to conference rules. In science, there are "science fairs" where one student is competing against another student. In art, talent is judged and prizes are awarded for excellence. In all of these areas, the group or the individual is representing a school. Why do we forbid girls to compete in physical activities? The girl today who is interested in sports is not a rarity. The girl desiring more participation, more practice in the world of competition, more practice in loyalty correctly placed, more practice in understanding the worth of the individual and the group, should be provided with these opportunities to the fullest extent possible. These experiences simply provide another frame of reference for living a meaningful life. The teachers of physical education should be given the opportunity, and should accept the challenge, to provide the leadership for a well-balanced and well-functioning program leading to these experiences.

Let us remember that permanency is merely an illusion. We are faced with economic and technological changes, and rapid changes in

---

*From Illinois Education **54**:126, November 1965. Used by permission.

our culture. This fact should influence the educator and the student. Can physical educators say they have done all they can to provide situations conducive to the interaction of teen-age girls? Team games and individual sports promote opportunity for one individual personality to act upon another. Studies have shown that activity is enlivened by competition, that individuals strive harder to reach their potential. If a game is being played on the basis of "Apples against Bananas," the desire to excel in performance or to participate to the fullest, and the interest in the activity, is not as great as it is in a more competitive situation of school against school.

Our lives are filled with tensions, strains, and social amenities. Physical education must provide situations which will help the student adjust to her society. The extended program can do this by providing more opportunity for practice in competitive activities, providing opportunity for expanded knowledge and participation in carry-over sports, and instilling a desire for continued participation in sports after termination of school life.

Physical education contributes to the present maintenance and future improvement of physical fitness and therefore contributes to the health of the individual. Physical education also helps to build character and exposes the student to social situations which contribute to good sportsmanship.

The physical educator must provide the leadership. The swimming clubs, gymnastic clubs, and softball teams, sponsored by the community and by commercial enterprises, and usually coached or instructed by men, will take advantage of the skilled and interested girl if we do not provide her with some form of competition beyond that which is offered by the high schools today.

Consideration of the student's needs, interests, and abilities must determine the course of action. The understanding and insight of the physical educator must determine the value of an activity to those participating. The physical education teacher in Illinois is capable of assuming leadership of the expanded program in physical education for the high-school girl. She has the foresight and integrity.

This proposal to the Girls Athletic Association of IHSA for a Sports Day program carries with it no mandate. It is not a requirement of membership that Play Days be provided. Sports Days would not be a requirement, either, but would simply provide more opportunity for participation in activities included in the physical education and intramural program. The teacher, in any one school, is cognizant of the amount and type of program which can be offered because of facilities, equipment, staff, and students. The teacher, through her association with students in the regular program and in intramurals, is aware of the needs, interest, and abilities of each student. Not all schools, not all programs, and not all students would or should be included in the Sports Day program. Should those students needing, desiring, and having the ability to participate in such a program be denied the opportunity if the feelings of the school administration and the physical educator, and the facilities and equipment available, make it possible and advantageous? Even though the number wanting to or being able to take advantage of the opportunity to participate might be small, should we eliminate this learning situation because of fear?

Fear that such a program would develop into an interscholastic program patterned after a boys program seems to be uppermost in the minds of those administrators on the IHSA legislative commission and of some of the physical educators within the state. Semantics plays a large part in the misunderstanding of the desirability of the Sports Day program. Many do not understand the Sports Day concepts and can only be guided by the competitive program offered to boys in the state.

No one is interested in starting an "interscholastic" league. No physical educator who is interested in the girl of today is going to "load" the schedule with Sports Days. Actually the Sports Day, by its informal structure, eliminates the possibility of scheduling games weekly, monthly, or on any regular basis as is being done in the already approved program of interscholastics—in which opportunity is provided to participate in badminton, golf, archery, and tennis. Tennis schedules are made up; badminton schedules are made up on a league basis by the participating schools. Sports Days are not scheduled; they are occasional events provided when weather, facilities, equipment, and desire by student and teacher make them advisable. Give the physical education teacher the opportunity to provide the leadership in the Sports Day program—a learning situation.

If unity is ever to be reached, it may well be through the realization that all parts belong to the whole. The physical education program's success depends on all its phases: the regular program, the adapted program, the intramural program, and the extramural program—just as the educational program's success depends on all its phases, one phase being the physical education program. If an expanded program of activities is not provided when deemed advisable, we are not contributing to the success of the whole—the educational curriculum.

I hope that in the not-too-distant future administrators and teachers, trained in the teaching of physical education and desiring to develop and to promote an expanded program, are able to see "eye to eye" on the regulations, controls, and methods of enriching the existing program of the Illinois League of Girls Athletic Association.

No

Margaret Johnson
Director of Elementary Physical Education,
District No. 175, Belleville, Illinois

The Illinois High School Girls Athletic Association program as now presented gives all girls of all Illinois high schools an equal opportunity for participation in the activity of their choice. The program encourages competition through intramural and Play Day activities and challenges all instructors of girls physical education to meet the demands of a changing, highly charged world and to develop physical fitness to meet the tensions, social adjustment, and emotional stability of each student.

The facilities of the average high school in Illinois are limited. Often there is one gymnasium and crowded outdoor space which must be shared with many other high-school organizations. These areas can be used to the greatest advantage for the majority of girls through the present program by grouping those of nearest age and ability for a particular activity.

The activities offered by GAA are unlimited and varied. They may include all competitive team sports for girls, as well as individual sports. There is a place for all levels of ability and interest for each and every high-school girl. Many girls are challenged by team games and wish to continue with these in their college careers, or they develop individual skills which may well be continued into a more highly competitive area after high school. One of the benefits universal to all girls is learning to use their leisure time profitably as adults.

The GAA activity hour during the school year is one opportunity for girls to release accumulated tensions of the heavy academic school day. Furthermore it is a time for fun

and relaxation, for meeting friends in a friendly atmosphere with friendly competition rather than one of preparing for a Sports Day meet with more tensions added to an already busy day. It is a time of give and take, a time of adjusting to situations as they arise, and a time for laughs. This is where the desire for learning to be a girls' physical education teacher can be aroused. Group leadership is developed through officiating, serving as a captain of a team, scheduling tournaments, and scoring, among other things.

Play Days have many advantages, so many that they overbalance the advantages offered by Sports Days. Play Day gives the host school an opportunity to use its local GAA organization to its utmost capacity and ability. Arranging a day of activity for 150 to 200 girls uses the many talents available in such an organization. Here is an opening for theme discussions for choosing and assigning teams, for planning sports, and for innumerable other talents. All of this provides the basis for a group to work together in order to learn cooperation on a smaller scale, to be applied in getting along with others throughout life. Individual abilities are recognized through selection of team captains and officials for each sport.

Competition is important. More important is the opportunity to develop lasting friendships between girls from different high schools, with no tensions and no fears of failing to represent their high schools to advantage. It might be claimed that friends are made through Sports Days; but in competitive sports there is never time to make lasting friendships. The pre-game time is spent in preparation for the game or contest. Afterwards there is joy and jubilation if the game is won, or disagreement, perhaps even hard feelings, if the game is lost—with neither situation one of real congeniality. Play Day provides each girl with a day of competition, fun, social activity, and personal satisfaction—fulfilling the needs of the girls and furthering their social adjustment. Such get-togethers bring about a better understanding among students of various high schools and promote better sportsmanship, especially in the area of the boys interscholastic program.

The term "Sports Day" in reality means interscholastic competition. The present GAA program permits Sports Days for interscholastic competition in archery, tennis, golf, and badminton. This would seem quite sufficient. The schools requesting any change should first use the media available to them through the existing bylaws to prove the need for or advantage of more interscholastic competition, and to uncover the problems which will arise and for which controls will be necessary.

Few schools have the facilities or staff to carry on both a strong intramural program and a Sports Day program. A good, competent teacher could not permit a girl to participate in a game or contest unless she was fully prepared and in good physical condition in order to be at her best. This takes time away from the intramural program thus weakening it. With Sports Days, local pressures from students and adults—to say nothing of the press—would likely limit such competition to the same schools which make up the boys athletic conference. The pressure on students of representing their high school would be very strong, and high-school students are very much aware of these pressures.

The financial obligations of the school district would be increased by the obvious and necessary physical examinations, insurance, provisions to care for injuries, transportation, awards, teacher's salary, officials' fees, custodian's fees, and many other incidentals. With few exceptions, boards of education in Illinois are faced with ever-increasing budgets and difficulty in gaining support for increased taxation within the district. Increasing enrollments continually force greater financial demands on all phases of education. In view of this, it is most unlikely that a board of education, or the taxpayers, would approve a request for an added and unneeded expense.

The present GAA program is an educationally sound school program. It stresses participation for all girls, not just those of special ability; it encourages participation in many activities, both team and individual; it emphasizes leadership and social graces. Regardless of size, all schools now participate on an equal basis in Play Days, workshops, and summer leadership camp.

Most other states envy the Girls Athletic Association of Illinois because it has succeeded in fulfilling the educational objectives in girls and women's sports which are most desirable. Let's keep GAA and intramural sports without the rivalry and pressures of interscholastic Sports Days.

38 ᵇ SHARED INTRAMURAL SPORTS*

DON R. ANDERSEN
DISTRICT COORDINATOR OF PHYSICAL EDUCATION,
WINNETKA (ILLINOIS) PUBLIC SCHOOLS

For the past two years Wilmette [program refers to Howard Junior High School and St. Joseph School, Wilmette, Illinois] has been the scene of a unique experiment in interschool relations. Seventh- and eight-grade students of one of the community's parochial schools are now included in the intramural athletic program sponsored by a public junior high school. As a result, these boys and girls are participating in sports and skills areas which were previously denied them.

The Wilmette public schools have long maintained a highly diversified program of intramural sports and activities. Due to a number of factors, such as shortage of facilities and instructional staff, the parochial schools have not been able to offer such varied experiences to their students.

Although interscholastic athletic competition is stressed at St. Joseph elementary school, physical education is offered only one-half hour per week. In addition, the intramural program was seriously lacking in depth.

Because the parochial school youngsters were not receiving as broad a background in sports skills and experiences as their public school counterparts, a group of parents and St. Joseph administrators sought the advice of Millard D. Bell, the public school superintendent. He suggested that the seventh- and eighth-grade parochial school youngsters be integrated into the existing program of intramural sports at Howard Junior High School, located less than a half block from St. Joseph.

All intramural activities are conducted in the junior high school; the public schools furnish the equipment and administer the program. The danger of overtaxing the facilities and staff or of crowding the public school youngsters out is minimal. Outdoor activities are seldom a problem, due to the size of the athletic fields; and even those sports which must be conducted inside may be accommodated by judicious scheduling of games or practices.

The greatest problem has been the disparity

*From Illinois Education 54:128, November 1965. Used by permission.

in basic athletic skills. Youngsters who have physical education for one 30-minute period per week are competing alongside another group who has 40 minutes of physical education daily. Obviously, the parochial school student's experiences are somewhat limited. However, his mastery of skills and concepts grows perceptibly as he participates in the intramural program.

Since the public school has assumed the responsibility of seventh- and eight-grade intramurals, the parochial physical education staff is able to devote more time to their fifth- and sixth-grade intramural sports. In the future this should lessen the difference in athletic skills between the students of the two schools, when they reach junior-high age.

So thorough is the integration of students on the various teams that interschool rivalries seldom occur. Leagues are determined by ability grouping in basketball and softball. In tackle football the boys are rated by age, height, and weight and are placed in appropriate categories. Volleyball is the only sport in which St. Joseph players participate on a non-integrated basis.

Included in the girls' intramural program are such activities as soccer, volleyball, basketball, archery, badminton, softball, tumbling, and folk and modern dancing.

The intramural program is scheduled from 3:30 until 5 P.M. for four days one week and five days the next. Boys and girls each have two days of intramurals every week, with the boys getting the extra day the second week.

Such a project would not be possible without assistance from sources outside the physical education departments. The school board pays an extra-duty stipend to junior-high faculty members who assist with the coaching and officiating responsibilities. Communications between the schools could pose a problem, so two members of the Howard physical education staff are responsible for interschool liaison.

A program of integrated intramural athletics would not be practicable in every school system. Consideration should be given to whether or not the public schools can accommodate such an increase in participants; the availability of enough staff and the adequacy of facilities also warrant appraisal. Finally, the attitude of the public school administration must be determined. The difference between "shared time" and "integrated program" is probably only one of semantics.

The underlying philosophy of the Wilmette public schools is to provide the best in educational experiences to *all* children of the community. Since the public schools are better equipped than their sectarian counterparts, it is incumbent upon them to take the initiative and to offer a complete program of integrated intramural athletics.

PROJECT AND THOUGHT QUESTIONS

1. Prepare a list of administrative principles that you feel are essential for the successful administration of intramural and extramural programs.
2. Why have intramurals and extramurals sometimes been referred to as laboratory periods for the basic instructional physical education program?
3. What are some of the values that accure from corecreational intramural and extramural program?
4. Arrange for a Sports Day at your school. Appoint committees, invite schools, plan the program, and implement the day.
5. What are the objectives of intramurals? Of extramurals?
6. Prepare a position paper on "Intramural and Extramural Programs Should be the Only Type of Athletic Program in the Junior High School."
7. What should be the relationship between the intramural and extramural programs and the interscholastic and intercollegiate athletic programs?

SELECTED READINGS

American Association for Health, Physical Education, and Recreation: Girls sports organization handbook, Washington, D.C., 1961, The Association.

American Association for Health, Physical Education, and Recreation: Intramural sports for college men and women, (revised edition), Washington, D.C., 1961, The Association.

Anton, T., and Toschi, L.: A practical approach to intramural sports, Portland, Maine, 1964, J. Weston Walsh.

The Athletic Institute: Intramurals for the senior high school, Chicago, 1964, The Institute.

Bucher, C. A.: Administration of health and physical education programs, including athletics, ed. 5, St. Louis, 1971, The C. V. Mosby Co.

CHAPTER 8 INTERSCHOLASTIC AND INTERCOLLEGIATE
ATHLETIC PROGRAMS

Varsity interscholastic and intercollegiate athletics represent an integral part of the total physical education program. They should grow out of the intramural and extramural athletic programs.

Athletics, with the appeal they have for youth, should be the heart of the physical education program. They should be an important part of education and an aid in attaining goals that will benefit all persons who participate in such programs.

The challenge presented by varsity interscholastic and intercollegiate programs is one that all physical education personnel should recognize. The challenge can be met and resolved if physical educators aggressively bring to the attention of administrators, school and college faculties, and the public in general, the true purposes of athletics in a physical education program. It is important in the administration of such programs to stress the importance of having an athletic program that meets the needs of all, that is organized and administered with the welfare of the individual participant in mind, that is conducted in the light of educational objectives that are not compromised when exposed to pressure from sports writers, alumni, and townspeople, and that requires leadership trained in physical education work.

In actual practice the organizational and administrative structure of athletic programs takes two forms. At times the programs are organized as integral parts of the physical education administrative structure and at other times as separate units apart from physical education. Some departments of athletics that operate as separate units evolved from the nineteenth century, at which time athletics were not considered an integral part of the educational program. If athletics are looked upon as intrinsically related to education, then the administration should give careful consideration to incorporating them as part of the physical education program. This practice should always be the case on the precollege level.

The readings in this chapter discuss many features of athletic programs, including the value of programs for girls, the need for a new type of athletic program, crowd control, ad-

ministrative problems, certification of coaches, and sportsmanship.

Charles A. Bucher, in the first selection, writes that athletic programs should not be determined by sports-minded citizens and parents who desire to reap glory from their youngsters' achievements. Sports and varsity programs should be used as a means of individual self-improvement for the participants.

Charles E. Forsythe's article expresses the same theme; local-level administration is the key factor in the success or failure of interscholastics. The prime consideration should be competition, school interest, skill improvement, friendships, good sportsmanship, and the right to play and compete.

Good sportsmanship, the conduct of the coach, spectators, and the treatment of officials are the responsibility of the administrator, according to Jack H. Marcell, author of the next article. Coaches determine the tone of the crowd and players, in the expression of their own attitudes. Administrators, Marcell believes, should ensure improvements in the quality and effectiveness of the sports program through professional cooperation with their coaches.

Who is best qualified to coach a varsity sport? Arthur A. Esslinger writes that the best qualified person should have a physical education major background with experience as a member of the varsity sport to be coached. Twenty-five percent of all coaches today do not have these qualifications. A proposed program for the certification of future coaches includes courses in medical aspects of athletic coaching, principles and problems of coaching, theory and techniques of coaching kinesiological foundations of coaching, and physiological foundations of coaching.

The article from the American Association for Health, Physical Education, and Recreation on crowd control points out some of the possible causes of problems in this area. Of concern to administrators should be lack of communication, lack of involvement, lack of respect for authority, and outsiders. Possible solutions would be to develop written policies, provide adequate facilities, teach good sportsmanship, intensify communications to inform the community, and involve law enforcement.

Bonnie Jo Bevans devotes the next article to a discussion of a sound philosophy in respect to the involvement of girls in interscholastics. Administrators, she believes, must be concerned with establishing a set of principles for planning and controlling the competitive experiences of girls, with adherence to the local guidelines governing interscholastics for girls.

Research studies, as surveyed by Paul K. Reger, show that programs in competitive sports for women are less than fifty years old. The woman's place in society and the concept of femininity are changing quickly. Physiological and sociological research show that there is no danger to women engaged in interscholastic competition, but rather that there is a gain of a new dynamic concept that cannot be attained elsewhere.

The Iowa girls' track and field meet, an interscholastic meet reported by E. Wayne Cooley, involved 18,000 girls in 1968 as compared to 1,500 girls in 1962. It was learned that the girls were proud to create an identity within the school and the community in this expression of athletic ability.

Andy Bakjian describes the successful interscholastic program for boys in the Los Angeles high schools. Twenty-five percent of all the boys in this district are engaged in interscholastics. The success of this program is based to a great degree on the functions of the Policy Determining Committee, which sets rules and regulations governing players, practices, competition, coaches, and responsibilities of all parties involved at competitive events. The school district administrators believe that control is the key to a successful program.

39 ᔭ NEEDED: A NEW ATHLETIC PROGRAM*

CHARLES A. BUCHER
PROFESSOR OF EDUCATION,
NEW YORK UNIVERSITY, NEW YORK

Athletics, as played in college and professional ranks, have no place in the junior and senior high schools of this nation. Yet, there are some secondary schools in this country where the athletic pattern is very similar to the more advanced forms of competition found in institutions of higher learning and among the professionals. Sports-minded citizens rather than educators determine the program and the stress is on the spectator rather than the student. Such practices are preventing excellence in education for many communities.

Educators have lost the battle for a sound sports program in many of our colleges and universities where administrators have been forced to yield to the pressures of alumni and other groups. If there is any consolation that can be derived from such a dilemma it is that the participants at least are adults. Immature youngsters in the nation's senior high schools and particularly in the junior high schools of this nation should never be subjected to such practices. Furthermore, the commercial interests who have reaped a bonanza from a gi-

gantic sports boom, the sports writers who have found a gold mine in copy for their newspaper, radio and TV programs, and parents who have found pleasure in basking in the limelight of their children's athletic achievements, must never be permitted to determine the type of programs that exist in the schools. Educators must assume the leadership role just as they do in other aspects of the school program—in mathematics, history, science, and foreign language.

We need a NEW ATHLETICS in our schools today. We have a New math, a New science, and a New English. We also need a NEW ATHLETICS—one we can rightfully label _Educational Athletics,_ as contrasted with the highly competitive spectacular form involving juggernaut athletes who are selected and trained to please the rabid customers in the stands, rather than using sports as a means of individual self-improvement.

Since Sputnik, the lay public and the academicians have insisted upon a faster academic pace for our students, greater depth in subject matter content, and more inspiring teaching. It is ironical, therefore, that they have not been more active in vigorously encouraging re-emphasis of sports in an educational direction,

---

*A speech given before the National Association of Secondary School Principals in Cleveland, Ohio. From Physical Educator **23**:99, October 1966. Used by permission.

even though sports have many times been responsible for distorting the other aspects of the educational program.

Too often the persons who have spoken out against highly organized athletic competition in our schools have been completely ignored and sometimes treated with scorn and ridicule. The well-respected Dr. James B. Conant's recommendations regarding the Junior High School academic program were received with great enthusiasm, but his labeling of athletics as the "poison ivy" of our schools, went almost unnoticed. After I wrote one article on the subject some time ago, I was told publicly by a sports writer that I should change opium dens.

Many of us who counsel against highlycompetitive sport programs in the schools are not against athletics. Instead, we want to see *more* not less athletics, *more* not fewer participants, and *more* not less money channeled by Boards of Education from the general fund into this area. But we want athletics used in an educationally sound manner. Many of us have played sports ourselves, some of us have coached, and we have seen the potential that sports have for helping our young people to become better human beings. Our mission, therefore, although not a popular one in many quarters, is to bring about a NEW ATHLETICS with the emphasis upon the educational values.

I have always had great admiration for school administrators-superintendents of schools and principals. I am aware of the many pressures placed upon them by the community, parents, teachers, and students. I recognize that sometimes it is very difficult to take a strong stand when it comes to an area such as sports because every red-blooded American considers himself an expert in this area. The public always seems to feel they are qualified to second-guess the quarterback, manager, coach—*and educator*—and say "If he had called this particular play, we would have won the game," or, "I know the best type of school sports program for our boys," or, "The kids are going to have to compete when they get into business—let's give them a taste of it now—it's good for them."

The school administrator is the one responsible for the educational program in his school and, as such, he should be the expert in and the leader for educational athletics. He has within his power the potential to utilize athletics as an educational medium or have them serve as a means of entertainment for the multitudes, to stress knowledge and understanding or gate receipts, and to recognize the unique values of athletics as an educational experience for our boys and girls, or see them as a way of gaining newspaper headlines. School administrators are the persons responsible for the total in-class and out-of-class educational programs that go on in their schools. Such a responsibility cannot be relegated to the coach, the alumni, or the enthusiastic community-minded citizen.

Sports have captured the thinking of the American public. Our weekend television programs monopolize the coaxial cable. The more learned programs, such as "Meet the Press" are preempted by all sorts of games and sports. Millions of people are literally glued to their seats when football and golf are scheduled. Under its new two-year contract with the National Football League, the Columbia Broadcasting System agrees to pay $18.8 million annually for television rights to preseason and regular season games. In turn, CBS has set a new top price for sponsors of $70,000 a minute. Professional football paid 7 million dollars for 20 new stars in this years draft. Newspaper space devoted to sports consumes many pages. The *New York Times,* one of the most respected and supposedly best balanced newspaper in the world, devotes more space to sports than to all the arts combined. And, this interest in sports is not confined to the United States. I traveled around the world three years ago and marveled at the interest our teams have generated in other lands.

Since athletics were first introduced into the educational picture, there has been a continual pushing downward of these competitive experiences into the lower educational levels. Educational athletics started at the college level with a crew race between Harvard and Yale in 1852. Then, other sports were introduced to the campuses throughout the United States. As higher education athletic programs expanded and gained recognition and popularity, the high schools felt sports should also be a part of their educational offerings. As a result, most high schools in America today have some form of interscholastic athletics. In recent years, junior high schools have also felt the impact of interschool athletic programs. Consequently, today most of the junior high schools have athletic programs, many of them carbon copies of those that exist in the senior high school, grades 10–12 having previously aped the colleges. Furthermore, the elementary schools are now looking at the junior high schools and instituting their own brand of sports. Games are being pushed further and further down into the tender years of childhood. A colleague of mine at Ohio State facetiously has said that if the trend continues it won't be long before we will be having prenatal bowl games.

And, wherever these full-scale athletic programs are established in education there are problems: examples—stress on the gifted player at the expense of the dub, emphasis on the spectator rather than the participant, priority given to boys at the expense of girls, and facilities being usurped by the varsity at the expense of intramurals.

In other areas and fields of specilization in the schools we seem very much concerned about having a sound educational program which uses the developmental aspects of child growth as guidelines and we demand progression and sequential development of subject matter. Yet when it comes to athletics, we become indifferent, bowing to community pressures and ignoring the way children grow and develop. For example, one can hardly recognize the sequential development of our athletic experiences from the grades to college. They should progress gradually and smoothly from the informal type of activity, the low intensity of competition, fundamental skills, to the more highly organized activities, higher intensity of competition and more complex skills. The way the athletic program is conducted however, instead of being developmental and progressive in approach, it seems to follow an adult formula which is projected downward upon our children and youth.

A question that particularly disturbs me is "Where is the cut-off point on interscholastic competition?" There are some athletic people who advocate such programs for the elementary school level. Is this where we stop? Does it follow that if varsity athletics have educational value at the college level they also have value at the high school level? If they have value at the high school level, do they have value at the junior high school level? If they have value at the junior high school level, do they have value at the elementary school level? How much varsity interscholastic athletic competition does a young person need? Three years of high school and four years of college permits seven years of competition plus all the years after formal schooling has ended. Is this enough? If we add three more years for the junior high school this would mean ten years. Is this enough? Or, should we go into the elementary school and add a few more years? How much is needed? I think perhaps too many of us have decided that varsity interscholastic athletics are

a good thing and believe that all is needed are controls to ensure the proper educational outcome. Too few of us have thought through objectively a much more important problem—can we justify interscholastic athletics of a varsity type below the high school level? If so, what is the justification?

Another question that I feel we should ask is, "To what extent do we permit the public to dictate educational policy?" It is interesting to note that educators determine the content of the mathematics curriculum, the number of years of science that is offered, and the guides for the teaching of English. Yet, when it comes to the athletic program, the public, to a large degree through their interest and support, determines what sports will be conducted and, in their role as spectators, some of the rules that will make the game more fascinating and spectacular. The public likes athletics and it is difficult for many persons to distinguish between educational athletics and sports that are conducted outside the school. These persons do not understand that as educators we have certain goals toward which we are striving and all phases of the program, in-class or out-of-class, must be justified in light of the contribution they make to educational goals.

I feel strongly that educators must take over the reins and determine the nature and scope of the athletic program rather than permit some uninformed community-minded citizens to do it for them. We cannot afford to progress blindly onward in compliance with the often short-sighted desires of society. We must strive to inform and convince society of what must be done if athletics are to be a benefit to our youth and be educationally sound, "for without instruction," as Thomas Woody said, "a society may ignorantly choose the worse rather than the better reason." This is going to mean we need educators with strong convictions and thick skins. But the satisfaction of doing what is right educationally will not be without its rewards.

It is clearly evident there have been many problems ever since games became a part of the school program—problems that require much thought on the part of professional educators and especially school administrators, the persons responsible for giving leadership within the school and interpreting to the community a sound philosophy of educational athletics. This leadership is particularly important in the years of early adolescence when boys and girls are experiencing many physical changes, when values are being formed, when skills are being learned, and when there is a transition from childhood to adolescence. The words of Thomas Woody are worth thinking about:

"Games are evil
Games are good
Oft are games misunderstood."

Since the theme of this NASSP conference is *Education: Yesterday-Today-Tomorrow,* it seems most fitting as a concluding statement to this presentation, to project one's thoughts into the future and forecast what the role of athletics in secondary school education will be like in the years ahead.

Will this popular desire for sport be directed into constructive channels which will enhance the total fitness and character of our youth and contribute to the achievement of educational goals? Or, will the American love of sport detract from our educational achievements? The road that sports will follow will be determined largely by your efforts, *or* the absence of your efforts—you who are the leaders of our secondary schools. The degree to which you assume a dynamic leadership role, keep your eyes on the educational values of sport, and articulately interpret to the public the place that sports rightfully hold in our culture will determine the future course of sports in the secondary schools of this nation.

Educational athletic programs for the future should include such characteristics as the following:

1. Athletic programs organized on developmental pattern.
2. Athletic sports seasons and number of games played restricted in length—some school administrators feel that 10 weeks is a sufficient length of time for any one sports season.
3. Athletic practices limited to not more than 1 1/2 hours per day.
4. Major sports becoming the minor sports and

A small portion of this speech has been taken from The State Education Department. *Interscholastic Athletics at the Junior High School Level,* Albany, 1965. (By the author)

minor sports the major sports—the lifetime sports get special consideration.

5. Gate receipts eliminated with the cost being paid out of the general fund, the same as for English, Mathematics, History and other parts of the educational program.
6. Sport contests conducted only on school premises—the public arena with its gamblers, foul language, and rabid spectators is a thing of the past.
7. Coaches appointed on the basis of their education qualifications, not win-loss records. A knowledge of the participant physically, mentally, emotionally, and socially, is one of the most important qualifications.
8. Athletics an integral part of the total physical education program. The Director of Physical Education is assigned all the duties in regard to the athletic program.
9. All games played on weekday afternoons prior to days when school will not be in session—night games are out.

For those of you who think this is too ambitious an undertaking, I would like to say that it is the essence of leadership that your reach must exceed your grasp. As Carl Schurz, an immigrant to this country pointed out long ago: "Ideals are like the stars; you will not succeed in touching them with your hands. But like the seafaring man on the desert of waters, you choose them as your guides, and following them you will reach your destiny."

The National Association of Secondary School Principals has a destiny which challenges it to assume the reins of leadership in educational sports and athletics. You have a long way to go, the competition for such a leadership role will be keen and the pressures will be great, but with stout hearts, and a firm dedication to what you know to be right, you will achieve.

As the wise poet has said:

The Winds Blow East
The Winds Blow West
The Self Same Breezes Blow
'Tis not the gale
But the set of the sail
That will determine where you will go

40 ᔆ SPELL OUT POLICIES, PROCEDURES*

Charles E. Forsythe†
Formerly State Director of High School Athletics,
Michigan High School Athletic Association,
Department of Education, Lansing, Michigan

There are at least two basic considerations regarding policies and procedures in any interscholastic athletic program today. The first, obviously, should be the values to be received by and welfare of the product itself—the students. The second is the relationship of athletics to other phases of the school program and the general administrative policies and procedures.

First considerations will deal with policies which should be reasons why we have interscholastic athletics in our schools today and what they can do for the students—both contestants and spectators.

COMPETITION—We believe that the basic American urge for competition should be maintained. *It's one of the things that has made America great—let's keep it.*

"WHOLE SCHOOL" INTEREST—A good athletic program must provide "whole school" interest and activity. It should include students in its activities other than athletes, as well as enlisting many student school organizations in the program.

HEALTH, SAFETY, and SANITATION—There are no more important lessons to be learned in any program than the values resulting from the formation of good habits pertaining to health, sanitation, and safety. Athletic programs have tremendous potentials in these areas.

SKILLS—From a basic educational standpoint athletics provide opportunities to teach new skills and to improve those we now have. It is axiomatic that we like best to do the things we do well.

FRIENDSHIPS—Athletics provide opportunities for the formation of lasting friendships, both with teammates and members of opposing teams.

SPORTSMANSHIP—Good sportsmanship is good citizenship, and athletics provide op-

portunities for their exemplification and observation.

PLAY—Athletics make it possible for youth to enjoy one of America's greatest heritages, the right to play and compete under equitable standards.

PENALTY FOLLOWS A RULES VIOLATION—One of the most important lessons to be learned from athletic competition is that a penalty follows the violation of a rule. Our athletic fields and play courts are but segments of society where mutually accepted rules and officials insist upon fair play. If this doesn't occur, the guilty party is penalized.

PARTICIPATION A PRIVILEGE WITH RESPONSIBILITIES—Students participating in athletics should understand early that such an opportunity is a privilege which carries responsibilities. They represent not only themselves but their school and community.

ATHLETIC SQUADS-ADVANCED CLASSES—Today we are rightly giving increased attention to the gifted child as well as to those in the middle and lower quartile groups in our schools. There is no reason why athletic squads may not be considered as comprised of gifted individuals and that such squads actually are advanced classes in athletics or physical education activities. It should be kept in mind that such a policy now is in effect concerning bands, orchestras, dramatic clubs, debating teams, play productions, and others.

What are student needs?

Certain basic considerations are necessary to determine procedures to be followed in administering any interscholastic athletic program. In other words, an inventory of student needs and possibilities, facilities, personnel, finances, organization, and relationship of athletics to other phases of the school program is essential before any athletic program can assume its most beneficial role. In general, an attempt has been made in the first part of this presentation to consider the student and his needs and possibilities. The discussion which follows

---

*From American School Board Journal 153:24, August 1966. Used by permission.

†Deceased.

concerns factors which must be considered, and policies to be determined, involving procedural matters concerned with the administration of athletic programs.

EQUITABLE DIVISIONS OF FACILITIES AND PERSONNEL—In the establishment of intramural and interscholastic athletic programs, as well as for physical education, there must be an equitable division of facilities and personnel. Time allotment, gymnasiums and playfields, instructors, and student ratios are important considerations. All of these must be taken into consideration by the school administration prior to the establishment of any interscholastic athletic program.

SCOPE OF PROGRAM—While it is desirable for all students to have equal opportunities to compete in many sports, it is impossible. Varying interests of students will be a vital factor in this matter. Schools are of different sizes; thus, the number of student participants will affect the amount and types of competition available. In general at least three factors will be involved in determining the scope of a local school program: (a) Is the staff sufficient to provide proper teaching and coaching? (b) Is adequate equipment available to insure, as nearly as possible, that the highest safety standards for participants can be maintained? (c) Are the playing facilities safe? Again, is safety paramount as far as playing fields, gymnasiums, and pools are concerned? If it is impossible to answer affirmatively in each of these three categories in regard to the contemplated sponsorship of a sport, it should not be a part of the school's athletic program.

FINANCING ATHLETICS—The policy to be in effect in financing the athletic program must be a matter of record and fully understood by all concerned. It hardly seems sensible that local boards of education should invest tax funds in facilities and pay the costs of coaching personnel, and then demand that gate receipts from athletic contests support the operation of the entire interscholastic athletic program. Increasingly, boards of education are assuming part or all of the financial responsibilities for interscholastic athletics, and rightly so, if they are to be considered a part of the educational program.

GIRLS' ATHLETICS—Determination must be made by a local school system if girls' activities are to be a part of the interscholastic program. At present there is increased impetus being given girls' interscholastic athletic programs on the part of national and state women's athletic organizations and by women physical educators. In lieu of organized interscholastic programs for girls, sports days and sports festivals often are sponsored by schools.

Increase of junior programs

There is an increase in the number of school systems sponsoring junior high school athletics as well as a broadened scope in the programs offered. A school system must establish its own policy in this regard. If there is to be a junior high school program, it should be broad in its offerings, and instruction, coaching, equipment, and playing facilities of the best type should be made available.

CENTER OF RESPONSIBILITY—Where should the responsibility for the general control of the interscholastic athletic program be located in a school? Who should do the coaching—physical educators or academic teachers? What should be the student-faculty relationship in the school organization that controls the program?

Generally, it seems desirable that a school athletic council should be formed with the physical education department having the central administrative authority, subject to confirmation by the superintendent or principal. It should be possible to draw on any branch of the faculty for coaches, provided they are qualified. There must be a complete understanding, however, concerning authority to be delegated to the athletic or physical education director, coach, or faculty manager pertaining to signing of contracts, eligibility procedures, purchase of and responsibility for equipment, completion of schedules, and the hiring of athletic contest officials.

Spell out injury liability

It is important that a school determine its policy concerning the care and payment of costs for injuries received by athletic participants. This should be publicized so that parents and students know what to expect before, rather than after, injuries are received.

WELL-DEFINED ATHLETIC POLICY— Much has been said concerning specific procedures connected with the interscholastic athletic program. Of major importance, however, is a well-defined athletic policy which has the approval and support of the local board of education. *In the last analysis, a board of education is responsible for all phases of the programs in the school system.* Usually, the implementation of the athletic policy is delegated to the superintendent of schools, and through him to the high school principal and then to the head of the athletic department. It should be understood by all that this general policy statement is the result of united effort. It should be printed and available to those interested. By reference as needed for the athletic code or policy to which the school, or school system, subscribes, it will be invaluable in avoiding difficulties, resisting pressures, and keeping control of the program in the school and under the direction of school people.

Recommended league affiliation

In conclusion, it is realized that the "grass roots" or local level administration is the most important single factor in its success or failure. At the same time each of us can help the other. Most schools in the nation belong to a league or athletic conference. Exchange of ideas and problems of kindred groups is possible in such organizations and this is valuable. Many problems and unpleasantries are avoided before they develop.

League membership is highly recommended. There are athletic associations in all 50 states, administered by dedicated officers and school men who are members of state boards, councils, or executive committees. Local school authorities should know these people and make use of the facilities and help. The administration of an athletic program comprises a team involving students, coaches, athletic directors, principals, superintendents, board of education members, league officers, and state athletic association officials.

41 ❧ ADMINISTRATOR, COACHES, AND SPORTSMANSHIP*

JACK H. MARCELL
ASSISTANT PRINCIPAL,
MAGOFFIN INTERMEDIATE SCHOOL, EL PASO, TEXAS

Reading between the lines of a recent article in the *Interscholastic Leaguer* on the conduct of basketball coaches during a game, one can see where much of the blame for uncomplimentary behavior can be put squarely on the shoulders of school administrators.

Administrators of participating schools have definite responsibilities toward the conduct of the coach, spectators, and the treatment of the officials. It is certainly a bad reflection on everyone concerned when the official can look in the stands and see the administrator taking part in the unsportsmanlike activities of the rest of the crowd.

Officials—like players, coaches, and administrators—are of varying abilities. Regardless of how the administrator might question the ability of the official he has certain responsibilities toward this official. It should be unthinkable for him to abandon these responsibilities and revert to the needling, abusing attitude of the crowd. Why should a man take his life in his hands, literally and figuratively, when he puts on an official's shirt and walks onto the field or court? The administrator would certainly not want his job to be put on that same basis.

It is hard enough for an official to do a good job with the coaches "working" him over. This in itself is objectionable enough, however, when an administrator does not provide for control of the crowd and the behavior of the coach, it becomes unpardonable and indefensible. Administrators who consider themselves to be spectators at contests in which their school participates are ignoring an embarrassing and perverse problem.

There is a tendency, at times with some justification, for the administrator to keep away from the trials and tribulations of the athletic department. There has been, and is, a tendency to leave the responsibility of running this important phase of the school's program to others. But if the philosophy and purposes of the interscholastic sports program are to be fostered then the administrators should properly assume responsibility. The problem may be approached in two phases that affect crowd behavior: the administrator's responsibilities, and the coach's attitudes.

When a coach is hired his philosophy and attitudes should be determined as nearly as possible. There should be an understanding of what is expected of the coach as to attitude and deportment. It should be made clear that bellowing at the officials, rationalizing every defeat, or ignoring the value of an honest decision will not be tolerated.

If a coach steps out of line, the administrator should so inform him. An extra 15-yard penalty in football or a technical foul in basketball does not take care of the situation. If necessary,

*From The Texas Outlook 52:20, March 1968. Used by permission.

an administrator should be near enough to the coach so that his presence will deter unsportsmanlike behavior. And if it continues, the administrator should not only look at the coach, but should tap him gently on the shoulder as a reminder to control himself. A conference the next day with the coaching staff should be held and at that time the standards should be reaffirmed or established.

As long as physical education is an integral part of the curriculum, as it should be, coaches should be dealt with in the same forthright manner that the principal assumes in handling teachers' problems in music, English, homemaking, or art. No administrator allows teachers to storm and rave around a classroom. Why should the coach be an exception to this rule?

It takes more than talk to control the actions of a crowd at a ball game. It also takes more than sufficient policing to insure a job well done by an administrator. Many things dovetail into making the entire situation harmonious. An administrator might follow these 10 rules for a successful evening at game time:

• Coaches should be advised to attend sports clinics and officials' meetings. Time should be set aside by the administration, and in-service credit given for attending such meetings.

• Student bodies should be instructed *constantly* on proper behavior in the stands and on crowd attitudes. Stress should be given to the idea that any decision, however adverse, is made by an impartial person and is to be accepted.

• The faculty should be briefed on how to control crowds at evening games. The area of responsibility and supervision at night differs markedly from that of an afternoon ball game. When the community is invited and encouraged to attend, additional problems arise which are not overcome by the hiring of two or three policemen.

• Avoid the officials' dressing room, especially if you have a complaint of some kind. There is always time after a day or two to write a report, if you are dissatisfied.

• Maintain and insist that regular time schedules be followed.

• Prescribe standards of sportsmanship and respect of authority on the part of the coaches and players. Spectators will pick up the trend and carry it forward.

• Arrange for officials to be notified in ample time so they may share rides to the game.

• Make sure that dressing facilities for officials are adequate and private.

• Make certain that the delegation of responsibility for the sport event is carried out in the proper manner.

• Standardize some method of paying officials so they need not wait around after the game for reimbursement.

Coaches influence the behavior of the crowd to a great extent. Every time a coach kicks a chair, throws his hat, sails his clip board, slams a towel, or jumps up and yells derogatory remarks at the officials, the crowd reflects his sentiment and a feeling of hostility is thus created.

The effect is most undesirable. The decision cannot be changed. The players become upset, the spectators grow more boisterous, and the official starts mopping his brow. It is ridiculous for coaches to say that they are not complaining about a particular decision but merely want the referee to be more careful on the next one. Any official worth his salt is not affected by the coach's antics. The spectator should be allowed to enjoy a ball game without infantile exhibitions by the coaches.

It should be remembered that coaches have a part in selecting the list of officials. It is from approved lists that assignments are made, and seldom are officials sent to cover a ball game for a coach who has scratched their names or has given them unfavorable reports.

These lists of competent officials are becoming increasingly harder to compile as pressure from the unsportsmanlike segment causes good officials to drop out. Officials have to pass tests, learn interpretations, and employ proper mechanics before their names are placed on the list for approval. Unfortunately, it is impossible to teach calls based solely on judgment.

Coaches should join officials associations to review and to learn the rules and their interpretations. The fact that a coach was once a high school athlete or "pro" player does not guarantee his knowledge.

The administrator is the key figure to insure major improvements in the quality and effectiveness of the sports program. He should keep in mind that officials are not infallible or perfect, and for that matter neither are administrators. But it does not mean that striving for perfection should be thrown aside. The administrator, the coach, and the official are professionals and they must work as professional individuals.

42 ❧ CERTIFICATION FOR HIGH SCHOOL COACHES*

ARTHUR A. ESSLINGER
DEAN, SCHOOL OF HEALTH, PHYSICAL EDUCATION, AND RECREATION,
UNIVERSITY OF OREGON, EUGENE, OREGON

The major problem confronting interscholastic athletics in the United States is the fact that approximately one-fourth of all head coaches of junior and senior high school teams have had no professional preparation for such a responsibility. Their sole qualification is their participation on a college or university team in the sport concerned. While such participation experience is advantageous, it does not begin to constitute an adequate preparation for coaching a secondary school athletic team.

It has been generally conceded that the best preparation for the position of head coach of a high school athletic team includes the combination of a physical education major plus participating experience as a member of the varsity team of the sport to be coached. Participating experience plus preparation as a physical education minor has been considered the minimum acceptable background. Yet nearly one out of four of our head coaches does not meet this standard.

The implications of this situation are serious. It has long been recognized that competitive athletics have exceptional educational potentialities. Their inclusion in our secondary schools has been justified on the basis of their significant contributions to educational goals. It is erroneous to assume, however, that untrained leadership can elicit the potential educational values which are inherent in athletics. Optimum results cannot be obtained by the coach whose only qualification is that he was a letter-winner in college. If we are to have quality education then we must have quality leadership. Our entire educational system is predicated upon the concept that educational outcomes depend upon professionally prepared leadership.

The coaches who lack professional preparation are handicapped in obtaining the social, moral, ethical, mental, and physical values inherent in interschool sport, and they are also not capable of protecting the health and well-being of the participants. They do not understand the dangers of violent body contact sports upon the human organism. Their lack of background in the structure and function of the human body is a serious liability which keeps them from knowing how to prevent injuries and other damage, to recognize and to evaluate injuries, and to follow the proper course of action when they occur.

It is regrettable that all coaches are not physical education majors who have competed in intercollegiate athletics. This represents the ideal which, unfortunately, cannot be attained. In most secondary schools it is not practical to man all head coaching positions with physical education majors. The reason is that most secondary schools compete in from seven to ten sports and field junior-varsity and freshmen as well as varsity teams in most, if not all, of them. The number of physical education staff members which are needed to handle the physical education program is not adequate to provide head coaches for each of these squads. In this situation the principal must call upon academic teachers to coach some of the teams.

Another problem is that some letter-winners on college teams want to enter a teaching career and to coach but they do not want to major and teach in physical education. They prefer to prepare themselves as teachers in other subject matter areas. The solution to this problem is to provide such teachers with the minimum essentials which all coaches should have.

The AAHPER Division of Men's Athletics has long been aware that many coaches were not adequately prepared for coaching assignments. To attack this problem, a Task Force on Certification of High School Coaches was appointed. The members are:

Ted Abel, Pittsburgh, Pennsylvania, Public Schools
Milton Diehl, Madison East High School, Madison, Wisconsin
Jack George, Roslyn, New York, Public Schools
Robert Jamieson, Grimsley High School, Greensboro, North Carolina
M. G. Maetozo, Lock Haven State College, Lock Haven, Pennsylvania
Don Veller, Florida State University, Tallahassee, Florida
Arthur Esslinger, University of Oregon, Eugene, *chairman*
Roswell Merrick, AAHPER consultant

Arthur A. Esslinger, chairman of the AAHPER Division of Men's Athletics Task Force on Certification of High School Coaches, introduces the report of the Task Force.

*From JOHPER 39:42, October 1968. Used by permission.

The Task Force came to the conclusion that the best way to "liquidate" unqualified coaches is for each state to establish certification standards for teachers of academic subjects who desire to coach. Such standards should be designed only for coaching—not for teaching physical education. The standards should represent the basic understandings and competencies without which no individual should coach. It is not intended that these standards apply to coaches now in service; rather, the recommendations are designed for future coaches.

Out of its deliberations the Task Force has developed a program which includes the minimum essentials which every secondary school head coach should possess. If such a program were required in every state for certification of coaches, interscholastic athletics would be appreciably improved over what they are today. The courses and course outlines follow.[1]

Semester Hours

Medical Aspects of Athletic Coaching	3
Principles and Problems of Coaching	3
Theory and Techniques of Coaching	6
Kinesiological Foundations of Coaching	2
Physiological Foundations of Coaching	2

Medical aspects of athletic coaching

The athletic program can never be termed educational unless the health of the participant is a primary objective. Medical and safety aspects are the heart of good athletic administration. Consideration of the individual's well-being must involve related safety factors.

In order to give the health and safety aspects proper emphasis in the preparation of a coach, the following areas are recommended.

   I. Medical aspects

      The medical aspects of the athletic program must be under the direct supervision of physicians.

      A. Preparation of the athlete for participation

         Physical examination

         1. "Team" approach—physicians, school nurses, coaches, and athletic director; dentists, when needed

         2. Importance of administering an efficient and well-planned examination

[1] In the development of these courses and course outlines, many competent, experienced authorities in the various areas were consulted. After completion, they were submitted to eleven leading physical education departments for review, criticisms, and suggestions. The replies received from these sources were incorporated in the final draft.

      B. Prevention of injury and illness

      C. Perception—early recognition of injury

  II. Protective equipment and facilities

      A. When the participant has been medically approved, proper fitting of the best equipment is necessary. Eliminate "hand-me-down" system

      B. Facilities

         Use of padded walls, sponge rubber for jumping pits, proper mats, turfed areas, proper maintenance

 III. Training

      A. General measures relating to health

      B. Use of tape or bandaging and other protective equipment

      C. Emergency care of injuries

      D. Physical therapy

      E. Prevention of overtraining

      F. Psychological counseling

 IV. Injuries

      A. Injury prevention

      B. Procedures when injury occurs

      C. Post-injury care

  V. Medical and safety problems

      A. Sources of information

      B. Importance of the coach having proper knowledge of sleep and rest, vitamins, drugs, smoking, drinking, tetanus immunization, hot weather training rules, fads, and fallacies

 VI. In-service training—care of the athlete

      A. Arrangements for seminars and in-service courses for coaches

      B. County and state clinics

 VII. Medical research related to athletics

      A. Organizations—information

      B. Conference proceedings

      C. Journals

Principles and problems of coaching

Because of the immensity of this area, some pertinent items may not have been included. The individual instructor is encouraged to develop any additional items deemed necessary.

   I. Personal relationships

      A. Qualities of the coach

         1. Positive attitude

         2. Pride in players

         3. Concern for interests of other people

         4. Firm but pleasant

         5. Golden Rule

      B. Influencing and controlling behavior in athletes

         1. Be yourself

         2. The private talk

3. The grapevine method
4. Setting the example
5. Handling individual differences
C. Creating and maintaining discipline and desire
   1. Necessity for hard work
   2. Goal setting
   3. Traditions
   4. Spreading enthusiasm
   5. Use of captains
D. Vital relationships
   1. The principal
   2. Teaching colleagues
   3. Parents
   4. The janitor
   5. Community—booster clubs, PTA, churches, etc.
E. The coach and his assistants
   1. Choosing assistants
   2. Loyalty
   3. Delegation of responsibility
   4. Delegation of authority
   5. Bilateral relationship
F. Athletes and their emotional problems
   1. Problems in the home
   2. School problems
   3. Girl problems
   4. Jealousies
   5. The extrovert
   6. The introvert
   7. The status seeker
   8. The "psyche" case
   9. The prima donna
   10. Case histories

II. Organization
A. Organizing and planning for practice
   1. Season objectives
   2. Weekly objectives
   3. Daily plans
   4. Time
   5. Weather
   6. Staff
   7. Equipment and facilities
   8. Helpful hints
B. Athletic contest management
   1. Importance of efficient management
   2. Before-game preparation
   3. Game responsibilities
   4. Post-game responsibilities
   5. Preparation for out-of-town contests
   6. General management duties and policies
C. Athletic equipment

1. Purchase of equipment
2. Marking of equipment
3. Issuing of equipment
4. General care of equipment
5. The equipment inventory
D. Athletic finances and budgets
   1. Finances and athletic programs
   2. Methods of raising funds
   3. Ticket selling problems
   4. Purpose of an athletic budget
   5. Preparing the budget

III. Important considerations
A. Training rules and how to enforce them
   1. Good training—a must
   2. The policeman-type
   3. No-rules-at-all type
   4. The scapegoat approach
   5. Squad-oriented type
B. Selection and evaluation of personnel
   1. Comparison to industry
   2. Individual sports
   3. Team sports
   4. Being objective
   5. Types of evaluation
   6. Past performances
   7. Getting the right man in the right job
C. Motivation and special inducements to athletes
   1. Awards (letters, trophies, etc.)
   2. Publicity
   3. Championships
   4. Scholarships
   5. Special "gimmicks"
D. Coaching ethics
   1. Players
   2. Opponents
   3. Officials
   4. School colleagues
   5. Coaching colleagues
   6. Public
   7. News media

Theory and techniques of coaching

I. Educational implications of the sport
A. Role in education
B. Role in physical education
C. Philosophy
D. Objectives
   1. Of the sport
   2. Of the coach
   3. Of the player
   4. Of the spectator
E. History
II. Fundamentals detailed

A. Teaching methods in performance skills
B. Drills for developing basic skills
  1. Offensive
  2. Defensive
III. Technical information
  A. Offensive tactics
  B. Defensive tactics
  C. Strategy
  D. Use of teaching aids
IV. Scouting
  A. Film analysis
  B. Pre-scouting check list
  C. Game scouting check list
  D. Post-game scouting check list
  E. Individuals
  F. Team
  G. Player performance rating systems
V. Conditioning for a specific sport
  A. Developing
  B. Training
  C. Conditioning
  D. Emotional aspects
  E. Educating (conceptual content)
VI. Organization and management
  A. Pre-game preparation
  B. During event
  C. Post-game aspects
  D. Outline of duties for team managers
VII. Practice sessions
  A. Daily
  B. Weekly
  C. Seasonal
VIII. Safety aspects of particular sport
  A. Rules and regulations
  B. Facilities, grounds
  C. Officiating
  D. Supplies and equipment
  E. Prevention of injury
  F. Legal aspects
IX. Rules and regulations
  A. Of the sport
  B. Penalties
  C. Local
  D. State
  E. National
X. Evaluation
  A. Season in retrospect
  B. Collection of appropriate materials
  C. Plans for following year
  D. Preparation of reports to administration

Kinesiological foundations of coaching

I. Anatomical factors
  A. The coach must have sufficient knowledge of human anatomy to:

1. Recognize any symptoms of ailments or deviations from normal health in order to provide first aid when such care is indicated and to secure the services of a physician when they are needed
2. Select equipment which will fit best and offer maximum protection
3. Conduct an adequate physical conditioning program for the squad as well as for the individual players needs
4. Establish a program for the prevention of injuries (By being aware of the parts of the body which are most subject to injury such as the knee, shoulder, ankle and the parts of the body subject to the most serious injuries such as the head and spine, the coach can more intelligently take measures which will reduce injuries)
5. More effectively tape and bandage his players

II. Mechanics of movement
  A. A knowledge of the mechanics of movement is indispensable to the coach and such information helps him to:
  1. Recognize more readily individual differences in the performance of a particular motor skill
  2. Develop more fully the individual student's potential in performing a motor skill
  3. Recognize more readily typical body alignments and their influence on motor performance
  4. Eliminate much "trial and error" in giving correct "coaching tips," producing more effective results in a shorter period of time
  5. Teach his students to use good and efficient body mechanics in all movement, thus reducing the number of injuries and the amount of fatigue
  6. Make more efficient use of coaching time
  7. Understand better the problems of efficiency and economy of movement
  8. Analyze performance more scientifically and base recommendations for improvement on sound anatomical and mechanical principles

Physiological foundations of coaching

I. Physiological factors
  A. The following areas of physiology are essential to the coach in order to provide him with an understanding of how the human organism functions.
    1. Central nervous system: motor functions
    2. Nervous system: sensory functions
    3. Properties and constituents of the blood
    4. Physiological mechanisms involved in the circulation of the blood and lymph
    5. Respiration
    6. Body fluids and kidney
    7. Metabolism and nutrition
    8. Endocrine system
    9. Growth and development
II. Exercise physiology factors
  A. Circulatory and respiratory adjustments
    1. The heart
    2. Heart rate and exercise
    3. Circulation of the blood
    4. Circulatory adjustments during exercise
    5. Body fluid changes in exercise
    6. Pulmonary ventilation
    7. Gas exchange and transport
  B. Environment aspects
    1. Environmental and body temperatures
    2. Cooling power of the environment
    3. Effects of external heat
    4. Effect of cold
    5. Effect of altitude
    6. Effect of humidity
  C. Metabolism and exercise
    1. Oxygen requirement and oxygen intake
    2. Aerobic and anaerobic metabolism
    3. The steady state
    4. Oxygen debt
    5. Influence of training on oxygen intake and debt
  D. Nutrition
    1. Elements of adequate nutrition
    2. Planning the athlete's diet
    3. Fluids
    4. Distribution of meals
    5. The pre-game meal
    6. Half-time feeding
    7. Making weight
    8. Weight loss in athletics
  E. Drugs
    1. Drugs affecting the autonomic nervous system
    2. Drugs affecting the central nervous system
    3. Drugs affecting the circulatory system
    4. Drugs affecting metabolism and nutrition
    5. Hormones
  F. Conditioning
    1. Chronic effects of athletic training
    2. Warming up
    3. Practice schedule
    4. Maximum training capacity
    5. Recuperative ability
    6. Pre-season
    7. Early season
    8. League competition
  G. Strength training
    1. Factors in strength
    2. Physiological basis of strength training
    3. Weight training exercises
    4. Weight training regimen
    5. Isometric training
    6. Circuit training
    7. Weight training hazards and benefits
  H. Endurance training
    1. Physiological training
      (a) Anaerobic training
      (b) Aerobic training
      (c) Heat training
      (d) Rhythm training
    2. Pace
    3. Training programs
      (a) Over and under training
      (b) *Fartlek* training
      (c) Interval training
      (d) Repetition training
      (e) Circuit training

Among the appropriate bibliographical references are:

1. American Medical Association. Protecting the health of the high school athlete. Chicago, Ill.: AMA. n.d.
2. Bender, James B. How to be a successful coach. Englewood Cliffs, New Jersey: Prentice-Hall, Inc., 1958.
3. Forsythe, Charles E. Administration of high school athletics. Englewood Cliffs, New Jersey: Prentice-Hall, Inc., 1962.
4. George, Jack F., and Lehmann, Harry A. School athletic administration. New York: Harper & Row, 1966.
5. Lawther, John D. Psychology of coaching. Englewood Cliffs, New Jersey: Prentice-Hall, Inc., 1965.
6. Ryan, Allan J. Medical care of the athlete. New York: McGraw-Hill, 1962.

43 ᴈ❧ APPROACHES TO CROWD CONTROL*

Summary of reports: small group discussions

CITY AND COUNTY DIRECTORS OF HEALTH, PHYSICAL EDUCATION, AND RECREATION
AMERICAN ASSOCIATION FOR HEALTH, PHYSICAL EDUCATION, AND RECREATION

The nature and seriousness of the problems in crowd control have recently become more drastic and bizarre as they have occurred in increasing frequency. They take on the collective character of a deliberate attempt either to ignore or confront the system. This social problem may be impossible to eliminate completely, but an attempt must be made to cope with the immediate symptoms. Our only hope is for imaginative and coordinated efforts by the school administration, the majority of students, and community authorities to promote standards of conduct conducive to continuing spectator sports in comparative tranquility. The alternatives are to allow a disruptive element to completely negate the nature of school athletics, to play with no spectators, or to abandon the activity.

The following will present some causes of crowd control problems and some approaches to solutions.

Some causes of problems

• Lack of anticipation of, and preventive planning for, possible trouble
• Lack of proper facilities
• Poor communication resulting in lack of information
• Lack of involvement of one or more of the following: school administration, faculty, student body, parents, community, press, and law enforcement agencies
• Lack of respect for authority and property
• Attendance at games of youth under the influence of narcotics
• Increased attitude of permissiveness
• School dropouts, recent graduates, and outsiders

Some approaches to solutions

Develop written policy statements, guidelines, and regulations for crowd control.
  1. Consult the following before writing policy statements or promulgating regu-

*From Summary of Conference Reports, City and County Directors of Health, Physical Education, and Recreation, December 1968, p. 17, American Association for Health, Physical Education, and Recreation. Used by permission.

lations: school administration, athletic director, coaches, faculty members involved in the school sports program, school youth organizations, local police departments.
  2. Properly and efficiently administer regulations and provide for good communications.
  3. Constantly evaluate regulations and guidelines for their relevance and effectiveness.
  4. Make guidelines and regulations so effective that the director of athletics who follows them is secure in knowing he has planned with his staff for any eventuality and has sufficient help, appropriately briefed, for any situation that may arise.

Provide adequate facilities.
  1. Plan and design stadiums, fieldhouses, and gymnasiums for effective crowd control.
  2. Provide for adequate rest room facilities.
  3. Establish a smoking area when indoor contests are held.
  4. Complete preparation of facilities before game time.

Teach good sportsmanship throughout the school and the community.
  1. Begin education in good sportsmanship in the earliest grades and continue it throughout the school life.
  2. Make frequent approving references to constructive and commendable behavior.
  3. Arrange for program appearances by faculty members and students jointly to discuss the true values of athletic competition including good sportsmanship.
  4. Make use of all news media through frequent and effective television, radio, and press presentations and interviews, commentaries, and frequent announcement of good sportsmanship slogans.
  5. Distribute a printed Code of Ethics for Good Sportsmanship.
  6. Include the good sportsmanship slogan in all printed programs at sports events.
  7. Urge the use of athletic events as an example in elementary school citizenship classes, stressing positive values of good

conduct at games, during the raising of the flag and singing of the national anthem: courtesy toward visitors.

8. Involve teachers in school athletic associations, provide them with passes to all sports events and stress the positive values of their setting an example of good sportsmanship.

Intensify communications prior to scheduled games.

1. Arrange for an exchange of speakers at school assembly programs; the principals, coaches or team captains could visit the opposing school.

2. Discuss with appropriate personnel of the competing school the procedures for the game, including method and location of team entry and departure.

3. Provide superintendent or principal, athletic director, and coach with a copy of written policy statement, guidelines and regulations.

4. Meet all game officials and request them to stress good sportsmanship on the field.

5. Meet with coaches and instruct them not to question officials during a contest; stress the importance of good sportsmanship and the fact that their conduct sets the tone for spectator reaction to game incidents.

6. Instruct students what to expect and what is expected of them.

7. Schedule preventive planning conferences with local police to be assured of their full cooperation and effectiveness in spectator control.

Inform the community.

1. Request coaches and athletic directors to talk to service groups and other community groups.

2. Stress the need for exemplary conduct of coaches at all times.

3. Invite community leaders (non-school people) to attend athletic events.

4. Post on all available notice boards around town, in factories and other public places, posters showing the Sportsmanship Code of Ethics and Guidelines in brief.

5. Release constructive information and positive statements to news media and request publication of brief guidelines on sports pages.

6. Provide new media with pertinent information as to ways in which the community may directly and indirectly render assistance in the crowd control problem.

Involve law enforcement personnel.

1. Police and other security personnel should be strategically located so as to afford the best possible control.

2. Law enforcement professionals should handle *all* enforcement and disciplining of spectators.

3. Strength in force may be shown by appearance of several policemen, motorcycles, police cruise cars, et cetera, at and near the site of the game.

4. Women police may be stationed in women's rest rooms.

5. Civil Defense organizations could patrol parking areas.

6. A faculty member from the visiting school may be used as a liaison with police and local faculty in identifying visiting students.

7. Attendants, police, county sheriffs, deputies should be in uniform. Uniformed authority figures command greater respect.

Use supervisory personnel other than police.

1. Select carefully teacher supervisors who are attentive and alert to signs of possible trouble.

2. Identify faculty members by arm bands or other means.

3. Provide for communication by means of walkie-talkie systems.

4. Assign some faculty members to sit behind the visiting fans; this reduces verbal harassment of visitors.

5. Employ paid ticket takers and paid chaperones to mingle strategically among the crowd and to remain on duty throughout the game, including half-time.

6. Issue passes to junior high physical education teachers to provide more adult supervision.

Plan for ticket sales and concession stands.

1. Arrange for advance sale of student tickets to avoid congestion at the gate.

2. Sell tickets in advance only to students in their own schools, and avoid sale of tickets to outsiders and non-students.

3. Provide for a close check at the gate or entrance.

4. Arrange for concession stands to be open before the game, during half-time and after the game, but closed during actual play.

5. Channel the flow of traffic to and from concession stands by means of ropes, or other means; keep traffic moving.

Prepare spectators and contestants.

1. Encourage as many students as possible to be in the uniforms of the athletic club, pep club, booster clubs, band, majorettes, cheerleaders.
2. Bus participants to and from the site of the game.
3. Have participants dressed to play before leaving for a game or contest.
4. Adhere to established seating capacity of stadiums and gymnasiums.
5. Request home team fans to remain in their own stands until visiting team fans have left.
6. Try to arrange for a statewide athletic association regulation prohibiting all noise makers including musical instruments except for the school band or orchestra under professional supervision.
7. Request the assistance of visiting clubs.
8. Educate cheerleaders, student leaders, band captains, pep squads, and faculty supervisors by means of a one day conference program.
9. Keep spectators buffered from the playing area as much as practical.
10. Request that elementary school children be accompanied by an adult.

Miscellaneous
1. Inform and involve school superintendents fully when problems arise in connection with sports events.
2. Impose severe penalties on faculty and student leaders guilty of poor conduct.
3. Publish the identity of offenders at games and notify parents, if possible; any penalties inflicted should also be noted (Note: If the offense leads to Juvenile Court action, care should be taken not to contravene laws about publishing names of juvenile offenders).
4. Consistently enforce rules and regulations; this is a necessity.
5. Work toward the assumption of responsibility for strong regulation and enforcement of team behavior on the part of the state athletic associations.
6. Attempt to work with the courts toward greater cooperation.
7. Avoid overstressing the winning of games.
8. Discontinue double headers and triple headers.
9. After-game incidents away from the proximity of the stadium or gymnasium are out of the control of school officials, but cause bad public reaction.

Summary

Sound safety controls and crowd controls at school athletic functions are a must! Greater concentration on treating the causes of the problem is essential. Preliminary groundwork is the key to good crowd control. Coordination and cooperation of school and law enforcement agencies is the key to success.

Youth should be taught to know what to expect and what is expected of them. Consistent enforcement of rules and regulations is a necessity if youth is to respect authority. Adult behavior should be such that it may be advantageously and admirably emulated by youth whose actions hopefully may result in deserving praise instead of negative criticism and disapproval.

The athletic program is a constructive and valuable school activity. It should be permitted to function in a favorable, healthful, and friendly environment.

44 ᴈᴗ THE FUTURE OF INTERSCHOLASTIC SPORTS FOR GIRLS*

BONNIE JO BEVANS
CHAIRMAN, GIRLS PHYSICAL EDUCATION DEPARTMENT,
VENTURA (CALIFORNIA) HIGH SCHOOL

The future of interscholastic sports programs for girls will be determined by what women want to have happen. The future is not independent of what individual teachers, states, or schools want to have occur. It is the direct result of their actions.

*This article was prepared at the request of the Periodicals Committee of the Division for Girls and Women's Sports. From JOHPER 39:39, March 1968. Used by permission.

A review of articles about interscholastic sports for girls from 1957, the year AAHPER's Division for Girls and Women's Sports first published a statement on interscholastic sports, through the present time indicates that crucial areas are
1. securing quality leadership at all levels
2. developing well-defined guidelines, principles, controls
3. educating administrators about competition for girls

4. implementing programs for each school and league.

These four action areas, which carry the key to future successes, are outlined and discussed here.

Leadership

The future of any program is directly related to the quality of leadership involved in its development. If women want anything to say about interscholastic competition for girls then they must assume some of the leadership positions to help organize and develop rules governing this form of competition.

The success these programs will find depends upon the extent to which qualified women are heard and are able to implement such principles as the DGWS guidelines for interscholastic competition. Women will have to assume leadership roles at the school, league, section, and state level, along with the men, if they want to have control of their programs. This does not mean that the valuable help of the men should be ignored. On the contrary, we should work together and can do so very effectively and with mutual benefit.

Women must begin now preparing themselves to teach, coach, and officiate the highly skilled girl in addition to preparing themselves to teach beginners. We can first ask the assistance of experts—the men. How better can we learn than from those who are actively coaching the highly skilled athlete? Those women who are now qualified to coach the highly skilled girl must also assist by providing clinics and workshops for women seeking help.

Officiating interscholastic competition is a most important area of leadership development. Highly skilled competition requires highly qualified officials. DGWS has a well-organized training program just for this purpose. More needs to be done by individual teachers at the high school level to develop qualified student officials for effective current use in physical education classes and for future recruitment as officials for interscholastic competition. More teachers need to take the time to become officials, at whatever level of skill they can develop, to help fill the gap and to better prepare their students for officiating. As interscholastic sports programs for girls expand, officials will be better paid for their time and effort, and an adequate supply of officials will become less of a problem.

Principles, guidelines, controls

There is real concern by many teachers when the subject of interscholastic sports for high school girls is discussed. They fear that teachers are being forced into becoming involved in interscholastic sports programs, that DGWS standards are being cast aside, that physical education instructional programs and intramural or extramural programs will suffer irreparably, and that departments will be forced into interscholastic sports competition when their intramural programs are barely able to exist.

None of these things have to occur now or in the future. The DGWS *Statement of Policies for Competition in Girls and Women's Sports* (1963) and the DGWS *Guidelines for Interscholastic Athletic Programs for High School Girls* (1965) provide every concerned teacher with a sound philosophy and a solid set of principles for planning and controlling the competitive experiences of girls.

If the women sit back and do nothing to assure that these DGWS policies and guidelines are being incorporated in controls governing interscholastic sports for high school girls, then there should be serious concern for the future.

Women have long provided instructional and intramural experiences for the less skilled and the average player, but we have ignored our responsibilities for providing instructional and competitive experiences for the highly skilled girl. To aid teachers in correcting this negligence, DGWS has formulated minimal guidelines with the recommendation that more stringent requirements be established at the local level.

Our obligation as teachers is to provide programs for every girl, including the highly skilled girl, *not* just to promote interscholastic sports programs DGWS strongly urges that if minimal conditions for the instructional program do not exist then interscholastic sports programs should not be attempted.

Controls or by-laws should be based on statements of belief or philosophy. The foundation of interscholastic sports programs and their future success will be dependent upon the integrity of the teacher-coaches in carrying out these beliefs and their dedication to the values of all areas of their instructional physical education programs.

Key principles in developing a statement of philosophy for an interscholastic sports program are these: (1) of primary importance is a sound and well-balanced program of physical education, (2) the program should be based on needs and interests of the highly skilled and include only those activities for which qualified leadership, financial support, and adequate facilities are available, (3) the responsibility for the intramural, extramural, and interscholastic sports programs should be delegated to the girls physical education department, (4) it should be financed by school district and/or student body funds, and (5) it is scheduled so that teachers, serving as coaches and officials, need not be released from their regular schedule of instructional responsibilities.

Educating the administration

Communication of information and ideas is the best way to secure acceptance and assistance from the administration. A working relationship must be established with the principal. He should know what is being provided in the physical education program and the values accrued from the intramural activities and extramural experiences which the students are receiving.

A meeting with the principal should be arranged for the sole purpose of discussing the policies and guidelines of interscholastic athletics for girls, how these policies might relate to the school situation, and what might be anticipated as future goals and aspirations for the instructional and extramural programs. A folder should be prepared for his files which contains copies of statements of beliefs, DGWS leaflets informing him of their purposes and standards, officiating information, and a copy of the intramural and extramural program of activities. He should receive copies of journals carrying articles on competition for the highly skilled girl, medical evidence regarding girls sports competition, current concepts about the role of girls and women in our society today, and values of competitive programs for girls. If and when the school is ready to enter into a program of interscholastic sports competition for girls, the principal will be able to assume a more positive role and will be more inclined to give his assistance in setting up and implementing a program.

Implementing an interscholastic sports program

If the state has a set of guidelines governing interscholastic sports for high school girls, implementation will necessarily include (1) agreement within the physical education department that the necessary leadership is available without jeopardizing your present instructional and extramural programs, (2) willingness of other schools in the area to enter into a program of interscholastic sports, (3) formation of a set of league or section by-laws governing the schools which wish to compete, (4) determination of sports each school can provide with leadership and finances, and (5) development of an interscholastic schedule mutually planned with the boys program to assure facilities. These requirements may mean starting with only one sport on an interscholastic basis, adding others as they can effectively be provided.

If programs are entered into without thoughtful consideration of all the problems and benefits, the cause of interscholastic sports could be set back many years. Women could lose all that has been gained in the past ten years. The future success of interscholastic sports programs for high school girls depends upon the ability of women leaders (coaches, officials, advisory committees, ethics committees) to proceed in a well-planned, dedicated manner.

COOPERATION WITH HIGH SCHOOL ATHLETIC ASSOCIATIONS

An encouraging development in many states is the increased cooperation between women physical education teachers and the state athletic association for boys. While in some states the boys athletic association does not administer, and occasionally prohibits, interscholastic competition among girls, in others they are now actively supporting girls athletics events. DGWS state chairmen have been requested to approach the state high school athletic association to discuss the formation of a women's advisory committee in the state association. In California, for example, the California Interscholastic Federation has approved a set of "Bylaws Governing Interscholastic Sports for High School Girls," which went into effect in September 1967. This does not, of course, mean that California has an ongoing, statewide program of interscholastic sports for girls or that all the problems of providing competition for high school girls have been solved. It does, however, provide something solid to build on and is an important first step in the right direction.

45 ∂ PHYSIOLOGICAL AND SOCIOLOGICAL ASPECTS OF GIRLS' ATHLETICS*

PAUL K. REGER
NORTH ROYALTON (OHIO) HIGH SCHOOL

Statement of purpose

The purpose is to analyze the values gained from athletic competition for high school girls.

We must have a basic knowledge of the physiological and sociological aspect of women in athletics.

The problem of the female in athletics should consider that:

1. Competitive sports for women is a new development, less than 50 years old,

2. It pre-supposes a new fundamental concept of the place of women in society.

3. The femininity concept had to be overcome. It stems from the victorian period, with little or no scientific facts to base their beliefs on.

4. The scientific assessment of the physiological fact leaves no doubt that women can participate in athletics virtually the same as men. Of course there are differences, but these differences are not categorical.

5. The physiological and sociological analysis reveals the desirability of the greater scope, athletics for women, as compared to a limited scope, or limited competition.

In dealing with this problem, we can readily see the need for more athletic competition for women.

Introduction

The aspect of athletic competition for girls is one of the problems physical educators are confronted with today. Many societies have expressed their reasons for and against it.

In our present society, the manifestation of competition has ascertained the idea of a modernistic civilization and womanhood has played a very important part in this movement. We live in a dynamic society of competition for social prestige, monetary gains, and for competition for competition sake. This being the case, then what are the physiological and sociological aspects of athletic competition for high school girls?

The physiological aspect

One of the main arguments against athletic competition for girls has been the physiological

dangers involved; the idea of difficulty or the impossibility of childbirth. They were told that sports would produce "a masculine type of woman", "that exercise makes girls muscle-bound" and developmental malformations will occur. (1) It is not proven fact that there is any physiological danger stemming from athletic competition for women.

One of the main arguments against competition has been the childbirth aspect. In a study on labor duration of athletes, it was found that women who had not previously participated in competitive sports had a harder time than participants. The mean totals were, athletes 17 hours 27 minutes as against 21 hours 26 minutes for non-athletes. (2) In the athletes there was no disorder in uterine contractions nor any indication that the elasticity of the cervix was lessened. A similar study was done by another physician who discovered that some olympic champions improved their physical efficiency after childbirth. (3) In dealing with Caesarian section, the ration of non-athletes to athletes, the athletes again had the lowest percentage of Caesarian sections.

The other phase of the physiological argument against athletic competition for girls is, should they participate during their menstrual period? If they do, will it be harmful to them? A girl with regular, well-established periods which occur about 28 to 30 days apart, though the interval may be from 21 to 35 days, and the flow is moderate and lasts from 4 to 7 days or short as 2 to 3 days, may participate. (4) Some activities [sic] that may be harmful during menstruation is heavy jumping. This may stretch the uterus which is heavy with blood during menstruation and may cause future flow to be difficult.

In a study done on olympic athletes, it was found that 29% of the competitors produced their best performances during menstruation. (5) In 63%, menstruation had no effect upon performances, while in 8% a slight drop of efficiency was in evidence.

A study done on 702 girls, 15 to 20 years of age, who worked under the mental strain of compulsion during World War II, as compared to 543 European female track and field, hockey,

---

*From School Activities **39**:19, December 1967. Used by permission.

tennis players, swimmers and gymnasts, showed 19.2% of the compulsive workers reacted with abnormalities of the menstrual cycle; and even after two years of regaining their freedom 3.4% had failed to recover. Not one of the athletes encountered any menstrual abnormalities. (6)

The last phase of the physiological aspect of athletic competition disproves there is any danger in women's childbearing traits or any developmental malformation caused by participation in athletics. We must assume, however, that a girl who competes in sports, does so voluntarily.

In respect to competition, let's examine the woman's progress in comparison with the male in certain events. A track and field team consisting of Mesdames Jackson, Hasenjager, Strickland, Browner, Blanker-Koen, Golubichnaja, Sander, Williams, Chudina, Cawley, Brand, Lerwill, Zybina, Ramaschkova, Bagrjaveeva, Dumbadge, Zatopkova, and Gorschakova would in 1952 have beaten 907 of all boys high school and university teams throughout the world. The women's 400 metre free style swim won by Miss V. Gyange, of Hungary, in 5 minutes, 12.1 seconds was faster than every swimmer of the men's 400 metre free style swim from the beginning of the games in 1896 up to Weissmuller's world record of 5 minutes, 6.6 seconds in 1922. Miss Hveger of Denmark swam the distance in 5 minutes and .1 seconds which could easily have beaten Weissmuller. How would the records compare had women been allowed to compete in athletic competition for a longer period? (7)

The sociological aspect

The female athlete has had to shake off the millenia of prejudice and ignorance which societies have placed on her.

This concept of femininity in womanhood stems from the victorian period in history. During this period, the status of the woman was placed on a high plateau. Society controlled what was the accepted way for her to act. In many places today, we still cling to this idea. The folkways and mores of the community dictate the accepted practices for the whole of the female population of the community.

When we think of the concomitant values derived from athletics, we are prejudiced in our thinking to deny female competition. Sociability is gained through teamwork and fair play.

To emphasize the social values gained from athletics, we can observe the change in garb or athletic wear of women. From regular dress, the female has progressed to the level where society allows her to wear garb that allows her freedom during movement for the sport in which she is participating. In the past it was considered unlady-like to appear in public unless standard clothing was worn, regardless of the activity.

Summary and conclusion

What are we trying to gain from competitive athletics for women? We should be trying to educate women through this medium of competitive athletics. Physical education for girls in high school cannot be successful if it is limited to the required class program. (8) The values derived from competitive athletics probably cannot be gained through other means.

The Physiological and Sociological values gained from athletic competition for women presents the effects of a new dynamic concept, which the athletic movement itself introduces on an increasing scale into mankind. (9) A concept which has come forth with force. In competitive athletics girls gain status which adds to their dignity, freedom, happiness, and personal satisfaction through these means: Excerpt A—1. Ease in childbirth; 2. Social Status; 3. Respectability; 4. Adaptability to life's problems.

BIBLIOGRAPHY

1. Ernest Jokl, Some clinical data on women's athletics, Journal of The Association for Physical and Mental Rehabilitation, I (March 1956), p. 11.
2. Ibid., Jokl.
3. Ibid., Jokl.
4. Margaret Bell, The doctor answers some practical questions on menstruation, American Association for Health, Physical Education and Recreation, 1952, p. 3.
5. Jokl, loc. cit.
6. Ibid., Jokl.
7. Ernest Jokl, Sports and world culture, British Medical Journal, (October 12, 1957), p. 875.
8. Ibid., Dr. Martha G. Carr.
9. Elizabeth K Zimmedli, Girl's interscholastic athletics, Pennsylvania Journal of Health, Physical Education and Recreation, (March, 1956).

Iowans believe in

46 GIRLS INTERSCHOLASTIC ATHLETICS *

E. Wayne Cooley
Executive Secretary, Iowa Girls' High School Athletic Union

A warm May afternoon; 1200 junior and senior high girls from throughout the state of Iowa; splashes of rainbow colors throughout the infield and around the running track; a display of medals and trophies in bronze, silver and gold; officials in white hats and red coats; hurdles standing in place to be mastered by the finest; three thousand spectators, including many anxious parents, boyfriends and track buffs—this is a typical girls' track and field meet in the spring or summer in the State of Iowa.

Reasons for a girls' program

The picture of girls' track and field in Iowa is significant for several reasons—it is a highly competitive activity; performances approach national and international records; entires dened with participants; the quality of performance attracts the real track buffs, and each meet carries newspaper, television, and radio appeal. This has become a reality in Iowa in a short period of six years because Iowa girls love track and field.

The people of Iowa do not differ in their outlook or interest from that of any other state, nor are the physical facilities utilized in track and field different from that of any other state. The great development in Iowa is a product of the outstanding interest developed by the individual interscholastic girls for running, jumping, hurdling and mastering use of field implements.

Prior to 1962, there was no organized track and field activity within the state. National and state athletic administrative leaders had totally ignored a participation interest that had existed within school bodies of the state. A plea was filed with the State Athletic Administrative Office, Iowa Girls' High School Athletic Union, in the winter of 1961, for a spring program of selected track and field events for high school attendance centers. Why should there be a track and field program for high school girls? The simple and justifiable answer is "girls love track and field."

Upon receiving approval from the State High School Athletic Administrative Agency for de-

velopment of a program, the choice of events in which the students might participate had to be established. At the outset it was determined that girls could effectively run a distance no greater than 110 yards; therefore, at the start of the 1962 season there were no running events longer than the 110 yard distance. Within two weeks after the start of the track and field season, it became apparent that that judgment had been in error, and there was an immediate change to a maximum distance of 220 yards. One year later the allowable running distance was moved to 440 yards and in 1965 the 880 Yard Run was incorporated into the high school schedule of events. In 1966, distance running was incorporated with a maximum running distance of one and one quarter miles.

Why distance events were increased

For the person who is seeking information as to why the maximum running distance has been increased from year to year, the answer is, it was requested by the participating students. In presenting their case to athletic authorities, girls indicated they conducted their personal workouts by running back-to-back 440's, thereby suggesting they would enjoy and were capable of a competitive event of 880 yards. Girls track team members of necessity must love track if they condition themselves for an 880 run in the time of 2:20, where the average high school half-miler of Iowa is performing today, or if the 80 Meter Hurdle participant will work the long hours necessary to master the technique needed for achieving a 12 flat hurdle time.

18,000 girls in competition

The first year of high school track and field in Iowa found 1500 girls participating from within the eligibility records of the State Athletic Administrative Office. Six years later, in the spring of 1967, in excess of 18,000 girls were carried within the eligibility records and reflected as participating in track and field throughout the state. In order to serve the interest of so many participants, invitational, conference, county, dual, quadrangular, and triangular meets were held weekly as sanctioned by the Iowa Girls' High School Athletic Union, from March 11

* From School Activities **39**:13, December 1967. Used by permission.

until the first of September of each year. The high point of the entire track and field season becomes associated with the State High School Team Championship held in late May on the famous Drake Relays Track, and the Iowa Track and Field Federation Outdoor Meet the following weekend.

Do girls really love track and field? A Track and Field Coaches Advisory Committee composed of professional teachers from schools within the state analyzed this question and in turn suggested participant practices as an obvious answer to the question. Students ran outside in the Iowa winter months and during the hot sultry months of the summer season in order to maintain strong physical condition. They arose early in the morning to work out before school in order to capture two workout periods per day.

Students attended out-of-state track and field clinics during the summer months, thereby giving up normal summer time pursuits with friends and family. A strong pursuit of temporary work jobs in the late school day hours helped earn money to pay personal expenses involved in track and field meets both in and out-of-state. Students were content to sleep in camp tents on out-of-state meets involving great travel distance in order to save valuable money to be applied to further participation in track and field meets. Students were content with long school days involving an early morning work out, a crowded schedule for class preparation for the following day, participating in a meet in the evening hours, with a late return home, all without complaint. The state high school Champion Quarter Miler in January of 1967 sustained a broken hip in another ath-

letic activity, subsequently giving strong request to consulting doctors for muscle exercises that could be utilized to maintain muscle tone during the period of hip recovery, and at the end of the following March, this same student won the State High School Indoor 440 Yard Dash. It is not uncommon to read feature newspaper accounts of a parent or both parents working out with the daughter in the early morning hours.

Why this strong devotion and commitment to the activity of track and field? Teenage girls by tradition and history are proud to create identity within the school and social community through the medium of outstanding achievement.

The receipt of a medal or trophy for a job well done in a running or field event is a medium of strong satisfaction for the preceding hours of hard work and preparation. Strong friendships are created in the competitive area of track and field, friendships beyond the participant's residential community.

The State of Iowa has proudly watched interscholastic participating girls reflect their interest in track and field. According to their ability level, the Iowa students have successfully met record objectives. Those capable of competing only on the state level have consistently outperformed the participants of a previous year. Those capable of national and international competition have closed in on such records until they are recognized today as future Olympic Game contestants. This has all been created because of the love of the individual for personal participation in a sport where no associated team member can assist, the total responsibility being that of the actual participant.

SHOWING CHANGES IN GIRL'S TRACK AND FIELD RECORDS IN IOWA FROM 1962 TO 1967

Events	1962	1967
80 meter low hurdles	12.2	11.4
60 yard dash	7.4	7.0
100 yard dash	11.6	10.9
220 yard dash	27.5	24.3
440 yard dash	62.8	55.5
880 yard dash	2:32.6	2:12.0
320 meter shuttle relay	43.3	41.6
320 meter shuttle hurdle relay	54.4	52.0
440 yard relay	54.5	48.2
880 medley relay	1:58.5	1:45.9
880 yard relay	1:53.7	1:45.9
4 kilo shot	37' 6-1/2"	40' 8-1/4"
Long jump	15' 8-1/4"	18'5"
Distance run (1 and 1 quarter mile)	7:30.0	7:08.0

47 OPERATING A MASSIVE CITY SPORTS PROGRAM*

ANDY BAKJIAN
COACH, JEFFERSON HIGH SCHOOL,
LOS ANGELES

While the NCAA and AAU are loudly and bitterly airing their differences, one of the largest school systems in the country, the Los Angeles City School District, is quietly and efficiently administering an interscholastic athletic program that embraces over one-fourth of the boys enrolled in its 50 high schools.

The program covers four divisions in basketball, three divisions each in football, track, swimming, and cross-country, two divisions each in baseball and tennis, and a single division in both golf and gymnastics.

How can such a massive program function so smoothly? The answer lies in the Los Angeles City H.S.'s Athletic Policy Determining Committee. Its rules and regulations, compounded in its famous "Brown Book", have been evolved over many years and have helped achieve the original purpose expressed by the 1931 Codification Committee:

"Uniformity of direction and control in our interscholastic activities will encourage and stimulate wholesome, worthwhile competition and develop a spirit of friendly relationship and cooperation between schools and leagues."

The Policy Determining Committee was established in 1921. Created by the city's Senior H.S. Principals Assn., it operates within the framework of the California Interscholastic Federation and is directly responsible to the Principals Assn. and the Superintendent of Schools.

A Supervisor of Athletics serves as a liaison between the P.D.C. and the various leagues, schools, and coaches. The P.D.C. is responsible for all rules and regulations, and serves as a committee of appeals on all matters brought to its attention. It also has authority on all matters of eligibility.

The P.D.C. consists of one principal from each athletic league (8 leagues now, soon to be increased to 10) appointed by the Senior H.S. Principals Assn.; three vice-principals, appointed by the Senior H.S. Vice-Presidents Assn.: one representative from the Los Angeles City H.S. Coaches Assn.; and the president of

the Senior H.S. Physical Education Chairmen's Assn.

Ex-officio members include the Area Supt. in charge of athletics, a representative from the Physical and Health Education, Safety and Youth Services Branch, and a representative from the Athletic Coordinators Assn.

The P.D.C. members serve for three years, with a third of the membership being appointed each year. All appointments must be made by the opening of the fall term. If no appointments are made by then, the incumbents continue in office until the appointments are made. It takes a two-thirds vote of the P.D.C. membership to amend or repeal any part of the constitution.

All communications pertaining to high school athletics are referred to the P.D.C. Each communication is prepared in duplicate; the original copy is forwarded to the chairman of the P.D.C. and the duplicate is sent to the Supervisor of Athletics.

No city high school team or athletic organization may leave the state for a contest, tour, or exhibition unless authorized by the P.D.C. All teams must travel by train or bus; the use of private cars is prohibited. If the contest involves on overnight stay, it must be approved by the P.D.C., the Area Supt. in charge of athletics, and the Board of Education.

Each sport in the city program has a League Manager, usually the vice-principal of one of the schools in the league, assisted by the head coach of the particular sport. The job is rotated every year among the schools in the league.

The chief function of the League Manager is to make up the schedule for all league contests. The schedule must be approved by the secretary of the P.D.C., after which it is submitted to the Supervisor of Athletics. Whenever a change in time, date, or location is deemed necessary, the principal of that school must submit a request in writing to the chairman of the Calendar Committee and the Supervisor of Athletics.

Schedule details for all-city championship contests are determined by the P.D.C. Schools may schedule league contests at night, but must have the approval of the Supervisor of Athletics, who'll make sure that the proposed site is suitable.

---

*From Scholastic Coach **37**:49, April 1968. Used by permission.

Exponent	Age	Height	Weight
13			79–84
14			85–90
15			91–96
16			97–103
17			104–109
18			110–115
19			116–121
20			122–128
21			129–134
22	10:9–11:2	47 down	135–140
23	11:3–11:8	47$^1/_2$–49	141–146
24	11:9–12:2	49$^1/_2$–51$^1/_2$	147–153
25	12:3–12:8	52–53$^1/_2$	154–159
26	12:9–13:2	54–55$^1/_2$	160–165
27	13:3–13:8	56–57$^1/_2$	166–171
28	13:9–14:2	58–59$^1/_2$	172–178
29	14:3–14:8	60–62	179–184
30	14:9 15:2	62$^1/_2$–64	185–190
31	15:3–15:8	64$^1/_2$–66	191 up
32	15:9–16:2	66$^1/_2$–68	
33	16:3–16:8	68$^1/_2$–70$^1/_2$	
34	16:9–17:2	71–72$^1/_2$	
35	17:3–17:8	73–74$^1/_2$	
36	17:9–18:2	75 up	
37	18:3–18:8		
38	18:9–19:2		
39	19:3–19:8		
40	19:9–20:2		
41	20:3–20:8		
42	20:9–21		

Class D—sum of exponents 79 or below.
Class C—sum of exponents 83 or below.
Class B—sum of exponents 88 or below.
Class A—sum of exponents 89 or above.

Example:	Age 15 years, 8 months, 20 days	Exponent	31
	Height 68 inches	Exponent	32
	Weight 136 pounds	Exponent	22
	Sum of exponents	Class B	85

A team cannot play more than two games per week. This applies to either practice or league games, or any combination, but not to All-City Tournament play or play-offs. All high school practices and contests must be held on high school premises, unless special authorization is granted by the Supervisor of Athletics.

Whenever it becomes impractical to adhere to the starting times, the Supervisor of Athletics will confer with the teams involved and make necessary adjustments.

The principal of each school is authorized to excuse members of the athletic teams in accordance with the principles established by the P.D.C., to insure the prompt start of the contest. The student body may also be excused early in order to reach the site of the contest and be seated by the starting time.

Teams cannot have any organized practice, scrimmage or contest on Saturdays, Sundays, holidays, or vacation periods, except as regularly scheduled and approved by the P.D.C. Athletes also are forbidden to report to the physical education plant (gymnasium) before school hours or the start of the last school period, and practice periods must be concluded two hours after the normal closing time of the school concerned.

During the last three weeks of any semester, screening is permitted, but it must not exceed two hours per day for a period of not more than 10 days. The purpose of this is to provide coaches with an opportunity to preview prospective candidates, who may request assignment to the last physical education period of the day during the succeeding semester.

Contestants in all sports must be fully and properly attired, and the responsibility for this rests with the school principal. The principal or his selected representative is also responsible for seeing that the athletes are properly groomed (clean shaven and hair trimmed in conformance with accepted standards). Athletes are permitted to participate in only one contact sport each semester.

Team members are forbidden to participate on outside teams in the same sport during the season of the sport. Anyone violating this rule is declared ineligible for interschool athletics for a period of one year.

The only way he can be reinstated is by action of the P.D.C., which may reduce the period of ineligibility to the remainder of the season or the semester if it can be proven that the boy unknowingly violated the ruling. All games in which the offender played are forfeited.

All athletes are covered by insurance set up by the P.D.C. and the Board of Education. The athletes are required to take a physical examination (includes the teeth) each semester before he can engage in practice, with the exam being administered at his school by a staff physician from the Health Services Branch of the L.A. city schools.

If an athlete is absent from school or practice for five days or more due to illness or injury, he must take another exam before he can continue in athletics. In cases of injury, the coach must fill out the necessary insurance forms and forward them to the proper sections.

Faculty overseer

Only properly certificated employees of the L.A. City School District are allowed to coach. When a team travels to another school, a member of the faculty must accompany the team and remain until the contest is over and all the the team members have left the dressing room. A faculty representative is present at all contests.

The seating on the players' bench is limited to players in uniform, members of the physical education staff, the principal, athletic coordinator, the physician, and not more than four student managers. The coach is responsible for the conduct on and in the vicinity of the bench.

Student spectators are forbidden to have any artificial noise makers such as horns, cowbells, whistles, and megaphones, or to wear or display pom-poms, leis, or rooter's caps. Both the visiting and home drill teams may use such items while marching during half-time intermission, but must discard them upon returning to the bleachers.

A school whose students sponsor or are associated in any way with demonstrations or other activities that violate this rule is subject to immediate disqualification from further interscholastic competition, and only the P.D.C. has the power to reinstate it.

Schools are held responsible for the conduct of their students, alumni, and other community groups who attend their contests. Any school which incurs a suspension by the P.D.C. relinquishes the right to compete in the specific sport at the conclusion of the regular schedule and is placed on probation in all sports for a period of one year, during which further penalties can be imposed by the P.D.C. if they feel that circumstances warrant them.

During the suspension period, the schools involved cannot meet each other in dual competition or substitute other opponents on these dates. Each school receives a loss in the league standings for the suspended game.

The home school is also responsible for the following details of the event; supervision, seating, parking arrangements and traffic control, dressing facilities and towels, preparation of the field, and supplies and equipment.

The vice-principal of each school, or his representative, is responsible for the amateur standing and eligibility of his teams and must certify that each member has been interviewed and has had his records examined. Before the first league game in any sport, the vice-principal must send an alphabetized certificate of eligibility for each boy to the Supervisor of Athletics. The Certificate contains the athlete's address, birthdate, height, weight, and number of semesters in attendance in high school.

When a boy reaches his 19th birthday, he becomes ineligible for interscholastic sports. If this birthday falls after September 2, however, he retains his eligibility. This rule also applies to the spring sports, where the birthday falls after February 1.

To compete in varsity football, basketball, track (events of 440 yards or more), or cross-country, a boy must be at least 15 years of age. There's no minimum age for other sports, events, or classifications. But a student cannot participate in any sport unless he attended school for at least 10 weeks in the preceding semester.

He must also have passing grades for the preceding semester in at least 20 periods of new work leading to the completion of his high school course. Five of these periods must be in physical education, and the marks must cover 10 or more weeks of actual class attendance.

If a student is ineligible scholastically on the first day of the semester, he's ineligible for the entire semester. But if he has had to drop out of school because of a serious illness or injury, he has the right to petition the P.D.C. for eligibility.

147

An athlete who's not currently making passing marks in at least 20 semester periods of new work, including physical education, cannot compete in interscholastic athletics until the next five weeks' scholastic check.

All students are informed that athletics is a privilege and not a right. The athlete must maintain high standards of citizenship within his school and community. Each school is charged with seeing that its athletes are in good standing. Any boy regarded ineligible because of poor citizenship will, upon transferring to another school, remain ineligible for a period of one semester, or for as long as he would have been ineligible at his original school.

To represent a high school in athletics, a boy must be a resident of that district when he registers. If he registers at a school other than the one in whose district he legally resides, he's ineligible to represent that school unless he attends on a permit carrying athletic privileges or a Statement of Residence.

After filing a Statement of Residence, he remains ineligible until he puts in 20 weeks of attendance at his new school. His legal address is where his father or legal guardian resides.

A prospective athlete must also file with his vice-principal an affidavit signed by his parents or guardian to the effect that he is not a member or a pledge of any unauthorized club. False information will incur ineligibility.

To compete in a contest on any given day, the athlete must have attended at least two class hours of school, exclusive of the lunch hour and the athletic period. In case of death in the family, court orders, or extreme emergencies, the principal has right to make exceptions. A boy is entitled to athletic competition during only the first six semesters of school attendance at a three-year high school.

If a school plays an ineligible student, knowingly or unknowingly, in any contest involving team play, such as football, basketball, or baseball, the contest will be forfeited.

All students who plan to participate in athletics are classified for competition by class (A, B, or C).

If a school's athletic budget is low, the P.D.C. will provide the school with the necessary equipment. The school must furnish a request form containing an inventory of all athletic equipment, its financial operation, and an itemized athletic budget.

Each school has the power to determine its letter awards. To earn a letter, a boy must be passing 20 semester hours of school work, including physical education, and be in good standing as a citizen in school.

To provide the maximum number of buses with minimum interference with the school schedules, the L. A. School District has found it necessary to regulate team travel.

When a bus is furnished for away games, only those boys traveling in it will be eligible to compete. Athletes assigned to travel by bus must return by bus.

A school system as large as the L. A. School District requires an harmonious relationship with all its auxiliaries. The Los Angeles City H. S. Coaches Assn. (400 members) work closely with the P.D.C. in solving mutual problems.

Our coaches could be the highest paid in the U.S., and as a result they are very carefully selected. Each coach is aware of his obligations to his school and community, and is constantly seeking to instill in each boy the high standards inculcated in the P.D.C.'s "Brown Book".

Good athletic programs, we feel, make good citizens.

PROJECTS AND THOUGHT QUESTIONS

1. Why are interscholastic athletics an integral part of the physical education program and, therefore, administered by physical education personnel?
2. What are some of the qualifications needed by a director of an interscholastic or intercollegiate athletic program?
3. Do a job analysis of an athletic director's position.
4. What are the pros and cons of including interscholastic athletics at the junior high school educational level?
5. Develop a practical program for crowd control that could be instituted in a large city high school athletic program.
6. Debate the question: "Should girls engage in interscholastic and intercollegiate athletic programs?"
7. What differences should exist between the administration of a high school athletic program and the administration of a city recreational athletic program? Give reasons for your answer.

SELECTED READINGS

American Association for Health, Physical Education, and Recreation: Secondary school athletic administration, Washington, D.C., 1969, The Association.

Bucher, C. A.: Physical education for life. A text for high school boys and girls, St. Louis, 1969, Webster Division, McGraw-Hill Book Co.

Bucher, C. A.: Administration of health and physical education programs, including athletics, ed. 5, St. Louis, 1971, The C. V. Mosby Co.

Bucher, C. A., and Dupee, R. K., Jr.: Athletics in school and colleges, New York, 1965, The Center for Applied Research in Education, Inc., The Library of Education.

Division for Girls and Women's Sports, American Association for Health, Physical Education, and Recreation: Philosophy and standards for girls and women's sports, Washington, D.C., 1969, The Association.

George, J. F., and Lehmann, F. A.: School athletic administration, New York, 1966, Harper & Row Publishers.

Hixson, C. G.: The administration of interscholastic athletics, New York, 1967, J. Lowell Pratt and Company.

Proceedings of the Sixth National Conference of City and County Directors: Approaches to problems of public school administration in health, physical education, and recreation, Washington, D.C., 1968, American Association for Health, Physical Education, and Recreation.

PART THREE THE HEALTH EDUCATION PROGRAM

The health education program is rapidly gaining stature in American educational institutions. The body of scientific knowledge that has been developed concerning that which constitutes proper health habits is affecting our way of life. Radio and television advertising relating to cigarette smoking is being controlled. National and state legislation is being passed, to prevent the sale of harmful drugs and to provide an educational program that orients the nation's children and youth to the hazards of drug abuse. False claims for commercial health products are being scrutinized.

Probably the most significant advance in the health professions today is the recognition of the need for education in respect to health matters. As a result, educational programs are becoming mandatory in some states and are being instituted voluntarily in others. In addition to health science instruction, there has been increased attention given to the health services, not only for the school and college population, but also for older people. Further-

more, there is a great forward movement to ensure a healthful environment for every American, whether within the school plant or on the college campus, or in relation to such problems in our communities as air pollution, water pollution, noise, and insecticides. Never before in our history has there been so much concern for each person's health, whether it be his physical, mental, or social health.

Health educators are spending considerable time in their school and college settings and in their professional associations, planning curricula, developing teaching materials, and becoming professionally involved in other ways, in order to upgrade health programs.

An important part of a book of readings on the administration of school health and physical education programs is the significant contributions from the professional literature that relate to health science instruction, health services, and a healthful enviornment. An attempt has been made to include some of this significant literature in this part of the book.

CHAPTER 9 THE HEALTH SCIENCE INSTRUCTION PROGRAM

The health science instruction phase of school and college programs refers to the provision of learning experiences that will influence knowledge, attitudes, and conduct relating to individual and group health. Today, there is a great amount of scientific health knowledge available that every person should have. The elements of good nutrition, the hazard of drug use, the dangers of tobacco and alcohol, mental health, first aid, environmental health, the anatomy and physiology of the human body, health services, sex education, and the causes of disease are a few health areas for which we have much scientific information. This knowledge, if passed on to the youth of today, can help to shape their attitudes and influence their health practices. A sound health science instruction program will help to ensure that students are intelligent citizens on matters of health, that they understand the values of possessing good health, and that they are wise, healthy consumers.

There are many new developments in the field of health education that augur well for the future of this field of endeavor. There is increased emphasis upon health teaching in our schools and colleges today. Professional preparing institutions are placing greater stress on the preparation of teachers for their responsibilities in this area. There is closer cooperation between the school or college and community health officers. Medical doctors, dentists, and other representatives of professional services are taking greater interest in public health. School and college administrators and their teaching and professional staffs are voicing increasing concern about students and their health. More research in the health area is providing new and better directions to help the schools and colleges in changing the health behavior of many boys and girls.

The articles selected for this chapter discuss the guidelines for health instruction programs in schools and colleges, the need for instruction in such critical areas as drugs and sex, and other significant health information that requires the attention of both health educators and physical educators.

In the first article Harold J. Cornacchia writes that administrators need, want, and should receive help to better understand the nature and organization of programs of health instruction. California held a health education conference of forty-five selected educational leaders to develop guidelines and discuss programs, curriculum, time allotment, teachers, and community involvement. These guidelines were developed by administrators and for administrators, to aid in curriculum development and administrative decisions.

The program in Washington, D.C., as described by Bernice W. Wade, is designed to make health teaching more meaningful, practical, and adaptable for the students. It seeks to change attitudes and improve the health practices of youngsters. The program, as outlined, can be successful only if time for counseling is permitted, if all faculty help in teaching moral and spiritual values, and if teachers are selected according to training, personality, interest, and capabilities.

Patricia Schiller devotes her article to an explanation of a conceptual approach to sex education. Educators, she believes, should present sexuality, sexual identity, self-image, and social roles, and not "sex," as the crucial learning content. Program planning in this area involves parental support, appropriate subject content for all grade levels, and the use of teachers certified in the area of sex education.

Concern for another crucial area of health education, that of drug education, was surveyed by Mickey C. Smith, Robert L. Mikeal, and James N. M. Taylor. The authors conducted a national survey of drug education programs and concluded that major improvements are needed in this area on a national level. Crash programs are not sufficient; drugs need their own emphasis and place in the educational structure, with outside experts, printed matter, and audiovisual aids being used to supplement the program.

The health science instructional program, in its broadest scope, includes safety and driver education. In the next article, Norman Gesteland describes a driver education program that is different in scope and subject content. The program includes night driving exercises with simulated dangers. It also enrolls mentally retarded students. The program is fully supported by the teachers, students, local citizens, and board of education.

Because of the nature of physical education, students are exposed to risks. A national conference on safety, described by C. Albert Long, was held, to formulate suggestions for accident prevention. The causes of accidents were found to be inadequate leadership, faulty equipment, irresponsible student behavior, insufficient skill, poor physical condition, and the inherent risks in the activity. Long urges promotion of safety through the good example set by the instructors.

In the last article in this chapter, Fred V. Hein describes the impact of sports and athletic programs on the health knowledge of students. Competitive sports discourage smoking, and students tend to emulate the behavior of athletes. The Committee on the Medical Aspects of Sports of the American Medical Association believes in teaching health and nutrition through sports, employing both the public mass media and the organized instructional programs of schools and colleges. Linking nutrition with athletics and other energy-demanding activities is a motivating factor in health education.

48 ◆ GUIDELINES FOR SECONDARY SCHOOL HEALTH EDUCATION*

HAROLD J. CORNACCHIA, ED. D.
PROFESSOR OF HEALTH EDUCATION, SAN FRANCISCO STATE COLLEGE,
SAN FRANCISCO

Health educators agree it is necessary to reach the school superintendent to increase or improve health education programs. The superintendent or administrative head of a school district is the key to sound instructional programs.

Over the years, attempts to reach top school officials have met with limited success. Perhaps the lack of results was because health educators talked to themselves or did little to actually involve administrators. Superintendents have not always been interested, supportive, or well-informed regarding the nature and organization of appropriate or adequate health instruction programs. However, in recent years, administrators have become more concerned with health because they have been confronted in their schools with a variety of health problems of youth such as venereal disease, drug abuse, alcohol abuse, smoking, teen-age pregnancies, and teen-age promiscuity. These problems have often resulted in community pressures for health education programs which have not always been identified as such.

In California, for example, the demand for instruction has resulted in a variety of administrative actions and problem areas at the secondary school level. These include—

1. The development of instructional programs on alcohol, tobacco, drugs, and family health and their introduction without careful consideration to grade placement, subject placement, teacher competency, teacher resistance, teaching methods, instructional materials, clearly defined objectives, and others. Health education has often been fragmented into the curriculum.
2. The passage of state laws mandating into the curriculum such areas as drugs. This action has resulted in further health education fragmentation. Recent California legislation, however, permits broader interpretation to include a total program of health education.
3. The extension of health education curriculum fragmentation because of administrative expediency and ease of curriculum inclusion of health problem areas. Numerous districts have concluded that health is best organized into the school program solely through integration or correlation with social studies, science, physical education, and other subjects.
4. Development of "crash" programs. Special assemblies with special speakers presenting information related to school, tobacco, and drug abuse have taken place with the belief such activities constitute adequate educational programs.
5. Variation in the amount of time devoted to health in the curriculum. This has contributed to curriculum fragmentation. Administrators have been faced with the decision of what to squeeze out in order to squeeze in something new.
6. The need for financial support for curriculum development and reorganization, teacher preparation, and instructional materials.
7. The extent or participation of the community in health instruction programs. Should parents be consulted and should public and voluntary health organizations and agencies be involved?
8. The selection and qualifications of teachers to teach the health problem areas. Some districts have hired special itinerant teachers who spend several weeks in a junior or senior high school to present special units.

*From School Health Review 1:22, November 1969. Used by permission.

The administrative decisions to resolve the health problems identified in California schools have generally resulted in poor quality instructional programs. The "crash" programs, the integration and correlation approaches, and other actions have accentuated the fragmentation of the health education curriculum. It is this writer's opinion that the fragmentation concept of health education is extremely difficult, if not impossible, to justify philosophically principally because of the problems of evaluation, coordination, and teacher competency.

The present health problems of students and community curriculum demands, together with the questions and actions of California superintendents, indicate administrators need, want, and should receive help to better understand the nature and organization of health instruction programs. Top school officials apparently are and must become more ready to receive guidance to ensure quality programs. The climate for involvement of school administrators and their acceptance of responsibilities for health education has never been more opportune.

Capitalizing on this favorable atmosphere, a conference of 45 selected educational leaders, including twelve secondary school principals, nine physicians, three school board members, seven health educators, and two professors of education administration, was recently convened by the author for two days at Asilomar, California. School representation came from school districts of varying sizes, geographically distributed. The purpose of the meeting was to develop administrative guidelines for secondary school health education for California schools that would aid in the increase of, and lead to, quality instructional programs.

Unique features

The significantly different features of the meeting were:

1. The conference was officially sponsored by seven groups—
   California Association of School Administrators (superintendents)
   California Association of Secondary School Administrators (principals)
   California School Boards Association
   California Medical Association (School Health Committee)
   California State Department of Education
   California School Health Association
   San Francisco State College
2. The selection of representatives from the sponsoring groups was made by the organizations themselves.

3. Health educators had an opportunity to talk with and to administrators and school board members.
4. The conference was generally conducted and and planned by administrators with health educators serving as consultants to help guide the proceedings.
5. Physicians had an opportunity to discuss health education with educators.
6. The guidelines were the product of all participants.
7. Financial aid was provided by the California Medical Association and the Easter Seals Society for Crippled Children and Adults of California.
8. The meeting was held at a pleasant location away from schools so those in attendance could work in a relaxed, informal, comfortable, and sociable atmosphere free from telephones and other interferences.

In essence this was a conference for administrators, by administrators, and with administrators. It was not the usual type of meeting where health educators found themselves talking to themselves. The guidelines that emerged from the meeting are presented here.

Programs

1. Health education should be identified as a separate subject in the school curriculum.
2. School districts have an obligation to make provisions for health education as an integral part of general education.
3. Health education should be a planned sequential program in grades K-12; crash programs emphasizing special health topics should be avoided.
4. Adequate time and resources for health education should be provided.
5. Districts should be encouraged to explore innovative organizational patterns for instruction, such as flexible scheduling, in order to provide for effective health education.
6. Districts should also offer pre-school and adult health education programs, if not otherwise available.

Curriculum

1. Curriculum development should focus on student achievement of desired behavioral objectives.
2. Relevant health concepts should be included at the most appropriate developmental levels of children and youth.
3. Health education should be responsive to the needs of students and the demands of society and should reflect current scientific knowledge.
4. The curriculum should focus on the positive aspects of health.
5. Students and the community should be involved in curriculum development to ensure

the inclusion of instruction based on health needs, interests, and problems.

6. Districts should be encouraged to explore innovative and creative instructional methods which actively involve students in the achievement of established behavioral objectives, such as small discussion groups, independent study, and team teaching.

Time

1. Health education should receive equal consideration with other subject areas in the curriculum.
2. Adequate time should be provided to achieve the established behavioral goals and program objectives.
3. Specific time allotment should be given to the treatment of health education in depth as well as recognizing it as an inherent portion of several other disciplines.
4. Time allotment will vary depending on individual and community needs.

Teachers

1. Health education in schools should be taught by an adequately prepared teacher with a demonstrated interest and aptitude in health education. Wherever possible, the teacher should have specific preparation in health education, preferably a major or minor.
2. Desirable teacher qualities should include ability to interact meaningfully and honestly with students, to act capably as a resource for students, and to be sensitive to individual differences and needs.
3. Districts should provide continuing programs of in-service teacher preparation in health education that should also reflect current scientific information.

Coordination

1. Responsibility for the development, coordination, and implementation of health education in the school district should be assigned to a specific person.
2. Districts should be encouraged to seek and utilize consultant services from county schools offices and from medical sources.

Community

1. School districts should be responsive to and involve the community in planning, developing, and implementing programs in a variety of ways, including the establishment of and/or the participation in school-community health councils.

2. Districts should never assume permanent acceptance of health education by the community but should constantly assess and revise the program in accordance with changing needs and attitudes.
3. Districts should enlist the help and support of community leaders.
4. Available community resources should be utilized to augment and enrich the instructional program.

Financing and facilities

1. Sufficient financial support should be provided to ensure adequate facilities, personnel, and instructional materials to achieve objectives.
2. School districts should seek resources which may be available from a wide variety of community agencies and organizations.

Evaluation

1. The program should be periodically evaluated in terms of effectiveness based on realistic and measurable criteria.
2. Pupils, teachers, parents, and others should be involved at regular intervals in the evaluation of the program in terms of relevance to pupils.

As a follow-up to the guidelines that were developed, plans are now under way to (1) obtain formal adoption by the various organizations that sponsored the conference and (2) conduct state regional meetings of school administrators and school board members for implementation.

The guidelines prepared do not by themselves provide new content or new approaches to health instruction. However, they were developed by administrators and for administrators. As such, they allow for self-determination and local autonomy in curriculum development and administrative decisions. This flexibility is especially important to small school districts. In addition, the material prepared provides evidence that school administrators are interested and can be involved in the development of quality health education programs if they are provided guidance.

The time for action to increase and improve health education programs has never been more opportune. The conference procedures can be duplicated by anyone who wishes to put forth the effort to do so. Health educators have a unique opportunity to demonstrate leadership and to act now.

49 ❧ HEALTH EDUCATION IN THE DISTRICT OF COLUMBIA*

In spite of what headlines seem to imply, there are thousands of young people in the District of Columbia who are eager to grow up strong and decent. And there are hundreds of inventive and devoted teachers who are determined to help them reach this goal.

BERNICE W. WADE
DIRECTOR, DEPARTMENT OF HEALTH AND PHYSICAL EDUCATION OF THE DISTRICT
OF COLUMBIA PUBLIC SCHOOLS

For many years we have been teaching facts related to health and family living, and our students have been listening to us in the classroom and returning home to follow the same family patterns they have followed for generations. I thought my mother could do no wrong, and the young people of today think and feel the same toward their mothers. They may listen to our teaching, but little or nothing we teach seems to penetrate their pattern of everyday living.

We need to make our health teachings meaningful, practical and adaptable. We need to change attitudes and improve the health practices of our young people. The success of this depends largely on the teachers, the emotional climate of the classroom, and the separation of health education from physical education.

The climate of the classroom needs to be friendly, supporting and safe for each student; it should be a place where the student has a sense of belonging, a feeling of security, affection, and recognition. When this kind of climate is established, students feel free to express their needs, their interests and are willing to exchange experiences. Unless this type of climate exists, few behavior changes will take place—in health or anything else.

Separation of health from physical education

It has become increasingly evident that health education is distinctly separate from physical education. Teachers of health education require specialized training, and in the secondary schools of the District of Columbia, we are establishing a policy of separating health education from physical education.

In the fall of 1966, the Department of Health and Physical Education of the District of Columbia Public Schools instituted a pilot project in which health education and physical education were separated in four junior high schools. In the fall of 1967 Ballou and Roosevelt, two senior high schools, entered the pilot project. Experienced teachers were assigned to the pilot projects in all six schools; eventually, the Department hopes to have all health education taught by specialists.

In the spring of 1966 planning meetings were held with principals and teachers in the junior high schools in the program and the following agreements were reached:

1. Five periods of health education would be taught per week on the eighth-grade level, with one half of the eighth-grade students to receive health instruction the first semester and the other half to receive instruction the second semester.
2. One-half credit would be given for each semester of health education.
3. Boys and girls would be taught together.
4. A health test would be given to students before and after they took the course.
5. A take-home textbook would be available for each student.
6. Wherever possible, the health education class would meet in a room with blackout curtains for use in showing films and filmstrips.
7. Necessary equipment would include a film projector, a filmstrip projector, a tape recorder, charts and other visual aids, Curriculum Resource Bulletins and Curriculum Kits.
8. In-service workshops would be held for teachers of the classes in health education.
9. Organization of a functional Health Council in each pilot school.

At Garnet-Patterson Junior High School, all of the classes were coeducational. At the beginning of the year there was some giggling and self-consciousness among the students, but this soon vanished. At the end of the school year, all of the teachers believed that teaching health education to mixed groups was worthwhile and should be continued.

An outstanding example of team teaching is being carried on by Mrs. Jean George and

*From National Association of Secondary School Principals Bulletin 52:(326):100, March 1968. Used by permission.

Mr. Charles S. Tibbs, both teachers of Health Education at Rabaut Junior High School. On one occasion, for instance, smoking was the topic of discussion. An appropriate film was shown, pictures of Nat King Cole, who died of lung cancer, were displayed. Then followed a serious and sensible discussion of the whole subject of smoking.

In the senior high school pilot project, which began this school year, students will have one year of Health Education at the eleventh-grade level. Three teachers have been assigned to teach Health Education exclusively. The following guidelines were established for this program in the two senior high schools participating:

1. Boys and girls are taught together.
2. Approximate class size is 30.
3. Health education teachers have no other assignment except health instruction.
4. Students receive credit toward graduation for the eleventh-grade physical education.
5. Homework is kept to a minimum.
6. Students are encouraged to take part in intramural program, since this is the only physical education activity offered them during the year.
7. The Supervising Director responsible for the Health education program will spend considerable time with the teachers in planning and preparation.
8. Since many adolescents need opportunities to talk about their problems with an understanding adult, teachers will provide an opportunity for counseling the young people they teach.

Our ultimate objective is to expand this program into all of the secondary schools. We want to hire fully trained and certified health educators to teach all courses.

Our approach is to recommend that among physical education teachers now teaching health, those best qualified by interest, training, and judged competence be given full-time assignments in health instruction and be freed of physical education responsibilities. This shift would be balanced by having other teachers freed to take full physical education responsibilities, so that at this point a large number of additional teachers would not be required. An additional benefit of this arrangement would be that a number of male teachers who teach health but cannot attend meetings, seminars, and workshops because of coaching responsibilities would be freed to devote their full attention to this field.

When we have established this policy of separating health instruction from physical education, we will have greatly improved our instruction in the classroom and have far superior teaching in the gymnasium and on the athletic field.

Method of teaching

There is no one best method of teaching, but a combination of many best methods. There are, however, some points concerning methodology which deserve emphasis.

For one thing, health and family life education must be practical, meaningful, and adaptable. In particular, the urgency of the need for sex education is apparent from the fact that in 1966 there were 4,958 live births to unwed mothers in the District of Columbia. Of these, 2,257 live births were to unwed mothers in the 15-to-19 age group. There were 2,259 cases of gonorrhea in the 10-to-19 age group.

The school must contribute to the rehabilitation of the family. Family breakdown is all too prevalent. The school must make it clear to young people that there is nothing more important than a strong family unit. The significance of family living must be taught young people.

Since 1958, we have been teaching Health and Family Life education from kindergarten through twelfth grades. We are now beginning to realize that we must go beyond the four walls of the classroom, if we expect to raise the standard of behavior of our young people in the Washington area. We must get into the community and work with parents if we hope to attain our goal.

Too much moralizing and preaching tend to kill interest. We should at all times, however, be concerned with developing and improving standards of good conduct. We urge our teachers to take their pupils as they are and build the program around their outstanding needs and interest. The skillful teacher is able to lead a discussion group in which pupils will air their personal problems. In some cases, a question box is used, where pupils drop their unsigned slips suggesting subjects for discussion.

Evidence now available suggests that the procedure most likely to be effective in teaching moral and spiritual values is to weave these concepts into the entire life of the school and to make them a vital part of all subjects of instruction in the school program. This we are trying to do.

As a result of program experience, curriculum materials have undergone several revisions. In previous guides, a section on "Moral Standards" was introduced following the unit on Family Living. However, several years of experience with the program indicates that the learning of moral and spiritual values depends less on logical presentation of a body of material and more on the ability of the teacher to present pupils with experiences that are really meaningful. In our revised resource bulletin, learning about values is not reserved for a single section, but is introduced throughout the bulletin so that it may be a significant and integral part of the entire program.

The junior high school

We introduce the junior high school course with the less sensitive areas of learning: Cleanliness and Grooming, Exercise, Rest and Sleep, and Eating Habits and Food Needs. This provides an opportunity for the teacher to establish rapport with his or her students. Then we are ready to go into more vital and sensitive areas: Understanding Ourselves (Mental Health); Adjusting to Adolescence (Sex Education); Living with Others (Interpersonal Relationships); The Effects of Tobacco, Alcohol, and other Habit-Forming Drugs; and The Prevention and Control of Disease Including Venereal Diseases. We finish the course with units on Community Health, Safe Living, and First Aid.

We believe it is important that young people accept sex as a natural part of life. Each should know about the physiology and anatomy of both sexes and appreciate the need to treat his own body and the bodies of others with care and respect. In learning to satisfy his own needs he must be encouraged to take the long view and to consider life as an ongoing process in which present behavior affects future happiness and successful living. Sex education does not arouse the pupil's curiosity or produce an over concern about sex when it is embedded in a course of health instruction and when it is properly conducted.

The senior high school

In the senior high school, Health and Family Life education is taught in grades 10, 11 and 12 two periods a week for the full year. The major topics in each of these years are:

Tenth grade: Physical Health, which includes the reproductive system and first aid and safety

Eleventh grade: Mental Health, Marriage and Family Life Education

Twelfth grade: Home Nursing, Community Health

Marriage and family living

We regard family life as the most fundamental and satisfying of all our relationships and as an area of living which has the major influence on all other life relationship patterns. We have been training our young people for many years in mathematics, science, English, social studies, music, art, and so on, but we have failed to train them to live, work, and play effectively and comfortably with each other and with a partner in marriage.

Our objective is not only to impart knowledge, but the larger goal of helping young people gain self-respect, purpose, and direction in life. The areas covered in the District course in Marriage and Family Living are:

1. The family: (a) purpose; (b) responsibilities of members; (c) parent-child relationships; (d) brother-sister relationships
2. Making and keeping friends
3. Dating
4. Choosing a mate: (a) physical love; (b) intellectual love; (c) moral love
5. Enemies of marriage
6. Engagement
7. Marital adjustments: (a) financial; (b) in-laws; (c) sex relationships; (d) social activities and recreation; (e) associating with friends; (f) religious life; (g) training and disciplining of children
8. Divorce and separation
9. Parenthood

Young people need to understand how the family affects total development, that the satisfaction of basic needs in family living provides a springboard for adjustment and effective action in other areas. At the same time, there should be an awareness that although one may not be a member of a strong family unit, he has the opportunity to develop into a fully functioning adult and have satisfying family relationships of his own in the family he will create himself.

Venereal diseases

Controlling venereal diseases involves the major educational task of changing sexual behavior. In both the eighth grade and again in the tenth and twelfth grades we teach about this very vital area. In the eighth and tenth grades we teach about venereal diseases from a personal viewpoint and in the twelfth we add the community health angle. The basis of both approaches is the intimate personal sex behavior most often demonstrated in premarital and extramarital sexual relations.

We stress venereal diseases as diseases of irresponsibility, which depends largely upon the company one keeps and on the development of sound moral attitudes which we hope will result in desirable sex conduct.

Evaluation

The following are some of the answers we received when we asked twelfth grade students, "What Have You Gained from the Course in Health and Family Life Education?"

- "I can understand and appreciate my parents better now that I have had this course."
- "I have stopped resenting the fact that my parents were divorced."
- "Family Living taught me more responsibility in what is expected of me and what is each person's part at home."
- "I learned a basis for choosing a right husband so that our marriage will last and how to bring up our children."
- "Thanks to my Marriage and Family Living course, I did not make a terrible mistake."
- "I have more respect for some things, to be nice to your wife and to be more careful about girls and getting a girl's disease."
- "Marriage and Family Living prepared me more for life to come. It showed me what stones to leap over, step on, go around, pick up and put aside or get rid of."

As time goes on we need better evaluation of our program, and more research studies will be made. Meanwhile, we do know that

1. Most of the principals state that the program is good and is needed. Teachers report a greater respect for authority and a greater effort by students to exhibit self-control. Both teachers and principals report an improvement in attitudes.
2. Parents report to the teachers that their children seem more willing to assume responsibilities within the family circle.
3. Specialists and consultants have visited and evaluated the program and found it to be sound and worthy of note.
4. Interest in the course continues high. Students ask for the course to be continued. They bring

their personal problems to the teachers more freely and in greater numbers as a result of the program.

Although we do have as yet rather meagre objective evidence to prove this program is successful, we are convinced that this course in Health and Family Life Education is a vital part of the education of every pupil in our schools.

Looking to the future

1. *We need a time for counseling.* Adolescents need some strong ties when they are trying to stand on their own feet and form their own beliefs. They need friends and acceptance.

They need strong, stable warm adults for whom they have respect, in whom they have confidence and upon whom they can rely, but who will not dominate them. They need opportunities to talk about their problems with a sympathetic, understanding adult, who listens well and who will take them seriously. We need a definite time and place for counseling students who have intimate personal problems.

2. *We need the help of every member of the faculty in teaching moral and spiritual values.* There are many opportunities in subject areas other than Health and Family Living for stressing wholesome family relationships and responsibilities and acceptable standards of behaviors. Good character education must permeate the entire school program.

3. *We need to have more care taken in the selection of teachers as to their training, personality, interest, and capabilities.* Now we are beginning to realize that we must go beyond the four walls of the classroom in Health and Family Life Education and involve the parents and the community if we are to raise the standards of behavior of the young people in the Washington area.

---

50 ◆ SEX EDUCATION THAT MAKES SENSE*

PATRICIA SCHILLER
CLINICAL PHYCHOLOGIST, DISTRICT OF COLUMBIA PUBLIC SCHOOLS;
EXECUTIVE DIRECTOR, THE AMERICAN ASSOCIATION OF SEX EDUCATORS
AND COUNSELORS

People are becoming increasingly aware of the need for sex education for their children. Episodes running the gamut from premarital pregnancy to adolescent homosexual play strike terror in the hearts of parents and accelerate the pressure on the schools to hurry up and get a sex education program going.

What often results from this crisis climate is one or two lectures about menstruation and reproduction. Usually the school nurse or a doctor is brought in to help the teacher in this "sensitive" area of education. The teacher or the expert proceeds to give the children all the correct terms, using slides and anatomical charts. Sometimes a movie depicting the development from girl to woman and boy to man is

*From NEA Journal 57:17, February 1968. Used by permission.

shown. The students are permitted to ask questions, but the answers they get are often limited to the anatomical and functional aspects of growth, development, and reproduction.

What is wrong with this kind of sex education? Aren't the youngsters being taught the "facts of life" in an objective, unemotional way, with the correct use of terms, and aren't they receiving vital information about their bodies?

Let me answer on the basis of 14 years of professional experience in dealing with sexual and family living problems of children, adolescents, and married couples.

The short answer is that the information they are learning is necessary to the development of healthy sex attitudes, but this is only one aspect of such development.

It is sexuality, not sex, that is crucial. Human sexuality is what is personally important to the growing child, the adolescent, and the adult. Sexual identity is an important part of the self-image and affects every aspect of life. For example, sexuality involves the name we are given at birth, the toys we play with as a child, the clothes we wear, the friends we have, the things we like to do, the courses we take in high school and college, the careers we choose, the way we see our roles and responsibilities in our homes, and last but not least, the ways we satisfy and cope with our sexual needs and urges as responsible and committed human beings.

Asking other questions may reinforce the point: Is it enough to teach a sixth grade boy how one becomes a father without teaching him what it means to be a respected man? Don't we also need to teach him attitudes and behavior that will help him, on reaching manhood, to be a sympathetic, kind, and understanding husband and father? As upset and panicky as we get at the thought of youngsters' having premarital relations, how much more critical and upsetting is the crisis that will be caused later on if they marry and have children only to end up with divorce and family disintegration.

During adolescence, when youngsters need to discuss their conflicts and concerns with adults other than their parents, it is particularly important for them to have teachers who understand their emotional and social problems. During the transitional ages, particularly in early adolescence, children may have trouble accepting their sexual identity. Some girls feel no pride in their sex and actually fear being women. Many boys, especially when they are smaller than their contemporaries, fear that they may not be able to be real men because they associate masculinity with physical size and development.

Some questions that youngsters frequently ask reflect the real worries of youth and indicate that it is mainly their attitudes about sex that constitute a problem for them, for their parents, and for teachers.

How can we help them with their bewilderment as to whether the sex urges they feel mean they are in love? How can the young boys or girls sort out the various emotions that accompany sexual desires to hug, to kiss, to pet? Are their tumultuous feelings the real thing or just puppy love? Is there a way to work out sex needs, other than in sex play? What are young adolescents to do about the fantasies, fears, and dreams that they experience along with their sex urges?

Human sexuality includes the social roles that men and women play. Many young children have difficulty understanding and learning these roles. Those most enmeshed in the dragnet of uncertainty are usually children brought up in a one-parent home, especially where they have little contact with adults of the sex of the missing parent or where parents are passive, resentful of the children, or unable to accept the responsibilities of parenthood.

In recent years, many leading sociologists have stressed the need for young boys to develop a strong male image early in life in order that they can later take on their role as head of the house. Psychologists and sociologists have emphasized the importance of providing male substitutes for absent or rejecting fathers. Whenever possible, male teachers, coaches, relatives, older brothers, recreation leaders, and scoutmasters should be encouraged to act as models and substitute fathers.

Since over 75 percent of our population marries at one time or another, the teacher should give young people an opportunity to discuss dating, going steady, engagement, marriage, and family life. A trained sex educator can help students explore the pros and cons of going steady and the sexual behavior appropriate in dating.

In a ghetto school, during an eleventh grade class in personal and family living recently, the students, a boy and a girl, spontaneously role played a problem that the class was discussing —should a girl ask the boy into her house after her first date with him? The scene was set at the door of the girl's house and the young man, age 17, asked whether he could come in. The girl, also 17, said she was tired and would like to say goodnight. She added that she had enjoyed being with him.

The young man looked forlorn and disappointed. In an awkward but angry manner he mentioned that the least she could do was to invite him in because he had taken her to the movies and for a hamburger and coke later and that this cost him $5. He felt he wasn't getting his money's worth from her.

The girl wisely answered that she thought the good time they had and the progress they had made in becoming friends were more important than paying back by kissing and necking.

The class talked over the issues involved in the scene enacted and concluded that a "real man" respects his girl friend's wishes.

The class discussed the fact that the sex urges of boys and girls are quite different in nature and degree—for example, that girls should be aware that their behavior can sometimes be painfully provocative to boys. Boys are readily stimulated by a girl's figure, her flirtatious remarks, and the way she wears her clothes, while girls are stimulated more by romantic feelings of love, an atmosphere of tenderness, and music and soft lights.

With what has been discussed thus far by way of background, let us turn now to practical considerations.

How, what, and by whom should sex be taught in the schools? No ideal model will fit all schools, neighborhoods, or cities. However, a few general guidelines may be helpful, especially those that have proved useful in a variety of school situations.

As a first step, the school should enlist parental support and involvement throughout the planning and operation of the program. [See "Planning for Sex Education: A Community-Wide Responsibility" by Mary S. Calderone, M.D., in the January 1967 NEA Journal.] With parental consent and involvement, the school can proceed with confidence in developing a sex-education program.

Educators should be sensitive to parents' concerns. Many parents are fearful that new values, standards, and behavior patterns contrary to their own will be taught their children. In the process of cooperating in planning a program, educator and parent can learn to trust and understand each other—all to the benefit of the children under their care.

Regardless of the length of the program for students, parents need to be involved in separate group discussions, study groups, lectures, or seminars on human sexuality while their youngsters are receiving sex education. (Involving ghetto parents is hard but worth trying. For one hour a week during a whole semester, I worked with a nucleus of four mothers of elementary school children. The next year there were 25 parents, including some fathers. The word had been spread.)

This kind of parallel education enhances communication between the parent and child at home and within peer groups as well. Many a sex education program has suffered because when the children came home with new insights and understanding, they were met by parents who still clung to many outmoded or uniformed concepts and attitudes.

A second step involves developing a sex education program appropriate for each age level and making it an integral part of the curriculum from preschool to college level. Children in special education classes and schools should be involved as well as those attending regular classes. (A principal pointed up this need recently when he reported the pregnancy of a 14-year-old special-education student who is confined to a wheel chair. She had never received sex education at home or at school.)

Sex education should encompass human sexuality rather than merely the reproductive aspects of sex. It should deal with the psychological, sociological, economic, and social factors that affect personality and behavior as well as with human reproduction.

Team teaching appears to be the most effective approach to sex education. In urban centers, opportunities abound for enlisting the help of experts in the community. Even in small towns or in suburbia, the schools can invite a doctor, social worker, or psychologist from outside the school system to supplement the efforts of teachers, counselors, and other school personnel. If the budget will allow it, schools might well bring in paid consultants occasionally to discuss with parents and teachers new trends in and classroom approaches to sex education.

The team approach is used in the Webster Girls' Junior-Senior High School in the District of Columbia, where I was the clinical psychologist and group therapist. This D.C. public day school for pregnant teen-age girls was originally funded by the U.S. Children's Bureau as a pilot project. The school provides continuous education for the girls during pregnancy and returns about 90 percent of them to regular schools two months after childbirth. A multidisciplinary approach is used—teachers, a psychologist, an obstetrician, a public health nurse, a social worker, and a nutritionist participate in the sex education and family life program.

A comparison of girls who attended Webster with those who were unable to attend because of lack of space indicates that those who attended had fewer second pregnancies, did better in their academic studies, found better jobs on graduation, and appeared to have more stable marriages when they did marry.

The project has demonstrated the need for sex education as an integral part of school curriculum beginning in the early grades. (Many of the girls at the Webster School reported feeling that if they had studied human sexuality with understanding teachers during elementary school, they would not have become pregnant. They felt their parents needed help too.) It has also shown that teachers at all levels, but particularly at the elementary school level, need special training in the presentation of sex education in order to make it succeed.

Since a comprehensive school program in sex education should be multidimensional, it needs to involve teachers in all subject areas as well as such staff members as the counselor and school nurse.

Sex and sexuality ought to be dealt with in many courses in the curriculum rather than be confined to one course labeled Sex Education, Personal and Family Living, or the like. It can be introduced in courses in biology, sociology, health, history, literature, economics, and psychology.

The preschool curriculum can deal with plant and animal growth and care of the young.

In addition to providing appropriate information about puberty and reproduction, the elementary school curriculum can deal with family roles and relationships; understanding one's emotions (especially feelings of love, anger, aggression); and how anxiety and guilt affect relationships between family members and friends.

The junior high school curriculum can deal with customs, values, and standards in dating and in boy-girl group relationships; with emphasis on the meaning of masculinity and femininity; and on the economic, social, legal, and psychological factors involved in carrying on the responsibilities of adulthood.

In high school, sex education should include consideration of marriage, family planning, infant care, vocational choices and opportunities, divorce, unwed motherhood and fatherhood, masturbation, homosexuality, and conflicts confronting young men and women in their social and personal relationships.

The course work should be taught by certificated teachers who are comfortable with the material and interested in teaching. Classes need to be tailored to the students' needs, and students should be encouraged to express their feelings and differences. Panel discussions, role playing, group discussions, films, exploration of case studies, and listening to recordings of individual problems help create a comfortable atmosphere where students enjoy participating and learning.

In my opinion, the important thing in sex education is to deal with human sexuality openly and fully in a classroom climate that makes the student feel safe and free to express his feelings of wonder, pride, and concern about his sexuality.

51 ᴥ DRUGS IN THE HEALTH CURRICULUM: A NEEDED AREA*

Mickey C. Smith, Ph.D., Robert L. Mikeal, Ph.D., and James N. M. Taylor
Respectively, Professor and Chairman, Department of Pharmacy Administration, Assistant Professor of Pharmacy Administration, and Graduate Student in Pharmacy Administration, School of Pharmacy, University of Mississippi, University, Mississippi

ᴥ *Those drugs thou hast, and their adoption tried,*
Grapple them to thy soul with hoops of steel,
But do not dull thy palm with entertainment
Of each new-hatched, unfledged remedy

Polonius to Laertes
Hamlet

*Presented to annual meeting of the American School Health Association, Detroit, November 10, 1968. From The Journal of School Health 39:331, May 1969. Used by permission.

It would be hard to improve upon the counsel of that early "health educator," Polonius. He has given us such an excellent balance of positive and negative in drug evaluation. Indeed, if it were possible to impart his two basic principles, the problem of teaching the young about drugs would be much nearer solution. Unfortunately, the young (and some who are not) seem very often to take just the opposite attitude.

Mary Poppins has told us that "a spoonful of sugar makes the medicine go down." A large number of adolescents and adults, apparently applying a modern interpretation, have found a sugar *cube* a most effective means of exploring the world of that new "medicine," L.S.D. How can we fathom this paradoxical distaste for medicines with all of their potential benefits and eagerness for illicit drugs with all of their potential for harm?

We believe that some of the explanation lies in the knowledge and perceptions of young people toward drugs. We further believe that answers to some of our current problems relating to drugs may lie in changing the methods of instruction about drugs and their nature in our nation's schools.

What is a "drug?" In their widely-used pharmacology textbook, Goodman and Gilman define a drug as "any chemical agent that affects living protoplasm." (1) This definition is so broad, however, that it has little value. Barber takes a different view: "The social and psychological definitions of materials of all kinds are highly relevant to their being named 'drugs.' We might even say that nothing is a 'drug,' but naming makes it so." (2)

What is the nature then of the drug problem? Is it drug abuse, and limited to misuse of illicit drugs such as "speed," "pot," and "acid?" Does it not also include drug *misuse* including self-administration of legitimate drugs for their supposed abortifacient effects, trading prescription drugs not prescribed for the recipient, unnecessary use of products as a result of over-zealous promotion?

Certainly any misuse of drugs is bad, and the potential for drug misuse is much greater than may be commonly recognized.

Drug use by school-age children

While a lot has been written about the abuse of narcotic and stimulant drugs by the young, not a great deal of attention has been devoted to sanctioned use of drugs by the same group.

The National Center for Health Statistics found, in 1967, that children under age six suffered from the following number of acute conditions per 100 students:

Upper respiratory conditions	163.0
Infective and parasitic diseases	62.4
Influenza	47.2
Digestive system conditions	15.8

For young people aged 6 to 16, the incidence figures were:

Upper respiratory conditions	97.4
Infective and parasitic diseases	37.3
Influenza	34.6
Digestive system conditions	9.5

In many cases of illness, the youth will receive prescribed drugs from his physician. The leading prescribed pediatric drugs in 1965, according to the National Disease and Therapeutic Index, were biologicals (20% of pediatric prescriptions), antibiotics and sulfonamides (18%), penicillin (16%), cough-cold preparations (9%), and non-narcotic analgesics (5%). Although similar data were not available for the older children, we have some information concerning their drug use.

During the summer of 1967, we conducted a three-month observation of pharmacy purchases in four community pharmacies. More than 4,800 customers were observed. Almost fifteen percent of those entering the pharmacy were high-school age or younger. As might have been expected, many of their purchases were ice cream and candy. Nevertheless, approximately ten percent of the prescriptions were for this group. They also purchased some products for self-medication. Table 1 provides a summary of the types of drugs used for these legitimate purposes. These prescriptions and proprietary products were not necessarily used by the young, but school-age young people made the purchases and, therefore, did have contact with them.

We know, then, that our youth are exposed to and take legitimate drugs for legitimate purposes and illicit drugs for illegitimate reasons. In addition, there is a sort of "gray" area of drug use which may include use of available products when such use is based upon misconception or misinformation.

Many teenagers, for example, will mistakenly state with considerable authority that a good dose of quinine will promote abortion. Probably as many "know" that aspirin and Coca-Cola, when taken together, will provide a "buzz." Pharmacists have reported a variety of other regional and national instances of teen-age misuse of both reputable products for self-medication as well as some of the more questionable patent medicines. (3) Statistics also show that persons under fifteen years of age tend to purchase their proprietary drug products more frequently outside regular drug outlets and therefore away from professional supervision. (4)

At any time one can predict that a number of the students in any moderately-sized elementary or high school class is taking or has recently taken a prescription or non-prescription drug for a perfectly legitimate purpose. The chances are good that the class will contain diabetics, epileptics, or other chronic disease sufferers who make daily use of proper drug therapy. Statistics from the National Center for Health Statistics indicate that more than one in five of the population under seventeen years of age suffers from one or more chronic conditions.

All of the above use of drugs is the submerged part of the iceberg. The visible use tends to be, because it is dramatic, much more frequently discussed and includes the abuse of narcotics and stimulants. Intelligent use, perception of, and attitudes toward drugs require more knowledge than that the average school child is apparently getting at present.

Table 1. Prescribed and non-prescribed drugs purchased by and for children under 15 years of age

Prescription drug type	*Number of purchases*
Antiinfectives and antibiotics	10
Tranquilizers and sedatives	4
Hypotensives	4
Vitamins and minerals	4
Appetite depressants	4
Antihistamines	3
Hormones	3
Analgesics	
Narcotic	3
Non-narcotic	3
Diuretics	2
Anticonvulsants	2
Miscellaneous	7

Non-prescription drug type	
Topical antiseptics and	5
analgesics	3
Laxatives	2
Wart remedies	2
Asafoetida	1
Antacid	1
Oral analgesic	1
Douche powder	1
Insulin	1
Miscellaneous	3

II. *Teaching about drugs*

As a start toward determining the instructional needs about drugs, we conducted a survey of state departments of education in an effort to determine something about their approach to health education. We found that all states allow for the teaching of courses in health, however only thirty-eight require such courses. It was also found that there is considerable variation in the grade levels at which health courses are taught, ranging from kindergarten to high school with a variety of combinations between.

A number of states combine the health course with other courses, with home economics (11), physical education (19), and science (19) the most frequent combinations.

We were interested in the authorities' evaluations of drug problems in their schools and particularly the relative severity of these problems. It became apparent from this survey that problems associated with the use of drugs rank high. Only mental health and general hygiene received more first-place mentions in the survey, and drug abuse actually ranked first in total mentions.

Since special problems usually evoke special attention, we also asked for information concerning the use of guest lecturers to supplement the regular instruction in health courses. We found that most states use some outside lecturers, with physicians, nurses, and public health workers the most frequent guest speakers.

As a start toward evaluating instruction on drugs, we have made preliminary examination of available state health curriculum guides as well as the most frequently used health textbooks. The results of these preliminary examinations are summarized in Tables 2 and 3. It can be seen that considerable attention is devoted to the negative aspects of the drug use and the drugs which are most frequently abused, but that the more positive aspects of drug therapy received less emphasis.

Not every state presently has established guidelines for health education. In addition, a number of states are currently in the process of revising their guides. Table 2 contains a brief summary of the recommended curricular treatment on drugs in those states from which current guides were available.

Of the guides studied, that of the state of Washington seems to present the most balanced and comprehensive approach to drug education; and we urge interested health educators to examine this guide.

Table 2. Suggested treatment of drugs in state health education curriculum guides (eleven states included)

State	Grade level	Outline of content
A	7–12	Suggests collecting popular magazine articles on drugs and discussing reasons for A.M.A. acceptance or rejection (sic). Suggests pointing out the dangers to consumer health of over-gullibility to patent medicine advertising, and that the danger of patent medicines is delay in proper diagnosis and treatment. One of twelve content areas deals with stimulants and depressants.
B	1–12	Primary level—dangers in the incorrect use of medicines Junior high level—effects of alcohol, drugs, and tobacco on body and social functions Senior high level—analyzing effects of narcotics, drugs, tobacco and alcohol, and the use of patent medicines
C, D, E	7–12	Grades 7–9—suggests discussion of hazards of self-diagnosis and self-medication, review of medicine chest contents, evaluation of drug advertising Grades 10–12—suggests more comprehensive practice of the above and guest lectures on drugs by physicians and pharmacists
F	7–12	Discusses the importance of following prescription directions under the topic "Home Nursing." Mentions narcotics and stimulants with alcohol.
G	K–12	Defines the responsibility of informing students of dangers of drug abuse
H	K–12	Mentions narcotic drugs only in conjunction with alcohol and tobacco
I, J, K	1–12	Nothing on drugs

One of the characteristics of these guides which seems to stand out is the continuing negative role applied to drugs. Although most devote some time and emphasis to some

Table 3. Content analysis of health textbooks

Aspects of drugs	Per cent mentioned
Negative	45%
Neutral	32
Positive	23
Total	100%

Drugs mentioned	Per cent mentioned	
Abused drugs		57%
Narcotics	33%	
Depressants	14	
Stimulants	8	
Hallucinogenics	2	
Other drugs		43
Unspecified	12	
Biologicals	10	
Vitamins	8	
Antiseptics	4	
Antibiotics	3	
Minerals	3	
Antituberculars		
Hormones	1	
Total		100%

category with a general title such as "prevention of control of disease," it is seldom, if ever, that drugs appear in this discussion, although the term describes well their major positive role. Discussion of drugs occurs much more commonly either with "smoking and alcohol" or in discussions of consumer health aimed at alerting the student to the dangers of over enthusiastic advertising claims.

In an extremely detailed analysis of high-school textbooks completed in 1960, Greenslade (5) recommended *inter alia:*

1. "Additional information on modern medical developments for health can be included to keep up with the rapid number of achievements in the field of science and medicine. . . ."
2. "A . . . study (similar to hers) limited to the one of alcohol, tobacco, and narcotics for all health textbooks published for grades 9 through 12."

We would echo Cronbach's statement that "at the center of the present day educational scene in America is the textbook." (6) Accordingly, we are presently engaged in a formal content analysis of elementary and secondary health textbooks as they relate to drugs and drug therapy.

165

III. Discussion

We do not believe that crash programs for combating drug abuse, as necessary as they may be at present, are an acceptable substitute for a well-balanced instructional program on both the positive and the negative characteristics of drug use. The S. H. E. S. conceptual approach is a good one, but it will require some time for broad implementation. In the meantime, we suggest that statewide use of outside speakers on the subject of rational drug use be employed.

We suggest the need for research into students' perceptions and knowledge of drugs and their use. What differentiates a "drug" from a "medicine," for example. More information is needed also on the informal communications which affect these perceptions. Legitimate, commercial, traditional, and illicit channels of communication should be studied. Unlike smoking and alcohol use, the proper use of drugs has a beneficial effect on the individual. This can be a decided advantage in instruction concerning drugs and the positive values serve as a point of departure in any effort to curb illicit use.

We feel that limiting discussion of drugs to a section shared with alcohol and smoking is wrong for two reasons:

1. It fails to point up the very positive benefits of drugs properly used;
2. It sets up in the student's mind a relationship between use of drugs and such "pleasurable" practices as smoking and drinking.

Drug discussions in the context of "consumer health" may also run into snags. We have observed efforts to discourage self-medication entirely. While it is certainly true that the young patients should have guidance of parents, and that the parents should be discriminating in their use of drugs and information about drugs, efforts to curb self-medication entirely are likely to be dismissed as unrealistic.

In summary we would recommend the following:

1. Greater depth in presentation of instruction about drugs in the health curriculum —particularly the more positive aspects of their use;
2. Attempts to make these presentations more meaningful by relating the material presented to conditions and drugs by which the students are most frequently actually affected;
3. Disassociation of drugs from tobacco and alcohol in instruction;
4. Formal planning to utilize drug experts as guest lecturers;
5. Research to determine the relationships between drugs as agents for healing and as tools for abuse in the perception of the young to guide future instruction.

It is not too surprising that education about drugs should take on a negative character. It is much easier to issue a blanket warning against misuse, than to provide a thorough grounding in the proper use of drugs. Nevertheless, the use of outside experts as well as the increasing amount of printed matter and audiovisual aids on the subject of drug use should make it possible to provide a more positive approach to drug education. We would support the statement of Dr. Morris Fishbein that "people should be educated for their own good about health . . . , and that the vast majority of people, given such education, use their knowledge wisely."

REFERENCES

1. Goodman, Louis S. and Alfred Gilman, The pharmacological basis of therapeutics, Third Edition, New York: The Macmillan Company, p. 1, 1965.
2. Barber, Bernard A., Drugs and society, New York: Russell Sage Foundation, 1967, p. 166.
3. eg. Day, Robert L., O–T–C medication for menstrual problems, Journal of the American Pharmaceutical Association, N58, No. 9, p. 479 (September, 1968).
4. National Center for Health Statistics, Series 10, November 33, (1965–1964).
5. Greenslade, Margaret Milne, The type and amount of health information in selected health textbooks for grades nine through twelve, Doctoral Dissertation in Health and Safety, Indiana University, 1960.
6. Cronbach, L. J. (Ed.) Text materials in modern education, Urbana: University of Illinois Press, 1955, p. 1

52 ♥ DRIVER EDUCATION THAT'S DIFFERENT*

NORMAN GESTELAND
CHAIRMAN, DRIVER EDUCATION DEPARTMENT,
JANESVILLE (WISCONSIN) HIGH SCHOOLS

This school term the Janesville, Wisconsin, public schools are offering an expanded driver education program. Students will have both classroom (theory) and on-the-road, behind-the-wheel (laboratory) instruction during the regular school year.

For some time in the past, classroom driver education has been required for all tenth grade students, but on-the-road, behind-the-wheel instruction has been offered as an elective in the summer, and only about 70 percent of the eligible students were able to take advantage of this instruction.

However, when Congress passed the Highway Safety Act of 1966 and the Wisconsin legislature enacted a law requiring driver education for people under 18 who wish to apply for a driver's license, the staff and administration of Janesville's two high schools felt the need of an expanded program. They recommended instituting a driver education course during the school year that would be able to handle nearly 100 percent of the eligible students for both classroom and behind-the-wheel instruction.

Some townspeople thought tax money should not be used to provide any driver education in the high school. As with so many other communities, our city was facing a rather stiff tax increase. The local school board, at a regular meeting, held a public hearing on whether to continue driver education or discontinue it at the end of the school term.

Although the meeting was held in a rather small room, several hundred people were on hand to defend driver education. Influenced by many parents, students, teachers, and other interested persons who spoke in behalf of our program, the school board voted unanimously not only to retain driver education but to expand the program as recommended by the administration. The City Council—the final authority in determining the total school budget—was also persuaded to approve the budget without reduction of the driver education portion proposed by the school board.

Much of what is taught in Janesville's driver education course is typical of similar courses in high schools throughout the country. Attitudes, laws, and theory are covered in the classroom phase of driver education. Community resource people are a valuable part of this phase. In a panel discussion, a local policeman, a deputy sheriff, and a state highway officer explain the operation and jurisdiction of their departments. They also stress highway safety procedures.

In addition to use of filmed sequences in simulators (devices that resemble the driving compartments of cars), the on-the-road, behind-the-wheel phase of the course includes several important exercises that are, we believe, somewhat out of the ordinary.

One entire lesson is devoted to entering, traveling on, and leaving a freeway. Another exercise is the wheel drop. Students are instructed to drive off the edge of the road onto the shoulder and then to drive back onto the road several times at various speeds to get the feel of how the car reacts. The teacher talks the pupil through the first trial and then helps with advice if necessary on the others. In addition to the wheel drop, students practice panic stops until they learn to stop in the shortest possible distance.

How to handle a car in the event of a high-speed blowout is another important lesson. A special device inside the training car enables the instructor to suddenly let the air out of a tire through special holes—producing a "blowout" equivalent to one caused by a three-inch gash in a sidewall. After taking a student through several dry runs in a closed area to familiarize him with the correct response when a tire is blown, the instructor trips the valve on the device.

Another unusual aspect of the driver education program at Janesville is our night-driving exercise.

Begun in 1965, it consists of a three-hour drive through several small towns and two cities of over 40,000 population. Cars are usually sent out in groups of three, with four students

*This article was obtained through the joint efforts of the NEA National Commission on Safety Education and the American Driver and Traffic Safety Education Association, an NEA department. From NEA Journal 58:60, September 1969. Used by permission.

to each car. Each student drives about 45 minutes.

An amber light on the top of each car helps identify our vehicles. Instructors are in voice contact at all times with the cars through a two-way radio system. This system is the heart of the night-driving exercise. (It is also a very valuable safety aid. One calm day we had to alert our entire 17-car fleet to a tornado warning; within two minutes, all cars were on their way to cover.)

During a typical night exercise, each group encounters a series of problems, all of which are designed to test the students' ability to cope with driving dilemmas.

• To give students practice in yielding to an emergency vehicle, a sheriff's deputy assigned to us stops each car. He then checks the learner's permits.

• Each small group of cars comes upon the scene of an "accident." A wrecked car (donated by a local dealer) is in a ditch against a tree with smoke pouring from the engine compartment. Two "bleeding" victims are in the car.

Our students go into action. Some set up flares and road guards to warn oncoming traffic; others rush for the fire extinguishers in the car trunks. Students check the victims' pulse; try to determine the seriousness of their injuries; and treat for shock, covering the victims with newspapers, blankets, and a seat cover. Two students head for the nearest farmhouse to call for help and identify the location of the accident. The instructor may offer advice, but generally he merely observes how the students put into practice what they were taught in the classroom.

• In another incident, the students come upon pedestrians walking along the edge of a county trunk road—one dressed in light clothing, the other in dark. Invariably, the driver notices only the pedestrian clad in the light clothing.

• Later on in the evening, each car meets an automobile with only one lighted beam. This car (driven by one of the supervisors) crowds the oncoming student vehicle to the shoulder of the road. An automobile also follows the student car with its lights on bright to see if the young driver can properly adjust his mirror to reduce the glare.

While all these situations present a certain degree of danger to the student, we feel that it is realistic preparation for the hazards he will face later on when he is driving alone.

A unique aspect of our driver education program is our work with the mentally retarded. Many citizens of Janesville are interested in this project—and so are some out-of-towners. Muriel Humphrey, the wife of the former Vice President and the grandmother of a retarded child, visited our driver education classes for the retarded.

The special students who participate in this program receive many hours of instruction on the simulation equipment. They also drive cars, trucks, and vans on our large multiple-car driving range and have some experience on the road as well.

One mother told me that driver education has finally given her son an interest in life. After completing the course, he was able to get a job as a stock boy and delivery truck operator. He takes pride in his work and is a very careful driver—an attribute his employer wishes each of his employees possessed. For the first time, the boys feels equal to his classmates: "I have the same driver's license as anyone else."

This boy also takes pride in helping with family expenses. Since this program began, several other special students have also gained employment and have been able to help provide family income.

Driver education is regarded as a valuable part of the curriculum at Janesville High School. The board of education decision—backed by so many teachers, students, and local citizens—to offer both classroom theory and on-the-road, behind-the-wheel training to almost all our students indicates that driver education will be held in even higher regard.

53 ᔓ INTEGRATION OF SAFETY IN THE PHYSICAL EDUCATION CURRICULUM*

C. Albert Long
Professor of Health and Physical Education,
Fairmont State College, Fairmont, West Virginia

ᔓ *The need for safety in work and in play*
is essential for each from day to day.
So serious a matter cannot be given a glance
for most such important factors can't be left to chance.
Since education helps prepare us for effective living
The area of safety must be a part of this giving.
Without a consciousness in safe ways of human action
trouble and disaster would be a common infraction.
As a teacher and part of the system of schools
we must educate for safe living to eliminate the fools.
Life is too precious and should be enjoyed
Long

The need for safety

By the nature of the physical education curriculum students are exposed to risks which are not normally found in the regular classroom. Since the activities within the curriculum, with good leadership, aid in fulfilling the physical, social, and emotional needs of the young school age population it would hardly be feasible to curtail the program. The alternative is the inclusion of safety in physical education.

In order to cast the light of explanation upon this subject a closer examination is necessary. This can be started with the following definitions of terms which will be used throughout this presentation:

Safety—the actual doing or applying of knowledge and skills learned to aid safe and effective living

Integration—(pertaining to safety education) relates to planned and incidental teachings in other curricular areas

Before any part of a curriculum can be justified there must be a need. Is there a need for safety in physical education?

The need for making safety a part of the physical education program is essential to the point of having a national conference on the subject. The Conference on Accident Prevention in Physical Education, Athletics, and Recreation was held in December, 1963. The object was to formulate suggestions for accident prevention in the areas concerned. This indicates there must be a need if national concern is present.

Safety is an essential element in courses connected with gymnasiums and laboratories.[1] The National Safety Council has studied various areas of the school system to get a better understanding of the problem and of how to deal with the problem of accidents. The studies have reported findings in various safety education texts as well as other publications including *Accident Facts*.

To add statistical significance to the justification of safety in physical education, one of the Council's publications reports that nearly one-half of all school accidents occur in the gymnasium or on the playing field. Relatively few casualties result from unavoidable risks inherent in the activity itself. In relation to specific activities the following lead in the percentage of injuries: Touch Football, Heavy Apparatus, Football, Wrestling, Tumbling.[2]

Excluding the above activities is not solving the problem but merely evading the issue and depriving students of certain experiences. This responsibility of problem solving involves each individual physical educator. Many such activities add to the school program with adequate leadership.

The National Safety Council has studied the causes of the various accidents associated with physical education and found them to be in-

---

*From The Physical Educator 25:82, May 1968. Used by permission.

[1] National Safety Council, Safety education methods, (National Safety Council, Education Division: Chicago, Illinois) p. 17.
[2] Florio, A. E. and Stafford, G. T., Safety education, (New York: McGraw-Hill, 1962) p. 33.

adequate leadership, faulty equipment, irresponsible student behavior, insufficient skill, poor physical condition, and the last factor would be risks inherent in the activity itself.

A closer study of the situation indicates poor leadership has been the big cause of participation accidents. This might indicate a lack of knowledge of safety procedures or a lack of concern for them. In either instance the correction of the situation should be of great concern.

Recent studies have shown a direct relationship between the teacher's organizational abilities, knowledge of specific safety techniques, and familiarity with these phases of safety inherent in the presentation of skills, and how well he is able to instill habits of safe behavior in his students.[3] This places a great responsibility on the field of physical education and on each physical educator. There are implications for teachers on the job and for teacher preparation programs.

An article by Mr. Hunter in the *Journal of Health, Physical Education and Recreation* aptly states:

> "If physical education believes in the maintenance, conservation, and improvement of human resources, we cannot deny the contribution of safety education. We should recognize the worth of it as its inclusion in our program."[4]

The final representation of need for safety in the physical education curriculum is the law in loco parentis. This means that the teacher must act as a parent in relation to the student's welfare. This should motivate each physical educator to be concerned with safety in every activity to avoid possibly being negligent. Naturally the best way to do this is to do a good, proper, and conscientious job of instruction and supervision.

How can we promote safety?

Certain subjects such as industrial education and physical education lend themselves to the integration or correlation of safety learnings. Instruction in these subjects considers actual hazards that are inherent in the courses and makes a contribution to the preparation of you

for meeting dangers faced at home, work, and outside the classroom.[5]

There are certain procedures which can be followed in safety promotion which are not necessarily peculiar to a specific activity. Since physical education activities are taught for the purpose of growth through movements, physical educators will want to consider whether they are placing adequate stress on the skills and knowledge that are essential for continued participation in selected sports.[6]

In order to have a clearer concept of the role of safety in physical education the following aims have been formulated:

1. To train students to accept responsibility for their own safety and that of fellow participants.
2. To provide safe equipment and facilities.
3. To help students develop a degree of physical fitness and skill commensurate with safe participation in athletic activities.
4. To institute the administrative controls necessary to ensure optimum protection for participation in the physical education program.
5. To recognize and guard against the particular hazards associated with each activity.[7]

Specific measures can be taken to help accomplish the aims which have been previously mentioned. A factor which could aid the promotion of general safety is the attitude of the group and each individual student. The atmosphere and conditions which perpetuate the desirable attitude depend on the instructor. For example, the student is not likely to adhere strictly to a listing of "forbidden actions." The adherence would probably be effective only when supervision is direct.

It must be explained, through action and verbalization, that safety measures increase the possibilities for enjoyment; this in no way implies removal of the more hazardous activities which are highly beneficial. Carrying on an activity without constant fear of being injured because of certain safety precautions is certainly more enjoyable.

The instructor can do a great deal to promote safety by setting a good example. His attitudes are reflected in his actions and in turn imparted

[3] A physical educator looks at safety, Elizabeth Williams, Journal of Health, Physical Education, and Recreation, Vol. 35, Nov-Dec., 1964, p. 43.

[4] The Safety Component of education, Journal of Health, Physical Education, and Recreation, Vol. 34, May 1963, p. 18.

[5] Strasser, M. K., Aaron, J. E., Bolin, R. C., Eales, J. R., Fundamentals of safety education, (McMillan Company: New York, N.Y. 1962), p. 167.

[6] National Commission on Safety Education, N. E. A., Safety education, Reprint from Journal of National Education Association, October, 1960, p. 7.

[7] Florio, A. E., and Stafford, G. T., Saftey education, (McGraw-Hill Book Company: New York, 1956), p. 276.

to the students. If students are to develop a safety consciousness, they should not be constantly exposed to unsafe behavior.

Students tend to develop a sense of personal responsibility in proportion to the opportunities given them to plan, execute, and appraise their own conduct.[8] The best way of developing the ability to choose the proper and safe method of action is more forthcoming when exposed to the proper or safe methods.

The teacher who uses good teaching techniques will be in better control of the situation; and, therefore, safety will accure. This is quite aptly expressed in the following comment:

> A class that is conducted efficiently is so busy performing necessary and worthwhile activities that there is little or no opportunity for "cutting capers." Disorder arises when interest and action begin to lag or when confusion exists.[9]

We stated previously that a great many school accidents occur in organized and unorganized games. This means a major responsibility for the physical educator. The teacher must instigate action with knowledge concerning the following principles:

1. The instructor must ascertain how well a participant performs before further progression.
2. There must be proper instruction at all times.
3. Rules concerning the program and specific activities must be obeyed. These rules must be for the benefit of the student.
4. The value of protective equipment must not be under estimated.
5. There must be supervision for all phases of the program with closer attention given to the more hazardous activities.

Perhaps an action which might evolve from the preceding principles is the inclusion of activities related to efficient ways of lifting, moving, pushing, and pulling. Instructing students in how to fall would be highly profitable and could be easily incorporated in a unit on tumbling.

Another aspect of safety integration in the physical education curriculum is striving to accomplish the established goals of the program. Objectives of physical education include skill and strength development. Even a superficial analysis reveals that these qualities play a major role in efficient, safe performance of actions. This is stressed further in a statement

by the Safety Research Projects Committee of the National Safety Council which states that the development of alertness, agility, and body control are a contribution to the school safety program.

In another related instance the inclusion of swimming in the curriculum has an inference toward safety integration. Development of skill in this curricular phase facilitates safe living. If a critical situation did arise where the skill had to be used, the application for safe living would be apparent.

The screening of students by medical examination has definite health benefits, but there are safety facets concerned also. Having a student in a class working in weight training or working through a circuit training schedule with a defective heart valve would certainly not be safe for him or his classmates. So the health examination may be a type of incidental or indirect safety examination.

Each individual can facilitate the integration of safety with physical education by concerning himself with the following factors:

1. Techniques of organization
2. Progressive skills
3. Conditioning
4. Grouping in team activities
5. Sportsmanship
6. Rules and regulations
7. Understanding of risks involved
8. Individual limitations
9. Regular evaluation of procedures

To further discuss the place of safety in the curriculum let us look at the procedures which should be taken in a specific activity. Gymnastics would be a good example of highly hazardous curricular offering which must integrate safety education. Some of these factors which must be included in the activity are the following:

1. Careful placement of apparatus with sufficient mats
2. Spotting apparatus (hand and overhead spotting belts)
3. Teaching individual spotting
4. The use of chalk on the hands
5. Progression in stunts
6. Encouraging participants never to use apparatus alone
7. Careful explanation and demonstration of stunts

The safety implications above could also have effective teaching implications for the physical educator. The careful placement of apparatus facilitates better organization and control.

---

[8] Ibid. p. 277.

[9] Staley, Seward, Sports education (New York: A. S. Barnes and Company, 1939), p. 240.

Spotting apparatus being used allows the performer to go through a movement without worrying about falling or injury. Teaching students how to spot aids in having him share the responsibility for his safety and other participants. It also allows more participation in that each student need not wait for the instructor to help him through a stunt. Careful explanations and demonstrations of all stunts are good teaching procedures to make sure each student understands fully what is to be done. Explaining the stunt in parts and in relation to body aids understanding and safety.

Each activity could be taken individually to show the implications for efficient teaching and safety education. It should be understood that any factor which makes learning more complete is profitable. If these procedures promote safety and better learning, then they should be given careful consideration in planning.

The consideration of needs and characteristics of students actually has safety implications, and this is necessary for planning and instituting curricular offerings.

A physical education teacher who does everything within his power to better the learning situation, to motivate the student, and to teach as effectively as he can will come nearer to accomplishing known objectives and will do more for effectively integrating safety in physical education.

As teachers of movement in a variety of skills
Should we be concerned with safety or consider it a frill
Since our objectives point in the direction of health
Should we not be concerned with protection of self?
If we look at each skill and give it some thought,
There would be agreement the safe way should be taught.
Safe measures protect us and each one that we teach
So let students learn safety through action and let others preach.

Long

BIBLIOGRAPHY

ARTICLES

American Medical Association Committee on Exercise and Fitness, Health problems revealed during physical activity, Journal of Health, Physical Education, and Recreation, Washington, D.C.: AAHPER, Vol. 36, September 1965, p. 6.

Fitch, Fredrick, Seven areas of consideration for playground safety, Safety Education, Vol. 33, January, 1954, p. 16.

Hunter, O.N., The safety component in education, Journal of Health, Physical Education, and Recreation, Vol. 34, May, 1963, p. 18.

National Committee on Safety Education, Reprint from National Education Association Journal, Washington, D.C.: National Education Association, October, 1960, p. 7.

National Safety Council, Accident facts, Chicago: N.S.C., September, 1960, p. 91.

Staton, W.M., and Butler, L.C., Fitness and safety, Journal of Health, Physical Education, and Recreation, Washington, D.C.: AAHPER, Vol. 31, September, 1960, p. 31.

Williams, Elizabeth, A physical educator looks at safety, Journal of Health, Physical Education, and Recreation, Washington, D.C.: AAHPER, Vol. 35, November-December, 1964, p. 43.

BOOKS

Florio, A.E. and Stafford, G.T., Safety education, New York: McGraw-Hill Book Company, 1956.

Hyde, F.S. and Slown, R.C., Safety programs and activities, Chicago: Berkley-Cardy Company, 1952.

National Safety Council, Safety education methods for secondary school, Chicago: National Safety Council Educational Division, 1949, p. 17.

Seaton, Don and Stack, Herbert, Safety in sports, New Jersey: Prentice-Hall, Inc., 1948.

Stack, Herbert and Elkow, Duke, Education for safe living, New Jersey, Prentice-Hall, Inc., 1957.

Staley, Seward, Sports education, New York: A.S. Barnes and Company, 1939.

Strasser, M.K.; Aaron, Janus; Bohn, Ralph; and Eales, John, Fundamentals of safety education, London: Macmillan Company, 1964.

54 ❧ IMPROVEMENT OF FOOD SELECTION THROUGH PHYSICAL EDUCATION AND ATHLETIC PROGRAMS*

FRED V. HEIN, PH.D.
SECRETARY, COMMITTEE ON THE MEDICAL ASPECTS OF SPORTS,
AMERICAN MEDICAL ASSOCIATION

Sports and athletics are now a definite part of our culture and have a particular appeal to our young people. They are especially absorbing to the participants in varsity sports, of course, but their influence on youth as a whole is greater than is commonly realized.

To illustrate, take the case of 200 students recently studied with respect to smoking habits. (1) The single most important factor in discouraging smoking was found to be participation in competitive sports. Even regular smokers tended to discontinue the habit during the sports seasons in which they competed.

This suggests a compelling reason for instituting broad programs of athletics and physical education for both boys and girls throughout the school and college years. To be most effective as a motivating force and in terms of other values, such programs should include a great variety of activities. (2)

The more sports that are included, the more likely that the program will catch the interests and meet the needs of the greatest possible proportion of students. So the goal is to include as many sports as can be supervised safely and as many students as can be involved healthfully.

The influence of sports on the health behavior of students is not confined entirely to those who participate. Other students tend to emulate the health behavior of players and particularly of those who excel. (3) So our "gatekeepers" for health education with respect to the student body are often the star athletes.

It is dangerous to assume that the health education effects of sports and athletics will always be on the positive side. If athletes are encouraged or allowed to eat quantities of honey, swish down yogurt, or gulp up vitamins with the idea that these products are endowed with some special values for improved performance, the effects will be decidedly negative.

Not only will such practices influence the health attitudes of the youths that are indulging in them, but they will also influence the health attitudes of youngsters observing the practices.

*From the Journal of School Health 37:340, September 1967. Used by permission.

A well-known Olympic shotputter a few years ago is a case in point.

This particular shotputter, who at that time held the world's record for his event, was a great believer in honey as a "high-energy" food and the "quick-life" theory. So this athlete would bring honey with him to the shotputting ring and right before he put the shot take a huge swig in front of everyone including, at times, a TV audience.

No wonder young shotputters and for that matter discus throwers, javelin throwers, and other athletes took to the honey habit. "If the champ took it, won his event, and even set records, it must be the thing to do. And if it works for the Olympic champ, it should work for me."

This story is not told to discredit honey, which is a perfectly good food. It is told to discredit the theory that there is any super-food that can somehow give an athlete super-energy for super performance. It is told, also, to point up how wrong it is to teach an athlete, and/or those watching him, that he can rely on anything else but his own resources developed through carefully conditioning his body, diligently practicing his skills, responding well to coaching, and fully marshaling his mental and physical resources during competition.

Another hardy misconception in the area of nutrition and sports relates to the so-called high protein diet. Some coaches are still convinced that their athletes need steak at least twice a day and that their meals should be crowded with other protein foods. It should be said in this connection that the athletes themselves have done nothing to discourage this practice.

Studies have not shown such a diet to be advantageous in either vigorous sports or heavy work. (5) Perhaps the persistence of this misconception may relate to a mental mirage linking up muscle, maleness, and meat in terms of virility and athletic performance.

The problem here and the negative teaching is that again the idea of some special food or food types being of special and unusual benefit is fostered. This may lead the athlete and those who emulate him to overemphasize one food group in their diet to the detriment of the diet as a whole and to the neglect of, or even exclusion of, other needed nutrients.

Still another misconception in sports that has been very difficult to deal with is the myth that water must be withheld from the athlete during practices and games. This belief has been extremely widespread; if the athlete was allowed any water at all during play, he was required to rinse his mouth only and then to dispel the water.

In recent years the start of the football season has gradually been moved up with practices started earlier and earlier. In many parts of the country this has meant hot weather football, particularly at the beginning of the season. This coupled with the withholding of water during play had some disastrous results.

In a number of instances, deaths from heat illness have occurred that are directly linked to football. Until the 1966 season there were as many as five or six fatalities annually from heat illness. (6) Now we are hoping this problem is being brought under control.

During the last seven summers the AMA Committee on the Medical Aspects of Sports, with the cooperation of allied health organizations and school and college athletic associations, has conducted an intensive publicity campaign with respect to heat illness.

This publicity, utilizing all the professional and public media, has been aimed at team physicians, athletic trainers, coaches, the players themselves, and the general public. Emphasis was placed on the need for water and salt replacement during hard, hot weather, physical activity. The need for light clothing, rest periods, proper scheduling of practices, and other precautions during hot weather activity was also pointed out.

This year (1966) only one death has been recorded in football attributed to heat illness. We intend to continue the campaign and hope that before long the unnecessary deaths from this athletic misconception will be a thing of the past. Only a continuing program of professional and public education can accomplish this objective.

Turning from the negative aspects of instruction about nutrition and sports to more positive phases, what are some of the basic principles we might be able to teach in connection with physical education and athletics? Among some of the most significant are the following:

• Calorie intake and physical activity output are interdependent in maintaining desirable weight. An active football player, for example, might consume 5,000 calories a day without putting on excess pounds while a sedentary student would soon become obese were he to eat at the same daily rate.

• In general, the athlete needs substantially the same balance and variety of foods as his peers. He needs more calories than some of his less active friends, but he needs nutrients from each of the food groups in about the same proportions.

• No specific foods or vitamin supplements can in themselves upgrade athletic performance. Claims to the contrary are not supported by clear-cut evidence and the conflicting results of studies in this area suggest that the alleged benefits are probably psychological.

• Improvement in the performance of athletes and the efficiency of industrial workers as the result of eating a good breakfast have been demonstrated. Almost without exception, the performance of subjects in such demonstrations shows that breakfast does make a difference.

• Studies show that the athlete needs at least three meals a day for optimum performance. There is also some evidence to suggest that more frequent spacing of meals might be desirable in some cases.

• For best performance, particularly in hot weather, there should be regular replacement of the water lost from the body through perspiration. In hot weather salt needs daily replacement, which ordinarily can be done satisfactorily by a little extra salting of foods at meals.

• "Going heavy" on proteins in the training diet serves no useful purpose. Protein, as was formerly believed, does not seem to be the chief source of muscular activity.

• Recent research suggests that an emphasis on carbohydrates may be warranted particularly for endurance events. These studies show that in strenuous activity there is increased utilization of carbohydrates if these are available.

There are many other principles that could be cited, but these examples are sufficient to show that athletes, their coaches, and the sports-minded public will be interested in them if they are properly presented.

The idea would be to replace fallacy with fact; to rid athletic circles of the bizarre ideas and misconceptions that still persist. Fortunately, a good start has been made by a growing group of nutritionists and interested physicians who are writing, speaking, and conducting in-service education in this area.

As a result, there is, in turn, a growing group of coaches, trainers, and athletes who have been exposed to the facts about nutrition and sports. Once they become "believers," they are almost as militant as nutritionists in spreading the gospel, quashing the quack, and fighting the fad. At this point I would like to make a plea to the nutritionist readers to join the ranks of those who are helping to teach nutrition through sports. You will have a highly motivated group to deal with and a receptiveness in your audience that is both surprising and pleasing.

To do this teaching through sports, we need to employ both the public mass media and the organized instructional programs of our schools and colleges. Both approaches are already being used, but both need to be sharpened and stepped up markedly.

Public media available to us include pamphlets, popular periodicals, professional journals, radio, TV, exhibits, and meetings of various kinds. You may be interested in a few examples illustrating how we have used these media for education about the health aspects of sports at the American Medical Association.
• In cooperation with the National Federation of High School Athletic Associations, the AMA publishes a monthly article on some aspect of sports medicine. In the area of nutrition some of the titles have been "The All American Diet," "Winning and Weight," "Food Fads and Facts," "Hot Weather Hints," and "Quackery in Sports." These articles, through the Federation, reach high schools throughout the United States.
• After the articles are prepared, a companion news-release is written, which is sent to some 2,500 newspapers throughout the country. For one current release, we checked through a clipping service and found that more than 1,000 papers used the release.
• Appropriate articles are also converted into short radio and TV spot announcements for use on public service time. These are forwarded periodically to radio and TV stations, and we know through evaluation procedures that these materials are widely used.
• We have invited coaches and trainers as well as interested physicians to attend our meeting on the Medical Aspects of Sports. Some of the more sophisticated of these have had places on the program within their areas of competency. In turn, many physicians have been invited to appear on the programs of their organizations.
• Like the Food and Nutrition Section of APHA, we have included discussion of nutrition and sports within the programs of AMA meetings and conferences. Also, we have encouraged the inclusion of this subject in state and local meetings of medical and allied health groups.

The organized instructional program of schools and colleges offers a unique opportunity to teach about nutrition through sports. Physical education classes are required for all students in most schools. Where there are good programs including intramural sports, the young people are almost as interested in their participation as are the varsity athletes.

The physical education teacher, like other teachers, has an obligation to teach those aspects of health in his classes that naturally relate to his subject. For physical education these include both elementary physiology of exercise and health practices relative to physical activity. Obviously, instruction in both of these areas involves nutrition education.

It involves the principles discussed earlier and others with which you are all familiar. A good example relates to an interested [sic] energy expenditure table that was recently published.

This would make ideal teaching material for physical education, because it shows the energy equivalents of food calories expressed in minutes of activity for swimming, running, and other sports. While exercise should not be thought of merely as the way to walk off a piece of cake or swim off a doughnut, this is an interesting aspect of nutrition and physical activity.

In today's bountiful society, one of the major problems in the country is "creeping overweight." Many young people fail to balance their calorie intake with adequate physical activity.

Studies show that these overweight young people become the obese adults and interestingly that they often eat less than their peers of normal weight. (9) The problem is that they also exercise less and some consciously or subsciously avoid physical activity.

Inner feelings or attitudes about food and physical activity act like a "catalyst" to determine eating and exercise practices. These feelings are more likely to relate to immediate objectives than to long-term goals. (10)

As Dr. Roswell Gallagher, the well-known student of adolescent medicine, has so aptly said: The aspiring adolescent athlete will accept good habit advice, because he knows he needs extra energy for his activities and is willing to do anything that will bring him success.

Doctor Gallagher has suggested that the best solution to nutrition teaching for adolescents is to guide them into activities which require zest and will yield them acceptance. This will be more rewarding, he believes, than merely telling them why they ought to eat properly.

Linking up nutrition with athletics and other energy-demanding activities in which young people want to excel can pay big educational dividends. Youth is a time when acceptance in the peer society is all important and teachers, coaches, and other adults involved in the guidance of young people should take full advantage of this motivating factor.

The absorbing activities of physical education and athletics provide bright, sharp tools for nutrition education. Only a broad and varied program of physical education and athletics can attract the interest and meet the needs of the majority of students. The relationship of proper nutrition to success and acceptance should be used to motivate young people to improve their nutrition practices. Nutritionists have an obligation to ally themselves with physical education teachers and coaches to make sure that practices and instruction relative to nutrition and sports are in keeping with current knowledge in the field.

REFERENCES

1. Haynes, W. F., Jr., et al. Smoking habits and incidence of respiratory tract infections in a group of adolescent males, American Review of Respiratory Diseases, 93:731, May, 1966.
2. Committee on Exercise and Physical Fitness of the American Medical Association, Need for varied activities in physical education, Journal of Health-Physical Education-Recreation, 36:6, 8, June, 1965
3. Committee on the Medical Aspects of Sports of the American Medical Association, Athletics and health education; in Tips on athletic training III, American Medical Association, Chicago, 1961.
4. Personal communication with Allan Ryan, M.D., Team Physician, University of Wisconsin, and member of the AMA Committee on Exercise and Physical Fitness.
5. Mayer, J. and Bullen, B. Nutrition and athletic performance, Physiological Reviews, 40:369, July, 1960.
6. National Alliance Football Committee, Fatality report, National Federation of State High School Athletic Associations, Chicago, (Issued Annually) and, American Football Coaches Association, Fatality report, The Association, Chapel Hill, North Carolina, (Issued Annually).
7. Committee on the Medical Aspects of Sports of the American Medical Association, Food facts and fallacies; in Tips on athletic training VII, AMA, Chicago, 1965.
8. Konishi, F. Food Energy equivalents of various activities, Journal of the American Dietetic Association, 46:186, March 1965.
9. Johnson, et al. Relative importance of inactivity and overeating in energy balance of obese high school girls, American Journal of Clinical Nutrition, 4:37, 1956.
10. Hein, F. V. Teenage gap in knowing and doing, School Lunch Journal, 18:42, April, 1964.
11. Gallagher, J. R. and Harris, H. Emotional Problems of the adolescent, Revised Edition, 1964, Oxford University Press, New York.

PROJECTS AND THOUGHT QUESTIONS

1. Prepare a topical outline for a health science instruction program for grades kindergarten through college. Indicate the topics you would cover in each grade and the rationale for your plan.
2. Prepare a position paper on the subject: Sex education should be a part of each child's education. Present it to your class.
3. Select a health program that has been written up in the Journal of School Health during the last five years and critically evaluate its worth.
4. Write an essay on the relationship of health education to physical education including (a) objectives, (b) qualifications for teaching, (c) program, and (d) facilities.
5. Prepare a simple test of health knowledge concerning such topics as nutrition, disease, and mental health. Administer the test to your class and determine their knowledge of these areas.
6. What are some common misconceptions on the part of students in regard to health subjects.
7. Identify some problems in regard to the administration of a health science instruction program, and set forth your proposed solution for each of these problems.

SELECTED READINGS

Anderson, C. L.: School health practice, ed. 4, St. Louis, 1968, The C. V. Mosby Co.
Bucher, C. A.: Administration of health and physical education programs, including athletics, ed. 5, St. Louis, 1971, The C. V. Mosby Co.
Bucher, C. A., Olsen, E., and Willgoose C.: The foundations of health, New York, 1967, Appleton-Century-Crofts.
Grout, R. E.: Health teaching in schools, ed. 5, Philadelphia, 1968, W. B. Saunders Co.
Joint Committee on Health Problems in Education, National Education Association-American Medical Association: Health education, Washington, D.C., 1961, National Education Association.
Mayshark, C., and Irwin, L.: Health education in secondary schools, St. Louis, 1968, The C. V. Mosby Co.

CHAPTER 10 THE HEALTH SERVICE PROGRAM FOR STUDENTS, INCLUDING ATHLETES

School and college health service programs are essential to the maintenance of good health by school children, college students, and athletes. Without satisfactory health services, the health of students and athletes cannot be adequately developed, maintained, and protected.

The history of health services shows that in early schools and colleges the stress was mainly on providing sanitary facilities and a clean environment. This goal was accomplished through a system of inspections and procedures. In recent years there has been greater attention given to those measures essential to the maintenance and improvement of a student's health. As a result, physicians, dentists, and other specialists have become more closely related to the schools and colleges. In turn, this has meant better detection of health defects, a more complete follow-through to ensure the correction of such defects, more adequate means for preventing and controlling communicable disease, an increased realization of the potentialities of the medical examination as an educational tool, and more attention to the eyes, throat, ears, nose, and teeth. As the need for better health services was recognized by the public at large, state laws were passed to provide these services. These laws required such procedures as periodic medical examinations and regular checking of vision and hearing. They also stressed the need for nurses who were trained not only in their particular field but also in education. Today there is a feeling that, in order that the student be adequately educated, health services must be an essential part of the program.

Health services cover a broad area. They include the procedures established to (1) appraise the health status of students, athletes, and educational personnel, (2) counsel students, parents, and other persons concerning appraisal findings, (3) encourage the correction of remediable defects, (4) help plan for the health care and education of handicapped (exceptional) children, (5) help prevent and control disease, (6) provide emergency care for the sick and injured, (7) promote environmental sanitation, and (8) promote health of school and college personnel.

In the first article in this chapter, an administrator, Harry P. Day, views the health service program as a challenging problem area. The problems he describes are the findings of an able physician-director for the health service program and the educating of the physician-director in the nature of this all-encompassing job. The job entails personnel administration of school services, meeting of student needs, and maintenance of a working relationship with the teaching and research areas of the school program.

The objectives of the health service program, as outlined by Ruth A. Frary, are education, environment, and services. The programs should be person-centered rather than program-centered. School health services should also be concerned with prevention rather than treatment and should deal with community health needs.

The Committee on the Medical Aspects of Sports explains the role of the team physician in the total picture of the health service program. The team physician ensures pre-season examinations and health guidance of the athletic team members throughout the season. He makes judgments relating to participation and supervision in school sports. The Committee believes that it is best for one physician to serve in this capacity.

Citing cases of high school football and wrestling teams, Allan J. Ryan shows the need for medical supervision of high school athletic programs. The coach must cooperate with the team physician and must be willing to accept his decisions and recommendations. The physician must understand rehabilitation of athletes, and both he and the coach must serve the causes of youth and sport.

55 ❧ UNIVERSITY ADMINISTRATION VIEWS THE HEALTH SERVICE*

HARRY P. DAY, ED.D.
DIRECTOR, THE NEW ENGLAND CENTER FOR CONTINUING EDUCATION,
DURHAM, NEW HAMPSHIRE

Some of you must be wondering why a dean of students has been asked to view the health service on behalf of the university administration. You would have good reason to wonder since in some institutions the line of administrative responsibility offers no direct connection between the health service and the office of student affairs. It just happens that this administrative link is provided at Florida State and, as a result, an opportunity has been afforded for me to observe our health service at close hand over a period of years. As a consequence, I have come to have a profound respect for the work done in this area, and I have learned a great deal by viewing the student in all of his mysterious ways through the eyes of the trained physician and his staff.

Before getting to the business of documenting in a practical fashion some of the insights about student life provided through the health service, let me touch on the complexity of the administrative arrangements which alone make the health service rather unique. First, the university administration seeking a health service director must be patient and sort among the small band of able physicians interested in college health work for an administrator capable of supervising a staff, running a hospital, doubling as a fiscal officer and performing as a physician. For added measure it should come as no surprise if there is an expectation that supervision will be given as well to the athletic medical program, to the planning necessary for a new infirmary building, and to budget projections for a legislative biennium based on a growing student population that no one wishes to predict in exact numbers. If I left anything out it was likely the assignment of periodic meetings with student senate committee members who plow the campus at least once each semester looking for a major scandal in the infirmary. Surely there is reason enough for the good man to be found occasionally looking over his shoulder to see how things are progressing on the outside in the private practice of medicine.

The important thing for the university administration to realize is that once the able director-physician has been found, every effort should be made to allow him to run his show in the light of the special needs of his staff and the special services to be offered students through his program. The dividends to be gained by the university as a result of the effective functioning of a student health service are great and should be prized by those ultimately responsible for the total welfare of the institution.

The identification, then, of an individual capable of performing a variety of assignments as director of the health service is a number one responsibility for the university administration. Once the director has been selected, there should be clear understandings as to institutional policies that affect the health service. Appropriate guidelines are sometimes hammered out over a period of years, depending on the growth and change in scope of the institution, but surely there is no better backbone provided the health service than the clear understanding of those responsibilities, and special burdens, to be carried by the service. I will give two illustrations to show what I have in mind—obviously, there could be many more examples given. First, there is the important area of confidentiality of records. All of you know that the demands of the institution often impose a burden on the physician who bears a special relationship to his patient. In spite of the difficulties which sometimes develop, I believe it is clear that the special relationship between physician and patient must be recognized and respected. The university physician must closely adhere to all the ethical and professional tenets of medicine, perhaps even more carefully than other specialties. This responsibility should certainly include professional self-discipline and possible removal of fellow physicians who are unable or unwilling to achieve a satisfactory level of medical practice. Of course, there are areas of common responsibility whereby the counseling personnel who share concern with the physician over a particular student case may be assisted in their work. I will return to this point later.

*Presented at the Annual Meeting of the Southern College Health Association, Tallahassee, March 24-26, 1966. Used with permission from the Journal of the American College Health Association, 15:140, December 1966.

The second illustration of a policy area which I should like to identify is that of athletic medicine. It is my belief that overall supervision of this aspect of student life should be the responsibility of the health service. Clearly, the large, well developed and well funded intercollegiate athletic program generates considerable flexibility and independence for itself, but as long as the students involved are a responsibility of the university I believe it is in the best interest of the student, and the athletic program, to link the athletic medical service to the university health service.

Coming now to the student and his needs, I'd like to examine some of the special insights provided through the health service. First, it is my belief that the more selective admissions requirements set by most universities have given us a student population with characteristics we must understand if we are to deal successfully with the student's total educational experience. We have highly capable young people who face the complexities of the large campus at the same time society at large imposes distinct limitations on the role of the young, unmarried adult. Cross currents of opinion beset the student at a time when he is attempting to find himself intellectually as well as morally and physically. In this confusion between the private world of the individual and the conflicting demands of society, the student has need of help at times which is best given by the physician. In displaying the physical stress and strain, or potential for it, which frequently goes along with mental disturbance, the student opens a window to the health service professional—whether he be physician, psychiatrist or clinical psychologist—a window which is essential to viewing the total person. The snapshots of the student's total personality thus revealed are essential to student personnel people attempting to understand and cope with the entire fabric of student life in an academic community. I never look at the monthly report of the health service without asking myself what story is being told through the nature of the cases handled by the Infirmary. I would not want a meeting of personnel staff members to review student life broadly unless I could have representation from the health service. The pressures of the classroom pace will produce cases for the Infirmary just as surely as will the restraints, whether they be reasonable or unreasonable, which are imposed by the university community and society at large.

A second point to be made about special insight into the student's needs has to do with sexual problems. It is my belief that the confusion of young people over questions of morality and the frankness that prompts them to speak more freely of their problems in this area have placed a special burden on the health service. Because of the confidential nature of the patient's relationship with the physician and because of the physician's technical knowledge in dealing with questions about sex, I fully support the role played by the health service in reaching students who might never seek help otherwise, or who might seek help outside the university in situations fraught with all kinds of danger. There is a counseling role to be played by the health service which is greatly needed, which would be difficult to duplicate anywhere else on campus, and which students respect as they learn the interest of the health service is in the student's welfare and not in taking punitive action for misbehavior. It is my opinion that the university administration is in need of the feedback about student problems in the area of sexual behavior which can be provided out of the counseling experiences of the physician, but at the same time the administration must relinquish any claim to direct access to the record and the identification of the student who has come to the physician on a confidential basis. If the physician feels the university's interests are best served by raising questions as to the student's health or mental well being, the university administration should accept the recommendation of the health service as to those steps deemed best in dealing with the student. It is at this point that the physician and other personnel workers need to support one another, preferably through the formal channel of a health committee and its recommendations.

Moving on from the student and his concerns, I should like to focus attention on the relationship of the health service to other student personnel offices. I believe the best way I can sum this up is to say that plenty of work needs to be done by all people providing student services. We should recognize what special competencies are held by professional people engaged in different aspects of student personnel service. Each professional group should attempt to stress training necessary for an individual to gain competency in his chosen field. There should then be a willingness to share in the business of providing the best student service possible with each specialist playing his appropriate role. Frequently, the problem in getting a team approach to providing student service is due to poor communication among specialists. Errors are easily committed on all sides. The counselor with limited clinical experience may fail to recognize the point where a specialist could help him. Certainly, the educational counelor who fails to recognize limits between counseling and psychotherapy is vulnerable. The clinical specialist, on the other hand, may be so condescending in his approach to working with the counselor that no rapport is possible. The person who loses out in such a situation is the student.

To sum up, I'd like to emphasize again the major contribution to be made to a total university environment by a resourceful, well-trained staff working through the health service. The daily service function has received most of my attention because the need for it is so evident. On the other hand, there is so much to be done through the training and research com-

ponents of the health service. In the absence of staff to carry on these related functions, the health service should seek to form a strong professional relationship with those campus units engaged in teaching and research. The profit to both should be evident. Also, out of such natural ties should come better team approaches to pressing student problems. It is the integration of all these functions which will make the student health service even more attractive to those specialists on the outside who now gaze in some wonderment at those who chose university health work. One of these days these same individuals may discover what a challenge is presented through this field and what a measure of personal dedication is required for the individual who succeeds in the field of student health service.

56 ﾠ SCHOOL HEALTH SERVICES: KINDERGARTEN THROUGH COLLEGE *

RUTH A. FRARY, M.D.
DIRECTOR, UNIVERSITY HEALTH CENTER, UNIVERSITY OF CALIFORNIA AT SANTA CRUZ

Health knowledge and the application of new health practices are not being generally applied by individuals in this country in spite of the expenditure of considerable time, effort, and money in public health programs including school health services. The avowed purposes of health programs in schools, kindergarten through college, have been laudable and aimed at definite objectives set forth by many national groups.

According to School Health Services, the publication of the Joint Committee on Health Problems in Education of the National Education Association and the American Medical Association, the reasons for health services will include consideration of their relationships to (a) facilitating learning, (b) encouraging pupils to obtain needed medical or dental treatment, (c) adapting school programs to individual pupil needs, (d) maintaining a healthful school environment, and (e) increasing pupils' understanding of health and health problems.

A report of Health Services in California Junior Colleges states that the health services usually included (1) individual health guidance

(health counseling) and health appraisal procedures (2) health protection (prevention and care of emergency illness, injury, communicable disease, and encouragement of healthful environment); and (3) working with others in the college and in the community to attain health education objectives.

The "Recommended Standards and Practices for a College Health Program" of the American College Health Association states that:

"The ultimate objectives of any college or university health program are to maintain a state of optimum health, both physical and emotional, among the student body and staff, to indoctrinate each student with proper attitudes, and to instill good habits of personal and community health. An adequate health program assures a healthful and safe physical and emotional environment, health education, and health care." The objectives for all schools then include the triumvirate: health education, healthful environment, and health services.

College and University Health Services aim to meet the students' need for prompt medical service, and preventive medical activities under circumstances that will be least likely to interfere with academic progress. The chief differences between services at the college level and those in elementary schools, is the provision of some forms of medical care on the campus itself. Only about 20% of colleges have

*Presented at the Eleventh National Conference on Physicians and Schools, sponsored by the Department of Health Education of the American Medical Association, Chicago, Illinois, Oct. 6, 1967. From The Journal of School Health 38:207, April 1968. Used by permission.

a fully developed health program; however, this percentage includes most of the larger universities. Moore and Summerskill (1953) found that institutions with the highest standards of health care also had the highest academic standards.

All of these objectives are laudable in themselves, but in their application, they have tended to be program-centered rather than person-centered. This is regrettable when one considers that in a few years, nearly 50% of our population may be attending schools of some kind.

The new pre-school or Head Start programs have had health programs as a very important part of their emphasis. Of 1400 pre-school children examined at five university affiliated hospitals in Boston, one third were found to be seriously ill and in need of medical attention. The logical question to ask is "How come no one spotted their problems sooner—and did something about them?"

This same question had been asked previously when large numbers of our youth were rejected for military service. It will be asked again when studies are made of unemployment and school dropouts. As the physical fitness program received impetus from the military rejection rate, so school health services may be asked to play a role in these problems as well as the many other identifiable health problems of today. The schools along with other institutions in our society have a real responsibility to help meet this challenge, but to do so the whole focus of health services may have to change.

This is the decade of *the individual,* of emphasis on *self-discovery,* "self identity", *ego-centered psychology.* This may be at least partly a reaction to depersonalizing influences in our society—such as all digit dialing, zip codes, numbers for identification. We have all experienced the fear of being relegated to the numbered society typified by the prison inmate in his dehumanizing uniform.

Two concepts which I would like to suggest for school health services are that they take a holistic approach to the child (student) and they be person-centered rather than program-centered. This latter point can be emphasized by pointing up the increasing value observed in doing fewer routine examinations and more referral examinations.

A negative example of the person-centered approach is that the "Quack", who appears to meet the needs of some people by providing emotionally gratifying reassurances and guarantees. As Viola Bernard, M.D. said at the Second National Congress on Medical Quackery: "The degree to which the administering and distribution of medical services meet the patient's needs as a person would seem crucial to reducing the public's receptivity to quackery."

To use an analogy more directly related to a health "service" program, one only needs to compare the former method of "clobbering" pediatric patients with strong drugs prior to coming to the operating room so the anesthetist waiting there could clamp an ether mask over his unsuspecting face; to the modern and much safer and less traumatic method of having the anesthetist meet the patient in advance, establish a warm friendly relationship and explain each procedure as performed.

These are strong statements and surely not meant to indicate that the majority of health service programs in schools ignore the individual. These examples were used to emphasize the importance of considering the person rather than the program.

The services must also be seen as a continuum which places the responsibility for the health of the young child almost solely with the parents —the adolescent should be assuming increasing personal responsibility—the college student even more—and the college graduate should be able to assume full responsibility for his own health.

Schools should place more emphasis on accomplishing these goals, rather than continuing programs of doubtful value in health appraisal, communicable disease control, and maintenance of elaborate health records. As Carl Shultz, M.D. has pointed up (1965) a great deal more research is needed to prove the value of some of the time honored approaches to school health. Among these, he mentions the following as never having been adequately tested:

1. Health impairments adversely affect scholastic performance.

2. Because the teacher is in close contact with school children and can observe them throughout the day, she is in an ideal position to make an estimate of a child's health status.

3. The failure of parents to seek medical care for their children after referral from school health programs is largely a product of insufficient medical facilities and services.

4. Because health records of children contain medical information, they must be maintained and examined only by professional health personnel.

One hundred years after periodic examinations were first recommended as a means to uncover causes of ill health, doctors are still not in complete agreement as to their value, except perhaps in early detection of disease. The periodic examination as practiced by many institutions may be a waste of physician and patient time, may produce a false sense of security and accomplishment, and may when ineffective produce only a volume of statistics.

The University of California campuses for years have done routine admission physical examinations on all entering students. As long as a student remained continuously enrolled, which could be as long as nine or ten years, chances are he would never be seen again. Many of the students admitted had been under the care of physicians or had undergone routine physicals for many purposes during their pre-college years.

The newer campuses of the University of California are requiring physical examinations by a private physician before admission. The University of California at Los Angeles this year is trying a new plan of the students filling out a health history form, being screened for tuberculosis, being interviewed by a physician at the time of admission and referred only for indicated examination. This type of appraisal is being used in many other colleges with some modifications.

There are undoubtedly many persons who will be offended by these remarks—who honestly and sincerely feel that routine physicals are valuable if one *septal* defect is picked up a year. A number of studies on the periodic examination have been summarized in a pamphlet published by HEW: "Periodic Health Examinations", a compilation of abstracts from the literature by Gordon S. Siegel, M.D.

Perhaps as the findings of the Headstart medical program has shown, there are large segments of our population for whom routine, screening type of examinations would be very revealing, but they must be done in a situation which permits something to be done about the findings. The same situation may exist at the college level when we begin to get more entrants from disadvantaged backgrounds. The experience with foreign students has shown us that they need more services than our own middle class youth.

All school health services must be viewed in the context of their total community health picture. The astronomical cost figures for health care and the duplication, fragmentation, and overlapping of services in most every community, makes it mandatory for each institution offering health care to look carefully at its role and function.

Let me give you one example. The community of Palo Alto, California, home of Stanford University, and the Palo Alto Clinic, with most of its middle class citizens under very adequate care of private physicians, for many years had a school immunization program. Can one measure the effect of this program in terms of prevention of diphtheria, tetanus, whooping cough, or small pox, against its probable effect in suggesting to these children and their parents— "someone else takes the responsibility for preventing disease—you won't have to think about it". The overlapping of services in this instance is also very apparent.

As Knutson (1965) says: "Is public health practice adapting as quickly as it might to emerging concerns of the people served: Are we in some situations attempting to guide people to be concerned about what we believe to be important rather than focusing program efforts to equally significant areas to which they are striving?" Are the recipients of services (and their parents) being consulted? Have the schools and the health professionals become too objective in their thinking?

The findings of the research conducted in Manitowoc, Wisconsin as reported in "The Manitowoc Story" suggest some ways in which school health programs might take a fresh look at themselves. The study team consisted of a school health consultant, a dental health consultant, a nutritionist, and an advisory public health nurse. A psychologist acted in an advisory capacity. The team worked closely with a group of administrators from the school system studied.

Positive findings were mentioned in the report as well as suggestions for improvement. The readiness-for-school programs and the orientation of pupils entering junior high school were cited, and the team felt that additional preparatory efforts could be made for these two transition experiences which appeared to have great meaning for parents and children.

The team made practical suggestions for recognizing the individual during group activities. For example, in discussion of a health film, the pupils could be given opportunity to satisfy their curiosity and express their feelings and the meanings this experience has had for them.

They found too much reliance on conformance to what "we" (the authority figures) think is good for people, rather than on their right to make their own decisions. Coercion has frequently been observed to produce complex reactions of conformance-rejection.

The team observed little expression of warm,

affectionate interaction between teachers and pupils. They found the teachers felt a little threatened by this suggestion. I have had the same experience recently in dealing with teachers of intermediate grades in an in-service education session on sex education. It is a basic premise that people grow, develop and maintain a healthy status only when their relationships with other human beings, the people that they live with everyday, fulfill their needs for affection and security. This type of relationship is the key channel for learning.

Conclusions of the study regarding teaching about health centered around preparing children for change, rather than the simple teaching of facts.

The Manitowoc story may not sound to you like a school health services program. You are used to hearing about health examinations, screening tests, emergency care, disaster plans, provision for handicapped students, immunization levels, dental examinations, teacher-nurse conferences, and referrals for medical care.

Milton J. E. Senn in "The Role, Prerequisites and Training of the School Physician" (Pediatric Clinics of North America, Nov. 1965) said "If the educational system is based on recognition of the individual child and his needs, that system will have a well-functioning health team composed of school physician, guidance counselor, psychologist, psychiatrist, and social worker. The school physician would be a component of the school administration and a direct participant, not an outsider looking in."

Dana Farnsworth in describing the administration of college health services states that the appropriate position of a health service in the administrative structure of a college or university is that of a separate department of division, more or less parallel with the organization headed by the dean of students, with the director reporting directly to the president or, in the very large university to the vice-president in charge of student affairs.

When school administrations (be they public, private, lower schools or universities) give this kind of status to health services, they will be doing it because they believe that the health of every child and every staff member is important.

When school health personnel can approach school health services with a philosophy of prevention rather than treatment, in other words, if they are constantly looking for the strengths in peoples more than defects to be removed, some of the goals may be reached.

This has been a very philosophical approach to the subject so let me close by saying that health services at every level should be evaluated in the context of total community health. Eliminating duplication, fragmentation, and overlapping should be a goal of every health service.

BIBLIOGRAPHY

1. School health services, publication of the Joint Committee of Health Problems in education of the National Education Association and the American Medical Association, Ed.: Charles C. Wilson, M.D.
2. Health, physical education and recreation in California junior colleges, a study of programs, services and facilities: Bulletin of the California State Dep't of Educ. Vol. XXLX, No. 6, May 1960. Prepared by Louis E. Means, Consultant in School Recreation, Bureau of Health Education, Physical Education and Recreation, California State Department of Education.
3. Recommended standards and practices for a college health program, American College Health Association, reprinted 1964.
4. Research in community health, U.S. Department of Health, Education and Welfare, Public Health Service Publication No. 1225, July 1964.
5. National aspects of school health, Carl S. Shultz, M.D. and Perry Lambird, M.D. in pediatric Clinics of North America, Volume 12, Number 4, November 1965.
6. The role, prerequisites and training of the school physician, Milton J. E. Senn, M.D., ibid.
7. Knutson, Andie L. The individual, society and health behavior, New York: Russell Sage Foundation, 1965.
8. Manitowoc story, a team approach to a school health study, Virginia Hull, Betty Krippene, Frances Porter, Wisconsin State Board of Health, 1966.
9. College health services in the United States, Dana L. Farnsworth, M.D. Student Personnel Series No. 4, The American College Personnel Association, Washington, D.C. 1965.
10. The preparation and the role of nurses in school health programs, guidelines for the use of administrators, educators, and students, prepared by Helen Goodale Florentine, National League for Nursing 1962.
11. Proceedings: Second National Congress on Medical Quackery, sponsored by the American Medical Association and the Food and Drug Administration 1963.
12. Siegel, Gordon S., M.D., M.P.H.: Periodic health examinations, abstracts from the Literature U.S. Department of Health, Education and Welfare Public Health Service, Washington, D.C.

57 ᔢ THE TEAM PHYSICIAN*

COMMITTEE ON THE MEDICAL ASPECTS OF SPORTS OF THE AMERICAN MEDICAL ASSOCIATION

It is now well accepted that a preseason medical evaluation which extends beyond an actual examination to include a careful health history is an integral aspect of an athlete's preparation for participation in sports. The basic goal is to assure for each candidate the best possible health guidance with respect to his particular interests and capabilities.

It is also well accepted that the athlete merits the season. The assurance of the services of a physician for all athletic contests in which injuries can be anticipated is an important provision in a school's coordinated medical supervisory plan. Other provisions include enabling the attending physician to handle on-site injuries under desirable conditions, arranging to obtain emergency medical care during practice sessions as needed when a physician may not be in attendance, and establishing policies and procedures that provide the best possible protection to the athlete.

Colleges and universities often meet these goals by retaining a team physician under the auspices of the student health service or on a consultant basis. High schools ordinarily do not have such resources; but since a school bears primary responsibility for the conduct of its activities, it has a duty to establish and maintain an effective program for the health supervision of its athletic activities.

The task therefore is to formulate a plan for the best possible use of the community's medical personnel. One desirable plan is for appropriate representatives of the school to seek the assistance of the local medical society in working out arrangements that are mutually acceptable and that offer optimum medical guidance for each athlete. Any arrangement must include the development of school health policies that provide sound practices and procedures in the health supervision of the student participants. The ideal arrangement would include the appointment of a physician to serve as team physician for the school's sports program. This arrangement does not absolve the school of its responsibilities in this area of concern; rather, it provides an effective and efficient fulfillment of its responsibilities.

The dual responsibility of the team physician

The title "team physician" denotes a physician who is vested by the school with authority to make medical judgments relating to the participation and supervision of students in school sports. Without such a categorical designation of responsibility, there cannot exist the continuing medical assistance the athlete deserves. To put the responsibility of on-site medical decisions on the shoulders of non-medical personnel—or physicians who are removed from the scene—serves no one effectively.

Having accepted the responsibility of acting in behalf of the school, the team physician faces a dual responsibility of ensuring: (1) that the athlete is not deprived unnecessarily of the opportunity to participate if an injury or other clinical condition is not potentially serious and does not interfere with the player's performance; and conversely (2) that the student's future in athletics and in life is not jeopardized by unwarranted eligibility for a particular sport or by premature return to competition in any sport after injury or illness.

This dual responsibility of the team physician is direct and unavoidable and needs the full support of all school personnel involved. The team physician's personal task within this responsibility is to develop an ever-increasing sharpness in on-site diagnostic and prognostic assessments. His competency can be enhanced by review of current literature on athletic medicine, inquiry of medical authorities about unresolved questions, and, where possible, participation in conferences on the medical aspects of sports.

The advantages of personalized supervision

Even a highly qualified physician cannot be at his best if he is unfamiliar with the peculiarities of the sport to be supervised, the characteristics of the athletes who are the subject of his decisions during the season, or the special health problems of the visiting team's personnel with whom he will be involved.

Coordination of the preparticipation health examination is basic. Familiarity with the individual athlete's characteristics come from personal acquaintance, observation, and review

---

*From The Journal of School Health **37**:497, December 1967. Reprinted with the permission of the American Medical Association.

of his medical history. At stake is a workable understanding of the individual's "norm" with respect to his general behavior, capabilities, problems, interests, and responses to success and failure. From such an understanding of the individual, the team physician can gain a more prompt awareness of any deviation from normal and a better sensitivity as to its significance in athletic competition.

Periodic conversations with the coaching staff about their plans, problems, and programs are also helpful. Similar conversations with game officials about rules and the enforcement of rules have been found to be of mutual value. Moreover, discussion of common concerns with team physicians serving other schools—especially those on the particular conference or league schedule—is a definite asset; plans for caring for injured athletes on the visitor's team would be a strategic agenda item.

A bonus comes to the school which involves the team physician in the overall administrative preparations. His familiarity with the school's general health policies and overall athletic operations yield a better protected athlete. In addition, welcome economies through avoiding the purchase of unneccessary supplies and substandard equipment may be realized. The physician's familiarity with the medical and insurance resources in the community also may bring cost-reducing policies and practices in these areas of school responsibility.

In-season care

The school should cooperate with the team physician in having at his disposal during the season: (1) proper equipment for on-site emergency care; (2) an adequately equipped off-site medical station for evaluation and care of athletes whose injuries may not require immediate hospitalization; (3) pre-arranged means for obtaining immediate medical consultation and transportation when time is of the essence. The details of these recommendations differ widely from community to community because of the variables of proximity to a hospital, the preferences of the physician, and the nature of the school's facilities.

There is a distinct difference between on-site medical treatment and first aid care. The first requires a physician's competencies for diagnosis and decisions; the second requires an educated recognition of the problem and appropriate temporary actions until medical services can be obtained. Arresting a simple nose bleed is within the realm of first aid, assuming the delay is insignificant. At the other

extreme, the proper emergency first aid care of an athlete's suspected neck or spinal injury is to take no action except to obtain the assistance of a physician immediately.

Between these two extremes are the injuries that require off-site medical treatment of athletes who are removed from play. An emergency medical station, near but not at the site of action, will give the team physician the opportunity to make a prompt but unhurried initial evaluation of the injury.

Whatever the arrangements, conditions should be such as to foster public respect for the purposes of sports and confidence in the protection of the athlete through responsible health supervision of sports. Any injury that appears sufficiently serious to receive more than simple first aid care merits an unhurried evaluation that is difficult to provide in close proximity to excited fans and competitors. On-site medical treatment of the athlete has a potent psychological impact, especially in sports such as wrestling or basketball, where the spectators are looking over the shoulders of the physician and the athlete under treatment. Moreover, treatment is more satisfactorily administered under the more clinically desirable conditions of a medical station.

There are instances where on-site treatment is medically advisable. The physician may elect to reduce a dislocation on the spot, for example, if intense pain or the risk from delay in reduction is too great. Obviously, these decisions and actions presuppose a team physician whose degree of skill and experience is matched by discretion.

Relationships

Communication among all parties involved in health supervision of sports is of the utmost importance if satisfactory cooperation and coordination is to be achieved. The team physician with both the authority of the school to act in its behalf and the involvement of medical society representatives in the program's planning has the best opportunity to fulfill his responsibilities ethically and effectively. Of special significance is the relationship of the team physician to his medical colleagues who are the family physicians of his athletes and the specialists with whom he may consult. Unless by coincidence or by advance agreement with particular colleagues, the athletes for which the team physician is responsible are not his patients in the long term sense. Therefore, pre-existing relationships must be respected and preserved.

The team physician's role thus is related to immediate health supervision and to referral for follow-up medical treatment, the particulars of which have been spelled out in that school's health policies. The school can further assist in this distinction by stipulating in the parents' "authorization to participate" form that approval is given for emergency medical care by the team physician at the time of participation.

The team physician, however, will have a responsible interest in seeing that his athletes obtain appropriate followup treatment. This interest may be pursued appropriately by

- discussing the progress of a disabled athlete with the attending physician;
- assisting his colleagues (individually or in conference session) in becoming oriented to authoritative principles of athletic medicine;
- evaluating periodically the approaches to total care of the athlete with officials representing the school, the medical society, insuring agencies, and other appropriate groups;
- helping the parents and athletes to understand their respective responsibilities in the conduct of the coordinated program.

Nonmedical coordinator

The duties of the team physician are best carried out if a member of the school faculty has the responsibility for coordination with the physician. Such a person is needed to help consolidate the athletic and health considerations involved in advance planning, on-site supervision, road trips, direct communication with the athlete, and administrative liaison with the school nurse or health officer.

Road trips, for example, usually cannot be expected of the high school team physician. Incorporated into the schools' procedures should be a definite mechanism for the home team physician to meet the visiting team's nonmedical coordinator for mutal consideration of pertinent information.

Preferably, this person would be a qualified athletic trainer; his competencies are directly related to both the school's and physician's responsibilities. However, few high schools have a qualified athletic trainer. The alternatives include an assistant coach assigned to handle trainer responsibilities or a faculty safety coordinator who can attend all athletic sessions.

Summary

The team physician's function relates to decisions of medical eligibility of youthful participants in athletics. This involves consulation during the advance preparations for the season, requires competent management of emergencies, and includes appropriate referral and followup of athletes with conditions requiring further treatment. He is also concerned with the recording and collation of pertinent information bearing on the decisions he must make.

Such functions can be handled by a series of alternating physicians if such a course of action is essential. It would certainly be better, however, for a single physician to function regularly in this capacity. The advantages of such a plan with respect to his knowledge of the athletes and his understanding of the job are obvious.

MEMBERS OF THE COMMITTEE

Donald B. Slocum, M.D., *Chairman*
Eugene, Oregon

Jack C. Hughston, M.D.
Columbus, Georgia

Jack W. Kennedy, M.D.
Arkadelphia, Arkansas

William D. Paul, M.D.
Iowa City, Iowa

Alexius Rachun, M.D.
Ithaca, New York

Kenneth D. Rose, M.D.
Lincoln, Nebraska

Richard C. Schneider, M.D.
Ann Arbor, Michigan

Thomas E. Shaffer, M.D.
Columbus, Ohio

Fred V. Hein, Ph.D., *Secretary*
Chicago, Illinois

Kenneth S. Clarke, Ph.D., *Staff Coordinator*
Chicago, Illinois

58 ᔕ ESSENTIAL ASPECTS OF PROVIDING MEDICAL SERVICES FOR ATHLETES*

Current practices often are cruel and inhuman

ALLAN J. RYAN, M.D.
UNIVERSITY HEALTH SERVICE, UNIVERSITY OF WISCONSIN,
MADISON, WISCONSIN

This presentation was made at the 1967 National Conference for State High School Coaches Association. It is a direct and forthright discussion of a matter which is of utmost importance to both the administrator and coach of interscholastic athletics.

Basic questions remain

For the past 10 years we have been talking together—physicians, coaches, trainers, physical educators, athletic directors, school administrators and parents—about the provision of medical services for high school athletes. It is time to take stock of what we should work together for in the future.

Is there a need for medical supervision of high school sports? You would find relatively few people who would answer this question with a direct, "no". Yet how much medical supervision of high school sports, with the exception of football, really takes place? Where such supervision does exist, what is the extent and quality of this supervision? These are not really different questions, but related to the answer to the first since they bear on the results which are one of our principal means of determining need.

A few horrible examples

Allow me to draw from some personal experiences, which are not unique since my colleagues tell me of very similar situations which they are experiencing, to suggest some answers to the question of the need for good medical supervision. At the University of Wisconsin we have a program of adaptive physical education for those undergraduates who seek personally or through their family physicians to be excused from the one semester required program. In one semester recently we had 27 male freshman enrolled who were suffering from defects in the musculo-skeletal system. Eighteen of these had defects which were the result of sports competition in high school. Of these eighteen, eleven had occurred in football, three in basketball and one in ice hockey.

To cite a few examples, one boy first injured the "ligaments" of his knee in 1961. In 1962 he suffered what was called a "subluxation" of the knee. Finally, in 1965 he suffered an injury to a "cartilage" in the same knee. The lateral semi-lunar cartilage was removed. When he was examined by us the knee was still markedly unstable and hyperextensible in spite of fairly good strength in the thigh muscles. Two boys had been allowed to suffer three occurrences of dislocation of the kneecap before surgery. Both showed marked atrophy of the thigh muscles on the operated leg and instability of the kneecap on the opposite leg. Two other boys had suffered repeated injuries to one knee and had been treated by "whirlpool" therapy only and brief periods on crutches. Both have had recurrent "locking" of the knee, a sure sign of old injury to the meniscus, and both also show loss of the anterior cruciate ligament and partial ruptures of the medical collateral ligament.

Boys may hide information

We have two boys who were recruited to play football who had both suffered recurrent dislocations of both kneecaps in highschool. One had participated as a freshman the year before I arrived at Wisconsin and suffered dislocations in both fall and spring practice. The second boy concealed the history of his previous injuries and it was not uncovered until he had suffered another dislocation in freshman practice. Neither of these boys will play any more football at Wisconsin. Another freshman dislocated his shoulder on the football practice field and popped it back again before the trainer could get across the field to him. Although he had denied previous injuries on his admission history-taking and physical examination for football, he admitted at this point to 15 dislocations of one shoulder and 10 of the other suffered while playing basketball and football in high school. He refused reconstructive surgery for both shoulders and subsequently left college.

Another freshman dislocated his shoulder on

*From School Activities **39**(3):17, November 1967. Used by permission.

the second day of practice. It was easily reduced, indicating a previous injury. He then admitted to a previous dislocation in his senior year at high school. How was it treated? "I came off the field to the sidelines, the coach pulled it back in and I went back into the game on the next play." Was there any subsequent treatment? "I played every game for the rest of the season." This boy had reconstructive surgery for his shoulder but because of family reasons left school at the end of the term and did not return. Cases such as these could be multiplied endlessly but I will not tax you further with them.

The statistical evidence

Take the twentieth annual report of high school football fatalities, the most recent year for which complete figures have been released publicly. There were 20 fatalities, not a great number considering the estimated one million senior and junior high school participants covered by the survey. Nineteen of these were due to injuries to the head and the neck. The report goes on to say,

> Since 1960 almost all of the direct fatalities have been caused by brain and neck injuries. It becomes more evident each year that there is an increasing need for the teaching of 'heads-up' tackling and blocking. Head and neck fatal injuries must be reduced. Continuous studies divulge that coaches will need to teach their players to block and tackle so that their heads do not contact the opponent first. The practice of 'spearing' or 'goring', which is driving the head directly and with force into the chest, stomach and kidney of an opponent when blocking or tackling, is condemned by all responsible persons truly interested in the game of football and the welfare of its participants. The human head is not fashioned to serve as a battering ram. When it is so used, there is danger of hyperflexion, hyperextension or compression of the cervical bones, as is the possibility of concussion. The opponent who receives the blow is in equal or perhaps greater danger of being injured.

Schneider's study confirms

Ample confirmation of these observations is afforded by Dr. Richard Schneider, Professor of Neurosurgery at the University of Michigan who has collected with the aid of his colleagues over 100 cases of head and neck injuries in football which have resulted fatally or in permanent neurologic damage or paralysis. Many of these cases are documented by movies of the games in which they took place, showing the mecha-

nism of driving the head forward into the opponent.

One might fairly ask the question as to where communication has broken down between physicians and coaches so that we are unable to get rid of this dangerous practice. Rules committees have attempted to legislate against it but have succeeded only in placing an almost impossible burden of judgment on the official. There must not only be understanding on the part of the coaches but a strong desire to eliminate this technique of play before we are rid of it.

Heat stroke

Turning to another aspect of the report of the National Federation, it may be noted that there were 14 so-called "indirect" fatalities in the same year. Four of these were definitely attributed to heat stroke, but in an additional five cases there was strong evidence that indicated that heat stroke could have been the sole of a contributing cause of death. The methods of preventing heat stroke in athletes should be well-known to football coaches by this time. They have been widely publicized all over the country for the past seven years every summer, and have been the topic of numerous discussions at Sports Injury Prevention Conferences. Yet one of these boys died after practicing on a field where the air temperature was 98°. What the practices had been in the individual cases with regard to giving salt to the players beforehand, allowing water freely during practice and games, taking rest breaks and so on we don't know. What is apparent in these cases is a breakdown of communication between physicians and coaches, and a lcak of the medical supervision of the sports program.

The situation in wrestling

Lest it be thought that all the problems exist in football, let us shift our attention to another sport of increasing popularity throughout the country—wrestling. Here there is certainly no lack of injuries, here are problems with regard to physical examinations and medical attendance at matches, but above all we have the weight-control problem. Most coaches think of this as a problem only from the standpoint of how to balance their representation in the allowable weight calsses with the boys available. Did you ever stop to think, by the way, about one of the most important reasons why we have only nine weight classes in most states for high school wrestlers? Because nine boys and a coach just fit comfortably into two cars for the purposes of travel.

Regulations ineffectual

A majority of our states today have regulations which are supposed to eliminate the abuses of crash dieting and dehydration. They are so full of loopholes that in effect they amount to no more than pious resolutions. Again, as in the case of "spearing" in football, effective elimination of these practices depends on the willingness of coaches to stop them. Where has communication broken down here between physicians and coaches?

I have received dozens of letters from distressed parents in different parts of the country, some of them physicians, asking what can be done to put an end to these practices. Cases of serious illness in young boys who have followed them are recounted in these letters. In one community in our state not far from Madison, a newspaper write-up of a local high school wrestler who has been quite successful for the past three years appeared this last fall. It stated that this boy has cut his weight as much as 23 pounds to wrestle in certain meets, and he wrestles in the lower weight classes. He lives with his coach all during the week during his competitive season in order to accomplish these feats of weight control and only goes home to his family who live in the same town, on weekends. These facts were personally attested to me by an official who works in the conference in which this boy wrestles and knows him.

Warnings were given

The American Medical Association has made many public statements about these abuses, the most recent being a very complete summary of the situation entitled. "Wrestling and Weight Control" issued in January of this year. The health hazards to the competitor are pointed out. The disadvantages as far as competition are [sic] concerned are made clear. Specific references to scientific studies corroborating the statements made are given and the elements for a sensible weight control program are outlined. Yet when I attended the weighin for our state high school wrestling tournament just a month ago, there was a "sweat-box" standing right next to the scale, and it was being used. Kids were running around in rubber jackets and suits over their sweat clothes. Some of the boys looked so dehydrated I really felt sorry for them. One boy told me he had nothing but an egg and a glass of grapefruit juice each day for the preceding week.

So much for as the kids say today, "what is happening". It is not because of lack of effort to improve the situation on the part of both schools and physicians. Indeed, in spite of the bad examples referred to, there has been considerable improvement in almost every part of the country: Just to take one of many examples let us look for a minute at West Virginia.

West Virginia has done something

Five years ago a state committee on the Medical Aspects of Sports was organized with a membership of ten team physicians from different areas of the state and representatives from the school and college associations in the state. This committee works closely with the secondary school activity commission. They made a survey of the state's high schools and found that all of the 118 high schools reporting had physical examinations of their football players made before the season. Sixty-three had regular team physicians and 52 had good game coverage and on-call service of physicians. Only three had inadequate coverage.

The committee recommended in 1965 that a preseason conditioning program of one to two weeks without contact should precede regular football practice. A subsequent survey indicated that 119 of 128 schools accepted this recommendation and 100 reported fewer injuries than during the previous season. They have asked all county medical societies to be responsible for seeing that every school with a sports program has good medical coverage. The chairman of this committee has recently been elected to honorary life membership in the state coaches association, indicating the degree of cooperation and teamwork which is present.

What do you really want?

What can the individual coach do to improve medical supervision of sports? First I would suggest that you ask yourself frankly if you really want good medical supervision and all that goes with it. Are you willing to accept constructive criticism with regard to the medical aspects of training and conditioning including diet? Do you feel that a boy is being "molly-coddled" if he is kept out of a practice or a game by a physician for an injury or an illness which still allows him to attend his regular school classes? Incidentally, I came across a high school conference recently that had to adopt a rule that if a boy were too sick or injured to attend classes that he could not practice or play in an interscholastic sport! Do you resent it if a boy who has had a concussion without being unconscious is held out for the rest of the game by a physician who has doubts as to whether a fairly severe injury may not have occurred? Would you argue with the best judgment of a physician who feels that a boy with only one testicle or one serviceable eye should not play in a contact sport? If you can answer the first question "yes" and the other three "no", then you are ready on your part to undertake a cooperative program with a team physician.

Selecting a team physician

Probably your school already has some arrangement with a physician to provide medical supervision for its athletes. Are you satisfied that you are getting the coverage and attention you would like to have? Does your physician show a real interest in sports and a good understanding of the problems that you have to face as a coach? Is there something more that you can do on your part to foster this interest?

Some of the things that can happen to impair a physician's effectiveness as a team physician are a growing and too-busy practice, loss of interest due to several unfavorable or unfortunate experiences arising from conflict between parents' and athletes' wishes and medical recommendations which have been made, or misunderstanding arising from the ill-advised attempt of the physician to trespass into the area of the coach's authority. If you have reason to believe that the physician is not following practices that are commonly accepted according to what you have been able to read about or have heard in sports injury conferences, then you might have reason to look for a change.

Sometimes a tactful suggestion to an older man that he should accept a younger man as an assistant to take on some of the burden of coverage will accomplish a great deal if the right young man who has the time and interest can be found. Beware of taking a physician simply because he is a friend or a father of one of your athletes, unless there is no other way to get one. Actually your friend might be ideally suited by his training, experience and interest to do the job, in which case you would want to have him, but try to see to it that he is appointed by the school and that his selection meets with the approval of the local or county medical society. Neither of you should feel mutually obligated except to provide the best possible supervision for the athletes.

Ask the medical society

Where you don't have a physician and don't know where you are going to get one put the matter in the hands of your local or county medical society. If it is not possible for them to recommend one man to do the job they will try to arrange some sort of joint coverage until you can make a more satisfactory arrangement.

The essential medical facilities

What should you be looking for in the way of medical supervision? Well, depending on the circumstances you may have to settle for something less than what you might consider ideal, but don't compromise on what you consider to be essential, no matter what it is. Remember that your success in getting it may depend not only on your willingness to be cooperative but also, to some extent, on the facilities you have to offer. It is not necessary in a high school program to have a fancy training room with elaborate equipment. What your physician would like to have is a small room into which you can fit an examining table, treatment table, desk and a couple of chairs. This equipment can be very simple and plain. It is the privacy and the availability of proper space and light to work with that are valuable.

You would certainly like to have a short medical history and physical examination for each of your athletes every year. Even if these are not all done by your team physician they should be available for his review. You would want him to check every athlete with a disabling injury that causes him to miss a practice or game, even if the athlete goes to another physician for his treatment. You would want him to say when an injured athlete was ready to return to competition.

You would want him to be present for competition in body contact sports or at least available on immediate call. You would probably like to have him drop around after or during practice sometime in these sports to look at some players and discuss the progress of the team as a whole. You would like to have his advice regarding the athlete's nutrition, their conditioning program, their protective equipment, and their psychological problems individually and collectively if they are difficult.

You want someone who understands the importance of the rehabilitation of the athlete following injury and that it is a matter of teamwork which must begin from the time the injury takes place. Finally, you want someone who you can respect and who will respect you and your athletes. When you have all these things, the implementation of the details of your cooperative effort is not difficult and should be a pleasure.

We have come a long way on this road together, physicians and coaches, and yet we still have a long way to go. By continuing to meet together and talk together about our mutual interests and problems the way will be made smoother and our traveling more pleasant as we seek to serve these two causes which are so important to us all, youth and sport.

PROJECTS AND THOUGHT QUESTIONS

1. What are the essential health services that each school system and each college and university should provide for its students?
2. Survey the health services provided in your school, college, or university. Critically evaluate the services offered.
3. How can an outstanding health service program contribute to a good athletic program? What health services should be provided for athletes?
4. List the procedures that should be followed in a thorough medical examination.
5. What administrative problems are commonly involved in the health service program, and what solutions would you propose for each.
6. Identify the persons who are responsible for and carry out the health service program in a school, a college, or a university. Do a job analysis on the duties performed by each of these individuals.
7. Prepare a case study of a student who utilized the health services of a school or college and thereby contributed to his health.
8. What administrative measures do you feel should be taken to ensure that adequate precautions are taken in case of injury or accident?

SELECTED READINGS

Bucher, C. A.: Administration of health and physical education programs, including athletics, ed. 5, St. Louis, 1971, The C. V. Mosby Co.

Eiserer, P. E.: The school psychologist, New York, 1963, The Center for Applied Research in Education, Inc., The Library of Education.

Ferguson, D. G.: Pupil personnel services, New York, 1963, The Center for Applied Research in Education, Inc., The Library of Education.

Joint Committee on Health Problems in Education, National Education Association and American Medical Association: School health services, Washington, D. C., 1964, National Education Association.

National Committee on School Health Policies: Suggested school health policies, ed. 3, Chicago, 1962, American Medical Association.

CHAPTER 11 THE ENVIRONMENT FOR HEALTH EDUCATION AND PHYSICAL EDUCATION PROGRAMS

The environment for health education and physical education programs has two facets: the physical and the psychological. Included in the physical considerations is the provision for facilities that take into account physiological needs of the student, such as proper temperature control, lighting, water supply, and noise control. Another consideration would be the provision of facilities that take into account protection against accidents. The facilities should be planned so that the danger of fire, the possibility of mechanical accidents, and the hazards involved in student traffic would be eliminated or kept to a minimum. A third consideration would be protection against disease. Attention to such items as proper sewage disposal, sanitation procedures, and water supply would be required. Many of these considerations are discussed in Chapter 12, "The Physical Plant."

In order to have a mentally healthful and educational environment, we must be concerned with more than the physical aspects such as facilities. It is necessary to take into consideration the administrative practices that involve the psychological environment and that play an important role in providing for the total health of the student. The number of emotionally disturbed students in our society, for example, shows the necessity for coming to grips with this problem. Health educators and physical educators should be especially concerned with mental health and emotional health because of their close relationship to physical health and illness.

Good mental health is a state of mind that allows the individual to adjust in a satisfactory manner to whatever life has to offer. Good mental health cannot be thought of as a subject that is included in the school or college curriculum. Instead, it must permeate the total life of the educational institution in that programs are flexible and geared to individual needs, a permissive climate prevails, and students are allowed considerable freedom and become responsible for their own actions.

School and college programs are excellent laboratories for developing good human relations, democratic methods, responsibility, self-reliance, and other essentials for happy and purposeful living. The degree to which these laboratories are utilized for such purposes depends upon administrative officers, teachers, custodians, and other staff members. Such important considerations as administrative policies, teachers' personalities, program, human relations, and professional personnel will determine to what extent educational programs justify their existence in human betterment.

The articles in this chapter point up considerations for a healthful environment for students.

Beeman N. Phillips conducted a study in which he developed a school anxiety scale to determine the extent to which school anxiety is a function of school experience and to determine the degree to which school behavior is a function of school anxiety. Phillips believes that the results indicate that school anxiety and school motivation define characteristic reactions to social and academic demands of schooling.

In the next article, Matthew W. Gaffney states that the purpose of the secondary school is the building of self-directed students. In Cold Spring Harbor, New York, the students' free period allows a chance for guidance, quiet study, group study, language practice, or a visit to a teacher's office. Students have this choice every day, and the program has been successful, based on the fact that repeated violations of school policy have been few and far between.

Gene Jordan expresses the fact that teachers of other disciplines feel that physical education is fun time and play time, and he says that punishment for common misdemeanors often comes in the form of withholding students from physical education classes. Jordan thinks that this form of punishment deprives a child of an important phase of the educational process and of life's process, since physical education is part of the educational process, which includes physical activity, which is most important to a growing child.

Student rioting, common to many school campuses, is explained by Robert E. Calmes as a questioning, by youth, of our educational institutions and the concepts they teach. This unrest can be avoided if teachers present a democratic model, show a willingness to examine generally accepted ideas, and develop student respect for mores that constitute mature behavior. Teachers, Calmes believes, must present an attitude of trust and genuine interest.

59 ✌ THE NATURE OF SCHOOL ANXIETY AND ITS RELATIONSHIP TO CHILDREN'S SCHOOL BEHAVIOR *[1]

BEEMAN N. PHILLIPS
THE UNIVERSITY OF TEXAS AT AUSTIN

Several years ago a project[2] was initiated which had several major purposes. One was to develop a school anxiety scale. Another was to determine the extent to which school anxiety is a function of school experience. A third was to determine the degree to which school behavior is a function of school anxiety. And finally, we were interested in the extent to which these foregoing relationships held for children with different socio-cultural backgrounds.

The subjects in the major portion of the project included more than 500 fourth graders in eight elementary schools selected to represent the socio-culturally diverse groups in a city of 225,000. Approximately half of the sample was split between middle class Anglos and upper-lower class Anglos, and the remainder was split between lower class Negroes and Mexican-Americans. Data were gathered at the beginning and end of fourth grade, and again at the beginning and end of fifth grade, from the children themselves, from teachers, from standardized tests, and from cumulative records. In peripheral studies, some additional data were gathered from these children as sixth graders, and from other samples of children in the city.

Conception of school anxiety

Originally, we conceived of school anxiety in two ways: as a function of a disposition to be anxious, and as a function of the anxiety evoking potential of school situations. This conception is summarized in Figure 1. We patterned our thinking partly after the work of the Yale group (Sarason, Davidson, Lighthall, Waite, &

Ruebush, 1960), and justified the extrapolation from test anxiety to school anxiety on the grounds that other school situations share the characteristics of test situations, although perhaps not to the same degree.

In developing the concept of test anxiety, the Yale group have emphasized the role of evaluation in test and test-like situations; and since most school situations are explicitly or implicitly evaluation-oriented, essentially the same theoretical framework can be applied to the concept of school anxiety. Also, granting that school situations have many common characteristics, learning theory suggests that an original anxiety response in a school situation is likely to be extended or generalized to other school situations through similarity of associated cues, and through stimulus generalization. Thus, utilizing the terminological distinctions of Levitt (1967) and Spielberger (1966) in their recent books on anxiety, our definition of school anxiety appears to lie somewhere between the usual definitions of situational and trait anxiety.

At the same time, considering the implications of studies which indicate that response styles account for a significant proportion of the variance in personality questionnaires, we conceptualized the major response styles as aspects of defensiveness, and considered it conceptually logical to think of defensiveness as leading to, or as being manifested in, two styles of coping as indicated in Figure 2.

Also, it may be argued that anxiety and defensiveness differ in significant ways, and that the effects of anxiety and defensiveness in school depend on the nature of the situation. Specifically, it is likely that children have developed characteristic responses to anxiety evoked by school situations, and that these reactions generally are unadaptive rather than adaptive in school situations. Furthermore it is likely that children differing in anxiety will exhibit greater differences in unadaptive behaviors in evaluative, academic, and structured school situations than in permissive, social, and unstructured school situations. However, it is likely that children differing in defensiveness will exhibit greater differences in adaptive and unadaptive behaviors in permissive, social, and unstructured school situations than in evalua-

---

*From Psychology in the Schools 5:195, July 1968. Used by permission.

[1] Presented at American Psychological Association Symposium on "Anxiety and School Behavior," (Janet Taylor Spence, Chairman) Washington, September 1967.

[2] The project was supported from 1964–1966 by a grant from the USOE Cooperative Research Branch; and of the many graduate students who have been involved, it is necessary to single out Keith McNeil, Russell Adams, and Ed Gotts as professional collaborators.

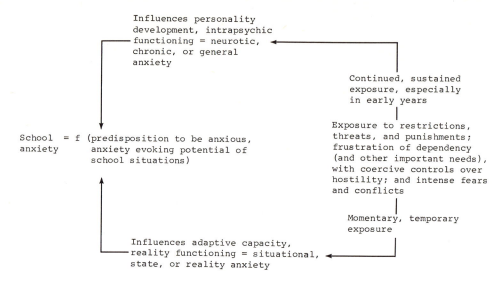

FIGURE 1. The nature of school anxiety schematically represented.

tive, academic, and structured school situations. And it is anticipated that defensive children with an approach style of coping will generally exhibit adaptive behaviors, while defensive children with an avoidance style of coping will generally exhibit unadaptive behaviors, in these social aspects of schooling.

Factor analysis of the children's school questionnaire

The children's School Questionnaire was developed to measure school anxiety and coping style, and it consists of 198 orally administered items randomly assigned to three forms which were administered about a week apart. Most of the items were taken from research instruments previously appearing in the literature, including items representing defensiveness, test, audience, recitation, and generalized anxiety, in addition to a number of items prepared by the project staff. CSQ item responses in the Fall, fourth grade, and the Fall, fifth grade, were factored using image analysis; and clearly replicated school anxiety and coping style factors were obtained. The school anxiety factor had 74 items, and the coping style factor had 37. "Factor scores" for these scales were obtained by assigning unit weights to the items and summing. Based on Horn's (1965) observations, this simple method seemed preferable to more elaborate factor scoring techniques. These separate sets of items were subjected to subsequent factor analysis, but time would not permit a consideration of those results. The stability of school anxiety scores across

the school year was high: for fourth grade it was .63 and for fifth grade it was .68. The stability of coping style scores was lower, being .37 for fourth grade and .48 for fifth grade.

Some other project variables

As previously noted, a number of different kinds of information on children was obtained in the project. And in some instances, variables were derived from instruments developed in the project. These and other school behavioral variables need to be briefly described; and where variables stem from project-developed instruments, representative items are presented.

A. Representative items for school anxiety, approach coping style, avoidance coping style, sex-linked interests and attitudes, and self disparagement in relation to peers, which were derived through factor analyses of the Children's School Questionnaire, are:

School anxiety scale (SA)
Factor 1 (negative valuation by others)
Do your classmates sometimes make fun of the way you look and talk?
When you recite in class do you often wonder what others are thinking of you?
Are you frequently afraid you may make a fool of yourself?
Factor 2 (taking tests)
After you have taken a test do you worry about how well you did on the test?
Do you worry a lot while you are taking a test?
Do you worry about being promoted, that is, passing from the . . grade to the . . grade at the end of the year?

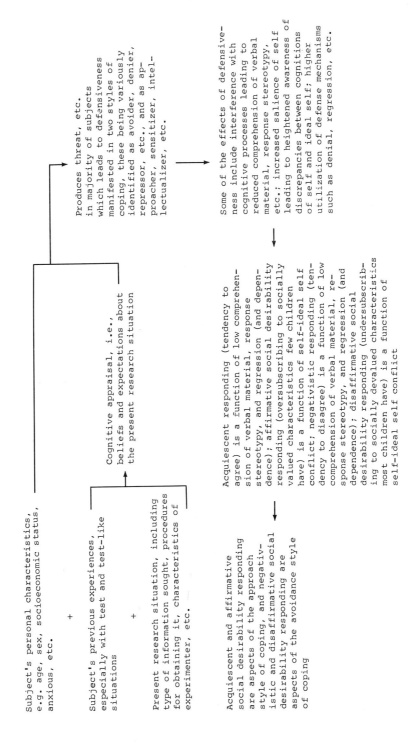

FIGURE 2. Response styles schematically represented as aspects of approach and avoidance styles of coping. (Adapted from Lazarus, 1964.)

Factor 3 (lack of confidence in meeting expectations of others)

Do you have a hard time keeping up with the other students in class?

In your school work, do you often forget; or do you feel sure you can remember things?

Is it hard for you to have as good a report card as your parents expect you to have?

Factor 4 (physiological reactivity)

Do you sometimes shake all over when you are asked to recite in class?

Do your knees shake when you are asked to recite in class?

Do you sometimes have a fear of fainting in class?

Sex-linked interests and attitudes scale (S)

Are you as good in games like kickball as other students in class?

Would you rather listen to music; or ride a bicycle?

If two children were fighting on the playground, would you go tell the teacher; or let them fight?

Would you rather read a book; or play ball?

Self disparagement in relation to peers (SD)

Can others do things better; or can you do most things well?

Do people think you make many mistakes' or few mistakes?

Do your classmates make fun of you for the way you play in school games?

Do you generally do what your friends like to do even though you sometimes want to do something else?

Coping style scale (CS)

Approach coping style (PCS)

To get others to like you do you try to find nice things to say about them?

When you have done well on something, do you feel pleased with yourself even when no one else in the class notices what you have done?

Do you always raise your hand in class when you know the answer?

When you are working in a group, do you usually volunteer for more work than anyone else in the group?

Do you always think that mother's way of doing things is better; or do you sometimes think your own way is better?

When the teacher gives an assignment, do you get busy on it right away?

Avoidance coping style (VCS)

Do you ever worry?

Are you ever unhappy?

Has anyone ever been able to scare you?

When you make something in class, do you try to make sure that all the other children see it?

Do you wish that your teacher paid more attention to you?

Do you get angry when you are working on something important in class and someone interrupts you?

B. Representative items for the eight problem behavior variables are:

Variable	Items or sketches
Aggression, with independence strivings (AI)	(3) Cruelty, Bullying; (11) Impertinence, Defiance; (22) Resentfulness; (44) Fights with little provocation; (62) Stubbornly resists the will and authority of the teacher
Active withdrawal (AW)	(13) Inattention; (16) Lack of interest in work; (17) Laziness; (43) Uses real or imagined inferiorities as an excuse for not really trying; (72) Uses laziness as a means of attracting attention
Emotional disturbance with depression (ED)	(10) Fearfulness; (25) Sensitiveness; (37) Unhappy, depressed; (39) Unsocial, withdrawing; (70) Is sad and apathetic
Self enhancement through derogation of others (SE)	(19) Overcritical of others; (33) Tattling; (41) Clings to teacher and seeks to be near her and hold her hand; (45) Exhibits righteousness, snobbishness
Diffuse hyperactivity (DH)	(7) Disorderliness in class; (23) Restlessness; (52) Is a compulsive talker; (65) Attracts attention by being a nuisance; (66) Exhibits constant movement of fingers or hands, persistent perspiring of parts of the body
Feelings of inferiority (FI)	(2) This child is sensitive to criticism. He is unable to react constructively to criticism; and he devotes much effort to prove his solutions to problems are the correct ones. (6) This child overresponds to flattery. He is easily led by those who praise him; and because he feels a great need to prove his adequacy, anyone who supports it gets a warm reception.
Neurotic symptoms associated primarily with academic tasks (NA)	(8) This child has a spotty performance record, in that while achievement in most areas is average or better, achievement in one or more specific areas is unaccountably low. It almost seems that he "blanks out," or has a mental block for some things. (15) This child has unrealistically high expectations for himself, more

than could be expected from past performances or scores on aptitude tests. He responds to test scores and report card grades with remarks similar to "I can do better."

Neurotic symptoms associated primarily with social relations (NS)

(17) This child generally does not get along very well with children his own age or in his own class. He usually plays with children who are younger and in lower grades, and the games he plays are those appropriate for younger children. (23) This child gives the impression of always having his guard up, so that it's difficult to know how he feels and what he's thinking. He is unlikely to share secrets with anyone, especially an adult. He rarely expresses either pleasure or displeasure about what happens to him.

For the first five variables listed, a pool of 72 overt, discrete school problem behaviors were orginally collected—40 from the series of studies initiated by the classic research of Wickman, and the remaining 32 from the literature on children's school learning and behavior difficulties. Teachers' nominations of children for these 72 characteristics on all four testing occasions were combined and a factor analysis of these results produced the five problem behavior variables listed. (This classification system for discrete pupil behaviors utilizes the teachers' own underlying observational categories; it does not necessarily provide the most psychologically interpretable and useful classification system, and Gotts (1968) discusses an alternative procedure for classifying these discrete pupil behaviors.) The sketches on which the remaining three problem behavior variables are based were derived from psychoanalytically-oriented studies of children's school learning and behavior difficulties by Blanchard (1946), Klein (1949), and Pearson (1952).

C. The basis for the school motivation variable, which was defined as desire and effort toward, as well as pleasure in, doing well in school academically and socially, was forced-distribution ratings by teachers of children on eight behavioral characteristics. These characteristics rated are: shows evidence of strong pleasure in good work; enjoys working with others and participating actively in groups; concerned with lessons and careful about work; eager, energetic, and frequently volunteers; frequently helpful and sympathetic to others with problems; tries hard to make friends and to be accepted; seeks social recognition and likes offices and leadership roles; strikingly attentive to tasks.

D. Peer acceptance and peer rejection were based on a typical sociometric instrument with one exception, that being that only same-sex choices were allowed. (It should be noted, also, that peer acceptance and rejection are considered as separate psychological "dimensions," a decision supported both conceptually and empirically in this project.)

E. The Metropolitan Achievement Test and the California Test of Mental Maturity also were administered on the four occasions, and in addition, teacher grades in academic subjects were obtained during both school years.

Stability coefficients across each school year were computed for all these variables, and

internal consistency estimates were obtained for most, and these results generally were satisfactory.

Correlates of school anxiety

The validity and generality of our school anxiety scale has been investigated in several studies peripheral to the project's main purposes. At the end of the first year of a four year previously unreported study of non-graded versus graded patterns of organizing children for instructional purposes in a homogeneous, upper middle class school, it was found that non-graded children had decreased in school anxiety, while graded children had not (Otto & Phillips, in progress). In a study of early school experience using information from the cumulative record, we found that school anxiety in fourth grade can be predicted as early as first grade, sometimes with surprising accuracy (Phillips, 1967). In a study of over- and under-achievement, using Thorndike's suggestion for computing a measure of over- and under-achievement in which the effects of intelligence are partialled [sic] out, it was found that school anxiety was related to under-achievement (Adams & Phillips, 1968). In a study of the degree of socialization into middle class culture, based on the semantic differential, small negative correlations between degree of socialization and school anxiety were obtained.[3] In a study of birth order, there was no difference in school anxiety between first-born and later-born children, but as predicted from Schachter's theory, there was a tendency for high-anxious first-born to pick popular peers more often and to reject disliked peers more often than high-anxious later-born.[4] Finally, in a study based on developmental

[3] McNeil, K. A., & Phillips, B. N. Scholastic nature of responses to the environment in selected subcultures. Unpublished manuscript, 1967.

[4] Adams, R. L., & Phillips, B. N. Motivational and achievement differences among children of various ordinal birth positions. Unpublished manuscript, 1967.

theory, it was found that masculinity-femininity was significantly related to the school anxiety of boys, but not girls (Gotts & Phillips, 1968).

Multivariate analysis of school anxiety and coping style in relation to school behavior

As Levitt (1967) has pointed out, multivariate theories of anxiety do not exist, and the results of multifactor studies sometimes are confusing and ambiguous. Yet, it is a psychological truism that human behavior is determined by complex constellations of factors, and the further development of anxiety theory requires multivariate investigations. We generally proceeded from this premise in our research on school anxiety, and in the multivariate analyses to be discussed next, a fixed-model analysis of variance was employed with Anglo versus Non-Anglo, high anxiety versus low anxiety, high motivation versus low motivation, and approach coping style versus avoidance coping style as the fixed effects, and with the other variables being considered as the dependent variables. High anxiety, high motivation and approach coping style included the subjects with scores above the median on three of the four testing occasions; and low anxiety, low motivation, and avoidance coping style included subjects with scores below the median on three of the four test occasions.[5]

As to the results for the main effects, high and low anxiety consistently differentiates between adaptive and unadaptive behavior in school. High-anxious children generally engage in more problem behavior, are disliked more by peers, see themselves in more disparaging ways, and are lower in school achievement and aptitude. Not surprisingly, approach and avoidance coping style also consistently distinguishes between adaptive and unadaptive behavior. In fact, coping style actually is more discriminating than school anxiety with respect to problem behaviors. However, there are few differences between approach and avoidance coping style in school achievement and aptitude where differences for school anxiety are highly significant.

As to the main effects of high and low moti-

vation, we expected these to be consistently significant, partly because there is a lack of independence between school motivation and some of the other variables, although this effect is diluted somewhat since two different teachers' observations are averaged. Also, Non-Anglos generally have slightly higher problem behavior means with the exception of emotional disturbance with depression where Anglos have the higher mean; and, of course, Non-Anglos have lower school achievement and aptitude means, as expected. It should be added that it is likely that the procedures for obtaining teachers' nominations for the problem behavior variables reduced somewhat the Anglo-Non-Anglo differences on these means.

Taken together, therefore, these results for the main effects indicate that school anxiety and school motivation define characteristic reactions to both the social and the academic demands of schooling, while coping style primarily defines characteristic reactions to only the social demands of schooling.

As to the interactive effects of these variables, since high motivation produces adaptive reactions to school situations, when the joint effects of school motivation and school anxiety, and school motivation and coping style, are considered, the circumstances are indicative of conflict which may be conceptualized in terms of approach and avoidance tendencies (Miller, 1959). And summarizing the joint effects of school anxiety and school motivation as well as the joint effects of coping style and school motivation, the presence of conflict appears to be more deleterious to Non-Anglos than Anglos. That is, high anxiety combined with high motivation, and avoidance coping style combined with high motivation, appear to increase, relativity speaking, the problem behavior means, and to decrease, relatively speaking, the school achievement and aptitude means. These deleterious consequences possibly occur (especially for Non-Anglo children) because the adaptive tendencies associated with high motivation (in the *absence* of high anxiety or avoidance coping style) are debilitated by the *presence* of high anxiety or avoidance coping style. But, possibly they occur because the unadaptive tendencies associated with high anxiety and avoidance coping style are facilitated by the presence of high motivation. Also, it is possible that high motivation differs in such a way among Anglos and Non-Anglos that the highly motivated Non-Anglo is more vulnerable to both of these potential effects of conflict. For example, fear of failure, ambivalence toward success, and

---

[5] Supplementary tabular material has been deposited with the American Documentation Institute. Order Document No. 9746 from ADI Auxiliary Publications Project, Photoduplication Service, Library of Congress, Washington, D.C. 20540. Remit in advance $1.25 for photocopies or $1.25 for microfilm and make checks payable to: Chief, Photoduplication Service, Library of Congress.

compensatory tendencies may be more a part of the high motivation of Non-Anglos than Anglos.

Multivariate analysis of school anxiety and coping style in relation to changes in school behavior during the school year

Earlier, school anxiety as a source of differences in school behaviors was considered in the context of learning theory and the Sarason position regarding the effects of anxiety on learning, and the results reported appear to be in general agreement with expectations based on those theories. However, the date analyzed represented averages over the period of two school years, not changes in school behavior; so the results, therefore, are only indirectly or circumstantially relevant. In the multivariate analyses to be discussed next, changes in school behavior from the beginning to the end of the school year were examined, using a repeated measures analysis of variance design (See Footnote 5). Summarizing the results, the following generalizations may be noted:

A. School problem behavior trends to increase more for high-anxious than low-anxious subjects, primarily among Anglos, since there is a tendency for low-anxious Non-Anglo subjects to increase in problem behavior more than high-anxious Non-Anglos.

B. School achievement and aptitude behavior tend to increase more for low-anxious subjects than for high-anxious subjects, especially among Anglos.

C. School problem behavior tends to increase with high motivation more than it does with low motivation, especially for Non-Anglos.

D. School achievement and aptitude behavior tend to increase more for low motivation than for high motivation, especially for Anglos.

E. School problem behavior increases more for subjects with avoidance coping style than for subjects with approach coping style, especially for Non-Anglos.

F. School achievement and aptitude behavior tend to increase more for subjects with approach coping style than for subjects with avoidance coping style, especially for Anglos.

G. Finally, comparatively speaking, school anxiety is involved in more interactions relating to change in school behavior than in interactions relating to overall status in school behavior.

A methodological problem highlighted in these analyses is that increases in school behavior during the school year may be due either to factors which depress these school behaviors at the beginning of the school year, or to factors which elevate these school behaviors at the beginning of the school year, or to factors which elevate these school behaviors at the end of the school year. The problem, therefore, is how to distinguish the two types of factors so that factors which depress school behavior at the beginning of the school year are not interpreted as factors which facilitate increases in these school behaviors during the school year.

A substantive point highlighted in these analyses is that there are both similarities and differences in the school behavioral correlates of school anxiety and coping style, with the particulars being that, while differences in coping style lead to greater differences in the incidence of school problem behaviors, only differences in anxiety lead to systematic differences in school achievement and aptitude behaviors. Therefore, it appears to us that defensiveness and anxiety have somewhat different effects in evaluative (academic) and permissive (social) school conditions. While the results help to illuminate this hypothesis, checking it is a task for the future.

REFERENCES

Adams, R. L., & Phillips, B. N. Factors associated with under- and over-achievement among socio-economically and racial-ethnically different elementary school children. Psychology in the Schools, 1968, 5, 170–174.

Blanchard, P. Psychoanalytic contributions to the problem of reading disabilities. In Anna Freud et al. (eds.), Psychoanalytic study of the child, 1946. Pp. 163–187.

Gotts, E. E. Levels of school anxiety in relation to child personality variables in school. Psychology in the schools, 1968, 5, 217–222.

Gotts, E.E., & Phillips, B.N. The relation between psychometric measures of anxiety and masculinity-femininity. Journal of School Psychology, 1968, 6, 123–129.

Horn, J. L. An empirical comparison of methods for estimating factor scores. Educational and Psychological Measurement, 1965, 25, 313–322.

Klein, E. Psychoanalytic aspects of school problems. In Anna Freud et al. (eds), Psychoanalytic study of the child, 1949. Pp. 369–390.

Lazarus, R. A laboratory approach to the dynamics of psychological stress. American Psychologist, 1964, 19, 400–411.

Levitt, E. E. The psychology of anxiety. Indianapolis: Bobbs-Merrill, 1967.

Miller, N. E. In S. Koch (ed.), Psychology: a study of a science. Vol. 2. General systematic formulations, learning, and special processes. New York: McGraw-Hill, 1959, Pp. 196–292.

Pearson, G. H. J. A survey of learning difficulties in children. In R. S. Eissler et al. (eds.), Psychoanalytic study of the child, 1952. Pp. 322–386.

Phillips, B. N. Anxiety as a function of early school experience. Psychology in the Schools, 1967, 4, 335–340.

Sarason, S. B., Davidson, K. S., Lighthall, F. F., Waite, R. R., & Ruebush, B. K. Anxiety in elementary school children. New York: Wiley, 1960.

Spielberger, C. D. Anxiety and behavior. New York: Academic Press, 1966.

60 ∂ STUDENT BEHAVIOR: VITAL PART OF THE INSTRUCTIONAL PROGRAM IN THE SECONDARY SCHOOL*

MATTHEW W. GAFFNEY
DISTRICT PRINCIPAL, COLD SPRING HARBOR
(NEW YORK) SCHOOLS

The discipline and control of students in the secondary school deserves considerable attention. The American high school is a complicated social institution. Anyone even remotely connected with such an institution, bringing together as it does a large number of growing adolescents for the purposes of education, shortly realizes that such a task cannot be accomplished without clear and concise patterns of teacher and pupil movements within the buildings and within the allotted time span. The issue soon becomes clear that the operation of the school will either result in a controlled environment in which the activities of the school can proceed successfully, or it will be a disorganized disaster.

Impending disaster is such an ever-present fear, that the administrators in charge often create rules and conditions for student movements and control which operate for the purposes of the administration and teachers without taking into consideration the ulterior purposes of the school—the building of a self-directed student; a truly maturing adolescent.

The basic philosophical position from which a policy regarding student discipline and control originates is quite simple. The only purpose of the secondary school is the education of students. The students come to high school just growing out of childhood and it is expected that they will leave six years later quite mature, capable of self-direction and, ultimately, self-instruction. It is important that the basic climate be established and maintained that the school is a workshop. It is a place to get a job done. It is expected that the rules will be reasonable and will be directed toward the ultimate welfare of the students. The school takes the position that the students wish for the success of the school and that they will live within its reasonable rules.

The nonconforming student, violating the

basic rules of the school, must be brought to realize that he is acting in such a way as to injure his own educational opportunity. In addition, he must see that his acts may prevent the school from reaching its purposes for the other students. Discipline, therefore, will take the posture of correction, not punishment. The disciplined student must be brought to realize that the aim of the corrective experience is to create an experience whereby he will learn to be self-directed and to conform to reasonable rules. The school is the last chance for society to help the undisciplined. No opportunity to help should be overlooked.

Self-direction through free periods

The nature of the secondary school with the self-directed assignment of one, two, or more free periods in the course of each instructional day, offers to the school administration the opportunity to establish a setting in which the student may learn the important lesson of self-direction. The older practice of an assigned study hall with a study monitor taking roll and enforcing silence in a confined and sometimes sterile atmosphere falls short of providing this opportunity for self-direction. In its place, the following practice has been instituted.

The central office is provided with the names of students who are not assigned to a specific class instruction for each period of the day. Students who are free in a particular period may elect each day the area to which they wish to report. For students who desire to go to a library area, a language practice room, an independent laboratory, or to the office of a particular teacher who is free at the same time, this choice is open. On arriving at this location, they sign a sheet noting the area and the particular period. This sheet, shortly after the opening of the period, is sent to a recording clerk in the central office.

Students wishing to go to a room where absolute silence is guaranteed and large enough table space is available so that their books and

*From The Clearing House 42:222, December 1967. Used by permission.

papers may be laid out, can choose the study area noted as the "Independent Study." Here a teacher is in charge and is responsible for guaranteeing the contract of silence; silence from teachers and custodians as well as fellow students. Students in this area also sign a sheet which is forwarded to the recording clerk in the central office.

Students wishing to converse with fellow students or to work with groups of four to six where no restrictions are placed on conversation in a normal tone of voice, can go to the "Cooperative Study Area." Here the rules are those of ordinary decorum. Students are expected to select a table of four but may move around freely from table to table as the occasion arises. Talking is permitted at normal voice levels. Students also sign the entry slip which is forwarded to the recording clerk.

Students who have chosen either an independent study area or the library, but do not conform to the rules of quiet studious application are immediately asked (i.e., sent) to the Cooperative Study Area where their impulsive desire to talk with neighbors may be exercised without restraint.

These three areas of choice are open during any free period during the day and may vary from day to day as the desires of the student dictate.

The task of the recording clerk in the central office is to match the students lists arriving from each of the study areas against the list of students who are unassigned according to the particular period. In the event that a student failed to sign into a particular area, he is presumed to be loose within the building or to have taken French leave. The name of the student is then reported to the assistant principal in charge of discipline and the student, when found, is brought before him. His case is reviewed as to whether there has been some error in reporting.

If the student is found to have been unable to assign himself to a particular area and wanders loose, he is now recognized as a student in personal difficulty and unable to operate within a free-choice situation. He is then assigned to a "Directed Study Area."

A Directed Study Area operates each period of the day in the charge of a teacher who is to make sure that the student arrives promptly, that he stays in the room in a condition of absolute silence. No excuses are permitted for leaving the study area except for a dire emergency. The minimum time of assignment to this area is one full school week. At the end of one school week the student may petition for release from this area in a letter of petition addressed to the assistant principal and forwarded to the principal with the approved endorsement of the teacher-in-charge of the Directed Study Area.

Each student who has been assigned to the Directed Study Area is asked to discuss this with his parents. The office of the school sends to the parents an explanation of the assignment of the student to the Directed Study Area. This letter explains its purposes and invites the parents to discuss with their son or daughter the importance of developing self-control and good study habits.

Warning notices of unsatisfactory scholastic success are prepared monthly and at each of the marking periods a list is prepared of the students receiving such notices. This list is placed in the hands of each of the teachers in charge of the cooperative study areas. The students who are on this list and are in regular attendance and seem to appear more than a few times in this study area, are asked to discuss with the teacher-in-charge as to whether they are making the proper choices of their free time.

In addition, the records clerk, who has on file the names of the students who have elected the cooperative study area, makes a tabulation of the number of times the failing or warned student has studied there. A form letter is sent to the parents of the student informing the parents of the continued choice of the student in the Cooperative Study Area and requests the assistance of the parents in reminding the students that this choice may be one of the reasons for their lack of success in their scholastic endeavors. The individual guidance counselor of each of these failing students is given a copy of the letters sent to the parents and is kept informed of the frequency of the non-succeeding student's presence in the Cooperative Study Area.

Minor violations of school rules

School tardiness and tardiness in arriving at assigned classes repeated for more than a relatively few occasions is viewed as evidence of a personality defect. Persistent school tardiness is reviewed by the assistant principal with the offending student. The cause of the tardiness is reviewed and examined on an individualized basis. Where it appears that the home is contributing to the tardiness of the student, a letter to the parents is formulated requesting their assistance. Where the problem of school tardiness appears to be the individual student's personality pattern, a full dress review of the situation is made using the guidance counselors and, if necessary, the services of the parents. The student evidencing a regular pattern of tardiness to school, unexplainable through any outside force, is required to report regularly every day to the assistant principal for discipline. If a penalty seems in order, it is worked out on an individualized basis depending upon the circumstances.

Tardiness to class is charged to the attention of the individual classroom teacher. The tardy student is noted by the classroom teacher and an individual discussion with the student is required. Frequent tardiness to class on the part of the student is reported to the assistant principal for discipline who calls the offending student in for a discussion of the cause of the tardiness. Punishment or penalty are here also worked out on an individual basis.

Major violations of school rules

There are certain actions of students which give evidence of serious social sickness on the part of the student. In addition, certain of these actions profoundly affect fellow students and, if continued unchecked, could well destroy the fabric within which the institution is able to continue. Among these acts are truancy, leaving school in the middle of the session without formal dismissal, insolence to a faculty member, deliberate acts of insubordination to the administration or the faculty, fighting ending in physical violence, the use of tobacco or alcohol, and deliberate destruction of school property.

The discovery of a student engaging in any of these major violations requires immediate action. The offending student is referred to the assistant principal in charge of discipline. It is extremely important that at this point the student not be reprimanded as being a bad person or as one with whom the school must disassociate itself, or one from whom the school authorities will extract penalties and punishment as restitution to the school. Rather, the initial conference with the pupil should search for the cause of the action, inviting the pupil to enter into intellectual search for the reason for his or her actions. In serious cases, the parents are contacted and invited to come to the school and discuss the matter with the school authorities.

The discipline action takes the form of placing the student on probation. A student under probation is required to carry with him throughout the school day and for as long as the probation needs to be continued, a complete schedule

of his or her locations in the building at all times. Each subject matter teacher and each study hall teacher is required to initial for each period for each day under the heading of satisfactory or unsatisfactory conduct. In the event that the student has lost time in school, there is a requirement that the time be made up at the close of school in the afternoon by working silently in one of the school libraries for a minimum period of one hour each day. In the event of destruction of school property, the parents and pupil are requested to make restitution for the amount of damages the school has suffered.

Each student placed on probation has sent to his home a letter to the parents explaining what probation is, the reasons for placing the student on probation, and a determination of the minimum length of time which the student should be on probation. At the conclusion of the probationary period, the student may come into the office of the high school assistant principal and request release from probationary status. His sheets are reviewed and he must next request and receive an interview with the principal of the school. At this time the entire case is reviewed: the causes of the action, the penalties and punishments extracted, and whether the student understands completely the reasons for probation. This is the opportunity for the principal to make sure that the student understands that conduct of this sort cannot be condoned, for the welfare of the pupil and the school system is at stake. The principal alone can remove the student from probation. A follow-up letter is sent to the parents at the time of the removal of the student from probation.

Actual suspension from school for any period of time is used only in the most serious of circumstances and when it is absolutely necessary to protect the school from the presence of a seriously disturbed individual. The services of the school psychologist and other experts are brought in for a full case conference leading to a discussion of and preparation for permanent expulsion.

Does the system work?

The evaluation of a program of discipline is quite easy. How many repeaters are found on probation? How about the percentage of students in the "directed study halls." An "opinion poll" of teachers, parents, and most important of all, students, can easily be prepared and evaluated. If the repeaters are few and far between, if the percentage in the directed study areas is under 2 per cent, and if it is the opinion of the students that the system is fair but firm, then the system works!

61 ᘒ PROPER PUNISHMENT*

GENE JORDAN
PUBLIC SCHOOLS, MARYVILLE, MISSOURI

Is punishing children by keeping them out of physical education time a good practice? Is this the only time and way the teacher can punish the offender for such misdemeanors as chewing gum in class, talking, or not having assignments completed on time?

Perhaps this means of discipline is employed more in grade schools than junior or senior high schools. It is easy for the teacher to tell Johnny he is going to stay in from recess or physical education as punishment. Is this best for the child?

Don't misunderstand me. I'm not opposed to discipline for those deserving little darlings who can't be still or can't remember to do an assignment, but I'm convinced that a better way should be found.

From a legal standpoint a grade teacher may withhold recess privileges from one or more students when he is in charge of the classes' recess, but how can one teacher justify withholding a student from another teacher's class by not allowing a student to go to physical education which is taught by the other teacher.

Suppose physical education teachers refused to send a student back to a grade teacher or academic class because he was rowdy or couldn't do what was required of him in the physical education class. I'm sure the teacher would immediately be jumping down the physical education instructor's throat or bending the principal's ear with his tale of woe.

Too often teachers think of physical education as a playtime or recess which the children enjoy, and withholding them from it is proper punishment. They fail to recognize it as a class where the learning process is taking place just as it takes place in their own classroom and is just as important in its own way as math, art, science, etc.

Just try measuring the value of instilling the importance of good health practices and exercise into youth. Men in their 50s and 60s who exercise, play golf, tennis, hike and swim—where did their interest begin? In an age where we now have more free time, these activities are important.

Many of these older citizens began an interest in these activities through participation in physical education classes, or perhaps, even during recess at a younger age. I'm sure this leaves a lasting impression and I would not want them to remember physical activity as a way of punishment for not doing homework.

Physical education is important, and in some schools where the classes only meet two or three times a week, it is even more important for a child to attend as often as possible. To some children this may be the major share of physical activity that they receive during the day. Far too many will go home and sit in front of the television set until it is time to go to bed.

Punishing a child by keeping him from physical education not only creates ill feeling among teachers, but most important, deprives the child from physical activity which is important to the growing boy. Also, it can disrupt a physical education class by taking members away from teams which have been organized for tournament play or scheduled team game.

Before you refuse to allow a student to go to his next scheduled physical education class, think. Are you doing the best for all concerned?

*From School and Community 53:94, November 1966. Used by permission.

62 ᘒ DISSENT: THE TEACHER'S ROLE*

ROBERT E. CALMES
PROFESSOR, COLLEGE OF EDUCATION, UNIVERSITY OF ARIZONA,
TUCSON, ARIZONA

Student rioting on American campuses must certainly be attributed in some part to the sincere questioning by youth of the value of our

*From Today's Education 57:10, January 1969. Used by permission.

educational institutions and the concepts they teach. These are the same values and concepts which, by and large, many adults have accepted without a great deal of anxiety and have incorporated into a way of life.

Student questioning becomes student dissent

and dissent becomes active disagreement, civil disobedience, rioting and the other manifestations of discord with which we in America have grown familiar.

While a certain degree of dissent has become acceptable and even commendable as a healthy manifestation of a country's freedom and vigor, many people have become concerned over its extent in the United States today. Many likewise cannot comprehend the not infrequent violence and the tendency toward anarchy on some campuses.

It would be impossible in a magazine article to define just what moral precepts must gain universal approval for America to continue its democratic experiment. But nearly everyone would agree that there are limits to civil disobedience. To put it another way, there are restrictions on one's freedom when one is a member of a society.

What then can a teacher do in order to help his students become aware of these restrictions, these moral precepts which one must either impose on his own conduct or accept as impositions—in the form of law—by the society as a whole? What does the available research seem to suggest teachers might do to help the student develop within himself a system of character which would manifest itself in respect for the rights of a society?

It should go without saying that the first need is for the teacher himself to present a democratic model. If the teacher is perceived as living a full and enjoyable life within the framework of a democratic society, it is easier for the student to view such a life, with its composite of freedom and restriction, as ideal.

A teacher encounters students in a relaxed, less defensive, psychologically more receptive mood outside the classroom. If, for example, a teacher displays anger at a referee's decision during a football game—genuine anger that is unrelated to the normal sportsman's displays—he is confusing the students at the game. The teacher has shown a basic disregard in his own life style for the discipline he preaches in the classroom. The students could then conclude rightfully that the way to structure one's life is to do what one is told only at certain times. The teacher has unwittingly served to endorse the cause of civil disobedience.

Secondly, teachers must display a consistency in their willingness to examine generally accepted ideas. If the teacher challenges the students to observe natural phenomena and derive scientific principles from their observations, then he must also allow students to observe *social* phenomena and draw conclusions. The teacher, in other words, cannot simply proclaim that his own interpretation of history, of governmental actions, of varying religious viewpoints and other critical areas of thought, is the correct viewpoint. He must, instead, allow the students, through open classroom discussions, to derive their own conclusions. The consistency—which in turn can give a student a sense of stability and dependability—is found in the willingness to judge *all* philosophies in a critical light.

A third necessity for developing in students a respect for the mores which constitute mature behavior is to display a reasonable, logical spirit of inquiry into the various courses of action that are possible. It is certainly a mark of the American democracy that one is presented with choices of action in a given situation. A totalitarian government tends to remove the choices and substitute an officially endorsed course of action.

Why is it that a teacher demands a certain type of conduct within the classroom? Would other behavioral approaches be equally justified and supported? If when a teacher is confronted by the student on the necessity for a certain course of action, the two can rationally, logically and reasonably discuss the matter, the student will have inherited, perhaps, a new approach to his own dealings with others.

Fourthly, evaluation of a student's behavior, after the fact, can produce in him an appreciation for the freedom of choice that is inherent in a democracy. If the teacher lets his students know how their behavior is perceived by others in a rational dialogue, he may be training them to engage in feedback sessions with others whom they encounter. Later, the ability to react to another's thought or action in a reasonable discussion might aid them as taxpayers, parents, teachers, administrators, supervisors, coaches, secretaries, etc.

When behavior is, in the teacher's view, undesirable, the teacher should be careful to point out that it is the behavior, not the person himself, that is objectionable. And further, it must be made abundantly clear why such behavior is to be avoided. This, of course, takes time and energy; yet, such behavior on a teacher's part greatly aids in the development of a level of character which comes ever closer to what most people would agree is necessary for a successful democracy. When punishment is necessary in the extreme cases, its severity must be guided by the importance of the case rather than by the emotional state of the punisher. Untempered punishment serves only to induce resentment and can even cause the student to exaggerate his objectionable behavior.

Finally, an attitude of trust and genuine interest on the part of a teacher can give the student the incentive to guide his own conduct toward an ideal which includes many democratic principles. Such trust is shown in utilizing honor systems, in allowing students to carry out their own research projects or other activities without unnecessary supervision, and consulting the students on curriculum decisions and on administrative details. The interest is likewise manifested in similar attitudes as well as in familiarity with names (both within the classroom and outside the school setting), in participation in activities that are not strictly educational and in congratulating students for successful ventures.

These factors—interest and trust—are of great importance in the development of a person's moral system. Such support helps to convince youth that the teacher believes they can effectively regulate and control themselves.

A teacher who attempts these types of links with his students may even alter his own character in the process.

PROJECTS AND THOUGHT QUESTIONS

1. Prepare a list of guidelines that you feel are essential for administrators to follow in order to provide a healthful physical environment for their students.
2. Prepare a list of guidelines that you feel are essential for administrators to follow in order to provide a healthful psychological environment for their students.
3. What are the implications for a healthful environment of student dissent in today's educational institutions? As an administrator what plan would you follow in order to act in the best interests of the total health of all persons concerned?
4. What forms of punishment do you feel are proper in a health education or a physical education class when students disrupt the class?
5. Define what you mean by a permissive climate for students.
6. Describe the procedures that you would establish for emotionally disturbed students in a school or college.

SELECTED READINGS

Bucher, C. A.: Administration of health and physical education programs, including athletics, ed. 5, St. Louis, 1971, The C. V. Mosby Co.

Bucher, C. A., Olsen, E., and Willgoose, C.: Foundations of health, New York, 1967, Appleton-Century-Crofts.

Joint Committee on Health Problems in Education, National Education Association and American Medical Association: Healthful school environment, Washington, D. C., 1969, National Education Association.

Oberteuffer, D., and Beyrer, M. K.: School health education, ed. 4, New York, 1966, Harper & Row, Publishers.

PART FOUR ADMINISTRATIVE FUNCTIONS IN HEALTH EDUCATION AND PHYSICAL EDUCATION PROGRAMS, INCLUDING ATHLETICS

The administrative functions that are involved in the conduct of health education and physical education programs are numerous. They include such tasks as planning and maintaining facilities, budgeting, purchasing and caring for supplies and equipment, managing insurance and legal liability, planning curricula, maintaining and promoting good relations with the public, and evaluating pupil, staff, and programs. These functions take up much of the time of directors of health and physical education programs and also of many of their staff members.

To carry out administrative functions effectively and efficiently, health educators and physical educators must be knowledgeable about and possess expertise in these special areas. For example, it is important to know the best procedures for purchasing and caring for equipment, in order to save the taxpayer's money; to know if a student is properly insured so that an accident will not result in financial hardship; to understand the legal processes and the importance of avoiding negligence in the conduct of a program so that lawsuits will not develop; to be aware of the process by which

the most effective curriculum is created; to recognize the need for good public relations and for the media, which are most important for getting a message across, in order to obtain public support; and to be familiar with the manner in which a pupil's or staff member's effectiveness can be most objectively determined, in order to provide the best environment for learning and working. Knowledge and skill in carrying out these functions are important considerations for organizing and administering outstanding programs in health education and physical education.

Part Four contains more articles than any other section of this book because of the many administrative functions that are included and also because it seemed necessary to provide the reader with many significant points of view relating to these functions. An intensive search was conducted to find articles that would be most helpful, not only for the administrators themselves, but also for the many health educators and physical educators who are teachers and professors and who want to be aware of significant new developments in these specialized areas.

207

CHAPTER 12 THE PHYSICAL PLANT

The construction, supervision, and maintenance of facilities are very important administrative responsibilities. In this day and age in which enrollments in schools and colleges are growing, much construction is taking place, and new ideas are being introduced pertaining to such items as partial shelters for physical education facilities, swimming pools, indoor and outdoor sports facilities, and health suites, it is important for the administrator and also the health education teacher and the physical education teacher to be well informed about facility management. This is an important consideration if the educational needs of students and others who pursue programs in these specialized areas are to be met and if the need for economy in construction costs is to be achieved.

Facility planning and maintenance should stress an environment that is safe, attractive, comfortable, clean, practical, and adapted to the needs of the program and the individual and also should include a consideration of the recreational and health facilities of the community at large. The programs and facilities of the community are an important part of its total welfare. Since school and community programs are closely allied, they should be planned coordinately and based on the needs of both. Other considerations in facility management include attention to the need for future expansion; to proper allocation of space for activities, offices, and service units; to geographical and climate conditions; and to safety and health.

The articles selected for this chapter provide the reader with a discussion of current trends in facilities; the broad outlines of facility management; and examples of outstanding indoor and outdoor physical education facilities, health facilities, joint school and recreation park facilities, and other phases of school and college physical plants.

Indoor facilities for the physical education and athletic program at the University of California at Irvine are described by Wayne H. Crawford in the first article. Planning for this facility was accomplished by considering the proposed figures for projected enrollment, the number of students per section, the number of sections per day, intramural and intercollegiate programs, multiple use of facilities, and use of facilities for nonsports events.

John Padjen and Lillian Castner describe the physical education plant at New Trier High School West. The facilities include three two-level buildings for boys' facilities, girls' facilities, and the natatorium.

In the next article James V. Sullivan and Robert H. Weatherill point out that, when school boards and architects do not seek the advice of physical educators, serious errors in construction are inevitable. The University of Maine facility shows cooperation and planning for the future in its designs. The authors believe that physical educators must review literature on gymnasium designs and must travel to survey other facilities. The outcomes of research are the determining factor in the architectural sketches and in good building design for all.

The President's Council on Physical Fitness recommends at least fifteen minutes of rigorous activity per day for all school youth. James B. Delamater points out that outdoor facilities for physical education have been built to encourage the participation urged by the President's Council. Through the use of obstacle courses, aquatics centers, hard-top surface areas, and all-weather tracks, many educators have enriched their overall program offerings.

Harold B. Gores describes future designs for physical education facilities, such as field house bubbles, climate control, and varieties of floor surfaces that are sometimes layered. These new facilities are aimed at improving the quality of teaching in our programs. Gores thinks that programs still dependent on the weather are primitive.

In the next article, George T. Wilson explains that the use of park facilities for education began in the 1930's. Today, schools are turning to direct contact with nature through the use of nearby parks providing the ideal settings for outdoor labs or classrooms. School camping programs have been very successful with the use of this innovative method.

Harold K. Jack, author of the final article in this chapter, believes that health education facilities should have the latest innovative devices and teaching aids. The classrooms should be equipped for formal and informal situations. The laboratory or resource center for individualized activity should contain a health library, special equipment, and displays.

63 ❧ THE LATEST IN INDOOR PHYSICAL EDUCATION FACILITIES *

WAYNE H. CRAWFORD †

FORMERLY, DIRECTOR, PHYSICAL EDUCATION AND ATHLETICS,
UNIVERSITY OF CALIFORNIA AT IRVINE

In 1962 the Regents of the University of California initiated plans for the establishment of a new campus on the vast Irvine Ranch in rapidly mushrooming Orange County. The master plan for campus development with architect William Pereira as consultant, called for 2,000 students in 1965, with a systematic increase until a maximum enrollment of 27,500 is attained in the late 1980's. Strong programs of physical education, intramural, and recreational sports, and intercollegiate athletics were envisioned as a part of the total campus development. Because of previous experience and research in the problems involved, it was my good fortune to be invited to work with architects and engineers in the development of space and facilities for the physical education and athletic program.

The first information needed was a projection of student body enrollment figures for each year from 1965–1990, to determine space and facility requirements for each point in time. Of particular importance were: (1) activities to be included in the physical education instruction program; (2) the maximum numbers permitted in each class section; (3) the number of class sections required daily in each activity; (4) specific sports offered in intramural and intercollegiate athletic programs, and the estimated number of participants each year over a 30-year period; (5) multiple use of facilities by both sexes; and (6) special problems of planning facilities for non-sports events such as lectures, concerts, dances, and dramatic productions.

Considerable study and research was devoted to the problems of site location. It was important that facilities be removed from the academic core of the campus, yet readily accessible from classroom buildings and residence halls. Sufficient land was required for future development of additional buildings, pools, fields, and courts. In order to ideally locate outdoor facilities in relationship to accessibility from dressing rooms, orientation to the sun, and protection from prevailing winds, the position of the sun and wind gauge readings were

plotted at various hours daily over a nine-month's period.

The main building

The initial building, designed by architects Blurock, Ellerbroek & Associates, was envisioned as a multi-purpose structure to house all indoor activities of the physical education and athletic program but, additionally, to serve as the center for non-sports campus functions until such time as an auditorium, student union, and theater were available. Planning was centered around the following units: (1) main gymnasium floor areas; (2) auxiliary gymnasiums and activity rooms; (3) handball and squash courts; (4) swimming pool; (5) dressing rooms and service facilities; and (6) offices and classrooms. A brief description of the planning features of each unit is presented below.

Main gymnasium floor complex

The main gymnasium floor is 114' by 114', providing an intercollegiate basketball court, two regulation cross-courts, three volleyball courts, and six badminton courts. On one side and fifteen feet above the main floor is a 100' by 30' mezzanine, designed for classes in fencing, tumbling, and recreational activities such as table tennis and shuffleboard. On the opposite side is a 70' by 45' area, raised 3½ feet above the main floor and planned as a combination stage-dance room. An electrically-driven, sound-proof partition permits isolation of the facility as desired.

Several unique and interesting ideas are carried out in the planning of this multi-purpose area. Because of the various activities to be accommodated the floor surfaces of the three areas are different. The main gymnasium floor is of first-grade hard maple with a penetrant finish called "lignophol." This is superior to the usual wax-type treatment where street shoes are permitted on the floor. Pressure-sensitized tape lines in different colors and widths are used rather than painted court markings.

The stage-dance room is of hard maple, but no surface treatment is used other than weekly buffing with steel wool and vinegar. A finish of this type is ideal for modern dance and ballet. The floor surface of the mezzanine is

---

*From American School and University **39**:81, May 1967. Used by permission.

†Deceased.

non-slip asphalt tile, as the area is primarily used by persons in street shoes and refreshments are served here at various events.

Spectator seating is designed to serve the requirements of all functions in the building yet not decrease activity space. Various seating arrangements are possible: (a) For intercollegiate basketball games, telescopic bleachers on the mezzanine and main floor provide a solid bank from the edge of the intercollegiate court to the mezzanine ceiling. Similar type bleachers mounted on wheels provide an additional 500 seats on the stage. (b) Where a large crowd is anticipated for events such as a symphony concert or graduation ceremonies, the solid bank of bleachers is supplemented by theater-type folding chairs on the main floor. (c) To offer maximum seating comfort for stage events in which less than 1,000 spectators are in attendance, telescopic bleachers are recessed and theater-type chairs placed over the entire main floor. A storage system is designed under the stage for ease in handling chairs.

The multi-use concept of the stage presented many perplexing moments for those involved in the planning. Obviously, it is not ideal for each specific use, yet the finished product is a pleasant and functional compromise. Provisions for dance instruction include 6-foot high mirrors along the entire rear wall; portable dance bars which are easily installed in floor plates; a built-in sound system including record player, record storage racks, tape recorder, and 14 recessed speakers over the entire ceiling.

Lighting of the main gymnasium and mezzanine is accomplished by means of recessed 8-lamp, 4-foot square fluorescent fixtures over the entire ceiling. Any measure of light intensity from five to 100 foot candles is easily controlled from key-operated switches inside all entrances. Modern fluorescent lighting is ideal for sports activities as it has a low brightness factor at source (volleyball and badminton players can look directly up into the fixture without glare), does not cast shadows or glare on floor surface, and has far greater longevity than other types.

Gymnastics, combatives and weight training unit

Although separate rooms are provided for each of these popular activities, they were considered as a unit in early planning deliberations. Located adjacent to the main gymnasium floor, and constructed as a three-room complex, it is possible to take advantage of several common functions and requirements. On occassion, each activity uses all three facilities.

Apparatus, mats and equipment can be quickly moved to the main floor for intercollegiate competition. The area can be isolated from the rest of the building, thereby permitting its use when events are in progress on the main floor or when other facilities are locked. A large, centrally located storage room serves the needs of each room, thus saving valuable building space. Direct access to the unit from dressing rooms below is made possible by a separate stairway. Forced-air ventilation is extremely important in these areas to promote comfort and carry off odors. A brief description of each room is presented below:

Gymnastics

An unobstructed floor 95' by 30' with a 22' high flush ceiling offers an ideal environment for all gymnastic activities. The location of cross beams, floor plates, overhead suspensions and all apparatus was determined after consultation with Olympic team gymnasts and coaches. Artificial light is by means of recessed fluorescent fixtures, and natural lighting is through narrow tinted-glass openings on the upper part of outside walls.

Combatives

The combatives room was planned to meet the needs for instructional classes in wrestling and judo and for intercollegiate wrestling team practice. The 50' by 25' floor is of plywood panels installed on subfloor and sleepers. It was not considered important to provide a first-grade hardwood surface, as two 25' by 25' wrestling mats cover the entire area. All walls are covered with ensolite padding to a height of 6'. A recessed wrestling timer is mounted on one wall.

Weight Training

A facility of this type is of paramount importance in the modern program. Weight training has become increasingly popular as a physical education activity, as a recreational hobby, and as a training device for many of the intercollegiate athletic teams.

The room features a unique 3" by 3" endgrain block flooring, designed to withstand the abuse of dropped weights. Plywood panels to a height of 6' serve to eliminate marks and scratches. All walls are strengthened with structural steel for the attachment of chinning bars, pulleys and other training equipment. Upper walls and ceilings are treated with acoustical tile to reduce irritating noise. Lighting is by means of recessed fluorescent fixtures in two columns the length of the ceiling.

Classroom and audio-visual storage room

A large classroom is located in a corner of the building, convenient to all activity areas and outdoor facilities. It is specially planned for audio-visual instruction, having no windows and being air conditioned. A large pull-down projection screen is mounted on the front wall, and electrical outlets for all types of equipment are at the base of all four walls.

A spacious storage closet with built-in cabinets to house projectors, film library, tape recorders, record players and other audio-visual equipment is at the rear of the room.

Handball-squash courts:

One of the finest facilities of its kind in the world, the handball-squash structure is showcased on the modern Irvine campus. Planned as a wing of the physical education building, it extends the entire length of the outdoor swimming pool deck.

Housing six 20' by 20' by 40' combination handball-squash courts, the facility is designed for class instruction or national championship competition. All floors are of select hard maple, front walls are of precast concrete panels, side and rear walls have a concrete core with an outer shell of lath and hard-finish plaster.

A small balcony overlooking this court is specially equipped for tournament umpire, scorekeeper, and public address announcer. Microphone connections to ceiling-recessed speakers above the court and spectator bleachers are available for either class instruction or tournament play.

Swimming pool

Brief mention will be made of the outdoor pool at this campus because many of the planning features apply to both indoor and outdoor pools. Designed as a multi-function facility for class instruction, water polo, driving and competitive swimming, it has proven to be more than satisfactory.

The pool is of the L-shaped type, being regulation NCAA distance of 25 yards in one direction and 25 meters across the "L". Depth of water is from 4' to 6^1/$_2$' down the racing lanes and 12' in the diving area.

Special features of the pool include underwater observation windows, a complete above and below water sound system, above and below water lighting for night swim meets and water polo games, electric heaters mounted along one wall for the comfort of swimmers during inclement weather while resting between events, and a water-spray device recessed in the gutter under diving boards. Automatic filter chlorination and heating systems provide ideal conditions for the health and comfort of swimmers.

Dressing rooms and service facilities

All too often given only perfunctory attention in planning of new buildings, the facilities of this area are the "heart" of a successful physical education and athletic program.

Occupying the entire ground floor of the initial structure at the Irvine campus, locker-dressing-shower-equipment rooms suites are provided for men and women. Long-range plans call for inclusion of dressing facilities for men only in the next building, at which time the total present area will be altered for sole use of the women's program.

A forced-air ventilating system in the floor pulls air through all lockers, facilitating rapid drying of apparel and removing offensive odors. Floors of the entire area are heated by an underfloor radiant system. Women have their choice of gang showers or individual dressing-shower cubicles.

A separate building houses offices of the physical education department and student health service. Long-range plans call for construction of a new health service facility in the near future, at which time the entire present building will be occupied by physical education personnel.

On either side of a central lobby are located the general office suites for receptionists and clerical staff. Window openings and long, formica work counters provide an efficient method of handling such routine functions as ticket sales.

64 ❧ NEW TRIER HIGH SCHOOL WEST*

JOHN PADJIN
PHYSICAL EDUCATION DEPARTMENT, NEW TRIER HIGH SCHOOL WEST,
NORTHFIELD, ILLINOIS

LILLIAN CASTNER†
FORMERLY, PHYSICAL EDUCATION DEPARTMENT,
NEW TRIER HIGH SCHOOL WEST

An old township with a rich educational tradition, both academically and athletically, New Trier is justly proud of its exceptionally handsome and functional new high school.

New Trier H. S. West consists of a cluster of six buildings centered around the library and administration building. Linked to the center structure by glass-enclosed corridors are the mathematics-science, English-art, and language-social studies buildings. The fifth building is a music-drama-speech structure with an 800-seat auditorium. And the sixth is an ultra modern gymnasium-pool complex designed to express and develop the physical well-being of every student.

This complex incorporates a new, dynamic and eye-appealing design adapted to a functional and flexible program. The instructional staff played a primary role in the planning of this facility, and their recommendations prevailed in most instances.

The physical education area embraces a group of three two-level buildings, which form a separate campus from the academic and administrative areas. The buildings include the boys physical education, girls physical education, and natatorium units.

The facilities and eqiupment establish the framework for excellent programs in four major areas—boys and girls physical education, boys and girls intramurals, interscholastic athletics, and community recreation for youth and adults.

Basically, the boys and girls departments have similar facilities, with the boys area being slightly larger in square footage. *Each* has three gyms, *each* has a specialty room (a wrestling-weight training room for the boys and a dance room for the girls), *each* has an adapted physical education room, and *both* share the swim pool on a semester basis. Each department has a total of 5 1/2 teaching stations.

In addition, *each* has separate locker rooms and offices in the natatorium, physical educa-tion locker room facilities, an equipment cage and storage, staff offices and locker room facilities, separate offices for the department chairman, intramural offices and meeting rooms, and a first aid room. The boys department also has a classroom and a varsity locker room.

Ground level of boys gym and natatorium

The ground level of the boys gym provides a departmental staff office with an adjacent staff locker room and shower facilities. There are separate offices for the physical education chairman, boys intramural director, two athletic directors, and the student sports editor. Adjacent to the intramural director's office is the student intramural staff meeting room.

The physical education locker room utilizes the pedestal combination cubicle–full-length locker arrangement with a central duct exhaust system. At one end of the locker room is an athletic equipment storage cage which runs the full length of the room and separates the physical education locker room from the varsity locker room. The latter (16' x 63') contains 90 extra-large pedestal lockers. Five stall showers and drying areas are provided, with washroom facilities at each end to serve both locker rooms.

An exit from the varsity locker room leads to the mud room (for cleaning muddy equipment prior to entering locker room) and an outdoor corridor. The mud room is adjacent to the athletic training room. Adequate physical education storage is located in the physical education locker room. The intramural equipment room is located in the main locker room adjacent to the student intramural staff meeting room.

The first-floor lobby is terrazzo floored and adequately equipped with trophy display cases and bulletin boards.

The ground level of the natatorium provides offices for the aquatic director and swim staff, and has adjacent locker room and shower facilities.

The natatorium locker room consists of 135

---

*From Scholastic Coach **37**:12, June 1968. Used by permission.

†Deceased.

floor-model full-length lockers, washroom facilities, and storage bins for bathing suit distribution. The showering area includes a preliminary rinse stall, a sudsing stall, a secondary rinse, and a final rinse upon entry to the pool deck.

Second level of boys gym and natatorium

Two stairways lead to the terrazzo-floored second level, which also is adequately furnished with trophy cases. There are two inside entrances to the principal gymnasium facility, which consists of three teaching stations.

These areas are classified as the Intramural Gymnasium, the Main Gymnasium, and the Gymnastics Gymnasium. The first two are on the floor level, while the third is on stage level. Each of these three areas can be partitioned by folding door dividers.

The floor level gyms are equipped with eight baskets each, thus permitting three cross-court games in each gym. Each of the three gyms has four badminton courts (total of nine).

The Intramural Gym is used throughout the day as a physical education teaching station and is converted into an intramural area for an hour and a half after the school day before being turned over to athletic teams.

The Gymnastic Gym is used primarily for gymnastic activities throughout the season and then is used for volleyball and badminton. As a gymnastic station, it is complete with the finest of equipment and folding bleachers for gymnastic meets.

The Main Gym becomes the primary area for varsity basketball and wrestling, with the folding bleachers extending from the intramural and gymnastic gyms' side walls, permitting seating for 2,300 spectators.

The raised stage nature of the gymnastic gym also provides for multi-purpose use. It is used for graduations, stage productions, and student assemblies. The area under the stage also permits storage of chairs and wrestling mats.

The second level of the natatorium provides entry to the pool balcony and seating for 888 spectators. The west underside of the pool balcony is used as a temporary weight station during the winter season.

Girls physical education

As mentioned earlier, the girls facilities are similar to those of the boys. The gymnasia-pool complex also has two stories. On the ground level are the locker rooms, offices, smaller activity spaces (dance studio and adapted gym), equipment rooms, rest rooms, first aid room, and a 22' x 12' office for the girls A.A.

The second level is almost entirely occupied by the gymnasia and the equipment storage areas.

The dance studio is roughly 40' x 52' and has mirrors on one wall and a handrail. The storage space within the room is adequate for a piano and recording device.

The adapted gym (22' x 35') has stall bars and a storage cupboard for blankets and other equipment used for adapted students.

The three 78' x 44' gymnasia (with solid walls) form the second story of the complex. The floors are marked for one basketball court, two volleyball courts, and three badminton courts.

The storage areas are just outside the gyms or (for field events) on the way to the field. The storage cupboards for hockey sticks have vertical divisions so that the sticks may be separated by size. Between classes the hockey shin guards are hung on a peg board in the storage area under the pool balcony. The same peg board serves for the storage of fencing equipment between classes.

The gym locker room (72' x 72') contains 1,764 baskets and 200 full-length lockers.

Outdoor facilities

Outdoor facilities at present include a quarter-mile composition track around a practice football field, eight football-soccer-field hockey practices fields, and eight asphalt tennis courts.

Swimming pool

The size of the total area (pool and deck) is 104' x 73', with the pool itself being 75' x 45'. Other vital statistics:

Water capacity: 175,000 gallons, recirculated once every six hours.

Temperature: water 78–80 degrees, air 84–86 degrees.

Type of filters: three pressure type sand filters.

Type of chlorination: HTH solution (calcium hypochlorite—70% available chlorine).

Swimmer capacity: 171 persons.

Lighting: 50 footcandles.

Locker room (24' x 52'): 135 full lockers for boys, 117 for girls.

Pool shower area: 24' x 40'

Dimensions of boys facilities

Main gym (2,300 seating): 62' $\times$ 102'

Gymnastics gym (800 seating): 55' $\times$ 102'

Intramural gym: 48' × 102'

Practice wrestling room—weight training station: 38' x 80'

Adapted physical education gym: 40' x 60'

Utility room—class or meeting room: 25' x 30'

Boys physical education locker room (1,500 phys ed lockers, 150 sport lockers): 70' x 88'

Varsity locker room (90 extra-large lockers): 16' x 63'

Shower and drying area, five stalls with nine heads each: 20' x 80'

Training room: 20' x 22'

Intramural equipment room: 15' x 20'

Physical education staff office: 19' x 21'

Department chairman office: 9' x 11'

Sports news director's office: 9' x 11'

Athletic director office: 9' x 11'

Athletic equipment cage room: 12' x 64'

Physical education storage: 15' x 20'

Mud room: 12' x 12'

Intramural staff meeting room: 16' x 18'

Intramural director's office: 9' x 16'

Temporary weight station, under pool balcony: 12' x 95'

Aquatic director office: 11' x 21'

Mud room

The mud room is a 12 × 12 area that leads into the locker rooms from the outdoors. It has bench seats around its perimeter, a water outlet, hoses, and a tapered floor with a large grated drain in the center.

Upon coming in from a wet and muddy play area, the student can take off his shoes and hose them down. Athletes (especially football players), after a muddy practice or return from a muddy game, can hose themselves down in this room. This simplifies the maintenance of the locker room areas and increases the life of the equipment.

65 ᐛ GYM DESIGN AND CONSTRUCTION*

JAMES V. SULLIVAN
ATHLETIC DIRECTOR, UNIVERSITY OF MAINE,
PORTLAND, MAINE

ROBERT H. WEATHERILL
ARCHITECT, PORTLAND, MAINE

Most physical education and athletic specialists have only a limited knowledge of the design, construction, and maintenance of their facilities. What's more, since they don't anticipate any involvement in facility development, they're not particularly interested in acquiring such information.

Small wonder, then, that architects and school boards fail to seek their advice. The results are obvious: Since the specialist knows little about functional design and construction, and the architect knows even less about physical education, serious errors in construction are inevitable.

For best results, the architect and the specialist must pool their knowledge. That is what the authors did in designing a multi-purpose building for the University of Maine. They feel qualified, therefore, to offer some sound suggestions on the design and construction of a conventional gym.

Several major factors must be taken into consideration at the outset: What activities will be conducted in the building? How large will the physical education classes be—now and in the future? Where will the heavy traffic areas be? How much money will be available? Where should the building be located?

Before undertaking any preliminary planning, the physical education and athletic administrators should take two steps. First, they should review all the recent literature on gym construction and design. Second, they should travel as widely as possible to survey other facilities and confer with the staff members of these schools.

After completing this personal investigation, they should form a planning committee to work out a program with the architect. At the first meeting between this committee and the architect, the former should offer its suggestions on what should be included in the building. These suggestions should form the architect's bases for preliminary sketches.

Following are the areas that must be considered in the conventional gym building:

The main floor will undoubtedly receive the heaviest traffic in the gym. It will be used for physical education classes, intramural sports,

*From Scholastic Coach 37:7, January 1968. Used by permission.

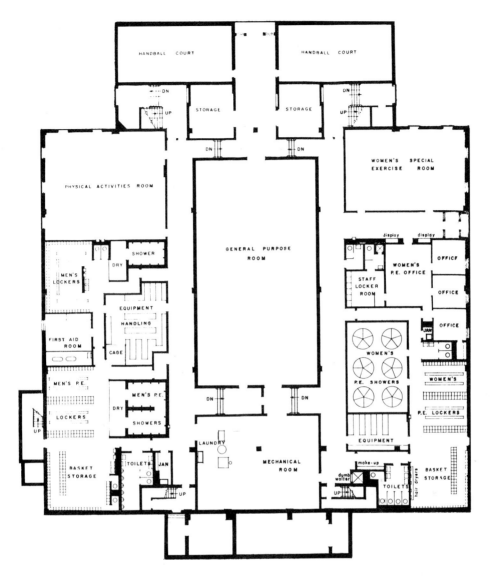

and recreation, as well as varsity events and other extra-curricular activities.

For classes, the main floor may be divided into at least two teaching stations, one for girls and the other for boys. The latest concept, however, is to divide the main floor into three teaching stations. The major station will be a regulation basketball court that also can be used for volleyball, indoor tennis, indoor track, and badminton.

The other two stations, though substandard in size for basketball, will accommodate regulation-sized courts for volleyball, indoor tennis, and badminton. One of these substandard stations could also be designed for gymnastics.

The way to obtain the three teaching stations is to divide the whole main unit alongside the basketball court. Two sliding or moving parti-

tions, which can be operated electrically, can divide these units for physical education classes, intramurals, or athletic purposes.

The athletic program will benefit from this three-divisional idea, as the main floor will be able to accommodate capacity attendance for basketball by making use of all the folding bleachers.

The main station also can be used for wrestling meets, with one or both sets of the bleachers being used. Gymnastic events may be presented on one of the substandard stations, with the spectators being seated on a partially extended set of bleachers.

It would also be possible to hold some type of event at one end, with the spectators being seated on folding chairs on the floor itself. This arrangement would be ideal for graduation

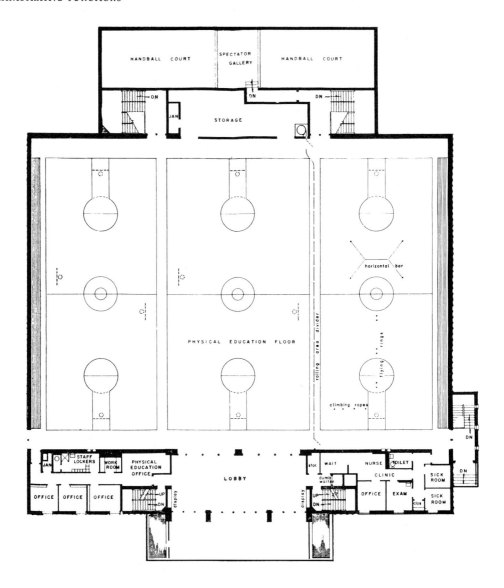

exercises, concerts, plays, clinics, and school assemblies.

The floor of this main area can be constructed of some type of hard wood. The writers have found that a mechanical bend of wood to the sub floor usually is more practical than the adhesive or chemical bond. Wood floors on grade must be protected against the intrusion of moisture, which is very damaging.

The synthetic type of floor is currently gaining wide acceptance. It can be used for many purposes without fear of damage.

The ceiling of the main area should be at least 22 feet high, its composition being left to the architect. A high-quality speaking system is essential for athletic events and other extra-curricular activities, and the advice of an accoustical specialist should be sought.

The lighting system for the main unit should provide at least 50 foot-candles of illumination. Fluorescent lighting is recommended for evenness of illumination and lower cost. For heating and ventilation, the specialist must again depend on the architect's recommendations. Since this area will be used all day for classes and intramurals, and for heavily attended events on selected evenings, the heating and ventilation are extremely important. Attention should also be given to the sound of the heating equipment.

The bleachers should be of the folding, or telescopic, type. They may be made either of wood or a vinyl-covered steel, and should recess into a compact unit requiring little space.

Manufacturers of vinyl-covered steel bleachers claim that they're easy to maintain and are splinter-proof. Repair kits are available for the vinyl cover.

Sight line diagrams are provided by the manufacturers. Caution is necessary in installing bleachers over synthetic floors. If the bleachers are too heavy and the rollers too small and narrow, they may damage the synthetic material.

The locker rooms should be located in strategic areas accessible to both the teaching stations and the outdoor areas. The size and shape of the rooms will depend upon the maximum number of students who'll use them during any one period.

The floor should be made of a material that won't deteriorate or become slippery when wet. Tile or concrete usually is the most suitable material for floors. The floor drains should be located in the areas where excess water usually accumulates.

Because of the amount of moisture in locker rooms, all the ceilings, wall, doors, etc., should be moisture-proof. The ceiling should be 10 feet high, and the lights should provide approximately 30 to 40 foot-candles of illumination. The heating should be sufficient for comfort when walking barefooted and unclothed.

At Maine, the locker alcoves are separated by steel mesh and rolling grill doors which drop from the ceiling. This makes it possible to furnish private alcoves for visiting teams, and to lock the doors for the security of the visitors' valuables.

The shower room should be located in an area which allows a free circulation of traffic and which is convenient to the locker rooms, teaching stations, and outdoor areas. Gang type showers are recommended for the boys, and individual showers with adjacent dressing stalls for the girls.

The size of the shower rooms will depend upon the maximum number of students using them at one time. It's also important to remember that some of these showers will be used for intramurals, and that some schools will want a separate shower room for varsity teams.

The floors should be of ceramic mosaic tile, and the walls of ceramic tile to a height of at least six feet. If possible, the tile should go right up to the ceiling. A nonpeeling epoxy paint may be applied to concrete or cinder block walls. The ceramic tile or epoxy paint will eliminate the possibility of moisture or bacteria penetration.

It's important to locate the drains in the proper locations and to be certain that the floor pitches to the drains in order to facilitate the removal of excess water.

The lights should be moisture-proof, with their switches located outside the shower rooms. There are arguments for and against the use of liquid soap dispensers. The "againsters" say that such dispensers may leak after a period of time, causing the soap to run down the wall and spoil the wall's appearance. The recessed soap dish has merit and should be considered.

The drying area should be adjacent to the shower rooms and be large enough to allow several students to dry off at the same time. The flooring should be the same as that for the shower rooms, and the drains should be located close to the focal points of excess water.

The equipment rooms must be carefully planned. They should be large enough to accommodate all the physical education, intramural, and athletic equipment, and should contain storage shelves, have aisle space between the shelves, and be accessible from both sides.

The room should be convenient to the locker and shower rooms. Thus, a Dutch door facing the locker rooms will make it possible to dispense the towels for physical education and intramurals, easily and without traffic congestion.

The ceiling should be at least 10 feet high, permitting the suspension (and storage) of clothing from it. The walls can be made of concrete blocks, and the floor of concrete. Ventilation is important, as excessive moisture will affect the stored materials.

The general activity room can accommodate many diversified activities, including a corrective physical education program. If large enough, the room could also be used for wrestling practice.

The corrective and adaptive equipment can be located on the walls and at one end of the room. The room at Maine includes such equipment as stall bars, chin bars, chest pulley weights, regular weights and racks, a rowing machine, a bicycle, benches, and wall mirrors.

The room may also be used for fencing, small free-exercise classes, tumbling activities, judo, karate, etc.

The ceiling should be at least 10 feet high to allow for such weight-lifting exercises as the military press. The walls and the floor can be of concrete block, with a wooden platform extending over part of the floor for the weight work.

The floor should be free of any permanent fixtures, thus making it possible to move around mats and other equipment—giving the room maximum flexibility.

The dance room is an important teaching station for the girls' physical education program. It can also be used for instruction in free exercise, fencing, posture improvement, and class subjects. The room will require wall mirrors to enable the girls to study their dancing form, and hand rails (barres) for preliminary exercising.

The room should be at least 25' x 30' and have excellent acoustics and a quality sound system.

The ceiling should be at least 10 feet high, and the floor should be of medium, resilient wood. The walls can be made of painted concrete block, with fittings for tack-boards and bulletin boards. The heating and ventilation will depend upon the number of students using the room, the time of year, climate, etc.

The first aid rooms should be located near the locker rooms. Since the boys' room will be used for the treatment of both athletic and physical education injuries, it should be a little larger and more fully equipped than the girls' room.

Some high schools have eliminated the need for a girls' first aid room by using the nurse's health room for this purpose. The school nurse often will tend to the girls' injuries, thus relieving the physical education teacher of this duty.

The dimensions of these rooms will depend upon the total student enrollment and the size of the physical education classes. The ceiling should be at least 8 feet high, and the walls should be of concrete block painted with moisture-resisting epoxy. If possible, the lower portion of the wall should be faced with ceramic tile to prevent the steam from the whirlpool from peeling off the regular paint.

The light system should provide 40 to 50 foot-candles of illumination, and have several grounded electrical outlets on the walls. The floor should be of concrete or ceramic mosaic tile, with drains in the proper places—one of them being located near the whirlpool. A wash sink and mirror should also be included.

The heating and ventilation should receive particular attention; and the equipment should include plinths, heating lamp, whirlpool (for boys), cabinets for medical supplies, and a refrigerator.

The laundry room can double as a drying room by including racks and clotheslines. The minimum size should be 10' x 10' with a 10' ceiling.

Inserts should be provided in the ceiling for the clotheslines. Drainage placement is very important. The floor should be of concrete and the walls of concrete block painted with moisture-resisting paint. The lights should provide 40 to 50 foot-candles of illumination.

The equipment for a high-school laundry room must include two automatic washers and one or two electric gas dryers, the size of which will depend on the amount of washing and drying that will be done. A good laundry can serve both the boys' and girls' programs and save the school a large amount of money.

The staff offices should be large enough for lockers, a desk, chair, book cases, file cabinets, and extra chairs for visitors. Toilet facilities should be nearby.

The ceilings should be 8 feet high, the walls may be of concrete block, and the floors of vinyl asbestos tile. The lighting should come from overhead, with outlets for desk lamps and electric typewriters. Each office should be able to regulate its heating and ventilation.

The offices may be located adjacent to the locker rooms, thus giving the physical education instructors a view of the whole locker room area, or may be located next to the main gym floor for supervisory purposes.

The lobby requires careful planning. Its size will depend upon the gym's spectator capacity. The ticket area or window may be recessed into the wall or may protrude from it. Some designers believe that a permanent ticket booth is a waste of space, and that a portable booth not only saves space but is less costly.

The trophy display cases should be located where they can be seen by everyone entering the lobby area. The ceiling should be 10 feet, the walls may be of painted concrete block, and the floor can be made of natural stone, ceramic quarry tile or some resilient material. In any event it must be nonslipping and easily maintained, as this is a heavy traffic area that requires frequent attention.

Recessed floor mats can be placed just inside the doors, and public toilet facilities must be located nearby. The lights should be chosen for their attractiveness. A high level of illumination is unnecessary; 20 or 30 foot-candles are minimum.

Storage and janitor areas are essential for the storage of all the heavy physical education, intramural, and athletic equipment, as well as chairs, tables, and other furniture. In short, everything that cannot be handled by the equipment rooms.

66 ᐃ A LOOK AT TODAY'S OUTDOOR PHYSICAL EDUCATION FACILITIES*

JAMES B. DELAMATER

HEAD, DEPARTMENT OF PHYSICAL EDUCATION, NEW MEXICO STATE UNIVERSITY, UNIVERSITY PARK, NEW MEXICO

We are fortunate to be living in an interesting and challenging era—a period of rapid change and infinite opportunity. This is especially true for those of us in positions of leadership in physical education and recreation.

Challenge courses

Any list of objectives for physical education would be incomplete without a high ranking for vigorous muscular activity. During recent years those who may have yielded to the always-present animal urge to take the easy and pleasant course, avoiding undue exertion, are reminded that there is no easy way to the maintenance and improvement of physical health and vigor.

A few years ago, the President's Council on Physical Fitness recorded, as a national standard, a minimum of 15 minutes per day of vigorous physical activity for all school youth. The emphasis was on the word *vigorous,* and the recommendation was not intended to reduce the length of the normal activity period, but rather to have *at least* 15 minutes of that period devoted to vigorous physical workouts.

For this purpose, the challenge course (sometimes known as the obstacle course) and other running courses of varying lengths and descriptions have been constructed and put to good use. While professional understanding and some ingenuity are necessary requisites for the design of this facility, there is no standard course. Rather, it can and should be designed and constructed to carry out the particular program requirements of the school.

Among apparatus and equipment available are pegboards, parallel bars for dips and traveling (including the "roller-coaster" type), overhead ladders, scaling walls, vaulting bars and steeplechase obstacles, dodging and agility equipment, ropes and poles for climbing, and, of course, paths for running.

The challenge course can present obstacles interesting enough to excite red-blooded young American youth; it can be as vigorous as it need be to provide abundant, hard physical work and, with good sense, can be used to enrich the complete program of physical education for boys and girls.

Aquatic activities

Instructional and competitive physical education programs in our schools and colleges require facilities which will insure a program uninterrupted by weather conditions. Therefore, an indoor swimming pool is desirable in most localities.

However, the outdoor pool, and the outdoor pool equipped with a portable roof or "bubble" for use during cold seasons, continue to be included in the plans of educational and recreational organizations as a feasible means of launching swimming programs and as an economical means of providing for aquatic activity during peak seasons of use.

The 50-meter pool with provisions for 25-yard and 50-meter competitive courses, competitive and recreational diving, water polo, and large areas of 5-foot maximum depth for instructional and recreational swimming provides a nearly ideal facility for outdoor education and recreation. The new California Junior Colleges (Foothill, San Mateo, Chabot, Cerritos, Rio Honda, and others) have excellent outdoor facilities. Many institutions with much less favorable weather conditions utilize limited indoor facilities for swimming during cold months together with well planned outdoor pools for use during the remainder of the year.

For the institutions and communities which may not be able to finance the kind of facility described above, an inexpensive portable pool is now available commercially. This pool is 16 feet by 24 feet by 36 inches, and the normal water depth is 30 inches to enable instruction for youthful beginners in maximum safety. The water treatment system designed for the portable pool provides excellent clarity and sanitation.

This pool can be dismantled and transported from one location to another in a 2 1/2-ton truck and can be assembled, filled, and ready for use in five and one-half hours. It is sturdy and comes equipped with a vandalproof cover which can be placed over the pool and locked in about 15 minutes.

The portable pool will accommodate 16 chil-

*From American School & University 39:82, May 1967. Used by permission.

dren in beginning swimming classes, and in at least three large city systems where used—Los Angeles, Brooklyn, and Dayton—it has been judged most satisfactory. This innovation suggests one manner whereby elementary schools—where basic swimming instruction should be provided—may be able to move forward in an important program area.

It has always been difficult to finance and otherwise provide the kinds and numbers of indoor teaching stations needed for a modern program of physical education and community recreation. Educational leaders have, therefore, turned to the out-of-doors where many "indoor" activities can be conducted healthfully and economically.

Outdoor gyms serve well

The outdoor gymnasium certainly does not, nor should it be expected to, take the place of an indoor facility. Nevertheless, much can and should be done in the out-of-doors to decrease the total cost of facilities and to provide the variety and number of spaces needed to enrich the physical education program.

For many years "hard top" of one kind or another has been used to provide all-weather surfacing for outdoor physical education activities. Today, tar asphalt and cement concrete have been joined by many new materials which can be used to provide excellent surfacing for most indoor or outdoor court activities.

Outdoor areas require shelter from cold and gusty breezes and this can be achieved by locating buildings or walls on the north and/or prevailing wind sides of such areas. The heat from the sun will also add to the comfort of students during outdoor periods.

Proper grading of surfaces will result in rapid drainage, and smooth finishes and resilient materials mean comfort, safety, and efficiency in use. Attention to the proper design of goal and net posts, and other equipment and lines, can make the outdoor gymnasium a real asset in the promotion of physical education and outdoor recreation.

There are even possibilities for multiple-use which outdoor facilities provide. At the University of California at Berkeley, for instance, the roof of a parking area is designed to include eight fine, outdoor all-weather tennis courts. The courts are heavily used for instructional, competitive, and recreational play. Floodlighting of these facilities at night to extend the outdoor education and recreation day is a most important feature.

All-weather tracks

The all-weather track is a necessity wherever track and field activities are to be promoted efficiently and economically. Such a track is graded to enable rapid drainage, and even the normal rainstorm need not curtail activity. The all-weather track has permanent lines, distant

---

Outdoor Skating Rink at Gordon College

A ten-year planning projection was completed in 1963 for Gordon College and Divinity School—a privately controlled, accredited institution in Wenham, Mass.

The result—three new buildings were in use by September of 1965.

Several leaders in the community, who themselves had been hockey stars in their college days, became interested in providing an ice skating rink for Gordon College since such a facility was not part of the master plan.

One enthusiastic planner discovered a used rink for sale in Virginia, and needed funds were pledged for the project.

The rink was to be solely owned, operated, and controlled by Gordon College, but three other private schools in the area would help defray operating expenses in return for regularly scheduled ice time for their students.

A consultant supervised the move of the equipment from Virginia and laid out the building to house it.

This included refrigeration plant, piping, checkroom equipment, several hundred pairs of rental skates, a public address system, and a "Zamboni."

"For the uninitiated," explained Gordon College's business manager L. J. Cone, "a Zamboni is a jeep equipped with a Rube Goldberg array of tanks, valves, scrapers, conveyors, and remote driving controls, and costing about $10,000 new. Its key function is to resurface the skating ice."

Separate contracts were let for site preparation, building construction, overhaul and installation of the refrigeration plant, and the carpentry for side boards and benches. Lighting was specially designed with the help of the lamp manufacturer and a representative of the local utility company.

The rink is a valuable addition to the physical education programs of the college and local schools.

Construction costs reached $200,000, with operating expenses approximating $10,000 to $12,000 per season.

[sic] markers, and hurdle locations and requires a minimum of maintenance, thereby reducing long-term costs and enabling its continuous and constant use. There are many excellent new materials available for this facility, with initial costs far from prohibitive.

Outdoor education and recreation are in their infancy insofar as modern public education and community recreation are concerned. Nature study areas where many species of trees, bushes, plants, bird and animal life, and flowers can be observed and studied by young and old alike are being and will be developed in ever increasing numbers.

Facilities for a variety of social outings, including outdoor cooking and eating, camping, social games and sports, boating and other water sports, dramatic, musical, and dance activities, outdoor assemblies and religious activities, will be common.

Many far-sighted educators have altered the face of a previously unused corner of the school grounds, campus, or adjacent community to develop such facilities and thus have enriched their overall offering and contribution to the total education of their clientele. The Outdoor Education Project of the American Association for Health, Physical Education, and Recreation offers abundant assistance to those who wish help in planning such activities.

In conclusion, it is important to emphasize that this report is only a sampling of what is new and exciting in outdoor education. Hopefully, these ideas will provide worthy food for thought, but for a real experience, I urge the reader to take each and every opportunity to visit neighboring schools and colleges to see what they are providing in the way of outdoor physical education and recreational facilities. There will always be at least one good idea worth consideration.

67 ⮞ NEW TRENDS IN ATHLETIC FACILITIES*

Harold B. Gores
President, Educational Facilities Laboratories, Inc.,
New York

I am the head of a small foundation called Educational Facilities Laboratories. We have $2,000,000 a year to help schools and colleges with their physical problems. We are a laboratory; we do not make gifts, but we do put quite a little money into the athletic side of education.

I am presently writing a chapter for a book entitled *High School 1980* which will be coming out next year. The chapter is on high school facilities, and presented here is a preview of the section having to do with physical education, health, and recreation facilities of the future.

Nearly a hundred years ago, thanks to the demonstration of rhythmic gymnastics by German and Scandinavian gymnasts at the World's Columbia Exhibition in Chicago in 1893, schools purchased wands and dumbbells and began to build the American student's body.

At the turn of the century, schools were well on their way to improving the physical well-being of their students when the game of basketball arrived. This game, invented at Springfield College in 1891, involved an inflated ball which was dropped through an elevated peach basket hoop. So great was this game's

natural charm and its potential at the box office that the wands, the dumbells, and related apparatus went promptly to the school's attic. (In fact, two different high schools at which I served in the 1930's still had an attic full of wands and dumbbells left over from this earlier age.) Any high school seeking respectability and public confidence had to have a basketball box, still called a gymnasium, in which to develop the skills of its already best-coordinated youth.

In small towns everywhere, but in the Midwest especially, the game of basketball captured the public interest and, alas, became an acceptable substitute for physical education in many schools. Later there was even a rich professional future for boys whose pituitary derangement endowed them with stature approaching seven feet.

By 1970, interscholastic baseball had died at the gate; football was losing to the competition of professionals playing on television. Only basketball, in a special facility designed to its requirements and frequently costing as much as a fourth of the total cost of the school, had the economic viability to survive into the 1970's as the last vestige of education's sports biz. In many schools, basketball bore the same relation to education, as Robert Hutchins once

*From *Secondary School Athletic Administration*, January 1969, p. 19, American Association for Health, Physical Education, and Recreation. Used by permission.

said about college football, that bullfighting does to agriculture.

But in the 1970's, as urbanization and affluence increased, as more persons were jogging for their lives, as the medical profession spoke out more clearly on the relation of good health to cardiovascular tone, education was moved to provide programs and facilities for physical fitness and lifetime sports for all.

Not the least of the thrust came from the students themselves (I am talking 1980 now) who, being taken increasingly into partnership in educational policy planning, were aghast to discover, and promptly set out to fix, the maldistribution of funds spent on the development of so few for the entertainment of the declining many.

By 1980, the basketball box will have been replaced or supplemented by a new art form, the outlines of which began to emerge in the late '50's as the field house. Many of these earlier field houses were little more than basketball floors stuffed into domed circular containers. Yet, they represented an advance if only that the change in nomenclature implied the intent to serve more than gymnasts.

Just as the gymnasium had progressed to the field house, the latter, without dropping the name, became in the 1970's a great simulated outdoor area. Depending on the severity of the climate, these new field houses will be rigid shells or partially air-supported membranes— great scoops of the sky providing universal space uninterrupted by interior posts. Goodyear Rubber is working on this intensively. Their object eventually is to cover four acres with a membrane, the cost of which should be about $1.50 a square foot and 5 cents a square foot annual maintenance, partially air-supported, partially cable-supported and capable of being patched without deflation.

Irrespective of the region, whether North or South, the field house will be climate controlled against heat or cold. It will be an acre of June. Within, the floors will be whatever surfaces are appropriate to the chosen activities. Plastic ice for skating, artificial turf for field games, composition floors for track, hard floors for basketball and dancing. Some of these surfaces will be layered to enable quick change and to achieve multiple use of space. Savings on the shell of the building will go to offset the cost of the variety of floor surfaces, the air conditioning to enable year-round use, and the lighting. The overall cost per use, day and night, will drop substantially; and cost per use, not cost per square foot, is the criterion for econ-

omy. Moreover, the field house, with its multiple use of space and its artificial surfaces (which, unlike natural grass, never have to be rested) offer substantial economy for urban schools located on expensive land.

The economy of the field house is in its accommodation of a wide range of activities for the student body and the whole community, day and night, irrespective of the weather. Barnaby Keeney, former President of Brown University, in seeking all-weather facilities for physical education, athletics, and recreation, said, "Here in Providence, Rhode Island, it is primitive to let the weather determine the program. We don't play lacrosse at Brown; we only cancel it."

In Bethesda, Maryland, seven years ago, Educational Facilities Laboratories put up the $25,000 that enabled the geodesic dome field house to be in competition in the open market with the standard and conventional basketball box gymnasium. The school board agreed that if the dome came in reasonably equal, they would build it. The question was who would pay for two sets of plans—certainly not the taxpayers of Maryland. So we put up the additional money. The dome came in at $2.37 a square foot less than the conventional box against which it was bid.

Early in the 1960's EFL helped with the planning of a high school in Kansas which was one of the first to use a domed roof for physical education. EFL has also supported some of the experimentation in air-supported bubbles at the Forman School in Litchfield, Connecticut. It came about simply because the headmaster needed a gymnasium and had only $25,000. The longer he talked, the clearer it was that he really didn't need a gymnasium; he needed a space for certain types of activities other than basketball. Basketball could be played in the existing facility. So we gave him the money to go on the road and to see whether and how close he could come to a $25,000 gymnasium in which—from September to June—he could run a physical education and athletic program. He finally wound up with a bubble, putting the first one over a swimming pool, the second one over a field of artificial turf, and more recently, a third one over a hockey rink.

This, obviously, is the poor man's answer to covered space. It is the cheapest way to set a membrane between the people and the weather.

In Greeley, Colorado, EFL helped to experiment with a semi-enclosed shelter. Many of the days there are delightful, but there are some days when the wind sweeps across the plains and an enclosure is required. We sought a building that would open and close, that literally could turn its back against the wind, from whichever direction it came and, under certain circumstances, turn its back against all four directions of the compass.

We need more experimentation with this building type. Perhaps some one has an idea of how to construct a building that opens up when the weather is benign but closes itself on any or all sides in bad weather. The plastic industry, certainly, should be altered to this need.

EFL has worked with artificial turf and in 1959 we made a grant to the New York City Schools to investigate the use of rooftops for additional facilities. The typical inner-city school is a great masonry fortress afloat on a sea of blacktop and surrounded by a chainlink fence and two basketball hoops. If it were our intention to devise the kind of school that would drive the middle class out of the central city toward the suburbs or into private education, today's inner-city school is the ideal instrument.

Because city land is so expensive, we looked to the rooftops, designing the schools like a flattop—anything that must jut through the roof will be stacked to one side as on an aircraft carrier. One school in England has real grass on the roof, but no one is allowed to step on it. The grass had been put on the roof only to please those living in adjacent high-rise apartment buildings.

Because natural grass could not withstand continuous use on a roof-top playground, we turned to the textile industry, asking that they create artificial grass. Several corporations responded, especially American Biltrite Rubber and Monsanto. American Biltrite Rubber's product was put in the Forman School's bubble, and Monsanto's product, which later was named Astroturf, was installed in the Moses Brown School in Providence, Rhode Island. From the Moses Brown installation in 1964 has come a whole new industry. Our cities are building more enclosed stadiums not only to increase their utilization but to reduce knee and ankle injuries in football. One company has a market target of 40 outdoor fields for next year; another has 10. Artificial fields are emerging and will eventually get to the American high school as soon as enough people realize the economy of having a field that never has to be rested.

The old formulas for size of school sites—20 acres plus an acre for every hundred children— are based on a suburban concept of what a school is. If 20 acres plus an acre for every hundred children were applied in some parts of Manhattan, the student body would be wiped out.

Such formulas are now made obsolete by the playing surface that does not have to be rested. Instead of taking more land and razing the houses on it at great expense, schools should try methods that will give higher utilization.

For the last three years EFL has contributed to the salary of Dick Theibert, former director of Athletics at Brown University, now at Chapman College in Orange, California, in order that he be released to work with industry in developing the new materials. Nothing is too experimental for him to consider. Not long ago he asked my opinion about an aluminum bat. "We have a company," he said, "that can make an aluminum bat that is guaranteed by the engineers not to alter batting averages or home run output. Furthermore, it won't sting the hands, and it won't splinter. How do we get this thing started?"

We have put money into an experiment to use cold air instead of brine-filled pipes to make ice. Two such rinks are already in use and I am told by one manufacturer that 10 more are in prospect this year. We have just started another experiment at Purdue, trying to make ice by passing Freon gas through thin aluminum tubes in much the way trucks are refrigerated. The target cost is $3.50 a square foot.

About eight years ago I said that some day the plastic industry will find a way to make a product on which you can skate. This now appears to be happening. A plastic product called SLICK is being developed. It comes in 3-foot by 8-foot sheets and shows great promise. Though not yet slippery enough for hockey, it is good for general skating.

These new facilities are aimed at improving the quality of teaching health, physical education, and recreation. But those in the profession must also contribute toward that improvement. First I would suggest that the profession improve its public image. Too many people in this country associate physical education with poms poms, whistle tooting, and the marching bands of televised collegiate football. The profession should also associate itself as closely as possible with the medical profession and let the public know that physical education, health, and recreation are more than competitive games and gate receipts. It must be demonstrated that the work in school is but an extension of the family doctor's concern about the health and physical well-being of any individual child.

Secondly, I believe the profession should

reach out toward the field of science and conservation education. Believing this to be true, EFL has just commissioned Dr. Eugene Ezersky of the New York City Public Schools, Assistant Supervisor of Physical Education for Boys in New York City, to study the feasibility of establishing out-of-city camping experiences for children who go to school and live and eat in the inner city. I believe that camping experience for inner-city youth will come soon in our big cities. At the moment there is a vacuum in leadership and, in my view, physical education is the logical source of leadership when the money becomes available.

And third, new schools should be built not just for children, but for people. To be sure, the school must serve the children well but, especially if the school is in the central city, it must serve people of all ages. It is especially incumbent on physical education, health, and recreation that its plant and program operate year-round, day and night. Just as the school is interested in the health of a fourteen-year-old boy, it should be equally interested in his middle-aged father who is jogging for his life. Moreover, if the program has something for everybody, the bond issue for the needed facilities and personnel is more likely to be passed.

Finally, the profession must accept the fact that a program of physical education, recreation, and health, which is still dependent on the vicissitudes of weather, is primitive. Help hasten the day when the program is conducted indoors. EFL will do its best to develop inexpensive, poor man's astrodomes if they will be put to use day and night, summer and winter. America's health is too important to leave to the weather.

68 ⮞ JOINT SCHOOL-PARK FACILITIES OFFER ADVANTAGES—NATURALLY*

Dr. George T. Wilson
Assistant Superintendent of Schools, Milwaukee, Wisconsin

Our national parks, monuments, and reservations are among America's greatest assets. However, it wasn't until early in the 20th century that educators and park administrators began to realize that the greatest gains from these resources could best be obtained through a program of wise use and public information.

The educational implications and advantages of using our outdoor resources judiciously were impressed upon the public by school teachers and administrators, and were interpreted by park naturalists. Soon, thereafter, some colleges and universities acted quickly to reap the educational benefits of our rich natural heritage by conducting field classes in the parks or at other suitable locations set aside as part of the extensive campus areas of land grant schools.

Used field trips in 1930's

In the 1930's state park and forest areas frequently were used successfully by secondary and elementary schools for specialized field trips, conservation education classes and projects, and in some instances (notably Michigan) for school camps. During this period the teaching of conservation and outdoor education as part of a state's public instruction requirements was passed into law by several state legislatures.

Among the noteworthy pioneers in the newer concepts of outdoor education and school camping and how these concepts could be implemented through cooperative school-park use were Reynold Carlson, L. B. Sharp, Julian Smith, and William G. Vinal.

Building-centered facilities

At the root of education "through and for" the wise use of the outdoors was the basic concept that nothing is so well learned or so well retained as direct contact with nature. Aldo Leopold strengthened this basic idea of John Dewey's "direct experience" school of learning by further emphasizing the importance of development of perception through sensory educational contacts with the out-of-doors.

Teaching in the classroom and in the outdoors those things that can best be taught in each element requires both building-centered instruction and outdoor laboratories.

The past quarter century of population explosions called for nearly all available educational construction and acquisition dollars to be channeled into classrooms and school buildings. New demands for outdoor education laboratories and a growing conservation curriculum also sought out additional resources in national and state parks and forests, and in lands held for this purpose by universities and colleges.

In some instances, private donors provided suitable areas needed as outdoor education centers. A new source was discovered in those

---

*From American School Board Journal 153:37, August 1966. Used by permission.

more extensive county, regional, or municipal parks that had retained natural areas or had developed naturalist programs. This increased use of the regional, county and municipal parks by schools, and the subsequent development of cooperative school-park programs, are some of the truly significant outdoor education developments of recent times. Programs in this field can be developed and written into curriculums by large and small school systems alike.

Modern educators are faced with an anomaly in which time, distance, and space are shrinking. The demand on educators to include new and varied subjects in the curriculum increases daily; accelerated speeds reduce great distances, and unspoiled space, in terms of land, pure water and air, decreases daily.

Open space and natural areas whose terrain and character is available and suitable for outdoor education is gobbled up by the thousands of acres for highways, subdivisions, and buildings to meet man's insatiable appetite for development. The freeways generate more of the same problems they seek to solve. Open spaces virtually are destroyed by development, and those remaining become increasingly insensitive to the sensitivity built in by nature. Here lies the greatest challenge for education and parks.

Schools have turned increasingly to nearby parks to complement the classroom with outdoor laboratories to help Americans enjoy to the fullest their rich outdoor heritage and recapture everyone's close tie to the soil.

Since public education for wise and discriminating use of parks is vital to the recreation and parks movement *cooperative school-park programs become a mutual benefit partnership.* School-park programs offer exceptional advantages to pupils in regular and special education divisions.

The outdoors also can be brought into the classroom to motivate, stimulate and prepare students and teachers for followup field experiences. School systems using recreation and park outdoor education programs that carry over educationally oriented programs during the summer actually become 12-month schools.

Parks ideal outdoor labs

Parks with extensive natural areas provide ideal settings for the outdoor laboratory or classroom. This especially is true to the degree that parks have unspoiled areas, natural terrain, and provide at one site a meadow, low and upland areas, woods, and a stream or lake.

School planners who are foresighted enough to locate school buildings adjacent to rich outdoor laboratories in large parks enable administrators, teachers, and park or recreation personnel to develop successful cooperative programs.

Since all schools obviously cannot be located adjacent to such areas, the alternative which has proven quite satisfactory is the renovation or construction of a park facility large enough for one or more outdoor education classes. Such facilities made available to schools by the park need not be ornate, but basically ought to provide space for multiple-use classroom, a pure water supply, separate toilet and lavatory facilities for boys and girls, a simple kitchen to supplement bag lunches and provide for refrigeration of milk or other perishable food products, and a dining area.

One section of the facility, or preferably a separate building, could house a nature museum to assist the teacher or other resource personnel to interpret the area. Nature trails often start at and return to such a facility.

"Every season has a reason"

Since buildings will be used mostly by classes during the usual academic year, some form of heat ought to be installed so they may return frequently in order to learn that "every season has a reason." The primary classroom, of course, is the out-of-doors itself. For the most part, park departments have found that an outdoor education facility has a relatively low initial cost and very little maintenance is required. When not used by the schools, it can be "headquarters" for other youth groups having closely related objectives in outdoor education.

When the facility is large enough to accommodate additional classes and sleeping quarters for boys and girls may be used for overnight camping, the outdoor experience is greatly enriched through outdoor group living experiences for teacher and pupil alike.

Some of the major guidelines to cooperative planning of school-park programs are:

1. The development of the educational program specifically ought to meet the needs of the class instructional units. Such needs, units, programs or curriculums are best determined by the school system itself. The subject matter of the outdoor laboratory, whether interwoven with other subjects or made the focus of a unit of elementary or secondary instruction, essentially is determined by the school.

2. Programs proposed by the school must fall within the framework of park capabilities

to provide needed facilities, area, and resource personnel. These are determined largely by park budgets, although in some instances per pupil use costs act as an assist to park budgets.

3. The park administration should gain an understanding of the concept of the community school and how it reaches out to bring knowledge into the school and looks at the entire area as its educational laboratory.

4. The planning, implementation, and administration of the program, while primarily a school responsibility, should provide opportunity for involvement of members of both staffs.

5. Cooperation must be evident on all levels from policy-making bodies to field personnel.

6. There must be a realization that one of the major problems in an outdoor education program is the economical transportation of pupils. (Outdoor areas on a regional, county, or local level are easily accessible by school bus and usually can be reached economically.)

7. Park lands should not be taken away for other public buildings, including school construction, because such lands are at a premium. Where adjacent vacant lands are available for school use, construction on these school sites could be highly desirable.

8. Population and land pressures require a high degree of cooperation among public agencies such as schools and parks to attain the optimum use of available dollars for outdoor education.

Programs serve conservation

Some of the most desirable and effective school-park programs successfully implemented have been concerned with erosion control, providing food and cover for wildlife, growing horticultural stock, and the planting of school forests or arboretums. School camping is a particularly significant program since it combines the values of outdoor learning with 24-hour social living.

Other projects that can flourish under cooperative programs are all those programs considered to be interpretive, i.e., observations of flora, fauna, soil, air, water, landscaping and gardening, nature museum and trail development, outdoor oriented sports, i.e., archery, boating, casting, hiking, shooting, conservation projects and demonstrations; special field trips and recreational outings; day and overnite camping, and the emphasizing of family camping skills.

Cooperative school-park programs in outdoor education benefit all Americans in many ways.

69 ᔏ RESOURCE ROOMS FOR HEALTH EDUCATION*

Recommended requirements for the classroom and the learning center for school health

HAROLD K. JACK
CHAIRMAN, DEPARTMENT OF HEALTH, PHYSICAL EDUCATION, AND RECREATION, TEMPLE UNIVERSITY, PHILADELPHIA

Modern education has become dependent upon a number of complex and sophisticated procedures—not the least of which are the facilities needed for conducting modern instruction. The curriculum in all disciplines is dependent upon the latest innovative devices and teaching aids. Health education is not an exception. Facilities for health education include lunchrooms; health suites; adequate lighting, heating, and ventilation; classrooms; and laboratories or resource rooms, which are designed for self-teaching experiences.

A basic concept in planning facilities for health education is that the teaching-learning facilities should be considered primarily as resource rooms. Such rooms consist basically of two types, or a combination of these types of rooms. The types are:

The classroom. In the classroom, provisions should be made to teach in both an informal and a more formal class situation. Further provisions should be made so that demonstrations, audiovisual material, teaching machines, and the like could be easily incorporated into the process.

The learning center for class resource use and individual use. The learning center should be

*From JOHPER 40:46, November-December 1969. Used by permission.

considered as a type of laboratory or resource center for complete teaching of health education. The learning center is essential in schools which use the modular scheduling type of organization. Such a center makes it possible for students to come for short periods of time and engage in individual study. The associated learning center should be situated adjacent to the work conducted by the more specific classroom situation. Ideally, the classroom and learning center should be situated adjacent to each other.

The learning center could be in combination with a health classroom (one room) in case space is at a premium. However, if such is the case, individualized study could not be scheduled during the time that specific classes in health education were being conducted. The most desirable plan is for the learning center to be a separate installation.

Health education may be grouped with physical education as an administrative device and, if such an arrangement exists, the learning center could serve both health and physical education. In other situations, the learning center for health education might be a part of a larger learning center or a special section of a larger center. Another approach might be to include the health education learning center with the total school learning center, or to have a total school center as a part of the library. In every school, the need for some kind of learning center is basic. Ideally, learning centers should be set up for specific departments, particularly if modular scheduling is to be used.

Basic concepts for a learning center for health

1. It is a resource area for health education and for all students interested in health education.

2. It is a library which contains common references which students in health education would normally use.

3. It is an area in which any student can make use of any of the special equipment, such as record players, microfilm or microcard readers, tape recorders, individual film viewing machines, and office machines. It should be used for the making of teaching materials and exhibits and any other project which would be associated with the individualized work or study which would be of benefit to the student.

4. It is an area where committee work could be carried on and special assignments could be developed. It also provides for display of

posters, charts, and similar materials. All teaching aids would be included.

Built-in equipment

Health education classroom

(Recommended: 1,000 sq. ft.)
Science laboratory demonstration table, equipped with gas, water, and electrical connections
Large floor model lectern equipped with lighting controls, projector controls, microphone, and speaker as well as sound controls
Projection screen, electrically operated
Rheostat for lights (dimming)
Booster lights for TV and videotape filming up to 100 foot candles
Closed circuit TV cable and outside antenna connections
Electrical outlets (all four walls)
Speaker system connected to lectern
Chalk boards in front and rear of room
Tack boards on one entire side of room
Carpeted floor and acoustical ceiling
Bookcases or book shelves for current class reference books
Closet for storage of supplies, models, charts, textbooks

Learning center

(Recommended: 1,000-1,500 sq. ft.)
Book shelves along one wall
Work counter along opposite wall with storage cabinets below and above work counters
Control counter
Combination work-storage room to be located near entrance to center
Individual cubicles (carrels) for listening to tape recorders, record players, audio tapes; viewing of films, slides, film strips; administering hearing and vision tests with equipment; reading and individual research; use of office machines.
Eight-twelve carrels are suggested. Each should have a work surface 4' x 2'; each carrel 6½' in height, 4' deep and 4' wide. Interior of carrel should be sound conditioned. Counter to be at table height and a double electrical outlet at counter. Individually controlled lighting in carrel which is adequate for sustained reading.
Acoustical treatment on ceiling
Carpet on floor
Two reading areas, arranged by using book shelves or carrels as dividers

Furniture

Classroom
Teachers desk and chair
Work table 6' x 3' with matching chairs
Projector stand
40 tablet arm chairs or tables and chairs to seat a class of 40
Coat and hat rack
Waste paper baskets (2)

Supply and equipment lockers if no storage closet is provided

TV receiver for closed circuit or roof antenna

Two four-drawer filing cases

Pencil sharpener

Learning center

Chairs for carrels and work tables, plus six extra chairs

Waste paper baskets

Coat and hat rack

Chair for control counter

Six stools for work at counters

Equipment

Classroom

Scientific equipment for demonstration including glassware table

Qualitative scale for experiments

Overhead projector

Slide projector

Film strip projector

Movie projector

Charts and diagrams on roll-up equipment

Demonstration models

Sample teaching machines

Refrigerator

Pencil sharpener

Learning center

All of the items listed above in duplicate except for demonstration table equipment and refrigerator

Ditto machine

Copy machine

Tape recorder

Record player

Film viewers

PROJECTS AND THOUGHT QUESTIONS

1. Plan a health suite that you would recommend to your superintendent of schools for your high school.
2. What are some of the new trends in facility construction? What are the advantages and disadvantages, if any, of each trend you mention?
3. Prepare a sketch of what you consider to be an ideal physical education plant. In your plans, consider both outdoor and indoor facilities.
4. Visit a nearby school or college and do an evaluation of the health facilities and the physical education facilities in light of each of the following considerations: (a) safety and health of students, (b) space allocations for various activities, (c) office space, (d) locker rooms, (e) outdoor areas, and (f) equipment storage areas.
5. Develop a list of standards for facilities in the following areas: (a) lighting, (b) heating and ventilation, (c) school plant sanitation.
6. What considerations should be made in school or college facilities for recreational activities?
7. Prepare a list of references for obtaining information on various aspects of facility construction and maintenance.

SELECTED READINGS

American Association for Health, Physical Education, and Recreation: Planning areas and facilities for health, physical education, and recreation, Washington, D.C., 1965, The Association.

Bucher, C. A.: Administration of health and physical education programs, including athletics, ed. 5, St. Louis, 1971, The C. V. Mosby Co.

Dickey, D. D.: Athletic lockers for schools and colleges, Minneapolis, 1967.

Joint Committee on Health Problems in Education, National Education Association and American Medical Association: Healthful school living, Washington, D.C., 1969, National Education Association.

Leu, D. J.: Planning educational facilities, New York, 1965, The Center for Applied Research Inc., The Library of Education.

CHAPTER 13 BUDGETING, ACCOUNTING, AND PURCHASE AND CARE OF SUPPLIES AND EQUIPMENT

Budgeting and accounting are necessary administrative considerations for requesting funds, making monies available to areas and individuals, and then exercising control so that funds are used in a right and efficient manner. The administration is responsible for carrying out these functions. They are major duties and require special qualities of integrity, foresight, wisdom, and firmness.

Fiscal management reflects the administrative program. It shows where the emphasis is, what is considered important in long-term planning, and what the activities are that need developing and emphasis. The administration must therefore closely coordinate program with budgeting and accounting. They go hand in hand.

The providing of services by a school or college system, whether in the form of personal help, facilities, instructional materials, or other items, usually involves the disbursement of money. This money must be secured from proper sources, expended in the light of educational purposes, and accounted for in detail. The budget—the master financial plan for the entire school or college system or any subdivision—is constructed with this purpose in mind.

Health educators and physical educators should know the procedures for handling such funds with integrity, the basic purposes for which the educational program exists, the laws governing education, and the codes and regulations concerning fiscal management. Only as the funds raised are used wisely and in the best interests of the students and all people concerned, can the large outlay of monies be justified.

Health and physical education programs utilize many supplies, as well as equipment, that cost thousands of dollars. Supplies are those materials, such as shuttlecocks and adhesive tape, that are expendable and need to be replaced at frequent intervals. "Equipment" is the term used for those items, such as parallel bars and audiometers, that are not considered expendable but are utilized over a period of years.

Since there is a large investment in supplies and equipment, which are vital to school and college health programs and the safety of participants, to good playing conditions, and to values derived from the programs, it is important that the administration give careful consideration to their purchase and care.

Many different sources exist for purchasing supplies and equipment, many grades and qualities of materials are available, and many methods of storing and maintaining materials are utilized. Some of these sources, grades, and methods are good and some are questionable. In order that the greatest values may be obtained for the amount of money spent, basic principles of selecting, purchasing, and maintaining of supplies and equipment need to be known and understood. Although it is impossible to cover all these principles, several of the most important are included in the discussion provided by the articles included in this chapter.

In the first article, J. Alan Thomas explains how administrative decisions are related to finances. He analyzes the nature of decisions upon which the budget is based. There are three dimensions to these decisions he believes: economic, technical, and political. Future budgets, he says, will be based on anticipated revenues, expenditures, and pupil performance.

Edwin Long describes the use of data processing in preparing athletic budgets. The method is accurate, simple, fast, and economical; copies are easily prepared; and inventory is easy. The step-by-step process is included in the article.

Purchase of supplies and equipment often requires a competitive bidding system. Lee O. Garber explains that the competitive bidding system does not require that schools purchase from the lowest bidder, but rather from the "lowest responsible bidder." He cites court cases that have arisen over what constitutes a "responsible bid." The results of these cases can prove to be beneficial to administrators and educators alike.

In a brief article, John C. Kaczmarek writes that athletics involve the health and safety of *all* participants and that purchase and care of equipment must therefore, meet high, rigid standards of workmanship, quality, and safety. Included is a list of guidelines for selecting equipment and considerations for the personnel assigned to handle equipment.

Schools have been held legally responsible for providing a safe environment for school functions. Andrew Grieve cites court cases that show how legal decisions have been made against schools in cases of negligence. It is the responsibility of those concerned with athletics to be certain that equipment and facilities provide participants with the optimum of safety.

In the next article, C. Phillip Selway describes how the efficient, smooth-running, and econo-

mical service in equipment and laundry rooms is necessary in schools and colleges today. The program at the University of Delaware offers suggestions for a good operation.

North Carolina has solved the problem of inventory control by means of a perpetual inventory, which is outlined by Frank J. Murray in the concluding article in this chapter. The program, headed by a specialist in this area, saves considerable time normally spent on the yearly inventory.

70 EDUCATIONAL DECISION-MAKING AND THE SCHOOL BUDGET*

J. ALAN THOMAS
DIRECTOR, MIDWEST ADMINISTRATION CENTER,
UNIVERSITY OF CHICAGO

Most administrative decisions in any organization are related, in some way, to finances. The financial aspects of these decisions are summarized in the budget. Thus, the budgetary document is a statement of the manner in which resources are allocated to achieve the goals of the organization. The preparation and execution of the organization's budget is therefore a central administrative task.

The purpose of this paper is to analyze the nature of the decisions upon which the budgetary document is based. The analysis suggests that there are three dimensions to these decisions: (1) the economic dimension, which involves using available resources in an attempt to maximize goal achievement, (2) the technical dimension, which is based on our knowledge of teaching and learning, and (3) the political dimension, related to the political aspects of resource allocation, both between the public and private sectors, and among and within public institutions.

Most administrative decisions involve more than one of these dimensions. For example, a decision to introduce team teaching into a school has economic aspects (since the cost of the innovation should be calculated, and compared with the anticipated consequences), technical aspects (since the decision to introduce an innovation results in part from our knowledge of processes of teaching and learning), and political aspects (since political support, both within the school and in the larger community, must be mustered, in order to make innovation possible). Another example,

this time with important economic and political implications, would be a decision to de-emphasize athletics in the program of a high school.

These three ways of viewing administrative decision-making have a power of explanation beyond implications for budgets. They may also, for example, be used to depict three images of the school administrator: the efficient manager, the instructional leader, and the politician. Again, these images do not necessarily describe different kinds of people; rather, they are dimensions of a complex set of decision-making behaviors.

Economics and the school budget

When the budget is regarded as a statement of anticipated expenditures and revenues, it is primarily an economic document. There is another way in which it is related to the science of economics. In order that the schools may best serve society, money should be spent so as to obtain the greatest possible educational benefit. This is the criterion of efficiency, the use of available resources in such a way as to maximize goal achievement.[1] As an *efficient manager,* the school administrator will attempt to achieve the best possible results with the funds at his disposal.

In the case of business enterprises whose primary aim is, at least in theory, to maximize profits, the efficiency criterion is clear and explicit. In education, two major types of prob-

*From Administrator's Notebook 12:4, December 1963. Used by permission.

[1] Throughout this paper, efficiency is defined as the relationship between valued output and valued input. See Robert A. Dahl and Charles E. Lindblom, *Politics, Economics and Welfare* (New York: Harper and Brothers, 1953), p. 39.

lem render the meaning of efficiency somewhat obscure.

The first set of problems results from the fact that it is difficult to assign priorities to educational objectives. These objectives are, in the main, value judgments, and opinions about their relative importance vary, both among and within communities. For example, it is difficult to establish priorities when one segment of a community favors that the home economics program be expanded, while another segment advocates that it be abolished. Furthermore, it is difficult to measure the degree to which many objectives of education have been attained.

In the case of those objectives which can be measured, the result is a number of individual indices, which can neither be compared with one another nor combined into a single index. Finally, while businessmen can compare costs with sales in order to determine the amount of profit, it is usually impossible to express educational outcomes in the same units as costs. The single exception to this problem is the measurement of the economic productivity of education, where costs of education are related to the increased earning power of individuals, and to the economic growth of the society.[2] Even here, some serious measurement problems remain.

Even if we agree on objectives and their priorities, and upon some conventions by which they may be measured, there remains the second problem, selecting the "best" means to achieve these ends. This problem has two major aspects. The first is that we usually do not have enough information about the nature and magnitude of educational inputs and outcomes. For example, educational decision-makers usually lack sufficient information about the post high-school academic and vocational success of their graduates. Furthermore, they do not usually have enough data concerning the influence on learning of the out-of-school environment.

The second aspect of the problem is that we do not have adequate information about relationships between inputs and outcomes in education. For example, we would find it difficult to predict what changes in achievement would result from small increases or decreases in the pupil-teacher ratio.

In summary, the economic dimension of educational budgeting requires that we agree upon objectives and their priorities, and that we select the means by which we can best achieve these objectives. In practice, however, given the complexity of large educational enterprises, this is a counsel of perfection. The number of value choices to be made is too great for agreement to be readily reached, and the problem of selecting the best means to achieve the valued goals is an extremely complex one. In order to partially overcome these difficulties, a method called "incrementalism" has been proposed. This method will be discussed at a later point in this paper.

Technical decisions and the budget

Only a fine conceptual line separates what we have called the economic dimension from the technical dimension of educational decision-making. In the preceding section we have shown that the efficiency criterion demands the selection of best means for accomplishing given ends, given limits on the availability of resources. The selection of procedures is also a technical matter, since it must be based on the present state of our knowledge concerning processes of teaching and learning.

As a result of the increasing complexity of large educational enterprises, no one person is in a position to make the technical decisions for the entire school or school system. The assumption is made that teachers and department heads, as well as staff and line personnel, possess the expertise necessary to make technical decisions within their domain of action. Hence, technical decision-making in education is, of necessity, decentralized.

The administrator, as *instructional leader*, helps to create the setting within which "good" decisions may be made. Furthermore, he helps to coordinate decisions concerning educational technologies (or methods of instruction), creating patterns of technologies, which we may call "strategies of education." For example, while a particular style of pupil-teacher interaction which is operative in the teaching of social studies may be called a technology, the organization of the school into groups of various sizes to permit a variety of types of student-teacher interaction may be called a strategy.

The various educational strategies which are implemented in a given school will, inevitably, be reflected in the educational budget. At the same time, limits on available resources which are imposed by external political forces will set some bounds on the strategies which are feasible in a given situation. Hence, technical decisions both determine and are determined by the educational budget.

---

[2] Theodore W. Schultz, *The Economic Value of Education* (New York: Columbia University Press, 1963).

The budget as a political document

The above sections have demonstrated that the school budget is an *instrument* for implementing educational purposes, and for obtaining economic efficiency. The budget is also a *product,* which is developed by procedures which are essentially political.

In the first place, the magnitude of the budget which sets some limits on the educational program, is determined by political processes. At the national, state, and local levels, legislatures make decisions which determine levels of educational expenditure in school districts.[3] These decisions are influenced by interest groups, through lobbying or other political activities.[4]

Within the school system as well, bargaining among groups and individuals at all levels of the organization affects resource allocation. The budgetary allocations result from a compromise among the demands of the organizational units and the academic departments. One of the major functions of administration is to mediate among the groups which make demands, both within the organization, and in the larger community.

The administrator as *politician* will therefore mediate among opposing demands and will utilize political influence in mobilizing support for himself and his program. One device he may utilize is the budgetary document itself, which has a public relations function, as well as an information-giving purpose. This argues for care in the construction of a budget which presents information meaningfully to the interested public. Furthermore, the public's perception of the school's success, as judged by an estimate of the educational output, affects its willingness to provide resources. For example, the number of National Merit semi-finalists which a school can produce no doubt has a salutory effect on the willingness of a community to support its high school. As one administrator remarked, "One of the biggest jobs of the administrator is to develop pride in the schools." This also is a political activity.

Incrementalism

It would be exceedingly difficult to apply the above analysis to complex organizations such as large school systems. In actual practice, however, the situation is much simpler than would, at first glance, appear. The major part of the organization and the budget remain the same from year to year, and attention is focused on small changes or increments which occur as the system grows or as new strategies are developed.

The method of incrementalism involves an analysis of the decisions that accompany these changes.[5] As year-to-year changes in the budget are proposed, the value premises which lie behind the changes in resource allocation are examined. For example, a decision to spend more money on the physical sciences, as opposed to spending additional funds to improve instruction in English, or a decision to build a large library at the expense of an elaborate gymnasium, is based on certain value premises. These premises may be examined—by the school faculty, the administrators, the school board, and the parents—and an attempt may be made to reach some sort of consensus with respect to them.

Once agreement on values is reached, problems of measurement may be considered. Again, it is easier to consider the measurement of the results of minor (or marginal) changes in the school program, than to consider immediately all the measurement problems which the program presents. Minor increments in performance may be compared with the additional costs which are involved, and judgments may be made as to the worth of the program changes.

The technical aspects of decision-making can also be managed more readily when we are considering marginal program changes. The alternative possible ways of achieving the desired outcomes can be compared through research into the cost and effectiveness of alternate educational strategies.

Finally, political decisions made by the community may be more rational when the incremental method is properly applied. For example, in voting on an increase in the tax rate, citizens can be made aware of the marginal increments in performance which are anticipated, as well as of the increased cost. The judgment as to whether anticipated benefits warrant the added taxes may then be made by a more adequately informed electorate.

[3] See the publications in *The Economics and Politics of Public Education Series* (Syracuse: Syracuse University Press, 1962 and 1963).
[4] David B. Truman, *The Governmental Process* (New York: Alfred A. Knopf, 1953).

[5] Charles E. Lindblom, "Decision-Making in Taxation and Expenditures," in *Public Finances: Needs, Sources, and Utilization* (Princeton: Princeton University Press, 1961).

The performance budget

The preceding analysis suggests that some new kinds of budgets may, in the future, be developed. It is possible to draw a parallel here with the use at various levels of government of the so-called performance budget, which Burkhead defines as: "a budget classification that emphasizes the things which government does, rather than the things which government buys."[6]

The performance budget in education would imply the allocation of funds according to anticipated increments in pupil performance. Thus a performance budget in education would include statements about anticipated revenues, expenditures, and pupil performance.

Many of the difficulties in applying this concept have already been commented upon. Educational enterprises are very complex, and they seek a multiplicity of objectives. It is difficult to identify, rank and measure the outcomes of education. However, rather than discarding the concept, we suggest three cases in which the performance budget may be both appropriate and useful to the administration of education. In each of these cases incrementalism decreases the difficulty of developing a performance budget.

The first such case is the budget for a special educational project. For example, a budget related to the development of a project for increasing educational opportunities of children in slum schools might be organized on a performance basis. The goals of the project would be stated in terms of budgeted performance increments, and these increments would be related to the expenditures which are required to produce them. This would of course require that we possess considerable knowledge of the relationships between inputs, educational technologies, and expected outcomes.

The second case where the performance budget may be useful occurs whenever marginal increments in expenditure are planned in a school district. For example, a proposal to increase the operating rate of taxation might have as a primary goal the improvement of written English, by employing theme readers. It seems in this connection to be both appropriate and feasible to suggest, in relatively precise terms, the changes in pupil performance which are anticipated as a result of the increased expenditures.

Finally, the performance budget concept may be useful in the analysis of specific aspects of the school's program. The program area to be examined in this way may change from year to year. For example, it is possible that in a given year the senior mathematics program might be budgeted on a performance basis. Alternately, the costs and benefits of an Advanced Placement program may be itemized in the budget. This kind of analysis forces teachers, department heads, and administrators to examine the consequences of expenditures in the various sectors of the school's program.

---

[6] Jesse Burkhead, *Government Budgeting* (New York: Wiley, 1956), p. 133.

71 ᑄ PREPARING ATHLETIC BUDGETS THROUGH DATA PROCESSING*

EDWIN LONG
DIRECTOR OF ATHLETICS, PHOENIX (ARIZONA) UNION
HIGH SCHOOL SYSTEM

Several years ago I became fascinated with the possibility of the use of data processing equipment in the construction of athletic budgets. Not only was I fascinated, I was over my head with work assignments and felt some method had to be devised to construct the athletic budget which could reflect a saving of time and a greater degree of accuracy than we had experienced in the past, when we had used the old-fashioned method of typing athletic budgets, then adding the columns reflecting the

*From Secondary School Athletic Administration, January 1969, p. 57, American Association for Health, Physical Education, and Recreation. Used by permission.

subtotals and eventually a grand total, and finally proofreading and double-checking each of these for accuracy, because it is almost impossible to go through an athletic budget without making an occasional error or two in the cross multiplying of unit costs versus quantity costs.

Furthermore, the fourth, fifth, and sixth carbons of the athletic budgets were frequently illegible, and the item that appeared on line one of the first copy would appear on about line three of the fifth or sixth carbon. When it came time to read and discuss budgets, it was a serious problem. Consequently, the Phoenix Union High School System embarked upon a method to construct the athletic budgets for its ten high schools through the use of data processing primarily to provide a savings of time and to achieve a greater degree of accuracy in the final product.

Reviewing some of the advantages of data processing budget construction which evolved from our experience, the first, which is one of the things we were looking for, is accuracy. Once the bugs have been worked out on trial runs in the use of this type of budgeting, achievement of accuracy becomes almost fool-proof. Along with accuracy comes the point that, if an error is made, it is repeated consistently at all ten schools and usually shows up immediately in the budget-reviewing stages.

The second advantage is simplicity. The forms we use in the budget-making process are simple; they are easy to fill out; they reflect a great amount of information; and they are easily understood by the many people involved in the construction of athletic budgets when you have ten high schools and some 13 different sports, including four girls' sports and the pom-pom and cheerleading activities.

The third advantage we have discovered is that budget making through the use of data processing equipment is economical. It saves time and I can think of no more important commodity these days. Very little time is spent by those who initiate the budgets and much less time is spent at my level in reviewing and recommending approval of the budgets. Even more important, much less time is spent in implementing the budgets once they have been prepared and approved by the board of education.

A fourth advantage are [sic] the by-products which result from having budgets set up on data processing equipment. Two of these by-products we have already implemented and use all the time. Two more bear serious investigation as, in my opinion, they can realistically be used in the future. The first by-product which we use in our district is typing of warehouse requisitions from the original budget. I will go into this in more detail later.

The second by-product is a vendor requisition which is produced in a seven-part copy all filled in and typed out by the machine, ready for the coach who initiated the budget to now initiate the requisition when he sees fit. These requisitions are printed according to code, that is, capital outlay items, supplies, transportation, repairs, and items purchased from gate receipt funds.

A third by-product I can foresee in the future is a purchase order for a vendor which can, I believe, be made from the budget in the same way the requisitions are made. I think this can be easily handled; all that would have to be identified or added to the purchase order or an extra copy of the requisition would be the purchase order number, the vendor's name and address, the unit, and the total price, and it would be ready to mail to the vendor, thus saving retyping of all the other information which goes on a purchase order.

Another by-product I can visualize is the inventory. This is important to all of us and easily adapted to this type of budget making. We could carry a running inventory at a particular school of a particular item to be identified on the budget form at the same time the coach initiates his budget requests for the coming year, by merely adding a second quantity column to reflect the present inventory. Certainly all of us respect the importance and use of inventories, and it can become useful and helpful in screening the athletic budget.

A fifth advantage is speed, which somewhat relates to economy. We can actually make the athletic budgets for ten high schools for 13 different sports—a budget which totals approximately $270,000—in a matter of a very few days. If it *had* to be done and you had access to the key punch operators and the running time on the data processing equipment, this could very easily be constructed in ten days. Our biggest hold up is the key punch time and the machine running time.

A sixth advantage is control of the requisitioning of items from the athletic budget once it has been approved and placed in the hands of the many coaches in a large multischool district. Whenever you have ten high schools and a large, comprehensive athletic program, if you can control the flow of the requisitions, it is really important to your buyers and your warehouse personnel as well as to you as the athletic director in reviewing the requisitions once more as they are processed. By having all the requisitions printed off the machine at the end of the school year and then separating them by sports, you are able to release a certain sport at a certain time with the instructions that these requisitions be processed immediately. Therefore, you are able to control their flow through the different business offices which may have to be used in your particular school district. In our case, it is budget control first, my office second, and the purchasing division third. By following this procedure, if I have had a change of mind or there is a change of specifications, I am able to adjust the requisi-

ID#	QTY	UN	DP	CODE	DESCRIPTION	UN COST	UNIT DESC	AMT
				ATHLETIC BUDGET 1965–1966				FOOTBALL
100050		1	73	2130	BELTS WEB CHAMP	$ .40 EA	24 REP	
					SIZES:....MED....LG....XLG			
					WIDTH:....1 IN....1¼ INCH			
S00075		1	73	2130	CHIN STRAPS, ADAMS PRO WHITE	$ .75 EA	40 REP	
S00125		1	73	2130	FACE BARS WILSON F2182	$ 1.75 EA	40 REP	
S00150		1	73	2130	FACE GUARDS RAWL 14NG	$ 6.75 EA	3 REP	
S00175		1	73	2130	FOOTBALLS PENNSYLVANIA PF6S	$ 12.00 EA	10 REP	
100200		1	73	2130	GAME JERSEYS CHAMP FB26	$ 4.00 EA	40 REP	
					.....STYLE.....SLEEVE			
					.....BODY COLOR...TRIM STYLE			
					.....TRIM COLOR. EXTRAS....			
					X CUT.....SDS.....OTHER			
					PUT SIZE BEFORE NUMBER...10...11			
					.....12.....13.....14.....15.....16			
					.....17.....18.....19.....20.....21			
					.....22.....23.....24.....25.....26			

Exhibit A. Athletic budget.

tions before they go to purchasing for issuing of a purchase order or a warehouse stock requisition.

The seventh advantage is that of making what I call a "composite" budget of all ten of our high schools, item by item, so I can get a quick bird's eye view of any one item on a district-wide basis. For example, the first item on the football budget might be athletic socks. By turning to the first page of the composite football budget, I can compare and see the quantities requested from all ten schools for this particular item. Each item reflects a total quantity for the entire district of ten schools along with the dollars and cents amount budgeted.

Many things can be related immediately and errors can be detected easily. For example, if you know that ten local charter buses will be needed for [a] varsity football team during the season and a school has only budgeted for five, it becomes immediately and easily obvious that a mistake was made in the budgeting. This can be pointed out to the school and corrected in time to avoid an embarrassing situation September first.

In the next few pages, I present the step-by-step process we use in the construction of our athletic budgets.

The first year of using this particular method of budgeting for athletics almost cost me and some of my colleagues our jobs for being so insistent in carrying it out. Our budget making was full of errors. We had changed some of the forms being used and people had difficulty in acclimating themselves to some of these changes. Requisition forms were oddly shaped because margins were needed on the sides for the machines to feed them through for printing purposes; therefore, they came out a little larger than the conventional requisitions. I pleaded that everyone who was upset and disturbed over this type of budget making should please be patient and give us one year to work out the kinks and bugs. They did, and we did, and I venture to say that if we turned budget making back to the old method of a more manual nature, I probably *would* be fired!

Exhibit A is page one of the athletic budget for one of our high schools in Phoenix. The first column on the left, identified by the heading ID#, refers to the identification number given each item on the budget. We use this number in discussing budget items from time to time over the phone with the buyers or with people at the schools so we can refer to a number rather than a description of an item or a name. Some numbers are prefixed with the letter "S" which indicates that this is a warehouse stock item. When requisitions are printed, the stock items are printed on separate requisitions from the nonstock items. We are very fortunate in Phoenix in that we have a tremendous warehouse system and are able to warehouse about 80 percent of our athletic equipment. As an example, last year we had all of our football jerseys in warehouse stock by the first of February.

The second column, QTY, is the only column left blank in the first step of our budget-making procedure. This item is filled in by the coach and is the key item in the first step of budget construction.

The next column is headed by the letters UN,

which means "unit" or "school." Any time that I see Unit 1, I immediately associate this with Camelback High School; Unit 2 is Carl Hayden High School; Unit 3, Central High School; etc.

The fourth column has a heading of DP, which represents "department," or the particular sport involved. For example, the number 73 appearing on this example immediately tells me this is a football budget; 74 represents cheerleaders, 75 baseball, and so on down the line with all of athletics being assigned the 70 and 80 series of any of our data processing work. Once acquainted with these numbers, you can read them as if they actually said "football," "baseball," "basketball," etc.

The next column is given the heading CODE. This merely reflects the state code that relates to that particular item, whether it is a capital item or an instructional item, a medical item or repair item, etc. Some items reflect the abbreviation ACT instead of a code number. This indicates that the item is purchased from athletic gate receipts. Each of the different codes can be given a subtotal which also gives a chance to compare different prices in different categories of one budget to another or one school to another and also separates tax budget funds from activity or gate receipt budget funds. When the many codes are added together into a grand total, the result is the total budget for that particular sport; and the sum of these figures gives a particular school's budget. The individual school budgets added together give a *grand* grand-total for the entire district's athletic budget. Having all these things in the machine on a code basis, a department basis, a unit basis, and a quantity basis, makes possible many different studies or breakdowns for comparing the athletic budget.

The next column, DESCRIPTION, describes the particular item presented on that particular line. Included is a complete description, and provision is made for the coach to insert on the requisition all vital information necessary to complete the requisition and send it to the buyer for purchasing purposes. I am referring to such things as sizes, colors, widths, trim styles, sleeve styles, and other information necessary to give a complete description of all pieces of athletic equipment. In some cases a single line description of all pieces of athletic equipment. In some cases a single line description is all that is needed; sizes, etc., are not vitally important. Other items, such as football game jerseys, require several lines to reflect the size in relationship to the jersey number, etc.,

to have the available information for the buyers or purchasing division.

This column is probably the key to the entire athletic budget because the description of the items must be completely accurate, and must be predetermined or the requisition part of the budget is of no value. Options can be offered here so that the coach can check one or the other of a certain description or style. We established our descriptions, or specifications, through a joint process of working in group meetings with the different coaching departments. We review these annually to meet our latest needs insofar as specification changes are concerned, but few changes have to be made each year.

The next column reflects the UNIT COST of each item. In some cases the unit cost may be a dollar and cent denomination which must be multiplied by the quantity required to come up with the total amount of money to be put in the budget for that particular line for that particular item. For example, to cover football laundry, the unit cost may be $25, and the quantity might be ten. The machine would then multiply ten times $25 to come up with a total of $250 as the amount the coach requests for laundry for football. Our previous year's buying experience dictates the unit costs used for the coming year.

The next column, UNIT DESCRIPTION, is a unit maximum purchase or the most that can be requested of any single item. In no case, however, is enough money provided for a school to purchase a maximum of all items in one budget. We have tried to place a control here by requesting that most of these are purchased only on a replacement basis (REP means replacement). If a coach requests a dozen of a certain item, he must come up with the old ones to be discarded or turned in for replacement.

The last column provides space for the insertion of the amount put into the budget for a particular item. This amount doesn't come out even when multiplying the quantity times the unit cost. Instead, the machine automatically adds 4 percent into each line to cover the Arizona sales tax or for payroll items where we have to add 4 percent matching funds.

The first step in budget preparation is to issue a budget information memorandum (Exhibit B), which goes out to each coach. This includes, of course, the date the memo is initiated and to whom it is addressed and reflects basically (1) the procedure to be followed, (2) a calendar schedule to be followed, (3) the

Date: December 13, 1967
To: Coaches, Administrative Assistants
From: Ed Long
Subject: Instructions for preparing the 1968–1969 Athletic Budget

The athletic budget procedure for 1968–1969 is basically the same as it was for 1967–1968. The data processing equipment of the System will be utilized to its fullest extent in assisting you in this process. The step-by-step procedure and timetable follow:

1. December 12: A printed, tabulated listing of the athletic budgets of each athletic department of each unit was distributed to each unit (through its Administrative Assistant). Duplicate sets of these budgets have been produced for unit distribution as follows:

   a. One (1) broken copy is for the coaches. This copy is to be filled in by the coach and returned to me through his Administrative Assistant.
   b. One (1) broken copy is to be retained at the unit in the office of the Administrative Assistant for reference.

Coaches are to insert the number of items they desire within the framework of the limitation that has been set forth under the heading "Unit Description". Please insert the quantities needed on the dotted line under the heading "QTY".

2. January 9: The Administrative Assistant is responsible for returning all athletic budgets to me on this date. Quantities needed should have been inserted on all budgets.

3. February 6: The priced budgets (quantities listed times price listed plus 3$^{1}/_{2}$% for applicable sales tax) will be returned to the Administrative Assistants. You will be asked to revise your budget if necessary to conform to the total dollar allocation given your unit from Tax Budget and Student Activity Budget funds.

4. February 13: All athletic budgets completed in final form are returned to me by this date. If any returned budget is not within the limit of the dollar allocation, I will make the necessary final cuts.

5. February 20: I will submit the athletic budgets to Mr. Burress, Director of Budgeting.

6. After the Board of Education has adopted the 1968–1969 budget for the System, four (4) copies of your final athletic budget will be forwarded to each unit. These copies will reflect all changes made while being processed. The Board of Education will formally adopt the budget at its first meeting after July 1, 1968.

Each page of the 1968–1969 athletic budgets has a "header" line. This identifies the school, the athletic budget date, the department of athletics, and the appropriate page number of the department's budget. A second "header" line follows, which contains the following descriptive information:

1. ID#—(item identification number) The numbers assigned to each item are printed immediately below this head. ID#'s preceded by the letter "S" are warehouse stock items.

2. QTY—(quantity) Dotted lines have been created immediately below this heading for the insertion of the quantity of items you wish to budget.

3. UN—(unit) The number appearing below this line is a code identification of the school.

4. DP—(department) Number appearing below this line is a code identification of the department.

5. CODE—Four digit numbers appearing below this line identify designated state code for budgetary purposes.

6. DESCRIPTION—The budget item is properly described below to include vendor's catalog numbers, sizes, colors, widths, etc. PLEASE DO NOT FILL IN THE BLANKS IN THIS SECTION. They will be used at the time the "tabulated requisition" is forwarded to you for completion.

7. UN COST—(unit cost) The expected cost to be incurred for the purchase of the unit(s) described is set forth in the column immediately below this heading. This cost will be used in all cases in extending the budget amount. Any substitutes in price or item will not be made unless it is deemed advisable for all units.

Exhibit B. Budget information memorandum.

8. UNIT DESCRIPTION—In the column immediately below this heading, <u>maximum</u> quantities or dollar amounts are set forth. In no case should there be a time when the quantities you set forth as your budget needs exceed the maximums found in this column. If they do, they will be reduced to the maximums stipulated.

9. Allocations for each unit:

    a. From tax budget funds: $15,500

    b. From activity budget funds (by sports):   7,500

  *(district level):   3,150

        Total: all departments . . . . $26,150 × 10 = $261,500

*car purchase and maintenance, post-season activities, awards, equipment man overtime, bleacher rental

1968–1969 Athletic Budget Guidelines

Tax budget funds (by sports): $15,500

Activity budget funds (by sports)   7,500 $23,000

District level

  Activity budget funds:

    Car purchase and maintenance $1,000

    Post-season activities   500

    Awards   1,000

    Equipment man overtime   200

    Bleachers   450   3,150 $26,150

                                    × 10 = $261,500

RECAP:

    Total tax budget funds   = $15,500 × 10 = $155,000

    Total activity budget funds = $10,650 × 10 = $106,500

    TOTAL BUDGET   = $261,500

Exhibit B. (Cont.)

inclusion of budget allocations for that particular school and (4) a breakdown of these budget allocations as to how much money is appropriated from tax budget funds and how much from student activity or gate receipt funds.

We also carry a portion of the budget at the district level, which merely means that the amount of money is kept in a lump sum for all ten schools to draw upon as needed. Some of the items purchased from this district-level fund are the annual purchase of previously allocated items such as station wagons and their maintenance, postseason activities (which is an item that can't always be foreseen), awards, some of the athletic equipment men's overtime, and bleacher rental.

For the benefit of new coaches, we also give a brief one- or two-sentence description of the several columns that are reflected in the budget worksheets.

The second step is to give each coach who will be filling out a budget request a complete budget which includes all the things mentioned in Exhibit A. He merely goes through the budget and marks the quantities of items he wishes for a particular sport, line by line, omitting those he does not want. At the end of the budget the coach may write in additional items not already listed but which he thinks he wants so I can review them and give consideration to approval or disapproval of them. Exhibit C shows the first page of the budget form completed by a coach.

Once this rough draft is finished, which doesn't take much time or effort on the part of the coach, it is forwarded to my office. We collect all ten budgets and turn them over to data processing where the recommended quantities are key punched, cross multiplied by the unit cost to reach the many subtotals and eventual grand total for each individual school. These figures are then added together to reach the grand grand-total for the district.

If, at this point, the total requested for a particular school exceeds their allocation, the budget is returned to the school with instructions to cut the budget to stay within the allocated figure. The coaches then go over it again with their own needs in mind, give and take one sport against another, until they cut the budget down to the figure we have allocated in the beginning. Then the budget is resub-

ALHAMBRA   ATHLETIC BUDGET 1965–1966   FOOTBALL

ID #	QTY	UN	DP	CODE	DESCRIPTION	UN COST	UNIT DESC	AMT
100025	12	14	73	2130	ATHLETIC SOCKS. CHAMPION 198	$ 8.00 DOZ	24 DOZ	99.36
100050		14	73	2130	BELTS WEB CHAMP	$ .40 EA	24 REP	.00
					SIZES: . . .MED. . .LG. . .XLG			
					WIDTH: . . .1 IN. . .1¼ INCH			
S00075	404014	14	73	2130	CHIN STRAPS, ADAMS PRO WHITE	$ .75 EA	40 REP	31.05
S00125	6	14	73	2130	FACE BARS WILSON F2182	$ 1.75 EA	40 REP	10.86
S00150	3	14	73	2130	FACE GUARDS RAWL 14NG	$ 6.75 EA	3 REP	20.90
S00175	10	14	73	2130	FOOTBALLS PENNSYLVANIA PF6S	$ 12.00 EA	10 REP	124.20
100200	40	14	73	2130	GAME JERSEYS CHAMP FB26	$ 4.00 EA	40 REP	165.60
					. . .STYLE . . .SLEEVE			
					. . .BODY COLOR . . .TRIM STYLE			
					. . .TRIM COLOR. EXTRAS.			
					X CUT. . . . .SDS. . . . .OTHER			
					PUT SIZE BEFORE NUMBER. . .10. . .11			
					. . .12 . . .13 . . .14 . . .15 . . .16			
					. . .17 . . .18 . . .19 . . .20 . . .21			
					. . .22 . . .23 . . .24 . . .25 . . .26			

Exhibit C. Completed budget.

CAMELBACK   ATHLETIC BUDGET 1965–1966   FOOTBALL

ID #	QTY	UN	DP	CODE	DESCRIPTION	UN COST	UNIT DESC	AMT
S00025	24	01	73	2130	ATHLETIC SOCKS. CHAMPION 198	$ 8.00 DOZ	24 DOZ	198.72
S00075	40	01	73	2130	CHIN STRAPS. ADAMS PRO WHITE	$ .75 EA	40 REP	31.05
S00125	15	01	73	2130	FACE BARS WILSON F2182	$ 1.75 EA	40 REP	27.11
S00175	10	01	73	2130	FOOTBALLS PENNSYLVANIA PF6S	$ 12.00 EA	10 REP	124.20
100200	40	01	73	2130	GAME JERSEYS CHAMP FB26	$ 4.00 EA	40 REP	165.60
100225	6	01	73	2130	GAME PANTS SOUTHLAND SP67	$ 13.50 PR	6 REP	83.83
100250	40	01	73	2130	GAME STOCKINGS. CHAMPION.	$ 2.65 PR	40 PR REP	109.71
S00275	24	01	73	2130	GRID PADS. WILSON 9420	$ 1.50 PR	24 RP REP	37.26
100300	15	01	73	2130	HEADGEAR PLASTIC. . . .STYLE.	$ 18.95 EA	40 REP	294.14
100325	2	01	73	2130	HELMET TAPE. . . . . . .COLOR.	$ 3.95 ROLL	36 YDS	8.17
S00350	12	01	73	2130	HIP PADS. RAWLINGS 17KP	$ 9.00 PR	12 PR REP	111.78
S00475	48	01	73	2130	INNER SOLES ASSORTED SIZES	$ .25 PR	48 PR REP	12.42
S00500	2	01	73	2130	JAW PADS HELMET ADAMS	$ 14.00 DOZ	24 DOZ PR REP	28.98
S00525	4	01	73	2130	KICKING TEE. VOIT	$ 2.10 EA	4 REP	8.69
S00550	40	01	73	2130	KNEE PADS P100	$ 4.00 PR	40 REP	165.60
S00575	2	01	73	2130	OFFICIALS SHIRTS. RAWLINGS 20KRS	$ 6.50 EA	4 EA	13.45
100625	108	01	73	2130	PRACTICE JERSEYS. CHAMPION NY56	$ 3.00 EA	108 REP	335.34

Exhibit D. Final print-out of athletic budget.

mitted to me. I check each one over once more before submitting them all to data processing for a second print-out.

The third run (Exhibit D) is our final print-out of athletic budgets for that particular school. At this step, we run multiple copies of the budgets in two formats. First they are run as in Exhibits A and C; then in Exhibit D, which is called a short form, which merely means that instead of including all the information under the DESCRIPTION column, we have used only the first line which describes the basic item. In other words, game pants, Southland SP67, is all that would appear on that budget,

not reflecting the color, body stripe, size, etc., which might be necessary to prepare the requisition. This shortens the length of the entire budget for each sport to a matter of two or three pages, making them easier to handle. The detailed information isn't really vital after this point, anyway.

Exhibit E shows page one of the composite print-out which I spoke of earlier. This reflects totals in the quantity column and totals in the amount column of each individual item for all ten schools. This is very helpful insofar as putting out the bid and being able to analyze and see how much is being spent on different

					ATHLETIC BUDGET 1965–1966			FOOTBALL
ID #	QTY	UN	DP	CODE	DESCRIPTION	UN COST	UNIT DESC	AMT
S00025	24.00	01	73	5611	ATHLETIC SOCKS. CHAMPION	8.00 DOZ	24 DOZ	199.68
S00025	24.00	02	73	5611	ATHLETIC SOCKS. CHAMPION	8.00 DOZ	24 DOZ	199.68
S00025	12.00	03	73	5611	ATHLETIC SOCKS. CHAMPION	8.00 DOZ	24 DOZ	99.84
S00025	24.00	04	73	5611	ATHLETIC SOCKS. CHAMPION	8.00 DOZ	24 DOZ	199.68
S00025	24.00	05	73	5611	ATHLETIC SOCKS. CHAMPION	8.00 DOZ	24 DOZ	199.68
S00025	24.00	06	73	5611	ATHLETIC SOCKS. CHAMPION	8.00 DOZ	24 DOZ	199.68
S00025	24.00	10	73	5611	ATHLETIC SOCKS. CHAMPION	8.00 DOZ	24 DOZ	199.68
S00025	14.00	14	73	5611	ATHLETIC SOCKS. CHAMPION	8.00 DOZ	24 DOZ	116.48
S00025	24.00	15	73	5611	ATHLETIC SOCKS. CHAMPION	8.00 DOZ	24 DOZ	199.68
S00025	24.00	16	73	5611	ATHLETIC SOCKS. CHAMPION	8.00 DOZ	24 DOZ	199.68
	218.00T							1,813.76T
100050	24.00	01	73	5611	BELTS WEB CHAMP	.40 EA	24 REP	9.98
100050		02	73	5611	BELTS WEB CHAMP	.40 EA	24 REP	
100050		03	73	5611	BELTS WEB CHAMP	.40 EA	24 REP	
100050		04	73	5611	BELTS WEB CHAMP	.40 EA	24 REP	
100050		05	73	5611	BELTS WEB CHAMP	.40 EA	24 REP	
100050		06	73	5611	BELTS WEB CHAMP	.40 EA	24 REP	
100050		10	73	5611	BELTS WEB CHAMP	.40 EA	24 REP	
100050		14	73	5611	BELTS WEB CHAMP	.40 EA	24 REP	
S00050		15	73	5611	BELTS WEB CHAMP	.40 EA	24 REP	
100050		16	73	5611	BELTS WEB CHAMP	.40 EA	24 REP	
	24.00T							9.98T
S00075	40.00	01	73	5613	CHIN STRAPS, ADAMS PRO WHITE	.70 EA	40 REP	29.12
S00075	40.00	02	73	5613	CHIN STRAPS, ADAMS PRO WHITE	.70 EA	40 REP	29.12
S00075	20.00	03	73	5613	CHIN STRAPS, ADAMS PRO WHITE	.70 EA	40 REP	14.56
S00075	20.00	04	73	5613	CHIN STRAPS, ADAMS PRO WHITE	.70 EA	40 REP	14.56
S00075	20.00	05	73	5613	CHIN STRAPS, ADAMS PRO WHITE	.70 EA	40 REP	14.56
S00075		06	73	5613	CHIN STRAPS, ADAMS PRO WHITE	.70 EA	40 REP	
S00075	40.00	10	73	5613	CHIN STRAPS, ADAMS PRO WHITE	.70 EA	40 REP	29.12
S00075	40.00	14	73	5613	CHIN STRAPS, ADAMS PRO WHITE	.70 EA	40 REP	29.12
S00075	40.00	15	73	5613	CHIN STRAPS, ADAMS PRO WHITE	.70 EA	40 REP	29.12
S00075		16	73	5613	CHIN STRAPS, ADAMS PRO WHITE	.70 EA	40 REP	
	260.00T							189.28T

Exhibit E. Composite print-out.

items on a school-wide basis. This is the only budget I really use in my office. I do not use the ten individual school budgets; I use the composite which is printed out in the short form.

It is easy to read and is the best way to review because all ten budgets can be checked at one time by a quick glance, item by item. I can get a quick comparison of what each school asks for and after a time you get to know the schools and the programs and know exactly what to look for in the way of mistakes. You can then make corrections so you don't get caught the following football season budgeted for only half enough money for officials, or transportation, or some fixed charge without which you cannot get by.

We now print out eight budgets for each school, but give only one to each school at this date of our budget season. The others are distributed at the end of the school year after the

board of education has approved the budget.

At the same time, we also print up the requisitions which are kept in my office until we decide it is the appropriate time to distribute them. For example, in the spring of the year we distribute the football budget, the cross country portion of the track budget, and the pompom and cheerleading budgets. We will process those and get them out of the way before school ends, so we can handle all of our purchasing and delivering to the schools during the summer and have everything ready to go when the coaches come back in the fall at the start of their season.

Our particular method has become so well liked in our school district that we are rapidly moving into it for all of the subject matter areas on a line budget basis, and I know it will become a standard procedure in our school district in Phoenix in the very near future.

72 ॐ SCHOOL LAW*

When schools can ignore low bids

LEE O. GARBER
DIRECTOR, EDUCATIONAL SERVICE BUREAU,
UNIVERSITY OF PENNSYLVANIA, PHILADELPHIA

School districts are not always compelled to accept the low bid—even though virtually every state has a law on its books demanding that districts use a competitive bidding system.

These laws—and this is the heart of the matter—nearly always specify that the contract be awarded to the "lowest *responsible* bidder," a statement that seems clear enough to avoid controversy.

Such has not been the case. A lot of litigation and painful argument has arisen over what constitutes "responsible" and who decides who *is* "responsible." Confusion can be cut down if these guidelines, established by the courts, are kept in mind:

1. The laws that specify "lowest responsible bidder" do *not* deprive school districts of their rights to exercise discretion in determining whether the lowest bidder can perform the tract satisfactorily.[1]

2. It is up to the school district, not the courts, to determine who is responsible and who isn't.[2]

3. The word "responsible" is not limited to financial or pecuniary responsibility, but includes the bidder's ability to perform the contract according to its terms. Courts in New York and Pennsylvania have made this clear.[3] The Pennsylvania supreme court told school districts they should "investigate the bidders to learn their financial standing, reputation, experience, resources, facilities, judgement and efficiency" and then make a decision.[4]

4. There's little likelihood that the courts will interfere with a district's decision. When it awards a contract to the lowest "responsible" bidder, a district is using discretionary, not ministerial, authority. In other words, the district is using judgment, a function specified by law and approved by the courts. In any case, it would have to be proved that the district acted arbitrarily or fraudulently before court action could be expected.[5]

"All that is required of officials," stated the Connecticut supreme court of errors, "is that they observe good faith and accord all bidders just consideration, thus avoiding favoritism and corruption."[6]

5. The school district can reject all bids and start all over again. This, too, is an act of discretion and has been upheld by the courts.[7]

6. There is very little a disappointed low bidder can do, unless state law specifically gives him the right to complain. Where the law does, however, the burden of proof is on the bidder. It's up to him to show that he was "a responsible bidder" and, said a Connecticut court, there is "no burden on the board to go out and investigate blindly as to the bidder's responsibility."[8]

It should be kept in mind, however, that in most states a taxpayer can bring a suit without benefit of a state law permitting such action. It is wise, therefore, to keep our community fully informed about your bidding procedures and decisions.[9]

7. In most states a school district can reject a bid without having to give the bidder a hearing. New Jersey, however, has held that before the district can reject a low bid on the grounds that the bidder is not responsible, it first must give "notice and hearing to the bidder affected."[10]

---

*From The Nation's Schools **74**:50, August 1964, copyright, McGraw-Hill, Inc. Used by permission.

[1] Fred C. McClean Heating Supplies, Inc. *v* Westfield Trade High School Building Committee, 186 N. E. (2d) 911 (Mass). (1962).

[2] Somers Construction Co. *v.* Board of Education, 198 F. Supp. 732 (originating in N.J.) (1961).

[3] Pacionne *v.* Board of Education of City of New York, 195 N. Y. S. (2d) 593 (1959).

[4] Hibbs *v.* Arensberg, 276 Pa. St. 24, 119 A. 727 (1923).

[5] Coward *v.* Mayor, etc. of City of Bayonne, 67 N. J. L. 470, 51 A. 490 (1902).

[6] Joseph Rugo, Inc. *v.* Henson, 148 Conn. 430, 171 A. (2d) 409 (1961).

[7] Prout Boiler, Heating & Welding, Inc. *v.* Dickson, 164 N. E. (2d) 423 (Ohio) (1959).

[8] Meyer *v.* Board of Education, 221 N. Y. S. (2d) 500 (1961).

[9] R. S. Noonan, Inc. *v.* School District of City of York, 162 A. (2d) 623 (Pa.) (1960).

[10] Edward J. Rose, Inc. *v.* The Board of Education of East Orange, 121 A. (2d) 549 (N. J.) (1956).

8. The courts will not tolerate the rejection of a low bid in favor of another if the favored bid is changed in any way. "The acceptance of an offer is always required to be identical with the offer," the Washington supreme court ruled, "or there is no meeting of the minds of the contract." This kind of action "is not an acceptance and consummates no contract," the court warned.[11]

9. Care should be taken when advertising for bids. If the advertisement is worded as to constitute an offer to accept the lowest bid, the lowest bid must then, of course, be accepted.[12]

10. While it isn't essential to take the lowest bid by price, it is essential that any law demanding competitive bidding be followed. The statute is mandatory in all cases and is binding on all districts. When it is ignored not only is the district subject to prosecution, the unlucky winner of the contract has no legal recourse for collecting his fees—even though he may have furnished materials and labor and completed the work.[13]

[11]Blue Mountain Construction Co. *v.* Grant County School District, 306 P. (2d) 209 (Wash.) (1957).

[12]Reams *v.* Cooley, 171 Cal. 150, 152 P. 293 (1915).
[13]Yoder *v.* School District of Luzerne Township, 399 Pa. 425, 160 A. (2d) 419 (1960).

73 ❧ EQUIPMENT CARE CARDINAL OBLIGATION*

John C. Kaczmarek
Commissioner of Athletics,
Milwaukee Public School System

The wise purchasing and maintenance of athletic equipment is the responsibility which school authorities cannot evade. The administrative responsibilities for selecting and purchasing athletic equipment must be clearly defined and delegated. Athletics in a school system involve the health and safety of all the participants, therefore the selection and purchase of such equipment must meet high rigid standards of workmanship, quality, and safety to protect each participant. It is most essential, therefore, that a harmonious relationship exist in all the facets of choosing and securing athletic equipment, namely, between the coach and the athletic director; athletic director and the school administrator or the person delegated to act in his behalf.

The tragedy of mistakes made in purchasing equipment is multiplied many times because of the lack of understanding, communication, and resourcefulness between administrators. No school system should be exposed to censure for spending public funds because it shows a lack of cooperation within the working structure.

Administrators would be wise to establish sharp lines and patterns of communication between all involved. Regular procedures must be followed. A school athletic council should be composed of athletic directors, all head coaches, the purchasing agent of the school, the principal and/or superintendent or the delegated authority, and the director of physical education. Regular meetings must be scheduled in advance to ensure perfect attendance. Discussion relating to budgeting, selection, care, maintenance, utility, and the inventory should be reviewed periodically. When individuals are well informed through good communication, problems have a tendency to be eliminated.

Quality is main factor

The selection and purchasing of equipment is developed only by diligent work and experience. In the final analysis, experience is one of the best teachers. Never purchase athletic equipment with only price in mind. Experience teaches that equipment which meets the rigid qualifications is top quality and is priced higher. In extending this experience when purchasing bear in mind the following guidelines when selecting athletic equipment:

1. The best designed item and the material it is made of.
2. How safe and what protection does it afford?
3. Is the workmanship and quality of the best?
4. Has the item proven utility and what is the estimated cost of maintenance?
5. Does the purchasable item afford a ready source of generous supply on demand?
6. What price must be paid for the item?

Maintenance of any athletic equipment is a cardinal obligation of the administration. Large

*From American School Board Journal 153:29, August 1966. Used by permission.

sums of public funds can be squandered on maintenance because of inefficiency, lack of good judgment, poor discipline by the coach, and the failure to teach participants the proper care and value of an item. Equipment is designed and manufactured to withstand hard play on any play area, provided it receives the proper care, cleaning, and storage.

Personnel assignment important

Assignment of personnel to handle equipment, storage space, and inventories must be administered properly if length of service of an item is to be realized. It is essential that guidelines be established. A policy in maintenance and administrative responsibility should be clear to all in the program. All directors or coaches must be made responsible for the basic care of equipment. Information must be given to those responsible as to the proper handling of leather goods, athletic shoes, inflated materials, all rubber equipment, fabric used in athletic uniforms, hard plastic protective equipment, and laundering factors. The "do's" and "don'ts" properly interpreted from the time equipment is unpacked until it is discarded as "worn out" are essential.

Purchasing, maintaining, and storage of athletic equipment is big business today. Consequently, administration must gear controls with the same attitude that business establishments have adopted.

74 ❧ LEGAL CONSIDERATIONS ON EQUIPMENT AND FACILITIES*

ANDREW GRIEVE
ASSISTANT PROFESSOR OF PHYSICAL EDUCATION,
STATE UNIVERSITY OF NEW YORK COLLEGE AT CORTLAND,
CORTLAND, NEW YORK

In any discussion of the legal aspects of athletic activities, it must be realized that there are variations in the statutes of the various states regarding the immunity of school districts. It is not the purpose of this article to discuss the various legal viewpoints which exist throughout the fifty states but it would be wise to mention the present trend toward the elimination of immunity for school districts in the area of negligence. Over the past few years, the tendency has been to hold the school district responsible for providing a safe environment for school functions. Each year legislative action in various states has indicated that school districts should be held liable for negligent acts, and athletics, due to the nature of the activities, has become a prime target for such legal action.

Although we intend to direct our attention specifically toward situations in athletics which have or may result in legal actions because of equipment or facilities, information will be presented which is based on other activities but could prove to be precedent-setting in nature. Due to the absence of previous legal actions in one particular area, the courts will often utilize decisions which were the outcome of legal actions with similar circumstances, even though the activity itself may be different. A few such cases will be mentioned in this article. The important point is that the courts will look to other legal decisions as guides before judgments are made.

A number of legal actions involving athletic activities have been the direct result of situations created by equipment and facilities. It is the direct responsibility of all those concerned with athletics to be certain that such equipment and facilities are proper for the activity and provide the participants with the optimum of safety.

Manufacturers of such items and facilities are constantly emphasizing the safety of their products and this is one of their main selling points. They realize safety is one of the factors with which coaches and directors will be concerned as they make decisions on the purchase of equipment and the construction of facilities. For this reason a large majority of these suppliers spend considerable money and effort on research in order to provide the maximum in protection. As a result, there can be no excuse for a lack of safe equipment or facilities.

In many instances, legal problems might not arise in the case of varsity teams, but rather at the lower levels such as junior varsity, freshman or even junior high school groups. In some instances, these groups are the recipients of hand-me-down equipment, which may fit poorly, be unsanitary, and in need of repair. If legal action were instituted, and it could be proven that the equipment worn by an athlete did not provide him with the optimum of protection, the court would obviously be inclined to feel that negligence might be indicated.

*From The Athletic Journal 47:38, February 1967. Used by permission.

There was a case in Pennsylvania several years ago where the judge in a lower court strongly indicated his opinion of football. Since the school district had governmental immunity no claim could be settled, but if such immunity had not existed there could be little question as to the judge's attitude. This case involved *Martini vs. School District of Olyphant,* in which a boy was injured when he was sent into a football game with defective headgear. The judge stated:

"There are many moments when a football game produces a commotion and violence which would make an Apache war dance seem like a Sunday School picnic in comparsion. In one of these moments (the injured youth) lost his battered headgear and was stepped upon, kicked and otherwise manhandled to the extent that his nose was broken and he was carried off the field as if dead."

Due to the existing statutes, however, the court held football was an educational activity and had to be considered a governmental function thus eliminating the possibility of liability.

Although there is no record of such a case, a relatively new mandatory regulation which requires football players to wear mouthpieces could create difficulties for the coach who is not conscientious in checking this situation. There are boys who will avoid wearing this important protective item if at all possible. Since such protection is mandatory according to the football rules, the coach is responsible for being certain that each boy is wearing a mouthpiece during all situations in which there is the slightest possibility of a tooth injury. It has been medically substantiated that the mouthpiece also aids in the prevention of concussions and other head injuries. Thus, if a boy receives this type of injury while not wearing his mouthpiece, then a coach might well be held liable for his negligence in not verifying that the boy had this protective device in proper position. We are not looking for situations in order to frighten members of the profession, but in the legal action which we have mentioned, and those mentioned later, the predisposing factors are usually the exception rather than the rule, and this matter of the missing mouthpiece will be an exception, but one which could result in legal action.

In one case on record the court decision was based upon a very minute point. A youngster was struck by a bat which had slipped out of the hands of a player who was swinging at a ball. It was pointed out that the bat in question did not have a knob on the end as do most bats,

and was a factor in the accident. As a result, the school was found negligent for using equipment which could be considered dangerous.[1]

During an indoor baseball drill a student was directed to hit a ball and run to a base in the gymnasium. Since the base was not anchored in any way, the student fell and was injured. The court felt that such an arrangement was negligent and found the school district liable for the injury.[2]

Due to the variations in statutes, which we mentioned previously, a legal action may be instituted against a school district in those states which do not hold such districts immune. In those states which do provide immunity, the legal action could be directed at the individual teacher because he can be held responsible for his negligent acts. The previous two cases occurred in New York where the school districts are not immune and assume the responsibility for the negligent acts of their employees or officers.

During athletic events numerous accidents occur due to the nature of the facilities, and such accidents might well result in legal action. Certain areas and activities are more prone to such incidents because of the equipment and facilities required. In dealing with this area, we must consider all of the possible facilities which might be utilized for athletic events including fields, tracks, gymnasiums, courts, and even locker rooms.

There is one incident which stands out in our mind where an existing hazard could have unquestionably resulted in a legal action for negligence. During a baseball game a first baseman was chasing a foul ball and was intent upon catching the ball. He failed to observe a guy wire which was supporting a telephone pole. He ran full force into the guy wire which caught him across the neck and felled him. There was no type of protective fence or padding about this wire to prevent such an accident. This condition had undoubtedly existed for a long time but no action had been taken to prevent such an incident. Fortunately, the boy was not injured seriously, but if he had been there is always the question as to what would have been the court's decision in an ensuing legal action. Situations do arise which cannot be prevented, no matter how much supervision or what protective measures may be taken. In

[1] Rapisardi vs. Board of Education of New York City, 273 N.Y.S. 360.
[2] Bard vs. Board of Education of New York City, 140 N.Y. Supp. 2d 850.

this particular case, however, this hazard had obviously existed for a long time and could have been rectified if it had been noticed as a potentially dangerous condition.

Although it did not involve an athletic activity, there was a suit in California which had comparable circumstances. A young girl was playing on a school playground and was injured when she tripped over a cement box which projected above the ground. The court found the school liable for negligence because this situation had existed for several years, and they considered this sufficient grounds to consider that the school had previous knowledge of the situation.[3]

Even though there was no question about negligence existing, the courts in Minnesota found that a school performing a governmental function cannot be held liable. This case involved a football player who had unslaked lime enter his eye and caused him to lose his sight. If this accident had occurred in another state where this immunity did not exist, there would have been no doubt that negligence was present. As the result of this and similar incidents, it is now illegal, according to the rules to utilize this type of material to mark fields.[4]

Indoor areas can prove to be as replete with dangerous conditions as outdoor areas. We usually find there are pieces of equipment and appliances which can lead to liability suits if it can be proved that some negligent act took place. In general, if an accident could have been prevented by careful inspection of the facilities or the equipment it would have to be considered negligence by the courts.

In one case, a student was injured when he fell in the gymnasium due to a defective floor. At first the courts indicated the plaintiff had no cause for action, but on appealing the case a higher court stated if the claim of a defective floor could be substantiated the school would be liable. The contention was supported and the court found for the plaintiff on the basis that the school district was responsible for the proper maintenance of their facilities to protect the youngsters.[5]

There was a similar case in Oregon but the school district was not held liable. In this case, the suit concerned an injury suffered by a youngster when he collided with a radiator in a gymnasium. In this state maintaining a radiator in a gymnasium was considered as a part of the governmental function of the school and thus could not be considered as negligence although it did result in an injury.[6]

In New York there was a case which involved the absence of mats on the gymnasium wall. A participant ran into an unprotected wall and was injured. The plaintiff contended that during an activity in which there is the possibility of a collision with a wall it should have protective covering. The courts indicated that protective covering on all walls of a gymnasium is not the usual practice and found the school was not negligent.[7]

There are several cases which involve the use of mats during certain activities. There was a question in one case regarding the use of mats against a wall which served as the finish of a foot race. In this case, it was once again considered as not being the standard practice and the school was not held as being negligent.[8]

On the other hand, there are conditions which may indicate that matting is necessary due to the existing circumstances. The use of a slippery balance beam on an oily floor with no mat under it was considered as a negligent act.[9]

Being familiar with or being notified of a dangerous situation which exists in athletic facilities or equipment will usually result in the courts deciding in the favor of the plaintiff if an injury occurs as a result of such a defect. A boy was injured when using a defective springboard of which the supervisors had been informed. Since the court felt that such information was in the hands of those responsible for the activity prior to the injury, they were negligent in allowing the use of this piece of equipment.[10]

During athletic activities there will always be extensive use of the locker room and shower facilities. It is imperative for those in a supervisory capacity to recognize that injuries sustained in these areas must be given consideration as they inspect the facilities for safety and the elimination of negligent situations.

[6]Spencer vs. School District No. 1, Oregon, 254, Pac. 357.

[7]Bradly vs. Board of Education of City of Oneonta, 276 NYS 622; 243, A.D. 651 (New York).

[8]Kattershinsky vs. Board of Education of New York City, 212 NYS 424.

[9]Bush vs. City of Norwalk, 122 Conn. 426.

[10]Kelly vs. New York City Board of Education, 191 App. Div. 251.

[3]Bridge vs. Board of Education of City of Los Angeles, 38 Pac. (2nd) 199 (California).

[4]Mokovich vs. Independent School District, 177 Minnesota 466; 225 N.W. 292.

[5]Katz vs. Board of Education of City of New York, 162 App. Div. 132.

We have observed a large number of such facilities which could be considered unsafe, but we all too often inspect only the area where the athletic action is to take place. There was a case in California where it was obvious the courts felt such prudence was imperative. A participant was seriously injured when a loosened locker attachment gave way. The courts judged that this condition must have existed for a length of time in order for the accident to occur and it was the responsibility of those in charge of such facilities to guarantee their safety. Thus, the school was found liable for the injury.[11]

Since a locker room can be the source of injuries, it would be wise for those in charge of an activity to provide some supervision in this area. However, it is not expected that a coach will have to remain in the locker room whenever it is occupied. This was the basis of a litigation in New York whereby the plantiff contended there should be adequate supervision whenever this area was in use. The courts indicated it should not be necessary for constant supervision under normal circumstances.[12]

Although the attitude of the courts may at times appear unusual, those in charge of athletic activities must be well informed and do their utmost to protect the school district and themselves from possible legal action. An aspect which we must understand is that of the *attractive nuisance*. By this term the courts have indicated it is the responsibility of those in supervisory capacities to eliminate as much as possible situations which will attract youngsters whereby they might be injured. The classic case in this area had to do with two youngsters who climbed a fence around a railroad yard and were injured while playing on a turntable. Even though the area was fenced the parents of the youngsters were successful in a suit against the railroad as the courts adjudged the turntable an *attractive nuisance*. It is not assumed youngsters are going to realize the dangers which exist in certain situations and cannot be held responsible for their thoughtless actions.

In New York we find the doctrine of the *attractive nuisance* has not been completely accepted by the courts as being applicable to every situation. In a recent litigation the courts decided that a school district was not expected to supervise playground facilities when school was not in session.[13]

In the same state, however, there is a case on record where a school district was found negligent because a teacher failed to lock a gymnasium door during an unsupervised period. A youngster wandered into the gymnasium and was injured, even though he was not supposed to be in the area. The courts felt since the youngster was able to gain admittance to the gymnasium this had created an *attractive nuisance* and the teacher must be considered as being responsible for the injury.[14]

Although our thinking on equipment is usually limited to the areas of negligence and liability, the legality of the school board using tax money to purchase athletic equipment has been the source of several court actions. The law concerning such expenditures will vary from state to state. In some, it is specifically indicated in the educational law that public money can be used to purchase such equipment since athletic activities are considered a part of the educational program. The statutes of other states, however, specifically prohibit the use of such money for the purchase of athletic equipment and to do so would be the basis for legal action against the board of education or the individual who permitted such an expenditure. If the state law prohibits such action and a school does desire to purchase equipment or facilities, or repair and maintain such, the athletic program would have to be self-supporting. In these situations, the athletic program would have its own budget and the money involved would be spent solely for expenses associated with athletics.

We do not wish to enter into a discussion of the pros and cons of the two methods because there are strong arguments on both sides. In several instances, we have noted there has been a trend away from the separate athletic budget. Just recently, for example, in New York State it was ruled that all gate receipts must be placed in the general fund of the board of education. It has been legal to use tax money to purchase athletic equipment but many schools still maintained a separate athletic fund. The Bureau of Finance and Control of the State Education Department recently indicated that all income from such activities must be considered

[11] Freund vs. Oakland Board of Education, 82 P (2d) 197, (California).

[12] Donohue vs. Board of Education of Mt. Pleasant, N. Y., N. Y. Law Journal, Oct. 19, 1938, p. 1204.

[13] Streickler vs. New York, 15 App. Div. 2d 927, 225 N.Y. Supp. 2d 602 (1962), rev'd. 13 N.Y. 2d 716, 191 N.E., 2d 903 (1963).

[14] Longo vs. New York City Board of Education, 225, N.Y. 719.

as an income of the school board rather than being earmarked specifically for the athletic department. Hamilton and Mort, in their book, "The Law and Public Education," state the school board has the power and the responsibility to control the income from athletic events and this cannot be delegated to school employees, officials or students. A specific question was brought before the courts in Pennsylvania on this matter. The district and country courts both held that the proceeds from school activities belong to school districts and must be accounted for as are other district funds.[15]

The legality of the purchase of athletic equipment by a school board has been questioned in court action. In Montana this question was brought before the courts, probably as a test case. The courts indicated that such a purchase was legal.[16]

A similar question was raised in Pennsylvania because there was some doubt whether a school board had the authority to purchase such special items. There is a list of special items which school boards can legally purchase, but there was no mention of athletic equipment as such. The court interpreted the existing statutes to be broad enough to include the purchase of such items. They also indicated that another statute which permitted school boards to use tax money to provide for gymnasiums and playgrounds was broad enough in scope to include the purchase of athletic equipment.[17]

On the other hand, there was a rather unusual interpretation in Massachusetts several years ago involving the purchase of basketball uniforms with public money. In this state it is legal to purchase athletic equipment in this manner, but the question involved the purchase of special athletic equipment, namely basketball uniforms. The law allows for the purchase of any equipment which is used on land under the control of the school board. This brought up the question of the use of such uniforms by the school team for away contests.

The court decided that such items could not be considered under the broad term *supplies* and there could be no legal payment for these uniforms.[18]

There was an interpretation of the State Law of Ohio in Opinion No. 635 by the attorney general of that state regarding the legality of using school funds to purchase athletic equipment. He stated the following:

1. "Boards of education are without power to expend public school funds under control to support or promote the competitive playing of games by picked teams from the pupils of the public schools.

2. "The authority granted by law to the Director of Education to prescribe or approve a course of physical education in the public schools does not authorize the inclusion within such courses of what is commonly termed interscholastic athletics or the competitive playing of athletic games by picked teams from the pupils of the several public schools.

3. "Interscholastic athletics as the term is commonly used, is not a proper public school activity under law.

4. "A board of education in Ohio is not authorized to pay from public funds under their control the expense of furnishing basketball, football or baseball uniforms for the high school basketball, football or baseball teams, as the case may be.

5. "A board of education is not authorized to pay from public funds for the expense of transporting their basketball, baseball or football teams to a distant point for the purpose of holding an athletic contest between that school team and a team representing another school."

Obviously, as a result of this opinion, high school athletic programs in this state must be self-sustaining.

With the numerous legal actions which have involved equipment and facilities, all those concerned with athletics in the school situation must give consideration to these factors. If there is the least possibility that existing equipment or facilities could result in legal action, it is an obligation of all personnel to rectify such situations.

[15] In re. German Township School Directors, 46 D & C 562, (Pennsylvania).

[16] McNair vs. Dist. No. 1 of Cascade County et al, 87 Montana 423, 288 p. 188.

[17] Galloway vs. School District of Borough of Prospect Park, 331 Pa. 48, 200 A 99.

[18] Brine vs. City of Cambridge, 265 Massachusetts 452, 164 N.E. 2nd 619.

75 ⁊ EFFICIENCY IN THE EQUIPMENT AND LAUNDRY ROOMS*

C. Phillip Selway
Equipment Manager, University of Delaware,
Newark, Delaware

With all the current emphasis on education and physical fitness, schoolmen would do well to re-evaluate their procedures in the equipment room and laundry areas.

It's important to modernize our methods to cope with the expanding physical education and athletic programs and to produce an efficient, smooth-running, and economical service.

Basically, this area must meet every need of the coach, supply the team with speed and efficiency, and serve the school to its fullest capacity. In order to meet these requirements, the plan must be flexible enough to adapt to every change in the physical education and sports program.

The University of Delaware is a land-grant institution attended by about 4,000 full-time undergraduates (the majority of whom are male students), who need a flexible program in the equipment room. This area serves 22 freshmen and varsity teams, as well as 800 physical education students who require daily laundry and equipment services.

Among the responsibilities of the area are identification, issuing, laundering, repairing, and storage of equipment. Realizing that all coaches and equipment managers have their own ideas on procedures, I'm not suggesting that you change your present system. My intention, rather, is to help you reconstruct any weak areas you may have.

First of all, you should try to standardize your equipment. By this I mean that you shouldn't use many types of articles made by different manufacturers. Purchase the material you believe to be the best for your participants as well as your budget. Encourage your coaches to join you in observing this pattern, as their cooperation is needed.

Since it costs as much to buy a large quantity of inexpensive equipment as it does to buy a few pieces of good standard material, I buy no equipment that hasn't been *tried on the field* and found to meet our specifications. I never sacrifice safety for economy.

After field-testing all the types you're interested in, make a decision based upon quality, safety, and cost. Consult your team trainer, since his opinions on safety are valuable. Another aid to your decision can be a reliable sporting goods retailer. It's to his advantage to supply you with all of his services.

After determining the equipment best suited to your program, continue with this product so that you can eliminate all substandard material. You'll soon find you're using one basic type manufactured by one certain company.

Naturally, all schools are constantly being approached by companies and vendors hoping to supply them with their products. The companies you select must be reliable in every respect, being able to supply you with the repairs and replacements you'll need in future years. Any deviation from the practice of standardization can produce immense problems in fitting as well as repairs.

Most cottons can be stenciled by the manufacturer for a nominal cost during the production process. This can eliminate many man-hours of work for the equipment manager.

The quality of the merchandise must be the primary consideration, as the constant, daily use of cottons demands top-quality materials. Every time these cottons are laundered, a certain percentage of the budget is washed down the drain. Therefore, you must choose top-quality materials that have been proven to withstand daily use.

In our program, all participants, including graduate students and faculty members, are provided with a complete change of clean clothing before working out. This can be done simply in the form of a roll—wrapping the socks, supporter, "T" shirt, and shorts in a towel.

Don't worry about individual sizes when making these rolls, since this can be done at issue by making the participant responsible for his specific size.

When purchasing socks, use the largest size that fits the majority of the users. Whereas it's easy for a person to get into socks that are slightly large, it's impossible for a large man to get into small socks.

During the initial issue, each student signs an Equipment Card (made in triplicate) for everything he receives. Also recorded is such information as school, home address, and locker combination.

---

*From Scholastic Coach **34**:30, January 1965. Used by Permission.

When a student changes his roll, he receives only the replacement for whatever he turns in. Any missing article is immediately replaced, if he so desires. If not, the missing article is recorded on his card. Under this system, you have either the articles issued or a record for future payment.

Laundering is effected very efficiently with two washers, two extractors, and two driers. Since we're washing out only the perspiration and light dirt, we use an ordinary household detergent. This speeds the washing cycles and reduces the chemical detergent costs. All synthetic fabrics are washed in cold or lukewarm water and hung neatly in the laundry area to drip-dry.

By using portable lockers close to this area, it's simple to have the game equipment laundered and set up ready for its next use. The lockers can be wheeled to the lockerroom, where the equipment can be placed in the permanent lockers.

In repairing equipment, we try to avoid outside agencies. These have proven to be very costly in some areas. Though there are times when schools must rely on one or more of these concerns, most of our repairs are made by our equipment men during the off-season.

Conveniently placed in our laundry area is an electric sewing machine that's used to repair all fabrics. During football season, after the clothes are laundered, we repair jerseys and pants as they're sorted. Ready-made knee pockets can be replaced and small repairs made before they're returned to the issue area.

For repairs to heavier articles, such as belts and leather, we use an old shoe-sewing machine. Since this is a manually operated device, we're limited to minor repairs.

Inside our equipment area is a specially constructed room for shoe maintenance and storage. For repair work we have a vice, wire brushes, and small hand tools; while for polishing, we have an electric machine with a wire brush and buffing wheel.

All game shoes are hand-polished and machine-buffed before every contest. Practice shoes are rinsed with water to remove dirt, allowed to dry, and given one coat of neats-foot oil to replenish the removed oil and to keep the leather soft.

Small tools are kept handy at the issue counter for minor repairs on many types of equipment. Any major repairs are made in our own small shop. Here we have electric saws, drills, and sanders (both table and portable). This shop enables us to build, repair, or refinish

almost all of our field equipment, as well as handle various jobs for the Department.

All new equipment starts its rounds on the varsity level. It's used here until the equipment manager decides it should be passed on to the freshmen level. This process usually takes about two years. After two more years, the equipment is discarded.

At the end of each sport season, we take inventory while cleaning and inspecting the equipment for storage. This gives us a complete set of facts and figures at all times, in addition to eliminating the need for an all-sports inventory at the end of the school year. After compiling our facts and figures, we send a copy to each coach.

During the spring, I begin ordering my new equipment for the next school term. By setting up a file of the clothing and equipment sizes of everyone participating in sports, we can order game and practice equipment far in advance of manufacturers' deadlines.

This is the time that our equipment field-testing program pays off. Without any reservations, I can select from the articles on trial those which meet our standards. This eliminates all questionable materials from the orders.

Our fair-trial selection also keeps us abreast of all new products being introduced by the sporting goods manufacturers. By combining the trainer's injury statistics from the past season with field-testing information, an equipment manager can have a solid basis for his orders.

I believe every equipment manager should be encouraged to aid in the purchasing of equipment. Being the closest person to the equipment, he can give valuable opinions, and he'll also develop a greater interest in his work.

For the actual purchasing of player equipment, I submit the order to our athletic department business procedures. All purchasing is done on a competitive basis, with the order going to the lowest bidder. My recommendations and specifications, based on field tests and past experience, are generally approved.

We use three basic colors for our "T" shirts and shorts—navy blue for fall, red for winter, and gold for spring sports. On the first day of the season, we issue the corresponding color for that season. We hence know that anyone wearing the color of the preceding season must possess unauthorized equipment. Since cottons represent a large portion of the budget, the reclamation of this unauthorized equipment is most important.

Another area where much time and labor

can be saved lies in the initial issue of lockers. Each combination is recorded on a master control board in the equipment cage. These may be issued without leaving the area, and the combinations recorded on the student's record for easy reference. No student has access to any locker other than the one assigned to him. All the lockers are cleaned and locked when not in use.

In summary, I'd like to point out that the foregoing ideas are just basic in nature. Each equipment area differs with respect to general location, overall layout, laundry facilities, and general operational system.

76 ❧ PERPETUAL INVENTORY*

FRANK J. MURRAY
PHYSICAL EDUCATION DEPARTMENT,
UNIVERSITY OF VIRGINIA,
CHARLOTTESVILLE, VIRGINIA
FORMERLY, ASSISTANT PROFESSOR, NORTH CAROLINA STATE COLLEGE

North Carolina State College is extremely proud of its required physical education and instructional program. It embodies some 20 different activities including touch football, baseball, softball, golf, tennis, swimming, life-saving, skating, volleyball, squash, bowling, riflery, handball, archery, wrestling, boxing, speedball, track, and soccer.

A program as varied as this will embrace more than 75% of the entire student body; and when you consider the astronomical amount of equipment needed to expedite this program, the vital necessity for a clear-cut and efficient system of accounting becomes obvious. Without it, the stock will gradually vanish into nothingness.

It has long been the feeling of the head of the Physical Education Dept., Mr. P. H. Derr, that a full-time specialist offers the ideal solution to the equipment problem. The specialist eliminates a duplication of responsibility and relieves the teachers of the harassment attending such duties.

At N. C. State, a faculty member (the writer) has been appointed to offer assistance to the equipment custodians whenever possible. The result has been most auspicious. From this harmonious relationship between the writer and the equipment room custodian, has evolved a time-saving perpetual inventorial system.

Whenever a boy comes to the gym to check out his physical education uniform, he's issued the following items: a pair of socks, a supporter, a pair of shorts, a T shirt, a sweat shirt, a pair of sweat pants, a towel, a basket, and a combination lock. These items constitute his wearing apparel and he must sign a master card professing his financial responsibility for them.

Whenever any of these items become soiled, he merely brings the article to the equipment room for a clean replacement. The opposite side of the card lists the boy's basket number, combination number, locker number, serial number, date issued, date returned, condition returned, and charges ("Locker Assignment Card").

Should an individual lose an item of issued equipment, he merely brings his school identification card to the equipment cage and signs a statement that he has lost an item of wearing apparel and will be financially responsible for it. This statement is used to debit his account, and he's then issued a replacement.

This information is reflected on his personal master record card, and a copy of his statement is filed in a folder that contains other similar statements. At the end of the month a voucher will be prepared, that will account for all items of equipment that have been lost or destroyed during that month. A typical voucher appears in the accompanying chart.

A detailed filing system is essential to assure maximum efficiency. We employ a cardex filing system, utilizing a separate perpetual inventory card for each item of equipment in the gym. A typical example of this efficiency is indicated in the accompanying illustration. It may be explained as follows.

1st entry—inventory showing 3,600 towels on hand.

2nd entry—in September shipment of 500 towels is received.

The figures in voucher #1 are then added, showing a total of 55 towels that were lost to the Physical Education Department, then the total number of towels still on hand (4,045) are recorded. The same procedure is utilized for each piece of equipment.

Whenever an item is discarded because it's worn out or unfit for use, it's shown on the

---

*From Scholastic Coach 31:20, January 1962. Used by permission.

| | | | | PERPETUAL INVENTORY | | | | | | | | | | #11P16 |
DATE	ORDER NO	QUANTITY IN	QUANTITY OUT	BALANCE	DATE	ORDER NO.	QUANTITY IN	QUANTITY OUT	BALANCE	DATE	ORDER NO	QUANTITY IN	QUANTITY OUT	BALANCE
INVENTORY				3600										
9-61		500		4100										
10-61	Vou #1		55	4045										

MIN   MAX   COST   SELLING PRICE **price**

NO	ARTICLE		SECTION	AISLE	BIN
	TOWELS, CANNON (seconds)	.7562			

TYPIST PLEASE NOTE - START ALL TYPING AT SAME POINT ON SCALE. THEN REMOVE THIS STUB. BE SURE YOU HAVE A WELL INKED RIBBON. CARE USED IN TYPING WILL IMPROVE REFERENCE DURING THE ENTIRE LIFE OF THE INDEX. TRY A FEW IN THE POCKETS TO SEE HOW THEY LOOK BEFORE TYPING THE ENTIRE LIST.

ACME VISIBLE RECORDS, INC.

RE-ORDER FORM NO. 11P16-6   CROZET, VIRGINIA   PRINTED IN U.S.A.

Voucher #1   Oct. 30, 1961

	Lost	Destroyed	Others	Total
Towels	55	6		61
Socks	7 prs.	8 prs.		15
Volleyball		1		1

I certify that the above items were lost or otherwise disposed of in the best interest of the Physical Education Department.

_____

Signed

---

monthly voucher signed and attested to by the equipment custodian at the end of each school month.

At the end of the school year, all students are required to turn in the equipment issued to them at the beginning of the school year. When a boy brings his equipment to the cage, his master card is scrutinized to ascertain whether a deficiency exists between the amount of equipment that he has checked *out* during the year and the amount that he checks *in*. Should a deficiency appear, the student will sign a statement as to the amount that he owes.

The equipment custodian will then consoli-date all the student statements and send it to the business office, which in turn will act as a collecting agent, crediting the account of the Physical Education Department with the amount stated on the bill. The voucher and personal statements are considered subsidiary records and must be filed and saved.

This system may appear somewhat elaborate, but when you consider the monetary savings alone, to say nothing of the time normally used to conduct a yearly inventory, you can see that it's a necessity. Due to the current high cost of physical education and athletic equipment, a system such as this will pay for itself in one year.

251

PROJECTS AND THOUGHT QUESTIONS

1. Collect budgets from two high schools or colleges, and critically evaluate them.
2. Outline the procedure that might be followed in the preparation of a budget in a department of health and physical education.
3. What are the criteria for a good budget?
4. What are the most common sources of receipts and expenditures in a health and physical education department?
5. Survey a school or college policy on the purchasing of supplies and equipment. Evaluate this policy in light of your knowledge of appropriate purchasing procedures. Discuss in class.
6. List and discuss five principles that should be followed in respect to the selection of supplies and equipment. Apply these principles to the procedure involved in selecting parallel bars for the gymnasium.
7. Prepare an administrative plan that you would recommend to the administration for checking, issuing, and maintaining physical education supplies and equipment. Be specific, pointing out steps and procedures, to ensure sound property accountability.
8. What are the legal requirements for purchasing supplies and equipment in your state public schools? For example, what are the requirements for letting bids for purchases?

SELECTED READINGS

Association of School Business Officials of the United States and Canada: Purchasing and supply management manual for school business officials, Bulletin No. 22. Evanston, Ill., 1962, The Association.

Bucher, C. A.: Administration of health and physical education programs, including athletics, ed. 5, St. Louis, 1971, The C. V. Mosby Co.

Casey, L. M.: School business administration, New York, 1964, The Center for Applied Research in Education, Inc., The Library of Education.

How to budget, select, and order athletic equipment: Chicago, Athletic Goods Manufacturers Association (805 Merchandise Mart).

Participants in National Facilities Conference: Planning areas and facilities for health, physical education, and recreation, Chicago, 1965, The Athletic Institute.

Roe, W. H.: School business management, New York, 1961, McGraw-Hill Book Co.

CHAPTER 14   LEGAL LIABILITY AND INSURANCE MANAGEMENT

Legal liability and insurance management represent administrative concerns in programs of health and physical education. The danger of accidents while students are participating in the various activities that comprise the programs, the use of special types of apparatus and equipment, excursions and trips, the need for first aid, and other items concerned with health and physical education, have implications for liability.

Leaders in the fields of health and physical education should be informed about what precautions are necessary in the administration of their programs so that they are not held legally liable in the event of accident. The fact that approximately 50 percent of accidents in which school pupils are involved occur in buildings, more than 40 percent in playgrounds, and 10 percent on the way to and from schools shows the implications for these specialized fields.

When an accident resulting in personal injury occurs on school property, the question frequently arises as to whether the cost of damages can be recovered. The National Commission on Safety Education points out that all school employees run the risk of suits by injured pupils on the basis of alleged negligence that causes bodily injury to pupils. Such injuries may occur on playgrounds or athletic fields, in science laboratories, or any place that students congregate.

The legal rights of the individuals involved in such cases are worthy of study. Although the law varies from state to state, it is possible to discuss liability in a general way that has implications for all sections of the country. The selections that are included in this chapter provide the health educator and the physical educator, as well as school and college administrators in general, with an understanding of their responsibilities under the law to provide for the safety and welfare of not only student's, but also other people's property and belongings.

In the first article in this chapter, Alvin W. Howard, through citing court cases, shows how teachers may be sued for negligence and that they should therefore be aware of the many situations and conditions in which liability exists. The teacher is expected to be present or to take steps necessary to safeguard the students as shown in the cases cited.

George F. Shroyer writes that no coach or board of education could possibly pay out large sums of money for liability in cases of negligence. The coach, therefore, should use good judgment, act prudently, have the physician present at all contests, and follow the first-aid textbook procedures, to avoid law suits.

Questions often posed in cases involving negligence are answered by Charles J. Frankel in the next reading. The questions answered are those regarding legal responsibilities of the team physician and the school physician.

Andrew Grieve, in the next article, discusses problems involved in transporting students. Transportation of children to and from athletic events involves a greater risk of accident than any other school activity. Policies are more liberal today than in the past. Guidelines offered by Grieve, based on court decisions cited, are that only bonded carriers or school-owned busses should be used, students should not be allowed to transport athletic teams, coaches should not be permitted to drive school-owned vehicles, and administrators should know the laws regarding such policies and procedures.

Spectator injuries are the subject of another article by Andrew Grieve. The safety of spectators too often is left to chance, and the result is numerous legal actions. The courts have ruled that spectators assume a certain amount of risk when they attend a contest. At the same time, administrators must provide proper supervision, equipment, facilities, medical care, and freedom of hazards to spectators.

In the last article in this chapter, Lawrence W. Grimes explains some of the changes regarding athletics and insurance trends in the last few years. Most school districts are required to provide general liability insurance for those involved in educational activities. Grimes says that administrators must have a realistic attitude toward accidents and must plan accordingly. Trends are changing in handling and processing insurance coverage; schools, therefore, should have the proper current understanding of the nature, benefits, and obligations of an insurance contract.

77 ☙ TEACHER LIABILITY AND THE LAW*

ALVIN W. HOWARD
MEMBER OF THE FACULTY, UNIVERSITY OF NEW MEXICO,
ALBUQUERQUE, NEW MEXICO

Litigation of all kinds appears to be on the increase and school litigation is no exception. Teachers are not expected to know all of the many laws, regulations, and court decisions pertaining to the operation of the public schools. However, the very nature and responsibilities of the teaching profession, involving as it does care and supervision of children, make it desirable for teachers to be aware of what may or may not be areas of liability.

Guidelines of a somewhat definite nature exist for many of the more common situations met by teachers, although it is obviously impossible to anticipate all occurrences. Various court decisions have emphasized that the teacher must exercise "reasonable" caution, an "average amount of foresight," and provide "adequate supervision." Negligence is considered to exist if harm befalls as the result of an action which could have been foreseen by a prudent teacher, using ordinary care, in a reasonable effort to avoid trouble. The courts have, in various cases, stressed "prudence," "intent," "reasonableness," and caution in a situation in which danger is inherent.

Keep this clearly in mind: teachers may be sued for their negligence. School districts, because of the principle of governmental immunity, cannot be sued for damages in most states, but teachers can be and sometimes are defendants in suits for damages. Teachers are personally liable to pupils for injuries occurring because of teacher negligence. Negligence is often defined as lack of taking such care and precautions as a responsible person, one who is reasonably prudent, should take in any given situation. Children cannot be expected to behave as mature adults, the courts have held, and teachers, by reason of their training and experience, must expect that children will act in response to childish motives and must take necessary precautions accordingly.

Precautions considered necessary may vary with the age, maturity, and intelligence of the pupils, and the question which must be decided, should the issue reach the courts, is that of determining what a reasonably prudent teacher should have done in this particular situation to forestall possible harm to any of his charges.

The teacher is held to stand *in loco parentis*—that is, in the place of the parents as regards the pupil while he is under the jurisdiction of the school. This position gives the teacher the authority to control the pupils, but carries with it the responsibility to safeguard them.

In point of fact, it is indeed a curious matter that teachers who frequently have several years experience are thoughtless and careless in the presence of potentially dangerous circumstances. For example: the physical education teacher who permits students to work out on a trampoline with insufficient training or, worse yet, leaves the class to "free play" while he occupies himself in his office or the locker room; or the industrial arts teacher allows students with little or no training to operate power tools without proper supervision; or the classroom teacher who is often late to class or who leaves before the end of the period while, in her absence, the students engage in throwing things, scuffling, and other kinds of horseplay—all of these teachers may be found guilty of negligence and liable.

The consequences of proven negligence can be disastrous for the teacher. In instances where negligence has been proven, the negligent one has been held liable for physical harm, results of fright, emotional disturbances, and shock to an injured party.

The teacher is expected to be present in all school situations although his presence alone is not enough—he must take such steps as are necessary to safeguard his charges. He must call attention to potential dangers and warn students to take those precautions as appear necessary under the circumstances.

A Wisconsin student was scraping wax off a floor in a storeroom containing chemicals. He knocked over a bottle of acid and was burned and the teacher found himself defendant in an action for damages. In deciding in favor of the teacher the state supreme court ruled:

> A teacher in the public schools is liable for injury to the pupils in his charge caused by his negligence or failure to use reasonable care . . . (but) it was found that the defendant did warn the plantiff . . . and the cork was in the bottle.[1]

*From The Clearing House 42:411, March 1968. Used by permission.

[1]Grosso v Witteman, 226 Wis. 17, 62 N.W. (2d) 386 1954 Supreme Court of Wisconsin.

An action for damages was brought against a California school district when a small boy, who was playing on a playground gate in the schoolyard, lost a finger when the gate was slammed by another child. The teacher, said the plaintiff, was negligent in not maintaining adequate supervision. The court ruled for the defendant teacher and stated:

> The accident occurred while the boy was climbing the wall (although he had been told not to do so). . . . There was no substantial evidence to show negligence on the part of the teacher and negligence could not be inferred from the mere fact that the accident occurred on school grounds while the teacher was not at the particular spot at that moment. [2]

A New York case involved an action for $45,000 damages against the Board of Education and the principal for injuries received by a child who was riding his bicycle across the school grounds. Since neither the school board nor the principal had made any rule or regulation prohibiting bicycle riding on that part of the school grounds, the court found for plaintiff and damages were awarded. [3] Obviously, specific warnings and precautions become more than desirable; they are essential.

Another example of the need for direct and specific precautions may be found in a California case where a pupil was injured in an explosion in a science class which was caused by student substitution of potassium chlorate for potassium nitrate in an experiment. The court ruled against defendant teacher saying:

> It is not unreasonable to assume that it is the duty of a teacher in chemistry, in the exercise of ordinary care, to instruct students regarding the selection, mingling, and use of dangerous ingredients . . . rather than merely hand them a textbook with general instructions to follow the text. [4]

Those warm and sunny spring days can create problems, too. A teacher who took his class out on the lawn failed to stop a student who repeatedly flipped a pocket knife into the grass. Eventually the knife ricocheted and struck another student in the eye. An action

for damages was instituted against the teacher, and the court ruled that the teacher could reasonably be expected to know that the knife throwing was going on. He was negligent either in not noticing that this was happening or negligent in failing to stop it. [5]

Failure to provide adequate supervision or to permit violent play activities can lead to disaster. The court found against defendant school district in a Pennsylvania case in which a child drowned in a swimming pool operated by the district as a part of a summer recreation program. The district was held liable for the negligence of its employees in that they failed to give adequate supervision and permitted rough and disorderly play in the water. [6]

A New York physical education teacher was found liable for negligence when he required two boys, both untrained, to box while he sat in the bleachers and watched. The court said:

> It is the duty of a teacher to exercise reasonable care to prevent injuries. . . . These young men should have been taught the principles of self defense, if indeed it was a reasonable thing to permit a slugging match of the kind which the testimony shows this contest was. The testimony indicates that the teacher failed in his duties and that he was negligent. [7]

Activities occurring in out-of-class circumstances are more likely to create situations conducive to pupil injury and to require increased teacher prudence. It is easier for matters to get out of hand since there is usually a feeling of excitement and also a somewhat relaxed control. Hazing is a rich source of trouble and, in spite of the incidence of injuries and even deaths, each year seems to see more tragedy caused by this horseplay. An initiation into a school athletic club, held on school property, sponsored by a faculty member, included as a part of the ceremony an electric shock which was given to each initiate. The power for this electric shock was provided by the regular lighting circuit with the result that one initiate died. The teacher was found liable for negligence. [8]

Field trips can provide a multiplicity of haz-

---

[2] Luna v Needles Elementary School District, 154 Cal. App. 803, 316 p (2d) 773 (1957) District Court of Appeal, Fourth District, Calif.

[3] Selleck v Board of Education, 94 N.Y.S. (2d) 318, 276 App Div 263, (1949).

[4] Mastrangelo v West Side Union High School District, 2 Cal. (2d) 540, 42 Pac, (2d) 634 (California 1935).

[5] Lilienthal v San Leandro Unified School District, 193 Ca. App. 2d 453, 293 P. 2d 889 (1956).

[6] Morris v School District of Township of Mt. Lebanon, 393 Pa 633, 144 A. (2d) 737 (1958).

[7] Le Valley v Stanford, 272 App. Div. 183, 20 N.Y.S. (2d) 460. N.Y. (1947).

[8] De Gooyer et al v Harkness et al, 70 S.D. 26, 13 N.W., 2d (1944).

ards for teachers and students. A common misconception of teachers is that a field trip permit slip signed by a parent or guardian relieves the teacher of responsibility. Such is not the case. The law does not permit a parent to sign away a child's rights nor discharge a teacher from providing adequate supervision. The field trip permit only indicates that the parent gives permission for his child to make the field trip.

Another practice fraught with hazard is that of teachers using their own automobiles to take students to such functions as musical programs and athletic events. The teacher can find himself liable for injuries to students who are riding in his automobile, and, even worse, the teacher who permits another teacher to use his vehicle for transporting students may be held liable for injuries suffered by passengers due to the negli-

gence of the borrowing driver.[9] If the teacher takes payment for transporting pupils he is likely to discover that he has no protection from his own insurance in a "for hire" situation. While it is often difficult to refuse to take students to some activity, especially if no other way seems to exist for them to get there, this is an instance when refusal is the best policy.

In any situation which results in pupil injury the teacher may find himself charged with negligence. The newer forms of personal liability insurance provide a degree of protection, but there is no substitute for adequate supervision, prudence, and the care which may be expected of a reasonable person.

[9]Gorton v Doty, 57 Idaho 792, 69 Pac., 2d, 136 Idaho (1937).

78 ❧ COACH'S LEGAL LIABILITY FOR ATHLETIC INJURIES*

Dr. George F. Shroyer
Kansas State University, Manhattan, Kansas

Studies indicate a large number of injuries in athletics, and that no coach or board of education has the financial wherewithal to pay out large sums of money because of their liability for a negligent act.

Coaches are well aware of the variety of injuries—mostly minor, but sometimes serious—which may befall the individuals under their supervision. But, despite their vigilance, some athletes will sustain injuries. When an injury does occur, the coach must attend to it in a reasonably prudent manner. He should render first aid only, and, if the injury warrants it, he should call a physician.

The coach will be the first to reach the individual. He must use his judgment to determine the seriousness of the injury. In the school building, the teacher in charge would probably call the school nurse. The coach, if out on the field or in the gym, cannot call the nurse every time a boy picks up a splinter or gets the wind knocked out of him. He should, however, take immediate action to relieve the pain and determine the extent of the injury.

If there's swelling in the area, say around the ankle or hand, the coach must use his judgment

to determine the best action. In most cases, he would send the boy for an x-ray of the area. This, of course, protects the boy's health as well as prevents a liability suit.

In these instances, the coach is motivated only by his sense of responsibility for the pupil; he tries to do what's best for the injury. The legal liability of the situation is probably the farthest thing from his mind.

These first-aid questions are sometimes perplexing to public-school coaches, since they can involve a court action. Is there a duty to render first aid? What is the scope of first-aid treatment? Does the state specifically prohibit teachers from giving anything other than elementary first aid?

If immediate first aid seems indicated, the coach is obligated to do the best he can. Either lack of action or unwise action in an emergency may lead to a charge of negligence against the coach. A coach, in his college preparation, usually has received first aid training. If he has had this training, he'd be expected to act as a reasonably prudent trained person, leaving the injury in a better condition than he found it.

But if further injury results because of his failure to act in a reasonably prudent manner— i.e., doing something which left the wound in a worse condition than he found it—the coach can be held personably liable.

*From Scholastic Coach **34**:18, December 1964. Used by permission.

If the coach has not had first-aid training, he'd be expected to act as a reasonably prudent layman. It would seem that a board of education which hired a coach without first-aid training would be placing itself in a precarious position because of the high frequency of injuries that occur in athletics.

After first aid has been rendered to a major injury, the coach should not continue treatment. Coaches should follow this rule to prevent the possibility of being held liable for negligence in treating the injury. Diagnosis, prescription, and treatment are duties for the physician.

There's always the question of how far one should go with first-aid treatment. From all indications, there's no set rule. The person administering the first aid must use his judgment. Coaches sometimes find it necessary to perform minor medical measures on blisters, sprained ankles, injured knees, ingrown toenails, etc. Research doesn't show any court rulings on such actions.

The things a coach should do in order to prevent the possibility of being held liable are: (1) use good judgment, (2) act prudently, (3) have a physician present at all contests, and (4) follow the first-aid textbook. If the coach follows the Red Cross *First Aid Textbook* and bears in mind that he may be held negligent for not acting as well as acting, he needn't worry about being held liable for negligence in administering first aid.

The following court cases will point out some of the decisions that have been rendered.

In a California case (Orgando v. Carquinez Grammar School District), a teacher was held liable for not rendering first aid to a pupil. The case involved a pupil who was cut severly on the arm and eventually bled to death. The teacher was held negligent for not taking proper action.

In a New Jersey case (Duda v. Gaines), a coach was sued for not seeking immediate medical attention for a shoulder injury sustained by a boy in football practice. The case was tried under a stipulation that the defendent's duty was limited to the summoning of medical aid in a situation where an emergency existed.

The boy threw his shoulder out of place; the coach put it back and sent the boy to a school physician. Several days later, the boy again threw his shoulder out, and again the coach put it back. This time the coach told the boy he couldn't play the rest of the year, but that it wasn't necessary to see a physician a second time.

In making the latter statement, the coach was skating on thin ice, but the court didn't hold him liable, ruling that the second situation wasn't an emergency and didn't indicate that the boy was in urgent need of attention.

In another case (Sayers v. Ranger), in which a boy broke his arm jumping over a gym horse, the teacher walked with the boy to the supervisor's office, where he was given first aid and taken to the hospital. One of the acts of negligence alleged in the case was that the teacher shouldn't have forced the boy to walk to the supervisor's office.

The court noted that the walk was only a short distance, and felt that sending the boy to the hospital was better than having him wait for a physician to come to the school. Therefore, ruled the court, the teacher was not negligent. Had the instructor failed to take prompt and proper care of the injury, he could have been held liable.

Another case in point (Welch v. Dunsmuir Joint H.S. Dist.), a boy suffered an injury to his back in a football game. The boy was unable to get up and walk off the field, but several other boys carried him from the field by his arms and legs. The boy became a quadriplegic.

The court ruled that the boy was removed from the field in a negligent manner which aggravated and worsened the original injury. The court, therefore, awarded the boy $206,804 for damages.

Permanent injury and payment for damages may have been prevented if proper first-aid measures had been taken. It seems that most people would agree that, first, the boy should have been placed on a stretcher in a proper manner and carried from the field, instead of having been carried from the field by outstretched arms and legs; and, secondly, a physician should have been in attendance and readily available to take charge of all injuries.

Need for physical exam

In a California case (Bellman v. San Francisco H.S. District), it was clearly pointed out that some sort of physical examination must be given to pupils entering athletic activities. The case pointed out that a coach would be negligent to compel pupils to participate in certain kinds of exercises without determining in advance their aptitude for the sport, especially when the coach knows of some condition, such as a knee injury. The court meant that the coach should have a physician examine the athletes prior to participation in a practice or contest.

No coach would want to take the chance of being party to a liability suit for a possible coronary disease or some other ailment with which a pupil may report. A physical examination, therefore, is the coach's only safe protection against this type of liable suit, as well as the athlete's only health protection.

In co-curricular activities such as football, basketball, and other competitive sports, constant physical examinations are a necessity. Playing a pupil who is ill is a negligent act by the coach. The coach who knowingly or *unknowingly* sends an injured player into a game is held negligent. If the coach doesn't know of the injury, he's negligent for his ignorance (Morris v. Union H.S. District).

In the past, one reason for holding the coaches as well as the school districts liable for injuries may have been the immunity of school districts as agents of the state. The courts have started to change their attitude on this issue; California, New York, Washington, Illinois, Minnesota, and Wisconsin have already held districts liable or have warned the districts that they will be held liable for their torts.*

Since the courts have started to change their attitudes toward the liability for torts, the board of education or the district and not the coach will probably be the party to be sued. The coach doesn't have the financial status as does the district; therefore, in most cases, it's hardly worthwhile to sue the coach.

With the changing of the courts' attitude may come more law suits, for the plaintiff will have a chance of getting some money. It would be advisable, therefore, for coaches and administrators to check with the individual state departments to determine the standing of the district on the liability issue. If it's warranted, the school district should consider an insurance policy.

As for the coaches of the nation, the old adage, "An ounce of prevention is worth a pound of cure," is worthy of attention.

_____

*Shroyer, George F., How's your liability insurance, School Management, September, 1963, pp. 91-96.

79 ɞ THE TEAM PHYSICIAN AND THE LAW*

CHARLES J. FRANKEL, M.D.
ASSOCIATE PROFESSOR OF ORTHOPEDIC SURGERY, SCHOOL OF MEDICINE,
UNIVERSITY OF VIRGINIA, CHARLOTTESVILLE, VIRGINIA

Emergency away from home

Question: If a boy is hurt in a game away from home and his team physician is not there, what is the legal position of the doctor for the other team who gives emergency treatment?

Answer: The team physician for the team away from home must, if he is going to render any treatment whatsoever other than first aid, have a consent of the parents. This may be made available to the coach of the home team so that the treating physician can be protected. The other alternative is for the physician to call the parents and obtain consent over the telephone, using an operator or some other non-interested party as a witness.

Question: In many high schools the team physician is supposed to give first aid treatment only, referring the injured athlete to his private physician for definitive diagnosis and care. Must the team doctor worry about exceeding his authority in doing such things as reducing a dislocated shoulder in the locker room rather than sending the boy to the hospital and having it done by the family physician?

Answer: If the team physician's duties are limited to giving first aid, then he cannot exceed the consent given him. He has been given, I would hope, consent by the parent group to render whatever service they want him to render. If it is limited to first aid, that is all that he has permission to carry out.

Liability in cardiac complication

Question: Suppose a team physician examines a high school athlete and finds a suspicious cardiac murmur. He sends the boy to a cardiologist who says it is all right for him to play football. The team physician gives his approval, and the boy has a cardiac complication during a game. Who is liable in case the parents sue?

_____

*From The Journal of School Health **38**:87, February 1968. Used by permission.

This article is reproduced from "Medicine in Sports" Vol. 7, No. 3, August, 1967 Newsletter of the Rystan Company with the permission of Dr. Frankel and Mr. Charles G. Stanton, the Editor of Medicine in Sports.

Answer: The team physician should have obtained a release from the parents subject to the findings of the cardiologist. It is assumed that the cardiologist examined the boy with the consent of the parents. If a cardiac complication occurs, the cardiologist may be liable, though expert testimony will be needed to prove negligence. The team physician may be sued, but it is not likely that judgment will be against him.

Question: The high school team physician examines a boy and discovers a condition which he feels should rule out contact sports. However, the boys wants to compete, and the parents sign a waiver allowing him to do so. If the boy is hurt because of the condition, can the parents sue the physician or the school?

Answer: No physician should allow a youngster to play who he feels is unfit, waiver or no. If a waiver has been signed and the boy is hurt, the parents will not be able to sue, but the youngster can sue in his own right when he reaches maturity.

Question: What should a team physician do when he is convinced an athlete is not getting adequate follow-up treatment by his family doctor, and that permanent damage may result?

Answer: The team physician should contact the family doctor and state his complaints. If he is ignored, then a copy of his letter should be sent to the family.

Salaried team MD and the volunteer

Question: Is there any difference in the legal responsibility of a team physician who is a salaried employee of the school board and one who serves as a volunteer?

Answer: There is no difference in the legal responsibility of an employed physician or a volunteer. Once the patient-doctor relationship is set up, the responsibilities are the same.

Errors in examination report

Question: We can no longer handle routine physical examinations of our athletes at the high school. They are done by the family physician, who fills out a form stating the boy is either in good general health or has certain deficiencies. The report is reviewed by me, and if the student is certified as fit to compete in a sport, I sign my name over that of the examining physician. What is my liability in this, as I have approved examination reports containing gross errors that were only discovered when the coach saw the boys? If he had not brought these to my attention, some of these boys could have suffered serious consequences.

Answer: The signature of the team physician over that of the family physician makes both physicians liable should injury occur because of gross errors in the initial physical examination.

If the team physician hasn't the time to handle routine physical examinations, then he needs help. There are many instances in which schools that have no team physicians rely completely on the reports of family physicians. It has been held in many jurisdictions that the school district or school board should have been aware of the need of medical supervision and that reliance on correspondence with doctors is not adequate. Several large judgments have been obtained against physicians as well as the school board.

REFERENCES

Arstila, M., and Koivikko, A.: Electrocardiographic and vectorcardiographic signs of left and right ventricular hypertrophy in endurance athletes, J. Sport Med. 6:166, 1966.

Castellanos, A., Jr. and Greer, P.: Organized football for pre-high school children, J. Sport Med. 6: 187, 1966.

Committee on Exercise and Physical Fitness: Is your patient fit? A simple supplementary test for evaluating a patient's fitness, JAMA 201:117 (July 10) 1967.

Erickson, J. G., and von Gemmingen, G. R.: Surfer's nodules and other complications of surfboarding, JAMA 201:134 (July 10) 1967.

Ginsberg, M., Miller, J. M., and McElfatrick, G. C.: The use of inflatable plastic splints, JAMA 200:180 (April 10) 1967.

Magel, J. R., and Faulkner, J. A.: Maximum oxygen uptakes of college swimmers, J. Appl. Physiol. 22:929 (May) 1967.

Rudd, J. L., and Day, W. C.: A physical fitness program for patients with hypertension, J. Am. Geriatrics Soc. 15:373 (April) 1967.

80 ❧ LEGAL ASPECTS OF TRANSPORTATION FOR ATHLETIC EVENTS *

ANDREW GRIEVE
ASSISTANT PROFESSOR OF PHYSICAL EDUCATION,
STATE UNIVERSITY OF NEW YORK COLLEGE AT CORTLAND
CORTLAND, NEW YORK

Legal attitudes in the case of accidents involving school transportation differ considerably from those generally indicated in other school accidents. This is undoubtedly due to the general feeling that the transportation of students involves a greater incidence of hazardous situations. We also find there is a distinct variation in various state statutes where school transportation is involved. The school districts in several states, which are immune from most legal action, find this immunity may not hold true in transportation accidents. Some states make it illegal to purchase liability insurance except for transportation protection. We also find states which have special funds set aside for just such incidents. Obviously, there is more apprehension about transportation accidents than there is about accidents in other areas of the school program. Our investigation seemed to indicate school districts feel more responsible for such incidents since it is compulsory for youngsters to attend school, and with the combining of school districts for more efficient units, it becomes necessary for many youngsters to ride school buses.

The court records are replete with litigations involving transportation but only a few of the examples will be used which may have application to the transportation of athletic teams, while others should be used as precedent-setting in similar situations.

Use of public funds for athletic transportation

It appears as though the present attitude toward athletic team transportation is much more liberal than it was in previous years. With the concept that athletics should be considered as an integral part of the educational development of the student, then it should be considered legal to expend public funds for the transportation of such groups so they may participate in this educational activity, whether it be called curricular, extracurricular or recreational.

Mort and Hamilton in their book, *The Law and Public Education,* indicated it was their feeling, as a result of extensive investigation, that school funds could be used on transportation for educational purposes if express legislative authority is granted. This would indicate that as an educational activity public money could be spent for the transportation of athletic teams.

There have been a number of legal interpretations, statutes, and even legal actions which involved this matter of transportation for athletic groups. One such legal action was brought before the Supreme Court of Iowa a number of years ago. Their decision indicated school districts could provide transportation for certain pupils to and from school, but they had no right to transport pupils to basketball games.[1]

The Supreme Court of Utah was faced with a similar case and their decision differed somewhat. They agreed in part with the Iowa decision but indicated transportation should be permitted if the students' presence was required after school hours. A broad interpretation of this ruling would therefore permit the transportation of athletic teams through the use of public funds.[2]

In South Dakota there is a statute which clearly indicates transportation can be provided for interschool athletic competition and other educational activities if the board of education approves. Minnesota has a law which is broader than even that in South Dakota because it states that transportation is authorized for curricular, extracurricular, and recreational activities.

Foresight in transportation

In the pamphlet, *The Physical Education Instructor and Safety,* there is a specific list of safety precautions which the supervisor must consider when he is arranging for athletic team transportation.

"1. Students be allowed to travel in only bonded common carriers or school-owned buses.

"2. If students are allowed to travel in private cars, the school administrator should adhere to the liability law requirements of his state.

---

*From The Athletic Journal 47:64, March 1967. Used by permission.

[1] Schmidt vs. Blair, 203 Iowa 1016, 213 N.R. 593.

[2] Bear vs. Board of Education of No. Summit School District et al., 81 Utah 51, 16P 2d 900.

"3. Students should not be allowed to transport athletic teams unless they are authorized drivers of school buses. Use of students to drive private cars used to transport athletic teams is considered undesirable from liability and other angles."[3]

If the school does use bonded common carriers, it is the responsibility of those making such arrangements to ascertain that the vehicles to be utilized are safe. At the present time most states have strict regulations regarding the inspection of vehicles which are to be used for public transportation, but there are situations where, for the sake of a few dollars, a school might not be too particular in its choice. If an accident did happen to occur, the school district, or the person responsible for obtaining such transportation, might well be held as being negligent. In those states which do hold that school districts are immune from liability action, the transportation company or even the driver himself might well be held for negligence.

The school employee involved in the hiring of such carriers would find it advisable to check on the type of insurance and the limits of such insurance carried by the transportation company. In the event of an accident, proper coverage could well save either the school district or individuals involved large financial losses.

One situation with which many of us may be familiar is that of the coach driving a school vehicle to athletic contests. This may be standard practice in some areas but we have noticed a definite decrease in this procedure during the past few years. If an accident did occur and the coach was called upon to testify, it might be proven the coach did not have the necessary experience in handling large vehicles to be considered as being competent. The courts could easily indicate that coaching and driving a bus are worlds apart and it would not be in the best interests of safety to have such an individual responsible for transporting athletic teams. This could possibly lead to either the coach or the school district being held negligent.

Court decisions

As mentioned previously, there are innumerable court cases which have involved school transportation, but we feel a few examples will indicate the attitudes which have been most frequently exhibited by the courts and, at the same time, denote cases which might be precedent-setting in nature.

There was an unusual situation which arose in Maryland regarding the violation of a particular statute. The courts found a school could not claim immunity if an accident occurred in which there was a definite violation of an existing statute. In this particular situation, a school bus did not contain a safety lock as was required by state law. As a result, a child fell from the bus and was killed. Due to the violation of this statute it was considered a proximate cause of the accident and it was, therefore, permissible to sue the school district.[4]

There have been several cases in which the courts indicated the driver of a school bus must exhibit the highest degree of care since his passengers are youngsters and may not be cognizant of the existing dangers. As mentioned earlier, in order to fulfill the school attendance regulations it may be necessary for youngsters to travel by bus and it is the responsibility of the school district and particularly school bus drivers to guarantee the safety of the students. The same interpretation could be applied to the transportation of athletic teams. If there is any question as to the prudence of the school bus driver, the courts have specified the school or its employees, depending upon the immunity provision, will be held liable.[5,6,7]

The transportation of athletic teams or spectators to athletic activities will oftentimes result in the overloading of buses. In the transporting of teams, it is not only the team personnel but the matter of equipment which may result in overloading. With spectator transportation it may be a lack of properly anticipating the number of students who desire to attend the contest. In either case, if it can be proven the bus was overloaded, there is no doubt the school district or its employees could be held for negligence in the case of an accident. This was the attitude of the court in a transportation accident in New York which involved an overloaded bus.[8]

There was an incident in New Hampshire which directly involved the transportation of athletes following a practice session. It was the usual procedure in this school to transport the athletes on a truck from the field to the school

[3] The Physical Education Instructor and Safety, High School Series, Bulletin No. 3, National Education Association (1948), p. 36.

[4] Parr vs. Board of County Commissioners, 207 Md. 91, 113 A 2d 397.

[5] Phillips vs. Hardgrove, 161 Washington 121, 296 p. 559.

[6] Davidson vs. Horne, 71 S.E. (2d) 464 (Georgia).

[7] Van Cleave vs. Illini Coach Co., N.E. (2d) 398 (Illinois).

[8] People vs. Casey, 33 N.Y.S. (2d) 1,263 App. Div. 342.

immediately after practice. The coach would supervise the loading of the truck and he blew a whistle when the truck was loaded and ready to leave. In this instance, the driver of the truck proceeded to have the boys climb onto the truck without the coach being present to supervise the loading. The driver assumed all of the boys were on and started to move. At that moment one of the boys was climbing onto the truck by putting his foot on a rear tire to reach the truck bed. When the truck started to move, he fell under the rear wheels and was severely injured. In the court action which followed, the defense counsel implied the boy should have known the danger and he contributed to the negligent act. The court felt the boy did not know the wheel would start to roll as he attempted to get aboard and the driver should be held liable for his negligent act.[9]

In Georgia a negligence decision was based on imprudent speed. The bus, which was traveling over the legal speed limit, skidded and a youngster was thrown from the vehicle and killed. The courts indicated the imprudent speed was a cause for negligence.[10]

There were two cases which involved situations beyond the control of the driver and in both instances the courts held a student injured or killed on a school bus due to his own negligence or an act of God was beyond the control of the driver. The driver should exhibit constant care to insure the safety of students but he cannot be expected to watch but one.[11,12]

Under somewhat similar circumstances the school or its employees may be held negligent if there has been a complaint regarding certain dangers which exist. In one such case there had been several complaints regarding mischievous conduct by certain children. As a result of this mischief, a youngster was injured and the plaintiff contended the accident could have been prevented. The courts indicated the complaints constituted a warning, the driver should have taken preventive measures, and his failure to do so constituted negligence on his part.[13]

In most cases where the school district is exempt from tort liability, this immunity is applied to bus accidents. There was a school bus accident in Virginia where a youngster was killed. The courts held the school district was immune, but found the individual driving the bus could be held liable if his actions proved to be negligent.[14]

Although there are several cases on record where individuals were held negligent there was a case in Iowa in which the courts did not follow this precedent. In a litigation involving a school bus accident, the courts indicated the bus driver was performing a governmental function and, therefore, had the protection of immunity and could not be held liable.[15]

There have been court cases which questioned the capability of the driver of a bus which was involved in an accident. A North Carolina case involved the proficiency of a bus driver who lost control of a bus while transporting school children which resulted in the death of one of the youngsters. The school board was named as the defendant by the parents of the youngster. The courts pointed out the school board could only be considered liable if they hired bus drivers in a non-prudent manner and since this was not the case the school board could not be held liable.[16]

Two similar situations occurred in Georgia where the school districts are considered immune. These litigations questioned the qualifications for school bus drivers as they are hired by school districts. The courts arrived at a decision similar to the previous case and even noted it was not negligence if the school board happened to hire poorly qualified personnel except if the board knew of the poor quality of the individual so hired.[17,18]

Although only one of these cases directly involved the transportation of athletic groups, the decisions would most certainly apply to such transportation. Transportation of school-age children would be considered from a similar viewpoint, whether it be to or from school, the transportation of an athletic team or the transporting of spectators to an athletic event. We did learn about many other cases but they were quite similar in nature and the court decisions were comparable.

Privately owned vehicles

The situation of transporting school-age youngsters in privately owned vehicles is more apt

[9] Beardsell vs. Tilton School, 200 A 783, (New Hampshire).

[10] Robets vs. Baker, 192 S.E. 104 (Georgia).

[11] Lewis vs. Halbert, 67 S.W. (2d) 430 (Texas).

[12] Harrison vs. McVeigh, 5 S.E. (2d) 76 (Georgia).

[13] Roberts vs. Baker, 57 Ga. 733, 196 S.E. 104.

[14] Krasner vs. Harper, 90 Ga. App. 128, 82 S.E. 2d 267.

[15] Hibbs vs. Independent School District of Green Mountain, 218 Iowa 841, 251 N.W. 606.

[16] Betts vs. Jones et al., 166 S.E. 589 (No. Carolina).

[17] Roberts vs. Baker, 57 Ga. 733, 196 S.E. 104.

[18] Krasner vs. Harper, 90 Ga. App. 128, 82 S.E. 2d 267.

to occur in those activities which we consider extracurricular. Music, athletics, and other such activities are of a nature whereby small groups of students may be transported in private cars either for participation in such activities or as spectators. How many coaches have transported a group of boys to observe an athletic event at another school, or taken a similar group to attend a college contest? We know this is not an uncommon practice and have done so on several occasions ourselves. What have been the views of the courts on this situation when a litigation developed?

One factor which will affect the decision of the court involves the statutes regarding injuries incurred while riding in the car of another. This will vary from state to state and it would be wise for anyone planning to perform such a function to review this area. In a case in Idaho, a coach directed a group of boys to ride with him to a contest in a car which he borrowed from another teacher. During the trip the coach had an accident and the car rolled down an embankment, resulting in an injury to one of the boys riding with him. The parents of the boy brought suit against the owner of the car contending the coach had been negligent and as an agent of the owner, the owner should be held liable. In Idaho a *guest statute* does exist whereby anyone who rides in a car in a guest status cannot sue the owner of the vehicle. In this instance, however, the coach had directed the boy to ride in the car to the athletic contest and was thus not a guest in the true sense of the word.[19]

A rather unpleasant situation occurred in a school district not far from our own area a few years ago which had a telling influence upon the attitudes of those transporting school-age youngsters either in their own cars or school vehicles to extracurricular activities. Although this activity was musical rather than athletic, many coaches in the area could well recall traveling the same route under similar circumstances. A group of youngsters was on the way to a music festival in a school station wagon driven by one of the teachers. The vehicle was involved in a fatal accident and all the passengers, including the teacher were killed. Although the actual cause of the accident was never specified in the ensuing litigation brought by the parents, the court felt the driver of the vehicle had been negligent and could be held liable for the accident. Since there is a *save harmless* clause in New York State the school

district was held responsible for the action of its employee. The school carried liability insurance for such accidents but due to the magnitude of the claims these even exceeded the amount of insurance coverage. The school district, in order to settle the claims for this horrible tragedy, found it necessary to increase the tax rate of the district an enormous amount for several years. The horror of the tragedy had a telling effect upon the community and a mention of the money involved may appear rather heartless but when discussing the legal aspects of such a case it is necessary to indicate all of the factors.

There was another recent litigation in Delaware which would definitely set a precedent in legal decisions regarding the transportation of students in privately owned vehicles. A child was injured on a school playground during the noon hour and a teacher drove the youngster home. The child was absent from school for several days and the teacher became concerned over the seriousness of the injury. On going to the youngster's home the teacher discovered there had been no means of transportation for the youngster to get to the doctor. The teacher volunteered to drive the student and his mother to the doctor and during the trip they were involved in an accident in which both the mother and the child were injured. Both of the injured were named in a legal action against the teacher. The counsel for the defense contended the teacher was performing an errand of mercy and the two passengers were guests in the teacher's car as it was not her obligation to perform this service. The court, however, inferred it felt the teacher had a moral obligation and due to this act of kindness she would be improving herself as a teacher. As a guest of the teacher in her car, the injured parties could not have sued the driver, according to the state's *guest statute,* but since the court did not consider these individuals as guests they were allowed to make such claims against the teacher. This may appear as a rather broad interpretation as to what will benefit a teacher in his or her professional development but it does stand on the court record as such.[20]

The use of a privately owned vehicle resulted in an unusual situation in Kansas. A girl was injured in an automobile accident while riding to an athletic contest at another school during school hours. The driver of the car, another student, had permission of his father to use his car for such a trip. The school became in-

[19] Gorton vs. Doty, 57 Idaho, 792, 69 P. 2d 136.

[20] Truitt vs. Gaines, 318 F. (2d) 461 (Delaware).

volved only because the girl was permitted to ride to the game. Although the school did not pay for the use of the vehicle it was still under their control and, on this basis, the legal action had to be instituted against the driver and not the owner of the car. School permission precluded the *guest statute* in this state.[21]

In a similar situation, a cheerleader was being transported to an athletic contest in a private car. The athletic director knew of the arrangement and implied school approval. However, the court felt that such passengers were *guests* and the school did not become involved.[22]

As coaches or directors of athletic programs,

we must realize the courts have some unusual views on this matter of transportation injuries. We can probably all recall incidents in which we have exposed ourselves to possible expensive legal action if even a minor accident had occurred. Most of us have transported groups of athletes to interschool contests in small school vehicles or in our own automobiles. In other instances, we may have offered to drive a group of boys to observe athletic events at other high schools or nearby colleges or universities. Although we believe these are worthwhile undertakings and they might provide youngsters with opportunities they might not have otherwise, it is only wise to check on insurance coverage and the laws involved in such a situation before proceeding.

[21] Kitzel vs. Atkenson, 245 P. (2d) 170 (Kansas).
[22] Fessenden vs. Smith, 124 N.W. (2d) 554 (Iowa).

81 ~ LEGAL ASPECTS OF SPECTATOR INJURIES*

ANDREW GRIEVE
ASSISTANT PROFESSOR OF PHYSICAL EDUCATION,
STATE UNIVERSITY OF NEW YORK COLLEGE AT CORTLAND,
CORTLAND, NEW YORK

The prudent coach and athletic director are constantly on the lookout for situations which may cause injury to those participating in athletic activities, and might possibly result in legal actions involving the school district, its officers or employees. Unfortunately, the safety of the spectator is too often left to chance, and this careless approach has resulted in numerous legal actions.

Court decisions are difficult to predict because numerous elements must be considered, including the immunity factor, legal precedence, a slight variation in circumstances which may cause legal precedence to be ignored, public, or proprietary functions. All of these will have an effect upon legal decisions.

A young girl was watching a high school baseball game while sitting on a fence 35 feet behind first base. The shortstop on making a throw to first threw wildly and struck the youngster in the eye, knocking her off the fence and causing her to strike her head on the ground. As a result of this injury, she lost the sight in one eye permanently and suffered possible permanent brain injury. Her parents brought suit against the school district for close to $80,000, contending there had not been enough protection provided to prevent such an accident. The plaintiff's lawyer implied the girl should not be considered as having to assume any

*From The Athletic Journal 47:74, April 1967. Used by permission.

risk while watching such a game as it was supervised by school authorities. The school board attempted to have the claim dismissed but the district judge refused to do so. The case was carried to the highest court in the state where the decision was that any spectator assumes a certain amount of risk when he attends a contest of this type and found in favor of the school district.

This situation and another similar in nature, both of which arose in our vicinity, made it quite obvious to all concerned how unpleasant it can be when an unfortunate injury involves a spectator. There are several cases on record which seem to indicate that court decisions in this area will depend upon a variety of factors.

In a community adjacent to our own, a young woman was watching an amateur baseball game on the high school field. This game was being played by a community team, not a school team. The woman in question, who was sitting a good distance behind the backstop, was struck on the head by a foul ball and required hospital treatment. The community team had charged no admission and the school district did not charge this group for the use of the field. The attorney for the injured party attempted to prove the school board had been negligent in not providing a backstop of sufficient height to prevent such an accident. He contacted several schools in the area in an attempt to support his contention. Unfortunately, he discovered there was no standard regulation for backstops and the sizes of the backstops in the area varied considerably. When all the facts were presented to the court, the judge found no grounds for negligence.

There are court cases where immunity did not exist but in which the school districts were not held as being negligent. These court cases have done a great deal in setting precedents for similar legal actions. One action, which is closely akin to the preceding two, concerned the matter of protective screening at a baseball game. An individual sitting in the bleachers in the outfield at a baseball game was struck by a ball. The plaintiff contended there should have been protective screening in the area to protect the spectators. However, the court indicated there were areas where it would be imperative to have such screening, but due to the location of the bleachers there was no great danger in this area and thus no liability existed.[1]

Despite the fact that the law in Washington does not permit legal action for injuries incurred as the result of the use of athletic apparatus, the courts felt this did not apply to spectators. A spectator at a baseball game was struck by a thrown ball and the courts found in his favor.[2]

The courts realize that there are certain situations over which the supervisors of an athletic event have no control. There was a case involving rowdyism at a contest in California where a youngster was hit by a thrown bottle. The court decision was based on the fact that those responsible for the activity could not foresee the possibility of such an action and could not be held responsible for the misconduct of others.[3]

In New York State the school districts are not immune in cases of negligence and an action was instituted against a school district when a youngster, who was observing a baseball game, was struck by a flying bat. The court found that the supervisor certainly could not anticipate such an occurrence and thus prevent it. The school district was held as not being liable for this accident.[4]

The possibility of foreseeing a hazard, on the other hand, can result in a successful lawsuit as

was the case in California, where school districts are not held as being immune. A spectator was injured by a piece of glass in the area of an athletic contest. The school district was held liable since it was considered the responsibility of its employees to verify that such areas are free from hazards.[5]

In a similar situation, a spectator at a football game fell into an unlighted ramp on the school's parking lot and was seriously injured. The courts felt the school district was negligent in not placing a light near this hazard.[6]

Injuries to spectators may take many forms and some are more unusual than others. In Minnesota a spectator, who had paid admission, was standing about five feet from the sidelines rather than in the stands which had been provided. During the action of the football game two players rolled over the sideline and collided with the plaintiff. He contended that fencing should have been provided to prevent injury to spectators. The court indicated the purpose of such fencing was intended to keep spectators back from the field of action, not necessarily to protect them from possible injury, and due to such circumstances the school was not held as being liable.[7]

There is always the question whether an activity is a public or proprietary function. This situation has and could have some effect upon future court decisions. A public function would be considered as one which a school would hold for the benefit of the public and particularly the student body. A proprietary function would be considered as one in which the school would have to be considered in a profit-making undertaking. Although the school may charge admission for high school athletic events, these activities have been considered by the courts as coming under public functions since they are sponsored largely for the benefit of the student body. There were two such court cases which attempted to prove that charging admission made a school athletic event a proprietary function. The courts, however, indicated such activities must still be considered as public functions.[8, 9]

[1] Adonnino vs. Village of Mt. Morris, 12 N.Y.S. (2d) 658.

[2] Barnecut vs. Seattle School District No. 1, 389 P. 2d 904.

[3] Weldy vs. Oakland High School District of Alameda County, 65 P. (2d) 851.

[4] Cambereri vs. Board of Education of Albany, 284 N.Y.S. 892.

[5] Brown vs. City of Oakland, 124 P. (2d) 369.

[6] Watson vs. School District, 324, Mich. 1, 36 N.W. 2d 195.

[7] Ingerson vs. Shattucks School, Minnesota, 239 N.W. 667.

[8] Thompson vs. Board of Education, City of Millville, 79 A (2nd) 100 (New Jersey).

[9] Reed vs. Rhead County, 225 S.W. (2nd) 49 (Tennessee).

Conversely, there are situations whereby a school district could be considered as providing proprietary functions even though it might involve a high school athletic contest. In 1955, there was a case in Arizona where a school district was held liable for the injury of a spectator as the result of a fall through a broken railing. In this instance, the school district had leased their stadium to another school for a fee and as a result the activity became proprietary since it was not an athletic contest for their own student body. Thus, they had entered into a profit-making enterprise and could be held liable.[10]

Oddly enough there was another similar court action in Virginia where the judgment was somewhat contrary. The activity involved was not athletic in nature but had so many similar aspects that we feel it bears mentioning. A school board leased its auditorium for a concert to a group from outside the school. A spectator slipped on a waxed floor and sued the board contending this was a proprietary function. The courts felt, however, that although the auditorium had been leased the nature of the activity, a concert, was for the improvement of the culture of both the students and the community and did not consider the activity as being proprietary. Therefore, there was no cause for holding the school liable.[11]

The construction of bleachers and stands has led to several court actions with varying outcomes dependent upon circumstances and existing statutes. Temporary bleachers were constructed in a school for a special athletic event and when they collapsed resulted in several injuries. The school district however, could not be sued for negligence due to their immunity in the State of Iowa.[12]

A court in Michigan handed down a similar decision in an action brought about due to the collapse of bleachers during a football game. They applied the doctrine of immunity, indicating athletics were to be considered as a phase of the overall educational program and the game was, therefore, a governmental function.[13]

There was a similar legal action when a poorly constructed bleacher collapsed at an athletic event at the University of Minnesota.

Despite the fact that there was negligence in such construction, the athletic association, which was named as the defendant, was considered as a part of the university and since this institution was a part of the educational system they were immune from such negligence suits.[14]

The exact opposite decision was arrived at in Michigan as the courts judged the athletic association did not represent the educational institution but rather the students and the officers of the organization itself. Stands constructed by this athletic association at the University of Michigan collapsed and the plaintiff was injured. Due to the interpretation of the relationship of the association to the university, it was held as being negligent in the construction of such stands.[15]

The state of Washington holds that a school district is immune from legal action for injuries which occur during the use of athletic apparatus or manual training equipment. A spectator was injured at a football game when a railing gave way on the bleachers. The school district contended that under these circumstances they should be immune. The court, on the other hand, indicated that a railing on a bleacher cannot be considered as coming under the immunity regulation, and if they were negligent in this situation, the school could be held liable.[16]

As can be seen, there have been numerous legal actions which have involved injuries to spectators. The court decisions, of course, will be determined by the prevailing statutes of the state. We must also remember that even though the school district may be immune from liability suits, if the responsibility for the negligent act can be attributed to an individual, then he might well become involved in the litigation. Spectator safety must be one of the first considerations of the director of athletics. Too often our considerations are limited to the participants and we could leave ourselves vulnerable for such legal action in by-passing the possibility of dangerous spectator situations.

Most states have included in their legal statutes specific regulations which are intended to protect any individual who may utilize school facilities. The laws must be considered as being

[10]Sawaya vs. Tucson High School District No. 1. 281 P. (2d) 105 (Arizona).

[11]Kellam vs. School Board of City of Norfolk, 202 Va. 252. 117 S.E. 2d 96.

[12]Larsen vs. Independent School District of Kane, 223 Iowa 691.

[13]Richards vs. School District of Birmingham, 348 Mich. 490, 83 N.W. 2d, 643.

[14]George vs. University of Minnesota Athletic Association, 107 Minn. 424.

[15]Scott vs. University of Michigan Athletic Association, 152 Mich. 664; 116 N.W. 624.

[16]Juntilla vs. Everett School District No. 24, Washington; 35 Pac. (2nd) 78.

applicable to the spectators at athletic events. In New York State, these laws appear in the Education Law, Article XX, Section 167:

"1.   Doors must swing out and have anti-panic bars.

"2.   Exit signs must be illuminated.

"3.   There should be no assembly area above the first floor in wooden buildings.

"4.   Exits must never be locked.

"5.   There must be grills over all glass doors that may be used as exits."

The courts have also clearly indicated that it is within the domain of athletic supervisors to determine who shall attend school functions. In order to guarantee safety and proper conduct at athletic events, those responsible for such activities may eject any spectators and refund their admission to protect the other spectators. Likewise, they may refuse admission to any individual for the same reasons. Legal opinion indicates the school has no obligation to admit or allow to remain any individual who may cause unpleasant or unsafe situations to develop.

This opinion was clearly stated by Hamilton and Mort in their book on school law:

It has been held that spectators at an athletic or other school function are only licensees and may be ejected from the exhibition upon return of the admission fee. By the same token, the school authorities may refuse admission to any person for any reason or no reason. In other words, there is no legal obligation upon the authorities to admit any person to school functions, or to permit him to remain after he has been admitted. [17]

As the result of many legal actions which have involved spectators, it is imperative that those responsible for the administration of athletic activities recognize the potentially dangerous situations. We often become almost completely involved in verifying that dangerous situations which might involve the participants are eliminated, such as providing proper supervision, equipment, facilities, medical care, transportation, and the like. But all too often we bypass an inspection of bleachers, fencing, and other areas where spectators will be located and exposed to danger. Coaches and school personnel should not create an unpleasant situation for themselves or the school district because of such an oversight.

_____

[17] Hamilton, Robert and Mort, Paul. The Law and Public Education. p. 127.

82 ᴈᴗ TRENDS IN SCHOOL ATHLETIC INSURANCE*

LAWRENCE W. GRIMES
EXECUTIVE SECRETARY, NEW YORK STATE HIGH SCHOOL ATHLETIC PROTECTION PLAN, INC.

The prerequisites for school athletic insurance are here to stay and will multiply in the future. Schools, pupils, athletics, together with ever-increasing "claim-conscious" parents are the reasons for its continued growth. There have been many changes in its philosophy with the growth of athletic insurance. The "style" has changed in keeping with the times and will continue to do so.

Most school districts are required by statute to provide for general liability insurance. This is defined as "to save harmless and protect all teachers, members of administrative staffs, or employees from financial loss arising out of any claim, demand, suit, or judgment by reason of alleged negligence or other act resulting in accidental bodily injury to any person with-

_____

*From Secondary School Athletic Administration, January 1969, p. 70, American Association for Health, Physical Education, and Recreation. Used by permission.

in or without the school buildings; provided such teacher, employee, etc., was acting within the scope of his employment." In brief, suit must be brought against the district and negligence proven for the injured to recover any loss. The key here is that negligence be proven. Negligence is the failure to act as a reasonably prudent person would act under the specific circumstances involved. In short, if one could or should have anticipated trouble, failure to take preventive action is imprudent, and therefore negligent. Each year more and more judgments are handed down by the courts, resulting from school injuries to "infants" while participating in physical education and athletics. Here, the style is more prevalent than ever as evidenced by the number and amount of such judgments. School districts are continually required to increase the limits of their liability coverage in view of these judgments.

The majority of athletic injuries do not involve liability. Therefore, we direct our attention to the topic at hand—medical indemnity insurance for athletic injuries. Prior to 1930, (1) only a small percentage of parents had any accident insurance; (2) the insurance industry was not active in school athletic insurance because of unavailable statistics as to its risk; and (3) only a limited number of schools self-insured, those primarily for football where gate receipts were available. The Wisconsin High School Athletic Association was the pioneer in the field of school athletic insurance. In 1930, it made available to its member schools insurance coverage for football. Other state high school athletic associations followed suit. Their success was evidenced in that over a period of a few years, these benefit plans expanded their coverage to provide medical indemnity for all interscholastic athletics and intramural and physical education activities. In the 1940's there were 25 states participating in their own nonprofit sponsored benefit plans. In the late 1940's and the early 1950's the insurance industry became aware of the success of these plans which was inviting enough to encourage commercial companies to enter the field. The commercial field became so competitive with such attractive premiums, together with the pressures of local taxpaying insurance agents, that many school administrators were sympathetic toward this type of coverage. They felt it relieved them of all responsibilities for the school insurance program inasmuch as the carrier contracted to pay unlimited sums for almost anything that even resembled a school-associated injury.

This brought about the first major change in "style." Some state associations terminated their benefit plans, for a variety of reasons: (1) their prime function being athletics and not insurance, in that it was now available to schools through the insurance industry; (2) the volume of underwriting was not sufficient to withstand any competition; and (3) insurance companies contracted with state associations to write policies for its member schools. Although the style changed, the result was more pupils insured, in that policies were available in all states.

Competition is good for any commodity. As a consequence, the basic philosophy of school athletic insurance was made more comprehensive in that most of the benefit plans included "pupil" coverage for all school activities, from kindergarten through twelfth grade. This change in style broadened the scope of coverage both in activities and in insurees.

Today there are eight state high school ath-

letic associations which still very successfully sponsor their own benefit plans. I assume that those responsible for assigning me the topic "Is Athletic Insurance Going Out of Style?" raise this question in view of the fact that the number at one time was 25. I believe that to a certain extent these benefit plans have been, and still are, most instrumental in controlling the cost factor of competitive policies in their own state as well as exerting some influence on nationwide rates. These plans have adopted many of the trends of the insurance industry: (1) nonallocated benefits compared to the original plans which were all founded on a scheduled indemnity basis, (2) catastrophic coverage, (3) group coverage, (4) nonduplication of benefits, and (5) premium rates based on individual school experience rating. Going out of style? No!—staying abreast of the style.

California is the only state in which the schools are required by statute to furnish accident insurance for their pupils. Originally school districts felt morally obligated to help parents defray medical expense resulting from interscholastic injuries. Now the attitude of the parent for any school injury is "Who's going to pay? how much? and when?" As a consequence, nearly all school districts nationwide purchase athletic insurance voluntarily as a service in the public interest or make such coverage available for purchase by the parent. A high percentage of these districts extend this coverage to include all school activities for all pupils.

I am unaware of any reliable statistical evidence, based on exposures, that overall there is any increase in the number of interscholastic athletic injuries. More claims? Yes! The many factors and variables that account for this increase in the number of claims and the cost of claims are too numerable to detail in this presentation.

In the discussion of any insurance, by definition, we must get firmly fixed in our mind what constitutes an accident. Ordinarily we mean by "accident" that some undesired or unintended event has taken place, resulting in damage to persons or to property, and is usually caused by factors which are outside of the system to which the event belongs. In our everyday usage, we resort to the word "accident" not merely to describe a misfortune, but also our apology in advance. In essence, we are saying that something unpleasant or even calamitous has happened, but we are not to be blamed. It is not our fault because it was an accident. It was inevitable and it would have happened to anyone. Thus we remove ourselves from personal responsibility.

In an attempt to understand accidents more clearly, authorities explain them in terms of failure of either systems or persons. As an example of a failure in systems, a school was held liable for injuries because of failure to develop a proper storage procedure. The failure of the system here was that turf building materials, caustic and noncaustic, which are virtually identical in appearance, were not clearly so identified and were kept in an area where they could become confused. This is exactly what happened. The football field had been treated with the caustic material in place of the noncaustic material and some 25 players sustained serious burns of various degree.

In theory, accidents could be eliminated by devising a perfect system and then fitting a perfect man into the system. Unfortunately, in this imperfect world, there are no perfect men. And since systems are the product of man's imperfect ingenuity, there are no perfect systems either.

Some criteria which can be used as guides in evaluating whether or not an accident is an accident are worthy of repetition. These facts are neither new nor listed in order of importance, but more or less follow in chronological order: physical readiness, equality of competition, facilities, equipment, coaching techniques, officiating and rules, and liability. Each of these items requires an interrelationship of understanding cooperation, responsibility, authority, accomplishment, and purposes between the school, the coach, and the physician.

We must accept a realistic attitude about accidents. If we label all of life's unpleasant surprises as accidents, then we come to perceive ourselves as the playthings of fate, and we cultivate a philosophy of carelessness and irresponsibility. On the other hand, if we look for causes and hold ourselves accountable for the mishaps in our lives, we become people of resource and confidence, increasingly able to control the direction of events. If these conclusions are true, it matters very much how we define the word "accident." An accident is not an accident, when it is preventable.

We experienced a new style in a football injury claim recently which, I believe, relates directly to the impact that television has on our school athletes. I quote: "In the course of the game, teammates congratulated each other on the completion of a successful play by slapping each other's hands." Result and claim—fractured metacarpal bone of hand.

Excessive losses, in some instances attributable to abuses by schools, parents, and physicians, have been instrumental in pricing some commercial companies out of the market. The other alternative has been to pay irate parents and argumentative doctors and increase the premium, when necessary, to keep all happy. This is not fair to the average policy holder or the insurance carrier, whether the premium is paid for by the school district or by the parent. About 80 percent of the families in the United States have some type of health insurance. The major portion of this coverage is written by the Blue Plans on a scheduled basis. Much is written with a deductible. Practically all have specified limits. Why then, should parents, and in some instances physicians, expect schools to purchase school athletic insurance which provides greater benefits than those of the individual policies purchased by parents or group policies written through industry?

Only one third of the costs of all family health care is paid for by insurance despite the fact that four out of every five persons have some type of health insurance. Nationally, insurance does pay for nearly three quarters of all hospital costs, and it pays for about one third of the cost of physicians' services in the hospital. Fortunately, more health care items are coming under the umbrella of insurance protection, with many policies paying increasingly more for regular or new benefits. The trend is to supplement basic coverage with a major medical policy. Most group insurance policies now require that you be asked, with each claim, if you have duplicate policies. It was never the intent that a parent make a profit from a claim for a school athletic accident. Supplement other coverages, yes, but not duplicate.

If athletic insurance is to remain in style with the necessary coverage based on realistic premium rates, the school must assume the initiative as management in the efficiency of its operation. How? Through proper cooperation between the insured and his carrier. There should be an understanding by the insured that he has become a partner, with his insurer, in the safety and accident prevention programs, in the handling and processing of claims, as well as in certain other features of his insurance coverage. To understand some of the factors involved, schools should have a proper conception of the nature of the insurance contract, its benefits, and its obligations. Private business and industry have long since found that safety and accident prevention make for more efficiency in production, less cost of production, and greater profits. Accidents can be reduced drastically by implementing a good accident prevention program, but they cannot be eliminated completely. The carelessness of the insured and that of the teacher or coach is often the uncontrollable factor.

PROJECTS AND THOUGHT QUESTIONS

1. Visit a library where there is a record of court cases and legal files. Determine if there are any court cases on record that have implications for or directly involve the fields of health education and physical education. Describe the circumstances and rulings surrounding each case.
2. Arrange a mock trial in your class. Have a jury, prosecutor, defendant, witnesses, and features that are characteristic of a regular court trial. Ask your instructor to state the case that has come before the court.
3. What are the defenses against negligence? Illustrate each, using the fields of health education and physical education as a frame of reference.
4. What are some safety precautions that should be taken by every physical education and health education teacher in: (a) elementary school, (b) high school, (c) college, (d) youth-serving agency.
5. Prepare a report form that you would recommend to a school or college administration for the purpose of reporting accidents that occur in health and physical education programs.
6. What are the legal considerations in respect to the purchase and care of supplies and equipment?

SELECTED READINGS

Blackwell, T. E.: College and university administration, New York, 1966, The Center for Applied Research Inc., The Library of Education.

Bucher, C. A.: Administration of health and physical education programs, including athletics, ed. 5, St. Louis, 1971, The C. V. Mosby Co.

Garber, L. O.: Yearbook of school law, Danville, Ill., 1963, The Interstate Printers & Publishers, Inc.

Gauerke, W. E.: School law, New York, 1965, The Center for Applied Research, Inc., The Library of Education.

Pierce, T. M.: Federal, state, and local government in education, New York, 1964. The Center for Applied Research, Inc., The Library of Education.

State school laws and regulations for health, safety, driver, outdoor, and physical education: Washington, D. C., 1964, Department of Health, Education, and Welfare.

CHAPTER 15 CURRICULUM DEVELOPMENT

The increased interest in education during recent years has brought about much curriculum reform. We now have a new mathematics, a new physics, a new English, and a new social studies. Many schools and colleges have felt the impact of change and the need to look at the times through which we are passing and to develop curricula that meet today's needs. The explosion of knowledge, the growth of education in America, the complexity of society, and the impact of social change make it imperative that educators and the public alike examine what they have been doing in the past, evaluate what they are doing now, and develop programs that meet the conditions that they believe exist.

Each subject matter field must relate to and help each student approach self-realization and effective social behavior through an involvement of pertinent ideas, people, and activities. Individual differences must be provided for. Each school and college should examine its curricula to see if they reflect the fact that learning is a continuous and individual process that proceeds at various rates and to various degrees in the attainment of each student's maximum potential.

The curricula in health and physical education programs function as vehicles for achieving such objectives as organic development, skill development, mental development, and social development. They provide for experiences in terms of courses, subject matter, and activities that will best achieve these goals. They help to create the environment that will enable sound and meaningful education to take place. The experiences provided are means to an end, that end being the realization of the broad goals that have been established for the profession and that enrich human living. Each student is, through the experiences provided, helped to develop his abilities and to realize his full potential.

In the first article in this chapter, Robert M. McClure writes about the forces guiding curriculum development procedures. Providing of environments in which a variety of outcomes can be achieved, promoting of inquiry as a way of thinking, discovery methods, and problem-solving are some of the approaches administrators must take toward building innovative curricula. "Restructure" and "update" are the key words administrators are using as a guide to achievement in this area of education.

In curriculum and course development, there are four basic factors or concerns facing administrators. As outlined by Wesley P. Cushman, they are the organized body of subject matter, the nature of the learner, the nature of the learning process, and the nature of society. Cushman presents a brief overview of curriculum and course construction for the secondary level in health education.

The Battle Creek (Michigan) Physical Education Curriculum Project, under the direction of Paul Vogel, is developing, implementing, and evaluating a model curriculum for physical education at the elementary and secondary levels. The program, as outlined in Vogel's article is aimed at stimulating other in-depth projects in curriculum development.

In the last article in this chapter, Louis Botwin discusses the use of the overhead projector and the loop projector as an example of the use of audiovisual material to enrich the physical education curriculum. Audiovisual materials have numerous learning advantages, and it is suggested that workshops and clinics be arranged for the training of teachers.

83 ❧ TRENDS IN CURRICULUM DEVELOPMENT*

ROBERT M. McCLURE
ASSOCIATE DIRECTOR, CENTER FOR THE STUDY OF INSTRUCTION,
NATIONAL EDUCATION ASSOCIATION

Among the trends being discussed by those concerned with curriculum development, three seem especially useful for health educators to consider as they shape a program for the future: (1) the curriculum reform movement, (2) rational planning of curriculum and instruction, and (3) more reasonable curriculum development procedures. In addition to these three emphases, which shape this article, it is good for us to keep in mind that there are certain forces pervading curriculum work today. The first of these forces has to do with providing environments in which a variety of learning outcomes can be achieved. Promoting inquiry as a way of thinking, discovery methods, problem solving, and other learning modes are constantly in the educational headlines of today. A second concern has to do with new ways of organizing the environment. We now have nongrading, team teaching, multigrading, small and large group instruction, study carrels, and other means to personalize education. Finally, a third effort is to restructure the content of the school program. There has been a great interest in science and mathematics and from this have grown new programs in physics, biology, chemistry, and elementary and secondary mathematics, which not only introduced new teaching methods but also restructured the content of the field and updated it. Lately, there has been much more interest in the social sciences, the fine arts, and language. Restructure and update are the key words.

The curriculum reform movement

How has the curriculum reform movement related to the issues and problems facing school people today? Even though the movement is about fifteen years old, it is fashionable to say that it started with Sputnik. A careful reading of the literature reveals that this is not true, that there were many national projects going on in this country before Sputnik. Sputnik obviously caused us to pour more resources into the projects and, therefore, make them have greater impact.

Ole Sand discussed the movement in this way:

> Illinois Math . . . PSSC . . . SMSG . . . the FLES program . . . the Economic Task Force—these and a bewildering number of other new terms are finding their way into the educational vocabulary. The projects to which these terms refer are major curriculum studies that merit thoughtful consideration. They have grown, in part, out of the need to bring the content of the school curriculum up to date so that new knowledge and specific disciplines can be incorporated and obsolete content can be eliminated. Most of the projects have focused on the development of materials for the elementary schools; few have given attention to the elementary school program.[1]

Since Sand wrote this, over two years ago, a great many projects have come on the national scene that are attempting to influence the elementary school program. It is still accurate to say, though, that the secondary school has received the most attention from the curriculum reformers.

All, or almost all of the projects, are similar in their intent; certain kinds of objectives seem to hold from one project to another. For example, there is a great emphasis on the Gestalt of the field—to understand the structure of the discipline. Also, it is important to the developers of the projects that boys and girls gather and gain skills, understandings, and attitudes that are similar to those of professionals in the field —students are asked to work and think as historians do, behave as a physicist does, look at the national scene through the political scientist's glasses, and so on. Growing out of this objective is another outcome—the emphasis on individuals contributing to the field and bringing new knowledge to the discipline. This has not always been the way that we have worked in schools before. In the teaching of history, for example, boys and girls have been led,

*The author was the keynote speaker at the AAHPER National Conference for School Health Education Curriculum Development held in Washington, D. C. in February 1967. The speech, pinpointing factors to which health educators must address themselves in the future, is presented here as condensed by the author. From JOHPER **38**:25, November-December 1967. Used by permission.

[1]Ole Sand, Current trends in instruction, in Comprehensive musicianship: the foundation for college education in music (Washington, D. C.: Music Educators National Conference, 1965), p. 80.

either consciously or unconsciously, to think that contributions to that field come after years and years of study and that it is not very easy for one to get into a field like history or political science and make any contribution. Let us hope that the work of the new projects has changed this.

In order to achieve the objectives, curriculum reformers want children to have the opportunity to "explore, invent, and discover; to develop some of the tools of inquiry appropriate to the field, and to experience some of the feelings and satisfactions of research scholars."[2]

The Changing School Curriculum by John I. Goodlad, from which this statement was taken, contains descriptions of illustrative projects which would be useful to planners of health education programs in getting a better idea of what the reform movement is all about. Section III of this book, "Problems and Issues," is a good guide for looking at the future.

Some criticisms can be made of the curriculum reform movement. A major emphasis has been to create materials for the classroom, and the reformers have a very special way of talking about their materials. Many call them "teacher-proof." This means that it is not possible for a teacher to dilute them or to get away from the original intent of the scholar who developed them. Actually, that is not true but to start out with this intent is damaging to the good teacher's program and, probably, is not very helpful to the poor one. A second criticism is the lack of a well-defined theoretical base from which to derive curriculum. Large central goals to which curriculum reformers can relate their work are noticeably absent in American education. In general, we have fallen down on the job of defining specifically and with any kind of creativity what the purposes of the school are. Curriculum reformers are, therefore, working only within the context of their own discipline and what its contribution can be to a liberal education. They have not considered other forces that must impinge on educational decision making.

Lawrence Cremin gives several considerations to be faced if the movement is to achieve maximum effect.[3] He cites the urgency of asking priority questions more insistently than ever. What knowledge is of most worth? What priorities *ought* to be taught to children at any given stage of their development? He agrees with others about the need for systematic testing for all new curriculum programs and continuing experiments with a variety of approaches to each field of study. And he warns against the unfortunate conclusion from Jerome Bruner's dictum that knowledge does not have to be recast for purposes of teaching.

Rational planning

At the NEA Center for the Study of Instruction (CSI) we have come to call phase two of the reform movement "Rational Planning in Curriculum and Instruction."[4] As you will see, a different set of questions are raised about curriculum.

Logan Wilson caught the essence of what this restructuring of the reform movement should be like when he said:

> Although many things can be done—and indeed are being done—to improve American education, basic decisions about its future still proceed rather haphazardly. It seems to me that the most needed single improvement is a more rational perspective of means and ends.
>
> Education is now the nation's biggest business. If it is to continue to yield increased dividends in human usefulness and happiness, we need to think more vigorously and systematically about such questions as these: What are our major objectives? Which means are best suited to their achievement? How do we assess the "payoff" of a greater investment in education as contrasted to other uses which could be made of human and material resources?
>
> In short, I believe that our faith in the powers of education as the chief means of social betterment needs to be bolstered by the sharpest reasoning we can bring to bear on what we do and how we can best go about doing it.[5]

Rational planning of curriculum and instruction is not a new approach to planning the school program. It has its genesis in the work of Ralph Tyler, John Goodlad, Ole Sand, Hilda Taba, and others. The report of the Project on Instruction, the precursor to CSI, was a major effort of the National Education Association to add the voice of the teaching profession to an ever-growing number of voices talking about what schools ought to be like.

[2]John I. Goodlad, The changing school curriculum (New York: The Fund for the Advancement of Education, 1966), p. 92.

[3]Lawrence A. Cremin, The Genius of American education, Horace Mann lecture of 1965 (Pittsburgh: University of Pittsburgh Press, 1965), pp. 56–57.

[4]See, for example, *Rational Planning in Curriculum and Instruction: Eight Essays* (Washington, D. C.: Center for the Study of Instruction, National Education Association, 1967).

[5]This Week Magazine, December 18, 1966, p. 4.

The substantive professional books[6] that grew out of the Project on Instruction raised important issues, four of which are:

> *Establishing priorities for the school:* What are the distinctive priorities of the school in contrast to those properly belonging to other youth-serving agencies; what responsibilities does the school share with other institutions; what, then, should be included and excluded in the school program?
> *Selecting content:* How can schools make wise selections of content from the ever-growing body of available knowledge?
> *Organizing content:* How should the content of the curriculum be organized?
> *Organizing the curriculum:* How should the curriculum be organized to give appropriate direction to the instruction process?

The recommendations made by the National Committee of the Project regarding these four issues are important sources of information for health educators to use in planning their program.

What are the characteristics of this kind of curriculum development activity? The first, as we have already said, is that all appropriate competencies will be available at the decision making table. The second is that we will deal in a rigorous way with the question of the school's role in the total educational enterprise for our citizens. The development and utilization of a variety of means to accomplish our goals will continue to demand the attention of curriculum developers. A large collection of tested alternatives from which we can prescribe for learners is our goal. Much more careful attention will be paid to the fact that schooling is a total enterprise and not a series of unconnected levels. The acceptance of this fact will cause us to pay much more attention to scope, continuity, and sequence of the curriculum. Finally, practitioners of rational planning will do a great deal to use the scientific base of teaching and become much more liberal in their interpretation of the art of applying the scientific base.

Why has rational planning thus far had less impact than phase one of the curriculum reform movement? It is relatively simple to develop a course or outlines for a course or material for a course, but infinitely harder to build a total program. It requires time—lots of time—and

self-discipline to tackle the question of total curriculum planning, and the rewards for such planning are slow to come. The lack of immediate rewards requires the reeducation of those who will support such activities.

In order to become truly rational in our planning we need to operate from a theoretical base. Ralph Tyler gave us the beginnings when several years ago he asked four questions.[7] Familiar as these questions are, it is important to continually re-ask them for they are significant questions from which a theoretical base must grow. What educational purposes should the school seek to attain? What educational experiences can be provided that are likely to attain these purposes? How can these educational experiences be effectively organized? How can we determine whether these purposes are being attained?

The Project on Instruction; recent work by John Goodlad;[8] the Montgomery County, Maryland, Public Schools; the School Health Education Study; and others have extended the meaning of these questions. The Project, for example, added another dimension to Tyler's work by talking about levels of decision making:

> Close to these students, teachers make daily *instructional* decisions; at a more remote level, teachers and administrators make *institutional* decisions; state legislators and federal officials make *societal* educational decisions.[9]

It has been said that health education, at least in the high school, becomes a part of the curriculum when inclement weather arrives. What procedures can one use to ensure a more sustained health education program in the curriculum? The School Health Education Study has proposed a "rational" way to go about this: (1) A survey to determine the state of the field—a definition of this part of the curriculum, (2) a statement of priorities—objectives stated in terms of behavioral outcomes, (3) organiza-

---

[6] *Deciding what to teach, Education in a changing society,* and *Planning and organizing for teaching* (Washington, D.C.: National Education Association, 1963).

[7] Ralph W. Tyler, *Basic principles of curriculum and instruction* (Chicago: University of Chicago Press, 1950), pp. 1–2.

[8] John I. Goodlad and Maurice N. Richter, Jr., *The development of a conceptual system for dealing with problems of curriculum and instruction* (Los Angeles: University of California and the Institute for Development of Educational Activities, 1966). Report of an inquiry supported by the Cooperative Research Program of the U.S. Office of Education with the University of Chicago.

[9] *Planning and organizing for teaching* (Washington: National Education Association, 1963), p. 21.

tion of the content—key concepts, scope, sequence, organizing elements, and the like, (4) development of experimental materials based on a careful analysis of the data and decisions made, and (5) concurrent development of means of evaluation, including pre- and post-test analyses of outcomes. The progress of this important project must be a continuing source of pride to health educators. At least in one field a rational approach to curriculum planning is being conducted with great care and thoughtfulness.

Curriculum development activities in the future

There are historic parallels between present activities in the national curriculum projects and those that took place in the 20's and 30's. Development by William S. Gray of the basal readers is the best example of this similarity.

The basal readers changed the reading program of the schools almost overnight. It took out of the teacher's hands the decision making process about what materials and tactics to use in order to accomplish reading objectives. It laid out specifically the fundamental skills and presented a set of materials to go with the procedures. Since the publication of the basal readers, reading programs in schools have become increasingly better. One might ask, then, has this improvement resulted because we restricted teachers to what the research indicated and provided them carefully controlled materials with which to put the research into action? Or did the results come about primarily because through this process teachers were superbly educated to teach reading? Probably both facts have something to do with the quality of today's reading program, yet the reading program today is often characterized by a movement away from the basal readers and into individualization. Teachers now are able to make good decisions about pupil progress in reading because of their experience in a program that was carefully designed. Let us hope that if we use national programs that allow for little

flexibility, the eventual result will be better educated teachers, more able to make wise instructional decisions from their experience with new content. Let us also hope that it does not take thirty years to make this happen.

Marshall McLuhan helps us to see the school setting for today and tomorrow more clearly. Perhaps his implications for the school of the future give us some lead about the setting in which the rational, decision making teacher will find himself.

[Mass education] reached maturity just at that historical moment when Western civilization had attained its final extreme of fragmentation and specialization and had mastered the linear technique of stamping out products in the mass.

It was this civilization's genius to manipulate matter, energy and human life by breaking every useful process down into its functional parts, then producing any required number of each. Just as shaped pieces of metal became components of a locomotive, human specialists became components of the great social machine.

In this setting, education's task was fairly simple: decide what the social machine needs, then turn out people who match those needs. That age has passed. More swiftly than we can realize, we are moving into an era dazzlingly different. Fragmentation, specialization and sameness will be replaced by wholeness, diversity and, above all, a deep involvement.[10]

We are being inundated with data about what schools should be like. These data force us to do the hard and uncomfortable. They force change and decision but in our activity there is opportunity and this makes our professional lives worth living.

In criticizing today's philosophers, *Time* magazine asks the question: "Will philosophy ever again address the heavens? Will it contribute anything to man's vision, rather than merely clarifying it?"[11] Indeed, we now ask the same question of our schools.

[10] Look, February 21, 1967, p. 24
[11] Time, January 7, 1966, p. 24.

84 ❧ AN OVERVIEW OF APPROACHES TO CURRICULA AND COURSE CONSTRUCTION IN HEALTH EDUCATION*

WESLEY P. CUSHMAN, ED.D.
PROFESSOR OF HEALTH EDUCATION,
OHIO STATE UNIVERSITY, COLUMBUS, OHIO

Our discussion begins with an overview of approaches to curriculum and course development as I have observed them over the last thirty years. Curriculum is being used in its narrowest sense, that is, subject matter curriculum which, in this case, is made up of a series of health courses offered at different grades or levels of learning. The discussion and illustrations will be limited to the secondary level since emphasis in health education in the elementary grades since the 1920's has been on the promotion of health habits, teachable moments, and correlated learning rather than on knowledge through a health class. Because this is an overview, only the big ideas are dealt with, so what is said is not as clear-cut as it may seem. In fact, if you visit enough schools, you will find all of the approaches discussed being used today.

In curriculum and course construction, we are concerned with four basic factors: the organized body of subject matter, the nature of the learner, the nature of the learning process, and the nature of society. In my experience with course-of-study development, the only change has been a matter of emphasis of these basic factors. In the 1920's emphasis was on subject matter and the anatomical and physiological approaches were used; in the late 1920's the emphasis was on the child and the interest approach to the health curriculum emerged; in the late forties and early 1950's, social needs received more attention; and at present, emphasis is on health as a discipline and the concept approach is current.

Before we discuss changing emphases, let us look briefly at our subject matter field. We have a most difficult time describing it since the term "hygiene" lost its popularity back in the 1920's. "Health education" is a process; and "health" is a state of well-being; and whether we like it or not, the term "hygiene" which means the science of health and the preserva-

tion of life—a system of principles designed for the promotion of health, best describes our teaching area. The principles of hygiene are drawn from many other sciences and so it must be recognized that our subject is inter-disciplinary and applied. That health authorities are agreed as to the content of our field can be illustrated by the following samples which demonstrate how continuity in various health curricula is obtained by using subject matter areas as the organizing elements:

1. Organizing elements used by Oberteuffer, 1932, in his interest approach curriculum: He has arranged these by "life functions" rather than by the systems of of the body. (10)

   High school—interest approach (organizing elements)

   Playing
   Eating
   Teeth
   Resting
   Keeping well (Colds and communicable diseases)
   Degenerative diseases
   Elimination and exercise
   Thinking and feeling
   Appearance
   Social relations
   Breathing
   Public welfare
   Health and living

2. Hoyman in the Oregon curriculum in 1945 used the following "organizing elements" by which to set up units for grades 7–12. (7)

   High school—needs approach (organizing elements)

   1. Structure and functions of the human body
   2. Personal hygiene (including mental health and the effects of alcoholic drinks, stimulants, and narcotics)
   3. Physiology of exercise
   4. Nutrition
   5. First aid and safety education
   6. Choice and use of health services and health products
   7. Communicable diseases (and non-communicable diseases)

---

*Presented at the 11th National Conference on Physicians and School, sponsored by the Department of Health Education, American Medical Association, Chicago, Illinois, Oct. 4–7, 1967. From The Journal of School Health **29**:14, January 1969. Used by permission.

8. Community health and sanitation
9. Mental health (and family-life education)
3. The School Health Education Study writers used conceptual statements derived from the subject matter areas: (6, p. 20)

Ten concepts (SHE Study)
1. Growth and development influences and is influenced by the structure and functioning of the individual.
2. Growth and developing follows a predictable sequence, yet is unique for each individual.
3. Protection and promotion of health is an individual, community, and international responsibility.
4. The potential for hazards and accidents exists, whatever the environment.
5. There are reciprocal relationships involving man, disease, and enviornment.
6. The family serves to perpetuate man and to fulfill certain health needs.
7. Personal health practices are affected by a complexity of forces, often conflicting.
8. Utilization of health information, products, and services is guided by values and perceptions.
9. Use of substances that modify mood and behavior arises from a variety of motivations.
10. Food selection and eating patterns are determined by physical, social, mental, economic, and cultural factors.

In all the curricula, subject centered, interest and needs centered or concept centered, the organizing elements reflect a common agreement as to the basic content of our field.

As I have said, prior to and during the 1920's emphasis was on subject matter, physiological hygiene, the learning of facts. Courses used the anatomical and physiological approach to health problems. The parts and functions of the body had to be memorized before personal health could be discussed.

But in the late 20's and 1930's, the leaders in the fields of curriculum development reacted strongly against "the sterile, arbitrary and often nonsensical adult-imposed subject curriculum." (12, p. 288) Curricula became child-centered. In health education, the reaction was reflected by the use of the needs and interest approach. D. Oberteuffer was an early leader in this move-

ment and his curriculum guide for Ohio junior and senior high schools was developed around the questions asked by pupils. I quote from the health guide developed in 1932:

> The modern graded program of health instruction finds its prototype in courses in physiology and hygiene. In subsequent chapters will be found complete and graded lessons which involve much of physiology and hygiene and yet which approach problems of living from an entirely different point of view. True to the general swing in all subjects from the formalized type of instruction of an earlier day to the more functional and vital approach of modern education, health instruction now reverses on the teaching method and uses the detail and generalities of physiology *in answer to* rather than *as sources of* the problems of life. (10, p. 126, 127)

The Ohio guide (1932) has this to say about interests and needs:

> *Student needs form the basis for the selection of subject matter most likely to affect conduct favorably.* By student needs is meant the actual problems of living, those problems appearing every day in students' lives, about which students have an active curiosity and desire for information, or which teachers may anticipate and so fore-arm students against an adverse environment.
> . . . The case in favor of using student interests in this way is strong and clear. People will not think vitally about a problem unless that problem is *vital* to them. (10, p. 127)

This point of view is illustrated by the outline of the curriculum guide that relates to *nutrition* for grades 7 and 12. Please realize the guide includes material for grades 8, 9, 10 and 11, plus teaching suggestions and activities. The following excerpts.

Eating   Ohio. Grade 7 Food
Balanced meals
1. What food should a normal person eat?
2. What effect does a balanced diet have?
3. How much sweet food should a person eat?

Eating habits
1. Is eating fruit between meals good for you?
2. Should we eat what is on the table or waste it?
3. If one eats food too fast, will it cause indigestion?
4. Is it good to play ball right after a heavy meal?

Eating habits   Ohio. Grade 12 Food
1. Does it harm one to eat irregularly?

2. It is necessary to eat three meals a day?
3. What makes people hungry?
4. Why do people's tastes differ?
5. What are the effects of over-eating?
6. Will the constant use of breakfast foods which promote digestion hurt the digestive organs in the end?
7. Are talking, reading, and thinking bad practices while one is eating?

The Detroit study, which began in 1945, is probably the most thorough attempt to establish an interest-oriented curriculum from K-12. (3)

An interest approach, though recognized as an important condition under which learning takes place, has been, over the years, recognized as but only one way of seeking a basis for understanding for what a health education curriculum should achieve. We have learned from psychological studies and experience that expressed interests are not necessarily deep interest, that if individual interests are followed there may be lack of common focus, and that, in practice, the interest approach sacrifices subject organization as it is weak in providing sequence and often times scope. (12, p. 128)

Though the curricula of the future may not be built on interests alone we must take off our hats to the health education leaders of the 20's and 30's who had the courage to depart from the anatomical and physiological approach to hygiene. Also, it would be foolhardy for us *not* to continue to recognize the use of the special interests and concerns of the learner as a potent motivating factor in effective learning.

Though needs and interests are not mutually exclusive, Oberteuffer and the Denver study emphasized interests in their approach, whereas Hoyman in 1945, placed greater emphasis on social needs in building the Oregon health curriculum.

> The framework of the new health curriculum for the Oregon schools has been built around the major health problems that are common to Oregon students and to Oregon communities. (7, p. 10)

> The Oregon health-instruction plan is to meet individual student needs and to capitalize on student interests without making these the sole criteria in developing the health curriculum. (7, p. 11)

Hoyman used a four cycle plan—a cycle was a three year period—so each of his eleven areas was emphasized four times in the twelve-year curriculum. Nutrition, for example, was dealt with in grades 2, 5, 8, and 11. These are samples of the outlines for grades 8 and 11.

Nutrition grade 8 (h.s.)
1. Recommended common basic content.
   a. Food needs of the 12–14 age group
   b. Relation of diet to adolescent growth, vigor, health, and attractiveness
   c. Food-borne diseases
   d. Common digestive ailments

Nutrition grade 11 (h.s.)
1. Recommended common basis content
   a. Basic nutritional facts and principles
      1. Review and summarize the basic information included in the unit for the junior high school grades (pp. 75–90) and estimate how well the students apply what they were taught.
      2. Amount of food needed by the body
      3. Kinds of food needed by the human body
   b. Application of basic facts and principles
   c. Relation of nutrition to health, vigor, and attractiveness

To avoid some of the confusion between interests and needs, and to give better order to learning experiences in the 1950's, health educators advocated using our increasing knowledge of growth and development as a means of identifying and organizing health learning experiences. Many of you are familiar with the curriculum guide developed by the AAHPER Curriculum Committee which appeared in the Fall, 1962 issue of *Panorama,* published by the World Confederation of Organizations of the Teaching Profession. This guide is typical of the guides based on developmental needs developed at state and local levels.

Though many curriculum authorities advocated use of developmental tasks as a means of meeting individual and social needs in a more orderly manner, I know of no curriculum so developed. Developmental tasks as a source of health problems have been investigated in depth by Kime and Steig at the secondary school level. (8, 11)

To refresh your memory, a developmental task is a "task which arises at or about a certain period in the life of the individual, successful achievement of which leads to his happiness and to success with later tasks while failure leads to unhappiness in the individual, disapproval by society and difficulty with later tasks." (4, p. 2) A task is midway between an individual need and a cultural demand. Tasks can be used to relate health knowledge to developmental goals. They bring together ideas about biological maturation, socialization and psychological development of drives and motivation. Tasks can serve as criteria to determine when it is best to use a particular health problem. They give sequence to the curricula. (2, 12, p. 97, 98) For purposes of illustration, I have developed some problems related to development tasks of early and late adolescence as they might be used in a nutrition unit in the 8th and 12th grades.

Nutrition for 8th grade (developmental tasks)
1. How does what I eat affect appearance?
2. How does what I eat affect athletic performance?
3. How can one lose or gain weight?
4. How can the adolescent select his food wisely during this fast growth period?

Nutrition for 12th grade (developmental tasks)
1. How do my eating habits affect my work performance?
2. What factors should guide my selection of meals eaten in commerical places?
3. How can I prepare nutritious meals on a limited budget?
4. How can I buy economically without sacrificing quality?
5. How should I adjust my eating and exercise habits after marriage to control my weight?
6. What agencies and professional groups are protecting the public against food fads, advertising, chemical additives and high costs?

The present trend in curriculum development is the concept approach. It originated before, but began to gain momentum after Sputnik in 1957, and is now beginning to reach the schools. It is discipline centered; that is, it emphasizes the structural elements: the concepts and key ideas of the particular field of knowledge. The assumption is based on the idea that these elements (rather than facts) enable a student to deal best with new and unfamiliar problems. The learning experiences selected for a particular unit must help the student develop or discover the important concepts. The following are concepts related to nutrition as developed by the AAHPER Commission on Curriculum and the School Health Education Study.

AAHPER—Curriculum Committee
Health Concepts: guides for health instruction.
Nutrition is the food you eat and how the body uses it.
Food is made up of different nutrients needed for growth and health.

All persons, throughout life, have need for these same nutrients, but in varying amounts. The way food is handled influences the amount of nutrients in food, its safety, appearance, and taste.

School Health Education Study
Food selection and eating patterns are determined by physical, social, mental, economic, and cultural factors.
Subconcepts:
Choice of foods determines nutritional balance.
A balanced diet affects well-being and the desire for well-being affects food choices.
Food selection and eating patterns serve social and psychological purposes as well as filling physiological needs.

Here are some learning experiences that might be used to aid high school students in developing these concepts.

Problems that lead to development of AAHPER Concepts on nutrition
1. How much sweet food should a person have?
2. Why do people's tastes differ?
3. Food needs of the 12–14 age group.
4. Relation of nutrition to vigor and attractiveness.
5. How does what I eat affect athletic performance?
6. What agencies are protecting the public against food fads, advertising, and chemical additives?

You recognize these problems as coming from the curriculum guides just reviewed. They were selected to emphasize the point that in the concept approach the classroom learning experiences are not necessarily different from our curricula of the past. Learning experiences related to needs, interests, and developmental task are not excluded by this approach. Though concepts are important criteria in helping us select learning experiences they allow for wide choice at the classroom level. As I see it now, the greatest contribution of the conceptual approach to health education will be that it better identifies our discipline, and gives us the needed framework for knowledge and ordering our learning experiences.

I have not touched upon the role of objectives in deciding how courses shall be built. All of the people responsible for the curricula reviewed have used them. In health education, we have expressed objectives in terms of knowledge, attitudes and habits. The Taxonomy of Education (1) has given us new and more meaningful terms: health educators are replacing the term "knowledge" with *cognitive domain,* which emphasizes thinking skills, including comprehending, relating, analyzing as well as knowing facts. The *affective domain* is more significant than attitudes including, as it does, awareness and accepting. Habits is replaced by the term *action domain* and includes examining, demonstrating, evaluating and *doing* as forms of overt behavior.

As far as I know, the taxonomy objectives have not been used in setting up objectives for health units except by the School Health Education writers, who use them most effectively. These are not unique, however, to the concept approach and were developed independently from it. They are useful in unit construction no matter what approach is used.

Problem solving as a method of teaching has gained in popularity in recent years. It can be used most advantageously in health education. The needs and interests approach to curriculum design facilitated its use and developmental tasks help the health educator to select problems that are timely. Problems can and should be used to help students develop concepts.

In conclusion, it must constantly be borne in mind that in curriculum and course development we are concerned with organized subject matter, the nature of the learning process, the nature of the learner, and the nature of society. Newer trends in curriculum development are a matter of changing emphasis rather than departures from basic concerns.

BIBLIOGRAPHY

1. Committee of College and University Examiners, Taxonomy of educational objectives, Handbook I: cognitive domain, (Benjamin S. Bloom, Editor), New York: David McKay Company, Inc., 1956.
2. Cushman, Wesley P., Developmental tasks—a source of health problems, Journal of School Health, XXIX (September 1959).
3. Denver Board of Education, Health interests of children, Denver: Denver Public Schools, 1954.
4. Havighurst, Robert J., Human development and education, New York: Longmans, Green and Company, 1953.
5. Health concepts, Curriculum Commission, Division of Health Education, Washington, D.C.: American Association for Health, Physical Education, and Recreation, 1967.
6. Health education, School Health Education Study, St. Paul, Minn.: Minnesota Mining and Manufacturing Company, 1967.
7. Hoyman, Howard S., Health guide units for Oregon teachers, Salem: Oregon State Department of Education, 1945.
8. Kime, Robert E., Feasibility of using developmental tasks as a source of health interests, The Research Quarterly, 36 (March 1965), p. 38.
9. Krathwohl, David R., Bloom, Benjamin S., Masia, Bertram B., Taxonomy of educational objectives, Handbook II: affective domain, New York: David McKay Company, Inc., 1964.
10. Oberteuffer, D., Health and physical education series, Columbus: State of Ohio, Department of Education, 1932.
11. Steig, Peggy A., A study to determine the use of developmental tasks as a source for the identification of health interests of adolescents in grades ten through twelve (unpublished dissertation), The Ohio State University, 1966.
12. Taba, Hilda, Curriculum development: theory and practice, New York: Harcourt, Brace, and World, Inc., 1962.

85 ❧ BATTLE CREEK PHYSICAL EDUCATION CURRICULUM PROJECT*

BATTLE CREEK PHYSICAL EDUCATION CURRICULUM PROJECT TEAM
BATTLE CREEK PUBLIC SCHOOLS
Paul Vogel, *Project Director,* Louis F. Guerra, Auke Van Holst, Dona Rae Vogel
MICHIGAN STATE UNIVERSITY
Vern Seefeldt, Arthur Steinhaus, Wayne Van Huss, Janet Wessel

Periodic criticism of physical education programs in the nation's schools suggests a need

*From JOHPER **40**:25, September 1969. Used by permission.

Paul Vogel, who prepared this progress report, is director of the Physical Education Curriculum Project for the Battle Creek Public Schools, Battle Creek, Michigan. The Project, initiated in September 1966, is supported by funds provided under Title III of the Elementary and Secondary Education Act.

for an assessment of their curricular content. A review of the literature which is pertinent to physical education reveals a substantial gap between what is known and what is currently practiced. It appears that a primary need in physical education is to establish a systematic method of selecting, organizing, and evaluating curricular content so that the relevant knowledges, skills, and values may be incorporated into the teaching-learning situation.

The Battle Creek Physical Education Curriculum Project is the result of a response to this challenge on the part of a public school system working in conjunction with a university. A Project Team consisting of selected personnel from the Battle Creek Public School System and the Physical Education Department of Michigan State University are currently engaged in developing, implementing, and evaluating a model curriculum for physical education at the elementary and secondary levels.

The Project Team initially consisted of a curriculum specialist, the city director of physical education, two growth and development specialists, a sociologist, a physiologist, and a specialist in educational measurement. Although interdisciplinary in nature, this group held common views in such matters as educational philosophy, the need for change in curriculums of physical education, and the desire to retrieve, organize, and incorporate the pertinent scientific literature into a program of physical education.

The major objectives of the Project Team were to: (1) systematically identify the elements necessary to develop a curriculum model, (2) organize the content which is representative of this model in terms of a philosophy, general objectives, student outcomes, and a hierarchy of behavioral objectives, and (3) develop an "exemplary" program in physical education by organizing, implementing, and evaluating the teaching-learning experiences derived from the model.

The sequence of procedures utilized in the development of a model and the organization of its curricular content was as follows: (1) recognition of the need, (2) tentative philosophy, (3) criteria for selecting the body of knowledge, (4) identification of the body of knowledge, (5) revision of philosophy, (6) master plan, (7) scope and sequence, (8) organizing ideas, (9) content units, and (10), sequential lessons. Examples of the content at each level of the curricular structure are provided in the figures on the following pages.

Identification of a body of knowledge

Identification of the body of knowledge became the first major endeavor in the process of constructing a model curriculum. Numerous staff members and graduate students assisted in the development of bibliographies and the retrieval of information. Their efforts were guided by criteria in the form of operational principles and questions regarding the interrelationship of man and physical activity, including the contributions which have commonly been attributed to participation in physical activity. The library search, conducted in accordance with the following criteria, resulted in approximately 2,000 documents and abstracted research reports.

Operational principles

1. The principle of integration of learning and behavior
   a. Physical education is concerned with the individual as a whole person. Attention must be directed to man's physical structure and function, to his mental and emotional behavior, and to his personal interaction with society.
   b. Physical education is concerned with physical activity as a means of fostering or maximizing human development.
   c. An individual should demonstrate an understanding of the effects of activity at various developmental levels and be able to utilize this information in selecting the kinds and amounts of activity required to enhance his total well-being.
2. The principle of integrity of a subject field in education
   a. Physical education is a profession which draws upon the basic sciences for its body of knowledge. Within the educational establishment physical education serves as a subject field in which the fundamental facts, principles, and skills are brought together in a logical pattern.
   b. The knowledges, skills, and values inherent in this content can be sequenced in accordance with the abilities, interests, and past experiences of the learner.

Questions which guided the identification of curricular content

1. What is the influence of activity on man's physical, motor, psychological, and social development?
2. What is the influence of human variation on activity patterns of an immediate and long range nature?
3. What is the interrelationship between culture, environment, and the activity patterns of man?

Contributions of physical activity

Contributions of physical activity to the social, physical, psychological, and motor welfare of man were listed in detail. The current status of research and teaching methodology in such areas as perception, learning readiness, somatotyping, etc., was provided through consultants who met weekly with the Project Team and representatives of the physical education staff of the Battle Creek Public Schools. Contributions which were based upon empirical evidence or speculation were also included at this stage.

It became apparent that the criteria utilized for retrieving information were not appropriate for organizing curricular materials. The premise that a logical sequence of knowledges, skills, and values existed and could be identified within the literature prompted a search for persistent themes within the body of knowledge. This attempt to organize the voluminous collection of scientific information resulted in the following four themes:

Theme I —Man's performance and health are modified by adaptations made in response to stressors.

Theme II —Human development is characterized by an orderly progression, but the age of onset and rates of progress within each phase are unique to the individual.

Theme III —The interrelationship of body structure and function sets the boundaries of man's potential for movement.

Theme IV —The interaction of the individual with culture and society influences his participation in physical activities.

The content of the themes was organized into key ideas, subkey ideas, statements, and substatements, as shown in Figure 1. All statements and substatements were accompanied by an indication of the current status of knowledge in that area. The pertinent literature was identified in situations where the evidence clearly supported the statement. Where evidence was controversial, speculative, or empirical the logic for including such materials was cited.

The research documentation of the theme content served four purposes: (1) It provided a means for critically examining the traditional content of physical education. (2) It served as a reservoir of information from which to draw the content of a physical education curriculum. (3) It provided a means for the assessment of the quantity and quality of the research which supports the body of knowledge in physical education. (4) It provided for the advancement of this body of knowledge in a systematic manner through the organization of content and

Example of Theme Format

Theme II Human development is characterized by an orderly progression, but the age of onset and the rates of progress within each phase are unique to the individual.

KEY Fundamental patterns or common elements of movement are combined to form complex patterns of movement which make up the skills of sports and dance.

SUBKEY All specialized activities have elements of movement which are common to other activities.

STATEMENT Complex skills are composed primarily of familiar patterns which require some specific adjustment to meet the demands of the new activity.

SUBSTATEMENT All sports, games and dances involve propelling the body and/or other objects. (84)

To meet new motor activities with success an individual must have mastered a variety of fundamental motor patterns. (85)

FIGURE 1

identification of areas requiring supportive evidence.

Philosophical position

Although the process of constructing a curriculum model was initiated by individuals who were in general agreement regarding a philosophical position, it seemed prudent to delay a final statement of philosophy until the retrieval of information had been completed. The following statement is a revision of the tentative philosophy which guided the initial efforts of the Project Team.

> Physical education is that portion of the educative process which utilizes physical activity as a primary means for influencing the psychological, intellectual, and social, as well as the physical development of the individual to effectively meet and adjust to the demands of a changing society.

The master plan

The process of selecting appropriate content from the body of knowledge required an additional organization of the reservoir of information. This was accomplished within the framework of a master plan which was defined

MASTER PLAN OUTLINE

GENERAL PROGRAM OBJECTIVES

| #1 | #2 | #3 | #4 |

OUTCOMES

MAJOR BEHAVIORAL OBJECTIVES

FIGURE 2

Outcome and Major Behavioral Objectives

GENERAL OBJECTIVE I: Acquisition of motor skills and knowledge of their practice.

OUTCOME: To be proficient in a variety of motor skills.

MAJOR BEHAVIORAL OBJECTIVES:

To acquire proficiency in a wide range of sports, games and dances.

To be able to move the body efficiently in all fundamental skills.

To be able to combine the fundamental skills into complex patterns of sports, games and dances.

To know the rules, strategy and ethics of various sports, games and dances.

To understand role of gross motor activity in intellectual development.

FIGURE 3

in terms of general objectives, program outcomes, and major behavioral objectives. A diagram of the master plan is shown in Figure 2.

The following *general objectives* describe the types of learning and behavior that should implement the stated philosophy. It is implied that these objectives are achieved through participation in the sequential experiences of physical education, grades K-12.

1. The acquisition of motor skills and knowledge of their practice
2. The acquisition of knowledge concerning the effects of physical activity
3. The acquisition of knowledge and skills concerning social competence
4. The acquisition of knowledge concerning the influence of human variation on motor performance and health

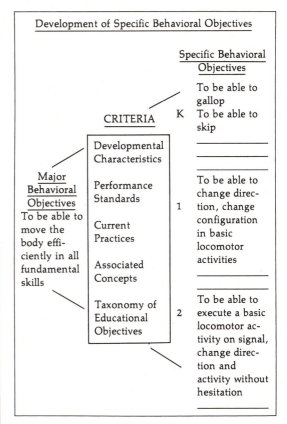

Development of Specific Behavioral Objectives

FIGURE 4

Program outcomes present terminal behaviors at grade 12 for students who have progressed through the physical education program in its entirety. *Major behavioral objectives* represent a series of increasingly complex behaviors which the students must achieve in their progress toward attainment of the program outcomes and general objectives (see Figure 3).

Scope and sequence chart

The process of developing a scope and sequence chart involved a proliferation of each major behavioral objective (see Figure 4). The product of this effort represents the content of the curriculum in specific behavioral objectives organized according to developmental level. Developmental sequences were well established in some areas, but in general these progressions were compiled by combining a comprehensive search of the literature, the advice of consultants, and empirical evidence. It was not the intent to establish firm and rigid sequences of behavior which would be specific to chronological age or grade level. Learning sequences for individualized instruction can only be assured when teachers can accurately diagnose the status of each pupil and plan instructional activities in accordance with such an appraisal.

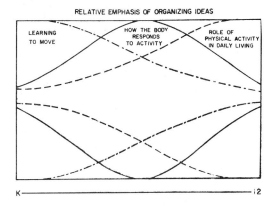

RELATIVE EMPHASIS OF ORGANIZING IDEAS

FIGURE 5

UNIT 1

EPISODE 1

1.SEGMENTS
2.
3.

EPISODE 2

1.SEGMENTS
2.
3.
4.

EPISODE 3

1.SEGMENTS
2.
3.

UNIT 2

FORMAT OF UNIT CONTENT

	CONCEPTS	ASSOCIATED CONCEPTS	SPECIFIC BEHAVIORAL OBJECTIVES	LEARNING ACTIVITIES
SEGMENT # 1				
SEGMENT # 2				
SEGMENT # 3				

FIGURE 6

The following resource materials served as a guide in constructing a scope and sequence chart:

1. A comprehensive review of developmental characteristics constructed according to modal age, including the age range of 0–17 years. Particular emphasis was given to growth standards, motor development, developmental tasks, and the predominant needs and interests of children.
2. The cognitive and affective domains as identified and sequenced by Bloom[1] and Krathwohl[2]
3. The teaching sequence of concepts and skills used in the biological and physical science curriculums
4. A development of social skills and values
5. The teaching sequence of health concepts
6. The vocabulary introduced at various levels in other subject areas

[1] B. Bloom and others, Taxonomy of educational objectives: Handbook I, cognitive domain (New York: David McKay Company, 1956).

[2] D. Krathwohl and others, Taxonomy of educational objectives: Handbook II, affective domain (New York: David McKay Company, 1964).

UNIT I LEARNING TO MOVE

EPISODE A: Body Awareness
   SEGMENT I. Identification of Body Parts

EPISODE B: Concepts of Space, Force, Time, Direction, Form
   SEGMENT I. Direction in Space

UNIT II LEARNING ABOUT PHYSICAL CHANGES AND DIFFERENCES

ASSOC. CONCEPTS	CONCEPTS	SPECIFIC BEHAVIORAL OBJECTIVES	LEARNING ACTIVITIES
Muscle Skeleton Bone Together Separate Segment Extremity	Head Trunk Arms Legs	To identify various parts of the body. To move specific parts of the body in various ways.	Problem Solving Movement Exploration Games: Simon Says Hokey Pokey
Space Direction Position	Toward— Away Up—Down Right—Left Over— Under Through	To move toward an object. To move through an object.	Obstacle Course Problem Solving

FIGURE 7

7. The results of an interest inventory administered to random samples drawn from the Battle Creek school population
8. A comprehensive collection of evaluation instruments and standards currently employed in schools throughout the nation

The transition from scope and sequence chart to content units was accomplished with the aid of organizational ideas (see Figure 5). The content was grouped according to units, episodes, and segments, each step representing a more detailed account of the objective to be attained by the student. These units were further delineated into concepts, associated concepts (drawn from other curricular areas), and specific behavioral objectives according to developmental level (see Figures 6 and 7).

The Project Team is currently involved in generating content units and a series of lessons for kindergarten and grades 1 and 2. Subsequent tasks involve the testing of these materials in selected schools, with the view toward revising the materials prior to incorporating them into other schools. Concurrently, a portion of the Project Team is developing similar materials for the later elementary and secondary levels. All materials will undergo feasibility testing and revision before they become available for general distribution.

A commitment

The present approach to curriculum development provides the foundation for an objective-centered program in physical education, matched to the developmental characteristics of learners in terms of their interests, needs, and goals. The scientific base of the content and the developmental characteristics used in sequencing the learning experiences provide a systematic plan for developing learning experiences. It is the hope of the Project Team that this interdisciplinary approach, cooperatively undertaken by a school system and a university, will stimulate other in-depth projects in curriculum development. Such mutual efforts should expedite the development and evaluation of curriculums and instructional materials now urgently needed in the physical education programs of the nation's schools.

86 ❧ THE MEDIA APPROACH, A HAPPENING IN PHYSICAL EDUCATION*

Louis Botwin
Teacher of Physical Education,
Park Intermediate School,
Westbury, New York

The employment of educational instructional media in our school programs have [sic] added many significant values towards new horizons in learning. Through the media made available today, we are able to solve many of our communication problems with our students by increasing our instructional and learning efficiency.

We physical education teachers must be made aware of the numerous learning advantages, through the utilization of such teaching equipment as the 8 mm single concept loop film and projector, as well as the overhead projector and transparencies. Next, we should develop within our own teaching techniques an understanding that instructional media must not be used as a supplemental enrichment device alone, but as a carefully planned and integrated part of the entire learning environment of physical education. We can then proceed to provide our students with the opportunity of gaining increased skill understanding and new learning experiences. We cannot depend on words alone to transfer our ideas and teachings. It would be advisable to look into the curriculum skill areas of our programs which we generally teach verbally with perhaps the use of a student or teacher demonstrator. Then we must ask ourselves could we do a better teaching job in this same program through the use of some audio visual treatment? (e.g. the utilization of the media previously mentioned).

Our next step is to add the ability to select ready made or their own instructional material, to transfer their ideas and teachings to specific visual forms. This can most effectively be developed through in-service programs or through the aid of teachers who are more familiar with the new teaching media and materials that are available. Therefore, it is important for physical education administrators to be familiar with the teaching aids and stimulate a desire among the staff to achieve an amount of skill and knowledge in using media.

The use of visuals in education is not at all new. Today's technological society has brought forth increasing availability and accessibility of new educational media and equipment. Other subject areas in our schools have been utilizing such equipment within their own departments. We have all experienced the values of using audio visual equipment in our program. It is about time we survey the field of media and learn just what is available and then plan our physical education curriculums employing the various instructional media of today. Physical education programs in our schools can serve as excellent springboards, therefore, making it possible for audio visual media to take on a vital and significant role in the development of an enriched, effective teaching and learning situation.

*From Physical Educator 25:116, October 1968. Used by permission.

Our physical education departments should develop their own media and curriculum centers. Here, all materials, guides, catalogues, equipment and listings would be made available. This phase of the program must be developed by the department chairman or director. The establishment of such a facility will enhance the entire physical education program. Teachers will be able to research, investigate, experiment and develop and improve their own teaching techniques with the availability of media materials contained in this center.

Since the area of media is so vast, only two comparatively new kinds of visuals which are both practical and essential to a sound functional physical education program have been selected.

8 mm single concept silent loop film features

The 8 mm silent loop film contains approximately 60 feet of film that operates on a speed of 16 frames per second, thus having a viewing time of about 5 minutes. This film loop is enclosed in a plastic cartridge. Each film loop deals with a specific topic and is quite concise in its content. Because of this plastic cartridge it now eliminates the old problem of film threading. You simply plug the cartridge into its model projector, turn the knob and film is set for viewing. One other outstanding feature is that the ends of the film are spliced together, therefore, making a continuous loop that permits the film to run over and over again. There is no longer any need to rewind, this cartridge film may be stopped, removed, changed and started in any portion of the viewing.

Since the film is enclosed in a plastic cartridge the operator never touches the film, thus eliminating the possibilities of damage through mishandling. This same plastic covering protects the film from outside agents and from collecting dust or dirt. The same cartridge provides for an ideal storage system, whereby each container is labeled and placed on shelves or racks as though they were miniature books in a case.

There is an ever increasing selection of films available today. Schools and districts can develop their own film libraries at an inexpensive cost. The current Athletic Institute Visual Aids Catalog has a listing of all the available film cartridges along with their corresponding prices. The Technicolor Company has developed their own special compact light weight movie projector, for which the cartridge films have been especially designed. Their projector weighs less than 8 pounds. They have several models with specific variations that are also illustrated in the Athletic Institute Catalog.

Two optional accessories for the projector are the zoom lens and the still picture button which allows a single frame to be studied without causing any film damage. The recent employment of the Super 8 mm film and matching projector has provided distinct advantages. Specifically, the film's bigger frame allows for brighter and sharper pictures on a large screen.

The compact projector may be utilized for rear screen projection as well as front projection. They have a console model that is a self contained unit, which projects a bright reflection free picture on its 20 inch rear projection screen. The advantage of this type of projection is that it may be viewed under normal lighting conditions in our gymnasium and classroom facilities, there is no need for darkness.

Also available for use are their rear screen projection kits that are of varying sizes. They may be utilized with the individual compact projectors, thereby providing a greater range of versatility for their implementation in school programming.

Large Rear Projection Screen and Mirror— Size 18" × 24", recommended for use with no more than 30 students.

Medium Rear Projection Screen and Mirror— Size 12" × 12".

Small Rear Projection Screen and Mirror— Size 5" × 7", recommended for study use up to 3 students.

The concept of this media [sic] is to provide a class, groups, or individuals with an opportunity to study a series of skills as in physical education, when, where and as often as they wish.

There is one additional feature; being able to have any existing 8 mm film set up in a cartridge. The cost is approximately $1.25 for splicing and setting the film in cartridge form. With this available, many teachers can make their own 8 mm concept films on specific skills in their area of instruction. Films can be sent directly to the Technicolor Company for this processing.

Dr. Louis Forsdale of Columbia University believes the 8 mm film is the only presently available vehicle, cheap enough, good enough and sound enough to make the motion picture accessible to the average teacher in the average school. He also states that the great contribution of the 8 mm film is that it can revolutionize the motion picture from the most difficult into being the simplest of all visual media to use.

Overhead projector

The overhead transparency projector is a reflected projection system that is used in front of audiences, classes and groups. Its unique feature is its effectiveness in a well lighted room. There is no need to darken the room in preparation to viewing overhead projection.

The operator places the materials to be projected on the flat stage surface above the lamp housing, with the bottom edge closest the screen. The material must be placed on the stage so that the operator is able to read its content when looking at the transparency which is to be projected. Following this procedure, the operator sees the material just as the viewers see the image on the screen, when the projector is turned on.

The transparency is a specially treated film or acetate sheet that projects the image. The common size for most transparencies is 10" × 10". The acetate rolls are used in a variety of ways especially as a continuous chalkboard. Grease pencils become chalk and a cloth serves as an eraser. The acetate rolls can move forward and backward and therefore can be used for developing new thoughts and referred to again for review purposes.

There are various ways of making a transparency. With new equipment, supplies and processes being developed so rapidly, the making of transparencies has become quite simplified. Representatives from various companies can be contacted to demonstrate and explain the entire process of making transparencies. The 3M Company has sales educational representatives that are especially available to come to the schools and meet with the interested staff members. There are also various books and guides available in preparing your own transparencies. An excellent handbook on this subject is Picture Power, it is available at no charge by writing to the Charles Beseler Company, East Orange, New Jersey.

Some practical hints

I would like to cite two particular experiences using the overhead projector in my physical education classes. The first was with a transparency made up showing the Volley ball court and outlining the official rotation system for a team. When this transparency was projected on the gymnasium wall I directed and taught an entire lesson to my class. It was easier developing the rotation concepts and generally the students were able to master this skill much sooner. The use of the overhead enables you to better communicate with your class concerning such a learning presentation.

My next example was using the overhead projector in conjunction with a trampoline program in rebound tumbling. Again copies were made of the various trampoline skills and developed a series of transparencies on this subject. [Sic.] When teaching the skills I would project a specific transparency on the gym wall and explain the various form and techniques required. Thus, each student would be able to actually understand visually what was to be expected of him regarding his position and form for these skills. To go a step further, the projection was focused on the gym wall directly in front of the trampoline so that when a youngster had his turn he was able to look straight ahead and view the actual skill as he was working on the trampoline. This technique was highly successful, and the many previous details that existed before the advent of the overhead projector did not have to be explained. The end result was, a highly effective learning and teaching situation.

Features of the overhead projector

1. The ability to project a brilliant image in a lighted room or gymnasium.
2. You can maintain good eye contact with your students, because of the normal front of the room position the overhead assumes.
3. The overhead may be used as a chalk board to write down information.
4. Through transparencies you can present various concepts, ideas and skill development to small, average or large size groups. Through selection of transparencies you can accomplish the best medium to meet the students' needs.
5. When you project a transparency, a pen or pencil pointer can be used with the projection, directing attention to various details appearing on the screen.
6. Points may be made through the use of a grease pencil, you can write over the transparency or on another acetate sheet.
7. You can control the rate of presenting information—an example being, a transparency on the shoulder roll, you can cover the transparency with a piece of cardboard and expose the progressions step by step as you discuss each point with your class.
8. Through the use of overlays you can superimpose additional materials, thereby reducing complex skills or difficult movements to its simplest design to teach skill progression.
9. Motion can be simulated on the transparency through the use of a polarizing spinner. This is a special effect to show the direction of movement perhaps in a transparency showing the entire cartwheel progression.

10. An accessory can be purchased to project 2″ × 2″ 35 mm color transparencies.

11. Through the use of copy machines we can duplicate the materials presented on the transparencies very inexpensively and give our students a ditto copy. This would serve as an excellent follow-up for a skill teaching situation in physical education.

The effectiveness of the overhead projector is primarily due to the increased introduction of the many supplemental materials being made available by the various manufacturing media companies. The 3M Company has to date, developed eight printed original packets for making transparencies for use in physical education. These contain approximately 180 transparency master sheets. Audio visual distributors have developed special kits for overhead projector use which contain various supplies and materials needed to get started in using the overhead projector.

Concluding statement

It is of utmost importance that various workshops and clinics be arranged, to help orientate and instruct our teachers in the implementation of media. To successfully inaugurate such a program leadership and interest must be generated from within our departmental staffs. Perhaps the individual taking on this vital role will be you. We must be prepared to provide and use such effective teaching techniques in our program in order to develop an enriched learning situation. As physical educators we must now take springboard approach to teaching with media and their related instructional materials if we are to make our subject more meaningful. This is our challenge!

MANUFACTURER OF THE 8MM PROJECTOR, EQUIPMENT AND ACESSORIES

Technicolor Corporation
Commercial and Educational Division
1985 Placentia Avenue
Costa Mesa, California 92627

For further information and specifications you can contact the above company.

PROJECT AND THOUGHT QUESTIONS

1. What is the relationship between curriculum development and the objectives of health education and of physical education?

2. Examine the *School Health Study* and summarize the main parts of this study in a presentation to your class. Identify the key concepts and subconcepts.

OVERHEAD PROJECTOR MANUFACTURERS

American Optical Company, Eggert and Sugar Roads, Buffalo, N.Y.

Bausch and Lomb Optical Company, 626 St. Paul Street, Rochester, N.Y.

Charles Beseler Company, 219 S. 18th Street, E. Orange, N.J.

Keystone View Company, Meadville, Pennsylvania

Minnesota Mining and Manufacturing Co., 2501 Hudson Rd., St. Paul, Minn.

Ozalid, General Aniline and Film Corporation, Binghamton, New York

Projection Optic Company, Inc. 330 Lydell Avenue, Rochester 6, N.Y.

Victorlite Industries Inc., 4117 W. Jefferson Blvd., Los Angeles, 16, Cal.

Write the above companies regarding any specifications for their overhead projections.

RECOMMENDED CATALOG

Visual Sports Instruction-Aids, The Athletic Institute, 805 Merchandise Mart, Chicago, Illinois 60654

RECOMMENDED READING MATERIAL

Audio visual materials and techniques—James S. Kinder, American Book Company, New York, 1959.

8 mm sound film and education—Louis Forsdale, ed., published by the Teachers College Bureau of Publications, New York, 1962.

Audio visual equipment directory—National Audio Visual Association, Inc., Fairfax, Virginia (annual publication).

Foundation for effective audio visual projections—pamphlet S-3, Eastman Kodak Company, Rochester 4, New York, 1962.

Making black and white transparencies for overhead projection, pamphlet S-7, Eastman Kodak Company, Rochester 4, New York.

Overhead projection—Horace Hartsell and Wilfred Veenendaal, American Optical Company, Buffalo, New York, 1960.

Planning and producing visual aids—pamphlet S-13, Eastman Kodak Company, Rochester 4, New York.

They see what you mean—visual communications with the overhead projector—Ozalid Audio Visual Department, Johnson City, New York, 1959.

Vu-graphics—Alan Finstad, Charles Beseler Company, East Orange, N.J.

3. State and support two key concepts for each objective of physical education, that is, (a) organic development, (b) skill development, (c) mental development, and (d) social development.

4. Secure a copy of a curriculum in physical education from a school or college and evaluate it according to criteria that you develop for this purpose.

5. Outline the steps that you feel should be followed in curriculum development.
6. Visit the library and examine three references on curriculum development. Browse through these references, and present to your class a brief overview of what each reference contains.

7. Prepare what you consider to be an acceptable curriculum for health and/or physical education in the elementary, junior high, senior high, or college levels. Analyze the steps you followed in constructing this curriculum, according to the steps recommended in item 5 above.

SELECTED READINGS

Bucher, C. A.: Foundations of physical education, ed. 5, St. Louis, 1968, The C. V. Mosby Co.

Bucher, C. A.: Physical education for life. A text for high school boys and girls, Manchester, Mo., 1969, Webster Division, McGraw-Hill Book Co.

Bucher, C. A.: Administration of health and physical education programs, including athletics, ed. 5, St. Louis, 1971, The C. V. Mosby Co.

Bucher, C. A., Olsen, E., and Willgoose, C.: The foundations of health, New York, 1967, Appleton-Century-Crofts.

Koopman, G. R.: Curriculum development, New York, 1966, The Center for Applied Research in Education, Inc., The Library of Education.

Mayshark, C., and Irwin, L. W.: Health education in secondary schools, ed. 2, St. Louis, 1968, The C. V. Mosby Co.

Nixon, J. E., and Jemett, A. E.: Physical education curriculum, New York, 1964, The Ronald Press Co.

Willgoose, C. E.: The curriculum in physical education, Englewood Cliffs, N.J., 1969, Prentice-Hall, Inc.

CHAPTER 16 PROFESSIONAL, SCHOOL, AND COMMUNITY RELATIONS

Health educators and physical educators have relationships with their colleagues, with other members of the faculty and administration, and with the community at large. The manner in which such relationships are handled will determine to a great degree the support, respect, and status that programs have within the school or college or with the public as a whole. Our relationships contribute to the image we reflect in the minds of others, as individuals, organizations, and a profession.

Good relationships take into consideration such important factors as consumer interests, human relationships, public understanding, and good will. In business enterprises, public relations departments attempt to show the important place that specialized enterprises have in society and how they exist and operate in the public interest. In education, public relations programs are also concerned with public opinion, the needs of the school or college, and the acquainting of constituents with what is being done in their interest. Such programs also concern themselves with acquainting the constituents with the educational problems that must be resolved, for a greater service to be rendered.

The opinion that the public, one's colleagues, or other group has of our programs represents a powerful force in ensuring the success or failure of our work. Programs can succeed or fail in terms of such influence. Therefore, in order to have good public relations, we must consider the interests of human beings and what is good for the consumers of our product and services.

As one public relations person stated, "Good relations is doing good and getting credit for it."

Charles Moser writes that "public relations" is selling your product, which in his case is athletics. The physical educator, he states, must sell his product to parents; he may visit the homes of his athletes, write letters to service clubs, contact news media, and most important of all, sell grades and athletics together.

In the next article, Daniel J. Scherer explains press relations to the educator. He points out that, when reporting to the news media, you should give current and accurate information; include pictures if possible, try to follow up your article, and when the story is published, circulate copies to people you need to impress in the educational setting.

John Sutthoff conducted a study of 301 P.T.A. members to determine their interest in school affairs on the local or the cosmopolitan level. In his article, Sutthoff describes the characteristics of the types of members—local or cosmopolitan—and the implications of their involvement in school affairs. The challenge facing administrators, he believes, is to raise the interest of those around them and prepare the citizens to accept change.

Too often photographs submitted to the news media never reach the public. Gordon G. Beld explains that these photos must be unique in interest, must have some life in them, must catch action, and must be appealing and somewhat different from most other pictures, in order to mean anything to community relations.

87 ❧ PUBLIC RELATIONS IS GETTING PEOPLE INVOLVED*

CHARLES MOSER
ATHLETIC DIRECTOR,
ABILENE (TEXAS) PUBLIC SCHOOLS

When I was a football coach, I was fanatic about quarterbacks, and since I have quit coaching football, I guess I have been fanatic about public relations. Public relations is selling your

product—athletics—and there has been no time that we needed to sell athletics more than now.

The selling of athletics through public relations needs to be done with honesty; it needs to be continuous, positive, accurate, indirect, and planned. Public relations is helping other people. It's extra work; it's pushing the good things about your program. Good public relations takes a lot of thought, and it develops slowly.

---

*From Secondary School Athletic Administration, January 1969, p. 47, American Association for Health, Physical Education, and Recreation. Used by permission.

Before we can develop a public relations program for athletics, we need to think about goals. The following are the goals we in Abilene, Texas, have adopted. First, we will never be satisfied until every boy is on an athletic team. We believe that every boy who is on a team gets something that he needs from the experience. Every youngster in America wants to be part of a gang, and we want every one of those youngsters in a gang, but we want it to be a football gang or a basketball gang. We want every boy on a team; perhaps this will never be possible, but we are proud to have over 2,000 boys playing football in Abilene, a town of 100,000 people.

For every boy on a team, there must be a good intramural program and a good physical education program.

As our second goal, we want sportsmanship. We feel that sportsmanship is everything, and we don't think we should have a team at all if we don't have it everywhere in this country.

The third thing we ask of our boys is that they be real competitors on the field and real gentlemen off the field. These are the ideas we are trying to sell to our boys.

Fourth, we ask every boy, and every coach, to improve each day. Do a little better the next day. Coaches aren't all Bud Wilkinson's, but we still can ask each of them to try to improve day by day.

The last thing we try to sell is the real reason we have an athletic program, that is, so we can have a better school system. Every time we talk to a service club, we stress that we want a tremendous athletic program so that we will have a tremendous school system. These are the five ideas we are trying to sell.

If you want a good public relations program you must plan, and you must think about it each week. We try not to go a month without sitting down with our head coaches and talking about public relations. "What do you want to sell this month?" We don't bother them during the season, but after the season we sit down together and decide what we want to sell. We may want to sell the kids on the idea of saying "yes sir." We may want to sell the idea of shorter haircuts or such, so we try to do a little research and then we try to communicate.

In public relations, we don't believe you should ever demand. The technique has to be indirect. You can't demand, but you can suggest, and we have lots of suggestions. You can suggest ideas to your coaches and when one of them does something you suggest, you can encourage him in front of the other coaches.

We think that has been the most successful way of making suggestions. One thing we do is ask the coaches to write a letter to the parents before, and at the end of, every season. We started off with two or three coaches doing it, and the parents loved it. Now we even have seventh grade coaches doing it. An example of our success—a mother called me and said her boy was in the seventh grade, and this was the first letter they had ever received from a teacher. She was thrilled that the seventh grade coach had written her and told her at the end of the season how much he enjoyed having her son in the football program.

To whom do you sell in public relations? There are about eight different groups to whom we try to sell our ideas in athletics. One of the first things I would do if I were coach is to meet with the sophomore girls early in the fall. They're new, and they're scared. You can tell them how glad you are to have them and what they can do to help in athletics.

If I were a junior high school coach, I would get the seventh grade girls together for the same kind of talk and really sell them on our ideas. I would also meet with the senior girls. They have a tremendous effect on the athletic program.

As soon as the cheerleaders are elected, you should meet and discuss what you and they can do the next year. You must know the cheerleaders and talk with them as often as you can, because they are usually the leaders in the school.

As for the players, we try to make our athletes the best citizens in the school. I know some people smoke marijuana; many people smoke cigarettes; many people drink—and I do not think all of these people are bad, by any means —but I know that every student is going to do all these things if the athletes start doing them. So we must urge the athletes to be good examples throughout the whole school system.

Young people want to be encouraged more than anything in the world, and many of us do not take time to sit down with them during the season. If I were a football coach, as soon as football practice was over, I'd try to have at least one athlete come to my office every day and just sit down and talk. Youngsters want to be encouraged, but too often it seems we only call them to the office when they are in trouble.

Taking care of injuries is the best situation for improving public relations, when you can really help a boy. And, too, we have study halls for our boys in high school, which the coaches handle during their off-seasons. Grades improve, discipline improves, and the teachers love it.

We help the athletes get jobs in the summertime. I believe in youngsters working in the summertime. If a kid will not work in the hot sunshine, he will quit in the fall, too. We help them get jobs so that they all will learn how to work.

We believe in disciplining the boys, but we also believe in being fair. You don't have to have four years of college and a master's degree to make a kid quit football for smoking one cigarette, but it requires a good coach to take a boy who is smoking and make him into a real man. We do not want to hurt any boy; we want to be fair, and we don't want to be wrong. This is the way I handle the smoking situation: if a boy smokes, I can't permit him on the team, because it hurts morale. I call him in and say, "I hear you're smoking." I don't ask him if he smokes. I have him sign a card saying he will quit the team if he smokes again. He carries the card in his wallet. Then if he does ever smoke again, I ask for his card. So I don't dismiss him: he quits. I think it's being fair with the boy; we are giving him every chance. And I have only picked up two cards in 28 years.

Write letters to parents and encourage your coaches to write to them. If every coach in the nation would write one letter a day, we could really sell athletics, but that's probably not possible. I try to write at least one every week. Every time I go to a basketball game, which is about three times a week, the next morning I write a letter to some fan, telling him how much I appreciate his supporting the program and attending the game.

Another aspect of good public relations is for the coach to visit the home of new students who come out for athletics. There is nobody who appreciates such a thing more than a new family in town. It's not hard to do; it's just a little extra. Another coach visits every ninth grade parent the summer before the students come into high school. This is also very effective.

When a boy is a senior, what do you do? Do you help him get into college? Are you interested in his future? We have a little form which we have each boy fill out that asks, "Where do you want to go to college? What do you want to major in? Do you want a scholarship?" There are eight or nine questions, and through this we know, when a college coach asks, whether the boy actually wants to go to college, whether he wants a scholarship, and so on. I had a group of parents ask me to speak to them about their sons going to college, so I developed a talk,

"What Parents Should Know About Preparing Their Boy for College." It contains statistics, costs, problems, and why a boy sometimes fails in college. Another idea that one of our coaches uses is the Booster of the Week. The Booster attends skill practice on Thursday afternoon. He rides on the bus with the team; he eats with the team in the dressing room; he sits on the bench; he comes home with the team. And these Boosters say it's the greatest night they've ever had.

These men never realized what a wonderful group the athletes are. Over a period of ten years, you've got 100 fellows that really believe in your coaches and your teams. And when the team loses, the Boosters realize how much it hurts a coach because they're really sort of part of it.

Concerning patrons, here are some of the things I have done. I send a letter to every motel and restaurant in town, where I know the management is interested in the team, telling them the different teams coming to our town, the date, the name of the coach to contact. Our restaurant and motel people appreciate this.

I write a letter to all the service clubs. There are 18 in our community—Kiwanis, Rotarians, Lions, etc.—and I tell them that our head coaches would be very glad to speak to their members. Our head coaches speak at every one of the service clubs during the month of August.

I like to sell the relationship of grades and athletes together. The five best athletes in our school with the five highest grade averages are honored in May each year. The seniors who have the five best averages—well into the 90's—are front page stories.

As for the faculty, you must help the teachers. Help the new teacher especially. Try to get your coaches to help him or her, and he or she will help you when you need it. Something that one of our coaches started organizing is very effective. Our lettermen present an assembly in May for the teacher who has had the best school spirit. The resulting good feeling is amazing.

Concerning the news media, we write a letter every Monday to our newspaper, radio, and television, telling them the important things scheduled for the week. You must get to know your news media; it's surprising what a coach or athletic director can do with a sports writer. Our first reaction is to gripe at him, but we can't do that with the news media. Sports writers come and go. Get to know the publisher or the editor.

As for coaches, it's helpful for them to join service clubs and work on the United Giver's Fund. Also we assign bulletin boards to one coach in each school or urge the head coach to assign one assistant to a bulletin board and compete to see who has the best one.

Self-evaluation inspires coaches. I have a self-evaluation sheet with ten different items: "Can you coach without criticizing a boy personally," and so on. The coach ranks himself on a one to five scale. The first year is not too good, because the weak coaches rate themselves too high, but what we look for in the second year is improvement. This is a good way to counsel the coach; you have a counseling "in," very personal, between the coach and you. Self-evaluation is a good motivation for your coaches.

You must inspire your coaches to work for good public relations, because you are going to have losing seasons; if you have good public relations, you can stand the losing seasons better. The way to achieve good public relations is to get people involved, one at a time— help them and get them involved.

88 ᴥ HOW TO KEEP YOUR DISTRICT IN THE PUBLIC EYE*

*Here are some basic steps you can take
to make sure your press relations program
is effective.*

DANIEL J. SCHERER
PROFESSIONAL PUBLICIST,
NEW YORK

"Sorry, I didn't hear about it. . . ." Those six words tell a tale of failure—a good idea dying from lack of interest, a worthy cause hampered because nobody heard what it was all about, a misconception never laid to rest because the truth was buried. Combating those six fatal words is the job of every schoolman with a story worth telling.

Almost everything that happens in a school district is "news," if somebody takes the trouble to tell the right people about it, at the right time and, most important, in the right way.

This is all part of "public relations," which is too often clouded with mystical jargon and mumbo jumbo. Getting down to fundamentals, what it really means is: press relations.

Lack of understanding

If school management executives and their aides are poor communicators—and, typically, they are—it is probably due in large part to lack of understanding of press relations and unfamiliarity with the minimal techniques needed to conduct a sound press relations program.

If your conception of the local newspaper editor is a squat, sullen monster with a heart of stone and arteries filled with ink, wearing a green eyeshade and sleeve garters, it's time you brought your thinking up to date.

The modern newspaper editor is a craftsman in a highly competitive field. And because the struggle for a place on the printed page is also competitive, the best approach for anyone with a story to tell the public is to match the editor's professionalism with a basic professional approach to your own publicity efforts. The following information will point you in the right direction.

As soon as you have decided you have news of interest to the local papers, you should inform the editors.

Call the newspaper and talk to the appropriate editor. Give him your information briefly. Remember, he's a busy man. He can tell you if he wants a prepared release or if he will take the information and write the story himself. Then again, he may decide to send a reporter out to conduct an interview. In this case, the interviewee must be fully armed with all the facts.

But the news release should be every school district's basic press relations tool. So pay particular attention to its fundamentals. Be sure it follows the very practical journalistic course, telling who, what, where, when and why:

Who are the people involved? (Remember, people make news.) Give names, titles, accomplishments and a meaningful quotation if one is appropriate.

What has happened? Is this a major event in the field? Has it taken place for the first time? Give details to show what is different about this situation, why it is newsworthy.

When did it happen? Or is it going to happen? Give exact date and time if it's needed to understand the story. Is this something that happened before or has been going on for a long time?

Where did it happen? Describe locale and other facts to properly position the event.

Why is it happening? Give the background of the event or situation.

Some do's and don'ts

When actually writing the release be careful to observe the basic do's and don'ts:

Do be sure your information is current. Events that took place yesterday, last week or last month are history. Editors do not publish history.

Don't send an article marked "Hold for release" to the editor more than two or three days ahead of the release date. He may forget he has it on his desk.

Do type your release, *double-spaced,* on *one* side of the paper only. Don't send editors articles written in longhand or on both sides of the paper.

Do put your name, organization name, address and telephone number at the top of the left-hand side of the first sheet of paper.

Don't write a headline for the article. The editors will decide the size of type to be used and will write their own.

Don't start the article at the top of the page. Put your first paragraph one third of the way down to leave room for a headline to be written on your story.

Do write "(more)" at the bottom of the page if the article continues to another sheet of paper.

Do put an end mark (#### or -30-) at the end of the article. This lets the printers know that no more copy is coming for that particular story.

Don't expect your article to be printed exactly as you wrote it. Editors often are short of space and must cut down all copy to get the news into the paper. Some editors rewrite every news release to avoid duplication in another newspaper.

Do be accurate. Make certain names are spelled correctly. Check addresses with the telephone book or city directory. Get all the facts right. Go over all information to catch any possible error before you send it. Errors on one or two releases will sour editors on subsequent material.

Your news doesn't get printed

A university professor once polled editors on their reactions to material submitted from outside. The most common reasons for not using such material: limited local interest; no reader interest; poor writing; material obviously faked; inaccuracy in story; material stretched too thin.

From this list of flaws, you can draw some obvious conclusions in planning your press relations effort.

It's also helpful to understand the problems of editors, reporters and the conditions under which they work. On a small city newspaper, a reporter may write from 10 to 40 stories a day, some running a column or more. On a larger paper, he will write less, but he has time to dig more deeply. Each is working a deadline and is under intense pressure. Thus, it is often impossible for a reporter to conduct an interview or come to your news conference or special event on a sudden call an hour or two before deadline unless the story is so important that it outweighs anything he is writing.

Don't get the mistaken idea that newspapers find it difficult to fill their columns and welcome anything. Major newspapers throw away scores of columns of copy for every column they use. Even on smaller papers, two dozen columns may be discarded for each one that makes it into print. Eighty percent of press releases generally make it only as far as the editor's wastebasket.

Yet, there is always room for a readable story with a good local angle. It's up to you, following the points outlined above, to take the time to identify stories in your schools, to define the local angle and to produce readable professional releases.

If you write a good release that doesn't get printed, don't get discouraged. Make a polite telephone inquiry to find out what was wrong with it. Editors appreciate this kind of effort to upgrade your material. And then, try again. Keep up a steady flow of *good* material to the newspaper and you'll strike gold more often than not.

What about bad news?

Trying to cover up bad news is a normal reaction. Most school districts have tried it, one time or another. But the greater their experience with the press, the more they realize that bad news cannot—and should not—be hidden. Instead, through cooperation with the press, it can often be made less damaging. You have to accept the fact that it is newsworthy when things go wrong. You can't hide your head in the sand and hope the bad news will just fade away.

The best policy is to cooperate fully with the press, radio and television in handling unfavorable news. They need more help in these situations, because adverse news does not announce itself in advance. Recognize that the press is basically fair and willing to print both sides of a story. Allowing its readers to be the judge of fully reported news is, of course, the basic function of a newspaper.

Candor is the keynote in such situations. This viewpoint is verified by a news wire service editor who says: "One of the most successful public relations men I know was the first, to my knowledge, to offer bad news as well as good of his own accord. The result is that he enjoys the respect and confidence of everyone and his forthrightness has paid many dividends to his organization."

Don't forget the picture

Special events are always picture-worthy. If a function deserves the title "special event" in the first place, photo coverage will be welcomed by local editors. Anything outside of your routine activities qualifies as a special event. A "junior Olympic" event, a bond election campaign kick-off, opening of a new school, dedication of a library or hospital wing—anything that doesn't normally occur once a week, every week, comes under the heading of special event.

While topnotch pictures tell their own stories, make sure each one has its own caption. Think of it as a brief release, telling, in simple form, just what the picture is all about.

Here are a few do's and don'ts for satisfying the picture editor:

Do plan any pictures you want to send with the article very carefully. Decide what view will best illustrate your story. Choose the details meticulously. Talk over each picture with the photographer before he makes a shot. Include people in the picture, if at all possible (but not too many). Editors are more inclined to use pictures with plenty of action and human interest. Avoid stiff poses.

Don't submit a picture of a row of smiling gentleman in business suits or ladies in flowered hats. Many similar pictures cross the editor's desk every day. If he printed all he receives, every page of the paper would look alike.

Do make use of the services of the best professional photographer you can find. His charge is worth every penny because his picture has the best chance of acceptance. Remember, your photograph is competing with many others for the same space.

If you can't afford this service, however, the editor may be willing to have a staff photographer cover the event—*if* you do a good job of selling him on your story idea. This puts the onus on you to do your homework and to "pre-write" the release for your presentation to the editor.

But the availability of staff photographers is limited and you'll be doing yourself and the editor a favor if you have someone available in the district who is proficient with a camera. Many districts have been very successful in getting a student or two to develop highly professional photographic skills. Another possibility: Your audio-visual director, or a teacher who is a photo bug.

Don't, however, expect editors to accept photographs made with a Brownie camera and flash attachment. Newspaper printing processes can blur even the sharpest print.

Do have 8-by-10 glossy prints made to send the editor. All publications use them and many will accept nothing else.

Don't offer the editor a negative instead of a print. An engraving cannot be made from a negative.

The follow-up

When yesterday's newspaper is gathering dust in the basement and this morning's news broadcast has passed into oblivion, you are ready to start again. For almost every story there is a follow-up possibility—a new angle, a logical future development, an updated situation. These are the pegs for your subsequent publicity efforts.

One last tip: Use your clippings! Not everyone in your target audience is certain to have read your hard-won publicity break. Make sure the right people see the story by sending copies of the item to your selected list of opinion-formers. They'll appreciate the courtesy. And you'll ensure deep penetration of your message.

89 ❧ LOCAL-COSMOPOLITAN ORIENTATION AND PARTICIPATION IN SCHOOL AFFAIRS*

JOHN SUTTHOFF

ASSISTANT TO THE PRESIDENT, CHICO STATE COLLEGE,
CHICO, CALIFORNIA

Citizen participation in school affairs is one of the unique characteristics of American public education. Yet there is little research on effective citizen participation in ways other than voting, and membership in voluntary associations.

A study completed recently at Stanford University identified and measured six forms of participation in school affairs (other than voting and organizational membership) and related them to the participants' orientation toward the local community.[1] Drawing upon concepts from reference-group theory developed by Merton and others,[2] it was hypothesized that the local or cosmopolitan orientation of an individual toward the immediate community was related to participation in school affairs. A person with a local orientation (termed local) was said to be preoccupied with the immediate community to the virtual exclusion of the larger social scene; while a person with a cosmopolitan orientation (termed cosmopolitan) was said to maintain a minimal tie to the community and world outside the local community.

In addition to identifying the existence of locals and cosmopolitans among a sample of 301 PTA members, indices were constructed which measured six forms of participatory behavior in school affairs. The indices were:

1. Activity in organization affairs: the extent to which the PTA member engaged in the work of the association:
2. Communicated interest in school affairs: the psychological closeness of the PTA member to the schools;
3. Loyalty to the organization: the extent to which the PTA member holds a firm attachment to the association;
4. Compliance with organizational policy: the extent to which the PTA member will go along with policies of the association;
5. Pride in the local schools: the extent to which anything concerning the local schools is a source of gratification to the PTA member;
6. Knowledge of organizational policy: the extent to which the PTA member is familiar with the policies and objectives of the association.

The first four indices met the criteria set by Guttman and Menzel for reliable scales.[3] The remaining two indices consisted of highly correlated item pairs.

Each form of participation correlated significantly with at least one other form of participation.[4] Loyalty correlated highly with all other dimensions of participation in school affairs. Communicated interest, organizational activity, and knowledge of organizational policy correlated with each other. The dimensions of pride and compliance were not significantly correlated with most other dimensions but were significantly correlated to each other. Correlations were found between communicated interest and pride and between loyalty and compliance.

It was found that locals and cosmopolitans differed in both the form and degree in which they participated in school activities. Locals were more likely than cosmopolitans to demonstrate loyalty to the PTA organization and to be involved in its activities. Cosmopolitans were closer to their schools psychologically as exhibited by more communicated interests in school affairs; they were considered to have read and to have talked more than locals about school issues and problems.

*From Administrator's Notebook 9:31, November 1960. Used by permission.

[1] John Sutthoff, "Local-Cosmopolitan Orientation and Participation in School Affairs" (Unpublished Ph.D. dissertation, School of Education, Stanford University, 1960).

[2] The concept is fully discussed by Robert K. Merton in his book, *Social Theory and Social Structure* (Glencoe, Illinois: The Free Press, 1957), pp. 387–436.

[3] Samuel A. Stouffer, *et al.,* "Measurement and Prediction," *Studies in Social Psychology in World War II* (Princeton, N. J.: Princeton University Press, Vol. IV, p. 11; and Herbert Menzel, "A New Coefficient for Scalogram Analysis," *Public Opinion Quarterly,* XVII (1953), 268–80.

[4] All differences reported are significant at the .05 level.

Characteristics of locals and cosmopolitans

Cosmopolitans tended to move to their present address from outside the community, while locals, who were less mobile, tended to move to their present address from within the community. Locals had less formal education, particularly beyond college; they held fewer professional positions: they held fewer organizational memberships; they belonged to more service clubs, but to fewer professional organizations and hobby groups; they participated less in children's organizations, such as Boy Scouts, Camp Fire Girls, and the like; they subscribed to fewer news and opinion magazines and to fewer daily newspapers published outside the community; and as PTA members they were more likely to have read the statewide *Parent-Teacher* magazine and less likely to have read the *National Parent-Teacher* magazine.

The data demonstrated that the experiences of a person in the immediate community affected his involvement in school affairs. The local, who was portrayed as a "great local patriot," showed greater loyalty and organizational activity within the PTA than his cosmopolitan counterpart. The cosmopolitan, a relative newcomer to the community, was less inclined to feel a close attachment to local institutions, but he did show his interest in school affairs more often by reading and talking about them.

The participant with local orientation to school affairs displayed greater loyalty to the school organization than did the cosmopolitan. The PTA was apparently included in the constellation of community referents with which the locals felt closely identified. Having lived longer in the community than the cosmopolitan, the local evidently established stronger ties with a number of institutions within the community, particularly the PTA. This was borne out by the local's expression of regret when asked how he would have felt if he had had to send his children to a school with no PTA. The cosmopolitan was by no means disloyal to the PTA. As a more recent immigrant to the community and with interests which extended beyond the city limits, he had neither the history of affiliation with the community nor the narrow perspective of the local which would have stimulated him to display a higher degree of patriotism to the PTA than the local.

If loyalty is necessary to maintain an organization, there is the likelihood that the extent to which its members are active will determine whether the organization carries out the functions for which it exists.

Both locals and cosmopolitans displayed a high degree of activity within the PTA. However, more locals than cosmopolitans held offices and committee memberships. Again the assumption may be advanced that the local saw the PTA as a community institution, and regarded his contribution of time and energy as benefiting not only the school but the community as well. The cosmopolitan, on the other hand, may have been less active in the PTA because he saw it as only one of the many groups concerned with the education of children. The fact that cosmopolitans exhibited more interest than locals in the Boy Scouts, Camp Fire Girls, and other children's organizations was evidence of broad interest in the welfare of youth.

The separate paths which organizational members followed in terms of their orientation were also suggested by an example of contrasting organizational memberships outside the schools. Locals tended to belong to service clubs, while the cosmopolitans tended to belong to professional associations.

Several reasons could be advanced to explain these differences. The cosmopolitan, because of relatively short tenure in the community, may have been considered an "outsider" by other organizational members. As a consequence, he had limited possibilities of being elected to leadership positions or committee memberships. Further, since the cosmopolitans were inclined to hold values and attitudes acquired outside the community, their suitability for carrying out school policies was subject to question by the locals.

It was clear that locals and cosmopolitans differed sharply in reading habits. Their newspaper and magazine reading both reflected and reinforced their divergent interests. The interests of locally oriented people were, by comparison, rather narrow. They read the local press and tended to ignore national magazines which presented broader views of news and opinion. If locals wanted to learn about PTA activities, they focused more on their home state than on the national level. Cosmopolitans demonstrated their interest in the larger society by subscribing to daily newspapers published in metropolitan centers. *Time, Newsweek, Atlantic Monthly, Harpers,* and other news and opinion magazines kept them abreast of national thought and trends. The *National-Parent-Teacher* magazine was preferred by cosmopolitans to the state magazine.

The fact that the cosmopolitan looked beyond the community for his views on education may account for his weaker loyalty and relative inactivity in parent organizations working with the schools.

While the local was relatively more absorbed than the cosmopolitan in displaying his interest in school affairs through organizational membership, the cosmopolitan was not standing by passively. He was busy reading and talking about school affairs. Because of his greater mobility, his more active interest in news and opinion from outside the community, and his higher educational attainment, he was better equipped than the local to communicate fresh ideas about educational practice and to compare the local educational system with other system.

Implications

The association between orientation and participation in school affairs illustrates in a limited way the application of the concept of local-cosmopolitan orientation to the analysis of social process. To the school administrator these findings should indicate that the participants in school affairs appear to be at least of two kinds—locals and cosmopolitans—each engaging in school activities in different ways with different motives.

In financial campaigns, the pupil census, or on citizen committees, the local could be expected to be a contributing and loyal participant. For discussing and disseminating information about the local schools' future plans and needs, the school administrator should probably turn to the cosmopolitan whose broader perspective and deeper insight enables him to bring fresher views to the situation.

Similarly, when the school administrator turns to the public for support for his educational program, he must appeal to two audiences who frequently hold conflicting values and interests.[5] The citizen who is locally oriented would be expected to assess the policies of the local schools in terms of their conformity to commonly accepted standards and values of the community. Ideologies and techniques

imported from the larger society would be suspect. Conversely, the more cosmopolitan layman would look principally to those clues which would tell him that the school system's educational program is in step with state and national trends. In many instances this divergence of views may lead to conflict. For example, many school board members consider rendering service to the community a civic duty. When change in personnel or curriculum is desired, the locally-oriented school board member would act to preserve the norms and values of the local community. The cosmoplitan may challenge this behavior on the basis of its narrowness; he may prefer that change should be consonant with educational developments at the state and national level. Oftentimes the school administrator must reconcile the differences between these two groups.

The extent to which the school administrator feels secure in his community is dependent upon a mutually acceptable definition of his role as educational leader between himself and the community. A close-knit community, homogeneous in population and with rigid values, may expect the administrator to maintain the status quo. The success of his attempts to institute change could depend upon his being considered a "native" or "close neighbor" by those in the community.[6] On the other hand, the administrator in such a community who desires to institute change solely upon the philosophies which are more characteristic of the "outside" could expect the hostility and the resentment which would face the "outsider."

The community with a more flexible value structure would offer a more attractive setting for this type of administrator. It seems likely that administrators with local orientations would be found in greater numbers in communities reflecting predominantly traditional values, whereas administrators with cosmopolitan orientations would be found in larger cities, newer suburbs, or younger communities with more heterogeneous and/or emerging values.

There may be an interesting relationship between administrator orientation and professional mobility. One may argue that as the school administrator gains a wider range of experience and achieves greater maturity, the local community no longer comprises the bounds of a secure and satisfying existence. He may tend to shift his orientation from local to

---

[5] "Emerging" and "traditional" value orientations toward education have been observed in American society by George Spindler, "Education in a Transforming American Culture," *Harvard Educational Review,* XXV (Summer, 1955), 145–56; Jacob W. Getzels, "Changing Values Challenge the Schools, "*School Review,* LXV (Spring, 1957), 92–102; and Roderick F. McPhee, "Individual Values, Educational Viewpoint, and Local School Approval, "*Administrator's Notebook* (April, 1959).

[6] Harry E. Moore, *Nine Help Themselves* (Austin, Texas: Southwest Cooperative Program in Educational Administration, 1955), pp. 53–67.

cosmopolitan and in so doing acquire a more remote frame of reference. The administrator may have to choose between trying to articulate new goals for his community's schools which reflect his changing orientation or move on to another community where the predominant orientation of the citizenry is compatible with his new, more cosmopolitan orientation. In many cases administrators with cosmopolitan orientations may accept an administrative assignment in communities with strong local orientations. When this occurs the administrator should be aware of these differences and modify his expectations accordingly.

While the local-cosmopolitan dichotomy carries with it the notion of "either local or cosmopolitan" this does not necessarily have to follow. An administrator with only a local orientation to school affairs may have a tendency to be narrow in his decisions and limited in the scope of his analysis of problems. This may work to the detriment of the school system for new ideas would be avoided, new notions of education would be neglected, and the educational program would lose its dynamic quality. On the other hand, an administrator with only a cosmopolitan orientation, because of his broad outlook and concern for the "world

scene," might ignore the unique needs of his school district, and as a consequence fail to meet the expectations and desires of the people of the community. It would seem that a proper balance between these two extremes should be achieved. The administrator should not only be oriented to the local situation but should also be closely attuned to what is happening on the larger scene.

The challenge to the administrator is great, for not only must he raise his own sights but he must also raise the sights of those around him. If he is to achieve a program which maintains a balance between the local needs and the broader requirements he must prepare his citizenry to accept change. His road to success will be much easier if he is aware of their orientation to school affairs.

The local-cosmopolitan orientation may have implications also for the analysis of organizational problems within the school. Research in the area of local-cosmopolitan orientations of teachers and administrators could contribute some better understanding of staff relations. Such factors as conflict, satisfaction, confidence in leadership, morale and the like, may in some measure be closely related to differences in orientation of teachers and administrators.

90 ∾ SCHOOL PHOTOS THAT GET INTO THE NEWSPAPER *

GORDON G. BELD
DIRECTOR OF INFORMATION SERVICES,
ALMA COLLEGE, ALMA, MICHIGAN

A picture in the paper is worth a thousand in the file drawer when you're publicizing school activities and events. But getting the picture into the paper isn't always an easy proposition.

Most of us believe that the editor needs a picture just like the one we're offering. Getting him to believe it is the problem.

The answer really is a simple one—make the picture so good that it sells itself. When it comes to matching a newspaper editor and a picture, it has to be love at first sight. If he doesn't like what he sees, there's not much chance that you're going to talk him into anything.

How do you get a picture so good that he can't resist it? Assuming that the quality of your photographic prints is good, it's a matter of presenting the subject matter differently.

The editor has seen thousands of class officers sitting behind tables staring at the camera. He's seen hundreds of cold, empty-looking

school buildings. He's seen scores of students handing checks for proceeds of the paper drive to the superintendent, and he's seen dozens of principals shaking hands with the school's honor citizen. He's probably seen plenty of students making posters for Saturday night dances, too.

Imagination is the key that will unlock the columns of your local paper to let your pictures in. Think of a different way to shoot them. If you're convinced there's no different way, try a few of these ideas and see if they don't improve your photos:

Put some life into it. If you're photographing a building or campus scene, be sure that the picture includes people. Want to kill a picture fast? Just put a finger over the two students in this one on the following page and see what happens.

Frame it. To add depth, it's a good idea to have something in the foreground or to use something or someone to frame the subject.

* From Michigan Education Journal 43:19, November 1967. Used by permission.

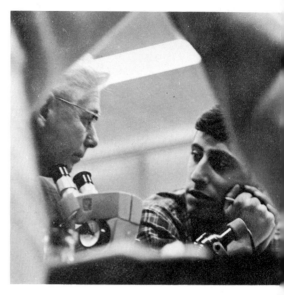

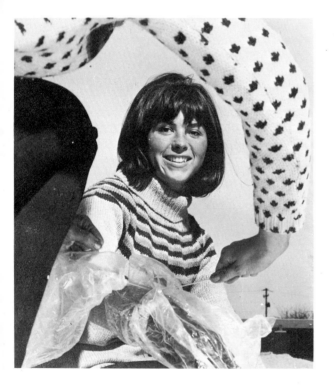

It's not as difficult as it sounds. Here are four examples:

The arm and body of a student leaning over a desk while awaiting his turn to talk to the instructor provide a frame for a view of the teacher and another student.

A young lady about to work on snow sculpture with a plastic bag tied over her mitten gets some help and framing from a friend.

Pillars of a building frame a student-teacher conference.

Watch the angle. Instead of shooting everything straight on, try to get some variety by occasionally climbing up on something and shooting down, or by crouching down and shooting up. For example, here's a different way to show the star of the basketball team. Note that the net in the foreground helps to provide depth, too.

Here's a new way to look at a groundbreaking ceremony. Probably only the worms have seen it from this angle before.

Catch some action. Obviously, action adds life to a picture. But action doesn't always mean something like a fullback crashing off tackle. It might be something as simple as a smile or a hand shooting up in the classroom.

And don't forget the background. Try to keep telephone poles, cluttered classroom corners, and other distracting elements out of the picture.

PROJECT AND THOUGHT QUESTIONS

1. Reflect on some of your business transactions. What were some public relations techniques used by business organizations that impressed you and left a good impression on your thinking? What were some techniques that left an unfavorable impression on you?
2. Prepare a set of guidelines that a faculty and staff associated with health education and physical education programs might follow in order to develop good relations with their (a) colleagues, (b) administration, and (c) community at large.
3. What are the various media that are valuable in communicating the value of health education and physical education programs to the public at large? Evaluate the effectiveness of each medium that you list and give some considerations for the utilization of each.
4. Prepare a news release on some event or phase of the department's program. Follow through and publish or broadcast.
5. Analyze the strengths and weaknesses of the present public relations program of the American Association for Health, Physical Education, and Recreation. Send this evaluation to the Association's headquarters.
6. Prepare a speech that is to be given before the entire faculty and student body in your school or college. The subject of the speech is: the contributions of health education and physical education to young and old alike. Present the speech in class.
7. Prepare a bibliography of films and other materials that might be used effectively to interpret either health education or physical education to the public.

SELECTED READINGS

Bucher, C. A.: Foundations of physical education, ed. 5, St. Louis, 1968, The C. V. Mosby Co.

Bucher, C. A.: Administration of health and physical education programs, including athletics, ed. 5, St. Louis, 1971, The C. V. Mosby Co.

Dapper, G.: Public relations for educators, New York, 1962, The Macmillan Co.

Douglas, K. R.: Trends and issues in secondary education, New York, 1962, The Center for Applied Research in Education, Inc., The Library of Education.

Jones, J. J.: School public relations, New York, 1966, The Center for Applied Research in Education, Inc., The Library of Education.

CHAPTER 17 MEASUREMENT OF PUPIL ACHIEVEMENT

Measurement and evaluation programs are increasingly becoming an important, recognized administrative responsibility in health education and physical education programs. In order that pupil progress may be determined, that these programs be conducted in the best way possible, and that the benefits be shown that are derived from participation in these programs, measurement and evaluation are essential.

In recent years, many measurement techniques have been developed in the fields of health education and physical education. Some of them have been carefully constructed in a scientific manner, but others fall far below acceptable standards. Administration has the responsibility for seeing that materials that give valid and reliable results are used. Some of the measurement techniques that are being utilized today are tests, rating scales, checklists, photographic devices, and controlled observation.

Measurement has several important purposes. It helps to determine the progress being made and the degree to which objectives are being met. It aids in discovering the needs of the participants, identifies strengths and weaknesses of students, aids in curriculum planning and shows where emphasis should be placed, and gives direction and helps to supply information for guidance purposes.

Measurement findings can also be utilized in other ways. They can be used for such purposes as the grouping of participants according to similar mental, physical, and other traits, which will ensure better instruction. They yield infor-

mation that can be used as an indication of a person's achievement in various skills and activities. These findings also provide information that can be used to predict future performance and development, provide data on attitudes that determine whether or not the participant has proper motivation, and focus attention on future action that should be taken in the program.

Clayne Jensen writes that, in order to teach effectively, educators must obtain information about the students' needs, interests, abilities and potential. Teachers, he believes, must have a well-designed testing program with careful selection and construction of appropriate tests. These tests must be valid, reliable, objective, and economical and must apply to the educational objectives.

In the next article in this chapter, Robert N. Singer expresses his belief that physical education does not readily lend itself to objective measurement. Close relationships with students may tend to alter a final grade, whereas grades should be as objective as is possible. Physical educators, he says, must attempt to achieve consistency in grading.

Lynn W. McCraw believes that every teacher, in order to achieve the goals of measurement, should be familiar with the basic principles of grading and then should formulate a plan consistent with these principles. Presented in this article is a plan for grading based on the premise that individuals like to receive some tangible recognition for attainment and achievement.

91 EVALUATE YOUR TESTING PROGRAM*

CLAYNE JENSEN
ASSISTANT DEAN, COLLEGE OF PHYSICAL EDUCATION,
BRIGHAM YOUNG UNIVERSITY, PROVO, UTAH

In order to design a teaching program and to teach effectively, certain information about students must be obtained. The more information a teacher has about students' needs, interests, abilities, and potentials, the better he can do his job. Much of the needed information must be gathered through testing, which calls

for a well designed testing program and careful selection and construction of appropriate tests.

According to McCloy, measurement in physical education has two purposes: a. to increase knowledge, b. to improve instruction. To increase the knowledge of the teacher and student is the first purpose of measurement. But little has been gained unless the second purpose is accomplished, that is, to use the increased knowledge to improve instruction.

*From The Physical Educator 21:149, December 1964. Used by permission.

Bookwalter claims that the more specific purposes of measurement are to:

1. Inform a student as to his progress toward objectives.
2. Serve as a basis for guidance of the student.
3. Serve as a basis for replanning lessons.
4. Inform the parents as to the student's progress toward objectives.
5. Provide the administrator with a partial basis for promotion, academic awards and guidance.
6. Furnish objective information for classifying students.
7. Furnish objective information on which to grade or mark students.
8. Diagnose specific difficulties.

With present emphasis on physical fitness, physical tests seem to be utilized by teachers more than ever before. There is a demand for teachers to measure abilities on a mass scale and with increased accuracy. As a result, physical testing has become more common place in our schools. In light of this fact, an important problem to physical educators is to recognize and select sound methods of measurement.

Measurement may be highly subjective or highly objective in nature. Subjective measurement may include some degree of objectivity, but it always involves a high degree of subjective judgment. An example of subjective measurement is a teacher's opinion of student attitudes. Objective measurement is based on exactness and precision. A measure is objective to the extent that two or more people will score it the same under the same conditions. Objective measurement is based largely on fact, while subjective measurement is based largely on opinion, which in turn should be supported by facts. Probably no measure in physical education is completely objective, and no measure ought to be completely subjective. Teachers should strive for a high degree of objectivity in measurement, and yet realize that not all important qualities can be objectively measured.

In selecting objective tests for use in the program, the following elements should be highly emphasized.

Validity is the most important quality of any measure. It is the degree to which the measure truthfully measures that which it purportedly measures. A valid measure of one characteristic is not necessarily a valid measure of another characteristic and tests are usually validated for only one purpose.

Not every measurable quality can be measured with the same degree of accuracy. For instance, ability to perform in the vertical jump can be very accurately measured, while ability to perform in soccer can be less accurately measured. Therefore, contrary to statements made by many authors, there can be no general rule concerning the degree of validity necessary for a measure to be useful. The only rules are, that the most valid measure available should be used, and that high significance should not be attached to results of tests which are not highly valid.

Reliability is the degree to which a test consistently measures whatever it measures, that is, the extent to which it measures the same thing every time. A test that is valid is also reliable, but a test can be reliable and not highly valid. Reliability is a quality of consistency and to this extent, reliability contributes to validity of a test.

Objectivity is the degree to which consistent results are obtained from the use of the same method of measurement by different persons. Essentially, it is the preciseness of the instruments and techniques used. Errors resulting from scoring a test result in consistency in the measure, and to this extent objectivity contributes to reliability.

Administrative economy is a serious consideration in selecting and constructing tests. In order for a test to be practical and justifiable it must be economical in terms of time and cost. It is difficult to say how much time and money should be devoted to any test or measure. But in every case, before the teacher decides to use a test he should critically weigh the value of the results in contrast to the expenditure of money and time.

Educational application is another factor which will cause the teacher to select some tests in preference to others, and in constructing his own tests, educational application should serve as an important guide. It should be noted that the type of program to be offered during the year dictates, to a great extent, the type of tests to be employed. The testing program must be in harmony with, and supplementary to the activities being taught. Thus, tests should be selected which can be most useful in the program.

Norms are valuable for certain kinds of tests, select one test in preference to another. *Standard instructions* for administration of standardized tests are very important if the results are to be reliable. Thus, some equally good tests may be rejected because standardized instructions are not available.

Some recognized testing authorities agree that the only measures that are highly useful in physical education programs are valid measures that can be administered to at least 40 students at one time or in one hour and require little equipment. Measurements are useful only if the results are capable of interpretation and can be practically applied.

It must be remembered that methods of mea-surement can be useful only if they are adminis-tered and interpreted correctly. "Figures do not lie, but liars figure," and likewise, measures that are highly valid prove useless when im-properly administered and interpreted.

92 ❧ GRADING IN PHYSICAL EDUCATION*

ROBERT N. SINGER
FORMERLY FACULTY MEMBER, MICHIGAN STATE UNIVERSITY,
EAST LANSING, MICHIGAN

Most areas of education have more or less standard methods of offering content material and then measuring its infiltration into resistant cerebral masses. Because of its peculiar nature, however, physical education does not lend itself so readily to objective measurement. Nor is there agreement among physical educators that measurement for grading purposes in physical education should be the same as in other edu-cational disciplines.

Many differences have tended to separate physical education from its place alongside the other education offerings. By no means the least important of these is the question of grad-ing student achievement. There is no consis-tency in grading by members of the profession and no consistency with the rest of education. Allowing for teacher differences in grading methods, and the right and necessity for this liberty, there nevertheless appears to be too wide a gap in grading procedures between edu-cation and physical education as well as among physical educators.

If we wish these inconsistencies to stop (and there is some disagreement in our field whether this is desirable), then we should take stock of what is happening and why.

The so-called "academic" courses, generally speaking, grade on achievement, regardless of student individuality and improvement shown in the course. Can or should the physical edu-cator do the same? An answer to this question has to be complex and well qualified by neces-sity. If one believes physical education to be distinct and unique from the other disciplines, then perhaps the approach to grading should also be unique. Then again, if it is thought that physical education should contain procedures as well as goals similar to other educational areas, perhaps adjustments in grading methods are necessary. Criticisms have to be met and overcome.

A major area of concern for the physical

educator is the difference in students' motor ability and coordination. Recent evidence has shed light to the effect that perhaps there is no such thing as general motor ability. A student can or will potentially perform well in activities that contain skills in which he has had previous experience. Therefore, just because one excels at basketball is no reason to expect that he will be an outstanding swimmer. Recent research has increasingly demonstrated the specificity of motor skill learning.

However, it is fairly obvious that some stu-dents possess such a low degree of coordination that they will probably never achieve satisfac-tory status, let alone excel in any sport. If we are to grade in accordance with academic sub-ject standards, achievement should be the important consideration, not improvement. The mathematics teacher does not provide his stu-dents with an initial test of mathematical knowl-edge, then observe and record how much effort each one puts into the course, and finally weigh these factors with a final test score in order to determine the final grade of each student. Does this mean that the physical educator should not?

In high schools, especially the larger ones, superior students are assigned to special classes. This homogeneous grouping provides those with greater intelligence capacities an oppor-tunity to penetrate deeper into study areas and offers the teacher a more ideal situation in which to grade fairly; he need grade only on achievement. In slower classes, the students have an opportunity to excel at their own level, and their interest and motivation is not lost as it would more than likely be if they were placed with more advanced students.

Would not certain physical and skill tests indicate those individuals at the lowest end of the continuum and with the least possible chance of success in any physical education classes? If these students, poorest in coordina-tion and fitness, were placed in special classes, physical education would not have to acknowl-

*From JOHPER 38:38, May 1967. Used by permis-sion.

edge these factors as part of the final grade in skill classes.

Obviously, certain individuals will come to an activity with greater skill than others because of past experiences. At the same time, some individuals will have had a more extensive background in mathematics than their fellow students and therefore will have an advantage in a mathematics course. Just as the more inferior mathematics students will have to do extra homework to compensate for their disadvantage, those individuals not possessing much tennis skill will have to work harder to stay with more advanced tennis players.

If it is the policy of the school or college to divide courses into beginning, intermediate, and advanced areas, then physical education should follow suit. Consideration of individual levels of motor coordination, fitness, and sport skills will result in a more homogeneous placement of students. This procedure will, in turn, result in a grading method more favorable to the students.

Improvement should not have to be considered to the extent it is in today's physical education classes. It is difficult enough to fairly evaluate students' achievement in skill, knowledge, and attitude, let alone improvement in these areas. We should remember that in the other educational areas, knowledge as expressed in a few written tests is the major if not the sole determiner of a final grade. It is no wonder, therefore, that to the sincerely dedicated physical educator, bogged down with so many evaluations of each individual in all aspects of the physical education experience, final grading poses such a trying and unhappy time.

Obviously, the physical education teacher who does not make enough evaluations of the student is just as guilty, if not more so, than one who accumulates too many. A fairer, more justified final grade is one based on a few measurements rather than only one. The final grade should consist of a written test, skill test, and subjective evaluation during play, with attitude and interest modifying the grade.

There is no reason why the student should not be responsible for rules, history, strategy, and other matter connected with the activity. For some reason, many physical educators feel that movement skill should be the only basis for the grade, that written tests are not a part of physical education. A good written test can be constructed for any sport, and there is no reason for its absence as an evaluation procedure. Excellent physical performance does not necessarily indicate abundant knowledge in the

activity, and there is no evidence to substantiate the belief that a strong relationship exists between written test scores and skill performance scores. Physical education should measure and reward both the skilled and the knowledgeable.

The greatest mistake is made by those few physical educators who feel that the students merely need to show up in class in order to receive a grade no lower than a "B." Grades can fall among the normal probability curve, if measurements are adequate and accurate. Distribution of grades, based on a firm foundation, is an important step toward bridging the gap between physical education and other education areas.

Physical educators must attain some sort of grading consistency among themselves before consistency can be reached with the other education areas. The following suggestions are offered to help overcome the problem.

1. All students should be tested for motor coordination and fitness, with the lowest placed in special classes.

2. If it is the policy in other educational areas, activities in physical education should be divided into different skill levels according to student competencies. Initial sport skill tests would determine student status for placement purposes.

3. The grading procedures should be clearly outlined by the teacher and made known to the students.

4. Final grades should be based on achievement on a written test, skill tests, and/or observation during play. These grades are to be modified according to the student's attitude and interest.

5. Because of the difficulty in the nature of grading on improvement, this procedure should be abolished or minimized.

Fair, high standards are respected by all. If we wish the respect of other disciplines, there is no doubt that our grading procedures must be reevaluated and strengthened. Ultimate achievement in the goals of the course must be the basis for grade. If tennis is the activity, then skill and knowledge demonstrated in tennis at the end of the term should comprise the final grade.

Probably one of the disturbing challenges to objective grading and yet at the same time one of the rewarding features of our profession is our ability "to get to know" our students. The closet relations between student and teacher are formed in the physical education class. This relationship is desirable in many ways, but unfortunately may tend to alter a final grade.

Grades should be as objective as possible, without concern to personality and friendships.

When the preceding suggestions are followed, when physical educators raise grading standards, when there is agreement as to the standards, when physical education and other fields in education become more closely related in their marking systems, physical education will have taken one of the necessary forward steps to gain the respect it deserves from the other disciplines.

93 ❧ PRINCIPLES & PRACTICES FOR ASSIGNING GRADES IN PHYSICAL EDUCATION*

LYNN W. McCRAW
CHAIRMAN, DEPARTMENT OF PHYSICAL AND HEALTH EDUCATION,
UNIVERSITY OF TEXAS, AUSTIN, TEXAS

One of the most perplexing problems with which physical education teachers are confronted today is that of evaluating student progress and assigning grades. There are few issues on which there are such divergent views or so much concern and interest. There are almost as many different plans for grading as there are teachers of physical education, but many grading practices are educationally unsound. Far too much variation exists among grading plans in schools today, and in too many instances no plan at all seems to be the situation.

Actually, while exploration and research are still needed, enough is already known to provide a sound basis for grading. Each teacher should first of all become familiar with the basic principles of grading and then formulate a plan that is consistent with these principles. Presented here are principles which merit consideration.

1. Grades given to students should be based on *all* of the objectives of the course, such as skills, physical fitness, attitudes, appreciation, and knowledge. These factors should be weighed according to the emphasis given in the instruction; however, a major portion of the grade should be based on skill and/or physical fitness with a minimum standard of achievement for each of the other objectives.

2. The grade for a student should be determined by the extent to which he attains the objectives with ample consideration given to attainment in terms of capacity and to improvement during the instructional period.

3. The grading procedure used for physical education should be consistent with that for other subjects in the school or school system. This includes the use of symbols (A, B, C, D, F: S or U; or Pass or Fail), distribution of grades, and the inclusion of grades in the computation for the honor roll.

4. The grade assigned to a student should be based on his performance in relation to the objectives of the course and not in comparison with other students. There can be no justification in applying the so-called curve system to assigning grades in physical education.

5. The same basic principles and plan should govern the grading procedure in all physical education classes in the school system. These principles and plan should be developed cooperatively by all teachers.

6. A variety of instruments, both subjective and objective, should be used in the evaluating process. The selection of these instruments should be in terms of: extent to which they are valid, reliable, and objective; ease with which they are understood, administered, and scored; economy in time and equipment; availability of norms and/or standards; and extent to which they serve a useful purpose, i.e., meet the purposes of tests.

7. Evaluative instruments should not be used solely or even primarily for assigning grades. Other purposes are to: provide a basis for classifying students for instruction; determine needs of students in terms of specific objectives or competencies; motivate students to attain objectives; provide a method of instruction, i.e., in taking the test the student is drilling on the skill; provide the teacher with material for self-evaluation of teaching effectiveness; provide the teacher with additional material for curriculum evaluation and revision; and provide data for reporting to parents, school administrators, and the public the achievement of students in physical education.

8. Students should be informed of the procedure to be used for assigning grades in physical education. Notification should be made in writing at the beginning of the unit, semester, or school year as appropriate.

To comply with the first principle of assigning grades in terms of all of the objectives of physi-

---

*From JOHPER 35:24, February, 1964. Used by permission.

cal education, it is necessary to select specific components to be used as a basis for grades and to determine their relative weightings. The chart presents a list of such components together with a suggested range of weightings and instruments that may be used in evaluating each component. This list is based on the commonly accepted objectives of physical education and the suggested weightings place emphasis on the attainment of skill and physical fitness. This is consistent with the belief that these are the most important of our objectives. However, the plan does not preclude placing emphasis on attitude, knowledge, appreciation, and behavior, for to comply with our basic principle there should be a minimum standard of achievement for each of the objectives. To do this the teacher might well adopt a procedure whereby to receive an "A" a student must have an overall average to justify such a grade and in addition have at least a "C" or even a "B" on each of the components.

One of the most difficult tasks in grading is to apply the principle of giving ample consideration to attainment in terms of capacity and to improvement during the instructional period. It is practically impossible to determine one's ultimate capacity to achieve in any quality. Nevertheless, it is possible to distinguish among students, particularly those at extreme ends of the scale, in the capacity to learn. An even more perplexing task is the decision for those who approach their own individual capacity. Some would advocate that everyone who reaches his own capacity should receive an "A" regardless of what that capacity might be. This practice would violate the principle of determining grades by the extent to which one attains the objectives of physical education. A suggested solution is to operate on this latter basic principle and then to use whatever subjective or objective evidence is available to make adjustments in individual grades. While a student at the lower end of the scale should not receive an "A," he might well deserve a "C" or even a "B" if he approaches his own capacity.

In the consideration of improvement during the instructional period, a common practice is to administer an initial test at the beginning of the unit of instruction and then a final test at the end. The evaluation is then based on the gain from the initial to the final test. There are at least two major objections to following such a procedure and basing the grade solely on improvement. There is the danger that students will deliberately do poorly on the initial test so that they can demonstrate more improvement

during the unit. A second problem is the difficulty in interpreting improvement from the initial to the final test, particularly when there is considerable variation among initial scores. For example, on shooting free throws in basketball, when the test is the number of goals made in ten trials, student X gets 2 on the initial test and 4 on the final test while student Y gets 8 on the initial test and 10 for the final score.

Both of these students have a gain of two goals, but many contend that student Y deserves more credit for his gain since he started with a much higher initial score. This is based on the premise that it becomes increasingly more difficult to improve in performance as one approaches his physiological and psychological limits. To give these two students the same grade for improvement would therefore be unsound. Even more deplorable is a percentage plan frequently used whereby the gain is divided by the initial score. By this method student Y has a percent gain of 25 and X one of 100. Obviously this procedure does just the opposite of what is desired and should not be used under any circumstances.

Considerable research has been directed toward the problem of interpreting improvement, and no satisfactory, practical method has been found. For this reason, the student's grade should first be determined by the extent to which he attains the objectives and then adjustments made on the bases of improvement. For example, a student who reaches only the standards required for a "D" might well be given a "C" if he has shown considerable improvement to reach these standards. In considering improvement, attention should be given to gains on all components on which grades are based and not just on skills alone.

Insofar as possible the teacher should utilize objective test instruments in assessing achievement of students in the various traits upon which grades are based. However, this does not preclude the use of subjective evaluation. In many instances the teacher's judgment may well be more valid and reliable than objective data. It should be remembered that most sport skill tests have been validated by using a criterion of judgment ratings; thus they are not likely to be any more accurate than are the ratings themselves. Too often teachers are reluctant to base grades on their own judgment for fear of being challenged by students and parents. They prefer to employ a statistical formula that utilizes scores obtained from a series of objective tests that may or may not be valid.

PROPOSED PLAN FOR GRADING

Components	Weightings	Instruments
Attitude in terms of	5–25%	Attendance and other records
Attendance		Teacher observation
Punctuality		
Suiting out		
Participation		
Skill in terms of	20–35%	Objective tests
Form in execution of skill		Teacher observation
Standard of performance		Student evaluation
Application in game situation		
Physical fitness with emphasis on	20–35%	Objective tests
Muscular strength and endurance		Teacher observation
Cardiovascular-respiratory endurance		
Agility		
Flexibility		
Power		
Knowledge and appreciation of	5–25%	Written tests
Skills		Teacher observation
Strategy		
Rules		
History and terms		
Behavior in terms of	5–25%	Teacher observation
Social conduct		Student evaluation
Health and safety practices		

This does not imply that tests should not be used in determining grades in physical education. On the contrary, tests are most important. Many valid and reliable batteries are available, and they should be used to the maximum extent possible. In fact, their use far transcends the assigning of grades. Testing is actually part of method and provides one of the many tools that the teacher needs to visit pupils in the learning process. It would be difficult indeed to justify administering tests solely for the purpose of assigning grades.

In solving the problems of grading, many persons advocate abolishing all grades or assigning "S" for satisfactory and "U" for un-satisfactory. This procedure merely alleviates the problem, for one must still use some basis for deciding whether the student receives "S" or "U" and this decision can be just as difficult as deciding between "A" and "B."

Assigning grades in school is consistent with our culture, for individuals like to receive some tangible recognition for attainment. It has become a well-established practice in schools and is not likely to be abolished. Grading is one of the most difficult tasks that the physical education teacher must perform; it is also one of the most important. Each teacher must accept the responsibility of devising and using a grading plan that is based on sound principles.

PROJECTS AND THOUGHT QUESTIONS

1. List the various purposes of measurement in health and physical education programs. Cite an example for each purpose that you have listed, for which a goal has been achieved in actual practice.
2. List as many measurement techniques as you can that are presently being used in (a) health education programs and (b) physical education pro-grams. What is each measurement technique designed to measure?
3. Develop what you consider to be a *minimum* program of measurement for pupils in health education and physical education programs that should be carried out in each school and college program.
4. Develop what you consider to be a *desirable* program of measurement in health and physical education programs.

SELECTED READINGS

Ahmann, J. S.: Testing student achievements and aptitudes, New York, 1962, The Center for Applied Research in Education, Inc., The Library of Education.

Bucher, C. A.: Administration of health and physical education programs, including athletics, ed. 5, St. Louis, 1971, The C. V. Mosby Co.

Clarke, H. H.: Application of measurement to health and physical education, ed. 4, Englewood Cliffs, N. J., 1967, Prentice-Hall, Inc.

Mathews, D. K.: Measurement in physical education, Philadelphia, 1963, W. B. Saunders Co.

CHAPTER 18 TEACHER, COACH, AND PROGRAM EVALUATION

In recent years, administrators, parents, teachers, and other persons have been concerned with developing ways and means of measuring teacher effectiveness for the purpose of making sound decisions in respect to retention, salary adjustments, and promotion, as well as for the ultimate goal of helping teachers to improve their effectiveness on the job.

Administration has an important role to play in the evaluation of teachers. Leadership needs to be provided in this area for the establishment of a planned program of evaluation. Teachers should be helped in improving their own effectiveness. Records should be kept for determining progress, and decisions should be made as to appraisal and program requirements. In-service programs should be planned.

Various means of evaluating educational programs have been devised. These range from very elaborate and detailed checklists, rating scales, and scorecards, to a list of questions that the administration should ask to determine the relative merit of certain administrative practices and programs.

Several important aspects of teacher evaluation and program evaluation are discussed in the articles that have been selected for this chapter.

With the touch of a science fiction writer, Ralph E. Billett projects into the future to the time when teacher evaluation may be computer-ized. Evaluation has not, however, reached that point yet and must be conducted on the present level of knowledge. Billett says that evaluation is essential since improvement and progress can only be made in light of the results.

In the next article, Nelson E. Wieters points out some flaws in teacher evaluation that often dampen teacher morale. The picture of personnel management is changing from what the administrator did "to" and "for" the teacher to what the administrator *does* and *how* he does it.

A study of 483 University of Oregon students was conducted by Alan F. Quick and Arnold D. Wolfe to determine what qualities constitute the ideal professor. The results showed that, of paramount importance, are encouraging of independent thinking, good organization of course content, and a deep and sustained enthusiasm for the subject.

In the last article in this chapter, John B. Crossley suggests a framework upon which evaluation of the coaching staff may be based, suggests an evaluative procedure, and "role-plays" the case of reemploying one coach and dismissing another. If the philosophy and objectives of education are known and accepted by the teaching and coaching staff, then administrators are professionally obligated to stand behind their evaluative decisions.

94 ᴥ EVALUATION: THE GOLDEN FLEECE*

RALPH E. BILLETT
DIRECTOR OF PERSONNEL,
RAMAPO CENTRAL SCHOOL DISTRICT NO. 2,
SPRING VALLEY, NEW YORK

Let us leap forward in time when the little school within a school has been refined so that one teacher is assigned to several students. Instruction is so individualized that teachers sit opposite students in fully automatic material center carrels. We arrive on the school scene just in time to witness an instruction coordinator (formerly principal) sit down with a classroom experience director (formerly teacher) for an evaluation conference.

The coordinator produces a pocket-sized uranium-activated differential interpolator. All is in readiness for the statistical feed-down. First the compatibility quotient of the instruction coordinator and the classroom experience director is inserted into the machine; next the classroom director's metabolic index, then the composite cephalic induction brain waves of the class members, and finally the professional and public relations numerical index of the classroom experience director.

After a 30-second interval, the tabulation key is pressed and a numerical instruction rating complete with a multi-colored item graph and the merit salary equivalent emerges

---

*From New York State Education 15:42, January 1968. Used by permission.

on a short contract form. The classroom experience director signs one copy and retains the other as his contract for the next school year. It is very neat, and simple, and without negotiation.

Today we continually search for that neat simple package solution to teacher evaluation. We hope for a universal formula of factors to convert that diversified human behavior known as teaching to a performance rating. Although it is very important that we continually strive to improve evaluative devices and our knowledge concerning the teaching-learning process, it is equally important that we utilize all information from our present plateau of evaluative knowledge rather than defer or half-heartedly apply it in anticipation that an educational alchemist will produce the perfect evaluation formula.

The case of teacher evaluation is in many ways similar to the problem of teaching reading. In reading we now generally accept the fact that no one method is best, but a method can be made to do its best by the practitioners' confidence in and willingness to conscientiously apply it. So it is with evaluation. The instrument cooperatively developed, with the confidence of the participants and with energetic and proper application, will succeed. Let us look at some of the factors on *Knowledge Plateau* concerning evaluation.

1. Evaluation is essential in the teacher-education program since improvement and progress can only be made in light of results.

2. The evaluation instrument should be cooperatively developed by administrators and teachers if it is to attain the confidence of all participants. It should be developed by per-colation rather than solely by the drip down or bubble up processes.

3. Administrators must use the evaluative instrument cooperatively upon common targets to "zero-in" evaluative determinations. A common error is to develop a fair evaluative device, and then have it unfairly applied because of diversity of points of view. Although complete uniformity is impossible, the diversity gap can be narrowed by trial evaluations.

4. Essential items and optimal brevity are mandatory if an evaluative instrument is to be conscientiously used.

5. Since improvement of instruction is the primary mission of evaluation, the core of evaluation devices must be classroom performance items. Principles of learning and teaching can be lost in the social and professional development forest.

6. An overall rating is important if an evaluative device is to be conclusive. An open-ended list of items is a "face-saving" and "decision-ducking" mechanism.

7. Administrators must divorce the heart from the head in the evaluative process to prevent difficult or impossible future surgery. Too frequently the old medical axiom can be applied to the evaluation process: The evaluation was a success but the teacher died.

Jason, in his quest of the Golden Fleece, spent years of tests and trials in what appeared to be endless wandering and frustrations. Certainly we in education need to hitch our wagon to the evaluation star, but we must be certain that the wagon is properly constructed and a useful vehicle along the way to that evaluation horizon.

95 ~ BUILDING MORALE THROUGH NEW TECHNIQUES IN STAFF EVALUATION*

NELSON E. WIETERS
ASSISTANT PROFESSOR OF RECREATION AND OUTDOOR EDUCATION,
GEORGE WILLIAMS COLLEGE, CHICAGO

We are concerned with a subject area in which as many new things are happening as are taking place in space technology. To the general public these changes and these new concepts are not so dramatic as moon trips, but to the field of modern management, to that now very highly specialized professional who

*From Secondary School Athletic Administration, January 1969, p. 40, American Association for Health, Physical Education, and Recreation. Used by permission.

turns mediocre operation into thriving enterprise (including our technological firms who produce for moon-shots), this subject is a crucial one.

I, like the teacher of physical science, have a difficult time keeping up with the new developments being researched, pioneered, and documented by a host of psychologists, sociologists, group-dynamics experts, management consultants, and so forth. To attempt in this short space to meet fully the demands implied by the topic "Building Morale Through New Techniques in Staff Evaluation" is a difficult task. However, I do hope to portray the changing picture of personnel management, and I hope to be specific enough to provide carry-over in the form of "take it home and try it" exercises.

One way to describe the new concepts is to say that they tend to challenge the sanctity of those techniques many of us still think of as new. By challenge I do not mean a denial of the validity of their existence, but the challenge that calls for an awareness of the variables that determine degrees of effectiveness. Let me begin by applying this to my topic as it is stated. The word "morale," though a relatively new concern in the field of supervision, is already almost impossible to find in the subject index of the new publications. It seems it has been replaced by words that describe the various components of that which we generalize as morale, words such as "self-actualization," "motivation," "communication," "organizational attitude," and "interpersonal relationships." I believe this says that modern management is becoming more sophisticated in terms of "what determines terms!"

For our purpose here, let me define what I believe the word "morale" means. It means that which would exist provided nothing comes along to destroy it. Equated with the word health, health means the absence of illness. There are things that destroy health; there are things that destroy morale.

One could accurately describe the modern approach to supervision as the human relations method, the subtle but powerful impact of man on man. The challenge to the traditional approaches is the simple question, "Are my actions producing what I think they are producing?"

If we continue this approach, we must next question the relatedness of the word "building." There are two ways to arrive at a state of health. One is to maintain it: the other is to rebuild it once it is destroyed. There are two ways to reach a state of morale. One is to maintain it; the other is to build it once it is lost. Listen to your coaches—they frequently say, "It's impossible to get the boys up for every game." I agree with the claim that morale-*building* is a superficial, temporary esprit de corps that can be reproduced to only a given degree.

If you can accept this frame of reference, at least in part, let me then go to step one, which is to determine those viruses which tend to destroy morale. I've taken a few of the modern principles, related them to the data received in my discussions with athletic directors and have

here a few examples of the "morale viruses" in your field.

Step one: analysis of causal-variables[1]

Virus 1. The athletic department historically suffers from a lack of status or prestige in comparison with other elements of the institution.

Virus 2. Athletic directors for the most part come from coaching ranks. They are therefore conditioned to a certain behavior model exemplified by statements such as: "Get in there and get 'em"—"I don't care how tired you are, you gotta go!"—"You're loafing."—"Drive, drive."

Understand, I am attaching no value judgment here, for this technique is, of course, an important one for sports. (One certainly does not advocate that sensitivity training replace signal calling in the huddle.) Perhaps, though, you can see the difficulty the athletic director might have in adopting new techniques. (Even the degree of similarity in the way athletic directors organize their speeches to quarterback clubs in astonishing!)

Virus 3. Overdependency on the athletic director by staff members because of the traditional division of labor within athletic departments, i.e., "you do the coaching and I'll handle the other decisions," leads to a lack of involvement in problem-solving. This in turn eliminates any tendency to share responsibility or satisfactions for either failure or success.

Virus 4. Diversity, because of the organic division of labor (each member coaching a different sport, for example), creates a situation where it is difficult for staff to identify their common goals as a group. Commonality in goals is essential to group unification. Group unity is an essential to staff morale.

Virus 5. Lack of the athletic director's ability to be influential upwards is a deterrent to good morale. All experts seem to agree that regardless of leadership techniques and working conditions, full staff morale never really exists unless they see their supervisor as part of the power structure.

Virus 6. The historical phenomena of attrition among coaching staffs (win or leave) prevents the administrators from ever establishing the closeness with staff necessary for modern management approaches.

Virus 7. Unknown diversity between goals of the staff member and those of the athletic director causes problems. For example, the

---

[1] Likert, Rensis. The human organization: its management and value. New York: McGraw-Hill, 1967.

new coach's goal is to improve last year's winless season. The administrator is expecting him to surpass the .500 mark. Revelation of this diversity then becomes rather traumatic.

These examples may be correct or incorrect; they may or may not apply to you, but the important issue is the organizational analysis of the causal variables as a first step. After all, how can you judge your staff's response (morale) to your evaluation techniques if you are unaware of the other factors that might be responsible? Did you ever get the feeling that despite your efforts "John always seems to disagree"?

Step two: diagnosis of administrative attitude

I have been using the terms "modern approach," "contemporary methods," etc. In the event you lack a full understanding of what I mean by these terms, the following model will perhaps clarify as well as provide the basis for evaluating your attitude. I refer here to the work by Douglass McGregor.[2] He states that staff members can be divided into one of two categories depending on the assumptions they have about human behavior.

Theory X. (Management by direction and control)

Assumptions:

1. The average human being has an inherent dislike of work and will avoid it if he can.
2. Because of this, most people must be coerced, controlled, threatened with punishment to get them to put forth adequate effort toward the achievement of organizational objectives.
3. The average human being prefers to be directed, wishes to avoid responsibility, has relatively little ambition, wants security above all.

Theory Y. (Management by integration and *self-control*)

Assumptions:

1. The expenditure of physical and mental effort in work is as natural as play or rest.
2. External control and the threat of punishment are not the only means for bringing about effort toward organizational objectives. Man will exercise self-direction and self-control in the service of objectives to which he is committed.
3. Commitment to objectives is a function of the rewards associated with their achievement.
4. The average human being learns, under proper conditions, not only to accept but to seek responsibility.

5. The capacity to exercise a relatively high degree of imagination, ingenuity, and creativity in the solution of organizational problems is widely, not narrowly, distributed in the population.
6. Under the conditions of modern industrial life, the intellectual potentialities of the average human being are only partially utilized.

Now let us apply the discussion thus far to a similar analysis of evaluation methods. Let us take several "standard" techniques employed by the progressive administrator, techniques such as use of formal-position description, close day-by-day supervision, periodic appraisal sessions, formal evaluation forms, and the observation visit. Using my term "virus" and McGregor's emphasis on the difference between theoretical assumptions and just "plain old assuming," let's analyze these five examples.

1. Formal Position Description
   Traditional Assumption: Provides the individual with a clear-cut guide for his job and an outline for his work.
   Potential Virus: Develops a robot-like response, forces him to alter or base his personal goals on techniques and even worse, someone else's.
2. Ongoing Supervision
   Traditional Assumption: Close, constant supervision and assistance will accelerate worker growth.
   Potential Virus: Produces behavior which has not been internalized, but has been externally produced by the constant presence of his major threat.
3. Periodic Appraisal Sessions
   Traditional Assumption: Periodic confrontation will allow interim freedom for movement toward interdependence, but will prevent complacency by "keeping them honest."
   Potential Virus: Too far removed from the behavioral incidents and the environment in which they occurred for any recall, learning, or motivation to take place.
4. Use of Formal Evaluation Forms
   Traditional Assumption: Allows for a more accurate recording than would be possible in the uncomfortable one-to-one confrontation, and provides an ongoing record of worker progress.
   Potential Virus: Allows uncontrolled expression of the evaluator's prejudices, and might not include a plan for reconciliation of differences or inaccuracies.
5. Observation Visits
   Traditional Assumption: Provides the opportunity for first-hand knowledge of the worker in action.
   Potential Virus: Presence of the administrator severely alters the entire environment, leading to the collection of unrealistic and inaccurate data.

---

[2] McGregor, Douglass. The human side of enterprise. New York: McGraw-Hill, 1960.

Get the point? The "new" technique in "Maintaining Morale Through Evaluation" is the asking of the simple question, "Is my behavior producing that which I intend it to?"

Step three: identifying organizational image

We have (in step one) analyzed the casual variables of the total environment and (in step two) diagnosed administrative attitude. There remains the important step of determining the degree of similarity between how the organization is seen by the administration and how it is seen by the staff.

During the conference I distributed a greatly digested version of what is commonly referred to as the "Likert Model." Likert provides in his book several full models, with questions and explanations, that can provide a system for answering many organizational questions. The superficiality of the form I distributed was purposely planned. The exercise was to transpose my presentation to this new set of words to transfer the understanding of my listeners.

These were the conditions: Each person was a member of the athletic staff of "John Doe High School, Anytown, U.S.A." They were to visualize that which they believed to be the average attitude toward the average administrative system (top, horizontal line) and in which of these four systems the organizational variables (left hand vertical column) would be placed by the average staff. I challenged them to a little role-playing. They had to forget that they were on the management side of the fence and take the role of the staff member, discuss it, and then place a check in the square they felt to be appropriate in light of both their personal opinion and the effect of the discussion upon them.

The responses, shown in Exhibit A, show the distribution of opinions on the way the participants felt the average athletic staff in the country feels about their organizational environment. Even though the participants were administrators (i.e., in a sense they were really rating them selves as they feel others see them), note the preponderance of opinion toward System #2.

The analysis of these results provide several other interesting elements:

> Leadership: 64 percent felt that staff members see the athletic administrator of their schools as being authoritative in nature.

Exhibit A. Results of table-exercise with the Likert Model

Organizational variable	System I: exploitive authoritative	System II: benevolent authoritative	System III: consultative	System IV: participative group
Leadership	IIIIIIIIII IIIIIIIIII III	IIIIIIIIII IIIIIIIIII IIIIIIIIII IIIII	IIIIIIIIII IIIIIIIII	IIIIIIIIII III
Motivation	IIIIIIIIII IIIIIII	IIIIIIIIII IIIIIIIIII IIIII	IIIIIIIIII IIIIIIIIII II	IIIIIIIIII IIIIIIIIII IIIII
Communication	IIIIIIIIII IIIIIIIII	IIIIIIIIII IIIIIIIIII IIIIIIIIII IIIII	IIIIIIIIII IIIIIIII	IIIIIIIIII III
Interaction	IIIIIIIIII IIII	IIIIIIIIII IIIIIIIIII	IIIIIIIIII IIIIIIIII	IIIIIIIIII IIIIIIIIII IIII
Decision-making	IIIIIIIIII IIIIIIIII	IIIIIIIIII IIIIIIIIII IIIIIIIIII I	IIIIIIIIII IIIIIIII	IIIIIIIIII IIIII
Goal setting	IIIIIIIIII IIIIIII	IIIIIIIIII IIIIIIIIII IIIII	IIIIIIIIII IIIII	IIIIIIIIII IIIIIII
Control	IIIIIIIIII IIIIIIIIII IIIIIII	IIIIIIIIII IIIIIIIIII IIIIIIIIII	IIIIIIIIII IIIII	IIIIIIIIII II

Motivation: The rather even distribution here (note that System #4 ranks as high as any other) seems to indicate that the administrators feel that motivation comes from the process of interpersonal relations. Perhaps they were saying that even though the "authority" dominated in most areas, this was one area left up to the staff.

Communication: System #2 obviously dominates here, indicating the prevalence of vertical-downwards (but put in a nice way) communication system.

Interaction: Whether the heavy emphasis on System #4 here is the result of *planned* participative approach versus this is *where* it is, is problematical. Comparing this with the communication category, one might get the impression that even though the "boss" is issuing the communiques, the grapevine is really "where the action is."

Decision-making: Note the correlation between the results here, and those in the communication's category.

Goal setting: Ditto!

Control: Compare with the first category—"Character of Leadership"!

Also important is the fact that those who felt closer to System #4 in more than one category, felt the same about *all* of the categories. There were 12 in this group, perhaps indicating that their past experience was atypically progressive. (This group represents only 13 percent of the total.)

The reader must realize that the comments above do not represent a careful, scientific analysis. In fact, the table exercise was not conducted as such, and was only an exercise. It did provide some interesting data, however. You interpret it as you see fit.

In closing, let me reveal an anxiety I have that there may be those among you who might say: "Where were all the goodies? Where were the 13½ heretofore unheard of and magical techniques for solving all my morale problems through evaluation?" If you have missed it, let me summarize the "new technique." The new technique is the recent shift from what the administrator does "to" and "for" the worker, to what the administrator *does* and *how* he does it. That is the new technique!

96 ❧ THE IDEAL PROFESSOR*

ALAN F. QUICK
DIRECTOR, STUDENT AND INTERN TEACHING, CENTRAL MICHIGAN UNIVERSITY,
MOUNT PLEASANT, MICHIGAN

ARNOLD D. WOLFE
ASSOCIATE PROFESSOR, SOUTHERN OREGON COLLEGE,
ASHLAND, OREGON

What qualities do college students believe would entitle the professor to the label "the ideal college professor?" In an attempt to answer this question, an instrument was developed to which 483 University of Oregon students responded during the winter quarter of 1963.

Some of the abundance of available literature pertinent to the question was surveyed. A number of ideas were adapted from the literature and were introduced into a graduate seminar at the University of Oregon concerned with the problem of improving college teaching. Following the seminar's consideration, ten items were selected to be used as the basis of a rating sheet designed to obtain the desired information.

Cooperating professors distributed the rating sheets to their respective classes. The instructions to the participants, included on each sheet, were:

Below are statements frequently used to describe the "Ideal Professor." *Read the entire list carefully.* Write a "1" in the space provided by the statement you consider *most* important. Place a "2" before the *second* most important statement, and a "3" before your choice for the *third* most important. Also, please place an "X" before the statement you feel is *least* important.

The 483 rating sheets returned represented 5.5% of the total university enrollment. Distribution ranged from 2.8% of the graduate students to a high of 7.5% of the junior class. Of those responding 47% were men and 53% were women. In processing the data the following weighting points were used: first choice, 3; second choice, 2; third choice, 1.

If every student had voted for all three choices, the total points possible, with 483 respondents, would have been 2,898. Since a few students failed to mark three choices, the maximum points to be treated totaled 2,849.

It is evident that the participating students at the University of Oregon would be willing

*From Improving College and University Teaching 13:133, Summer 1965. Used by permission.

to bestow upon an instructor the title "the ideal professor" if he: encouraged independent thinking, had his course well organized, and had enthusiasm for his subject. They considered it somewhat less important that the professor have an excellent speaking voice and that he be scholarly and actively engaged in research.

As indicated earlier, the students were instructed to place an "X" before the statement they felt to be *least* important. Thirty respondents, or 6.2%, did not follow this instruction. Several of them commented that they did not comply because, "I do not consider any of the statements to be unimportant."

Table 2 shows that three statements were selected by 88% of the respondents as being the "least important." The same three statements received the lowest rankings in Table 1.

Freshmen rated the statement "is a careful evaluator—his tests are fair, sound, and complete and his grading is impartial" as the third most important, whereas the other class groups rated it sixth or lower. This

might indicate that freshmen are more concerned with grades than the other groups. Graduate students rated the statement "is scholarly and participates actively in research" as seventh most important, whereas the other classes rated it in last position. This higher placement may have been due to the graduate students' closer association with research activities. Little variation was evident in the ratings of the ten statements among the sophomores, juniors, and seniors.

Conclusions

According to the majority of 483 students who responded to the rating sheet, a professor who desired to achieve the status of "ideal" would do well to: (1) encourage independent thinking, (2) have the subject matter and the course well organized, and (3) have a deep and sustained enthusiasm for his subject. Although these three statements should be considered of paramount importance, the professor ought to be aware of his need to develop the ability to explain clearly, to wel-

TABLE 1. WEIGHTED RATINGS OF THE IDEAL PROFESSOR

Total points	Percent of total	Statements
541	19.0	1) Encourages independent thinking, not memorized knowledge.
475	16.7	2) Has the subject matter and the course well organized.
440	15.4	3) Has a deep and sustained enthusiasm for his subject.
353	12.4	4) Has the ability to explain clearly.
345	12.1	5) Welcomes differences in points of view and does not expect students always to agree with him.
284	10.0	6) Is a careful evaluator—his tests are fair, sound, and complete and his grading is impartial.
209	7.3	7) Has a good knowledge of his subject.
140	4.9	8) Likes college-age youth and is interested in them as individuals.
36	1.3	9) Has an adequate and well-modulated voice. He speaks clearly and with good pronunciation.
26	.9	10) Is scholarly and participates actively in research.
2,849	100.0	

TABLE 2. RATINGS OF THE LEAST IMPORTANT STATEMENTS

Number of students	Percent of total	Statements
198	43.7	1) Is scholarly and participates actively in research.
107	23.6	2) Has an adequate and well-modulated voice. He speaks clearly and with good pronunciation.
95	21.0	3) Likes college-age youth and is interested in them as individuals.
12	2.7	4) Is a careful evaluator—his tests are fair, sound, and complete and his grading is impartial.
9	2.0	5) Has a deep and sustained enthusiasm for his subject.
9	2.0	6) Encourages independent thinking, not memorized knowledge.
9	2.0	7) Has the subject matter and the course well organized.
6	1.3	8) Welcomes differences in points of view and does not expect students always to agree with him.
5	1.1	9) Has the ability to explain clearly.
3	.6	10) Has a good knowledge of his subject.
453	100.0	

come differences in points of view, and to become a careful evaluator.

Though the respondents gave the lowest ratings to the statements dealing with a good delivery, being scholarly, and participating actively in research, it cannot be assumed that the students felt the statements to be unimportant. They merely felt that, in comparison to the other statements, that they were less important.

Whether the responses to the rating sheet would have been the same for a random sample, or for the total population at the University of Oregon, is speculative. The authors, however, have concluded that it is worthwhile to determine how much importance students attach to statements usually associated with an "ideal professor" and plans are being made to conduct surveys on two other campuses.

BIBLIOGRAPHY

Barr, Arvil S. The measurement of teacher characteristics and prediction of teaching efficiency. Review of Educational Research, 22 (June 1952), 169–74.

Bousefield, W. A. Students' ratings of qualities considered desirable in college professors, School and Society, 51 (February 24, 1940), 253–256.

Goodhartz, Abraham S. Student attitudes and opinions relating to teaching at Brooklyn College, School and Society, 68 (November 28, 1948), 345–349.

Hoffman, Randall W. Students portray the excellent teacher, Improving College and University Teaching, XI, No. 1 (Winter, 1963), 21–24.

Ludeman, W. A. A study of the qualities of the ideal college teacher, Teachers College Journal, XXXI, No. 5 (March, 1960), 125–26.

McGrath, Earl J. Superior teaching in the colleges of the sixties, Improving College and University Teaching, VIII, No. 3 (Summer, 1960), 76–83.

McKeachie, Wilbert J. Student ratings of faculty: a research review, Improving College and University Teaching, V. No. 1 (Winter, 1957), 4–8.

Morton, Richard K. What do students expect of a teacher? Improving College and University Teaching, XI, No. 1 (Winter, 1963), 19–20.

Ryans, David G. The investigation of teacher characteristics, The Educational Record, XXXIV (October, 1953), 371–396.

Tead, Ordway. Some questions on college teaching, Improving College and University Teaching, II, No. 1 (February, 1954), 3–4.

Yourglich, Anita. Study on correlations between college teachers' and students' concepts of 'ideal-student' and 'ideal-teacher,' Journal of Educational Research, XLIX, No. 1 (September, 1955), 59–64.

97 ᘒ GOODBYE, MR. COACH*

How to fire the mentor of a winning team

JOHN B. CROSSLEY
CHAIRMAN, DEPARTMENT OF EDUCATIONAL ADMINISTRATION,
UNIVERSITY OF HAWAII, HONOLULU

Mr. principal, why and how do you fire a coach? Gives you the shudders to think about it, doesn't it? Haven't you known administrators who were fired themselves because they fired or tried to fire a coach?

The purposes of this article are:

1. to suggest a framework upon which evaluation of the coaching staff may be based,
2. to suggest evaluative procedures, and
3. to "story-tell" or role-play the case of reemploying one coach, dismissing another.

Fortunately there are an ever-increasing number of school administrators who see and make known to the athletic department, the student body, and the community that the athletic program is an integral part of the educational program of the school, a part of the curriculum—not "extra" curricular. These administrators have already provided criteria upon which to evaluate the athletic program and teachers (coaches) of the program.

Any institution must have a reason for its being. Certainly those responsible for the administration of a school have either helped to developed or have inherited a philosophy of education for that institution plus stated objectives of the educational program. In general, a statement of purposes is in written form for most high schools in the country. These purposes or objectives of the educational program are quite clear and concise.

Whatever the educational philosophy of the institution may be, whatever the stated objec-

*From The Clearing House 42:152, November 1967. Used by permission.

tives of the program may be, since the athletic program is a part of the curriculum developed to carry out the objectives, these then become the evaluative criteria used in determining the contribution each course, each experience, provides in attaining these goals and the criteria upon which the evaluation of each staff member rests. In other words, how effectively does this course, this activity, this teacher, this coach contribute to the purpose of the educational program?

How does the administrator evaluate the athletic program?

First: He is responsible for interpreting to members of the athletic department and the coaching staff the overall purposes of the educational program of the school. In employing coaches, he shares with them his expectations for the athletic program—that it will provide every participant opportunities to achieve to his maximum the values and objectives of the school's educational program. He points out that in a broad sense the coach is a "teacher" first, a coach second.

Second: With every justification, he may look for high standards of contributions by coaches to these goals, for the direct and indirect influence of the coaching staff upon team members and upon the entire student body in many instances is greater than that of members of any other teaching department of the school.

Third: Recognizing and relating the importance of coaching and athletics in the life of students, it becomes clear that he is a firm believer in athletics and will provide support and assistance for each activity.

Fourth: He reminds the coaching staff that, as chief administrator of the school, he has the responsibility of evaluating and reporting his evaluation of both the program and the staff to his superiors and to the community. To be as objective as possible in his evaluation, he must observe at first hand each aspect of the program, including the effectiveness of each teacher. He makes it clear that by such observation he not only becomes more objective in his evaluation but also is more competent to be of assistance in providing all means for teaching to be effective—better equipment, better learning conditions, etc. He also can from firsthand observation report to the community the superior work of teaching and coaching he is sure he will see.

Thus he reports the necessity of his seeing the athletic program at work—by observing practice sessions, dropping into dressing rooms,

being on the bench at games. He reports that on such visits he will be only an observer, will not interfere with coaching; if he has any suggestion, it will be made privately to the coach. Hopefully, he can truthfully say that he anticipates that such visits will be due to his deep interest in athletics. By the expression of such interest, he also notes that it enables the administration to be identified by teams and student body as supporters of the athletic program.

Given a situation where the suggestions above have been carried out with agreement and understanding, let's "pretend" a case of reemployment of one coach, a request for a resignation (or if necessary, dismissal) of another.

The football and basketball seasons are over. The time has come for final evaluation of all members of the teaching staff, including coaches. While the conferences between the two coaches in our story are, of course, independent of each other and private, for the sake of comparison, they are reported together item by item.

Principal: "Mr. Football Coach—Mr. Basketball Coach, as you know, these last two weeks I have been having conferences with all members of our faculty, making our evaluations for the year. I have your file with me which has reports of my other conferences with you during the year, the reports of my observations at practices, games, etc. Of course you also have copies of all these and so nothing new will probably come up today; rather, we'll try to put the whole story together.

"*Mr. Football Coach,* you know how pleased I have been with the way you have handled the fellows on your team. I am glad I could get you the extra money to get additional team equipment so you could keep even the poorer players on the squad all year. Even though they got to play little, they gained a great deal both in physical development and in self-esteem by being members of the squad. I was glad to see you got each of them in at least one game—glad that you used your less able players in some games rather than win by a big score.

"*Mr. Basketball Coach,* I certainly can say you won some games by astronomical scores. I know that pleased the boosters' club, but as I urged you early in the season, I wish you had kept a larger squad and given more fellows a chance to play. You had the equipment, it would have cost no more in transportation, and I offered you a second assistant if you felt you needed one.

"*Mr. Football Coach,* I'm not sure you know,

but both Bill and Ed, the two fellows who were just able to stay eligible during the season, both now are 'out of the woods' and are going to have nearly a B average in all subjects this semester. I appreciate how much you did to encourage them in their school work. You not only made good players out of them, but, through your efforts, they are benefiting from their entire school program for the first time.

"*Mr. Basketball Coach,* do you know that I'm still having a rough time with Miss Smith and Mrs. Jones regarding their attitude toward our athletic program? They complain bitterly each time one of our tennis or baseball players has to be excused from their classes for an away game and are constantly 'digging' at the athletic program in the faculty lounge. I think they are winning some converts to their point of view. As you know, for we talked about it at the time, this is due primarily to your harsh criticism of them because they wouldn't change grades in their courses and keep two of your players eligible. I'm afraid you haven't helped us in our efforts to raise the respect of our student body for quality academic work.

"*Mr. Football Coach,* I want to tell you again how much I appreciated that letter a few months ago from Mr. and Mrs. Brown, expressing their appreciation of how you had helped Jim get himself straightened out in his attitude toward girls. Thanks to you, all is O.K. now. An example of how a coach can help a kid have not only a clean body, but a clean mind.

"*Mr. Basketball Coach,* perhaps you haven't heard, but two fellows who played for you this year were suspended from school last week for having and passing around at school obscene pictures. I guess you weren't very successful in ruling out the smut and foul language your gang was using in the dressing room so frequently.

"*Mr. Football Coach,* only this morning I saw the final results of the election for student body officers for next year. You will be pleased to know that that big tackle of yours will be student body president and your second-string center will be treasurer. I think this is primarily a result of your work with the Letterman's Club. I know that you and the club members helped them develop their platforms and plan their campaigns, which were both dignified and astute. Those fellows will help us have a better school next year.

"*Mr. Basketball Coach,* I'm sorry you couldn't find the time to assist in any of our student body activities this year. You coaches have a lot of influence on our students and we could have used you in any number of ways.

"*Mr. Football Coach,* I want to thank you again for your contribution in building up good sportsmanship on the part of our students and our patrons who come to our games. Your behavior on the bench, your attitude toward game officials, your pep talks to your squad, your talks at our pep rallies, all contributed to our school and community having an enviable reputation in regard to good sportsmanship.

"*Mr. Basketball Coach,* you know how disappointed I was regarding your behavior at our games. I think I talked with you after each game, doing all I could to help you gain better self-control. But I certainly failed, for in our play-off game for the conference title you behaved worse than at any time during the season. If I had been the referee, I would have ousted you from the bench. Your worst offense was the very evident use of sarcasm on Sam when he missed those two foul shots and you pulled him out of the game.

"*Mr. Football Coach,* well, that's it. I'm glad you are on our faculty. You have contributed much to the purposes of our total program. I'm glad you turned down the offer to go to X Community College next year. We need men like you at the high school level where perhaps you can do more for boys and the entire student body than at the collegiate level. I know you wish you had won that last game and third place in the league, but maybe we'll hit next year. Anyhow, keep giving us the full benefit of your total ability as a 'teacher'; we'll not demand championships.

"*Mr. Basketball Coach,* I'm sorry all of my summaries today have to be negative—except one—of course, we did win the league championship and the southern-conference title. However, you will recall our conference when you were assigned as head basketball coach and the description, which you have in writing, as to how we see sports contributing to all aspects of our objectives of an education program for boys and girls. I admire your 'coaching' ability, but am sorry I cannot recommend that you continue with us due to your failure as a 'teacher.' I'll be glad to recommend you as a coach for a professional team."

In summary, it is suggested that if the philosophy and objectives of education are known and accepted by the teaching staff, are explained to parents and the community, if the coaching staff is made aware of its responsibilities and its unique opportunity to assist each player to profit from attaining—to the best of his ability—all the established goals of the educational program, and if cooperative and meaningful techniques for evaluation of each coach's contribution to these purposes are

established and carried out, then the administrator is professionally obligated and equipped to make and stand behind his evaluative decisions. He *can* fire a "winning" coach!

PROJECT AND THOUGHT QUESTIONS

1. For evaluation of a program of health education or physical education, prepare a checklist that covers aspects of these programs such as philosophy, curriculum, leadership, time allocation, program components, staff, facilities and equipment, and measurement and evaluation techniques.
2. Survey five teachers of health education and five teachers of physical education, to determine what they feel constitutes the most objective and and best method of evaluating their performance on the job.
3. What contributions can evaluation make in helping the teacher grow professionally?
4. Assume the role of the teacher who has been

observed by a supervisor of physical education, and have another student assume the role of the supervisor. After the observation has taken place, the conference between the teacher and supervisor takes place in your classroom. Have the class evaluate the procedure that was followed in the conference, which was acted out for the class. Have the class evaluate whether or not they feel the conference helped the teacher grow on the job.

5. What areas of school health and physical education programs, according to your observations and evaluation, need the most professional upgrading?

SELECTED READINGS

Bucher, C. A.: Administration of health and physical education programs, including athletics, ed. 5, St. Louis, 1971, The C. V. Mosby Co.

Fawcett, C. W.: School personnel administration, New York, 1964, The Macmillan Co.

Goldman, S.: The school principal, New York, 1966, The Center for Applied Research in Education, Inc., The Library of Education.

LaPorte, W. A.: Health and physical education scorecard no. 1 and no. 2, College Book Store, 3413 S. Hoover Blvd., Los Angeles, Calif.

National Education Association: Methods of evaluating teachers, National Education Association Research Bulletin 43:1, February 1965.

PART FIVE RECREATION, OUTDOOR EDUCATION, AND CAMPING PROGRAMS

The work of health educators and physical educators is closely allied with the recreation, outdoor education, and camping programs. Professional organizations, schools, colleges, and youth-serving agencies frequently include the fields of health, physical education, recreation, camping, and outdoor education in their departments, divisions, schools, colleges, or other administrative units. Although each of these areas is a separate and distinct field of endeavor, several administrative functions cut across all of these areas. Such considerations as facilities, staff, professional meetings, and financial planning often dictate the need for all the areas to work very closely with each other. Therefore, it is important to include some significant articles from men in these allied areas, in this anthology of readings designed to cover the various administrative facets of health and physical education programs.

At some time in the distant future it may be practical to publish a book of administrative readings for the administration of programs in each special area. At the present time, however, if one uses, as a criterion for the preparation of such an anthology, the way programs are currently organized and administered in the overwhelming majority of schools, colleges, and youth-serving agencies in the nation, a textbook of readings needs to cover the material as it is presented in this book.

CHAPTER 19 RECREATION AND OUTDOOR
EDUCATION PROGRAMS

G. Leslie Lynch writes that public schools should be recreational and cultural centers. School recreation is concerned with students, and park departments are left with the responsibility of providing recreation for the rest of the population. In some cities cooperative arrangements have been made between school and recreation departments. The public Lynch believes, should benefit by gaining maximum recreation service.

In the next article, Carl E. Willgoose describes this era as one in which people have an increasing amount of free time and an abundance of leisure. Education for leisure is the key to richness and fullness of life. Willgoose says that recreational activities should include cultural, social, and physical objectives, and he suggests some activities that have these objectives.

Norman Marsh shows how one elementary school in Sacramento, California, has outdoor learning right on the school grounds. One acre of the school ground has woods, tall grasses, a meadow, and a bog of water for plants and animals. This allows the students a firsthand observation of natural phenomena close to home and at low cost to school districts.

98 Ϩ THE ROLE OF SCHOOLS AS RECREATION CENTERS *

G. Leslie Lynch
Recreation Planner, National Recreation and Park Association,
New York

America's public schools should be recreation and cultural centers as well as centers of learning. Increasing leisure time and the rapid growth and crowding of the population into urban areas has made it necessary for all levels of government to accept the responsibility of providing for the recreation of the people. The schools, too, must provide more recreation lands and facilities for all children.

Up to now, school recreation planning, for the most part, has been concerned only with providing facilities for students attending a particular school. The recreation and park departments of local governments were left with the responsibility of providing for the recreation of the rest of the population. There has been little correlation of the recreation planning of school officials and local government, but the importance of such collaboration can be readily seen. This working together is necessary if the schools are to become recreation and cultural centers for all the people.

Why is it desirable for the schools to be community recreation and cultural centers? The economic reason for making the public schools recreation and cultural centers for all the people

is a very important one, but not the only one. Wherever there is an outdoor area for active recreation, there should be nearby indoor recreation facilites because it is necessary for the program to move indoors during winter and even at times during the rest of the year. If schools and recreation and park departments of municipal governments proceed independently to provide lands and buildings, costly duplication will obviously result.

Another reason why there should be close cooperation between the two agencies where recreation is concerned is that public planning for recreation should include all the people, and not just segments of the population. Education is, of course, primarily for children and young people. But all of the people need wholesome recreation, and the children require it at times when school is not in session.

If the schools planned full time recreation programs for their children at school centers, and the recreation and park departments planned programs for the rest of the population at separate community centers, it would be a most unfortunate and unsatisfactory arrangement. Furthermore, the public recreation program should be family oriented insofar as possible.

Some school officials feel that recreation is

---

*From American School and University 38:33, July 1966. Used by permission.

education and should be the responsiblity of the schools. Others feel that the schools have all they can do to meet the educational needs of children without taking on the additional responsibility of providing public recreation service.

Recreation and park officials agree that the recreation service is, and should be, educational. But it is education from an entirely different point of view. Elementary and secondary school education is principally for children and young people and must be compulsory. Recreation is for all ages and compulsion cannot enter into it.

Even more importantly, play areas which include facilities for active recreation and which adjoin existing schools comprise only one-fifth of the total park lands available. A comprehensive recreation program spreads over far more area than the parks adjoining schools. School officials should not be expected, therefore, to assume responsibility for the total park system and recreation program.

The administration of recreation and parks is logically a governmental rather than a school responsibility. It is necessary, however, that the two agencies correlate their recreation programs. It is equally important that they work together in planning that portion of the park system which includes active recreation areas adjacent to schools, and in planning school buildings which will serve as community recreation centers. They need to cooperate in acquiring the sites, in planning the buildings and the sites, and in the use, maintenance, and supervision of both buildings and sites.

In a number of cities, cooperative arrangements have been worked out. In some cases, the schools lease the recreation portion of their sites to the recreation and park department for a dollar a year and this agency takes full responsibility for developing and maintaining the recreation area.

In Minneapolis, a definite line on the site is agreed upon for the division of responsibility. In Seattle, the two agencies in one case acquired adjoining sites and a new school building was so designed and located that the recreation portion was on city property, and the city paid for its acquisition, development, and upkeep. Under this arrangement, the recreation and park department takes full responsibility for the maintenance of areas of the school building devoted to recreation, as well as for the recreation park.

Recreation land needs of the future will be much greater than the needs of today—perhaps

in the same proportion that the recreation land needs of today bear to the needs at the beginning of the century. There is every reason to expect that the population will continue to expand and that people will continue to have more leisure time.

A conservative standard to be applied by local governments—municipal, county, and metropolitan—in order to adequately meet future needs is ten acres of recreation land per thousand of the ultimate population within the urban areas. An additional fifteen acres per thousand of the ultimate population should be set aside in large parks and reservations outside the urban area within an hour's drive of the urban population. One-fifth of this total of twenty-five acres per thousand of the ultimate population, or five acres per thousand population, should be in the form of sites for active recreation adjacent to schools. Another one-fifth, or five acres per thousand population, should be in large parks within the urban area.

The neighborhood is normally the urban area served by a public elementary school and usually consists of not more than a square mile so that children may walk to the school and its adjacent recreation park. The site should include two and a half acres for each thousand of the anticipated neighborhood population, plus the land required for the school building and its immediate environs.

For example, if the ultimate neighborhood population is expected to be five thousand, the recreation park should have twelve and a half acres. If the school building and its immediate environs will require another two and a half acres, the total site should have fifteen acres. Half of the recreation area should be playground and half should be park, with lawns and trees forming a buffer on at least one side between the playground and adjacent homes.

The neighborhood recreation park should include the active recreation facilities needed for elementary school children and some facilities for adults in the park portion of the site. The district recreation park should supplement the neighborhood recreation park by providing recreation facilities requiring more space for older children and adults. Both areas should be designed to encourage use by all ages and particularly families.

It is important that outdoor recreation facilities be located near indoor areas to promote use of the entire site in winter or bad weather. Therefore, the school building adjacent to a recreation area should be designed so the recreation area should be designed so the recreation rooms may be used and heated without heating or opening up classrooms.

Among the facilities that should be provided in the elementary school are a gymnasium; a small auditorium that may be used for dramatics and various cultural activities; a lounge that may be the lobby of the building; an arts and crafts room; at least one room for meetings and games; an office for the recreation director; recreation storage space; and rest rooms that are directly accessible from the playground and which may be left open when the building is locked.

Indoor facilities at the junior and senior high school level should include a gymnasium for boys and men and one for girls and women, or a very large gym with a folding partition; an auditorium with seating capacity for community-wide events; a swimming pool; a common room or lounge that may be the lobby of the building; shops that may be used for both school and recreation classes; at least three rooms for meetings and other activities; an office for the recreation director; recreation storage space; and rest rooms which are directly accessible from the playfield and which may be left open when the building is locked.

In conclusion, it is vital that the school building and the adjoining recreation park should be attractively designed and maintained. The architect for the building and the landscape architect for the recreation park should be employed at the same time and should collaborate in locating the building on the site and in securing the proper relationship of the recreation facilities.

A desirable procedure is for school officials to draw up a written agreement to insure close collaboration in the comprehensive planning of the two systems. This includes cooperation in acquiring sites with which both agencies are concerned and in planning, developing, maintaining, and using the facilities.

Through the close cooperation of school and municipal officials, the public should benefit by gaining the maximum recreation service together with the most effective use of available funds. Furthermore, this cooperation should result in more beautiful school buildings and recreation parks. It will do much to stimulate full time use of recreation facilities, and will go a long way towards making the urban environment a permanently more attractive place in which to live, and consequently a place with enhanced and stabilized property values.

99 ෴ RECREATION—OBLIGATION OF THE SCHOOLS*

CARL E. WILLGOOSE
PROFESSOR OF EDUCATION, SCHOOL OF EDUCATION,
BOSTON UNIVERSITY, BOSTON

Changes in society are coming so fast that the educator who is satisfied with his curriculum, even for a little while, may be left far behind in only a few short years.

This is a mass age, an age of routines and conformities by human cogs in an industrial and political maze. It is an age of science and scientists, dynamic labor leaders, business tycoons, and public relations experts.

It is an epoch of uncomfortable school populations, of overfed and underactive children, of value illness, and of psychological stress leading to ulcers, coronary heart disease, low-back pain, mental disorders, and the tension syndrome. And with it all are the battalions of "experts" and "wise men," pill-takers and tub-thumpers to leech us of our ills—both real and fanciful, clinical and subclinical.

Clear also to those who observe are the urge for speed and social status, and the innumerable

home and school compulsions and pressures on primary-graders to achieve high marks in the solid subjects in order to prepare for Harvard and Yale. It seems incongruous to note that, at the same time, this is an era with an increasing amount of free time and an abundance of leisure.

Perhaps the greatest need today is for a set of human values—values that permit man to live reasonably free from unnecessary illness, stress, and pressure, because he has learned to balance work with play and to discover satisfactions both on the job and during his increasing hours of leisure.

The new leisure

The key to the whole mechanism of balance may be tied up in education for leisure—a leisure which is freely chosen and pursued, reaping creative, artistic, and spiritual satisfactions which contribute to the individual's inner growth. Work alone is not enough to satisfy. Neither is free time, if it lacks significance.

*From The Instructor **75**:39, May 1966, © Instructor Publications, Inc. Used by permission.

Work and recreation together make for wholeness.

Leisure-time activities can rejuvenate and recreate; play can be therapeutic. To the Greeks, the "time for freedom of action" was a time to think, to create, and to act in a hundred personally rewarding ways.

Recreation is associated with the richness and fullness of life. It is more than a nonlabor block of time, or a game, or working a piece of pottery. It is a cross section af all human activities and interests, a viewpoint toward divergence and balance.

In short, recreation is an attitude of mind. In practice, it becomes an outlet to creativity, both physical and spiritual, particularly as work becomes more mechanized and routinized and ceases to be an outlet for original thinking and acting.

The education of children

John Huston Finley, former editor-in-chief of *The New York Times* and New York State Commissioner of Education, wanted others to live for adventure of the spirit and adventure in imagination. He spoke of the child's "rightful heritage of play" and stressed a *permanently satisfying use of leisure.* He asked that children have a real and full chance to play, unregimented and according to their own learnings. If the "heaven of men's dreams" is to have music, poetry, art, and dancing, why not experience such joy now?

The after-school way

The formal part of the school day is full, but the after-school day is practically untouched in thousands of communities. If there is a "program," it is frequently designed for secondary

RECREATIONAL ACTIVITIES

Games—Sports
*Archery
Fencing
Intramural sports
  (Grades 4, 5, 6)
Semiactive social games
Signaling and compass games
Skating
Skiing
Stunts and tumbling
*Swimming
Table tennis

Hobbies—Crafts
Bait and fly casting
Campcraft
Ceramics
*Cooking
Flower collecting
Gardening
Insect collection
*Jewelry making
Metalworking
*Photography
Rock finding
Sewing
*Woodworking

Dance
*Couple dances, mixers (folk)
*Modern dance
Rope skipping to music
Social dances
*Square dances
Tap and clog

Music
Action game songs
*Bands and orchestras
*Glee clubs
Group recordings
*Group singing
Records and tapes
Rhythm instruments
Small group ensembles

Drama
Charades
Choral speaking
*Puppetry
Radio time
*Short plays
*Storytelling
*Theater trips

Art
*Clay modeling
Finger painting
Oil painting
Sculpture
*Watercolor painting

Literature
*Adventure stories
Animal stories
Fairy tales
Humor and nonsense
Picture books
*Poetry

Cooperative activity
Combining all efforts of
music, art, crafts, and drama
to produce a single expression

Miscellaneous—Social
Croquet
"Dress-up" parties
Free play
*Hikes
Marshmallow roasts
*Mental games, quizzes, and puzzles
Parties
Picnics
Social mixers
Television (special programs)

school only, and is limited to bands and glee clubs, games and sports. Girls' programs, especially, lack imagination and planning.

Stimulating after-school programs can be fashioned for almost any elementary school. The offerings should be broad and varied. Whether they are essentially cultural, social, artistic, or physical, they must be diversified enough to tickle the interests of a large number of children. The thrill of mastering a crafts project or developing a photograph in the darkroom may be far more stimulating to the inventive and imaginative boy than music or a game of ball.

A good elementary program should provide an opportunity for the searching and feeling neophyte to try many activities. Wide experiences during the formative years set the stage for richer understandings and practices in later life. Research indicates that game, sport, and hobby skills developed before age twelve tend to carry over to adult life.

Looking beyond

To paraphrase Jay B. Nash, the happy child is a busy child—busy but not cramped, able to paint, sing a song, study the stars, see a great play, and dream of sagebrush and snow-capped peaks—active, but with sufficient glide for recuperation.

Finally, the day may come when the vision of John F. Kennedy (at a convocation at Amherst College, October 26, 1963) will come true: "I look forward to an America which will not be afraid of grace and beauty . . . an America which will reward achievement in the arts as we reward achievement in business and statecraft. I look forward to an America which will steadily raise the standards of artistic accomplishment and which will steadily enlarge cultural opportunities for all of our citizens."

Some of the more successful recreational activities which embrace cultural, social, and physical objectives, and which are appropriate for after-school programming for both boys and girls are shown on the preceding page. The asterisk indicates activities which are most significant in challenging the creative and artistic nature of children. Arrange now for early instruction, and plan a proper presentation.

100 ✍ OUTDOOR LEARNING ON THE SCHOOL SITE*

NORMAN MARSH
TEACHER, BOWLING GREEN ELEMENTARY SCHOOL,
SACRAMENTO (CALIFORNIA) CITY UNIFIED SCHOOL DISTRICT

As expanding urbanization and increasing mechanization move today's children away from meaningful contacts with nature, opportunities for outdoor learning become more and more important. Such opportunities are being provided to the pupils of Bowling Green Elementary School, Sacramento, right on the school grounds.

The nature area

Near the school building, native California shrubs surround an outdoor classroom furnished with redwood benches in a semicircle. A meadow serves as a transition area from the outdoor classroom to the school's nature center and arboretum, developed on little more than an acre of school property. In this small area are woods, tall grasses, a meadow, and even a bog for water-dwelling plants and animals.

In the upper corner of the meadow, a stream begins from a spring simulated by a tapped water pipe. As the stream meanders across the meadow to drain into the bog, it varies in depth and width. In some places it spreads into shallow pools; in others it falls over log dams into deeper pools. Along its course are opportunities to observe "rapids," undercutting of stream banks, deposits of transported sediment, and changes of plant life along the banks. Grasses are allowed to grow uncontrolled except for an occasional trail along the water's edge, where insects, amphibians, and some animals such as moles find food and shelter.

The bog at the end of the meadow is covered with tules, water lilies, pussy willows, and cattails. Gambusia fish, toads, and frogs were imported and make this their home. Mud puppies, collected this spring, have been added. An elevated boardwalk enables observers to walk out over the bog and to note how the change in the water-land ratio affects plants, insect and animal life, and soil.

The grove contains a variety of conifers and

---

*From California Education 3:11, May 1966. Used by permission.

broadleaf trees. It is as yet a very young forest. As the trees mature, their shade will discourage some of the present grassy areas. In the meantime, all the weeds and grasses afford excellent materials for studying seed dispersal, propagation, plant succession, insect and bird colorations, and adaptations to the environment. A brush shelter provides a bird sanctuary that meadowlarks find particularly attractive. Close to the brush shelter is a small blind, with a "one-way" window, which serves as an observation post for bird watchers. From the blind it is possible to photograph birds and tape-record outdoor nature sounds.

Narrow foot trails are laid out through the area, with occasional redwood benches in open spots for observation, contemplation, or small group discussions.

Outdoor learnings

Teachers have encouraged pupils to familiarize themselves with the details of this planned area in a number of interesting ways. For example, pupils are informed that a particular plant is to be found somewhere in the nature center, and they are assigned the task of finding it. Since no plants bear name tags, various classroom and library resources must be used to gather identification data. Armed with these facts, the pupils go into the center to do the necessary research. To be successful, they must pay careful attention to details, to important differences, and to the peculiarities that make the specimen what it is.

Occasionally, serveral stakes, upon which numbered cards have been tacked, are temporarily stuck into the ground beside certain plants selected by the teacher. Pupils then follow the stakes and write the names of numbered specimens or whatever other information is requested. When they return to the classroom, they exchange and discuss the information they have recorded.

Colored slides are taken from time to time, to be used as supplementary learning aids. Insect collections are not encouraged. Specimens are not killed for mounting or dissecting, for it is thought that this type of activity has limited value for pupils of these ages. Such practices do not lead to an appreciation and understanding of the interrelatedness and dependency of living things. Specimens are collected only occasionally for the express purpose of temporarily observing more accurately the insects' distinctiveness, habits, and reactions to a controlled environment.

The opportunities presented by the center for firsthand observation of natural phenomena have stimulated the science program of the whole school. Other subjects have profited also. In mathematics, particular skills, such as indirect measurement and calculation and the plotting of contours and graphing of land area, have been practiced. In the social sciences, early uses of plants by Indians and European settlers have been studied. Composition and art have also been stimulated by the center.

An on-going project

The idea for the center and arboretum was conceived in the fall of 1961. With permission from the school board, the principal and the sixth grade science teacher cooperatively planned and began to develop the site. The school's Parent-Teacher Association recognized the values of the project and contributed financial aid. Other community members donated labor and materials. The pupils have taken responsibility in helping with the planting and maintenance of the natural area.

The project and its still-developing program of outdoor education are "open ended." There will always be something new to plan or to alter. There will always be something to arouse and satisfy new curiosities. In the area of increasingly regimented, regulated, planned, and supervised living, the center provides children a place to come close to nature.

Other schools in the district and in neighboring counties have become interested in the instructional values of the center. Requests for information about how to plan and organize similar centers resulted in an inservice workshop for interested administrators and teachers.

The Bowling Green Nature Center and Arboretum is open to youth groups, school groups, and parents of the community. It demonstrates how children can have worthwhile outdoor education experience close to home and at low cost to school districts.

CHAPTER 20 CAMPING

Pat Martin tells the story of school camping experiences for fifth- and sixth-grade students in Tyler, Texas. All the work done on nature studies, classes, school farming, and outdoor living is accomplished by the students, with great success and rewards.

One community, described by Dale C. Johnson, purchased a limestone quarry for a community school outdoor laboratory for all students in grades kindergarten through 12.

The program as outlined includes a summer school program and school-year field trips, and it is still expanding.

A program of outdoor instructional experiences, including summer camping for youngsters, is described by Evelyn Watters in the next article. She relates the story of one youngster, who is socially disadvantaged, and what he has gained from the camping experience.

101 THE CAMP TYLER SUCCESS STORY*

*A new approach to
education in an
outdoor classroom*

PAT MARTIN
DIRECTOR OF PUBLIC RELATIONS AND PUBLICATIONS,
GRAYSON COUNTY COLLEGE, TEXAS

Fifteen years of success and more than 50,000 children benefited. These are facts and figures that school officials in Tyler quote easily.

They refer to Camp Tyler, a unique school-community outdoor laboratory located in a wooded area on the shores of Lake Tyler. It is operated as part of the school system, and during the school year fifth and sixth graders spend from two days to a week at the camp studying nature at her best.

Camp Tyler is the only outdoor facility of its kind in the state and one of the few in the nation. The idea for the camp was originated by the Tyler Kiwanis Club, and with the help and support of several organizations and individuals, the idea grew into the founding of the Smith County Youth Foundation. Backed by a considerable sum of money raised by voluntary subscription, this organization provided the leadership needed to see the camp become a reality.

The Tyler public schools became interested in the camp as a site for a school camping facility, and in 1949 an agreement was reached with the youth foundation. The schools would operate the camp 12 months a year in exchange for use of its facilities, which the foundation would

provide, 9 months of the year. During the summer months such groups as the Campfire Girls, 4-H Club members, and Future Homemakers are offered use of the camp.

Major facilities include bunk houses scattered over the low hills, special buildings for crafts, soil testing, and weather predicting, and a large main building. This central structure has a dining room, kitchen, refreshment stand, nature museum, and office space.

James Dudley directs the activities of the outdoor classroom. He has been a counselor at the camp for seven years. Before coming to Camp Tyler, he was an elementary teacher and taught conservation in a Camp Tyler workshop conducted under the sponsorship of NEA.

All teacher-counselors at the camp are certified classroom teachers. They live in the bunkhouses with the students, and at times they find themselves on duty as much as 75 hours a week. Dudley says that men and women of "physical stamina, emotional maturity, outgoing personality, genuine human empathy, rural background, and/or natural science background" are necessary to a successful outdoor program.

Almost all of the work at the camp is done by the students themselves. They operate the refreshment stand, set tables, clean up after meals, and keep their bunkhouses in order.

*From The Texas Outlook 49:32, December 1965. Used by permission.

They also set up a bank, deposit their spending money in it, and carry out all financial transactions while in camp by checks. A post office in the main building is operated by the students. They are required to write home often during their stay, and parents are encouraged to write to them.

"The most important part of our program takes place outdoors," Dudley says. "The students learn to identify trees and animals native to East Texas, use tools such as axes and saws, recognize major constellations, test soil, determine the reasons for and stop erosion, and recognize the importance of the conservation of nature's creations."

"We try to tie everything into what the students have been studying in the classroom," Dudley maintains. "We visit them in their schools and help them decide what they want to do while they are in camp. They set up their own schedule and establish their own goals. We just work with them to help them accomplish their own purposes."

Camp continues no matter what the weather. Buildings in the area around the main lodge provide shelter, and classes take advantage of the specific time of the year to learn how nature changes with the seasons.

Fifth graders spend two days and one night in camp, while sixth graders stay an entire school week. They pay a small tuition fee that takes care of food and transportation costs. Students are encouraged to earn at least a part of their tuition fee. However, no student misses camp because of lack of money. The Youth Foundation guarantees that every child who wants to can attend. Attendance is not compulsory, but participation is over 90 percent.

"Many students come to camp and suddenly find themselves away from home for the first

time," says Dudley, "but we have had very few cases of incurable homesickness in 15 years."

Another integral part of the outdoor program is the school farm located on Camp Tyler property. Operated as a laboratory for the Future Farmer chapters, the farm is visited regularly by camp students and is one of the most popular parts of the program.

Tyler citizens recognize the importance of the camp in their school program. Seven years ago more bunkhouses were needed. It took the local civic leaders only weeks to raise the necessary money to build them. Many people volunteered time to help construct the new bunkhouses while others helped build and repair other facilities.

This type of help is typical. When the camp was being built, one man donated a deep well. He sent his crews to dig it, install a pump and a storage tank, and pipe water to the buildings.

Camp Tyler enjoys a nation-wide reputation as one of the finest camps of its type. Visitors by the hundreds have inspected it in its 15 years, and many workshops and meetings have been held there. School officials credit much of the camp's success to George W. Donaldson, who helped establish it and directed it for 14 of its 15 years. He is now associate professor of outdoor education at Northern Illinois University.

Ed Irons, Tyler superintendent, is a strong backer of the outdoor program. "We consider the outdoor education program at Camp Tyler to be a continuation of classroom activities related to field experiences, study, observations, and projects in outdoor settings," he said.

But Tyler's students are the most enthusiastic backers of the camp. One high school senior recalled that some of his most pleasant memories from his childhood days were of how he "learned to work and like it" at Camp Tyler.

102 ❧ CAMP QUEST—AN OUTDOOR LEARNING LABORATORY*

DALE C. JOHNSON
PRINCIPAL, CENTRAL JUNIOR HIGH SCHOOL,
LE MARS, IOWA

"Camp Quest? It is a rejuvenating step in each student's perpetual search for answers— answers to situations which he feels are meaningful," philosophized Camp Quest Life Science Instructor Tom Bohan as he flicked a tenacious horse fly from his arm while he watched 33

seventh and eighth grade boys and girls busily preparing breakfast by the light of the sun-splashed eastern horizon.

"Camp Quest? Or do you mean Camp Headache?" countered a school custodian with a twinkle in his eye as he pried a broken blade from the school's best mower.

Camp Quest is many things to many people, but to the students who live in the area served

*From Midland School 80:20, May–June 1967. Used by permission.

by the Le Mars Community School District it is a co-educational setting that provides an innovational change from the traditional academic school programs of the past.

A humble beginning

On November 5, 1964, a newspaper headline informed the community that an abandoned limestone quarry located two and one half miles northeast of Le Mars was going to be purchased by the city council for use as an auxiliary city dump. Since this area had been used for many years as a location for field trips for science classes, this news kindled an interest in the transaction. A series of "coffee sessions" at the Central Junior High, a meeting with a co-operative city council, several sessions with an interested superintendent and school board, and the support of a number of leaders in the community combined to block the proposal and to give life to the idea of a community school outdoor laboratory for all students, grades K–12. The approval of the camp, as a project under the Elementary and Secondary Education Act, provided impetus through a grant for funds for equipment necessary to conduct a sound educational camp program.

Summer school program

There are three facets to the entire Camp Quest Program. One is the co-educational Camp Quest Summer School for students in grades seven and eight. Youngsters spend from one to two weeks living in tents, preparing their own meals, and working within an academic curriculum which is based upon the discovery method of learning. This should not be looked upon as a group of uninformed students groping around for solutions to problem situations. Rather, they are students who are drawing upon their prior learning and researching to add to their knowledge as they engage in problem solving activities. A typical day's schedule at Camp Quest includes the following activities:

5:00 a.m.	Reveille—raising of the flag
5:15- 6:00	Breakfast—prepared by students
6:30- 8:30	Swimming and swimming instruction, New Deal Park, Le Mars
9:00-11:30	Lecture and demonstrations
11:30-12:00	Review and discussion with staff
12:00- 1:00	Lunch
1:00- 4:30	Individual and group projects
4:30- 5:00	Camp clean-up
5:00- 6:30	Supper—lowering flag
6:30- 7:30	Recreation
7:30- 8:45	Swimming at New Deal Park, Le Mars
9:00- 9:30	Free Time
9:30 p.m.	Lights out except for students working in Herpetology and Mammalogy

Individual and group projects can be selected from any one of the following interest areas: astronomy, rocks and minerals, fossils, entomology, agronomy, forestry, aquatic life, and ornithology. In addition, some phase of each day's instruction stresses the importance of the conservation of our natural resources. Four areas emphasized are: water ecology, fish and wildlife, soil conservation, and timber management. Last summer, presentations were made by nine guest lectures representing the Soil Conservation Service, Isaac Walton League, Plymouth County Extension Service, and the U.S. Forestry Service. Topics discussed during the 1966 summer session included: Land Management, Soil Science, Glaciation of Iowa, Forestry and Succession, Weed and Grass Classification, and Contour Mapping.

Basically, the objectives of the Camp Quest Summer are:

1. To stimulate interest in the life and earth sciences.
2. To develop within each student an awareness of the group's dependence upon the contribution of each member.
3. To develop self-reliance by placing students in situations where they must think and act for themselves.

Academic school year program

Instead of bringing some of the outdoors to the laboratory, a second facet of the Camp Quest program brings the student to the laboratory of the great outdoors. A student gathers an assortment of rocks on a field trip to Camp Quest. As the student organizes, labels, and catalogs his collection he finds he must read to learn more about the classification of rocks. This learning is purposeful because it is necessary if he is to carry through his projects. This is learning at its best. The student studies because he wants to know. He "discovers" for himself that knowledge is only a tool for greater understanding. Contrast his opportunities for learning with the student who has been told to read the next five pages in chapter 12 and memorize the characteristics of five different forms of metamorphic rock.

The camp site has been used primarily during the regular school year by Central Junior High students. Since a team-teaching, block-of-time schedule is followed, it is a relatively simple matter to provide students with two and one half hours of time for work at Camp Quest. The following schedule is used in grade eight:

Language Arts & American History BLOCK—OF—TIME		
Period 1	Period 2	Period 3
SPANISH	ALGEBRA I	SCIENCE

SCIENCE	TYPING	MATH	ACTIVITY PERIOD
Period 4	Period 5	Period 6	Period 7
Language Arts & History BLOCK—OF—TIME			ACTIVITY PERIOD

On days when work at Camp Quest has been scheduled, the block-of-time classes are taught during the regular science class period and the periods normally reserved for block-of-time instruction are used for the field trip. Such trips can be taken as often as once each week and this schedule still permits each student to receive more than 550 minutes of instruction each week in language arts and social science. Three teachers accompany approximately 85 students on each of the two and one half hour field trips.

Black Hills field trip planned

A third facet of Camp Quest is being initiated during the summer of 1967 for students who will have completed grade nine this spring. Twenty girls and boys who have attended Camp Quest Summer School in seventh or eighth grade will be selected to take a one-week field trip to the Black Hills. All housing and transportation costs will be paid for by the Central Junior High Science Club. Arrangements for housing have been made at a guest ranch in the Black Hills area. Students will provide their own spending money and a share of their food costs.

The itinerary will include:
1. School of Mines—Rapid City, South Dakota

2. Badlands National Monument
3. Black Hills National Forest
   a. One day with the U.S. Forest Service
   b. One day with the U.S. Job Corps
4. Museum—Deadwood, South Dakota
5. Gold Mine—Lead, South Dakota
6. Harney Peak Look-out
7. Mount Rushmore National Monument
8. Custer State Park Zoo and Museum
9. Gavins Point—Yankton, South Dakota

The objectives for this trip are:
- To provide experiences that relate in a positive way to a student's curricular program
- To promote self-confidence and a feeling of personal worth through each youngster's sharing in exciting educational experiences
- To provide motivation for the study of American History in Grade 10.

Camp improvements scheduled

One of the weaknesses of the Camp Quest program has been the lack of a structure large enough to shelter all of the students in case of inclement weather. Another weakness has been the lack of an adequate enclosed work area where a library can be maintained, where equipment may be stored, and where students can carry out research and work on projects. During this past year, a school bus has been used to take care of these functions. To meet these needs, the Board of Education has voted to move an unused rural school house to the Camp Quest site. This move is being made this spring.

A more comprehensive report of Camp Quest and the summer school program has been compiled in booklet form by the Board of Education of the Le Mars Community Schools. Copies may be obtained without charge by writing to: Vance Stead, Superintendent, Le Mars Community Schools, Le Mars, Iowa 51031.

103 ⮞ CAMPING FOR THE DISADVANTAGED CHILD*

EVELYN WATTERS
WIFE OF A SACRAMENTO,
CALIFORNIA, PRINCIPAL

"Boy, this is keen," said Daniel in almost breathless awe. He was having his first look at a High Sierra meadow, grassy and moist, sprinkled with clumps of pastel flowers. A gurgling stream splashed its way through the greens-

ward. Encompassing the 50-acre circle were forested mountain slopes spotted with disappearing strips of sparkling snow.

Daniel and his campmates live in the big city, and come chiefly from homes of parents who have marginal occupations or no jobs at all, and where more often than not only the mother is responsible for the children's welfare. Most of

---

*From California Teacher Association Journal 60:28, October 1966. Used by permission.

the middle-class advantages that are taken for granted during the years of child-rearing, are nonexistent in these families.

There never have been opportunities for family trips to the wilderness. These children are almost totally confined to their own homes, to the city streets, and to the school.

Few schools have sponsored outdoor instructional experiences that include summer camping. This is an area that can provide exceptional therapy and opportunity for children whose everyday environment is far removed from nature. In the case of Daniel, a service club had provided the financial backing for his temporary liberation.

From what was Daniel liberated? Go with me to his home, which I visited one winter evening after my car lights had failed. Daniel's family lived in the area and it occurred to me that I could use their telephone, rather than risk an accident.

The mother was solicitous, and as we waited to complete the call, a half dozen small youngsters converged around my young son in almost instant communication, and were soon chasing him around the house in joyous abandon. Daniel, who had recognized me as the wife of the school principal, sat on the floor in a corner of the room, his face wreathed in smiles. A television set blared full blast, the dishes were piled in the sink spigot-high, the automatic dish-washer stood silent and unused, brimming over with another burden of unwashed pots and pans. Cockroaches walked across the ceiling. A cat and a dog scrambled among the children and over the torn and ragged mohair furniture. One of the many females of the house attended a pan of something on the stove that smelled both good and bad.

This mismanagement of property and lives is characteristic of most poverty-plagued peoples of the world, and exists no matter what the color of the skin. It is the life of despair.

At this crucial stage of his life, Daniel is extremely vulnerable to forces that will either submerge and destroy him, or to those that can support and direct him.

For three years he had tried unsuccessfully to get to camp. The first time he was too young to qualify for registration. The second summer he missed the required free physical check-up at the school when his mother mistakenly assumed that she would need to pay a regular physician, and refused to let him go. The third year Daniel was able to register, finished the physical and had the verification in his possession, but on the night before camp he was

allowed to stay up to watch television until two o'clock, and the next morning no one awakened him. A forlorn little fellow faced his disappointment alone when he discovered he had missed the bus for camp.

This year the obstacle course had been successfully executed and Daniel had made camp. A counselor's whistle signaled him from his trance at the meadow, and he rejoined his companions for washup time preparatory to lunch.

Eating out in the open under a canopy of pine trees, with squirrels and chipmunks scampering under the tables and mountain bluejays squawking overhead is surely a far cry from lolling around the treeless concrete pavements with nothing to do. The week rocketed by in experiences that far surpassed monotonous hours of lying on the floor watching endless processions of television cartoons, westerns, and ancient versions of situation comedies.

There were hours of absorption in the craft tent. There were hikes up mountain trails to crystal clear lakes. There was swimming every afternoon with a half-mile walk of anticipation through the cool green forest, culminated by a running leap for the drifting rafts. In the words of Daniel, adventures of this kind fill your lungs with fresh air so full they feel like "busting"—just like your heart—"it's so happy!"

The night star-gazing, the magic, moonlit Indian ceremonies that hypnotize the initiates, the songs and stories around the big campfire, and the silence of the forest after a boy pulls himself deep into the warmth of a borrowed sleeping bag—these things will sink into Daniel's subconscious and surely affect his life. Even if he is never again lucky enough to get to camp, this experience will make a difference.

Daniel has potential, but he has so many strikes against him that unless some helpful influences are exerted, he will probably become another casualty of modern society.

The life at home with all of its confusion probably will not change, but mitigating forces in the boy's life may give him a better chance, and there are some responses to a summer camp experience that may be reasonably anticipated.

He may have absorbed enough conservation instruction to begin an understanding and observance of fire prevention; he may guard against trash and tin can litter in the forest, and from disfigurement of nature's creations. This in turn, would hopefully help him to give a second thought to these things at home, at school, and in the city streets. We would hope also that Daniel may someday guide his family to the mountains for a time of renewal and an appreciation of nature.

Henry David Thoreau was a great believer in the healing and restorative powers of nature, and what he wrote is as pertinent today as it was a hundred years ago: "In Wildness is the preservation of the World. Every tree sends its fibers forth in search of the Wild. The cities import it at any price. Men plow and sail for it. From the forests and wilderness come the tonics and barks which brace mankind."

Daniel went to camp because someone cared.

PROJECTS AND THOUGHT QUESTIONS FOR PART FIVE

1. List and discuss the objectives of recreation.
2. Prepare a list of guiding principles for the achievement of the objectives that you have listed in item 1.
3. Develop a plan whereby health education, physical education, and recreation would work cooperatively together in a school and community program. Outline the specifics through which such cooperation would be implemented.
4. Read and critically review one article in a recreation magazine.
5. Describe a school camp program for elementary school pupils. Outline the objectives of the camp, the program you would install, and the outcomes you would expect.
6. Describe what you consider will be a community recreation program in the year 2000.

SELECTED READINGS

Bucher, C. A.: Administration of health and physical education programs, including athletics, ed. 5, St. Louis, 1971, The C. V. Mosby Co.

Carlson, R., Deppe, T. R., and Maclean, J. R.: Recreation in American life, Belmont, Calif., 1963, Wadsworth Publishing Co., Inc.

Commission on Goals for American Recreation: Goals for American recreation, Washington, D. C., 1964, American Association for Health, Physical Education, and Recreation.

Kraus, R.: Recreation today—program planning and leadership, New York, 1966, Appleton-Century-Crofts.

Shivers, J. S.: Leadership in recreational service, New York, 1963, The Macmillan Co.

Shivers, J. S.: Camping—Administration, counseling, programming, New York, 1971, Appleton-Century-Crofts.